VARĀHAMIHIRA'S

BṚHAT SAṀHITĀ

बृहत्संहिता

VARĀHAMIHIRA'S

BṚHAT SAṀHITĀ

बृहत्संहिता

with English Translation, Exhaustive Notes and Literary Comments

PART ONE

M. RAMAKRISHNA BHAT

SINCE 1903

MOTILAL BANARSIDASS
PUBLISHING HOUSE • DELHI

Email: naraina@mlbd.in • Website: www.mlbd.in

@mlbdofficial

8th Reprint: Delhi, 2023
First Edition : Delhi, 1981

ISBN: 978-93-5760-480-2 (Part-I) (Hardcover)
ISBN: 978-93-90064-53-3 (Part-I) (Paperback)
ISBN: 978-93-5760-470-3 (Part-II) (Hardcover)
ISBN: 978-93-90064-54-0 (Part-II) (Paperback)
ISBN: 978-93-5760-431-4 (Hardcover set)
ISBN: 978-93-90064-55-7 (Paperback set)

Printed & Published by
Rajendra P Jain *for*
Motilal Banarsidass Publishing House
A-44, Naraina Industrial Area, Phase I,
New Delhi–110 028 (INDIA)
Email: naraina@mlbd.in Website: www.mlbd.in
Tel.: (+91-11)4751 1592
Showroom:
4637/20, F-2, Hari Sadan, First Floor, Ansari Road, Daryaganj
Delhi–110 002 (Opp. Fire Station) ***Tel.*** : (+91-11)4559 7999

CONTENTS

INTRODUCTION

It is by sheer grace of the Lord Śrī Siddhi Vināyaka that this new and enlarged edition of the Bṛhat Saṁhitā with English translation and exhaustive notes, literary comments, etc. has been made possible, considering the vastness and pre-eminence of this extraordinary work as well as the unique position of Varāhamihira, one of the brightest stars in the galaxy of Indian astronomers and astrologers. Though we cannot claim to possess all the qualifications needed for undertaking this onerous task single-handed, yet we have ventured to do this work mainly for two reasons, viz., our innate love for the qualities of head and heart of the illustrious author that are visible like gems in the pages of this work, which really deserves to be designated as his *magnum opus*, and the fact that we had translated jointly this work in 1947.[1] There have been persistent demands on the publishers for a fresh edition of the Bṛhat Saṁhitā, since none of the previous English editions by Dr. Kern, Chidambara Iyer and our own is available at present. It is in the fitness of things that the world of scholars and lovers of ancient culture and wisdom long to probe this mine of wisdom, nay, the *Encyclopaedia of Indian Culture* in general and astrological lore in particular. In all countries of the world, especially in India, where astrology is held in high esteem on account of its being the 'Eye of Wisdom,'[2] this was an honoured discipline. No activity, however insignificant it might be in the social, political or religious sphere of man, would be permitted without due regard being paid to the injunctions of Jyotirvidyā. For, astrology is a Śāstra, Science, according to the wise men of the east, who had tested the veracity of this Śāstra in the crucible of their experience and penance of several centuries. If some rationalists of today were to decry this Science as superstition, we have to forgive them their unscientific attitude. For, they know not what they say.

In reality, astrology is an integrated science as well as Dharmaśāstra. It aims at synthesis of all branches of learning, as shown by

---

1. See the Bṛhat Saṁhitā translated by V. S. Sastri and M. R. Bhat.
2. Jyotiṣāmayanaṃ cakṣuḥ.

the contents of this work, which is really encyclopaedic in depth and extent. Generally it is divided into four categories, viz., mundane, horary electional and natal astrology. This remarkable science, in which man all over the world has implicit faith, has been handed down in India from time immemorial. There are other countries like China where this was practised in the remote past. In our country, the Vedas and its branches, which are the oldest records of human civilization, contain innumerable references to the Nakṣatras, seasons, months, etc. It is to be remembered that astrology-astronomy is reckoned among the *limbs* of the Veda. The Taittirīya Saṁhitā (IV. 4, 10, 1-3) and the Taittirīya Brāhmaṇa (III. 1-1, 2) mention the presiding deities of the asterisms. The Ṛg Veda (II-32, VIII-3,20, etc,) speaks of the Moon as the *measurer of time*. Likewise the Atharva Veda (Book XIX) refers to the Nakṣatras. The Śākalya Saṁhitā gives the configurations of the stars. The Kauśika-sūtra of the Atharvaveda contains a Nakṣatra-kalpa and a Śāntikalpa, both treating of the lunar mansions. Pāṇini has many Sūtras bearing on the constellations, months, seasons, etc.[1] The Taittirīya *Brāhmaṇa* says that the 'Spring is the Face of the year'. The *Śatapatha* Brāhmaṇa speaks of six (sometimes five also) seasons (Ṛtus).[2] According to P. C. Sengupta[3] at the earliest Brāhmaṇa period the sun reached the winter solstice at the New Moon of Māgha; the year was considered to be at its end at the Full Moon of Phālguna; the *Kṛttikās* rose exactly in the east; and the Spring set in one day after the New Moon of Caitra. The *Arthaśāstra* (300 B.C.) refers (XLI) to Grahacāras (planetary movements), especially of Venus. As late as the 4th century A.D. Nakṣatras were used for dates in the Singhala Chronicle *Dipavaṁśa*. It is learnt that a work entitled *Śārdūlakarṇāvadānam* deals with the Buddha's exhortations to an outcaste girl. The work was translated into the Chinese language in 170 A.D. This work contains many chapters dealing with the topics treated of in our *Saṁhitā*, such as Earthquake, Moles, Results of birth in different constellations, Portents, Dreams, and Palmistry.[4]

It is believed by some Western as well as Indian scholars that the weekdays were introduced into India from the West. This view is erroneous for the following reasons: In connection with Rūpa-

---

1. I 2-60 to 63; II 3-45; IV 2-21; III 3-9, etc.
. II Kāṇḍa 17-6 Brā. 27.
3. Indian Hist. Qly. Vol. X 3 1934.
4. Bṛhat Saṁhitā, Intro. pp. 18-19, Vārāṇaseya Skt. Vi. Vi. Edn.

satra (Worship of the Stellar Deity CV. 6), Sage Garga who is quoted by Utpala, mentions the weekday, *Candravāre*. It is undoubted that Sage Gạrga is one of the most ancient authorities on astrology, being the direct disciple of Svayambhū, the Creator.[1] Burgess states in his concluding remarks thus: "There is abundant testimony to the fact that the division of the day into 24 hours existed in the East, if not actually in India, before it did in Greece." About some common words like Horā, he is of the view that "they were passed from the Sanskrit to the Greek at a period of high antiquity." Prof. Wilson is more forthright in his statement about the weekdays. According to him, it was unknown to the Greeks and not adopted by the Romans until a late period. He adds that the Hindus appear to have at least as good a title *to the invention* as any other people.[2] Burgess replies to those scholars who maintain that Indian astrology has been borrowed from the Greeks, thus: "It is difficult to see what it was that they borrowed, since in no case do numerical data and results in the systems of the two peoples exactly correspond." He concludes that 'the course of derivation was from east to west rather than from west to east', and *the Indians were the teachers rather than learners*.[3] It is in the light of the above conclusions that we have to interpret Varāhamihira's statement (II.14) that 'the Yavanas are honoured like the Sages.' The bogey of Greek influence is laid to rest by the strong arguments of Swami Vivekānanda. He says: "There may be, it is true, some similarity between the Greek and Indian terms in astronomy and so forth, but the westerners have ignored the direct Sanskrit etymology and sought for some far-fetched etymology from the Greek. That such shallow and biased learning has been manifested by many orientalists in the West is deplorable. From a single Sanskrit Śloka that reads, 'The Yavanas are Mlechchas; in them, this Science is established; therefore, even they deserve worship like Rishis . . .' in the west, they have gone so far as to declare that all Indian sciences are but echoes of the Greek; whereas a true reading of the Śloka may show that the Mlechcha disciples of the Aryans are herein praised in order to encourage them to a further study of the Aryan Sciences . . . ."

Of late, people in the west, especially some astronomers and other scientists, have begun to take some interest in Hindu astrology,

1. See notes under I-5.
2. J. Roy. Asiat. Soc. IX. 84.
3. Transactions of R. A. Soc. I. 579.

as its findings on mental health come very close to their own. For example, William Bonyun, an eminent American astronomer, describes Hindu astrology as "the oldest science in the history of mankind," whose precepts and formulae were worked out in the remote past, according to strictly modern scientific methods. Sir Bernard Lovell, Director of Jordel Bank Observatory admits that there is truth in the ancient belief in the connection between the Moon and lunacy. Similarly, Count Bjornistjerne admires the greatest antiquity of Hindu astronomy and civilization.

Modern Scientists have now discovered that Sun-spots and Solar flares have a direct bearing on heart-attacks, irritability, headaches, nausea, mental and nervous illness, etc. For, the human body is affected by the natural electricity in the air around us. Professors Robert O. Becker, a medical doctor, Howard Friedman, a psychologist, and Charles H. Bachman, a physicist, have detected the sensitive electrical receiving apparatus in our bodies which they believe is affected by fields of electro-magnetic force given out by the sun. Both types of solar disturbance release into space untold myriads of highly charged electrons and protons. These space hurricanes are known as solar winds. As a consequence of this the earth experiences what is usually called a magnetic storm, which plays havoc with radio and telegraph communications. Whenever sun-spots and solar flares led to geomagnetic storms around the earth, traffic accidents rose 70 per cent, suicides jumped abnormally. For, it is largely the harmful positive ions that come through from the Sun to affect us in these ways. Probably all living things are in fact affected by the sun's magnetism..[1] Recently the National Geophysical Research Institute of Hyderabad had come to the same conclusion: "A strong positive correlation is found to exist between the disturbances of the earth's magnetic field and daily hospital admissions of heart cases in Hyderabad."[2]

Readers would be surprised to hear that ancient Sages had discovered a correlation between some disturbances on the solar disc and terrestrial happenings like dust-storms, earthquakes, famines, destructive tendencies among men, diseases, destruction of life on a large scale, etc. These are called Tāmasakīlakas, Dark Shafts appearing on the Sun's disc, by the Sages. There are also other comets or Ketus that cause the phenomena akin to the sun-spots and solar flares.

---

1. From an article "How Sun-Spots affect you" by David Gunston.
2. Article, "Heart attacks linked to solar disturbances", Sunday Standard of 8-8-76.

Author: Varāhamihira (505 A.D.) was a scientist of rare merits, who in spite of his regard for ancient traditions and Sages, followed always the scientific method. His scientific thinking is illustrated by what he says in connection with the commencement of the solstices in III 1-3 as well as with Rāhu and eclipse.[1] In view of his extraordinary and masterly treatment of the subjects of astronomy and astrology in all their ramifications, he was held in high esteem by scholars of ancient and medieval India. About his greatness Al-Birūnī, the Arab scholar and traveller says, "Varāhamihira has already revealed himself to us as a man who accurately knows the shape of the world . . . On the whole his foot stands firmly on the basis of the truth, and he clearly speaks out the truth."[2] He was considered, for this reason, to be an incarnation of the Sun-God[3] and one of the Nine Gems adorning the court of the legendary King Vikramāditya. Kalyāṇavarman, author of the Sārāvalī (650-725 A.D.) says that our author has bequeathed to posterity the unique wisdom of the ancient seers. So does Bhāskarācārya in his *Siddhānta-śiromani* I. 2. Śatānanda in his *Bhāsvatī Karana* (1098 A.D.) calls Varāhamihira's work as one on a par with the *Sūrya Siddhānta*, while Kṣemendra reckons him among the great poets.[4] It is well known that astrology-cum-astronomy is based upon the theory that the Sun[5] is the hub and driving force of the universe. The same sun who is eulogized in many a Ṛgvedic hymn, chief of which is the famous Gāyatrī Mantra, was the tutelary Deity of Varāhamihira, whose genius, it is reported, flowered as a result of the Sun's unique boon. His life's mission was to revive the ancient learning of astronomy and astrology which was fast disappearing. His father was a great devotee of the Sun-God and was appropriately named *Āditya-dāsa*. This also shows that the sun was the tutelary Deity of his ancestors. The word Mihira, meaning the sun, in the author's name points to the same conclusion. The author asserts that he obtained a special boon from the Sun-God at *Kāpitthaka* and that his Guru was his own father.[6] Utpala explains that Kāpitthaka was a village where the Āvantikācārya was born and where there must have been a temple of the Sun-God famous in those days. Scholars have identified this village

1. V 1-8, 13, 17, 25; IX. 7.
2. Vide page 119 Vol. II of "India."
3. Vide notes on page 1.
4. *Aucityavicāracarcā*, 26-79.
5. Sūrya ātmā jagatas tasthuṣaśca. (Ṛg)
6. Bṛhajjātaka XXVIII. 9.

with the present *Kayatha* or *Saṁkāśya* at a distance of about 12 miles from Ujjain. This conclusion is in consonance with the popular belief that Varāha was a resident of Ujjain and spent his life there, radiating his unsurpassed wisdom to the whole world.

However, Utpala calls our author *Magadha-dvija* in two places in the Bṛhat Saṁhitā.[1] This word poses a riddle to scholars inasmuch as an Āvantika could not at the same time be called one of Magadha country. So Dr. Kern surmises that Varāha or his forefathers might have migrated from Magadha to Ujjain in search of royal patronage. Monier Williams, on the other hand, explains the word Maga as 'worshipper of the Sun.' If we follow this explanation, we shall have to admit that the word *Magadha* means 'the place or country where reside worshippers of the Sun.' In that case even the village *Kāpitthaka* could be called *Magadha*. It is possible that the country of *Magadha* was so called because of the Maga Brāhmaṇas who had colonized it in the remote past. Is there any connection between the *Magas* and the Magi who were supposed to be the wise men hailing from the East? We are inclined to believe that possibly some of the ancestors of the *Magas* migrated to Persia and had a colony of their own there. That is why we find Mitra, Aryaman, etc., names of the Sun-God, prevalent in that country in ancient times. We have another doubt also on the basis of a quotation of the *Bhaviṣyapurāṇa*— "मगं ध्यायन्ति ये तस्मात्तेन ते मगधाः स्मृताः" (CXVII. 55). This would also entitle Varāha and his ancestors to be classified as *Magadhas*, as they were all intensely devoted to the Sun-God. Is it possible that *Maga* is a variant or another synonym of Bhaga, meaning the Sun ?[2] We are also told that Varāha was one of the *Sakadvipi Brāhmaṇas* whose *Gotra* was *Mihira*. We are in the dark about the whereabouts of this *Śākadvipa*. This will land us in greater confusion. There is only one way of getting out of this dilemma: In very ancient times some worshippers of the sun must have migrated from India to the *Śākadvīpa* and colonized it; and later some of their descendants returned to India, the land of their ancestors. Hence the name *Śākadvipa Brāhmaṇas*.[3]

It is not known exactly as to who was Varāha's patron king. Many theories have been put forward by scholars: Some say that

1. In the beginning of his Vivṛti and under LXXXVI 4 of Bṛ. Saṁ.
2. इनो भगो धामनिधिः Amarakośa.
3. According to the भविष्यपुराण, Sāmba, son of Śrikṛṣṇa built a temple to the Sun at Mūlasthāna (Multan) on the Candrabhāgā (Chenab) and had to bring from Śakadvīpa Maga Brahmins for the installation.

it was Harṣa Vikramâditya of Ujjain who ascended the throne in the 6th century A.D. Others hold that it was Vikramāditya who came to power in 544 A.D. According to the Pañcasiddhântikā (I. 8-10) epoch of 427 Śaka year *Caitra Śukla Pratipad*, Varâhamihira must have composed it in 505 A.D. This fits in with Al-Bīrūnī's statement in 1030 A.D. to the effect that the P.S. was composed 526 years before his time.[1] According to Āmarāja, Varāha is said to have died in 587 A.D. It is also held that Varāha visited the Yavana country, and, according to Persian tradition translated the *Pañcatantra* into the Pahlavi language at the instance of the then King of Persia (531 to 576 A.D.)

Al-Birūni and Varāhamihira : Al-Bīrūnī (born in 973 A.D.) came to India in 1030 A.D. with the object of studying Hindu astrology and culture. He is also reported to have translated into Arabic the *Bṛhat Saṁhitā* (B.S.) and the *Laghujātaka* (L. J.), some parts of which are also explained in the pages of his *India*. Though he has done a wonderful work, he has committed some errors in interpreting Varāha's works.[2] He says that the Hindus have no understanding of the motions of the fixed stars; and he reprimands the author for the statement in IV.7 of the B.S. Al-Bīrūnī does not realize that in the *Saṁhitā* the author first of all mentions the views of ancient Sages like Garga, and then gives his own conclusions. The Arab scholar takes our author to task for his statement on the solstices and remarks: "The solstice has kept its place, but the constellations have migrated, just the very opposite of what Varāha has fancied." Even here we have to say in defence that Varāhamihira refers at first to the views of ancient sages and then states his own views in unequivocal terms. If Al-Bīrūnī had studied the author's statements carefully, he would have found no contradiction between his own view and that of Varāha. The latter's scientific attitude is borne out by his advice to students to the effect that they should study the subject by means of systematic observations and markings on a circle. Al-Bīrūnī shows his intolerance for the Hindu practice of performing sacrifices at the rising of stars such as Agastya (Canopus). He says, "It is rather chaff than wheat." The Arab traveller could not realize that it was the chaff that protected the grain. Besides, he could not rise to the high level of the lofty ideals of Vedic religion. We need

1. "India" II. p. 7.
2. See Appendix II.

not go into the deep significance, spiritual and scientific, of the institution of sacrifices. We have also to remember, in this connection, that Varāha was also a poet *par excellence*, and his medium and subject matter are such that he is easily lifted by their magic from the sordid plane of science to the ethereal regions of inspired poetry. All the same, Al-Bīrūnī praises the Hindus for their perfect knowledge of the eclipses.

His works : Utpala calls him Ācārya (Teacher), who is *Jyotiśśāstra-saṁgrahakṛt* (one who has abridged the works on astrology and astronomy). He says that Varāha has already compiled the two *Skandhas*, viz., Gaṇita and Horā, and now he is trying to compile the 3rd one, viz., *Saṁhitā* or *Aṅgaviniścaya*. The author says in the *B.S.* CVII 14 and *Bṛhajjātaka* (*B.J.*) XXVIII 6 that he has composed *Bahvāścaryaṁ jātakam* (Natal astrology of many wonders), *Yātrā* (or *Journey*) and the *P.S.* that is *Bahu codyam* of many arguments or wonders). His works are available in two versions, viz., *Bṛhat* (major) and *Laghu* (minor). His *Bṛhad Yātrā* or *Bṛ. Yogayātrā* was also known as *Mahāyātrā*. It had the commentary of *Sūryadeva Somasut* of *Naidhruva Gotra*. The *Svalpayātrā* (Abridged work on Journey) is also known as *Ṭikaṇika Yātrā*.[1] Another work on "Journey," according to Utpala, is the *Yogayātrā*. Kern had edited nine chapters of this work; and now the entire work has been published. Bhaṭṭotpala refers[2] to the two versions of the *Vivāhapaṭala* and is reported to have commented on it. In B.S. I.10 as well as LI.7, the Ācārya says that he has already written the *Yātrā*. Utpala invariably quotes from it and calls it *Yogayātrā* (under XLIII.31). He explains that the author had already written *B.J.*, *Bṛ. Yātrā*, and *Bṛ. Vivāhapaṭala*. The author refers to it in many other places too.[3] B.J. mentions *Vivāhapaṭala* and *Yātrā* as future works.[4] Similarly in the *Bṛ. Yātrā* it is stated that *Jātaka* has already been written.[5] *Yogayātra* IV.52 and *Vivāhapaṭala* 16, 97 speak of *Jātaka* as an earlier work. In his *Vivṛti* on *Yogayātrā* Utpala gives the order of Varāha's works as follows : (i) P. Siddhāntikā, (ii) Jātaka, (iii) *Yakṣyeśvamedhiya Yātrā*, (iv) *Yogayātrā*, (v) *Vivāhapaṭala*, and (vi) *Saṁhitā*. But after writing all these works Varāha must have

1. The word Tikaṇikā must be a vernacular name for 'small.' Cf. Kannaḍa word, cikaṇi, in this sense.
2. Under B. J. XX. 10.
3. B. S. XLIV. 14, 18; XLVIII. 22, 29.
4. B. J. XXIV. 16; XXVIII. 3.
5. Vide India As seen in Bṛ Saṁhitā, p. 32.

revised them. For, in P.S.XV.10 he refers to *Saṁhitā*; in B. J. XXVIII.6 to *V. Paṭala* and *Saṁhitā* in the past tense.

Many other works are also attributed to the Ācārya. Al-Bīrūnī states that Varāha wrote *Horāpañcahotrya* and a work on architecture. The latter must be the chapters LIII, LVI and LVII of B.S. that deal with this subject.

Vaṭakaṇikā seems to be a work on portents. 120 verses of this work are quoted in Ballālasena's *Adbhutasāgara* as those of Varāhamihira. He is supposed to have written works on erotics and poetics too. Another work in manuscript entitled *Pañcapakṣi* is attributed to our author. It is a short work on divination through the five vowels अ, इ, उ, ए and ओ. It has a commentary too. Other works attributed to him are *Praśnamahodadhi*, *Praśnacandrikā*, and *Daivajñavallabhā*.

Subject matter : The term *Saṁhitā* connotes 'compilation.' As such it cannot be an original work. Its business is to condense many Śāstras. It should, therefore, include details of many subjects found in varied works. The *Saṁhitā,* in astrological parlance, is nothing but an encyclopaedia of astrological and other subjects of human interest. It is also mundane astrology with many scientific topics and other subjects in which human beings have an abiding faith. Hence the Saṁhitā can rightly be termed a work of social Science. For, social science should have reference to and explanation of almost all aspects of social life and those that have a human appeal. The structure of the Saṁhitā is such that it gives ample scope for the exhibition of the poetic genius and artistic talents of the author. For, to state a simple fact the author uses poetic language abounding in figures and hyperbole while describing Agastya (cf. XIX.13-15). When we go through this work, we are reminded of Homeric similes and the linguistic elegance and charm of Vālmīki, Vyāsa, Bhāsa and Kālidāsa. Whatever subject the author takes up for delineation, whether it is eclipse, planetary movements, rainfall, clouds, gemology, architecture, water-divination or some other topic, it is discussed with thoroughness and mastery based on the knowledge of ancient Śāstras.

Varāha had several predecessors in the field of *Saṁhitā*, whom he mentions by name, viz., Garga, Parāśara, Kāśyapa, Ṛṣiputra, Devala, Bṛhaspati, Nandīśvara, etc. He mentions both Vṛddha Garga and Garga. He shows great regard for ancient sages. In every chapter he invariably mentions the authorities on the topic to be discussed.[1] Whenever he differs from their views, he gives his

1. Cf. XXI. 2; XXXII. 1; XLVI. 1.

own reasons for it.[1] His knowledge is really encyclopaedic. For like the Mahābhārata there is no subject that he has not discussed in his *magnum opus*. The subjects may broadly be classified under the following heads : (1) Astronomy, (2) Geography, (3) Calendar, (4) Meteorology, (5) Flora, (6) Portents, (7) Agriculture and Economics, (8) Politics, (9) Physiognomy, (10) Engineering, (11) Botany, (12) Industries, (13) Zoology, (14) Erotics, (15) Gemology, (16) Hygiene, (17) Augurus and (18) Stellar lore. In the first section which consists of eleven chapters from III to XIII and XVII and XVIII the author describes the movements of planets both from the astronomical and astrological points of view. He mentions Pūrva Śāstra, Eke, Tajjñāḥ, Bahūnāṁ mataṁ which Utpala interprets as the works of Vṛddha Garga, Garga, Parāśara, Kāśyapa, Kaśyapa, Devala, Nandin, Ṛṣiputra, etc. In XI.1 he refers to Garga and others as the authority for Ketu's transit. This section has many an excellent poetical piece in the descriptions of Sage Agastya, autumn and the Seven Sages.[2]

In the second section he discusses the allotment of countries to the nine regions on the basis of constellations. Similarly different animate and inanimate objects are assigned to the jurisdiction of the asterisms, and countries, peoples, etc. to the domain of planets.[3]

In the third section he treats of the effects of years, months and days presided over by the different planets.[4]

In the next section subjects like cloud-formation, winds, rainfall, etc. are expounded.[5]

In the fifth section flowers and creepers are discussed.[6] The Sixth section deals with portents like earthquakes, glow at the horizon, meteors, halos, etc.[7] The next group treats of the growth of crops, commodities, prices and trade.[8] In the eighth section are explained rituals for the improvement of royal powers.[9] The ninth one explains signs of men and women.[10] The tenth one deals with architecture,

1. III. 1, 2.
2. See IV 1, 2, 30; XII. 8-12; XIII. 1, 2.
3. See XIV-XVI.
4. See XIX.
5. See XXI-XXVIII.
6. See XXIX.
7. See XXX-XXXIX.
8. XL-XLII.
9. See XLIII-XLIV, XLVIII-L.
10. See LXVIII-LXX.

sculpture, town-planning, water-divination, etc.[1] The next section treats of treatment of trees.[2] The twelfth one expounds the manufacture of cements, perfumes, etc.[3] The next one is connected with the description of various animals, cows, dogs, etc.[4] The next section relates to domestic felicity, erotic remedies, etc.[5] The fifteenth section describes gems and their values.[6] The next topic dealt with is the cleaning of teeth.[7] The seventeenth section delineates in detail various kinds of omens through birds and beasts.[8] The last section is devoted to the functions of asterisms, lunar days, etc.[9]

Our author is *Samāsoktipriya* (fond of brevity) and *Mahāgranthabhīru* (afraid of too much elaboration), according to his worthy commentator. He himself says in B.J. I.2, 'Svalpaṁ vṛttavicitram arthabahulaṁ;' 'Nātilaghuvipularacanābhiḥ' B.S.I.2; 'Samāsato mamotsāhaḥ,' Sārabhūtam, 'Svalpagranthena' XXIV. 3, 'Samāsataḥ' LXIX. 40. In XLVII he calls himself 'Samāsakṛt' and adds that he should not be accused of prolixity, but he cannot help it as *Mayūracitraka* is a necessary limb of the Saṁhitā. As he began so does he close the work with a prayer to the Sun-God, etc.[10] Rightly does he say that he has extracted the Science-Moon (Saṁhitā) from the ocean of astrological Science (CVI. 1). Being an advocate of correct and scientific method, he condemns bad astrologers.[11] He states that the 'gold of poetry becomes brilliant being heated by the fire of bad critics.' His humility is shown in CV. 5 in his appeal to scholars. He praises astrology and good astrologers whole-heartedly and asks kings to employ good astrologers for their own benefit.[12]

Varāhamihira expresses his indebtedness to ancient Sages, viz., Kapila, Kaṇabhuj, Auśanasa, Viṣṇugupta, Pūrvaśāstra, Garga, Vṛddhagarga, Parāśara, Asita, Devala, Siddhānta, Sūryasiddhānta, Munis, Kāśyapa, Vajra, Maya, Ācāryas, Āgama, Atri, Bhāguri, Baladeva, Manu, Sārasvata, Sāvitra, Bṛhadratha, Pūrvācārya, Śakra,

1. See LIII-LX.
2. See LV.
3. See LVII, LXXVII.
4. See LXI-LXVII.
5. LXXIV-LXXVI, LXXVIII.
6. LXXX-LXXXIII.
7. LXXXV.
8. LXXXVI-XCVII.
9. XCVIII-CII, CIV, CV.
10. See CVI. 6.
11. See II. 1, 2, 15-18, CVI. 4.
12. See II. 8, 11-14, 19, 20.

Śukra, Vāgīśa (Guru), Vasiṣṭha, Kapiṣṭhala, Garutmat, Ṛṣabha, Bhāradvāja, Viśvakarman, Nārada, Nagnajit, King Dravyavardhana, Saptarṣimata and Yātrākāras. His store of knowledge is very vast, having studied all works on the subject both in Sanskrit and Prakrit.

He has followed closely the Saṁhitās of ancient Sages like that of Vṛddha Garga. The *Vṛddhagargīya* contains practically the same topics with an additional chapter entitled *Yugapurāṇa*. Varāha's respect for a good astrologer is commendable. For, according to him, a country that does not possess a good astrologer is doomed. A good astrologer must be an all-rounder : He must know everything connected with the three Skandhas, astronomy, horoscopy and Śākhā or Saṁhitā. The last one like the Mahābhārata should treat of every subject under the sun.

This work holds the mirror to the social conditions and the cultural height attained by India in the author's time. Most of the arts and crafts were practised and encouraged by the rulers and the ruled. For example, architecture, sculpture, iconography, manufacture of cements, perfumes, cosmetics, medicines, umbrellas, ornaments, etc., construction of chariots, cots, etc. were practised with consummate skill. Metallurgy, weaving, painting, music, dancing, acrobatics, leather work, calligraphy, book making, etc. had reached a high standard of perfection. People used to hold cock fights for the delight of all. Rich people used to tend in their houses fishes, tortoises, etc. The practice of *Sutee* was in vogue. People knew veterinary science, botany (Vṛkṣāyurveda), movements of birds and beasts, water-divination, weather conditions and good and bad auguries. People were generally highly cultured and enjoyed good life. This is borne out by 'Praise of Women,' 'Erotic Remedies,' etc.

In mundane astrology, eclipses play an important role. The author refers to the ancient view about eclipses, and dismisses it as unscientific. We understand that Mercury has a major say in the matter of price-fluctuation. This work appears to be meant for the benefit of kings. For, Agastyacāra, Indradhvaja, Puṣyasnāna, etc. are specially meant for them. They are also advised to perform worship on these occasions In ancient times kings had human observatories. Without meticulous care and keen observation, how could they find out if Jupiter became visible at daytime or at night (VIII. 18).

Geographical details of Varāha do not depart much from those of his predecessors. He follows Vṛddha Garga in this field. Geographical details are met with even in Vedic literature: The *Śatapatha Brāhmaṇa* states that the land known as *Kuru-Pāñcālas* was the home and centre of Brahminical culture. It speaks of the *Madhyadeśa*, *Kosala*, *Videha*, *Kāśi*, *Gāndhāras*, *Śālvas* and *Kekayas*. The *Kuru-Pāñcāla* country was comprised of *Kosala*, *Videhas*, *Śivaknas*, and *Sṛñjayas*. The *Aitareya Brāhmaṇa* speaks of the *Kuru-Pāñcāla* country as comprising the *Vaśas* and *Uśinaras*. To the south of this *Middle Country* lay the *Sātvatas*; to the east, the *Prācyas* i.e. *Kāśi*, *Kosala*, *Videha*, and *Magadha*; to the west, the *Nīcyas* and *Apācyas*; and to the north, the Himalayas, beyond which the *Uttarakurus* and *Uttaramadras* (Oldenberg). According to Oldenberg the testimony of the *Ṛgveda* shows the *Bharatas* as the rulers of the regions around the *Sarasvatī* and *Dṛṣadvatī*.

In chapter IV the author mentions a number of kingdoms and peoples : *Pāṇḍyas*, *Pratyantas*, *Magadha*, *Yavanas*, *Pulindas*, *Nepāla*, *Bhṛṅgi*, *Maru*, *Kaccha*, *Surāṣṭra*, *Madra*, *Pāñcāla*, *Kekaya*, *Kulūta*, *Pūruṣāda*, *Uśinaras*, *Gāndhāra*, *Sauvīras*, *Sindhu*, *Kiras*, *Draviḍa*, *Trigarta*, *Mālava*, *Kulinda*, *Śibi*, *Ayodhyā*, *Kaurava*, *Matsya*, *Śukti*, *Yaudheyas*, *Prācyas*, *Arjunāyanas*, *Mathurā* and banks of the *Veṇā*, these being assigned to different quarters. Parāśara, however, assigns *Draviḍas* to the east.

Meteorology is an important and interesting topic discussed in this work. What is the purpose of this branch of Science? It is to subserve production of more food for all living beings. Let us remember here the grand Vedic dictum, "अन्नं ब्रह्मेति व्यजानात्," and the words of the *Bhagavadgitā*, "पर्जन्यादन्नसम्भवः." Our author too says rightly, "अन्नं जगतः प्राणाः" (XXI. 1). Modern man, in spite of his remarkable scientific and technological advancement, must be alive to the truth of this statement of our author, when the world is threatened with over-population and natural calamities. *Meteorology* was practised in the times of Garga, Parāśara, Kāśyapa, Vajra and Siddhasena. The author's statement (XXI. 3) to the effect that the words of an observant astrologer will never fail regarding rainfall is highly significant in this context. Observation of the symptoms of *pregnancy of clouds* should be made when the Moon passes through the lunar mansion *Pūrvāṣāḍhā*, from the first day of the light half of *Mārgaśirṣa*. One could expect good rains on the 195th day after the cloud-formation. The symptoms too have been stated in unequivocal terms in XXI. 14-24. It is interesting to note that the ancients had devised methods to gauge rainfall.[1] There are two other methods known as the *Flag-method* and the *Seed-method* for finding out the direc-

1. See XXIII. 2.

tion of the wind and crop prospects.[1] These experiments are done during the Moon's conjunction with *Rohiṇī* in the dark fortnight of the lunar month of *Āṣāḍha*, as well as with *Uttarāṣāḍhā* and *Svāti* in the bright fortnight. It is well known that planetary movements causing certain configurations in the heavens influence the weather and behaviour and health of living beings on earth. In this connection the author enumerates several colours, while describing the Sun's rays and dust. The following are the names of colours : (1) *Śukla* (White), (2) *Kalmāṣa* (Greyish), (3) *Babhru* (Tawny), (4) *Kapila* (Russet), (5) *Vicitra* (Variegated), (6) *Māñjiṣṭha* (Red), (7) *Harita* (Green), (8) *Śabala* (Spotted), (9) *Pita* (Yellow), (10) *Tāmra* (Coppery), (11) *Aruṇa* (Rosy), (12) *Dhūmra* (Smoky), (13) *Bhasma-sadṛśa* (Ash-coloured), (14) *Bandhūka* (Deep Red), and (15) *Kajjala-* (Collyrium-like or jet black).

The author's close acquaintance with Political Science (which is part and parcel of Arthaśāstra) is proved by his able exposition of logistics and rules of warfare.[2] In this connection we may remember the exposition of political principles by poets like *Kālidāsa*, *Bhāravi* and *Māgha*. In respect of *Ulkā* (meteors) he follows closely *Kāśyapa* and *Garga*[3]. It is not clear who this *Bādarāyaṇa* occurring in XL is, as he uses the *Āryā* metre in connection with *Sasyajātaka*. Chapters XL and the next are interrelated, as they deal with crops and prices. It is also interesting that eclipses have a large say in the matter of crops and prices.[4] Chapter XLI is very useful for astrologers and researchers in determining the prices of commodities and growth of crops, from the relative positions of planets to the respective signs. Prices are to be determined from eclipses and other factors at *Saṁkrāntis*.[5] Good tips are given here to traders for getting maximum profit.

In political theme (XLVI) portents play an important role. So kings are advised to perform propitiatory rites to ward off their evil consequences. In this context, the author aptly remarks : "The king is the very tap root of the tree of subjects (nation)." He also gives the definition of a bad king (in verse 76) : "He is one who encourages heretics and atheists, is himself not of righteous conduct, cruel, etc." Verses 97-99 are very significant in that the author attaches great

1. See XXIV. 9, 11, 26; XXVI. 10.
2. Vide XXXIV.
3. „ XXXIII.
4. „ V. 24.
5. Vide XL. 11.

importance to stray utterances of mad caps, etc. and says, "सत्या ह्येषा सरस्वती." He answers the question as to why portents appear, thus : "Sins accumulated by men through wrongful actions bear fruit, which is fore-shadowed by these portents. Dissatisfied with the conduct of men, Gods create these portents. Hence the necessity for propitiation." He mentions three kinds of portents, viz., *Celestial, Atmospheric* and *Terrestrial.* The main authority for this is an ancient sage called *Ṛṣiputra.* In L. 9 the author pronounces an important principle connected with human physiognomy, while speaking of symptoms of Swords, "वनितानामिव तिलको गुह्ये वाच्यो मुखे दृष्ट्वा." Like a *Dharma Śāstra* this Saṁhitā lays down rules of conduct for youngsters : They ought not to sleep with their feet against the head-side of elders etc. For, it would produce disastrous consequences. The chapters bearing on *Architecture* and *Water-Divination* are long and exhaustive so much so that they have been treated as independent works by later writers. In the latter as well as in LXXVI on *Erotic Remedies* he exhibits his wonderful mastery of botany and medical Science as well as *Kāmaśāstra.* On *architecture* his authorities are *Maya* and *Viśvakarman,* but chiefly *Garga, Manu,* etc. In LVI he mentions 20 types of temples. He gives good tips for selecting sites for temples, because Gods dwell with delight in places where there are gardens, plenty of water, lakes with swans, etc. This shows that religion or spirituality and geography are closely related. That is the reason why sages resort to the Himalayan caves for penance. They say that the Himalayan atmosphere is surcharged with spiritual vibrations.

The different types of houses mentioned (in LIII) for different classes of officials correspond to modern classification government quarters in Delhi. One drawback in this section is that the author does not speak of preparing the site and laying the foundation with its five parts. According to him the site is to be tested by one's inclination (*Manorati*), *Flower-test, Water-test, Wick-test,* etc. Here and elsewhere we come across a number of technical terms such as शाखा, उदुम्बर, रज्जु, शिरा, पाली, चय, कोश, कटि, गर्भ पिण्डिका, अण्ड, कपोतपालि, नीवि, चन्द्रशाला, करवीरक, अधिवासन, प्रोथ, प्रपाण, पेचक, रन्ध्र, उपरन्ध्र, वेध, बोध, विष्कम्भ, कुक्ष्य, कुक्षा, कुकुन्दरा, ईषा, शीर्षणी, काच्छिक, डोम्बा, डोम, उल्लेपिका, पाशान्त, तर्कुक, व्यायाम (for व्याम), सुकुमारक, मणि, अलुप, etc.

He speaks of three kinds of soil, viz., *Jaṅgala, Anūpa* and *Maru.* Water is predicted with reference to certain trees and anthills. Underground symptoms are also mentioned. In *Maru* the maximum depth of a water vein is 75 *Puruṣas* and the minimum 5 *Puruṣas,* whereas elsewhere they are 7½ P. and 1½ P. respectively. In LIV *Sārasvata's* treatment is more detailed, while *Manu's* is general. The latter alludes to conditions for different tastes of water. The author names nine varieties of water veins. It is regrettable that we have no means of knowing about *Sārasvata's* work except through Utpala's quotations. *Manu* speaks of types of stones that have water underneath. It is interesting that this sage gives recipes for breaking hard stones,[1] and sage *Uśanas* for making swords unbreakable.[2]

While speaking of tank construction our author states[3] that tanks should have long sides on the east and west. He gives a recipe[4] for purifying well-water. For rain-water *Varāha's* authority is *Baladeva*, but Utpala does not quote him. On the other hand, he quotes from the works of *Ṛṣiputra*, *Garga*, *Devala* and *Kāśyapa*. So we are in the dark about the work of *Baladeva*, which was available to the author.

It is felt that Chapters LVI to LX should have been arranged after LIII, but the author gives the reason for the change in LVI. 1. According to *Maya* and *Viśvakarman* the height of a temple-storey should be 108 and 84 digits respectively. *Maya* is the authority mentioned by our author for his treatment of adamantine glue.[5] In LVIII we are given units of lineal measurements: *Paramāṇu* (Atom), *Rajas* (Dust-particle), *Vālāgra* (Tip of hair), a Nit, Louse, Barley, and digit, each following measure being eight times the previous one. *Nagnajit* seems to have written on *Drāviḍa* architecture and sculpture. There was also a system of measurement known as *Drāviḍamāna*. But this science was prevalent in the south long before *Nagnajit*. It is not known whether he was a *Digambara Jaina* or one who had conquered them. Sage *Vasiṣṭha* wrote on sculpture[6]. Varāha describes in detail all the limbs of an idol from head to foot with their measurements. The description of *Śrīmahāviṣṇu* is very entrancing and reads like *Dhyānaślokas*[7]. In the list of Gods and Goddesses described here there is no mention of *Sarasvatī*, *Kālī* or the Planets. There are some common features between Chapters XLIII and LIX in respect of trees.

1. Vide LIV. 112-115.
2. „ L. 25, 26.
3. „ LV.
4. „ LIV. 121, 122.
5. „ LVII.
6. „ LVIII. 8, 15.
7. „ LVIII. 31-35.

The ceremony of consecration and installation of idols[1] is very interesting and significant in that it has great esoteric meaning. The Deity is treated like a new-born child or a king in respect of sleep, food, clothing, etc.[2] In Verse 19 Varāha states that the *Magas* are the accredited priests for installing the Sun's images.

Physiognomy and *Palmistry* are treated of in three chapters, LXVIII-LXX. In the first he speaks of thirteen elements in the case of men for predicting their past and future. The knower of this Science is called *Sāmudravid.* This lore is known as *Sāmudrika Śāstra.* It is held by some that *Samudra* means Lord Viṣṇu, while by others, Śiva. It may also be the name of a class of writers on this subject. It is the name of a work quoted by *Padmanābha. Varāha* does not mention any particular authority here except 'मुनिमतानि निरीक्ष्य.' Even sage Garga refers to *Samudra*[3] (LXVIII). Monier Williams mentions some later works like the *Sāmudratilaka* of *Durlabharāja*; *Sāmudrikakaṇṭhābharaṇa* and *Sāmudrikacandrikā*. The *Vīramitrodaya* of *Mitramiśra* (of about the 14th century A.D.) mentions the signs of men and women (*Puruṣalakṣaṇa* and *Strīlakṣaṇa*) among a variety of subjects included in this *Saṁhitā*. It quotes several works like the जगन्मोहन, समुद्र, विवेकविलास, स्कान्द, भविष्यपुराण, प्रयोगपारिजात, गरुड़पुराण, नारदीयसंहिता, गर्गसंहिता and हेमाद्रि. According to this work too the *Gargasaṁhitā* quotes *Samudra* on *Anūka* (heredity and previous life). *Garga* is quoted in this work in respect of *Mṛjā* or lustre. According to the *Bhaviṣyapurāṇa* thick and large thumbs indicate lack of luck. Garga, on the other hand, has given unusual importance to the eyes: एकतो दुर्लक्षणशतं सौम्यं चक्षुस्तथैकतः । दुर्लक्षणशतं हन्यान्नरः सौम्येन चक्षुषा ।। तस्मान्नेत्रे . . . पश्येत्कालवित् ।।"

According to *Prahlāda* the lines on the body constitute the *Mudrās* imprinted by Īśvara. Hence the body becomes *Samudra* or *Samudraka.* So this science is termed *Sāmudrika.* This Chapter (LXVIII) has many ideas that are common to the *Vālmīki Rāmāyaṇa.* This has been shown in appropriate places in the notes. *Halāyudha* must have written a work on *Sāmudrikaśāstra.* For, in his commentary on the *Piṅgala Chandaśśāstra* there are given a large number of illustrative verses bearing on this interesting subject. Verses 89 and 116 are excellent both as poetry and as portraits of truth. The latter giving four constituents of real happiness, viz., food, drink, conveyance and

1. Vide LX.
2. Interested readers may read an article on this subject in the *Ananta Vibhava* Souvenir, April, 1976, by us.
3. Vide LXVIII. 95.

protection when needed, is reminiscent of a *Subhāṣita*, viz.,"षड्जीवलोकस्य सुखानि राजन्." In LXX.23 there is a famous *Subhāṣita* or *Arthāntaranyāsa* which is reminiscent of Kālidāsa's famous line "यदुच्यते पार्वति पापवृत्तये न रूपमित्यव्यभिचारि तद्वचः" as well as Śūdraka's remark, "न ह्याकृतिः सु (स्व) सदृशं विजहाति वृत्तम्"॥[1] : This chapter contains many repetitions of ideas already explained in LXVIII.[2]

We find excellent erotic poetry and *Śṛṅgāra* in LXXIV with superb imagery, like *Sāra*, *Vyatireka*, *Kāvyaliṅga*, *Upamā* and *Arthāntaranyāsa*. *Manu's* testimonial for women's superiority in nine verses is highly dignified and unique in world literature. The simile in the last verse is very telling and full of humour—"Thieves, when caught red-handed, cry 'thieves, thieves." *Manu* opines that by and large, women have greater self-control than men. Verse 16 shows that Varāhạ honours the *Suttee* custom. "The quintessence of kingdom consists in dainty food and damsels" is a fine general statement. Verses 18 and 19 are still more erotic in nature: "Even in the world of Brahman one cannot hope to get the joy that is experienced by embracing a loving damsel." In LXXV our author makes a statement which deserves to be tested by psycho-analysts and those engaged in researches on genetics. For, he says that a woman gives birth to a child that will resemble wholly the man whom she thinks of at the time of sexual congress. In verse 3 he states some of the Upaniṣadic principles regarding the experience of sensual objects by the Soul. There are also some excellent poetic pieces as well as some nice pieces of advice for daily life. LXXVI tenders very good advice to newly married young men about food and what they should avoid. Verse 12 is also important from the point of personal hygiene. This proves the author's deep knowledge of medical science.

Chapter LXXVII apart from showing the author's mathematical genius, gives us a peep into the high level of civilization of the people of his times. For, wealthy people used to manufacture luxury materials such as hair-dyes, hair-oils, scents, cosmetic powders, incenses, bathing powders, *Sarvatobhadra* scents, *Pārijāta*, *Kesaragandha*, etc., powders for perfuming the mouth, tooth-powder, tooth-sticks, etc. Verses 35-37 describe the advantages of betel-chewing and method of using its constituents. The words *Turuṣka* and *Yāvana* throw light on the ancient trade relations that our country had with the west.

---

1 Vide *Mṛcchakaṭika*. IX. 16.

2. The chapters on *Cāmara* and *Chatra* could have been incorporated by the side of those on *Khaḍga*, *Paṭṭa*, etc.

Probably the Turks and Greeks were expert manufacturers of perfumes. The instances of feminine treachery mentioned in LXXVII, 1, 2, are repeated in Sanskrit literature like *Bāṇa's Harṣacarita.* There are some very good indications of conjugal harmony mentioned in verses 4-6, and of disharmony in verse 8. He advises people to guard women against certain classes of persons and occasions. He states that virtuous women are called gems. He does not hesitate in condemning bad women. This too proves conclusively the author's thorough grasp of the essence of *Kāmaśāstra.* He advises people with what type of women they should have sexual relations.[1]

In ancient India handicrafts were encouraged by kings and the aristocracy. Various kinds of cots were made for different classes of high officials. 'A cot made of sandalwood and covered with gold and decked with gems is envied even by Gods.' The decorations are generally done with ivory.[2] He speaks of *Karmāṅgula* (practical digit) in this connection, which is the distance of eight husked barley grains (verse 8).

Gemology is another important topic discussed in LXXX. He mentions in all 22 gems and describes the qualities and varieties of diamonds (verses 4, 5). In verses 12, 13 he enumerates units of weights of gems and their corresponding values. Here the weight of 8 white mustard seeds is considered as equal to one rice grain. The price of a diamond weighing 20 *Taṇḍulas* (rice grains) is said to be two lakh *Kārṣāpaṇas.*[3] In LXXXII. 6-11 he praises an excellent ruby and mentions its prices according to weight. He states here that the prices he has mentioned are based on the standards prescribed by *Pūrvācāryas.* In the previous chapter pearls are described. He says that best pearls are got from eight places headed by *Siṁhalaka.* These pearls differ from one another in shape and shade. They are also presided over by different Deities headed by Viṣṇu, on the basis of their colours. Their prices are given in Karṣas silver on the basis of weights in *Māṣakas.* Here the units of weights are *Kṛṣṇala* (Retti), *Māṣaka, Dharaṇa, Suvarṇa* and *Pala.* He speaks of 18 types of *Pearl-necklaces.* This is another proof of the high water-mark of workmanship attained by the artisans of those days.[4]

In LXXXV we find principles of public health and sanitation highlighted following Ayurvedic injunctions.

---

1. Vide LXXVIII. 16-18.
2. „ LXXIX. 19.
3. 80 silver coins make one *Paṇa* and 20 *Paṇas* one *Kārṣāpaṇa.*
4. For different binds of ornaments see XLIII. 41-49.

Chapters LXXXVI to XCVI form one vast section dealing with omens and auguries. The author mentions several authorities for this subject. A king of *Avantī* named *Śrīdravyavardhana* is also said to have written on this subject. Unlike portents which always bode ill these auguries presage both prosperity and adversity for those going on a journey, as a result of their good and bad deeds of a previous existence. Unless the ancients had been keen observers of the heavens, how could they have stated the several conditions of planetary warfare, *Tāmasakīlakas* (comet), eclipses, etc. ? Similarly, they observed carefully the psychological behaviour of birds and beasts as well as those caused by environments such as the seasons. This is borne out by the delineation of the multitudinous omens. This reminds us of Kālidāsa's statement, "सत्त्वानामपि लक्ष्यते विकृतिमच्चित्तं भयक्रोधयोः:." Hence these omens are an instance of the psychological study of animals and of their impact on human behaviour. Even trees and creepers are supposed to presage coming events. It is to be remembered that there are hundreds of references to auguries and portents in the *Rāmāyaṇa* and the *Mahābhārata*. It is claimed that even in the Vedas there are such references. *Pāṇini* refers to them in many places.[1] The ancients observed minutely the nest-building activity of crows in particular months in order to predict future prospects for the country. Prediction of rain and pests is made on the basis of these nests.

The author gives in this connection a useful list of synonyms of birds and beasts.[2]

During our author's time, it is presumed, women were practising astrology and sooth-saying. They were called *Īkṣaṇikās*.

We can make a fair surmise about the commencement of seasons during the author's time. According to him the year began with Śiśira (cold season).[3] But Garga opines that it begins with *Vasanta*, the spring. Among the months, the pride of place is given to *Kārttika* by the author, because of the importance of *Kṛttikā* from early times. According to *Suśruta* the months begin with *Māgha* and the *Ṛtus* (seasons) with *Śiśira*.

Among the Chapters CIV assumes special importance on account of its being a mini text book on prosody, though it treats of the effects of planetary transits. The author utilizes this opportunity to teach prosody to posterity. It is believed that he wrote a

---

1. Vide I. 4-39; III. 2-53; IV. 3-73, etc.
2. „ LXXXVIII. 4-9.
3. „ XXX. 22.

book on metrics. He studied the works of Piṅgala and other writers on the subject in Sanskrit and *Prākṛta.* He says that he has made a neat summary of metrics in a pleasing manner. He expounds sixtyfour metres in this chapter.

Though the whole work abounds in principles of *Dharmaśāstra,* scattered here and there, the Chapter CV dealing with rituals is specially connected with that Śāstra.

Varāhamihira as a poet

It is doubtless that Varāhamihira ranks among the greatest poets of Sanskrit literature. He seems to be a great admirer of *Kālidāsa* who is designated as the *Vilāsa* (grace) of the Muse of Poetry. We may be permitted to include our author in this list of honour as— "यस्याः प्रेमा मिहिरकुलजः श्रीवराहः प्रसन्नः"। It has been already pointed out that the great Kashmirian critic, Kṣemendra, holds him in high esteem. Though he (Varāha) is conscious of the fact that he is treating of scientific topics, yet the poet in him asserts himself and makes his work a work of art too, a piece of excellent poetry — a *Mahākāvya*—'which is a joy forever.' He is an adept in embellishing his statements with apt figures of speech. He is seen wielding mastery over the figures in the following instances :

1. *Alliteration* : XXIV. 1, 2, 18, 36; XXVI. 8; XXX. 6; XII, 1, 2, 7; XIX. 2, 4, 17, 18; XLIII. 7. 35, 38, 39; XLVII. 9; LXIV. 3; LXXI. 1-7; LXXVI. 6, 9; LXXVII. 36; LXXVIII. 2; LXXIV. 3; LXVIII. 37, 39, 43, 44, 47, 109; LXIX. 37; LXXIX. 27; LXXXI. 7, 21; LXXXII. 5; XCIV. 14; CI. 12.
2. *General Statement* (*Arthāntaranyāsa*). II. 2; LIII. 95; LXX. 23; LXXV. 1-4, LXXXVIII. 14.
3. *Kāvyaliṅga* : II. 24, 28, 29, 33; LXXIV. 2, 5; LXXV. 4.
4. *Dṛṣṭānta* : XLVII. 28.
5. *Sārālaṁkāra*: LXXIV. 1.
6. *Svabhāvokti* : XXVIII. 4, 5.
7. *Yathāsaṁkhya* : XLIII. 5.
8. *Pratīpa* : LXXIV. 2.
9. *Vyatireka* : II. 38, 40; LXXIV. 2.
10. *Utprekṣā* (*Fancy*) : II. 20; IV. 30; XII. 2, 11, 12; XIII. 1, 2; XIX. 14; XXI. 24; XXIV. 14; XLIV. 26; LXXIV. 5.
11. *Nidarśanā* : II. 15.
12. *Subhāṣitas* : LXVIII. 25, 116; LXXIV. 4; LXXIV. 5, 6, 8-10.

13. *Śleṣa* (*Pun*) : LVIII. 99; CIV. 1, 5-7, etc. 23, 39, 51, 58.[1]
14. *Samuccaya* : CIV. 1.
15. *Arthāpatti* : II. 25, 32; XII. 14; LXXI. 13; LXXIV. 20.
16. *Atiśayokti* : II. 17.
17. *Rūpaka* (*Metaphor*) : XII. 6; XLIII. 32; XLIV. 1; XLVIII. 1, 8-10; LVI. 4, 6, 7; CIV. 32; CVI. 1, 4.
18. *Punaruktavadābhāsa and Yamaka* : XII 3; XIX. 2, 5.
19. *Parikara* : XXIV. 1, 2; CV. 9-12.
20. *Viśeṣokti* : XII. 4.
21. *Upamā* (*Simile*) : II. 13, 26, 35; III. 36; V. 62; XI. 44, 62; XII. 5, 8, 10; XIX. 5, 16, 17; XXI. 23, 36; XXIV. 13-18, 22, 32, 33; XXVIII. 3, 4. 11, 14, 17; XXX. 18, 28, 29; XXXII. 17, 21; XEIII. 6, 33; XLIV. 23, 27; LIV. 1, 62, 107-110; LVIII. 36; LXX. 7; LXXIV. 15; LXXV. 2, 10; CIV. 4, 8, 11, 14, 17, 34,42, 51, 53, 56, 57, 59; CV. 9-12.

Varāha's Nature-description

The author's descriptions of nature, of the ocean, gardens, clouds, towns, mountains, forests, monsoon, autumn and the starry heavens, and of fish, frogs, horses, etc. of sage Agastya's feat, are both graphic and fascinating. We find in them sound echoing the sense, nay, both dancing, as it were, in unison.[2] It is also to be noted that like Kālidāsa, he makes *Nature* a vivacious damsel. He knows also how to get maximum effect by means of appropriate metres, containing alliteration. For example, in XXIV. 13 and 14 the *Puṣpitāgrā* metre heightens the grandeur of the theme in such a way that the reader feels as though he is about to be drenched by a heavy shower. Here the four elements, viz., description, jingling assonance, elegant diction and theme—all work in unison to produce maximum effect on the reader's mind. The following examples will illustrate the author's powers of description of nature.[3]

Erotic Sentiment is much in evidence in the description of the year presided over by Venus, of the rite for *Puṣyasnāna* and of erotic remedies.[4]

---

1. Practically every verse in this chapter has śleṣa which is a necessity.
2. Vide XII. 2-12; XIII. 1, 2; XXIV. 12-19.
3. „ IV. 30; XLIII. 6, 7, 25, 26; XLIV 23-26; XLVIII. 5-12, 14; LVI. 4-8.
4. „ XIX. 16, 18; XLVIII. 8, 10; LXXIV. 4, 17-19; LXXVI. 7.

Kālidāsa's influence is clearly discernible in the images, descriptions and language employed by Varāhamihira. In many places Vālmīki's phrases and ideas as well as analogies are re-echoed by the author. In our previous edition some examples of this were provided. In this edition, however, a larger number of parallelisms have been pointed out in the notes : Hereunder are given a few instances of striking parallelism :

(1) The descriptions of Śarat and clouds resemble those of Kālidāsa in the *Raghuvaṁśa* IV and the *Meghadūta* respectively.

(2) The description of clouds, "स्रवद्वारिदानै:" (XXIV. 18) is reminiscent of "स्रवन्मदवारिधारा: . . . सुखान्युपलेभिरे ते" (Raghu. XIII).

(3) "मनो हि मूलं . . ." (LXXVIII. 14) is very similar to Kālidāsa's "न कामवृत्तिर्वचनीयमीक्षते" and "मनोरथानामगतिर्न विद्यते" and to Vālmīki's "मनो हि हेतु: सर्वेषामिन्द्रियाणां प्रवर्तने" (V).

(4) "प्रलम्बबाहु: . . ." (CV. 9) reminds us of Kālidāsa's "युवा युगव्यायतबाहु . . ." (Raghu. III).

(5) "शरदमल . . ." (CV. 10-12) resembles Kālidāsa's "सर्वोपमाद्रव्य . . ." (कुमार I).

(6) "सरस्सु नलिनी . . ." (LVI. 4-7) is an echo of Vālmīki's "हंसकारण्डवाकीर्णा . . ." (V).

(7) "परदारद्वेषिण: . . . " (LXVIII. 25) is verily like" वशिनां तु परपरिग्रहसंश्लेष . . . " (शाकु०).

(8) "सर्वोपकारानुगतस्य . . ." (LXXV. 9) reminds us of " सर्वोपकारक्षममाश्रमं ते" (रघु० V).

(9) "विस्तीर्णं . . ." and "मध्यं स्त्रिया . . ." (LXX. 4, 5) are on a par with "एतावता नन्वनुमेयशोभि . . ." and "तस्या: प्रविष्टा नतनाभि . . ." (कुमार० I).

(10) "यत्राकृतिस्तत्र गुणा वसन्ति" (LXX. 23) and "प्राय: शरीराकारानुवर्त्तिनो. . ." (II. 2) echo "यदुच्यते पार्वति . . ." (कुमार० V).

(11) "देदीप्यमानं शरदीव सूर्यम्" (XLIII. 6) is similar to Vālmīki's "पोप्लूयमानं शरदीव हंसम्" (V).

(12) "उत्पतद्भिरिव खं . . . "(XLIV. 26) is analogous to "पश्योदग्रप्लुतत्वाद् . . ." (शाकु०) and also the description of the *Puṣpaka* in the *Sundarakāṇḍa* of the *Rāmāyaṇa*.

(13) "क्षमया क्रोध इव जित:" (XLVIII. 13) is an exact replica of Vālmīki's "य: समुत्पतितं क्रोधं क्षमयैव निरस्यति."

(14) "पुलिनजघनेषु . . ." (XLVIII. 8) echoes "या संकतोत्सङ्ग . . ." (Raghu. XIII).

(15) "पोप्लतहंसच्छत्रे . . ."(Do. 9) is like "पद्मा पद्मातपत्रेण. . "(Raghu. IV).

(16) "जलखगनखविक्षतेषु" (Do. 8) is similar in idea to "नखक्षतानीव वनस्थलीनाम्" (कुमार० III).

(17) "प्रोत्तुङ्गकुड्मलकुचाः" (Do. 10) resembles "आवर्जिता किञ्चिदिव स्तनाभ्यां . . . लतेव" (कुमार० III).

(18) "गुरुजघनोद्वहन . . ." (Do. 14) echoes "न दुर्वहश्रोणिपयोधरार्ता . . ." (कुमार० I).

(19) "स्त्री रत्नोज्ज्वला राज्यसुखस्य सार:" (LXXIV. 1) reminds us of Vālmīki's "त्रैलोक्यराज्यं सकलं सीताया नाप्नुयात्कलाम्."

(20) "नभः प्रसन्नं विमलानि भानि. . ." is similar to "प्रसन्नदिक् पांसुविविक्त. .." (कुमार० I).

His Language : Like *Kālidāsa* our author wields language with rare felicity as well as facility. His language is remarkable for its simplicity, lucidity, delightful diction and lilting alliteration. Though he takes poetic licence many a time in respect of grammatical construction, gender, etc., his style is distinguished by what are called *Drākṣāpāka, Prasāda, Mādhurya, Sukumāratā* and other poetic excellences. Where necessary he uses *Ojas* i.e. long compounds, also for effectiveness as in the description of Agastya (XII). *Ācārya Daṇḍin* praises Kālidāsa's 'प्रसादसुभगं वचः'. We can say, likewise, that the description of the Seven Sages (Pleids) is noteworthy for its pleasant, simple diction and enrapturing imagery. We can cite as examples the verses describing the sky (XXXI. 5), house (LIV. 125), man's physiognomy (LXVIII. 1, 89, 91), woman's superiority (LXXIV. 3, 5, 17), erotic remedies (LXXVI. 2) and the effects of Mercury's transit (CIV. 22). The descriptions of Gods like Viṣṇu contain the excellence called *Udāratā*. Of course the work is replete with *Samādhi* in the descriptions of nature and seasons.

Rare Expressions : Varāha uses some rare expressions invariably following the ancient Sages ; हादिः, अन्तिः, ईक्षणीक (for ईक्षणिका), भिक्षुणिका (Sanskritized form of the Pāli word), वणिजकाः. 'नद्यः पयो न स्रवन्ति' (XIX. 1), अध्वानरुचिः (LXVIII. 80), जिघ्रण and मानयितुः (XCV. 61). The word मानयिता is generally used in the sense of 'one who honours'; but the author uses it in the sense of 'one who believes or has faith'. In Hindi it is still used in that sense. So we can infer that Varāha uses it in its correct sense, which might have undergone a change over the centuries. The expression 'प्रियं चान्नम्' (XXXIV. 14) meaning 'scarce and costly' is still used in some parts of India like *Karṇāṭaka* in that sense. The word डोम्ब meaning *acrobat* must be very old, possibly designating a class of people. It is still used in the South in the same sense in the compound डोम्बराट (play of acrobats). Another peculiarity of his language is that he resorts to *Anuvṛtti*, as in grammar. For example, in XXI. 8 the subject, *Garbhāḥ*, is to be borrowed from the previous verse. There are many expressions like "धात्री वश्यं सागरान्ताऽभ्युपैति" (LXXXVIII. 18) that are rather strange. So is the one in "आखण्डलायां दिशि" (XXXV. 7). This shows that the author is carried away by his zeal for delineating the theme, and forgets the grammatical niceties. There are many other violations of Pāṇinian rules such as in प्रज्वालयित्वा and स्थाप्य, which are out of place in this appreciation of the master's genius. Many a time the author had to disregard grammatical rules for the sake of metre.

His Scholarship : His mastery over various Śāstras becomes apparent when we go through this vast *Book of Knowledge*. Let us first of all consider his scholarship of grammar, which again confirms our conclusion that he had to discard grammatical norms only under poetic licence. He uses the following scholarly expressions :

(i) *Desideratives*—पिप्रीषया, सञ्चिक्षिप्सुः, दित्सन्ति, युयुत्सतः (for युयुत्समानस्य), बिभक्षयिषुः, जुगुप्समानाः.

(ii) *Frequentatives* : पोप्लूयन्ते, पेपीयते, जेगीयते, बोभुज्यते, रोरूयते, बम्भ्रमीति, पापठद्भिः, देदीप्यमानम्, बोभुजीति, नरिर्नति (for नरीनर्ति).

(iii) *Taddhitāntas* (*with secondary suffixes*) : प्रास्थानिकम् शार्व्याम्, तान्तवम्, ज्यैष्ठी, ग्रोपयिकम् वैयाघ्रे, पार्वतीयाः (for पर्वतीयाः), ग्रौदीच्याः (for उदीच्याः), शाकुनी (for शाकुनिकः), कौप्यैः (for कौपैः).

(iv) *Nāma-dhātus* (*Nominal Verbs*): पुरीषणे, धूमायन् (for धूमायमानः).

(v) *Compounds* : अध्यक्षरम्.

His mastery over medical science, mathematics, *Dharmaśāstra*, music, veterinary science, architecture, sculpture, perfumeries, iconography, metallurgy, erotics, etc. has already been pointed out.

Metrics : This is another important branch of studies where he evinces exceptional originality and mastery. This is evidenced by his remark in the Bṛhajjātaka, viz., वृत्तविचित्रम् (I.2). His employment of metres is judicious and free from artificiality. His choice metres add charm to the subject matter under discussion. Chapter CIV on planetary transits is especially utilized by the author to teach *Prosody Without Tears* to his pupils (श्रुतिसुखदवृत्तसङ्ग्रह). His verses are more charming like जघनचपला (courtesan). He introduces through pun the names of metres employed in the verses. It is to be remembered that the basic metre adopted by the author in this work is the common variety of Āryā. Identification of metres has invariably been done in the notes under the verses of other chapters as well. According to the author even great Śāstras of yore suffer for want of a good metrical form, because they appear unattractive.[1] मणिगुण-निकर:" is an example of fine poetry.[2] In this chapter alone he employs seven varieties of the *Āryā* and 52 other metres. He has used three kinds of *Daṇḍakas*. In this connection we can remember that *Piṅgala* mentions *Rātamāṇḍavya* (or *Rāta* and *Māṇḍavya* ?) as a writer on prosody; and Varāha names Māṇḍavya. It is possible that *Rāta* and *Māṇḍavya* refer to one and the same writer; but according to Utpala they are two persons as Rātamāṇḍavya and Māṇḍavya. Another feature of this section is that he gives the definition of some of the metres. For example, in verses 50 and 51 he gives the rules for *Upagīti* and *Āryā*; in 57 for Śloka and in 58 for treating the last short syllable in a foot as long.

Our author uses many metres which are not found in any work on prosody. The two verses, viz., 5 and 13, of XLVII have not been named, though they come under the *Paṅkti* group. He resorts also to grafting of one metre on another and thereby creates a new metre : Verse 14 of XLVII has been effected by combining one foot of the *Rathoddhatā* (of eleven syllables) and the other of *Priyaṁvadā* (of twelve syllables). This has resulted in the creation of a new *Ardhasama* metre. In LXXXV. 6 he combines one of *Vātormi* with another of *Śālinī*; in LXXXVIII verses 19, 21 and 27 are in *Bhadravirāṭ* minus the last long syllable; verse 26 of XLVII is of a nameless metre, but it is a variety of *Upasthitā* where instead of the penultimate long syllable there is a short one; in XXXIII. 29 the metre cannot be identified; verse 31 of LXXXVIII is an amalgam of *Samānikā* and *Pramāṇikā*; verse 12 of LXIX is in an unidentified metre, but in a footnote of the *Piṅgalacchandas* the author of the note *Śrī kṛṣṇa* by name calls it *Snigdhā* metre; he uses *Prākṛta* metre in LXX. 18 and in another place. He gives entirely new names to certain metres : He gives a romantic name, *Vilāsinī*, to CIV. 32, which is found neither in *Piṅgala* nor in the *Vṛttaratnākara*. He calls the metre *Hariṇī* by the name *Vṛṣabhacarita* (CIV. 10). All these things suggest that Varāha had a more ancient source like *Māṇḍavya*, which must have been more thorough than either. In XIV. 6 (I half) out of 30 *mātrās* he has used 22 short syllables, thereby showing his mastery over metrics. In XXIV. 13, 14 he employs the *Puṣpitāgrā* metre with telling effect. He makes use of the *Āryāgīti* rarely as in XCV. 15, 33 and LVIII. 58. In a large number of instances

1. Vide CIV. 1.
2. „ 27.

he employs *Āryā* of the *Vipulā* type.[1] He uses longer metres for the purpose of description and condensing many ideas. The *Drutavilambita* in XXVIII. 11 is very happy and effective. His *Varṇaka Daṇḍaka* must needs be mentioned for its choice diction and charming assonance.

In Chapter II some parts of the prose passages are found to be metrical : "सांवत्सरोऽभिजातः"; "कुशलोऽव्यसनी शान्तिक . . ."; "व्रतोपवासनिरतः"; "ग्रहगणितसंहिताहो"; "पौलिशरोमकवासिष्ठसौरपैतामहेषु . . ." "सूर्याचन्द्रमसोश्च . . ."; "कक्ष्याप्रमाणप्रति . . ." "क्षेत्रकालकरणेषु"; "शास्त्रस्य वक्ता तन्त्रज्ञः" etc. In the above examples we can detect parts of *Āryā*, *Śloka*, *Daṇḍaka*, *Śārdūlavikrīḍita* etc. Similarly in some of the Āryā verses we can discover parts of the Śloka metre.[2]

No doubt, a few instances of metrical flaw have been detected in this work. Some of them may be ascribed to the carelessness of scribes; e.g. in XXXIV. 2 there is one *Mātrā* surperfluous in the second foot ending in "हरितशुक्लाः". The author must have written "हरिशुक्लाः". Varāha is aware of Piṅgala's rule regarding *Atihrasva* when a short syllable is followed by प्र or ह्र. The footnote under this[3] reads thus : "वस्तुतस्तु तत्र न गुरुत्वम्".

Varāha must have been acquainted with the works of ancient sages on prosody such as क्रोष्टुकि, यास्क, ताण्डि, सैतव, काश्यप, शत, माण्डव्य etc. who have been referred to by Piṅgala. Our author uses the word "छन्दोविचिति" in CIV. 64 like Daṇḍin. We cannot say definitely whether there was a popular work of that title before our author; or the science of metrics might have been popularly known as *Chandoviciti*.

The author's knowledge of the Vedas, sacrificial lore and propitiatory rites is stupendous. For, he summarizes, sometimes, some Mantras and at others, quotes their initial words : In XLIII. 55 he quotes the initial part of the Mantra, "त्रातारमिन्द्रमवितारमिन्द्र . . ." In LXXIV. 7 while quoting Manu's views with approval he exhibits his deep knowledge of both the Dharmaśāstra and Vedic Mantras such as "सोमः प्रथमो विविदे गन्धर्वो विविद उत्तरः . . ."[4] आपो हि ष्ठा. . .", "हिरण्यवर्णा . . .", "आयुष्यं वर्चस्यं . . ."[5] Similarly he demonstrates his close acquaintance

1. Vide *Vṛttaratnākara* II. 26.
2. Vide LXXXVII. 17, 21; XCV. 12, 21; LVIII. 45, 46, 48; LIV. 27, 91, 95; LX. 10; LXVIII. 61; LXIX. 1, 2; LXXVIII. 19; LXXIX. 22; VIII. 8.
3. Vide *Piṅgala* chandas page 5; and XXX. 9 for तनुह्रस्व.
4. ,, LXXIV. 7.
5. ,, XLVIII. 72, 74.

with the rule of *Dharma-Śāstra* regarding *Dārātikrama*[1] and with many sacrificial rites such as स्थालीपाक, "रुद्रेभ्यः···" षडेव होमाः, प्राजापत्यमन्त्र, "आ वायोः···" इति पञ्चर्चः, "देवाः कपोत···", "सुदेवा···", शाकुनसूक्त, "वा मनो···", अथर्वशिरः, महाशान्तयः, महारौहिण, कुबेरहृदय, समृद्धिऋक् and इष्टापूर्त ।[2]

His intimate acquaintance with the Āgama-śāstra is attested to by his scholarly treatment of iconography, installation of idols, temple architecture etc. He must have studied thoroughly all the six traditions of that *Śāstra*, of which the *Śaiva* and *Vaiṣṇava* schools stand out most prominently. It is interesting to note that there is close relationship between this Śāstra and the *Saṁhitā* literature in astrology. For, both of them treat of the subjects such as art, architecture, gemology, painting, sculpture, town-planning, gardening, etc., etc. We are able to infer that in his time there was a famous work on *Āgamaśāstra* entitled *Sāvitra*.[3]

We have already seen that the author was an expert in Āyurveda for human beings and trees. He mentions several recipes for health and long life. He evinces his close acquaintance with genetics and other subjects treated of in *Āyurveda*.[4] Chapter LXXVI is full of interesting recipes for the preparation of tonics and elixirs. In verse 11 he gives a very good prescription for digestive troubles. In the next verse he advises people to refrain from eating excessively sour, bitter, salt and pungent dishes. His advice regarding ghee[5] reminds us of the Vedic dictum, "आयुर्वै घृतम्." He explains how tanks should be constructed and what kind of trees planted on its banks, so that there may be pure water for drinking purpose.[6] As an intimate knowledge of herbs and trees is essential for a physician, the author shows his proficiency in that branch also.[7] His description of the preparation and benefits of tooth powder and chewing betel leaves would bear repetition.[8] His reference to Prāṇāyāma and the process of the soul's experiencing pleasure and pain confirms our belief in his acquaintance with *Pātañjala* Yogasūtras, *Sāṁkhya* and other systems of philosophy.[9]

---

1. Vide LXXIV. 13.
2. „ XLVIII. 71, LVI. 2.
3. „ LX. 22.
4. „ LXXVI. 1; LXXVIII. 23, 24, 26.
5. „ XLVIII. 52.
6. „ LIV.
7. „ XXIX. 2, XLVIII. 39-42; XLIII. 15; LIV; LV. 3, 4, 10, 11; LX. 8.
8. „ LXXVII. 31-33; 35-37.
9. „ XCV. 62; LXXV. 3.

The author shows his intimate knowledge of culinary art also, as he refers several times to sweets and other tasty edibles like मोदक, उल्लोपिका, पूप, शष्कुली, पायस, गुडाशन, त्रिमधुर, परमान्न, भक्ष्य, दधि etc.[1] His knowledge of ornithology is borne out by his detailed treatment of various species of birds in connection with auguries. In this connection we are tempted to refer again to the wholesome political tradition prevalent in ancient times, viz., at the end of the *Royal Ablution* the king should proclaim protection to the subjects, release animals from the hands of butchers and order a general amnesty to prisoners except those who endanger internal peace.[2]

Author's Temperament, Character etc. : Varāhamihira must have been a man of robust optimism, humanism, humour, jovial temperament and a high moral calibre. For, he says that men should not be thwarted by fate or dejected by his Karman whose effects are presaged by portents and evil omens, but he should try to undo or mitigate their evil consequences by proper and timely expiatory rites. The portents are said to affect mankind both individually and collectively. They affect kings especially as they are the very foundation of the State-edifice[3]. He must have enjoyed both royal patronage and domestic felicity. We can justly infer that he enjoyed good dress and cosmetics as well as chewing betel leaves. He seems to have closely studied the *Science of Erotics* (*Kāmaśāstra*), trade and commerce (*Arthaśāstra*), metrology, meteorology, poetics and philosophy. He appears to have taken keen interest in the worship of Gods, Viṣṇu, Śiva and others, though his chief Deity of worship was the Supreme Sun God. He must have been influenced by the Yoga of *Devotion* propounded by Lord Kṛṣṇa. His devotional fervour is apparent in his firm faith in the power of Agastya to remove all sins, and in his fine delineation of the features of Lord Viṣṇu, which is on a par with his *Dhyāna-śloka*.[4]

He was a psychologist *par excellence* too. He was a keen observer of external nature as well as human nature and knew the working of the human mind. His ethical standard was very high and his instructions on moral conduct are worth their weight in gold.[5]

---

1. Vide XLIII. 38; XLVIII. 31; LIX. 8; XCV. 20; XII. 17.
2. „ XLVIII. 81.
3. „ XLVI. 3; XLVIII. 3, 82-86; CIV. 48.
4. „ XII. 14; LVIII. 31-35.
5. „ LXXV. 6-10.

Commentaries

It is presumed that the *Bṛhat Saṁhitā*, which had attained great fame in olden days, had many scholarly commentaries. It is a well-known fact that scholarship was measured in India in terms of original writings and scholarly commentaries on famous works. However, we have no knowledge of any commentary on this work prior to that of *Bhaṭṭotpala*, from whose references we can conclude that there were at least two schools of interpretation on the *Bṛhat Saṁhitā*, for the reasons mentioned below :

(1) Under LXVIII. 2 he says : केचिद् रुचिर . . . इति पठन्ति.

(2) He condemns the reading तिर्यञ्चम् in 108 and prefers the ancient reading तिरश्चाम्.

(3) Under LXXVI. 11 he states "तरलं काञ्जिकम्, पय इति केचित्".

(4) Under LXVIII. 1 he dislikes the reading 'प्रकृतयश्च ततोऽह्यनूकम्' for its grammatical flaw, saying 'अपरे अन्यथा पठन्ति.' He refutes their arguments ably.

(5) In verse 57 again he says "केचिन्मृदु . . .'.

(6) In verse 63 he refers to more than one interpretation : 'एवं केचित् . . .', 'अन्ये पुनः . . .'

(7) Under LXXXVI. 68 and 78 he refers to two schools of interpretation and concludes 'एषैव व्याख्या ज्यायसी.'

(8) Under verse 12 he condemns the interpretation of some in respect of प्राप्तसूर्या दिक्, as 'अत्र केचित् . . . अयुक्तमेतत्' and quotes भगवान् गर्ग.

(9) Under verse 31 while construing the word शौण्डिक, he says 'मधुपानसक्तः, कल्यपाल इति केचित्.'

(10) Under verse 79 he refers to two interpretations : 'एवं केचिद् व्याचक्षते, अन्ये चतस्रो दिश इच्छन्ति.'

(11) Under LIII. 75 while referring to नवगुणसूत्र . . . he condemns outright some interpreters : 'अत्र केचिदनिश्चितबुद्धयो विकल्पांश्चोदयन्ति . . .' and quotes several authorities like नन्दी, गर्ग, etc. to prove his contention.

(12) Under verse 31 he says 'केचित् चतस्र इति वर्धयन्ति.'

(13) Under verse 41 he states 'केचिदविदितशास्त्रसद्भावा मन्यन्ते.'

(14) Under XI. 7 he refers to व्याख्याविप्रतिपत्ति (conflicting interpretations) and gives the correct interpretation.

(15) Under V. 26 he quotes another interpretation : 'अन्ये एवं व्याचक्षते.'

(16) Under LXI. 5, 6 he says 'अक्षिभ्यां शिश्नेन च सिञ्चतीति केचित्.'

(17) Under LXI. 19 twice he refers to other readings: केचित् ... पठन्ति.

(18) Under LXVIII. 12 he says: 'केचित् . . . इति पठन्ति.'

The name *Bhaṭṭotpala* itself proclaims that the commentator was a Kashmirian. Al-Bīrūnī too specifically states this fact.[1] *Varuṇabhaṭṭa* commentator of the *Khaṇḍakhādyaka* confirms the above statement. Utpala lived in the middle of the 10th century A.D. For, he states in his commentary on the Bṛ. Jātaka that he wrote his *Vivṛti* in Śaka year 888 (966 A.D.). It was a Thursday coinciding with the 5th lunar day of the bright fortnight of the lunar month Caitra. The *Bṛhat Saṁhitā* was commented upon by him towards the end of the same lunar year i.e. on a Thursday, *Phālguna Kṛṣṇa Dvitīyā*.

He has also commented upon the following works : *Yogayātrā*, *Bṛhajjātaka*, *Bṛhanmānasa*) a Karaṇa *grantha* according to Al-Bīrūnī I. 157), *Laghujātaka*, *Bṛhat Saṁhitā*, *Khaṇḍakhādya*, *Ṣaṭpañcāśikā* (of *Pṛthuyaśas*).

His original works : He appears to have written many an original work, some of which are the following : (1) *Praśnajñāna* in 70 Āryā verses on horary astrology.[2] (2) He seems to have written a work entitled *Bhaṭṭotpala-horā-śāstram* in 75 verses. (3) According to Al-Bīrūnī, Utpala wrote a work entitled *Rāhunrākaraṇa* (*Rāhunirākaraṇa* ?) and *Karaṇapāta*, whose authenticity cannot be vouchsafed. (4) He states that he has written a work on *Vāstuvidyā*—architecture, from which he quotes five lines in the Bṛhat Saṁhitā.[3] Al-Bīrūnī's statements about his authorship of a work called the *Śridhava* are conflicting.[4]

His Contribution : We have already pointed out Utpala's unique veneration for Varāhamihira. He has rendered yeoman service to the cause of Indian culture and Sanskrit learning by means of his vast knowledge and practical experience of many branches of learning. But for his erudition and able exposition many passages and technical terms in this work would have remained obscure to the readers. His quotations from many unknown works are a boon to the world of scholars. His language is simple and forceful. He is well informed about many technical subjects such as

1. 'India' I. 157, etc.
2. See the English translation of this work by this writer and V. S. Sastri, Bangalore.
3. Vide LIII. 57.
4. ,, 'India' I. 367 and 158.

astronomy, mathematics, poetics, *Āgama* or *Tantra*, perfumery, etc. His frankness about his lack of practical knowledge of perfumes is praiseworthy.[1] Even here his knowledge is by far above the average. For, he quotes from *Īśvara's* work in *Prākṛta* on this subject in order to explain the terms *Vedha* and *Bodha*.

He mentions several authorities and quotes extensively from their works : (1) Unnamed authorities; (2) *Āgamavidaḥ*; (3) *Ācāryaviṣṇucandra*; (4) *Āryabhaṭa*; (5) *Īśvara*; (6) *Ṛṣiputra*; (7) *Kapila*; (8) *Karaṇa*; (9) *Kaśyapa*; (10) *Kātyāyana*; (11) *Kāmandaki*; (12) *Kāśyapa*; (13) *Kiraṇākhya-tantra*; (14) *Kuśalāḥ*; (15) *Khaṇḍa-khādyaka*; (16) *Garga*; (17) *Caraka*; (18) *Chandaśśāstra*; (19) *Devala*; (20) *Nagnajit*: (21) *Nandin*; (22) *Nārada*; (23) *Nighaṇṭu*; (24) *Pañca-siddhāntikā*; (25) *Parāśara*; (26) *Pāṇini-sūtras*; (27) *Purāṇa*; (28) *Purāṇakāra*; (29) *Puliśācārya*; (30) *Balabhadra*; (31) *Bāhulaka*; (32) *Bṛhajjātaka*; (33) *Bṛhaspati*; (34) *Brahmagupta*; (35) *Bhaṭṭotpala*; (36) *Bhadrabāhu*; (37) *Bharadvāja*; (38) *Bhānubhaṭṭa*; (39) *Bhṛgu*; (40) *Manudharmāḥ*; (41) *Maya*; (42) *Mayūracitraka* (of *Garga*); (43) *Mīmāṁsakas*; (44) *Yama*; (45) *Yavaneśvara*; (46) *Yātrā* and *Yogayātrā*; (47) *Rāta-māṇḍavyau*; (48) *Lokokti*; (49) *Laukāyatika*; (50) *Vararuci*; (51) *Vasiṣṭha*; (52) *Viśvakarman*; (53) *Vīrabhadra*; (54) *Vīrasoma* (writer on *Elephants' Treatment*); (55) *Vṛddha Garga* (or *Bhagavān Garga*) ; (56) *Vyāsa*; (57) *Śakra* (*Indra*); (58) *Śālihotra*; (59) *Śruti*; (60) *Samāsa-saṁhitā*; (61) *Samudra*; (62) *Sārasvata*; (63) *Sārāvalī*; (64) *Siddhasena*; (65) *Siddhārtha*; (66) *Sūryasiddhānta*; (67) *Smṛti*; and (68) *Hiraṇyagarbha*.

His Learning : His vast learning is attested to by his explanations of the following difficult technical terms : *Vedha* and *Bodha* (mixture of liquids and powders respectively) ; *Pāśānta* and *Daśānta*;[2] *Samavṛtta* (cylindrical);[3] *Kukṣā* (middle of the stomach) ;[4] *Viṣāṇa* (tusk) ;[5] *Unmāna* and *Māna* (height and weight); *Īṣā* (frame of a cot)[6] *Kṣveḍa*,[7] *Ghoṣa*;[8] *Vaitālika* (*Nagnācārya* ?); *Diṇḍibhāṇḍa* (musical drum) ; *Devalaka* (Bhojaka, it may mean a temple-worshipper;[9] (*Domba*

1. Vide LXXVII.4.
2. „ LXXI.9. The initial and final parts of a cloth.
3. „ LXXVI. 6.
4. „ LXVII. 19. It may be an obsolete form of *kukṣi* or *kukṣa*.
5. „ LXVII. 9, 10.
6. „ LXXIX. 27.
7. „ LXXXVI. 39 sound produced by the mouth.
8. „ *ibid.* 78 a cavern. We cannot say if he is correct. It may mean a hamlet or noise.
9. „ LXXXVII. 16.

(acrobats); *Kācchika* (perfume manufacturer); *Cokṣa* (wicked); *Skandha* and *Aṁsa* (these are distinguished by him : the latter is the side of the neck);[1] he explains *three* kinds of *Aṅgula* formed by the distances of 8, 7 and 6 barleys; he also distinguishes the two intersecting diagonals as *Vaṁśa* and *Rajju*, while the Ācārya designates both by the generic term *Vaṁśa*; *Alupa* (the junction of the collar-bone and neck,[2] *Aṇḍa* (possibly means the dome);[3] *Sukumāraka* (the raised portion or ridge of the ear);[4] *Gocchā* (has not been explained by him); *Tristhānaṁ mehate* (has been explained by him as—*Nityaṁ galad-aśruṇi cakṣuṣi bhavata ityarthaḥ*); *Maṇi* (is construed by him as the bottom of a well, but we feel that it means an artificial tank); *Kukundarā*[is explained as *Nitambārūpakam* (Kūpakam?); it may be the depressions in the hips],[5] *Pecaka* (root of the tail)[6]; *Udumbara* (consists of *Dehali* and *Niṭāla*, the threshold and its counterpart above);[7] *Piṭha* (foundation); *Śirā* (one of the 10 × 10 cross lines in the *Vāstu* chart); *Karavīraka* (inner corner of the eye);[8] and *Tarkukāḥ* (those who look at others' faces).

As observed above, his contribution to a variety of subjects of human interest such as architecture, astronomy, water-divination, etc. is astoundingly vast and deep. In the context of perfumeries he says under LXXVII. 4: "All the ingredients must generally be washed either with *Kāñjika* or with pure water, some with cow's urine, and then cooked on gentle fire in an iron vessel along with *Nakha* (shell perfume) and gingily oil. The Ācārya has not given these details. We too have not given them for fear of making the work too big." Then under verse 8 he gives a special rule : "Wherever a scent is to be fumigated, first it should be done with *Haritakī* and then only with the particular substance prescribed. This is the tradition among the experts of this science." In this connection we are surprised at his becoming humility in spite of his vast knowledge and information that are both copious and remarkable. For, he says: "गन्धसंस्कारपाकवेधबोधधूपनादिकं नोक्तम् । एतत्तज्ज्ञेभ्य उपलभ्य कार्यम् ।. . . न चास्माकमत्र तथाविधं प्रावीण्यम्" (LXXVII. 4) and quotes from the work *Gandhayukti*

---

1. Vide XC. 3.
2. ,, LXVI. 2.
3. ,, LVI. 22.
4. ,, LVIII. 7, 9.
5. CV. 12.
6. ,, LXVII. 2.
7. ,, LIII. 26.
8. ,, LVIII. 13.

in *Prākṛta* by one *Īśvara*. His keen scientific attitude and mathematical genius are revealed by his calculation and explanation of the varieties of scents. He says that by *Gauṇavṛtti*, secondary method, the number is 174,720, but primarily 43,680. In this connection he quotes a long passage from a *Nighaṇṭu* of synonyms of substances. This shows that he was well acquainted with *Āyurveda* also.

His profound scholarship in astronomy and mathematics is attested to by the calculations and quotations he has given in Chapter II. Therein he quotes profusely the *Brahmasiddhānta*, *Pañcasiddhāntikā*, *Pauliśa-siddhānta*, *Āryabhaṭa*, *Bhaṭṭa Balabhadra*, *Brahmagupta* and *Garga* about the elements of calendar (*yuga* etc.), whose smallest unit is ¼ *Truṭi*. It is surmised that he has written an independent *Karaṇa grantha*. Under II.12 he explains that the earth hangs in space like an iron ball held steady between two magnets. He tells us, in this connection, about the divergence of opinion among the *Ācāryas* regarding the 'lord of the day and Horā.'

His extraordinary proficiency in architecture is clearly proved by his quotations and intimate knowledge of the various details of the construction of houses and temples as well as iconography. He supplements many statements of the Ācārya with lucid explanations and apt quotations. According to his own statement he had written a detailed work on architecture. He mentions three kinds of cubits and digits, viz., *Sādhāraṇa*, *Jyeṣṭha* and *Kaniṣṭha*, and technical terms, *Kāṇḍa*, *Pāṁsuka*, *Stara* and *Varāṇḍikā*. He makes profuse quotations from the *Kiraṇākhyatantra*, *Nandin*, *Caraka* and *Anyaśāstra* and mentions many things not given by the author[1].

His intimate knowledge of the *Purāṇas* is attested to by his explanation of the many stories and names such as that of *Tilottamā*,[2] *Revanta*,[3] the Mothers (the seven *mātaraḥ* described in the *Saptaśati*), *Kāla* (Time),[4] etc. His knowledge of *Dharma Śāstra* and kindred subjects is equally amazing : under LXXXVII.39 he explains who is a *Vrātya*; he quotes the *Manusmṛti* (under I.6) which is directly based on the *Nāsadiyasūkta* of the *Ṛgveda*; *Kapila's Sāṁkhya* philosophy, *Kaṇāda's Vaiśeṣika* system, *Mīmāṁsakas*, *Advaita* philosophy (LXXV); he tells us which weekdays are good for *Saṁskāra*, *dīkṣā*, *vrata*, *mekhalā*, etc[5]. His knowledge of the Āgamas becomes quite evident

1. Vide LIV. 37, 58, 64, 90.
2. „ LXXIV. 20.
3. „ LVIII. 56.
4. „ I. 7 where he quotes the *Paurāṇikas*.
5. „ XCVIII. 16.

from his reference to the *Vātula tantra* and *Pañcarātrāgama* regarding the installation of *Śiva's* image and worship of *Keśava*. In Chapter C he quotes a good deal from works on *Dharmaśāstra*. His explanation of the shape of the altar as a quadrilateral with its middle part contracted shows his proficiency in sacrificial Core.[1] He quotes *Smṛtis* regarding bath at night.[2] His intimacy with *Arthaśāstra* is discernible in his explanation of XIX. 11. His acquaintance with *veterinary science* is worthy of admiration. For, he gives a long quotation which explains the anatomy of horses[3], and from *Parāśara* and *Vararuci* who treat of this subject, which was very popular in the Vedic period when horses of good breed and features were required for the *Aśvamedha* sacrifice. Though the author does not mention the word *Āvarta* (hairy circle) in verse 2, *Utpala* supplies it on the authority of *Vararuci*.

His proficiency in metrics and poetics becomes apparent by his scansion of verses and definitions of all the metres employed by the author. In this connection he refers to the views of *Rāta, Māṇḍavya* and observes that the *Ācārya* has made prosody an attractive subject and that he himself has made his *Vivṛti* (exposition) 'Śiṣyahitāvahā' (beneficial to pupils), a remark which is amply borne out by his scholarly explanation.

He is a poet of no mean achievement. He could have achieved singular success as a poet like his ideal, had he only wished for it. His poetic talent is discernible in the two verses (2nd and 3rd) at the beginning of his commentary as well as in those which he has put at the end of important sections, viz., II, XIII, LIII, XCVI and CV as well as the penultimate verse, describing his *Vivṛti* as a boat for crossing the ocean of *Varāha's* deep learning. In all these verses he uses charming metaphors and puns (e.g. *Artha* meaning wealth and sense).

He was an adept in the *Sāmudrika Śāstra* (Human Physiognomy): He explains minutely all the features, quoting the authorities of *Samudra, Garga* and some unnamed author. In this section he quotes only a single verse of *Parāśara*. He is so thoroughly informed about this subject that he has no hesitation in condemning the previous interpreters who gave a wrong reading and held that *Prakṛti*

---

1. Vide LIX. 19; CV. 8.
2. „ XLIV.8; LVI.2
3. „ V. 13.
4. „ LXVI.

and *Sattva* meant one and the same ıing[1]. In this connection he brings to our knowledge what *Kātyāyana* says regarding *Unmāna* (height) and *Māna* (weight).

Regarding gems he says that Diamond, Pearl, Ruby and Emerald are the most important among the 22 varieties of gems. His observation about the origin of gems, viz., subterrannean pressure in course of time produces gems, is quite scientific and uptodate.[2] He is also well informed about the prices of gems based on their weights and qualities.

His scrupulous adherence to local traditions and general principles in the sphere of iconography is worthy of his vast learning and keen understanding of the spirit of art. For he observes : "किन्तु तासां स्तनशोभा मध्यक्षामता नितम्बवैपुल्यं कार्यं येन प्रकारेण स्त्रीरूपस्य शोभा जायते" and "अत्र प्रतिमालक्षणं देवानां देवतानां यल्लक्षणमाचार्येणोक्तं तेषां लोकप्रसिद्धा यथा यथा शरीरशोभा भवति, तथा तथोक्तवत्प्रतिमा कार्या लक्षणज्ञैः ।"

His acquaintance with the science of *Erotics* or *Kāmaśāstra* is equally intimate. Under LXXVIII.12 he quotes from a work entitled *Bāhulaka* the definitions of *Bhāvas*, etc. Not much is known about this work. His quotations from *Kāśyapa* show that his *Saṁhitā* too had contained matters relating to erotics which *Varāhamihira* must have utilized for his work.

His proficiency in lexicon is proved by his quotations from *Nighaṇṭus* (already referred to). He explains certain words, quoting relevant *Kośas* : *Kukundara* as the cavity of the loins; *Ḍiṇḍibhāṇḍa*, as a particular musical instrument; *Jatru* is explained as 'कुक्षयोः सन्धिः' which is palpably incorrect. The mistake must be attributed to the scribe. For, *Kṣīrasvāmin* says "अंसवत्सयोः (वक्षसोः?) सन्धिरुद्भिन्नास्थि जत्रु."[3] He explains the word *Viyadgā* as 'girdle.' Similarly about *Viṣāṇa* he quotes some Kośa to show that it means also 'tusk.'[4] He follows the same procedure to prop up his explanation of *Kapotapāli*.[5]

His scholarship of grammar is testified by his quotation of Pāṇini's authority for explaining words like *Hautabhuja*.[6] Similarly under LXVI.2 he says, "अत्र प्राण्यवयवत्वात्सर्वत्र समाहारः" which is permitted by Pāṇini's rule II.4-2.

1. Vide LXVIII.4.
2. „ LXXXIII.3.
3. „ Amarakośa II. 6.78.
4. „ LXVII. 9,10.
5. „ LVI. 30.
6. „ Pāṇini IV.3-120; VII. 2-117.

We have already given an account of his veneration for the *Ācārya* bordering on religious devotion. He, therefore, tries always to justify *Varāha's* statements, though, *prima facie*, they may appear to be mutually contradictory. For example, the author says that Āvartas or curbs are bad (in LXVI.2) in *Savyakukṣi*, and again in the next verse he says that they are good in the *Kukṣi*. This, says, Utpala, is not self-contradictory. For he says : "There is no inconsistency in the Ācārya's statements, inasmuch as he has condemned it only on the left side of the stomach, and not on its right side." Similarly, the word *Gala* occurring in both these verses is no repetition. For, in the first instance it means *Hṛtkaṇṭha-sandhi* (junction of the heart and neck) and in the second the *neck itself*. Likewise. he supplies words and information not found in the author's verses.

Another important feature of *Bhaṭṭotpala's Vivṛti* is that he alludes to various regional traditions and vernacular words, which should provide sufficient material for research in linguistics:

(1) He states that the *Mṛdaṅga* (tabor) is popularly known as *Maṇḍala*.[1] Probably it was known by that name in his region.

(2) We learn from his statement (under LXXII.4) that *Vitāna* (canopy) was known as *Kanaka* in the world (*Loke*) i.e. in his regional language.

(3) He mentions that *Kṣveḍa* (sound produced by the mouth) is popularly known as *Śoḍanikā*.[2] We are informed that in the Punjab and Mālava people use the word in that sense.

(4) He says, similarly (under verse 41), that the bird *Bharadvāja* is called *Lāṭā* by the people.

(5) The word *Ḍomba* (which has already been noticed) occurring in LXXXVII.33 was probably known to him as meaning acrobats because of popular usage, though he does not give any explanation. It looks like a vernacular or a foreign word.

(6) The word *Cokṣa*[3] was understood to mean a *Duṣṭa* or notorious fellow, in popular parlance, according to Utpala, though the dictionary gives just the contrary meaning i.e. *H* is not clear as to how this word came to connote the opposite sense. Somebody has told us that the word *Cokhā* is used in the sense of *Sharp* in Eastern Hind .

1. Vide LXVIII. 95.
2. „ LXXXVI. 39.
3. „ LXXXVII. 43.

(7) In his local dialect, we are told, the *Bhṛṅgāra*, Vase, was known as *Dāṁdāni* or *Damani* (LXXX.6). We are not in a position to affirm whether the word was in vogue in Kashmir or elsewhere. We have been told, however, that that word is used in Eastern Hindi for *Guldastā* (vase).

(8) He explains the North Indian custom of building earthen granaries in the following words "कुसूलं मृन्मयं यत्रान्नादिकं[1] स्थाप्यते." Even now we can see in the villages such mud granaries standing near fields. In Eastern Hindi it is called, they say, *Dehari* or *Bakhār*.

(9) He interprets the word *Śvapacāḥ* (in LIII.84) as *Ḍomāḥ*. Even now outcastes are called by this term in Eastern Hindi.

(10) The word *Sahāyān* (in CIV.35) meaning companions or helpmates, is construed by him as *Sārthinaḥ*. We cannot make out as to what exactly he means by this expression. According to the accepted connotation of the term, it should mean 'one having a caravan or flock of animals.' It must be a case of semantic variation. For, actually *Sāthi* is used in Hindi in the sense of 'companion.' Utpala, therefore, must have been influenced by local usage.

(11) He explains the word *Jānu-kapicchā* (Knee-cap) in LVIII.17 as "ये च लोके एक्कलके इति प्रसिद्धे." This also would help research-workers in identifying the regions traversed by the learned commentator.

(12) Under LXIII.2 he remarks that the popular name of a kind of fighting cock, whose neck is like barley corn in shape, is *Yavaśiras*.

The world of scholars must remain greatly indebted to *Bhaṭṭotpala* for giving it a peep into a realm of wonderful ideas, arts, crafts, beliefs, traditions, etc. of the ancient peoples of this land. In this connection, some people naturally entertain a feeling that *Vṛddhagarga* and *Garga* might, after all, have been one and the same person. That this notion is quite unfounded would be clear to us from the forthright statements of Utpala: "एवमाचार्येण गर्गऋषिपुत्रयोर्मतमङ्गीकृतम्। वृद्धगर्गपराशरकश्यपैः सह मतभेदः।" We find here the two Gargas in the opposite camps. The Ācārya has preferred the views of the junior to that of the senior[2]. He quotes both the sages under XXXII.1-2.

1. Note the peculiar usage of the word *Anna* here.
2. Vide XXXII. 8-11.

Moreover he refers to the elder sage as 'Bhagavān Garga' as *Vṛddha-garga* and as *Gargeṇa maharṣiṇā*. Incidentally the *Gargasaṁhitā* is also known as *Vṛddhagargīya*. The *Mahābhārata* too refers to the Elder sage. With regard to the identity of *Kaśyapa* and *Kāśyapa*, we may conclude that the two names may, after all, point to one and the same person. For, Utpala refers to the author's difference of opinion with *Kaśyapa* and quotes in support *Kāśyapa*. The difference may be due to the carelessness of scribes.

Regarding *Devala* and others too some interesting details can be called from Utpala's *Vivṛti*:

(i) It is quite evident from P.S.I. 22 that Varāha has given the effects of planetary years, etc. on the authority of ancient sages (*Munipraṇītam ālokya*). Hence it is intriguing why *Utpala* has not quoted the authority of sages like *Parāśara*, but quoted only a single verse of *Devala*. On the other hand, he quotes eight verses from each of *Yavaneśvara* and the author's *Samāsa-saṁhitā*. This leads us to suspect that by *Utpala's* time the literature of ancient sages on this subject might have been well nigh lost.

(ii) He quotes two verses (under V. 11) of the *Sūryasiddhānta*, which are not available in its modern version. This leads to the conclusion that the version that was studied by *Utpala* was materially different.

(iii) *Utpala* quotes *Rāṭamāṇḍavya* on prosody and *Māṇḍavya* separately. This name, however, has been mentioned by *Al-Birūni* (I. 157) as that of the author of a *Saṃhitā*, which is quite possible, since the commentator quotes him in the B.J.[1]. It is to be borne in mind that the name *Māṇḍavya* occurs in many *Purāṇas*, the *Rāmāyaṇa* etc. It is quite possible that there were many sages of that name in ancient times.

(iv) The author states in LIV. 125[2] that his authority for 'Rainfall' (XXIII) is *Baladevamatādi* (views of *Baladeva* and others). However, the commentator does not quote him even once. On the other hand, he quotes *Garga* thrice, *Kaśyapa* once, *Devala* once and the *Samāsa-saṁhitā* twice (3 verses in all). It is, therefore, a subject fit for investigation, both from the point of meteorology and authorship of *Baladeva*.

(v) The author asserts that his authorities for temple architecture are *Garga*, *Manu* and others (*Maya*, *Viśvakarman*, etc.);[3] but the

1. Vide VI. 6; XI. 3, 5, 6; XIII. 2; XV. 4.
2. This verse is not found in the *Vārāṇaseya* edition.
3. Vide LVI. 29, 31.

commentator quotes not a single statement of *Garga* or Manu. On the other hand, he quotes extensively *Kāśyapa*, a verse and a half from *Tantrāntara* (another scientific work), one line from *Viśvakarman* and one verse from Maya. Does this mean that the manuscript of *Garga saṁhitā* that was available to *Utpala* did not contain this subject ? However, he quotes both the *Gargas* in the chapter on architecture (LIII).

(vi) *Utpala* rightly concludes that the five chapters (LXXIV-LXXVIII) dealing with 'Praise of Women' and such other erotic subjects are meant for the use of royal personages in their harems (*Antaḥpuracintāyāṁ* . . .).

(vii) He identifies sometimes the author with the work. This may be intentional, since it is usually asked, "Have you read Shakespeare ?" meaning his 'works.' In Sanskrit too such a practice is prevalent. For, Māgha is identified with his *Śiśupālavadha* by *Mallinātha* : "माघे मेघे गतं वयः." Accordingly *Utpala* might have said, "तथा च भद्रबाहौ पठ्यते" (IX. 37) instead of 'भद्रबाहुना . . .' Likewise, he identifies *Samudra*, the author, with his work (cf. LXVIII) : 'समुद्रे प्रोक्तं सामुद्रम्' though he should have said. 'समुद्रेण प्रोक्तं . . .'. This *Bhadrabāhu*, a Jain astrologer, is said to have written a *Saṁhitā* entitled the *Bhādrabāhavī Saṁhitā* and a commentary on the *Sūryaprajñapti*.

(viii) *Bhaṭṭotpala's* extensive quotations from the author's *Samāsa-saṁhitā* have saved that work from total oblivion. For, we have no other means of getting at its contents than through these references, though incomplete. Altogether 122½ verses of this abridged *Saṁhitā* are quoted in his *Vivṛti*. That work must have been lost soon after Utpala's time, since Al-Bīrūnī says nothing about it. Similar is the case with the work of an ancient author named *Sārasvata* who had written on underground water-sources. *Utpala*, however, quotes only 31 *Ślokas* from the above work, which would, otherwise, have remained a mere name.

(ix) Utpala quotes, for the benefit of his pupils, 32 verses of the *Akṣarakośa* of *Yavaneśvara*, occurring in the *Bodhiyātrā* dealing with journeys and horary astrology.[1] Elsewhere he quotes five verses of a *Yātrākāra* named *Siddhārtha*.[2] It may be conjectured that some Buddhist saint, a *Bodhisattva*, had written a work on *Yātrā*, which *Yavaneśvara* might have expounded, adding his own knowledge and experience.

---

1. Vide XCVI. 13.
2. „ CIV. 60.

(x) He explains the expression 'प्रियसाहसत्वं यत् तन्न तेजः'[1] as 'न तत् तेजः शृङ्गारो भवति.' It is suspected that this too might be another instance of semantic variation. In his local dialect the expression *Śṛṅgāra* might have had the connotation of 'chivalry or heroism.' This line of argument on the part of the author reminds us of *Bāṇa's Śukanāsopadeśa.*

We have already expressed our high appreciation of *Utpala's* simple and graceful language. However, we cannot close our eyes to some of the gross errors he has committed in grammatical construction, gender, compounds and interpretation : *Srotriya* is construed by him as *Niyaminaḥ*—(observers of vows); *Mānyamānapitṛ* is explained as *Mānya* (worshipable) and *Mānapitṛs* or *Pūjakas*. This kind of interpretation sounds odd. He construes *Akiñcanāḥ* (indigent) as *Akiñcitkarāḥ puruṣakārahināḥ* (LXVIII. 29). He explains the word *Strīmṛtyuḥ* (verse 61) as *Strī tasya mārayati*, which is evidently wrong in grammar. The word *Śroṇīnibha* (resembling hips) is explained as *Stryadhararāgasadṛśam* i.e. like the red tinge of a woman's lower lip. *Lavalīphala*, according to him, is *Lavaṅga-puṣpam, tasya phalāsambhavāt*. Actually *Lavaṅga* is clove, while *lavalī* is *Cicca acida* which is called *Kirunelli* in Kannaḍa. Similarly he explains the compound 'Vrīḍāvimiśrālasā' a bit clumsily by changing the *Karmadhāraya* into *Bahuvrihi*. The word *Śākuni* (fowler) is *Dhīvaraḥ* (fisherman) for him; *Avagāhana* (plunging) is *Uttaraṇa* (crossing); *Parivrājakasya bhayam* (danger to ascetics) is changed to the ablative case (i.e. danger from ascetics); the word *Pāyu* (anus) means *Upastha* (genital organ); *Avalokayan ikṣan* (for *ikṣamāṇaḥ*). *Brahmavarcaḥ, Sragdāmaḥ, Ratnabhedāni* etc. are some other instances. In some places we have taken a different view from that of *Utpala*. For example he says: 'अपसव्यः प्रदक्षिण उच्यते' which is against the views of the ancients.

He ridicules the pseudo-astronomers who speak of the sun's victory and defeat in planetary war.

Utpala's commentary was abridged, we are told, under the naṃe, *Utpalaparimala* by one *Bhāskara*, son of *Kumāra*, grandson of *Rāma* of *Naidhruva Kāśyapa gotra* and *Vārṣagaṇya* family. This is not available in print.

---

1. Vide LXXV. 7.

The commentator speaks of some of the verses of the text as *Anārṣa* i.e. not based on ancient authority, indicating thereby that they are not genuine : They are XVII. 9, 10; XXV. 6 and XXVIII. 17, 23 and 24. He has not commented either on the last three verses. Similarly, he considers some of the chapters as not genuine : They are XXVII entitled *Vātacakra*;[1] XXXVIII *Rajolakṣaṇa*;[2] LI *Aṅgavidyā*;[3] LII *Piṭakalakṣaṇa*;[4] and CIII *Vivāhapaṭala*, when he says, अथ प्रसङ्गागतं विन्ध्यवासिकृतं विवाहपटलं व्याख्यायते.' Among these chapters he is not quite sure about the genuineness or otherwise of Chapter LI, because the *Ācārya* includes this topic also among the contents of the *Saṁhitā* (II. 23). Hence it is reasonable to infer that some scholar or scholars before Utpala, finding some elements missing in their manuscript of this work, composed this and such other chapters in order to make the *Saṁhitā* appear complete. It is not known as to who the author *Vindhyavāsin* was.

In this connection Utpala observes that the five chapters (XXVII, LI, LII, LXVI and LXVII) are not included in the list of 100 chapters which contain a total of verses equal to 3900 *Ślokas*. The last verse of CVI specifically states that the work has been completed, as it ends with a prayer. We would, on the other hand, prefer to exclude from the total number of chapters, viz., 107, printed in this edition, the following six. viz., XXVII, XXXVIII, LI, LII, CII and CIII, the last chapter, viz., CVII, being out of the purview of the regular work. However, it may be presumed that the original work of Varāha must have contained chapters on *Wind Circle* (XXVII), *Haze* (XXXVIII) *Limbs* (LI) and *Pimples* also (LII). For he had promised these subjects in Chapter II. But the 'Table of Contents' at the end (CVII) omits to mention chapters XXXVIII, LI, LII, LXVI, LXVII, XCII, CII and CIII. This leaves a deficit of two chapters, which can be made good only by taking into account the two chapters LI and LII, because these were considered as genuine by some predecessors of Bhaṭṭotpala.

Though the printing of this unique work was commenced early in 1974, yet, as ill luck would have it, it could not progress satisfac-

---

1. Vide 'तच्च वराहकृतं न भवति'।
2. This chapter is omitted by him.
3. Vide "अत: परं केचिदङ्गविद्यां पठन्ति," but comments upon it.
4. ,, 'अत: परमपि केचित् . . .' but comments upon it.

torily. Hence the publishers have been advised to publish this work in two volumes, of which the first is brought out now for the benefit of eager scholars and students of astrology and astronomy as well as Indian culture in general. We hope by Heaven's grace the second volume will be published without much delay.

Vittal
10-1-1981

M. Ramakrishna Bhat

श्रीसिद्धिविनायको विजयते

बृहत्संहिता

BṚHAT SAṀHITĀ

उपनयनाध्यायः ॥१॥

Chapter I—Introductory

जयति जगतः प्रसूतिर्विश्वात्मा सहजभूषणं नभसः ।
द्रुतकनकसदृशदशशतमयूखमालार्चितः सविता ॥१॥

The Sun—creator—flourishes supreme—He who is the source of the universe and of the nature of the universe (or, who is the soul of the universe), who is the natural (inborn) ornament of the firmament, and who is bedecked with innumerable rows of rays that resemble molten gold.

[The author who is an ardent devotee of the Sun-God is never tired of praising his Deity of choice in the choicest terms, as he is in the Bṛhajjātaka. The simile of 'molten gold' being so apt makes one believe that Varāhamihira must have delighted in meditating on the rising Sun. The metre of this and the following seven verses is Āryā.

Bhaṭṭotpala, the able commentator of Varāhamihira, makes obeisance, in the first verse, to the Trinity, Gaṇeśa, the Seven Planets and his preceptor, at the commencement of his *Vivṛti*. In this connection, he calls our author *Āvantika* (one belonging to Ujjain), who composed this *Saṁhitā* or Compilation, after his intellectual powers were awakened by the Sun-God's boon. In the second verse Utpala salutes the Sun in the form of Varāhamihira, who is called by the wise the Sun himself, who had incarnated on earth in order to save, in the Kali age, the triple Śāstra, consisting of the three *Skandhas* or branches viz. horoscopy, astronomy and *Saṁhitā*, which he wrote in an abridged form, after he had created (in the golden age) the science of astrology with the three branches in great detail.

Following the epic description of the Mahābhārata war which is compared to a turbulent river, the commentator calls, in the third verse, the author (i.e. his work) an *ocean* filled with the water of numerous ideas, abounding in aquatic animals viz. groups of planets and constellations (as well as the Signs of the Zodiac), and bright with the gems of multiple Yogas (planetary configurations). Men of little intelligenee greedily wander about this ocean in search of *Artha* (wealth, correct meaning). 'Hence, according to my light, I construct this raft of explanation (for their benefit)'. See also what the author says in his *Bṛhajjātaka* (I-2) "शास्त्रप्लवं प्रारभे".]

प्रथममुनिकथितमवितथमवलोक्य ग्रन्थविस्तरस्यार्थम् ।
नातिलघुविपुलरचनाभिरुद्यतः स्पष्टमभिधातुम् ॥२॥

Finding the truth of the great Science expounded at great length by Brahman (the first or Ancient Sage or by ancient sages), I am now engaged in explaining clearly the same truth in words that are neither too brief nor too elaborate.

[The expression *Prathama-muni* used here is synonymous with Kālidāsa's *Purāṇo-muniḥ*. The author's idea is to impress upon the readers that he is only condensing the vast store of astrological knowledge bequeathed by numerous Sages of yore, so that they may understand the abstruse principle without any doubt or difficulty.]

मुनिविरचितमिदमिति यच्चिरन्तनं साधु न मनुजग्रथितम् ।
तुल्येऽर्थेऽक्षरभेदादमन्त्रके का विशेषोक्तिः ॥३॥

It cannot be said that an ancient work must be good as it was composed by sages, whereas one written by an ordinary man (i.e. a house-holder) cannot be so. For, what difference would it make in a non-Vedic subject when the same meaning is conveyed by two different groups of words ?

[The potency and efficacy of Vedic chants would be adversely affected by substituting synonyms or translating them into other languages. The Mantras have a peculiar charm and symphony of their own.

Here the author reminds us of Kālidāsa's own fighting words for recognition in the Mālavikāgnimitra (prologue) as "Purāṇam ityeva na sādhu sarvam...." However, Bhavabhūti strikes a slightly different note in his *Uttararāmacarita* in the verse, "Ṛṣīṇām punar ādyānām vācam artho'nudhāvati."]

क्षितितनयदिवसवारो न शुभकृदिति यदि पितामहप्रोक्ते ।
कुजदिनमनिष्टमिति वा कोऽत्र विशेषो नृदिव्यकृतेः ॥४॥

What difference is there between the divine declaration of Brahman to the effect that the weekday presided over by Mars i.e. Tuesday, is not auspicious, and the human statement that Tuesday is harmful ?

आब्रह्मादिविनिःसृतमालोक्य ग्रन्थविस्तरं क्रमशः ।
क्रियमाणकमेवंतत्समासतोऽतो ममोत्साहः ॥५॥

I have been encouraged to write this book, having seen many works on this science starting right from Brahman being abridged by successive authors.

[The commentator, Bhaṭṭotpala, quotes the following verses from Sage Garga, which state that this science of astrology—astronomy was originally created by the creator as an Aṅga or ancillary of the Vedas and handed down to Garga :

स्वयं स्वयम्भुवा सृष्टं चक्षुर्भूतं द्विजन्मनाम् ।
वेदाङ्गं ज्यौतिषं ब्रह्मपरं यज्ञहितावहम् ॥
मया स्वयम्भुवः प्राप्तं क्रियाकालप्रसाधनम् ।
वेदानामुत्तमं शास्त्रं त्रैलोक्यहितकारकम् ॥
मत्तश्चान्यानृषीन्प्राप्तं पारम्पर्येण पुष्कलम् ।
तैस्तदा स्रष्टृभिर्भूयो ग्रन्थैः स्वैः स्वैरुदाहृतम् ॥]

आसीत्तमः किलेदं तत्रापां तैजसेऽभवद्धैमे ।
स्वर्भूशकले ब्रह्मा विश्वकृदण्डेऽर्कशशिनयनः ॥६॥

It appears that originally i.e. before creation, there was nothing but darkness everywhere. Then water came into existence. From that sprang a fiery golden egg consisting of the two parts of the shell viz. heaven and earth. Out of this arose Brahman, Creator of the universe, with the luminaries (the Sun and the Moon) as his eyes.

[This verse is an exact summary of the following nine verses of the famous Manusmṛti I-5-13 :—

आसीदिदं तमोभूतमप्रज्ञातमलक्षणम् ।
अप्रतर्क्यमविज्ञेयं प्रसुप्तमिव सर्वतः ॥
ततः स्वयम्भूर्भगवानव्यक्तं व्यञ्जयन्निदम् ।
महाभूतादिवृत्तौजाः प्रादुरासीत्तमोनुदः ॥
योऽसावतीन्द्रियग्राह्यः सूक्ष्मोऽव्यक्तः सनातनः ।
सर्वभूतमयोऽचिन्त्यः स एव स्वयमुद्बभौ ॥

सोऽभिध्याय शरीरात्स्वात्सिसृक्षुर्विविधाः प्रजाः ।
अप एव ससर्जादौ तासु वीर्यमवासृजत् ।।
तदण्डमभवद्धैमं सहस्रांशुसमप्रभम् ।
तस्मिन्जज्ञे स्वयं ब्रह्मा सर्वलोकपितामहः ।।
आपो नारा इति प्रोक्ता आपो वै नरसूनवः ।
ता यदस्यायनं पूर्वं तेन नारायणः स्मृतः ।।
यत्तत्कारणमव्यक्तं नित्यं सदसदात्मकम् ।
तद्विसृष्टः स पुरुषो लोके ब्रह्मेति कीर्त्यते ।।
तस्मिन्नण्डे स भगवानुषित्वा परिवत्सरम् ।
स्वयमेवात्मनो ध्यानात्तदण्डमकरोद्द्विधा ।।
ताभ्यां स शकलाभ्यां तु दिवं भूमिं च निर्ममे ।
मध्ये व्योम दिशश्चाष्टावपां स्थानं च शाश्वतम् ।।

This statement of Manu has its root in the नासदीयसूक्त of the Ṛgveda].

कपिलः प्रधानमाह द्रव्यादीन् कणभुगस्य विश्वस्य ।
कालं कारणमेके स्वभावमपरे जगुः कर्म ।।७।।

Sage Kapila, propounder of the Sāṅkhya system of philosophy, has declared Pradhāna or unmanifested Prakṛti (primordial matter) to be the material cause of the universe, while Sage Kaṇāda, founder of the Vaiśeṣika system or atomic theory of the origin of the universe, has stated that the seven categories headed by Dravyas or substances constitute its material cause. According to some Time is the root cause of the universe. There are others like the Laukāyatikas who have declared that nature or the inherent properties of substances were responsible for the emergence of the universe. There are also some who opine that actions of beings are its cause.

[Here the author alludes to five theories about the origin of the universe. There are six Padārthas or Categories according to the Vaiśeṣikas, twentyfive according to the Sāṅkhyas and twenty-seven according to the followers of Patañjali. The Dravyas or substances are nine i.e. the five elements, Time, Space, Soul and Mind.]

तदलमतिविस्तरेण प्रसङ्गवादार्थनिर्णयोऽतिमहान् ।
ज्योतिःशास्त्राङ्गानां वक्तव्यो निर्णयोऽत्र मया ।।८।।

Let me stop this otherwise very lengthy discussion of a vast and polemical subject which has been referred to only incidentally. I am now engaged, on the other hand, in expounding in a decisive manner, the various parts of the science of Astrology in this work.

ज्योतिःशास्त्रमनेकभेदविषयं स्कन्धत्रयाधिष्ठितं
तत्कात्स्न्योंपनयस्य नाम मुनिभिः सङ्कीर्त्यते संहिता ।
स्कन्धेऽस्मिन्गणितेन या ग्रहगतिस्तन्त्राभिधानस्त्वसौ
होराऽन्योऽङ्गविनिश्चयश्च कथितः स्कन्धस्तृतीयोऽपरः ॥९॥

The science of Astrology has many branches within its scope and is mainly divided under three heads or sections termed Skandhas viz. Gaṇita or Tantra, Horā and Aṅgaviniścaya. The treatment of this subject in its entirety has been designated as Saṁhitā, Collection or compilation, by the Sages. The first section or Skandha is called Tantra as it deals with the movements of planets through the signs of the zodiac that are arrived at by means of mathematical calculations. The second section treats of Horā or horoscopy. The third and the last is termed Aṅgaviniścaya—determination of the limbs—as it explains the method of ascertaining by calculation the ascendant and other houses in a natal chart.

[The word Saṁhitā has a religious halo about it, as it has been used in connection with the Vedic texts and other hoary Śāstras viz. ऋग्वेदसंहिता etc., चरकसंहिता and the like. It is to be understood that Saṁhitās are not meant to be original works, but collections of materials gathered from various sources. Varāhamihira faithfully follows this tradition and draws profusely from Garga's work. For, says Garga :

गणितं जातकं शाखां यो वेत्ति द्विजपुङ्गवः ।
त्रिस्कन्धज्ञो विनिर्दिष्टः संहितापारगश्च सः ॥

Here the Sage calls the last Section *Śākhā*. The verse is in the शार्दूलविक्रीडित metre.]

वक्रानुवक्रास्तमयोदयाद्यास्ताराग्रहाणां करणे मयोक्ताः ।
होरागतं विस्तरतश्च जन्मयात्राविवाहैः सह पूर्वमुक्तम् ॥१०॥

I have already expounded in detail in my astronomical work, the *Pañcasiddhāntikā*, retrograde and direct motions of the non-luminous planets viz. Mars, Mercury, Jupiter, Venus and Saturn, their combustion (as a result of close proximity to the Sun) and re-emergence and the like (i.e. ग्रहयुद्ध or planetary war). Similarly have I explained already in detail everything connected with birth, journey and matrimony in my works entitled *Bṛhajjātaka*, Bṛhadyātrā or Yogayātrā and Vivāhapaṭala respectively.

[The exact name of the last work is not known. The commentator has included in his edition of this work a chapter (CIII) on this topic written by one *Vindhyavāsin*. It may be presumed to be a faithful summary of our author's missing work. This verse shows that Varāhamihira had already written the पञ्चसिद्धान्तिका, बृहज्जातक, बृहद्यात्रा and a work on विवाह. However, some references occurring in the पञ्चसिद्धान्तिका to this संहिता make us believe that all these works were planned simultaneously or cross references were introduced after all the works had been completed. See पञ्चसिद्धान्तिका XV-10 on Rāhu.

This verse and the following are in Upajāti metre.]

प्रश्नप्रतिप्रश्नकथाप्रसङ्गान्स्वल्पोपयोगान्ग्रहसम्भवांश्च ।
सन्त्यज्य फल्गूनि च सारभूतं भूतार्थमर्थैः सकलैः प्रवक्ष्ये ॥११॥

Avoiding trivial matters of very little practical importance such as long-drawn queries and answers, interesting legendary stories as well as the origin of planets, I shall here explain the real facts in their essential features along with all their benefits.

[The commentator explains and illustrates in detail the questions put by Krauṣṭuki to Vṛddha Garga. The story narrated by Sage Parāśara is about the fight between the Gods and demons or Asuras, in which the Gods seek the help of Śukra, preceptor of Asuras. Sage Parāśara tells Kauśika how the planets originated, of course, according to the Purāṇas.]

सांवत्सरसूत्राध्यायः ॥२॥

Chapter II—Canons for Astrologer

अथातः सांवत्सरसूत्रं व्याख्यास्यामः ॥१॥

We shall now explain the aphorisms i.e. rules or qualifications for an astrologer.

[This chapter consists of both prose passages and verses in different metres. The first aphorism is in line with those of ancient writers on the Śāstras like Caraka. However, original writers like बादरायण do not use the word व्याख्यास्यामः, but employ the term जिज्ञासा or enquiry, instead. In this chapter the author enumerates a number of qualifications expected of a thorough astrologer.]

तत्र सांवत्सरोऽभिजातः प्रियदर्शनो विनीतवेषः सत्यवागनसूयकः समः सुसंहितोपचितगात्रसन्धिरविकलश्चारुकरचरणनखनयनचिबुकदशनश्रवणललाटभ्रूत्तमाङ्गो वपुष्मान् गम्भीरोदात्तघोषः । प्रायः शरीराकारानुवर्तिनो हि गुणा दोषाश्च भवन्ति ॥२॥

In this connection an astrologer should belong to a noble family, be good-looking, of modest appearance or dress, truthful, free from jealousy, impartial, with well-proportioned and strong limbs and joints, undeformed, with beautiful hands, feet, nails, eyes, chin, teeth, ears, forehead, brows and head, with handsome body and a voice deep and sonorous. For, virtues and foibles are generally dependent on good and bad physical features.

[The author here expects a true astrologer to be possessed of all possible virtues and good physical features mentioned in the सामुद्रिकशास्त्र. We are reminded of the long list of virtues expected of the नायक—hero—of a drama according to Sanskrit rhetoricians. Like Kālidāsa our author is an adept in similes and general statements. Here the last sentence is a beautiful instance of अर्थान्तरन्यास. He has put the statement of Kālidāsa in his own words. See what the poet has said in the *Kumārasambhava* Canto V-36 :

यदुच्यते पार्वति पापवृत्तये न रूपमित्यव्यभिचारि तद्वचः ।
तथाहि ते रूपमुदारदर्शने तपस्विनामप्युपदेशतां गतम् ॥]

तत्र गुणाः । शुचिर्दक्षः प्रगल्भो वाग्मी प्रतिभानवान् देशकालवित् सात्त्विको न पर्षद्भीरुः सहाध्यायिभिरनभिभवनीयः कुशलोऽव्यसनी शान्तिकपौष्टिकाभिचारस्नानविद्याभिज्ञो विबुधार्चनव्रतोपवासनिरतः स्वतन्त्राश्चर्योत्पादितप्रभावः पृष्टाभिधाय्यन्यत्र दैवात्ययात् । ग्रहगणितसंहिताहोराग्रन्थार्थवेत्तेति ॥३॥

Now the following are the virtues of an astrologer : He must be clean, efficient, bold, eloquent, possessed of genius or ready wit, knower of the time and place, sincere, not timid in assemblies, not to be overpowered by his fellow students, expert, free from vices, well-versed in the art of performing rituals of both curative and preventive types, as well as in that of magic and bathing, engaged in the worship of Gods, observances or austerities and fast; possessed of great power generated by the wonderful achievements of his scientific knowledge and capable of answering queries made by others and suggesting remedial measures for troubles other than the visitations of God. He must also be thoroughly conversant with works dealing with calculations of planetary positions etc., Saṁhitā (triple compilation) and horoscopy in their details.

तत्र ग्रहगणिते पौलिशरोमकवासिष्ठसौरपैतामहेषु पञ्चस्वेतेषु सिद्धान्तेषु युगवर्षायनर्तुमासपक्षाहोरात्रयाममुहूर्तनाडीप्राणत्रुटित्रुट्याद्यवयवादिकस्य कालस्य क्षेत्रस्य च वेत्ता ॥४॥

Among the astronomical calculations the astrologer should be conversant with the various sub-divisions of time such as the yuga, year, solstice, a period of two months, month, fortnight, day and night, watch (a period of an hour and a half), Muhūrta (one of fortyeight minutes or two Ghaṭīs), Nāḍī (equal to 24 minutes), Prāṇa (time required for a breath), Truṭi (a small unit of time equal to that of two winds)[1] and its further subdivisions as well as

1. According to the ancient seers the following table gives the measures of time :

Time taken to pronounce one syllable is a Nimeṣa.

2 Nimeṣas = 1 Truṭi.
2 Truṭis = 1 Lava.
2 Lavas = 1 Kṣaṇa.
10 Kṣaṇas = 1 Kāṣṭhā.
10 Kāṣṭhās = 1 Kalā.
10 Kalās = 1 Nāḍikā.

60 long syllables or 6 Prāṇas (Breaths) } = 1 Vināḍi or Vighaṭī
(one breath consists of one inspiration and one expiration).

Angles

60 Tatparas = 1 Viliptā or Vikalā (second).
60 Viliptās = 1 Liptā or Kalā (minute).
60 Liptās = 1 Bhāga or Aṁśa (degree).
30 Bhāgas = 1 Rāśi or sign :

with the ecliptic (or with geometry) that are treated of in the five Siddhāntas (ancient astronomical systems) entitled Pauliśa (taught by Puliśa), Romaka (of the Romans), Vāsiṣṭha (taught by Sage Vasiṣṭha), Saura (taught by Sūrya or the Sun-God, called the Sūryasiddhānta) and Paitāmaha (of Pitāmaha or Brahman).

चतुर्णां च मानानां सौरसावननाक्षत्रचान्द्राणामधिमासकावमसम्भवस्य च कारणाभिज्ञः ॥५॥

He should also be thoroughly acquainted with the reasons for the existence of the four systems of measurement of time, viz. Saura or the solar system, Sāvana,terrestrial or the time intervening between the first rising of any given planet or star and its next rising, Nākṣatra or sidereal and Cāndra or lunar, as well as for the occurrence of intercalary months and increaring and decreasing lunar days.

[A solar day is the well-known period intervening two successive risings of the Sun. The same interval at the Equator is known as the Sāvana day. Thirty such days make one Sāvana month. The Sidereal day is the time taken by the Moon to traverse a star completely. Similarly a Sidereal month is the time taken by the Moon to cover the entire circle of 27 stars. A lunar day is called Tithi in Sanskrit and is measured in terms of 12° per day after the conjunction of the luminaries at a New Moon. A lunar month is the interval between two successive New Moons. See Āryabhaṭīya III—5, 6. An Adhikamāsa or intercalary month occurs when a complete lunar month is contained within the period of a solar month i.e. between two Solar Saṅkrāntis. It means that the Adhikamāsa, which is a lunar month, has no solar Saṅkrānti (transit) at all. Consequently that lunar year comes to have thirteen months. On the other hand if a lunar month comes to have two solar Saṅkrāntis, which is a very rare occurrence, it is called Kṣayamāsa or Diminutive month. One such month had occurred in the Śaka year 1744 and the next was in 1885 (Śaka year).[1]]

षष्ट्यब्दयुगवर्षमासदिनहोराधिपतीनां प्रतिपत्तिच्छेदवित् ॥६॥

He should also be well-versed in the calculation of the beginning and ending times of the cycle of sixty years, a yuga (a five-year period), a year, a month, a day, a Horā (hour), as well as of their respective lords.

1. Cf. ब्रह्मस्फुटसिद्धान्त "शशिसावनदिवसान्तरमवमानि।"

[The names of the five years constituting a Yuga and their lords as well as those of the 12 Yugas are explained by the author in Chapter VIII—23 and 24 *infra.* For Horā see पञ्चसिद्धान्तिका XIII—42.]

सौरादीनां च मानानामसदृशसदृशयोग्यायोग्यत्वप्रतिपादनपटुः ॥७॥

He should also be capable of explaining by means of arguments the similarities and dissimilarities as well as the appropriateness or otherwise of the different systems of measurement of time headed by the solar system.

[The differences among the four systems are to be found out by calculations, while the propriety or otherwise of a particular system has to be learnt from the Dharmaśāstras, which lay down all the rules for different rituals and observances.]

सिद्धान्तभेदेऽप्ययननिवृत्तौ प्रत्यक्षसममण्डललेखासम्प्रयोगाभ्युदितांशकानां छाया-जलयन्त्रदृग्गणितसाम्येन प्रतिपादनकुशलः ॥८॥

Despite differences of opinion among the Siddhāntas (astronomical systems) regarding the expiry or ending time of an Ayana (solstice), he should be capable of reconciling them by showing the agreement between correct calculation and what has been actually observed in the circle drawn on the ground by means of the shadow of the gnomon as well as water-appliances.

सूर्यादीनां च ग्रहाणां शीघ्रमन्दयाम्योत्तरनीचोच्चगतिकारणाभिज्ञः ॥९॥

He should also be well acquainted with the causes that are responsible for the different kinds of motions of the planets headed by the Sun, viz. fast, slow, southerly, northerly, towards perigee and apogee.

सूर्याचन्द्रमसोश्च ग्रहणे ग्रहणादिमोक्षकालदिक्प्रमाणस्थितिविमर्दवर्णदेशा-नामनागतग्रहसमागमयुद्धानामादेष्टा ॥१०॥

He must be able to forecast by calculation the times of commencement, ending, direction, magnitude, duration, intensity and colour at the eclipses of the Sun and the Moon, as well as the conjunctions of the Moon with the five Tārāgrahas or non-luminous planets and the planetary warfare.

प्रत्येकग्रहभ्रमणयोजनकक्ष्याप्रमाणप्रतिविषययोजनपरिच्छेदकुशलः ॥११॥

He should also be expert in determining accurately the motion in Yojanas, orbit, dimensions etc. of every planet in Yojanas.

[The subject of this verse is treated of in astronomical works like the Sūryasiddhānta, Āryabhaṭīya, Brāhmasphuṭasiddhānta etc. The Golādhyāya, Chapter IV, of the Āryabhaṭīya with the translation of W.F. Clark throws much light on this.]

भूभगणभ्रमणसंस्थानाद्यक्षावलम्बकाहर्व्यासचरदलकालराश्युदयच्छायानाडीकरणप्रभृतिषु क्षेत्रकालकरणेष्वभिज्ञः ॥१२॥

He must be thoroughly acquainted with the Earth's rotation on its own axis round the Sun and its revolution along the circle of constellations, its shape and such other details, the latitude of a place and its complement, the difference in the lengths of the day and night (lit. diameter of the Day-circle), the Carakhaṇḍas of a place, rising periods of the different Signs of the zodiac at a given place, the methods of converting the length of shadow into time (in Ghaṭīs) and time into the length of shadow and such other things, as well as those to find out the exact time in Ghaṭīs that has elapsed since Sunrise or Sunset at any required time from the position of the Sun or from the Ascendant, as the case may be.

नानाचोद्यप्रश्नभेदोपलब्धिजनितवाक्सारो निकषसन्तापाभिनिवेशैः कनकस्येवाधिकतरममलीकृतस्य शास्त्रस्य वक्ता तन्त्रज्ञो भवति ॥१३॥

He should really be learned in the Science of Astrology whose words have attained the power (of carrying conviction to the hearers) as a result of his proper understanding of the various objections and queries, and who is capable of expounding the Science which has become in his hands all the brighter and more flawless like gold that has been subjected to the touch-stone, fire and hammer.

[The qualifications of an astrologer-cum-astronomer indirectly enumerate the subject-matter of this Science in all its ramifications. Thus the Viṣaya or subject-matter of this Śāstra among the four Anubandhas has been explained.

After this the author resorts to the metrical medium.]

न प्रतिबद्धं गमयति वक्ति न च प्रश्नमेकमपि पृष्टः ।
निगदति न च शिष्येभ्यः स कथं शास्त्रविज्ज्ञेयः ॥१४॥

If a person is unable to understand the real purport of the Science (by separating the essentials from the non-essentials by means of his intellectual acumen), nor to answer any question put to him, nor to explain the Science to his pupils, how could he be known as an astrologer, one well-versed in this Science ?

[This is the usual tirade against half-baked astrologers, hypocrites and quacks. The following verse too is in the same vein.]

ग्रन्थोऽन्यथाऽन्यथार्थकरणं यश्चान्यथा करोत्यबुधः ।
स पितामहमुपगम्य स्तौति नरो वैशिकेनार्याम् ॥१५॥

He is an ignorant fellow who interprets the text wrongly and whose astronomical calculations are utterly inaccurate. For, such a person is no better than one who goes to his grandfather or God Brahman and praises before him his grandmother or the Goddess Sarasvatī with the attributes of a courtesan.

[Through the figure of speech Nidarśanā the author condemns charlatans bitterly, of course, in a sarcastic manner.]

तन्त्रे सुपरिज्ञाते लग्ने छायाम्बुयन्त्रसंविदिते ।
होरार्थे च सुरूढे नादेष्टुर्भारती वन्ध्या ॥१६॥

If an astrologer has mastered the astronomical Science, and has brought about perfect agreement between the mathematical results and observations made by means of the shadow of gnomon and the water-appliance, and is well established in the science of predictive astrology, his pronouncements will never go wrong or fruitless.

[After ridiculing unworthy astrologers the author extols a worthy one here. This is similar to the Vedic text quoted by Patañjali viz. "एकः शब्दः सम्यग्ज्ञातः सुप्रयुक्तः स्वर्गे लोके कामधुग्भवति", and Daṇḍin's statement viz.

"गौर्गौः कामदुघा सम्यक्प्रयुक्ता स्मर्यते बुधैः ।
दुष्प्रयुक्ता पुनर्गोत्वं प्रयोक्तुः सैव शंसति ॥"

See also फलदीपिका XXVI-50.

The instruments employed in astronomy are enumerated in the सिद्धान्तशिरोमणि thus.

गोलो नाडीवलयं यष्टिः शङ्कुर्घटीचक्रम् ।
चापं तुर्यं फलकं धीरेकं पारमार्थिकं यन्त्रम् ॥

उक्तं चार्यविष्णुगुप्तेन—

अप्यर्णवस्य पुरुषः प्रतरन्कदाचि-
दासादयेदनिलवेगवशेन पारम् ।
न त्वस्य कालपुरुषाख्यमहार्णवस्य
गच्छेत्कदाचिदनृषिर्मनसापि पारम् ॥१७॥

It has also been declared by the revered Viṣṇugupta :—

Perchance a man might be able to reach the other shore of the ocean by swimming, being driven by the force of wind. On the other hand, never could one, who is not a Sage, even dream of crossing the great ocean that is known as Kālapuruṣa or the God of Time i.e. the Science of Astrology.

[Just as the mysteries of life and death are proved by Sages by means of penance and Yoga, even so this Science of astrology helps one to solve this eternal mystery, provided he equips himself both intellectually and spiritually. In other words, a true astrologer must lead a life of contentment, detachment and contemplation.

This verse appears to have been taken from some work, possibly on astrology, written by the famous politician stalwart, Cāṇakya, who was otherwise known as Viṣṇugupta as well as Kauṭilya. This verse is in वसन्ततिलका metre.]

होराशास्त्रेऽपि च राशिहोराद्रेष्काणनवांशकद्वादशभागत्रिंशद्भागबलाबलपरिग्रहो ग्रहाणां दिक्स्थानकालचेष्टाभिरनेकप्रकारबलनिर्धारणं प्रकृतिधातुद्रव्यजातिचेष्टादिपरिग्रहो निषेकजन्मकालविस्मापनप्रत्ययादेशसद्योमरणायुर्दायदशान्तर्दशाष्टकवर्गराजयोगचन्द्रयोगद्विग्रहादियोगानां नाभसादीनां च योगानां फलान्याश्रयभावावलोकननिर्याणगत्यनूकानि तत्कालप्रश्नशुभाशुभनिमित्तानि विवाहादीनां च कर्मणां करणम् ॥१८॥

And the Science of Predictive Astrology treats of the following topics: The Signs of the Zodiac, Horā (equal to 15°), decanate (equal to 10°), Navāṁśa (1/9 of a Sign or 3°—20'), Dvādaśāṁśa 1/12 of a Sign or 2°—30'), Triṁśāṁśa (30° degrees assigned to the five non-luminous planets), determination of strength and weakness of planets on the basis of these parts or Vargas, ascertaining the multifarious strength of planets due to their direction, position, time and motion, the humours, constituent elements of the body, substances, castes, functions and the like, represented by or allotted to the planets as well as the Signs, the time of impregnation and actual birth, forecasting wonderful and freak births, immediate death, total span of life contributed by the planets, the planetary major periods and sub-periods, Aṣṭakavargas of planets, Rāja-yogas, lunar Yogas, conjunctions of two or more planets, Nābhasa-yogas and such other Yogas and their effects, the effects arising from the occupation of Signs, houses etc. by the planets and those of their aspects, exit from the world and the region from which one had come and to which one would go after death, predicting good and bad results on sudden queries, good and bad omens (or good and bad prognostications indicating the answers to be given to a query made on the spot), and the performance of religious rites such as marriage.

[Here the author alludes to all the three branches of astrology viz. Predictive Horary and Electional. Hence it appears that the name Horāśāstra is a comprehensive term and not applicable to predictive astrology or horoscopy alone. It is, however, to be distinguished from *Grahagaṇita*, Astronomy.]

यात्रायां तु तिथिदिवसकरणनक्षत्रमुहूर्तविलग्नयोगदेहस्पन्दनस्वप्नविजयस्नान-
ग्रहयज्ञगणयागाग्निलिङ्गहस्त्यश्वेङ्गितसेनाप्रवादचेष्टादिग्रहषाड्गुण्योपायमङ्गलामङ्गल-
शकुनसैन्यनिवेशभूमयोऽग्निवर्णा मन्त्रिचरदूताटविकानां यथाकालं प्रयोगाः परदुर्गोपल-
म्भोपायश्चेत्युक्तमाचार्यैः ॥१६॥

The ancient teachers have also stated that the Science of Yātrā or Journey or Expedition comprises the following topics : Tithis or lunar days, week days, Karaṇas, constellations, Muhūrta (period of 48 minutes), Ascendant, Yogas (called Nityayogas), throbbing of limbs, dreams, ritual bathing for victory in battle, sacrifices performed for propitiating the planetary Deities, worship of the Yakṣas seven days, before the commencement of a journey or expedition, prognosis through the movement of the flame of the sacrificial fire, reading the mind of the elephants and horses through the movements of their limbs, talk of the troops (or military proclamations), their activities and the like as omens, auspicious and inauspicious auguries as well as the positions of planets for the employment of the six military expedients and the four political means, camping grounds for the army, colours of the sacrificial fires as auguries, employment of ministers, spies, ambassadors or emmissaries and foresters at the appropriate time and the plan for besieging and capturing enemy fortresses.

[From the above-named topics it is clear that Yātrā covers the five elements of the almanac that can be got through mathematical calculations, prognostications which are within the province of horary astrology, and electional astrology. Unless the astrologer has a rudimentary knowledge of the rituals as well as politics he cannot be a good adviser in respect of military expeditions.]

जगति प्रसारितमिवालिखितमिव मतौ निषिक्तमिव हृदये ।
शास्त्रं यस्य सभगणं नादेशा निष्फलास्तस्य ॥२०॥

The predictions made by an astrologer who has mastered both the theory and practice of the science of astrology, and astronomy, as if it were spread before his eyes in the world, inscribed in his intellect and firmly implanted in his heart, will never go wrong.

[This verse is but an elaboration of verse II-3 *supra*. These two could have been given together.]

संहितापारगश्च दैवचिन्तको भवति ॥२१॥

A true astrologer whose business is to divine man's fortune as determined by his past actions, should also be a thorough scholar of the Saṁhitā.

[For a brief description of Saṁhitā see I-9 *supra*.

In the following long prose passage a detailed list of the contents is furnished.]

यत्रैते संहितापदार्थाः ॥२२॥

दिनकरादीनां ग्रहाणां चारास्तेषु च तेषां प्रकृतिविकृतिप्रमाणवर्णकिरणद्युतिसंस्थानास्तमनोदयमार्गमार्गान्तरवक्रानुवक्रर्क्षग्रहसमागमचारादिभिः फलानि, नक्षत्रकूर्मविभागेन देशेष्वगस्त्यचारः । सप्तर्षिचारः । ग्रहभक्तयो नक्षत्रव्यूहग्रहशृङ्गाटकग्रहयुद्धग्रहसमागमग्रहवर्षफलगर्भलक्षणरोहिणीस्वात्याषाढीयोगाः सद्योवर्षकुसुमलतापरिधिपरिवेषपरिघपवनोल्कादिग्दाहक्षितिचलनसन्ध्यारागगन्धर्वनगररजोनिर्घातार्घकाण्ड-सस्यजन्मेन्द्रध्वजेन्द्रचापवास्तुविद्याङ्ग-विद्यावायसविद्यान्तरचक्रमृगचक्रश्व-चक्रवातचक्रप्रासादलक्षण-प्रतिमालक्षणप्रतिष्ठापन-वृक्षायुर्वेदोदकार्गलनीराजनखञ्जनकोत्पातशान्ति-मयूरचित्रकघृतकम्बलखड्गपट्टकृकवाकुकूर्मगोजाश्वेभपुरुषस्त्रीलक्षणान्यन्तःपुरचिन्ता पिटकलक्षणोपानच्छेदवस्त्रच्छेदचामरदण्डशयनाऽऽसनलक्षणरत्नपरीक्षा दीपलक्षणं दन्तकाष्ठाद्याश्रितानि शुभाशुभानि निमित्तानि सामान्यानि च जगतः प्रतिपुरुषं पार्थिवे च प्रतिक्षणमनन्यकर्माभियुक्तेन दैवज्ञेन चिन्तयितव्यानि । न चैकाकिना शक्यन्तेऽहर्निशमवधारयितुं

निमित्तानि । तस्मात्सुभृतेनैव दैवज्ञेनान्येऽपि तद्विदश्चत्वारः कर्तव्याः । तत्रैकेनैन्द्री चाग्नेयी च दिगवलोकयितव्या । याम्या नैर्ऋती चान्येनैव वारुणी वायव्या चोत्तरा चैशानी चेति । यस्मादुल्कापातादीनि शीघ्रमपगच्छन्तीति । तस्याश्चाकारवर्णस्नेहप्रमाणादिग्रहर्क्षोपघातादिभिः फलानि भवन्ति ॥२३॥

In this Science the following subjects are dealt with in the Saṁhitā :—The movements of the planets headed by the Sun, their nature and change, if any, their magnitude, colour, rays, lustre, shape, setting, rising, orbit, change of motion on their route, retrograde and direct motion; upward motion, conjunction with a star or planet, and their course among these; the division of the constellations among the countries and their effects on the latter; the movement of Agastya (Canopus) and its rise, the course of the seven sages i.e. the constellation called Ursa Major, and their effects; the assignment of countries, substances and living beings to the planets and stars; a triangular oonfiguration of the planets wherein all the three houses, viz. 1st, 5th and 9th are occupied and its wholesome effects; the effects of planets being at war, their conjunction with the Moon, the planet presiding over the year and its effects, indications of the approach of the monsoon, the Moon's conjunctions with the stars, Rohiṇī, Svātī and the two Āṣāḍhas, signs of immediate rainfall, prognostication through the growth of flowers and creepers, the misty circle around the Sun and the Moon, a bar-like row of clouds crossing the Sun at its rising or setting, effects of winds, fall of meteors, appearance of a blaze in the quarters, earthquakes, redness of the sky at twilights, clouds appearing in the form of a city, dust-storms, portent of thunder-bolts, fluctuation in the prices of commodities, growth of crops, Indra's banner worshipped by kings, rainbow, architecture, the science of foretelling effects from the movements of limbs or from the cawing of crows, omens in the circle of quarters, phenomena connected with the deer, dogs, winds blowing in the eight quarters, characteristics of temples and royal palaces, manufacture of images, installation of idols, treatment and fertilizers of trees, water-divination, ceremony of general purification by water done by kings etc., flight of the wagtail, expiatory ceremonies for warding off calamities presaged by portents, a colourful resume of the astronomical elements, royal bath under the Puṣya asterism, characteristics of swords, royal crowns, cocks, tortoises, cows, goats, horses, elephants, men and women, matters pertaining to harems, features of pimples, tearing of shoes and clothes, chowries, royal staffs, beds and seats, examination of gems, characteristics of lamps, materials derived from tusks, wood etc., good and bad omens in general applicable to the entire world as well as to each individual and the sovereign—all these ought to be considered by an astrologer every moment of his life with a single-minded devotion. And it is not possible for an astrologer to comprehend single-handed all the omens occurring day and night. Hence an astrologer who is well employed by a king should engage four other scholars of the science (to assist him). Each of them would be in charge of two directions : One to watch the east and the south-east, the second one for the south and the south-west and the third one for the west and north-west, and lastly the fourth one for the north and the north-east. For, the fall of meteors and the like take place suddenly and disappear quickly, and different effects are mentioned according to their shape, colour, viscidity or glossiness, size and the like, as well as to their striking, grazing etc. the planets and stars.

[The word कूर्मविभाग has interesting connotations : It should not be construed as Division of Tortoise. Instead, it means, the Division of the Globe, because the back or shell of that animal resembles a half of the globe. In this connection read what Dr. H. Kern remarks on this subject : "The word *Kūrma* is the specific Sanskrit form of a word once common to all Indo-European tongues, viz. *Kūrma*, Lat. *Culmus*, Teuton *holm*, etc. It does not originally denote the 'tortoise' itself, but its back, for the proper meaning is 'mound, buckle, half-globe, holm." Even in Sanskrit, in such compounds, as *Kūrmonnata*, the word signifies the form of the back of the tortoise. At the time when the word *Kūrma-Vibhāga* became current, *Kūrma* was taken in its proper sense. Yet in later times, they wholly mistook the meaning and made an absurd drawing, representing a tortoise, as if *Kūrma* could denote a level ! The rendering by 'Globe' is not wholly exact, since properly only a half-globe, a *holm*, is supposed to be raised above the waters." The *Planetary Triangle* is referred to in the *Bṛhajjātaka* as "शृङ्गाटकं नवमपञ्चमलग्नसंस्थैः ।"

He gives its effect as, "शृङ्गाटके चिरसुखी ।"

The Sārāvalī, however, states,—

प्रियकलहसमरसाहससुखिनो नृपतेः प्रियाः सुभगकान्ताः ।
आढ्या युवतिद्वेष्याः शृङ्गाटकसम्भवा मनुजाः ॥]

कृत्स्नाङ्गोपाङ्गकुशलं होरागणितनैष्ठिकम् ।
यो न पूजयते राजा स नाशमुपगच्छति ॥२४॥

A king, who does not honour an astrologer who is thoroughly proficient in the science with all its parts and minute subdivisions and who is wedded to Horoscopy and Astronomy, will surely come to grief.

[In this and the following fourteen verses the metre employed is the Śloka.]

वनं समाश्रिता येऽपि निर्ममा निष्परिग्रहाः ।
अपि ते परिपृच्छन्ति ज्योतिषां गतिकोविदम् ॥२५॥

Even ascetics who have resorted to forests and who are free from attachment (i.e. the sense of 'mine') and family ties, consult an expert astrologer (who can know people's fate through the movements of planets).

[It is extremely difficult even for sages and hermits to attain self-realization. As Śaṅkarācārya states 'ईश्वरानुग्रहादेव पुंसामद्वैतभावना', it is not given to all to attain the supreme bliss. Some may have to take several births for that. Hence, naturally even sages may become anxious to know from an astrologer how far the planets are favourably disposed towards them.]

अप्रदीपा यथा रात्रिरनादित्यं यथा नभः ।
तथाऽसांवत्सरो राजा भ्रमत्यन्ध इवाध्वनि ॥२६॥

Just as the night devoid of lights or lamps is utterly blind, and the sky without the Sun dark, even so will a king grope in life in the dark like a blind man on the way, if he is not guided by a good astrologer.

[This and the following verses extol the utility and greatness of a true astrologer in all spheres of life, especially in the political one. The author, who was a gifted astrologer, had realized the unusual importance of astrology as a social science. The similes employed here are striking.]

मुहूर्ततिथिनक्षत्रमृतवश्चायने तथा ।
सर्वाण्येवाकुलानि स्युर्न स्यात्सांवत्सरो यदि ॥२७॥

If there be no astrologer to guide a king's steps, Muhūrtas (auspicious periods), lunar days, stars, seasons and solstices would all be confused for him.

[In the absence of an astrologer-guide the king cannot understand the seasons, auspicious and inauspicious days etc. and so may commit serious errors leading to Adharma.]

तस्माद्राज्ञाधिगन्तव्यो विद्वान् सांवत्सरोऽग्रणीः ।
जयं यशः श्रियं भोगाञ्छ्रेयश्च समभीप्सता ॥२८॥

Hence a king who aspires for victory, fame, prosperity, enjoyments and spiritual progress ought to employ the best astrologer who is well-versed in the science.

[In the author's view the king has no better friend, philosopher and guide than a good astrologer. It has been already shown that the astrologer should be an ideal person, not a mercenary. See his extraordinary greatness in the following verses.]

नासांवत्सरिके देशे वस्तव्यं भूतिमिच्छता ।
चक्षुर्भूतो हि यत्रैष पापं तत्र न विद्यते ॥२९॥

One who wishes for prosperity ought not to reside in a country which does not possess a good astrologer. For, no sin can remain in the place where resides an astrologer who is the eye, as it were, of the society.

न सांवत्सरपाठी च नरकेषूपपद्यते ।
ब्रह्मलोकप्रतिष्ठां च लभते दैवचिन्तकः ॥३०॥

A person who studies astrology and divines the course of people's destiny will never be found in hell. On the other hand, he will attain a permanent status in the world of Brahman.

ग्रन्थतश्चार्थतश्चैतत्कृत्स्नं जानाति यो द्विजः ।
अग्रभुक् स भवेच्छ्राद्धे पूजितः पङ्क्तिपावनः ॥३१॥

A Brahmin who knows this science in its entirety both in letter and spirit deserves to be worshipped and fed as the chief guest at a Srāddha and he sanctifies the whole feast.

[Generally guests that are not related to the departed person are not invited to Śrāddhas. However, great personages and saintly persons, who may visit a house by chance on such an occasion, are honoured and fed before the food is offered to the *manes*. The word पङ्क्तिपावनः means that one purifies the 'entire row of eaters', though the row may contain some unholy persons and the food served may not be quite holy and good.]

म्लेच्छा हि यवनास्तेषु सम्यक् शास्त्रमिदं स्थितम् ।
ऋषिवत्तेऽपि पूज्यन्ते किं पुनर्दैवविद्द्विजः ॥३२॥

The Yavanas are, no doubt, non-Aryan in origin. Still this Science has found a stable position in them. When even they are honoured as Sages, how much more should a Brahmin astrologer be ?

[The realm of the intellect and spirit knows no barriers of time and clime as well as of religion and colour. Our author displays his catholicity by acknowledging the greatness of Greek astrology. This statement, however, does not prove that Indian astrology is derived from the Greek. It only shows that by the time of Varāhamihira the Greeks and Romans had a system of astrology akin to the Indian. This led to his quoting parallel views of foreign astrologers.

The commentator quotes the following verses to show that the science went from the east to the west :

यद्दानवेन्द्राय मयाय सूर्यः शास्त्रं ददौ सम्प्रणताय पूर्वम् ।
विष्णोर्वसिष्ठश्च महर्षिमुख्यो ज्ञानामृतं यत्परमाससाद ॥
पराशरश्चाप्यधिगम्य सोमाद्गुह्यं सुराणां परमाद्भुतं यत् ।
प्रकाशयाञ्चक्रुरनुक्रमेण महर्धिमन्तो यवनेषु तत्ते ॥

What the Divine Sun had imparted to the humble Maya, king of the Dānavas, in days of yore, the supreme nectarous knowledge that the great Sage Vasiṣṭha got from Lord Viṣṇu, and the wonderful secret knowledge of the Gods that Parāśara obtained from Soma, were all brought to light in course of time by these illustrious ones, and are now found with the Yavanas (Greeks).]

कुहकावेशपिहितकर्णोपश्रुतिहेतुभिः ।
कृतादेशो न सर्वत्र प्रष्टव्यो न स दैववित् ॥३३॥

One who makes predictions as a result of sorcery, spirit-possession and learning got by eavesdropping and hearsay, should never be consulted. For, he is no astrologer at all.

अविदित्वैव यः शास्त्रं दैवज्ञत्वं प्रपद्यते ।
स पङ्क्तिदूषकः पापो ज्ञेयो नक्षत्रसूचकः ॥३४॥

One who assumes the status of an astrologer without having any knowledge of the Science should be considered as a sinner that pollutes the holy company of eaters at a feast and a mere gazer at the stars.

[The compound नक्षत्रसूचक is a derisive remark against charlatans. There are similar digs at grammarians and ritualists viz. वैयाकरणखसूचि: and मीमांसकदुर्दुरूढ:.]

नगरद्वारलोष्टस्य यद्वत्स्यादुपयाचितम् ।
आदेशस्तद्वदज्ञानां यः सत्यः स विभाव्यते ॥३५॥

The prediction made by ignorant men (i.e. so-called astrologers) which might be fulfilled by a fluke is just like a prayer made to the brick of the city gate for a boon that is granted by blind chance.

[There is a world of difference between a road-side stone and an Emblem of the Lord Śiva which has been installed in a proper shrine with due solemnity and to the accompaniment of Vedic rites and chants done by great saints and seers.]

सम्पत्त्या योजितादेशस्तद्विच्छिन्नकथाप्रियः ।
मत्तः शास्त्रैकदेशेन त्याज्यस्तादृङ्महीक्षिता ॥३६॥

A king should reject an astrologer who is proud of his little knowledge of the Science, who claims success of his previous predictions, and who is fond of elaborating irrelevant matters.

यस्तु सम्यग्विजानाति होरागणितसंहिताः ।
अभ्यर्च्यः स नरेन्द्रेण स्वीकर्त्तव्यो जयैषिणा ॥३७॥

A king wishing for success ought to worship and secure the services of an astrologer who is a past master in Horoscopy, Astronomy and Saṁhitā.

न तत्सहस्रं करिणां वाजिनां च चतुर्गुणम् ।
करोति देशकालज्ञो यथैको दैवचिन्तकः ॥३८॥

A single astrologer i.e. one who studies the course of Destiny, who is familiar with the special features of times and climes can achieve what a thousand elephants and four times as many horses cannot together do.

दुःस्वप्नदुर्विचिन्तितदुष्प्रेक्षितदुष्कृतानि कर्माणि ।
क्षिप्रं प्रयान्ति नाशं शशिनः श्रुत्वा भसंवादम् ॥३९॥

All bad dreams, bad thoughts, bad sights and bad deeds of a person come to an end immediately on his hearing about the Moon's passage over the lunar mansions from an astrologer.

[It is well-known that astrology-cum-astronomy is a holy ancillary of the Vedas called the 'Eye' of the वेदपुरुष. As such its study must redound to one's spiritual progress. Yogins meditate on the Sun. So it is a tradition among astrologers, and some others too, to read the पञ्चाङ्ग—almanac—in the morning after ablutions and recite the following verse at the end :

तिथेश्च श्रियमाप्नोति वारादायुष्यवर्धनम् ।
नक्षत्राद्धरते पापं योगाद्रोगनिवारणम् ।।
करणात्कार्यसिद्धिं च पञ्चाङ्गफलमुत्तमम् ।
एतेषां पठनान्नित्यं गङ्गास्नानफलं भवेत् ।।

The commentator here quotes another verse :

श्रुत्वा तिथिं भग्रहवासरं च प्राप्नोति धर्मार्थयशांसि सौख्यम् ।
आरोग्यमायुर्विजयं सुतांश्च दुःस्वप्नघातं प्रियतां च लोके ।।]

न तथेच्छति भूपतेः पिता जननी वा स्वजनोऽथवा सुहृत् ।
स्वयशोऽभिविवृद्धये यथा हितमाप्तः सबलस्य दैववित् ।।४०।।

Even his own father, mother, kinsman or a friend would not be solicitous so much for the prosperity of the king and his army (or followers) as is a friendly astrologer who works only for his untarnished fame.

[In the *Viyoginī* metre the author explains the supreme importance and self-abnegation of a true astrologer, to whom work is worship.]

———

आदित्यचारः ॥३॥

Chapter III—The Sun's Transit

आश्लेषार्धाद्दक्षिणमुत्तरमयनं रवेर्धनिष्ठाद्यम् ।
नूनं कदाचिदासीद्येनोक्तं पूर्वशास्त्रेषु ॥१॥

There was indeed a time when the Sun's southerly course began from the middle of the star Āśleṣā and the northerly one from the commencement of the star Dhaniṣṭhā. For, it has been stated so in ancient works.

साम्प्रतमयनं सवितुः कर्कटकाद्यं मृगादितश्चान्यत् ।
उक्ताभावो विकृतिः प्रत्यक्षपरीक्षणैर्व्यक्तिः ॥२॥

दूरस्थचिह्नवेधादुदयेऽस्तमयेऽपि वा सहस्रांशोः ।
छायाप्रवेशनिर्गमचिह्नैर्वा मण्डले महति ॥३॥

At present the southerly course of the Sun starts from the beginning of Cancer and the other from the initial point of Sign Capricorn. The actual fact which goes against the old statement can be verified by direct observation. The Sun's change of course can be detected by marking everyday the position of a distant object either at sunrise or sunset, or by watching and marking the entry and exit of the shadow of the gnomon planted at the centre of a big circle drawn on the ground.

[The author's scientific attitude is discernible here. A true astronomer should not follow blindly the statements of ancient writers. For, without applying periodic corrections to the results obtained according to old rules, one cannot get at the true positions of planets.]

अप्राप्य मकरमर्को विनिवृत्तो हन्ति सापरां याम्याम् ।
कर्कटकमसम्प्राप्तो विनिवृत्तश्चोत्तरामैन्द्रीम् ॥४॥

If the Sun should change his course before reaching Makara (Capricorn), he would cause the destruction of countries in the west and south, while should he alter his course before touching Cancer, he would harm the countries in the east and north.

[Sage Garga says on this :

यदा निवर्ततेऽप्राप्तो धनिष्ठामुत्तरायणे ।
आश्लेषां दक्षिणेऽप्राप्तस्तदा विन्द्यान्महद्भयम् ॥

Sage Parāśara too echoes the same idea. This means that sometimes on actual observation the Sun must have been found to be changing his course causing the solstices before touching the initial points of Capricorn and Cancer respectively. This phenomenon was considered to be a bad indication.]

उत्तरमयनमतीत्य व्यावृत्तः क्षेमसस्यवृद्धिकरः ।
प्रकृतिस्थश्चाप्येवं विकृतगतिर्भयकृदुष्णांशुः ॥५॥

Should the Sun tarry a little longer in his northerly course and then retrace his steps towards the south, he would cause great happiness in the country as well as an abundant growth of crops. The same effect will follow from the natural movement of the Sun. But if it is contrary to the rule, there will be danger to the world.

[By the word प्रकृति the commentator means the absence of any difference between observation and calculation.]

सतमस्कं पर्व विना त्वष्टा नामार्कमण्डलं कुरुते ।
स निहन्ति सप्त भूपाञ्जनांश्च शस्त्राग्निदुर्भिक्षैः ॥६॥

The planet Tvaṣṭā darkens the solar disc on days other than the Parvans viz. 8th, 14th and 15th of each fortnight. As a result of this seven kings and their subjects come to grief through clash of arms, fire and famine.

[See what Sage Parāśara says on this :

अपर्वणि शशाङ्कार्कौ त्वष्टा नाम महाग्रहः ।
आवृणोति तमश्श्यामः सर्वलोकविपत्तये ॥]

तामसकीलकसंज्ञा राहुसुताः केतवस्त्रयस्त्रिंशत् ।
वर्णस्थानाकारैस्तान्दृष्ट्वाऽर्के फलं ब्रूयात् ॥७॥

There are 33 Ketus or Comets named Tāmasakīlakas (Dark Shafts) that are the offspring of Rāhu. When they appear on the Sun's orb, their effects will have to be declared according to their colour, position and shape.

[For details see footnote at the end of Chapter XI *infra*.]

ते चार्कमण्डलगताः पापफलाश्चन्द्रमण्डले सौम्याः ।
ध्वाङ्क्षकबन्धप्रहरणरूपाः पापाः शशाङ्केऽपि ॥८॥

These comets produce untoward effects, when they are seen on the Sun's disc, but are auspicious when seen on the lunar orb. However, when they take the shape of the crow, headless body and a sword (or any weapon), they produce only evil effects even in respect of the Moon.

तेषामुदये रूपाण्यम्भः कलुषं रजोवृतं व्योम ।
नगतरुशिखरामर्दी सशर्करो मारुतश्चण्डः ॥९॥

ऋतुविपरीतास्तरवो दीप्ता मृगपक्षिणो दिशां दाहाः ।
निर्घातमहीकम्पादयो भवन्त्यत्र चोत्पाताः ॥१०॥

When these comets make their appearance the following effects are observed : The water turns turbid; the sky is filled with dust; a storm arises carrying sand and breaking the tops of mountains and trees (or of mountain trees); the trees and creepers show effects contrary to the seasons; animals and birds get heated by the Sun; there appear flares in the quarters; and thunderbolts, earthquakes and such other unusual phenomena take place foreboding evil.

[Modern scientists connect the appearance of sunspots with some unusual occurrences on the earth. I feel that these Tāmasakīlakas might have been the same as the sunspots of today.]

न पृथक् फलानि तेषां शिखिकीलकराहुदर्शनानि यदि ।
तदुदयकारणमेषां केत्वादीनां फलं ब्रूयात् ॥११॥

No separate effects should be declared if these Tāmasakīlakas make their appearance during the eclipses of the luminaries. Their effects will have to be declared only when they become visible at other times.

यस्मिन्यस्मिन्देशे दर्शनमायान्ति सूर्यबिम्बस्थाः ।
तस्मिंस्तस्मिन्व्यसनं महीपतीनां परिज्ञेयम् ॥१२॥

क्षुत्प्रम्लानशरीरा मुनयोऽप्युत्सृष्टधर्मसच्चरिताः ।
निर्मांसबालहस्ताः कृच्छ्रेणायान्ति परदेशम् ॥१३॥

तस्करविलुप्तवित्ताः प्रदीर्घनिःश्वासमुकुलिताक्षिपुटाः ।
सन्तः सन्नशरीराः शोकोद्भवबाष्परुद्धदृशः ॥१४॥

क्षामा जुगुप्समानाः स्वनृपतिपरचक्रपीडिता मनुजाः ।
स्वनृपतिचरितं कर्म न पुराकृतं ब्रुवन्त्यन्ये ॥१५॥

गर्भेष्वपि निष्पन्ना वारिमुचो न प्रभूतवारिमुचः ।
सरितो यान्ति तनुत्वं क्वचित्क्वचिज्जायते सस्यम् ॥१६॥

In whichever country these Dark Shafts are sighted on the solar orb, the kings of those countries will have great suffering. Even sages with emaciated bodies owing to hunger will forsake their religious duties and righteous conduct, and emigrate to other countries with difficulty, carrying in their arms their children that are reduced to mere skin and bones. Virtuous people will be robbed of their wealth by thieves, will heave deep sighs and have drooping eye-lids and languid bodies, and will shed torrents of tears of great grief blinding their eyes. Famished people will feel disgusted being tormented by both their own king and by the kings of other countries, and will condemn their king's conduct (which causes their suffering) but not their own previous acts. Though rain-bearing clouds appear in the sky, they will not pour down sufficient quantity of rain on the earth. Rivers will become very slender and crops sparse (i.e. in a few places only).

[In the next two verses the author refers to the effects of the shapes of these Dark Shafts.]

दण्डे नरेन्द्रमृत्युर्व्याधिभयं स्यात्कबन्धसंस्थाने ।
ध्वाङ्क्षे च तस्करभयं दुर्भिक्षं कीलकेऽर्कस्थे ॥१७॥

If the Dark Shaft on the solar disc should appear in the form of a rod, the effect would be death to the king; if in the form of a truncated body, it would cause danger of diseases; if in the form of a crow, there would be serious trouble from thieves; and lastly if in the form of a nail or wedge; there would be famine.

[The ancients must have come to the above conclusions after long and minute observations. For, they have given different evil effects for the Shafts appearing in different shapes.]

राजोपकरणरूपैश्छत्रध्वजचामरादिभिर्विद्धः ।
राजान्यत्वकृदर्कः स्फुलिङ्गधूमादिभिर्जनहा ॥१८॥

If the Sun's disc be attacked by the Shafts in the form of royal paraphernalia such as the umbrella, banner, chowrie etc., it is an indication of change of rulership; and if the solar orb is covered with sparks of fire, smoke or something similar to that, there would be destruction of human life on a large scale.

[By स्फुलिङ्ग what is possibly meant is the solar flare spoken of by modern astronomers.]

एको दुर्भिक्षकरो द्व्याद्याः स्युर्नरपतेर्विनाशाय ।
सितरक्तपीतकृष्णैस्तैर्विद्धोऽर्कोऽनुवर्णघ्नः ॥१९॥

If there is one of the objects mentioned above on the Sun's disc, it will cause famine; and if two or more such objects are sighted, it bodes the king's death. If, on the other hand; the objects mentioned above have the colours, white, red, yellow and black, the destruction of the four classes viz. Brahmin, Kṣatriya, Vaiśya and Śūdra, respectively is indicated.

[White is the symbol of purity, learning and intellectual guide; red is that of power, strength, anger etc.; yellow is the colour of auspiciousness and prosperity; and lastly black stands for inertia, ignorance and sin. Similarly wind and fire are symbols of physical power and intellectual brilliance respectively.]

दृश्यन्ते च यतस्ते रविबिम्बस्योत्थिता महोत्पाताः ।
आगच्छति लोकानां तेनैव भयं प्रदेशेन ॥२०॥

In whichever direction of the Sun's disc these great portents make their appearance, from that direction will arise trouble to the people.

ऊर्ध्वंकरो दिवसकरस्ताम्रः सेनापतिं विनाशयति ।
पीतो नरेन्द्रपुत्रं श्वेतस्तु पुरोहितं हन्ति ॥२१॥
चित्रोऽथवापि धूम्रो रविरश्मिर्व्याकुलं करोत्यूर्ध्वम् ।
तस्करशस्त्रनिपातैर्यदि सलिलं नाशु पातयति ॥२२॥

If the Sun should look red with rays shooting upwards, it forebodes the commander's death; if yellow, the prince's end; and if white, the priest's demise. If the Sun's upward rays be variegated or smoky and if there be no immediate rain following, it would cause great disaster to the country through robbers and clash of arms.

ताम्रः कपिलो वार्कः शिशिरे हरिकुङ्कुमच्छविश्च मधौ ।
आपाण्डुकनकवर्णो ग्रीष्मे वर्षासु शुक्लश्च ॥२३॥

शरदि कमलोदराभो हेमन्ते रुधिरसन्निभः शस्तः ।
प्रावृट्काले स्निग्धः सर्वर्तुनिभोऽपि शुभदायी ॥२४॥

The Sun appears generally reddish or tawny in winter, of greenish yellow or saffron colour in the spring, pale or golden in summer, whitish in the rainy season, of the colour of the interior of the lotus in autumn, and lastly blood-red in the dewy season. These natural colours of the Sun in the different seasons would produce only beneficial results. However, even if the Sun is glossy or having the colours assigned to other seasons in the monsoon, only auspicious results would follow.

[The commentator quotes from the author's समाससंहिता :

ताम्रघृतकनकमुक्ताकमलासृक्सन्निभः शुभः सविता ।
शिशिरादिषु षट्सु ऋतुषु प्रावृषि सर्वर्तुसन्निभः स्निग्धः ॥

as well as from वृद्धगर्ग:

शिशिरे ताम्रसङ्काशः कपिलो वापि भास्करः ।
वसन्ते कुङ्कुमप्रख्यो हरितो वापि शस्यते ॥
ग्रीष्मे कनकवैदूर्यं सर्वरूपो जलागमे ।
शस्तः शरदि पद्माभो हेमन्ते लोहितप्रभः ॥
एतत्स्वरूपं सवितुर्विपरीतमतोऽन्यथा ।

It is to be remembered in this connection that in ancient India the year commenced with the Śiśira or winter season.]

रूक्षः श्वेतो विप्रान् रक्ताभः क्षत्रियान्विनाशयति ।
पीतो वैश्यान् कृष्णस्ततोऽपराञ्छुभकरः स्निग्धः ॥२५॥

If the Sun should appear in the rainy season rough and white, it would cause the destruction of Brahmins; if blood-red in colour, the ruin of Kṣatriyas; if yellow, calamity to Vaiśyas (trading class); and if black, destruction of the Śūdras (labouring community). Still if he is glossy, he will prove auspicious to all the communities.

ग्रीष्मे रक्तो भयकृद्वर्षास्वसितः करोत्यनावृष्टिम् ।
हेमन्ते पीतोऽर्कः करोति न चिरेण रोगभयम् ॥२६॥

Being blood-red in summer the Sun causes danger to the people; in the rainy season he causes drought, being dark in appearance; and being yellowish in the dewy season he leads to the outbreak of diseases in the near future.

सुरचापपाटिततनुर्नृपतिविरोधप्रदः सहस्रांशुः ।
प्रावृट्काले सद्यः करोति विमलद्युतिर्वृष्टिम् ॥२७॥
वर्षाकाले वृष्टिं करोति सद्यः शिरीषपुष्पाभः ।
शिखिपत्रनिभः सलिलं न करोति द्वादशाब्दानि ॥२८॥

If the Sun's disc is cut by the rainbow, it bodes evil to the ruler of the country. If the Sun looks quite bright in the rainy season, it betokens immediate rain. Similarly, if the Sun be of the colour of the Śirīṣa flower in monsoon, there will be immediate rain. If, on the other hand, the Sun has the colour of the peacock's plume, there will be no rain for 12 years to come.

[See what वृद्धगर्ग says :

मयूरचन्द्रिकाभो वा यदा दृश्येत भास्करः ।
पूर्णे तु द्वादशे वर्षे तदा देवः प्रवर्षति ॥]

श्यामेऽर्के कीटभयं भस्मनिभे भयमुशन्ति परचक्रात् ।
यस्यर्क्षे सच्छिद्रस्तस्य विनाशः क्षितीशस्य ॥२९॥

If the Sun looks dark, there will be danger to crops from pests like locusts; and if he looks ash-coloured, there will be trouble to the country from an alien army. If the Sun's orb should have a slit, it forebodes the death of the king whose natal asterism is currently occupied by the Sun.

शशरुधिरनिभे भानौ नभस्तलस्थे भवन्ति सङ्ग्रामाः ।
शशिसदृशो नृपतिवधः क्षिप्रं चान्यो नृपो भवति ॥३०॥

If the Sun up in the sky should have the colour of hare's blood, it presages wars, and if he should look like the Moon, the king would be killed and another installed in his place.

[cf. गर्ग :

शशलोहितवर्णाभो यदा भवति भास्करः ।
तदा भवन्ति सङ्ग्रामा घोरा रुधिरकर्दमाः ॥]

क्षुन्मारकृद्घटनिभः खण्डो जनहा विदीधितिर्भयदः ।
तोरणरूपः पुरहा छत्रनिभो देशनाशाय ॥३१॥

The Sun appearing like a pot would cause hunger and death; if he looks cut up, people will die in large numbers; without rays he will cause dangers; appearing in the form of an arch, he will destroy the capital or cities; and in the form of an umbrella, he will cause the destruction of the entire country.

ध्वजचापनिभे युद्धानि भास्करे वेपने च रूक्षे च ।
कृष्णा रेखा सवितरि यदि हन्ति ततो नृपं सचिवः ॥३२॥

The Sun appearing like a flag or bow causes wars. The same effect will follow if he is quivering or rough or sharp. If there is a dark streak across the solar disc, the ruling monarch will be killed by his own minister.

[In the last quarter there is another reading—'नृप: सचिवम्', which would mean 'the king kills his own minister.']

दिवसकरमुदयसंस्थितमुल्काशनिविद्युतो यदा हन्युः ।
नरपतिमरणं विन्द्यात्तदान्यराजप्रतिष्ठा च ॥३३॥

Should the solar disc be struck by a meteor, lightning or thunderbolt at sunrise (or sunset), then it should be understood that the ruling king would die and the king of a foreign country be installed as the ruler.

[See पराशर :

उदयास्तमये भानुमुल्का हन्यात्समुत्थिता ।
प्रज्वलन्ती तदा राजा क्षिप्रं शस्त्रेण वध्यते ॥]

प्रतिदिवसमहिमकिरणः परिवेषी सन्ध्ययोर्द्वयोरथवा ।
रक्तोऽस्तमेति रक्तोदितश्च भूपं करोत्यन्यम् ॥३४॥

If the Sun should have the misty ring around him, or be red at the time of both rising and setting, there would be another king in the country.

प्रहरणसदृशैर्जलदैः स्थगितः सन्ध्याद्वयेऽपि रणकारी ।
मृगमहिषविहगखरकरभसदृशरूपैश्च भयदायी ॥३५॥

If the Sun should be covered at both the twilights with clouds resembling weapons of destruction, it would lead to wars in the near future. And if the clouds appear like the deer, buffaloes, birds, asses, camels and the like, there would be danger to the people.

दिनकरकराभितापादृक्षमवाप्नोति सुमहतीं पीडाम् ।
भवति तु पश्चाच्छुद्धं कनकमिव हुताशपरितापात् ॥३६॥

It is true that an asterism is subjected to great torture as a result of its being burnt by the hot rays of the Sun; but it soon becomes pure and sparkling like gold purified in fire.

[Sage पराशर says :

ग्रहोपसृष्टं नक्षत्रं सवितुर्योगमागतम् ।
विशोधयति तत्पापं तुषाग्निरिव काञ्चनम् ॥

Here we can see the difference in the opinions of the sage and our author. For, the former says that an asterism involved in an eclipse gets rid of the sin arising therefrom through its association with the Sun. However, वृद्धगर्ग strikes a different note :

यथाग्निना प्रज्वलिते गृहे तप्यन्त्यदूरिणः ।
तथार्कस्याप्यदूरस्थमृक्षं तदपि तप्यते ॥]

दिवसकृतः प्रतिसूर्यो जलकृदुदग्दक्षिणे स्थितोऽनिलकृत् ।
उभयस्थः सलिलभयं नृपमुपरि निहन्त्यधो जनहा ॥३७॥

If the mock-sun be situated to the north of the Sun, there would be good rain; if to the south of the Sun, storm; if on both sides of the Sun, danger from floods; if over the Sun, the king would die; and if beneath the Sun, the people of the country would perish.

रुधिरनिभो वियत्यवनिपान्तकरो न चिरात्
परुषरजोऽरुणीकृततनुर्यदि वा दिनकृत् ।
असितविचित्रनीलपरुषो जनघातकरः
खगमृगभैरवस्वररुतैश्च निशाद्यमुखे ॥३८॥

If the Sun up in the sky should look blood-red, it would ere long destroy the king. The same effect would follow, if the Sun be reddened by a dry duststorm. If the Sun's colour be dark, variegated, blue or soiled (rough), many people would be killed. The same disaster would overtake the country, if birds and beasts should howl dreadfully at sunrise and sunset.

[Being a poet of great eminence like कालिदास our author changes the metre towards the end of the chapter as it is done in the *Mahākāvyas*. This metre is called नर्दटक.]

अमलवपुरवक्रमण्डलः स्फुटविपुलामलदीर्घदीधितिः ।
अविकृततनुवर्णचिह्नभृज्जगति करोति शिवं दिवाकरः ॥३९॥

The Sun with a spotless form, with his orb not crooked, with bright, plentiful, clear and long rays, and having a natural appearance, colour and features will confer all good things on the people of the world.

[Says Sage पराशर :—

श्वेतः शिरीषपुष्पाभः पद्माभो रूप्यसन्निभः ।
वैदूर्यधृतमण्डाभो हेमाभश्च दिवाकरः ॥
वर्णैरेभिः प्रशस्तः स्यान्महास्निग्धः प्रतापवान् ।
भावनः सर्वसस्यानां क्षेमारोग्यसुभिक्षदः ॥

The verse is in the अपरवक्त्र or वैतालीय metre.

———

चन्द्रचारः ॥४॥

Chapter IV—The Moon's Transit

नित्यमधःस्थस्येन्दोर्भाभिर्भानोः सितं भवत्यर्द्धम् ।
स्वच्छाययान्यदसितं कुम्भस्येवाऽऽतपस्थस्य ॥१॥

By the Sun's rays one half of the Moon that is always beneath the Sun is illuminated, while the other half becomes dark by her own shadow, just as one half of a pot exposed to the Sun is.

[The commentator quotes both ब्रह्मसिद्धान्त and सूर्यसिद्धान्त :

रविदृष्टं सितमर्द्धं कृष्णमदृष्टं यथातपस्थस्य ।
कुम्भस्य तथासन्नं रवेरघस्थस्य चन्द्रस्य ॥

and

महतश्चाप्यधस्थस्य नित्यं भासयते रविः ।
अर्द्धं शशाङ्कबिम्बस्य न द्वितीयं कथञ्चन ॥]

सलिलमये शशिनि रवेर्दीधितयो मूर्च्छितास्तमो नैशम् ।
क्षपयन्ति दर्पणोदरनिहिता इव मन्दिरस्यान्तः ॥२॥

The Sun's rays being reflected on the surface of the watery Moon dispel the darkness of the night on the earth, just as the solar rays reflected on a mirror kept outside illumine the interior of the house.

[The सूर्यसिद्धान्त says :

तेजसां गोलकः सूर्यो ग्रहर्क्षाण्यम्बुगोलकाः ।
प्रभावन्तो हि दृश्यन्ते सूर्यरश्मिविदीपिताः ॥

आर्यभट says :

भूग्रहभानां गोलार्द्धानि स्वच्छायया विवर्णानि ।
अर्द्धानि यथा सार्द्धं सूर्याभिमुखानि दीप्यन्ते ॥

This verse of the text is also found in the पञ्चसिद्धान्तिका.]

त्यजतोऽर्कतलं शशिनः पश्चादवलम्बते यथा शौक्ल्यम् ।
दिनकरवशात्तथेन्दोः प्रकाशतेऽधः प्रभृत्युदयः ॥३॥

As the Moon goes farther and farther away from the surface of the Sun, her back gets more and more illumined by the Sun. In the same manner the Moon's disc begins to shine from the bottom in an increasing measure.

[See what the सूर्यसिद्धान्त says :

विप्रकर्षं यथा याति ह्यधःस्थश्चन्द्रमा रवेः ।
तथा तथास्य भूदृश्यमंशं भासयते रविः ॥]

प्रतिदिवसमेवमर्कात्स्थानविशेषेण शौक्ल्यपरिवृद्धिः ।
भवति शशिनोऽपराह्णे पश्चाद्भागे घटस्येव ॥४॥

In this manner the Moon's brightness increases everyday in proportion to her distance from the Sun, just as the western side of a pot becomes increasingly illumined in the afternoon.

[This explains how the Moon's phases occur. The simile given in this verse makes the meaning quite clear : Till the noon the front part of the pot will be illumined by the Sun and not the western or hind part. However, in the afternoon as the Sun descends from the zenith of the sky, greater and greater portions of the hind part of the pot are illumined.

In the following verses effects of the Moon's transit are given.]

ऐन्द्रस्य शीतकिरणो मूलाषाढाद्वयस्य चायातः ।
याम्येन बीजजलचरकाननहा वह्निभयदश्च ॥५॥

When the Moon passes through the south of the stars Jyeṣṭha, Mūla and the two Āṣāḍhas (Pūrva and Uttara), there would be destruction of seeds, aquatic animals and forests as well as danger from fire.

[The Moon is invariably auspicious if she moves to the left of planets and stars. See XVIII—1 *infra.*]

दक्षिणपार्श्वेन गतः शशी विशाखानुराधयोः पापः ।
मध्येन तु प्रशस्तः पितृदेवविशाखयोश्चापि ॥६॥

If the Moon should pass through the south of the stars Viśākhā and Anurādhā, evil effects would follow. However, if she passes through the middle of Maghā and Viśākhā, only beneficial effects will accrue to the world.

[See the समाससंहिता on this—

भवति विशाखाद्यानां षण्णां याम्येन पापदश्चन्द्रः ।
उदगिष्टः सर्वेषां पित्र्येशविशाखयोश्चान्तः ॥]

षडनागतानि पौष्णाद् द्वादश रौद्राच्च मध्ययोगीनि ।
ज्येष्ठाद्यानि नवर्क्षाण्युडुपतिनातीत्य युज्यन्ते ॥७॥

The six constellations beginning with Revatī conjoin with the Moon before she has actually come to them; the twelve stars beginning with Ārdrā conjoin with the Moon only when the latter comes to their middle portion, while the remaining nine counted from Jyeṣṭhā conjoin with the Moon only after she has completely passed by them.

[Sage गर्ग says :

उत्तराश्च तथादित्यं विशाखा चैव रोहिणी ।
एतानि षडध्यर्द्धभोगीनि महाक्षेत्राणि ॥
मघाश्विकृत्तिकासोमतिष्यपित्र्यभगाह्वयाः ।
सावित्रचित्रानूराधा मूलं तोयं च वैष्णवम् ॥
धनिष्ठाजैकपाच्चैव समभागः प्रकीर्तितः ।
एतानि पञ्चदश समभोगीनि मध्यक्षेत्राणि ॥
याम्येन्द्ररुद्रवायव्यसार्पवारुणसंज्ञिताः ।
एतानि षडर्द्धभोगीनि स्वल्पक्षेत्राणि ॥

See also ब्रह्मसिद्धान्त :

केशादित्यविशाखाप्रोष्ठपदार्यम्णवैश्वदेवानि ।
पट्षड्ज्येष्ठाभरणीस्वात्याद्र्वारुणाश्लेषाः ॥
पञ्चदशात्रानुक्तान्येकाऽभिजिदुक्तमृक्षभोगोऽन्यः ।
तन्मानं नाक्षत्रं दुरधिगमं मन्दबुद्धीनाम् ॥
अध्यर्द्धार्द्धसमक्षेत्राणां मध्यगतिलिप्तिकाः शशिनः ।
अध्यर्द्धार्द्धैकगुणा भभोगलिप्तास्तदैक्योनाः ॥
मण्डललिप्ताः शेषा भोगोऽभिजितः... ... ।

Now the author refers to some unusual appearances of the Moon and their effects.]

उन्नतमीषच्छृङ्गं नौसंस्थाने विशालता चोक्ता ।
नाविकपीडा तस्मिन्भवति शिवं सर्वलोकस्य ॥८॥

When the Moon looking like a boat has her horns raised a little and far from each other, there will be trouble to sea-faring people, but happiness to all the rest.

अर्द्धोन्नते च लाङ्गलमिति पीडा तदुपजीविनां तस्मिन् ।
प्रीतिश्च निर्निमित्तं मनुजपतीनां सुभिक्षं च ॥९॥

When the Moon's northern horn be higher than the other by a half, then it is called Lāṅgala or Plough (in shape). The effect of this would be trouble to farmers, but cordiality among the rulers of countries without any apparent reason, as well as good crops and prosperity in the country.

[A question might be raised here : How could there be good food crops and prosperity in the land when the husbandmen are in trouble ? The answer would be that when food crops are available in plenty their prices fall down. So the agriculturists suffer in consequence. It is also possible that there might be some epidemic breaking out among the farmers.

See what वृद्धगर्ग says on this :

यदा सोमः प्रतिपदि नौस्थायी सम्प्रदृश्यते ।
उत्तरोज्ज्वलशृङ्गो वा लाङ्गली च मनोहरः ॥
क्षेमं सुभिक्षमारोग्यं सर्वभूतेषु निर्दिशेत् ।
राज्ञां च विजयं ब्रूयाद्वर्द्धन्ते शृङ्गिणस्तथा ॥

From the above quotation it appears that according to this Sage no untoward happenings are indicated by the lunar appearance in the form of a boat or plough.]

दक्षिणविषाणमर्द्धोन्नतं यदा दुष्टलाङ्गलाख्यं तत् ।
पाण्ड्यनरेश्वरनिधनकृदुद्योगकरं बलानां च ॥१०॥

If the southern horn be raised by a half, it is named *Evil Plough*, and will bring about the death of the Pāṇḍya king and will lead to the mobilization of armies for war.

[वृद्धगर्ग is again quoted here :

दक्षिणे च भवेत्स्थूलं हीनं शृङ्गमथोत्तरम् ।
दुष्टलाङ्गलसंज्ञं तत् प्रजाक्षयकरं स्मृतम् ॥

This means that the *Evil Plough* is brought into existence when the Moon's southern horn appears much thicker than the northern one. The result of this would be destruction of human life on a large scale.]

समशशिनि सुभिक्षक्षेमवृष्टयः प्रथमदिवससदृशाः स्युः ।
दण्डवदुदिते पीडा गवां नृपश्चोग्रदण्डोऽत्र ॥११॥

When the two horns of the Moon are of equal height and thickness, there will be happiness, good rains and abundant food crops in the land. These effects will be felt throughout the month similar to those experienced on the first day of the month. If the Moon rises in the form of a rod, there will be trouble to the cattle and the king will be very cruel and tyrannical in punishing the subjects.

[वृद्धगर्ग says :

समशृङ्गो यदा दृष्टः शशी क्षेमसुभिक्षकृत् ।
प्रतिपत्सदृशं तत्र वासवो वर्षते तदा ॥

चन्द्ररेखा यदा चोदूर्ध्वमृज्वी दण्ड इव स्थिता ।
उदक्श्रृङ्गाधिकसमो दण्डस्थानं तदुच्यते ।।
उद्युक्तदण्डा राजानो विनिघ्नन्ति समन्ततः ।
गवां पीडां विजानीयाद्दण्डस्थाने यदा शशी ।।]

कार्मुकरूपे युद्धानि यत्र तु ज्या ततो जयस्तेषाम् ।
स्थानं युगमिति याम्योत्तरायतं भूमिकम्पाय ।।१२।।

If the Moon should appear in the form of a bow, there would be wars, and victory would go to those that live in the direction of the bowstring. Should she be stretched like the yoke of a carriage from the south to the north, there would be earthquake.

[वृद्धगर्ग states :

उदये तु यदा सोमं पश्येद्धनुरिवोदितम् ।
धनुर्द्धराणामुद्योगो जगद्युद्धकरो भवेत् ।।
क्षत्रियाः क्षत्रियान् घ्नन्ति वर्णांश्चैव तथा परे ।
अग्रतश्च जयस्तेषां पृष्ठतश्च पराजयः ।।
चन्द्ररेखा यदा व्यक्ता दक्षिणोत्तरमायता ।
शुक्लादौ प्रतिपद्येत तद्योगस्थानलक्षणम् ।।
सैन्योद्योगा भवन्त्यत्र भूमिकम्पश्च जायते ।।]

युगमेव याम्यकोट्यां किञ्चित्तुङ्गं स पार्श्वशायीति ।
विनिहन्ति सार्थवाहान् वृष्टेश्च विनिग्रहं कुर्यात् ।।१३।।

If the *yoke* is slightly raised at its southern tip than at the other, the Moon is then said to be *lying on a side*, the effect of which would be drought and destruction of traders.

[Compare वृद्धगर्ग :

याम्यकोट्यायतः किञ्चिद्युगकाले यदा शशी ।
पार्श्वशायीतिसंज्ञोऽयं सार्थहा वृष्टिनाशनः ।।]

अभ्युच्छ्रायादेकं यदि शशिनोऽवाङ्मुखं भवेच्छृङ्गम् ।
आवर्जितमित्यसुभिक्षकारि तद्गोधनस्यापि ।।१४।।

If one of the horns of the Moon should appear turned downwards as a result of the other's elevation, it is called 'Bent'. It would then cause famine in the country affecting even the cattle.

[See वृद्धगर्ग :

अधोमुखं यदा श्रृङ्गं शशिनो दृश्यते तदा ।
संस्थानमावर्जितकं गोघ्नं दुर्भिक्षकारकम् ।।]

अव्युच्छिन्ना रेखा समन्ततो मण्डला च कुण्डाख्यम् ।
अस्मिन्माण्डलिकानां स्थानत्यागो नरपतीनाम् ॥१५॥

If the horns of the Moon should together appear like an unbroken circle, the figure is called Kuṇḍa or *Pit.* It would force the ruling chiefs to abandon their posts.

[Compare वृद्धगर्ग—

अच्छिन्ना मण्डले रेखा शशिनो दृश्यते यदा ।
कुण्डाख्यं नाम संस्थानं नृपविग्रहदायकम् ॥

See also पञ्चसिद्धान्तिका V-1-10.]

प्रोक्तस्थानाभावादुदगुच्चः क्षेमवृद्धिवृष्टिकरः ।
दक्षिणतुङ्गश्चन्द्रो दुर्भिक्षभयाय निर्दिष्टः ॥१६॥

If the northern horn of the Moon be raised and if she be devoid of any of the forms mentioned above, she would lead to increase of happiness, and prosperity and to timely rains in the country. On the other hand, with the southern horn raised she portends the threat of famine.

शृङ्गेणैकेनेन्दुर्विलीनमथवाप्यवाङ्मुखं शृङ्गम् ।
सम्पूर्णं चाभिनवं दृष्ट्वैको जीविताद्भ्रश्येत् ॥१७॥

One who sees the Moon with only one horn, devoid of the other, or with one horn bent downwards, or the fresh Moon as full, will lose his life before long.

[See the समाससंहिता—

उदयन्तमप्यसदृशं न शुभं बहुरूपताथवैकस्य ।
एकश्चन्द्रविकारं यः पश्येन्न स चिरं जीवेत् ॥]

संस्थानविधिः कथितो रूपाण्यस्माद्भवन्ति चन्द्रमसः ।
स्वल्पो दुर्भिक्षकरो महान्सुभिक्षावहः प्रोक्तः ॥१८॥
मध्यतनुर्वज्राख्यः क्षुद्भयदः सम्भ्रमाय राज्ञां च ।
चन्द्रो मृदङ्गरूपः क्षेमसुभिक्षावहो भवति ॥१९॥
ज्ञेयो विशालमूर्तिर्नरपतिलक्ष्मीविवृद्धये चन्द्रः ।
स्थूलः सुभिक्षकारी प्रियधान्यकरस्तु तनुमूर्तिः ॥२०॥

Details of the Moon's configurations have already been dealt with. There are yet other forms of the Moon that are explained below : The Moon appearing tiny indicates famine, whereas the big Moon good crops. It is called Vajra or Thunderbolt when the Moon is slender in the middle, which is indicative of trouble to the people from hunger and fright as well as of war-preparations among the kings. When she appears like the tabor, she causes happiness and abundance of food crops. The Moon with a broad disc leads to marked increase in the king's wealth, with a stout disc she brings about bumper crops and with a slender form she causes the growth of agreeable grains (or, she makes grains very dear).

[Compare वृद्धगर्ग—

विलग्नमध्यो मेघाभो वज्रसंस्थानसंस्थितः ।
मध्यच्छिद्रो विलीनो वा भयं च जनयेन्महत् ॥]

प्रत्यन्तान्कुनृपांश्च हन्त्युडुपतिः शृङ्गे कुजेनाहते
शस्त्रक्षुद्भयकृद्यमेन शशिजेनावृष्टिदुर्भिक्षकृत् ।
श्रेष्ठान्हन्ति नृपान्महेन्द्रगुरुणा शुक्रेण चाल्पान्नृपा-
ञ्शुक्ले याप्यमिदं फलं ग्रहकृतं कृष्णे यथोक्तागमम् ॥२१॥

If the Moon's horn is struck by Mars, kings living in the neighbourhood as well as the wicked ones will come to grief; if it is struck by Saturn, there will be danger from weapons and hunger; if it is by Mercury, drought and famine; if it is by Jupiter, destruction of leading monarchs; and if it is by Venus, exit of petty kings. These effects caused by the several planets will be mild, if the phenomena take place in the bright fortnight, whereas in the dark fortnight they will be felt in full measure as stated in the text.

[Compare the समाससंहिता—

प्रत्यन्तविनाशोऽन्नक्षयो महाराजपीडा च ।
सङ्ग्रामाश्चाभिहते शृङ्गे भौमादिभिः क्रमशः ॥

This verse of the text suggests that keen observations were conducted by the ancients to detect any grazing or touching of the Moon's horn by the planets during the two fortnights, especially in the initial part of the light half and the final one of the other.

This verse is in the शार्दूलविक्रीडित metre.]

भिन्नः सितेन मगधान्यवनान्पुलिन्दान्
नेपालभृङ्गिमरुकच्छसुराष्ट्रमद्रान् ।
पाञ्चालकैकयकुलूतकपूरुषादान्
हन्यादुशीनरजनानपि सप्तमासान् ॥२२॥

When the lunar orb is cut asunder by Venus, the people of Magadha, the Yavanas, Pulindas, the Nepalese, the Bhṛṅgis, the Marwaris, the people of Cutch, Surat, and Madra, the Pāñcālas, the Kekayas, the Kulūtakas (people of Kulu valley ?), the cannibals and the people of Uśīnara (Kandahar) will have great sufferings for seven months.

[Fourteen geographical units are mentioned here according to the ancient geographical subdivision of the country.

The metre of this verse is वसन्ततिलका.]

गान्धारसौवीरकसिन्धुकीरान्धान्यानि शैलान्द्रविडाधिपांश्च ।
द्विजांश्च मासान्दश शीतरश्मिः सन्तापयेद्वाक्पतिना विभिन्नः ।।२३।।

If the Moon's disc is cut by the conjunction of Jupiter, the people of Gāndhāra, Sauvīraka, Sindhu and Kīra, and all kinds of corn, mountains, kings of the Drāviḍa country and Brahmins will be troubled for ten months.

[Some more regions are mentioned here. It is to be remembered that Jupiter presides over the Brahmin community. The metre is उपजाति ।]

उद्युक्तान्सह वाहनैर्नरपतींस्त्रैगर्तकान्मालवान्
कौलिन्दान्गणपुङ्गवानथ शिबीनायोध्यकान्पार्थिवान् ।
हन्यात्कौरवमत्स्यशुक्त्यधिपतीन्राजन्यमुख्यानपि
प्रालेयांशुरसृग्ग्रहे तनुगते षण्मासमर्यादया ।।२४।।

If Mars should obstruct the Moon's orb, it would cause troubles for six months to kings who have mobilized their army for war along with their vehicles (such as chariots, elephants and horses), the Traigartas (people and kings of the Trigarta region), Mālavas, Kaulindas (those of Kulinda), tribal chiefs (or leaders of groups), the Śibis, Kings of Ayodhyā, the people and rulers of Kuru country, Kings of Virāṭa and Śukti countries and other important Kṣatriya chiefs.

[The metre is शार्दूलविक्रीडित.

As Mars presides over war and is the commander of the heavenly forces, his contact with the Moon presages harm to war-mongers etc.]

यौधेयान्सचिवान्सकौरवान्प्रागीशानथ चार्जुनायनान् ।
हन्यादर्कजभिन्नमण्डलः शीतांशुर्दशमासपीडया ।।२५।।

If the Moon's disc is cut by Saturn, the Yaudheyas, ministers, people of the Kuru country, rulers of the eastern countries, and the Arjunāyanas will undergo great suffering for ten months.

[The metre is शुद्धविराट्. The Yaudheyas are a people belonging to the northern division. So are the Arjunāyanas.]

मगधान्मथुरां च पीडयेद्वेणायाश्च तटं शशाङ्कजः ।
अपरत्र कृतं युगं वदेद्यदि भित्त्वा शशिनं विनिर्गतः ॥२६॥

When Mercury cuts the Moon and then departs therefrom, there will be trouble for the country of Magadha, the city of Mathurā and the people living on the banks of the river Veṇā. In other places there will be peace and plenty as in the Golden Age.

[The metre is वैतालीय].

क्षेमारोग्यसुभिक्षविनाशी शीतांशुः शिखिना यदि भिन्नः ।
कुर्यादायुधजीविविनाशं चौराणामधिकेन च पीडाम् ॥२७॥

When the Moon is obstructed by Ketu (meteor), it will destroy people's health, happiness and prosperity; and it will cause much destruction among fighters (those that are employed in the military) as well as intense suffering to the people through increase in robberies.

[This occurs in पंक्ति, but no name is available for it. Of course it is similar to the शुद्धविराट् with सगण instead of the जगण before the गुरु.]

उल्कया यदा शशी ग्रस्त एव हन्यते ।
हन्यते तदा नृपो यस्य जन्मनि स्थितः ॥२८॥

When the eclipsed Moon is cut by a meteor, the king, whose natal star is occupied by the Moon at the time, will soon die.

[See the समाससंहिता—

उल्काभिहतो ग्रहणे तन्नक्षत्रं नृपं हन्ति ॥

This metre occurring under उष्णिक् category has no name given.]

भस्मनिभः परुषोऽरुणमूर्त्तिः शीतकरः किरणैः परिहीणः ।
श्यावतनुः स्फुटितः स्फुरणो वा क्षुड्डमरामयचोरभयाय ॥२९॥

If the Moon is of ash colour, rough, reddish, devoid of rays, and of dark appearance, and looks broken or shaky, people will have danger from hunger, tumult, pestilence, disease and thieves in store.

[The metre is दोधक.]

प्रालेयकुन्दकुमुदस्फटिकावदातो
यत्नादिवाद्रिसुतया परिमृज्य चन्द्रः ।
उच्चैः कृतो निशि भविष्यति मे शिवाय
यो दृश्यते स भविता जगतः शिवाय ॥३०॥

Should the Moon appear white like snow, the Kunda (jasmine) flower, lotus and crystal, as if she were placed above by Goddess Pārvatī after polishing her carefully with the idea that she might get happiness at night through her, she would bestow all happiness and prosperity on the whole mankind.

[The Moon is one of the eight constituents of the Lord Śiva's form. She is also said to adorn the matted locks of the Lord. Here the poesy of the astronomer asserts itself, as he gives a fine example of poetic fancy in this verse.

The metre is वसन्ततिलका.]

शुक्ले पक्षे सम्प्रवृद्धे प्रवृद्धिं ब्रह्मक्षत्रं याति वृद्धिं प्रजाश्च ।
हीने हानिस्तुल्यता तुल्यतायां कृष्णे सर्वं तत्फलं व्यत्ययेन ॥३१॥

If the Moon waxes regularly in the bright fortnight, Brahmins and Kṣatriyas as well as all the people will enjoy power, prosperity and happiness. If her growth is meagre, the effect will be loss; and if it is moderate, the result too will be likewise. These effects will have to be declared in the reverse order in the case of the dark fortnight.

[The metre is शालिनी.]

यदि कुमुदमृणालहारगौरः स्थितिनियमात् क्षयमेति वर्द्धते वा ।
अविकृतगतिमण्डलांशुयोगी भवति नृणां विजयाय शीतरश्मिः ॥३२॥

If the Moon is as bright as the lotus stalk and a pearl necklace, if her digits increase or decrease proportionately to the number of lunar days that have elapsed, and if her motion, orb and rays remain natural, all people will enjoy success and prosperity.

[Here the author sums up what he has said already about the Moon.

The metre is पुष्पिताग्रा].

राहुचारः ॥५॥

Chapter V—Rāhu's Course

अमृतास्वादविशेषाच्छिन्नमपि शिरः किलासुरस्येदम् ।
प्राणैरपरित्यक्तं ग्रहतां यातं वदन्त्येके ॥१॥

Though the demon's head was cut off, it was not deprived of life as a result of his having tasted nectar, and, it is said, it assumed the form of a planet.

[Compare the following Purāṇic statement :

सिंहिकातनयो राहुरपिबच्चामृतं पुरा ।
शिरश्छिन्नोऽपि न प्राणैस्त्यक्तोऽसौ ग्रहतां गतः ॥

The reader may notice here the author's regard for the views of ancient Sages in spite of his own scientific thinking.]

इन्द्वर्कमण्डलाकृतिरसितत्वात्किल न दृश्यते गगने ।
अन्यत्र पर्वकालाद्वरप्रदानात्कमलयोनेः ॥२॥

They say that the Dragon's Head (Rāhu) being similar in form to the orbs of the luminaries and dark in colour, is not visible in the sky except on the Parvan days (i.e. New and Full Moon). As a result of the Creator's boon Rāhu is visible only during eclipses and not on other days.

[The Purāṇic story runs thus : Siṁhikā, one of the wives of Sage Kaśyapa, requested her husband for progeny at an unseasonal hour. Enraged at this untimely request, he gave her a son who was dreadful like the God of Death. This child came to be called Rāhu. Soon after his birth he fought with Aditi's son and was trounced. Humiliated by this, he performed severe penance for ten thousand divine years on a Himalayan peak. He asked Brahman, when the latter appeared before him, to confer on him the status of a planet, immortality, victory over the Gods and power to devour the two luminaries. At this, the Lord spoke smilingly thus : "You will find it extremely hard to digest these two; still, be it so." So saying, Brahman vanished. Then Rāhu rushed at the luminaries. But Lord Viṣṇu hurled his discus, cut off his head and said, "Let the Creator's words not go to waste. In your respective periods you may devour the two luminaries and thereby indicate good and bad things for the world."]

मुखपुच्छविभक्ताङ्गं भुजङ्गमाकारमुपदिशन्त्यन्ये ।
कथयन्त्यमूर्तमपरे तमोमयं सैंहिकेयाख्यम् ॥३॥

Some Sages declare that Rāhu i.e. son of Siṁhikā, is of a serpentine form with only the face and tail, while others hold that he is formless and of the nature of pure darkness.

[The commentator quotes from three authorities : वीरभद्र who says—

सिंहिकातनयस्यास्य राहोः पुच्छमुखादृते ।
नान्यदस्ति परं बाहुकटिपादकरादिकम् ॥

वसिष्ठ who says—

भषट्कान्तरितौ राहुः सूर्याचन्द्रमसावुभौ ।
छादयत्युरगाकारो वरदानात्स्वयम्भुवः ॥

and देवल who says—

अन्धकारमयो राहुर्मेघखण्ड इवोत्थितः ।
आच्छादयति सोमार्कौ पर्वकाले ह्युपस्थिते ॥]

यदि मूर्तो भविचारी शिरोऽथवा भवति मण्डली राहुः ।
भगणार्धेनान्तरितौ गृह्णाति कथं नियतचारः ॥४॥

In case Rāhu has a body, moves in the zodiac, possesses only the head and a circular shape, how is it that he seizes the luminaries who are separated from him by 180°, when his own movement is fixed and uniform ?

अनियतचारः खलु चेदुपलब्धिः संख्यया कथं तस्य ।
पुच्छाननाभिधानोऽन्तरेण कस्मान्न गृह्णाति ॥५॥

If, on the other hand, his motion is not fixed, how is it that his exact position is determined by calculation ? If he is to be identified only by his tail and face, why should he not seize them (the luminaries) at other intervals (instead of only when 180° apart) ?

अथ तु भुजगेन्द्ररूपः पुच्छेन मुखेन वा स गृह्णाति ।
मुखपुच्छान्तरसंस्थं स्थगयति कस्मान्न भगणार्धम् ॥६॥

If this Rāhu who is a big serpent in appearance actually seizes the Sun or the Moon with his tail or mouth, why should he not obstruct half of the zodiac that lies between his head and tail ?

राहुद्वयं यदि स्याद् ग्रस्तेऽस्तमितेऽथवोदिते चन्द्रे ।
तत्समगतिनान्येन ग्रस्तः सूर्योऽपि दृश्येत ॥७॥

If there should be two Rāhus, when the Moon is eclipsed by one Rāhu when she is rising or setting, the Sun who is 180° away from the Moon should also be eclipsed by the other Rāhu whose rate of motion is also equal (to that of the other Rāhu).

भूच्छायां स्वग्रहणे भास्करमर्कग्रहे प्रविशतीन्दुः ।
प्रग्रहणमतः पश्चान्नेन्दोर्भानोश्च पूर्वार्द्धात् ॥८॥

At a lunar eclipse the Moon enters the shadow of the earth, and at a solar eclipse she enters the Sun's disc. That is the reason why the lunar eclipse does not begin at the western limb, nor the solar one at the eastern limb.

वृक्षस्य स्वच्छाया यथैकपार्श्वे भवति दीर्घचया ।
निशि निशि तद्वद्भूमेरावरणवशाद्दिनेशस्य ॥९॥

Just as the shadow of a tree goes on increasing on one side as a result of the Sun's movement, even so is the case with the shadow of the earth every night by its hiding the Sun during its rotation.

सूर्यात्सप्तमराशौ यदि चोदग्दक्षिणेन नातिगतः ।
चन्द्रः पूर्वाभिमुखश्छायामोर्वीं तदा विशति ॥१०॥

In her course towards the east, if the Moon tenanting the 7th house from the Sun, does not swerve much either to the north or the south (when her declination is very little), she enters the earth's shadow.

[Compare the ब्रह्मसिद्धान्त—

भूच्छायां शशिकक्ष्यागां रवौ भार्द्धान्तरास्थिते ।
यदा विशत्यविक्षिप्तश्चन्द्रः स्यात्तद्ग्रहस्तदा ॥]

चन्द्रोऽधस्थः स्थगयति रविमम्बुदवत्समागतः पश्चात् ।
प्रतिदेशमतश्चित्रं दृष्टिवशाद्भास्करग्रहणम् ॥११॥

The Moon situated below and moving from the west obstructs the solar disc like a cloud. The solar eclipse, therefore, is different in different countries according to the visibility of the eclipsed disc.

[The सूर्यसिद्धान्त says :

इन्दुना च्छादितं सूर्यमधोऽविक्षिप्तगामिना ।
न पश्यति यदा लोकस्तदा स्याद्भास्करग्रहः ॥
तमोमयस्य तमसो रविरश्मिपलायिनः ।
भूच्छाया चन्द्रबिम्बं च स्थाने द्वे परिकल्पिते ॥

The ब्रह्मसिद्धान्त—

भूच्छायेन्दुं चन्द्रः सूर्यं छादयति मानयोगार्द्धात् ।
विक्षेपो यद्यूनः शुक्लेतरपञ्चदृश्यन्ते ॥]

आवरणं महदिन्दोः कुण्ठविषाणस्ततोऽर्द्धसञ्छन्नः ।
स्वल्पं रवेर्यतोऽतस्तीक्ष्णविषाणो रविर्भवति ॥१२॥

When the lunar eclipse takes place, the obstructing agency is very large, whereas in the solar eclipse it is small. Hence in semi-lunar and semi-solar eclipses the luminous horns become blunt and sharp respectively.

[The same idea is found in the ब्रह्मसिद्धान्त—

महदिन्दोरावरणं कुण्ठविषाणो यतोऽर्द्धसञ्छन्नः ।
अर्द्धच्छन्नो भानुस्तीक्ष्णविषाणस्ततोऽस्याल्पम् ॥]

एवमुपरागकारणमुक्तमिदं दिव्यदृग्भिराचार्यैः ।
राहुरकारणमस्मिन्नित्युक्तः शास्त्रसद्भावः ॥१३॥

In this manner have the ancient seers endowed with divine insight explained the causes of eclipses. Hence the scientific fact is that Rāhu is not at all the cause of eclipses.

[The above categorical statement of our author shows that though he has regard for religious traditions, he would not allow scientific truths to be diluted with popular beliefs.

The ब्रह्मसिद्धान्त says :

यदि राहुः प्राग्भागादिन्दुं छादयति किं तथा नार्कम् ।
स्थित्यर्द्धं महदिन्दोर्यथा तथा किं न सूर्यस्य ॥
किं प्रतिविषयं सूर्यो राहुश्चान्यो यतो रविग्रहणे ।
ग्रासान्यत्वं न ततो राहुकृतं ग्रहणमर्केन्द्वोः ॥]

योऽसावसुरो राहुस्तस्य वरो ब्रह्मणायमाज्ञप्तः ।
आप्यायनमुपरागे दत्तहुतांशेन ते भविता ॥१४॥

तस्मिन्काले सान्निध्यमस्य तेनोपचर्यते राहुः ।
याम्योत्तरा शशिगतिर्गणितेऽप्युपचर्यते तेन ॥१५॥

A boon was conferred on the demon Rāhu by the Creator: "Thou shalt sustain thyself by means of the oblations offered to the sacred Fire at an eclipse." Hence Rāhu's presence is assumed at that time. The Moon has two nodes, Northern and Southern, as a result of her declination (deviation to the north or south), which can be ascertained by astronomical calculations. The Ascending Node is called Rāhu.

[Here the author refers to the traditional aspect of Rāhu mentioned in the Purāṇas. The two nodes of the Moon are called Rāhu and Ketu respectively.]

न कथञ्चिदपि निमित्तैर्ग्रहणं विज्ञायते निमित्तानि ।
अन्यस्मिन्नपि काले भवन्त्यथोत्पातरूपाणि ॥१६॥

An eclipse can by no means be ascertained through omens and other indications. For, portents such as fall of meteors and earth tremors occur at other times as well.

[This refers to a popular belief that an eclipse is heralded by some unusual occurrences such as earthquake and terrific thunder.]

पञ्चग्रहसंयोगान्न किल ग्रहणस्य सम्भवो भवति ।
तैलं च जलेऽष्टम्यां न विचिन्त्यमिदं विपश्चिद्भिः ॥१७॥

Scholars should not believe the following traditional statement to the effect that an eclipse cannot take place except, when there is a combination of five planets in the same zodiacal Sign, and that a week before the eclipse i.e. on the previous 8th lunar day, its characteristics can be inferred from the behaviour or appearance of a drop of oil poured on the surface of water.

[Here two more popular beliefs are mentioned. वृद्धगर्ग too refers to the same:

ग्रहपञ्चकसंयोगं दृष्ट्वा न ग्रहणं वदेत् ।
यदि न स्याद्बुधस्तत्र तं दृष्ट्वा ग्रहणं वदेत् ॥
अष्टम्यां परिवेषः स्यात्तैले जलगते यदा ।
प्रसारिते विजानीयाद्यतः खण्डस्ततस्तमः ॥]

अवनत्यार्के ग्रासो दिग्ज्ञेया वलनयाऽवनत्या च ।
तिथ्यवसानाद्वेला करणे कथितानि तानि मया ॥१८॥

The magnitude of the solar eclipse should be determined through the Moon's deflection i.e. parallax. The direction of commencement of the eclipse is found out through the deflection and angles of the Moon known as Ayanavalana and Akṣavalana. The duration of the eclipse is got by noting the exact time of conjunction of the Sun and the Moon. All these have been explained in detail by me in my astronomical work Pañcasiddhāntikā.

षण्मासोत्तरवृद्ध्या पर्वेशाः सप्त देवताः क्रमशः ।
ब्रह्मशशीन्द्रकुबेरा वरुणाग्नियमाश्च विज्ञेयाः ॥१९॥

The Creator (or Brahman), the Moon, Indra, Kubera, Varuṇa, Agni and Yama (God of death) are in order lords of the successive half-yearly periods since creation.

ब्राह्मे द्विजपशुवृद्धिः क्षेमारोग्यानि सस्यसम्पच्च ।
तद्वत्सौम्ये तस्मिन्पीडा विदुषामवृष्टिश्च ॥२०॥
ऐन्द्रे भूपविरोधः शारदसस्यक्षयो न च क्षेमम् ।
कौबेरेऽर्थपतीनामर्थविनाशः सुभिक्षं च ॥२१॥
वारुणमवनीशाशुभमन्येषां क्षेमसस्यवृद्धिकरम् ।
आग्नेयं मित्राख्यं सस्यारोग्याभयाम्बुकरम् ॥२२॥
याम्या करोत्यवृष्टिं दुर्भिक्षं संक्षयं च सस्यानाम् ।
यदतः परं तदशुभं क्षुन्मारावृष्टिदं पर्व ॥२३॥

During the Period presided over by the Creator Brāhmaṇas and the cattle will prosper; and there will be happiness, and good health among the people as well as abundant crops. In the next period owned by the Moon the results would be similar to those in the previous Period, but there would be trouble to the learned as well as drought. In the Period presided over by Indra rulers will be at loggerheads, autumnal crops will be destroyed and there will be no happiness among the people. In the fourth Period belonging to Kubera wealthy persons will suffer loss of their wealth but there will be general prosperity or good crops. In the fifth Period owned by Varuṇa there will be trouble to kings, but others will enjoy happiness and abundant crops. The sixth Period of Agni, otherwise known as Mitra, will lead to good harvest, health and happiness, freedom from fear (or protection or security) and abundance of water (i.e. good rains). Yama's Period, which is the seventh, will produce drought, famine and destruction of crops. In case of an eighth Period coming after that of Yama as a result of unusual causes, it will be harmful by causing hunger, death and drought.

वेलाहीने पर्वणि गर्भविपत्तिश्च शस्त्रकोपश्च ।
अतिवेले कुसुमफलक्षयो भयं सस्यनाशश्च ॥२४॥

Should an eclipse take place a little earlier than the time arrived at by astronomical calculation, there would be abortions and clash of arms. On the other hand, if it should commence a little later than the calculated time, there would be destruction of flowers and fruits, panic would grip the people, and loss of crops would ensue.

[गर्ग says :

वेलाहीने शस्त्रभयं गर्भाणां स्रावणं तथा ।
अतिवेले फलानां तु सस्यानां क्षयमादिशेत् ॥
दृक्समे पर्वणि नृपा निर्वैरा विगतज्वराः ।
प्रजाश्च सुखिताः सर्वा भयरोगविवर्जिताः ॥

and काश्यप—

अनागतमतीतं वा ग्रहणं पर्व दृश्यते ।
गर्भस्रावमनावृष्टिः फलं पुष्पं विनश्यति ॥]

हीनातिरिक्तकाले फलमुक्तं पूर्वशास्त्रदृष्टत्वात् ।
स्फुटगणितविदः कालः कथञ्चिदपि नान्यथा भवति ॥२५॥

I have mentioned the effects of eclipses taking place a little earlier or later than the calculated time for the sole reason that the ancients have stated so in their works. However, if the astrologer knows the correct method of calculating eclipses, by no means can there be any difference whatsoever in the time of their occurrence.

[Again we see our author asserting his scientific attitude. For, if there is any difference between the actual time and calculated time of an eclipse, it should be understood that the person concerned does not know the science of astronomy properly. Still Varāhamihira would quote the opinions of the ancients for historical reasons as well as for making his Saṁhitā a true compendium of both modern and ancient knowledge.]

यद्येकस्मिन् मासे ग्रहणं रविसोमयोस्तदा क्षितिपाः ।
स्वबलक्षोभैः सङ्क्षयमायान्त्यतिशस्त्रकोपश्च ॥२६॥

Should there be two eclipses, one solar and the other lunar, in one and same month, kings would be destroyed as a result of revolt of their army; and there would be bloody battles.

[काश्यप says :

चन्द्रार्कयोरेकमासे ग्रहणं न प्रशस्यते ।
परस्परं वधं कुर्युः स्वबलक्षुभिता नृपाः ॥]

ग्रस्तावुदितास्तमितौ शारदधान्यावनीश्वरक्षयदौ ।
सर्वग्रस्तौ दुर्भिक्षमरकदौ पापसन्दृष्टौ ॥२७॥

Should the luminaries rise or set being eclipsed, there would be danger to autumnal crops as well as to kings. On the other hand, if the eclipse should also be total and the eclipsed orb be aspected by malefics as well, there would be famine and pestilence all over the country.

[वृद्धगर्ग says in this connection :

उद्गच्छति गृहीतश्चेदस्तं वा यदि गच्छति ।
शारदं तु तदा सस्यं जातं जातं विपद्यते ॥
ग्रैष्मेण तत्र जीवन्ति नरा मूलफलेन वा ।
भयदुर्भिक्षरोगैश्च तदा सम्पीड्यते जगत् ॥

and ऋषिपुत्र—

यावतोंऽशान्ग्रसित्वेन्दोरुदयत्यस्तमेति वा ।
तावतोंऽशान्पृथिव्यास्तु तम एव विनाशयेत् ॥
उदयेऽस्तमये वापि सूर्यस्य ग्रहणं भवेत् ।
तदा नृपभयं विन्द्यात्परचक्रस्य चागमम् ॥
चिरं गृह्णाति सोमार्कौ सर्वं वा ग्रसते यदा ।
हन्यात् स्फीताञ्जनपदान्वरिष्ठांश्च जनाधिपान् ॥
ग्रैष्मेण तत्र जीवन्ति नराश्चाम्बुफलेन वा ।
भयदुर्भिक्षरोगैश्च सम्पीड्यन्ते प्रजास्तथा ॥]

अर्द्धोदितोपरक्तो नैकृतिकान्हन्ति सर्वयज्ञांश्च ।
अग्न्युपजीविगुणाधिकविप्राश्रमिणो युगेऽभ्युदितः ॥२८॥

कर्षकपाखण्डिवणिक्क्षत्रियबलनायकान् द्वितीयांशे ।
कारुकशूद्रम्लेच्छान् खतृतीयांशे समन्त्रिजनान् ॥२९॥

मध्याह्ने नरपतिमध्यदेशहा शोभनश्च धान्यार्घः ।
तृणभुगमात्यान्तःपुरवैश्यघ्नः पञ्चमे खांशे ॥३०॥

स्त्रीशूद्रान्षष्ठेंऽशे दस्युप्रत्यन्तहाऽस्तमयकाले ।
यस्मिन्खांशे मोक्षस्तत्प्रोक्तानां शिवं भवति ॥३१॥

Should an eclipse, solar or lunar, commence when the disc has just half-risen, it would destroy low tribals, Caṇḍālas etc. as well as all sacrifices i.e. religious practices. Should the above phenomenon take place in the first division of the visible part of the sky, when it is divided into seven equal parts, those that live by working on fire like the goldsmiths, virtuous men, Brahmins and hermits would be affected. If this happen in the second part of the sky, agriculturists, heretics traders, Kṣatriyas and army chiefs would come to grief. In the third part it would harm artisans, artists, the Śūdras, Mlecchas and ministers. If the eclipse take place at midday i.e. the fourth division of the sky, the king and the middle country would suffer, but the prices of grains would be fair. In the fifth division animals that live on grass, ministers, inmates of harems, and Vaiśyas (or merchants) would suffer. An eclipse occurring in the sixth division of the sky would harm women and the Śūdras, and lastly one occurring at sunset or the last portion of the sky would destroy robbers and those that live in the border countries. In whichever part of the sky the eclipse ends, the people and things corresponding to that part would be benefited.

[Kāśyapa says—

उदितास्तमितौ ग्रस्तौ सर्वसस्यक्षयङ्करौ ।
सर्वग्रस्तौ यदा पश्येद्दुर्भिक्षं तत्र जायते ॥

प्रथमांशे विप्रपीडा क्षत्रियाणां द्वितीयके ।
शूद्राणां च तृतीयेंऽशे चतुर्थे मध्यदेशिनाम् ॥

वैश्यानां पञ्चमे खांशे षष्ठांशे प्रमदाभयम् ।
दस्युप्रत्यन्तकम्लेच्छविनाशः सप्तमांशके ॥

येषामंशे भवेन्मोक्षस्तज्जातानां शुभं भवेत् ।

Also वृद्धगर्ग—

येषां सोमो युगे ग्रस्तो विमर्दो यत्र वा भवेत् ।
तेषां पीडां विजानीयान्मोक्षे शुभमथादिशेत् ॥

In the case of a solar eclipse the daytime should be divided into 7 equal parts. One should then note down in which divisions the eclipse begins, becomes maximum and ends. The persons assigned to these will in order suffer, be destroyed and prosper. Same is the case with a lunar eclipse, where the night is to be divided. From the text it is clear that certain castes, avocations and countries belong to certain subdivisions of the visible sky or the day or night, as the case may be.]

द्विजनृपतीनुदगयने विट्शूद्रान्दक्षिणायने हन्ति ।
राहुरुदगादिदृष्टः प्रदक्षिणं हन्ति विप्रादीन् ॥३२॥
म्लेच्छान्विदिक्स्थितो यायिनश्च हन्याद्धुताशसक्तांश्च ।
सलिलचरदन्तिघाती याम्येनोदग्गवामशुभः ॥३३॥
पूर्वेण सलिलपूर्णां करोति वसुधां समागतो दैत्यः ।
पश्चात्कर्षकसेवकबीजविनाशाय निर्दिष्टः ॥३४॥

An eclipse (i.e. Rāhu) occurring in the northern (winter) solstice would destroy Brahmins and kings (i.e. Kṣatriyas), while in the southern (summer) solstice, Vaiśyas (traders) and Śūdras (labouring class). If the eclipse, solar or lunar, be sighted in the four quarters beginning with the north, people of the four classes beginning with Brahmins would suffer in order. Should it occur in any one of the four corners or semi-quarters viz. north-east, south-east, south-west and north-west, Mlecchas, attacking or marching armies and those who earn their living by means of fire like fire-worshippers and smiths would be affected. If it begins in the south, aquatic animals and elephants will be destroyed; and if in the north, cattle will perish. If it should begin in the east, the earth would be troubled with floods; and if in the west husbandmen, servants, labourers and seeds and seedlings would be destroyed.

[See what Sage काश्यप says—

पूर्वे सलिलघाती स्यात्पश्चाद्धान्यकृषीवलान् ।
याम्ये जलचरान्हन्ति सौम्ये गोनाशकः स्मृतः ॥
म्लेच्छान्यायिनृपान्हन्ति विदिक्स्थः सिंहिकासुतः ।

and the समाससंहिता—

उदगादिषु दिक्ष्वशुभो विप्रादीनां सितादिवर्णस्य ।
विदिगादिगतो हन्याद्राहुर्म्लेच्छान्सविजिगीषून् ॥
द्विजराजन्यान्हन्यादुदगयने दक्षिणे तु विट्शूद्रान् ।
समरामयाय राहुर्यदि पक्षान्ते पुनर्दृश्यः ॥]

पाञ्चालकलिङ्गशूरसेनाः काम्बोजोड्रकिरातशस्त्रवार्ताः ।
जीवन्ति च ये हुताशवृत्त्या ते पीडामुपयान्ति मेषसंस्थे ॥३५॥

If an eclipse takes place in the Sign Aries i.e. when the Sun or the Moon is eclipsed while passing through Aries, the people of the Pāñcāla country, Kaliṅgas, the Śūrasenas, the Kāmbojas, people of modern Orissa, hunters or foresters, those who wield weapons i.e. warriors, and those that work on fire will come to grief.

[In this and the succeeding seven verses the author discusses effects of eclipses taking place in the twelve houses beginning with Meṣa. The metre is औपच्छन्दसिक.]

गोपाः पशवोऽथ गोमिनो मनुजा ये च महत्त्वमागताः ।
पीडामुपयान्ति भास्करे ग्रस्ते शीतकरेऽथवा वृषे ॥३६॥

When the eclipse, solar or lunar, occurs in Sign Taurus, shepherds, cattle, owners of large herds of cattle, and men who have risen to prominence will be affected.

[As the Sign affected is called Vṛṣabha—Bull—cattle, their owners and virtuous men are said to be afflicted. This Section may well be read with advantage with what is given in chapters XIV—XVI *infra*.

The metre is Vaitālīya.]

मिथुने प्रवराङ्गना नृपा नृपमात्रा बलिनः कलाविदः ।
यमुनातटजा सबाह्लिका मत्स्याः सुह्मजनैः समन्विताः ॥३७॥

If the eclipse should take place in Sign Gemini, high-class women, kings and powerful ministers and the like, persons proficient in (fine) arts, people living on the banks of the Jumna, people of Balkh, the Virāṭas and the Suhmas would be affected.

[As the Sign Mithuna is entirely *Human* with artistic activities, it is but meet that such persons are affected. The metre is वियोगिनी with one difference viz. in the last quarter instead of the initial सगण two long syllabes are used, thereby giving the same number of Mātrās].

आभीराञ्छबरान्सपल्लवान्मल्लान्मत्स्यकुरूञ्छकानपि ।
पाञ्चालान्विकलांश्च पीडयत्यन्नं चापि निहन्ति कर्कटे ॥३८॥

If the eclipse should be in Sign Cancer, it would afflict the Ābhīras, the Śabaras (these are people of some mountain regions), the Pallavas, wrestlers, the Matsyas, the Kurus, Śakas, the Pāñcālas and those that are infirm. Food-grains also would be in jeopardy.

[The metre employed is *Śuddhavirāṭ*.]

सिंहे पुलिन्दगणमेकलसत्त्वयुक्तान्
राजोपमान्नरपतीन्वनगोचरांश्च ।
षष्ठे तु सस्यकविलेखकगेयसक्तान्
हन्त्यश्मकत्रिपुरशालियुतांश्च देशान् ॥३६॥

Should an eclipse occur in Sign Leo, it would destroy the tribe of hunters, the people inhabiting the Mekala mountain, heroic persons, rulers and their equals as well as the forest-denizens. Should it occur in Sign Virgo, it would afflict crops, poets, writers scribes, musicians, people of the Aśmaka and Tripura regions as well as countries abounding in paddy fields.

[The Sign Siṁha stands for a mountainous region, and Virgo is represented by a virgin holding corn etc. As this Rāśi belongs to Mercury, whose exaltation and Mūlatrikoṇa are here, his characteristics are naturally affected. The metre is वसन्ततिलका.]

तुलाधरेऽवन्त्यपरान्त्यसाधून्वणिग्दशार्णान्मरुकच्छपांश्च ।
अलिन्यथोदुम्बरमद्रचोलान्द्रुमान्सयौधेयविषायुधीयान् ॥४०॥

If the eclipse occurs in Sign Libra, people of Avantī and Aparānta regions (i.e. the western borders near the Sahya mountain), virtuous persons, traders, inhabitants of the Daśārna country, Maru and Kacchapa regions wlll come to grief. If it takes place in Sign Scorpio, people of Udumbara, Madra and Cola, the Yaudheya tribe, fighters that use poisoned weapons and trees will be destroyed.

[In the first line there is a variant reading सिन्धून्, meaning rivers, for साधून्. The metre is उपेन्द्रवज्रा.]

धन्विन्यमात्यवरवाजिविदेहमल्लान्
पाञ्चालवैद्यवणिजो विषमायुधज्ञान् ।
हन्यान्मृगे तु झषमन्त्रिकुलानि नीचान्
मन्त्रौषधीषु कुशलान्स्थविरायुधीयान् ॥४१॥

If the eclipse should happen in Sign Sagittarius, it would destroy chief ministers, horses, people of Videha, wrestlers, the Pāñcālas, physicians, merchants, those that are rough and tough and those who wield weapons. An eclipse occurring in Sign Capricorn would ruin fishes, ministers and their families, men of low classes, those who are skilled in charms and herbs, those that are old and infirm and the persons who live by weapons.

[This Sign Sagittarius is presided over by Jupiter, who is the minister or teacher of the Gods. Its form also is partly equestrian and partly human. Hence the suffering of particular persons and animals. The metre is वसन्ततिलका.]

कुम्भेऽन्तर्गिरिजान्सपश्चिमजनान्भारोद्वहांस्तस्करा-
नाभीरान्दरदार्यसिंहपुरकान्हन्यात्तथा बर्बरान् ।
मीने सागरकूलसागरजलद्रव्याणि वन्याञ्जनान्
प्राज्ञान्वार्युपजीविनश्च मफलं कूर्मोपदेशाद्वदेत् ॥४२॥

If an eclipse takes place in Sign Aquarius, it will harm people living on the mountains and in the west, bearers of burdens, thieves, Ābhīras (herdsmen), the Daradas, noble men, residents of Siṁhapura and the Barbaras. One taking place in Sign Pisces would affect the shores of oceans and the articles such as pearls obtained from the sea-bed, foresters, scholars and those whose profession is connected with water or water-products. The effects of eclipse occurring in the several constellations will have to be predicted according to the rules mentioned in the Chapter on the "Sphere of the Heavens or Starry Firmament."

[In chapter XIV the author discusses the geographical subdivisions of the country in relation to the constellations. So we have to apply the principles enunciated in this chapter to the peoples and things presided over by the different stars, when we have to predict the effects of eclipses occurring in the different stars, as we have done in the case of the different Signs of the Zodiac.

मान्यान् is a variant for वन्यान् in the third line of the verse. The metre is शार्दूलविक्रीडित.

See समाससंहिता—

कूर्मविभागेन वदेत् पीडां देशस्य वीक्ष्य नक्षत्रम् ।
सहितं ग्रहणं येन तद्देशश्चाप्नुयात्पीडाम् ॥]

सव्यापसव्यलेहग्रसननिरोधावमर्दनारोहाः ।
आघ्रातं मध्यतमस्तमोऽन्त्य इति ते दश ग्रासाः ॥४३॥

Eclipses are of ten kinds viz. *Savya*, *Apasavya*, *Leha*, *Grasana*, *Nirodha*, *Avamardana*, *Āroha*, *Āghrāta*, *Madhyatamas* and *Tamontya*.

[When the shadow appears in different parts of the lunar or solar disc, or when the shadow appears to behave in different ways, different designations are given to the eclipses. *Savya* means the southern side of the disc, while *Apasavya* means the northern side. In the case of a lunar eclipse south-east is called *Savya*, while north-east *Apasavya*. In the case of the solar eclipse these are respectively north-west and south-west. *Leha* means '*licking* with the tongue'. *Grasana* means *swallowing*. *Niroaha* is *blocking*. *Avamardana* is complete *crushing*. *Ārohaṇa* is *remounting*. *Āghrāta* is *smelt*. The other two terms are self-explanatory.]

सव्यगते तमसि जगज्जलप्लुतं भवति मुदितमभयं च ।
अपसव्ये नरपतितस्करावमर्दः प्रजानाशः ॥४४॥

When the shadow (Rāhu) is on the southern side of the solar or lunar orb at an eclipse, the world will be inundated by floods, but people will be happy and free from fear. If the eclipse occurs on the northern side, people will perish as a result of the tyranny of kings and depredations of robbers.

[It is to be remembered that the words *savya* and *apasavya* mean different directions in the case of solar and lunar eclipses].

जिह्वोपलेढि परितस्तिमिरनुदो मण्डलं यदि स लेहः ।
प्रमुदितसमस्तभूता प्रभूततोया च तत्र मही ॥४५॥

The eclipse is called *Leha* (Licking) when the eclipsed disc is enveloped all round (or licked) by the tongues of darkness. All beings will be happy and there will be plenty of water on the earth as a result of this eclipse.

[The highly imaginative and observant Aryans must have observed eclipses where like the flames (i.e. tongues) of fire the tongues of shadow or darkness gradually licked and enveloped the orb].

ग्रसनमिति यदा त्र्यंशः पादो वा गृह्यतेऽथवाप्यर्द्धम् ।
स्फीतनृपवित्तहानिः पीडा च स्फीतदेशानाम् ॥४६॥

If a part of the disc i.e. one half, one-third or one-fourth, is covered by shadow, it is termed *Grasana* (Swallowing). As a consequence of this there will be the end of a very powerful king, and destruction of wealth in the country, and prosperous countries also will have troubles.

पर्यन्तेषु गृहीत्वा मध्ये पिण्डीकृतं तमस्तिष्ठेत् ।
स निरोधो विज्ञेयः प्रमोदकृत्सर्वभूतानाम् ॥४७॥

When the eclipse starts all around and forms a thick lump of darkness in the centre, it is called *Nirodha* (Obstruction). All beings will be happy in consequence.

अवमर्दनमिति निःशेषमेव सञ्छाद्य यदि चिरं तिष्ठेत् ।
हन्यात्प्रधानभूपान् प्रधानदेशांश्च तिमिरमयः ॥४८॥

It is called *Avamardana* (Crushing) when the eclipse is total and lasts long in that condition. Its result will be destruction of prominent kings and leading countries.

वृत्ते ग्रहे यदि तमस्तत्क्षणमावृत्य दृश्यते भूयः ।
आरोहणमित्यन्योन्यमर्दनैर्भयकरं राज्ञाम् ॥४९॥

It is called *Ārohaṇa* or *Āroha* (Mounting) if after the termination of the eclipse the luminary be again covered with darkness. Consequently there will be great panic in the country as a result of mutual fighting among the kings.

दर्पण इवैकदेशे सबाष्पनिःश्वासमारुतोपहतः ।
दृश्येताऽऽघ्रातं तत्सुवृष्टिवृद्ध्यावहं जगतः ॥५०॥

It is called *Āghrāta* (Smelt) when the shadow appears on a part of the disc as does the vapours of the hot breath of the mouth on a mirror. This will bring in good rains and prosperity to the world.

मध्ये तमः प्रविष्टं वितमस्कं मण्डलं च यदि परितः ।
तन्मध्यदेशनाशं करोति कुक्ष्यामयभयं च ॥५१॥

The eclipse is called *Madhyatamas* (Darkness in the Centre) when the shadow appears in the Centre of the disc leaving the surrounding parts bright. It will destroy the people of the Central regions and afflict humanity with fear and stomach troubles.

[This phenomenon is possible only in a solar eclipse].

पर्यन्तेष्वतिबहुलं स्वल्पं मध्ये तमस्तमोऽन्त्याख्ये ।
सस्यानामीतिभयं भयमस्मिंस्तस्कराणां च ॥५२॥

When the shadow is very thick in the surrounding parts of the disc and very thin in the central portion, the eclipse is known as Tamontya (Dark in the edges). There will be trouble to the crops through locusts and such other pests, and people will have danger from thieves.

[There are six Ītibādhās as stated below :

अतिवृष्टिरनावृष्टिर्मूषकाः शलभाः खगाः (खलाः) ।
अत्यासन्नाश्च राजानः षडेता ईतयः स्मृताः ॥

It means—Excessive rain, drought, rats, locusts, birds (wicked persons) and hostile kings in the neighbourhood. Sage काश्यप says about these ten kinds of eclipses thus :

सव्यगे तु सुभिक्षं स्यादपसव्ये तु तस्कराः ।
लीढे प्रजाः प्रहृष्टाः स्युर्ग्रसनं लोकनाशनम् ॥

निरोधे जनहर्षः स्यादारोहे नृपसङ्क्षयः ।
आमर्दितं चापमर्दे स्वयं क्षुभ्यन्ति पार्थिवाः ॥

स्वच्छं वर्णप्रदेशं यदाघ्रातं तद्विघातयेत् ।
मध्ये तमसि सन्दृष्टे पीडयेन्मध्यदेशजान् ॥

दृष्टे तमसि पर्यन्ते सस्यानामीतिजं भयम् ॥

There is a difference of opinion regarding the effect of the Āghrāta type of eclipse between our author and Sage Kāśyapa who remarks that it will bring about destruction.

In the following seven verses effects of various colours of the eclipsed disc are given.]

श्वेते क्षेमसुभिक्षं ब्राह्मणपीडां च निर्दिशेद्राहौ ।
अग्निभयमनलवर्णे पीडा च हुताशवृत्तीनाम् ॥५३॥

हरिते रोगोल्बणता सस्यानामीतिभिश्च विध्वंसः ।
कपिले शीघ्रगसत्त्वम्लेच्छध्वंसोऽथ दुर्भिक्षम् ॥५४॥

अरुणकिरणानुरूपे दुर्भिक्षावृष्टयो विहगपीडा ।
आधूम्रे क्षेमसुभिक्षमादिशेन्मन्दवृष्टिं च ॥५५॥

कापोतारुणकपिलश्यावाभे क्षुद्भयं विनिर्देश्यम् ।
कापोतः शूद्राणां व्याधिकरः कृष्णवर्णश्च ॥५६॥

विमलकमणिपीताभो वैश्यध्वंसी भवेत्सुभिक्षाय ।
सार्चिष्मत्यग्निभयं गैरिकरूपे तु युद्धानि ॥५७॥

दूर्वाकाण्डश्यामे हारिद्रे वापि निर्दिशेन्मरकम् ।
अशनिभयसम्प्रदायी पाटलकुसुमोपमो राहुः ॥५८॥

पांसुविलोहितरूपः क्षत्रध्वंसाय भवति वृष्टेश्च ।
बालरविकमलसुरचापरूपभृच्छस्त्रकोपाय ॥५६॥

If the eclipsed disc looks white, there will be happiness and prosperity all round, but trouble to the Brahmins. If the colour looks like that of fire, there will be fire-outbreaks and those who work with fire will suffer. If the colour be green, there would be all kinds of diseases afflicting the people, and destruction of crops through *Ītis* i.e. excessive rain, drought etc. If the colour is tawny, there will be famine and destruction of Mlecchas and swift-moving animals like camels. If the colour resembles that of the rays of the rising Sun, there will be famine and drought as well as trouble to birds. If it is grey, there will be prosperity and happiness but limited rains. If the disc appears reddish, or of the colour of the pigeon, or of gold, or yellow-black, people will suffer as a result of famine. If it looks dark or is of the colour of pigeon, Śūdras will suffer from diseases. When its colour resembles that of the spotless jewel (topaz ?) or is yellowish, it will harm the Vaiśyas (traders), but will lead to prosperity. If it resembles the burning flame in colour, there will be fire-outbreaks; if it resembles the colour of minerals, there will be wars. If it looks dark like the Dūrvā grass, or yellowish, there will be epidemics. When Rāhu looks like the Pāṭala flower in colour, there will be risk from lightning and thunderbolts. When Rāhu looks reddish brown, there will be destruction of the Kṣatriyas (fighting men) and rains. If the colour resembles that of the rising Sun, the lotus or the rainbow, it will bring about wars.

[In the following two verses effects of the aspects of different planets on the eclipsed disc are given.]

पश्यन्ग्रस्तं सौम्यो घृतमधुतैलक्षयाय राज्ञां च ।
भौमः समरविमर्दं शिखिकोपं तस्करभयं च ॥६०॥
शुक्रः सस्यविमर्दं नानाक्लेशांश्च जनयति धरित्र्याम् ।
रविजः करोत्यवृष्टिं दुर्भिक्षं तस्करभयं च ॥६१॥

Should Mercury aspect the eclipsed Moon, ghee, honey and oils would become scarce and dear, and kings would come to grief. Should Mars aspect the eclipsed lunar or solar disc, he would cause outbreak of wars, risk from fire and trouble from robbers. Should Venus be the aspecting planet, there would be destruction of crops, and appearance of all kinds of troubles and miseries on the earth. Should Saturn aspect it, there would be famine, drought and trouble from thieves.

[In the case of Mercury and Venus the aspected eclipsed disc can be only the lunar one, and not the solar one. For, Mercury and Venus can never be at a distance of 180° from the Sun.]

यदशुभमवलोकनाभिरुक्तं ग्रहजनितं ग्रहणे प्रमोक्षणे वा ।
सुरपतिगुरुणावलोकिते तच्छममुपयाति जलैरिवाग्निरिद्धः ॥६२॥

Whatever evil effects have been mentioned here as accruing from the aspects of planets on the eclipsed disc either at the commencement or at the termination of the eclipse, would all be warded off by the benefic aspect of Jupiter, as the blazing fire is put out by the pouring of water.

[To ward off the evil effects of planets' aspect on the eclipsed luminary Jupiter should be posited in the 5th, 7th or 9th house from the luminary. The metre is पुष्पिताग्रा.]

ग्रस्ते क्रमान्निमित्तैः पुनर्ग्रहो मासषट्कपरिवृद्ध्या ।
पवनोल्कापातरजःक्षितिकम्पतमोऽशनिनिपातैः ॥६३॥

If at the time of an eclipse (lunar or solar) there should occur portents viz. a strong wind, fall of meteors, dust-storm, earthquake complete darkness, and fall of lightning, the eclipse will recur after 6, 12, 18, 24, 30 and 36 months respectively.

[The commentator here quotes...

उपरक्ते यदा सूर्ये (चन्द्रे?) प्रबलो वाति मारुतः ।
मासषट्के तदा विन्द्याद्राहोरागमनं ध्रुवम् ॥
उल्कायां द्वादशे मासे रजसाष्टादशे तथा ।
भूकम्पे च चतुर्विशे त्रिंशे तमसि निर्दिशेत् ॥
षट्त्रिंशेऽशनिपाते स्यात्सर्वेषु स्यात् षडुत्तरे ॥

This ancient authority mentions only the solar (lunar ?) eclipse. Now he speaks of conjunction of planets with the eclipsed luminary.]

आवन्तिका जनपदाः कावेरीनर्मदातटाश्रयिणः ।
दृप्ताश्च मनुजपतयः पीड्यन्ते क्षितिसुते ग्रस्ते ॥६४॥

If Mars be conjoined with the eclipsed Sun or the Moon, the people of Avantī, those living on the banks of the Kāverī and the Narmadā (rivers) as well as despotic rulers would be in trouble.

अन्तर्वेदीं सरयूं नेपालं पूर्वसागरं शोणम् ।
स्त्रीनृपयोधकुमारान्सह विद्वद्भिर्बुधो हन्ति ॥६५॥

If Mercury be the planet conjoined, the people living in the country lying between the Ganges and the Jumna, on the banks of the Sarayū, those living on the east coast and on the banks of the Sona, womenfolk, kings, warriors, princes (or boys) and the learned would come to grief.

ग्रहणोपगते जीवे विद्वन्नृपमन्त्रिगजहयध्वंसः ।
सिन्धुतटवासिनामप्युदग्दिशं संश्रितानां च ॥६६॥

If Jupiter is thus eclipsed, there will be destruction of the learned, kings, ministers, elephants, horses, those that reside on the banks of the Indus as well as those that live in the north.

भृगुतनये राहुगते दाशेरककैकयाः सयौधेयाः ।
आर्यावर्ताः शिबयः स्त्रीसचिवगणाश्च पीड्यन्ते ॥६७॥

When Venus is thus conjoined with the eclipsed luminary, the people of Dāśeraka, Kekaya, Yaudheya, Āryāvarta and the Śibi country, womenfolk, ministers and tribes will be troubled.

सौरे मरुभवपुष्करसौराष्ट्रिकधातवोऽर्बुदान्त्यजनाः ।
गोमन्तपारियात्राश्रिताश्च नाशं व्रजन्त्याशु ॥६८॥

When Saturn joins Rāhu, the people of Maru (desert), Puṣkara and Saurāṣṭra, minerals, people living in the regions of the Arbuda mountain, people of low-castes, cowherds, and the inhabitants of the Pāriyātra mountain will quickly come to grief.

[In the following 12 verses effects of eclipses occurring in the 12 lunar months beginning with Kārttika are described.]

कार्त्तिक्यामनलोपजीविमगधान्प्राच्याधिपान्कोसलान्
कल्माषानथ शूरसेनसहितान्काशींश्च सन्तापयेत् ।
हन्यादाशु कलिङ्गदेशनृपतिं सामात्यभृत्यं तमो
दृष्टं क्षत्रियतापदं जनयति क्षेमं सुभिक्षान्वितम् ॥६९॥

Should an eclipse, solar or lunar, occur in the lunar month of Kārttika, men who eke out their livelihood through fire, people of Magadha, eastern kings, people of the Kosala country, the Kalmāṣas, the Śūrasenas and those of Kāśī (Benares) will be put to great suffering. The Kaliṅga king along with his ministers and followers will be wiped out. All Kṣatriyas will be afflicted, but all the rest will enjoy happiness and prosperity.

[The metre is शार्दूलविक्रीडित.]

काश्मीरकान्कौशलकान्सपुण्ड्रान्मृगांश्च हन्यादपरान्तकांश्च ।
ये सोमपास्तांश्च निहन्ति सौम्ये सुवृष्टिकृत् क्षेमसुभिक्षकृच्च ॥७०॥

If an eclipse takes place in the month of Mārgaśīrṣa, it will destroy the people of Kashmir, Kosala, and Puṇḍra as well as the animals of the forests and the people of the western border. It will also harm the Soma sacrificers, but it will lead to good rains and to the happiness and prosperity of the people.

[The metre of this and the following verse is उपजाति.]

पौषे द्विजक्षत्रजनोपरोधः ससैन्धवाख्याः कुकुरा विदेहाः ।
ध्वंसं व्रजन्त्यत्र च मन्दवृष्टिं भयं च विन्द्यादसुभिक्षयुक्तम् ॥७१॥

If the eclipse happens in the month of Pauṣa, there will be trouble to Brahmins and Kṣatriyas. The people of the Sindhu regions, the Kukuras and the Videhas will also suffer. There will be scanty rainfall, famine and fear.

माघे तु मातृपितृभक्तवसिष्ठगोत्रान्
स्वाध्यायधर्मनिरतान्करिणस्तुरङ्गान् ।
वङ्गाङ्गकाशिमनुजांश्च दुनोति राहु-
र्वृष्टिं च कर्षकजनाभिमतां करोति ॥७२॥

An eclipse falling in the month of Māgha will afflict people who are devoted to their parents, people born in the Gotra (religious lineage) of Sage Vasiṣṭha, those who are engaged in their sacred studies and performance of religious duties, elephants and horses, people of Bengal, Aṅga and Benares, but will bestow good rains for the joy of the farmers.

[It is to be remembered that the month Māgha derives its name from the constellation Maghā which is presided over by the *manes*. Hence the statement पितृमातृभक्त. The metre is वसन्ततिलका.]

पीडाकरं फाल्गुनमासि पर्व वङ्गाश्मकावन्तिकमेकलानाम् ।
नृत्यज्ञसस्यप्रवराङ्गनानां धनुष्करक्षत्रतपस्विनां च ॥७३॥

An eclipse occurring in the month of Phālguna will prove harmful to the people of Bengal, Aśmaka, Avantī, and those that live on the Mekala mountain, dancers, crops, noble women, bow-makers (i.e. manufacturers of weapons), Kṣatriyas and hermits.

[The metre is उपजाति.]

चैत्र्यां तु चित्रकरलेखकगेयसक्तान्
रूपोपजीविनिगमज्ञहिरण्यपण्यान् ।
पौण्ड्रोड्रकैकयजनानथ चाश्मकांश्च
तापः स्पृशत्यमरपोऽत्र विचित्रवर्षी ॥७४॥

An eclipse falling in the month of Caitra would affect painters, writers, musicians, dancing girls, Vedic scholars, dealers in gold, people of Puṇḍra, Orissa, Kekaya and Aśmaka. There would also be erratic rainfall in the year.

[In all these effects one could discern factors that affect particular professions, regions, castes and types of beings. The metre is वसन्ततिलका.]

वैशाखमासे ग्रहणे विनाशमायान्ति कर्पासतिलाः समुद्गाः ।
इक्ष्वाकुयौधेयशकाः कलिङ्गाः सोपप्लवाः किन्तु सुभिक्षमस्मिन् ॥७५॥

An eclipse taking place in the month of Vaiśākha would destroy cotton, sesamum and green gram. Descendants of Ikṣvāku, the Yaudheyas, the Śakas and the Kaliṅgas would be in trouble, but there would be good crops in the land.

[The metre is इन्द्रवज्रा in this and the following verse.]

ज्येष्ठे नरेन्द्रद्विजराजपत्न्यः सस्यानि वृष्टिश्च महागणाश्च ।
प्रध्वंसमायान्ति नराश्च सौम्याः साल्वैः समेताश्च निषादसङ्घः ॥७६॥

An eclipse taking place in the month of Jyeṣṭha will destroy kings, queens, Brahmins, crops, rains, large groups of men, gentle people, the Sālvas and the tribe of hunters.

आषाढपर्वण्युदपानवप्रनदीप्रवाहान् फलमूलवार्त्तान् ।
गान्धारकाश्मीरपुलिन्दचीनान् हतान्वदेन्मण्डलवर्षमस्मिन् ॥७७॥

An eclipse falling in the month of Āṣāḍha will destroy the banks of wells, tanks etc., rivers, those who live on roots and fruits, the people of Gāndhāra, Kashmir, Pulinda and China. The rains too will not be evenly distributed.

[The metre is उपजाति.]

काश्मीरान्सपुलिन्दचीनयवनान्हन्यात्कुरुक्षेत्रजान्
गान्धारानपि मध्यदेशसहितान्दृष्टो ग्रहः श्रावणे ।
काम्बोजैकशफांश्च शारदमपि त्यक्त्वा यथोक्तानिमा-
नन्यत्र प्रचुरान्नहृष्टमनुजैर्धात्रीं करोत्यावृताम् ॥७८॥

An eclipse occurring in the month of Śrāvaṇa will harm the following: the people of Kashmir, the Pulindas (hunters or forest tribes), the Chinese, the Yavanas, people of Kurukṣetra, Gāndhāra, the Central region, and Kāmboja as well as the animals with uncloven hoofs and autumnal grains. All the rest and other places will enjoy happiness and prosperity.

[The metre is शार्दूलविक्रीडित.]

कलिङ्गवङ्गान्मगधान्सुराष्ट्रान् म्लेच्छान्सुवीरान्दरदाश्मकांश्च ।
स्त्रीणां च गर्भानसुरो निहन्ति सुभिक्षकृद्भाद्रपदेऽभ्युपेतः ॥७९॥

If the eclipse occurs in the month of Bhādrapada, it will destroy the people of Kaliṅga, Bengal, Magadha and Surāṣṭra, the Mlecchas, the Suvīras, the Daradas, the Aśmakas, and children in the womb. However, there will be plenty of food in the land.

[The metre is उपजाति.]

काम्बोजचीनयवनान्सह शल्यहृद्भि-
र्वाह्लीकसिन्धुतटवासिजनांश्च हन्यात् ।
आनर्तपौण्ड्रभिषजश्च तथा किरातान्
दृष्टोऽसुरोऽश्वयुजि भूरिसुभिक्षकृच्च ॥८०॥

When the eclipse takes place in the month of Āśvina, the people of Kāmboja, China, the Yavanas, the Vāhlīkas, surgeons, people living on the banks of the Indus, in the Ānarta country, the Pauṇḍras (residents of Puṇḍra), physicians and the Kirātas (hunters) will come to grief. But there will be plenty of food and happiness.

[Our author states succinctly in one verse the effects of eclipses taking place in several lunar months in his समाससंहिता thus—

अश्वयुजि माघकार्त्तिकभाद्रपदेष्वागतः सुभिक्षकरः ।
राहुरवशिष्टमासेष्वशुभकरो वृष्टिधान्यानाम् ॥

The metre is वसन्ततिलका. Next he speaks of the ten kinds of the end of eclipses. See also verse 43 *supra*.]

हनुकुक्षिपायुभेदा द्विर्द्विः सञ्छर्दनं च जरणं च ।
मध्यान्तयोश्च विदरणमिति दश शशिसूर्ययोर्मोक्षाः ॥८१॥

The end of an eclipse, solar or lunar, is of ten varieties : (i) *Dakṣiṇa hanu*, (ii) *Vāma hanu*, (iii) *Dakṣiṇakukṣi*, (iv) *Vāmakukṣi*, (v) *Dakṣiṇapāyu*, (vi) *Vāmapāyu*, (vii) *Sañchardana* (viii) *Jaraṇa*, (ix) *Madhyavidaraṇa*, *and* (x) *Antavidaraṇa*.

[The last is also called *Antyavidaraṇa*. The definitions and effects of these ten kinds of Mokṣa or release are given in the following nine verses.]

आग्नेय्यामपगमनं दक्षिणहनुभेदसञ्ज्ञितं शशिनः ।
सस्यविमर्दो मुखरुङ्नृपपीडा स्यात्सुवृष्टिश्च ॥८२॥

If the eclipse begins to leave in the South-eastern quarter of the lunar disc, it is called *Dakśiṇahanubheda* (Break of the Southern or right Chin). The effect of such a release would be destruction of crops, appearance of facial diseases, trouble to the rulers, and good rains.

[Sage Kāśyapa says—
दक्षिणो हनुभेदः स्याच्चाग्नेय्यां यदि गच्छति ।
सस्यनाशं च कुरुते नृपभङ्गं सुदारुणम् ॥]

पूर्वोत्तरेण वामो हनुभेदो नृपकुमारभयदायी ।
मुखरोगं शस्त्रभयं तस्मिन्विन्द्यात्सुभिक्षं च ॥८३॥

If the release of the lunar orb occurs in its North-eastern part, it is termed *Vāmahanubheda*—Break of the left chin. In consequence of this there will be trouble and danger to the king's son, facial diseases and fear of armed conflict. However, there will be plenty of food grains in the land.

[Cf. Sage Kāśyapa—
पूर्वोत्तरोऽपरो भेदो नृपपुत्रभयप्रदः ।]

दक्षिणकुक्षिविभेदो दक्षिणपार्श्वेन यदि भवेन्मोक्षः ।
पीडा नृपपुत्राणामभियोज्या दक्षिणा रिपवः ॥८४॥

If the release takes place on the Southern side of the lunar disc, it is called the *Dakṣīṇakukṣibheda*—Break of the right belly. In consequence of this there will be trouble to the princes and conflict with the enemies living to the south.

[Cf. Kāśyapa—
दक्षिणः कुक्षिभेदः स्याद्वामे मोक्षो भवेद्यदि ।
राजपुत्रभयं तत्र दक्षिणाशाद्विषां वधः ॥

वामस्तु कुक्षिभेदो यद्युत्तरमार्गसंस्थितो राहुः ।
स्त्रीणां गर्भविपत्तिः सस्यानि च तत्र मध्यानि ॥८५॥

If the end of the eclipse occurs on the Northern side of the Moon's disc, it is termed Vāmakukṣibheda—Break of the left belly. As a result of this women will have miscarriages and the crops will be moderate.

[Cf. Kāśyapa—

सौम्याशां तु यदा मोक्षो वामकुक्षिविभेदतः ।
स्त्रीणां गर्भविनाशाय सौम्याशाधिपतेर्यथा ॥

According to this Sage there will be in addition the destruction of the king who rules over the territory in the north].

नैर्ऋतवायव्यस्थौ दक्षिणवामौ तु पायुभेदौ द्वौ ।
गुह्यरुगल्पा वृष्टिर्द्वयोस्तु राज्ञीक्षयो वामे ॥८६॥

Should the liberation take place on the South-western side of the Moon's disc, it would be designated as *Dakṣiṇapāyubheda*—Break of the southern or right anus—while the one in the North-western side, *Vāmapāyubheda*—Break of the left anus. In both the cases the effect would be that people will suffer from diseases of the anus and the generating organs. There will be little rain. In the case of the *Vāmapāyu* there will be the death of the queen of the land.

[Cf. Kāśyapa—

पायुभेदगते राहौ वायवीनैर्ऋताशयोः ।
गुह्यरोगभयं विन्द्याद्वामे राज्ञीभयं तथा ॥]

पूर्वेण प्रग्रहणं कृत्वा प्रागेव चापसर्पेत ।
सञ्छर्दनमिति तत्क्षेमसस्यहार्दिप्रदं जगतः ॥८७॥

When the commencement and end of the eclipse are both on the eastern side of the lunar disc, it is called *Sañchardana*—Vomiting. It will lead to happiness, peace, goodwill and prosperity as well as good crops.

[Cf. Kāśyapa—

ग्रासमोक्षौ यदा पूर्वे छर्दनं तु तदा भवेत् ।
क्षेमहार्दिप्रदं ज्ञेयं सस्यनिष्पत्तिकारकम् ॥]

प्राक्प्रग्रहणं यस्मिन्पश्चादपसर्पणं तु तज्जरणम् ।
क्षुच्छस्त्रभयोद्विग्ना न शरणमुपयान्ति तत्र जनाः ॥८८॥

If in an eclipse the beginning is on the eastern side and the liberation on the western side of the Moon's disc, it is called *Jaraṇa*—Decaying. As a result of this people will be troubled by hunger and threat of weapons and consequently be utterly helpless.

[Cf. Kāśyapa—

पूर्वेण ग्रसते राहुरपरस्यां विमुञ्चति ।
क्षुत्तस्करभयं तत्र मोक्षस्तु जरणं स्मृतम ॥]

मध्ये यदि प्रकाशः प्रथमं तन्मध्यविदरणं नाम ।
अन्तःकोपकरं स्यात्सुभिक्षदं नातिवृष्टिकरम् ॥८९॥

If the liberation starts from the middle of the Moon's disc and if that part becomes bright at first, it is called *Madhya vidaraṇa*—cleaving in the middle. Its consequences would be disaffection in the king's army, and sparse rains, but good crops.

[Cf. Kāśyapa—

यदा प्रकाशो मध्ये स्याद् दुर्भिक्षमरकं तदा ।

In the light of Kāśyapa's statement it would be better if we interpret सुभिक्षदं etc. in the text with the न as applicable to both the preceding word and the following one. Then it would mean—Neither good crops nor good rains. For, good rains and good crops always go together.]

पर्यन्तेषु विमलता बहुलं मध्ये तमोऽन्त्यदरणाख्यः ।
मध्याख्यदेशनाशः शारदसस्यक्षयश्चास्मिन् ॥९०॥

If at first there appears brightness all round leaving thick darkness in the middle of the lunar orb, it is called *Antyadaraṇa*—Piercing at the end. Consequently the central region of the land and the autumnal crops would suffer destruction.

[Cf. Kāśyapa—

पर्यन्ते विमलत्वं स्यात्तमो मध्ये यदा भवेत् ।
मध्याख्यदेशनाशः स्याच्छरत्सस्यं विनश्यति ॥]

एते सर्वे मोक्षा वक्तव्या भास्करेऽपि किन्त्वत्र ।
पूर्वा दिक् शशिनि यथा तथा रवौ पश्चिमा कल्प्या ॥९१॥

All these ten kinds of liberations that have been mentioned with reference to the lunar eclipse should also be applied to solar eclipses as well, but the only difference between the two is that wherever the *east* has been stated for the Moon, *west* should be taken for the Sun. Similarly in the case of other pairs of quarters.

मुक्ते सप्ताहान्तः पांसुनिपातोऽन्नसङ्क्षयं कुरुते ।
नीहारो रोगभयं भूकम्पः प्रवरनृपमृत्युम् ॥६२॥

उल्का मन्त्रिविनाशं नानावर्णा घनाश्च भयमतुलम् ।
स्तनितं गर्भविनाशं विद्युन्नृपदंष्ट्रिपरिपीडाम् ॥६३॥

परिवेषो रुक्पीडां दिग्दाहो नृपभयं च साग्निभयम् ।
रूक्षो वायुः प्रबलश्चौरसमुत्थं भयं धत्ते ॥६४॥

निर्घातः सुरचापं दण्डश्च क्षुद्भयं सपरचक्रम् ।
ग्रहयुद्धे नृपयुद्धं केतुश्च तदेव सन्दृष्टः ॥६५॥

अविकृतसलिलनिपातैः सप्ताहान्तः सुभिक्षमादेश्यम् ।
यच्चाशुभं ग्रहणजं तत्सर्वं नाशमुपयाति ॥६६॥

If after the termination of an eclipse there should arise a dust-storm in the place within seven days, it will cause famine ; if there be heavy mist, there would be outbreak of diseases ; if there be an earthquake, death of a leading king ; if there be fall of a meteor, destruction of a minister ; if there appear clouds of many colours, extreme panic ; if there be thunder, miscarriages ; if there be lightning, trouble to kings and tusked animals (or from kings and snakes) ; if there occur a misty circle around the Sun or the Moon, outbreak of diseases ; if there be false fires in the quarters, risk to the king and danger from fire ; if there be fierce dry winds, trouble from robbers ; if there be a clap of portentous thunder, or rainbow or Daṇḍa (a rod-like appearance of the clouds), danger of famine and attack by an enemy's army ; if there be a planetary warfare, wars among the kings ; and if Ketu (Comet) be seen, the same effect, i.e., wars. If there should be normal rains (without any unnatural features) within these seven days, there would be prosperity and plenty of food, and whatever evil was indicated by the eclipse, all that would be completely warded off.

[Cf. the समाससंहिता—

परुषपवनाभ्रगर्जितविद्युत्परिवेषभूप्रकम्पाद्याः ।
सप्ताहान्तर्न शुभा ग्रहणनिवृत्तौ शुभा वृष्टिः ॥

also वृद्धगर्ग—

अथेन्दुग्रहनिर्मुक्ते सप्ताहान्तर्भवेद्यदि ।
पांसुवर्षोऽन्ननाशः स्यान्नीहारो रोगवृद्धये ॥
नृपनाशाय भूकम्प उल्का मन्त्रिविपत्तये ।
रोगाय परिवेषः स्याद्भयायैवाभ्रसम्प्लवः ॥

विद्युद्गर्भविनाशाय दिग्दाहोऽग्निविवृद्धये ।
निर्घातेन्द्रधनुर्दण्डा दुर्भिक्षाय भयाय च ॥
पवनः प्रबलो रूक्षश्चौरोपद्रवसूचकः ।
सर्वोपद्रवनाशः स्यात्सम्यग्वृष्टिर्भवेद्यदि ॥
यद्राहुचरितं प्रोक्तं चन्द्रग्रहणहेतुकम् ।
तदेव सकलं सूर्ये वेदितव्यं शुभाशुभम् ॥]

सोमग्रहे निवृत्ते पक्षान्ते यदि भवेद् ग्रहोऽर्कस्य ।
तत्रानयः प्रजानां दम्पत्योर्वैरमन्योन्यम् ॥९७॥

Should a solar eclipse occur at the end of the fortnight after a lunar eclipse, people would become unruly and unjust in their behaviour and couples would be at loggerheads.

अर्कग्रहात्तु शशिनो ग्रहणं यदि दृश्यते ततो विप्राः ।
नैकक्रतुफलभाजो भवन्ति मुदिताः प्रजाश्चैव ॥९८॥

Should a lunar eclipse take place at the end of the next fortnight after a solar eclipse, the Brahmins would perform many sacrifices and be blessed with the fruit thereof, and all the subjects would be happy and contented.

[When an eclipse, solar or lunar, takes place, all persons are advised to observe some rules regarding food, recreation, etc. Those persons whose natal star or sign is affected by this are, however, advised to perform some propitiatory rituals including gifts. These are explained in the Matsya Purāṇa, Chapter 67. Devout Hindus abstain from food, sleep, etc. during an eclipse. For, though they may not be aware of the scientific reason for it, yet they feel that the period of an eclipse is a critical one, when mysterious cosmic forces are released, which when properly attuned through prayers and meditations lead to beneficial results.]

———

भौमचारः ॥६॥

Chapter VI—Transit of Mars

यद्युदयर्क्षाद्वक्रं करोति नवमाष्टसप्तमर्क्षेषु ।
तद्वक्त्रमुष्णमुदये पीडाकरमग्निवार्त्तानाम् ॥१॥

If Mars should start his retrograde motion while passing through a constellation that happens to be the 7th, 8th or 9th from the one in which he emerged after his conjunction with the Sun (i.e. eclipse), it (the emerging face) would be called *Uṣṇavaktra* or *Hot Face*. It is harmful to those who work on fire, such as the smiths, cooks and sacrificers.

[Cf. वृद्धगर्ग—

उदयान्नवमे कुर्यादिष्टमे सप्तमेऽपि वा ।
निवृत्तिं लोहिताङ्गस्तु तदुष्णं वक्त्रमुच्यते ॥
नरोऽग्निजीविनो ये च पचन्ति च दहन्ति च ।
तेषामुत्पद्यते तापो जायते धनसङ्क्षयः ॥

The author mentions in all five *Faces* of Mars.]

द्वादशदशमैकादशनक्षत्राद्वक्रिते कुजेऽश्रुमुखम् ।
दूषयति रसानुदये करोति रोगानवृष्टिं च ॥२॥

If Mars begins his retrograde motion while passing through the 10th, 11th or the 12th star reckoned from the one wherein he rises after eclipse, it is called *Aśrumukha* or *Tear-Face*. Consequently, he will spoil all juices or tastes, and cause diseases and drought at his next emergence from combustion.

[Cf. वृद्धगर्ग—

दशमैकादशे वापि द्वादशे वापि वक्रिते ।
लोहिताङ्गे ग्रहे ज्ञेयं वक्त्रमश्रुमुखं च तत् ॥
तत्र वर्षति पर्जन्यो दूषयित्वा शुभान् रसान् ।
ते दुष्टा दूषयन्त्याशु नृणां धातूंस्तथा भृशम् ॥
बहवो व्याधयः क्रूरा उत्पद्यन्ते शरीरिणाम् ।
बहुभिः कारणैरेतैस्ततो लोकः प्रलीयते ॥]

व्यालं त्रयोदशर्क्षाच्चतुर्दशाद्वा विपच्यतेऽस्तमये ।
दंष्ट्रिव्यालमृगेभ्यः करोति पीडां सुभिक्षं च ॥३॥

If the retrogression referred to above starts when Mars moves through the 13th or 14th star, it is known as *Vyāla-Vaktra* or *Snake-Mouth*. It will fructify when Mars gets eclipsed next time. Consquently, people will be troubled by snakes (or tusked animals), wild elephants and beasts, but they will enjoy prosperity or abundant food.

[Cf. Sage गर्ग—

त्रयोदशे च नक्षत्रे यदि वापि चतुर्दशे ।
निवृत्तं कुरुते भौमस्तद्वक्त्रं व्यालमुच्यते ॥
भवन्ति प्रचुरा व्यालास्तेभ्यो लोकभयं वदेत् ।
नृपाणामशुभं विन्द्यात्सस्यसम्पत्तिमादिशेत् ॥

also पराशर—

त्रयोदशचतुर्दशयोः सस्यदंष्ट्रिव्यालप्राबल्यं हिरण्यसञ्चयं च ।]

रुधिराननमिति वक्त्रं पञ्चदशात् षोडशाच्च विनिवृत्ते ।
तत्कालं मुखरोगं सभयं च सुभिक्षमावहति ॥४॥

If Mars begins his retrogression while passing through the 15th or 16th asterism counted from the one occupied by him at the time of his emergence, that *face* is known as *Rudhirānana* or *Blood-Face*. This will produce immediately facial diseases and panic, but it will also bring about prosperity.

[Cf. गर्ग—

यदि पञ्चदशर्क्षे तु भूसुतः षोडशेऽपि वा ।
निवृत्ते कुरुते वक्रस्तद्विदुर्लोहिताननम् ॥
दीप्तिमन्तः पार्थिवाश्च भवन्ति प्रथिता भुवि ।
क्षत्रकोपश्च सुमहान् मुखरोगा भवन्ति च ॥

also पराशर—

पञ्चदशषोडशयोर्मुखरोगो नृपक्षोभः शस्त्रकोपश्च ॥]

असिमुसलं सप्तदशादष्टादशतोऽपि वा तदनुवक्रे ।
दस्युगणेभ्यः पीडां करोत्यवृष्टिं सशस्त्रभयाम् ॥५॥

When the retrograde motion of Mars commences when he passes through the 17th or 18th asterism from the one occupied by him at the time of combustion, it (the *face*) is called *Asimusala* or *Sword-Stave*. When Mars becomes direct after this, people will be troubled by bands of robbers, drought and risk from weapons.

[The reader would have noticed in verse 3 and onwards that the counting of asterisms is done not from the one in which Mars emerges from eclipse, but from the one in which he gets eclipsed. This is made clear by the use of the word 'अस्तमये' in verse 3. Now compare what sage *Garga* says :

सप्तदशेऽष्टादशे वा लोहिताङ्ग निवर्तिते
निर्स्त्रिशमुसलं नाम तद्वक्त्रं परिकीर्तितम् ॥
पशुपुत्रधनं धान्यमाहरन्ते तु दस्यवः ।
प्राणिनां जीवनं हन्ति जायते शस्त्रसम्भ्रमः ॥

also पराशर—

"सप्तदशेऽष्टादशे वा दस्युगणैः प्रजानामुपद्रवमवृष्टिं शस्त्रभयं च" ॥]

भाग्यार्यमोदितो यदि निवर्तते वैश्वदैवते भौमः ।
प्राजापत्येऽस्तमितस्त्रीनपि लोकान्निपीडयति ॥६॥

Should Mars begin his retrogression in the star *Uttarāṣāḍha* after being released from eclipse in the star *Pūrva* or *Uttara Phalgunī*, and get eclipsed again in the asterism Rohiṇī, he would afflict the three worlds with untold sufferings.

[After disposing of the effects of the five *Faces* or Vaktra of Mars, the author now deals with the effects of some of the asterisms connected with his retrogression and combustion or release.

Cf. पराशर—

फाल्गुन्यामुदयं कृत्वा वक्रं स्याद्वैश्वदैवते ।
प्राजापत्ये प्रवासश्च त्रैलोक्यं तत्र पीड्यते ॥]

श्रवणोदितस्य वक्रं पुष्ये मूर्द्धाभिषिक्तपीडाकृत् ।
यस्मिन्नृक्षेऽभ्युदितस्तद्दिग्व्यूहाञ्जनान् हन्ति ॥७॥

Should Mars emerge from his conjunction with the Sun in the asterism Śravaṇa and become retrograde in the star Puṣya, kings would be in jeopardy. Similarly the people, countries and things denoted by the star in which he re-emerges would come to grief.

[See chapters XIV and XV for the countries, peoples, etc. denoted by the stars.

Cf. पराशर—

उदितः श्रवणे भौमः पुष्ये वक्रं चरेद्यदि ।
मूर्द्धाभिषिक्ता राजानो विनश्येयुः परस्परम् ॥
यथा जनपदव्यूहे दिग्विभागः प्रदर्शितः ।
तस्य वै मोहितं कुर्याल्लोहिताङ्गस्तथा मुखम् ॥]

मध्येन यदि मघानां गतागतं लोहितः करोति ततः ।
पाण्ड्यो नृपो विनश्यति शस्त्रोद्योगाद्भयमवृष्टिः ॥८॥

Should Mars start his retrogression while passing through the cluster of stars comprising Maghā, the Pāṇḍya ruler would meet with his end, and there would be drought and panic resulting from fighting.

भित्त्वा मघां विशाखां भिन्दन्भौमः करोति दुर्भिक्षम् ।
मरकं करोति घोरं यदि भित्त्वा रोहिणीं याति ॥९॥

Should Mars first cut the star Maghā and then Viśākhā, there would be famine in the country. Should he cut the star Rohiṇī, there would be great mortality in the land.

दक्षिणतो रोहिण्याश्चरन्महीजोऽर्घवृष्टिनिग्रहकृत् ।
धूमायन्सशिखो वा विनिहन्यात्पारियात्रस्थान् ॥१०॥

If Mars should pass through the southern side of Rohiṇī, he would cause drought and slump in the market. Should he appear emitting smoke or flames, he would destroy the people living in the region of the Pāriyātra mountain.

प्राजापत्ये श्रवणे मूले त्रिषु चोत्तरेषु शाक्रे च ।
विचरन् घननिवहानामुपघातकरः क्षमातनयः ॥११॥

The transit of Mars through the following stars viz. Rohiṇī, Śravaṇa, Mūla, the three Uttaras and Jyeṣṭha, would destroy the formation of clouds.

[Here the author speaks of the harmful effects of the mere transit of Mars through the above esterisms. This is one of the methods of predicting drought.]

चारोदयाः प्रशस्ताः श्रवणमघादित्यहस्तमूलेषु ।
एकपदाश्विविशाखाप्राजापत्येषु च कुजस्य ॥१२॥

The transit and rising of Mars after conjunction with the Sun in the asterisms Śravaṇa, Maghā, Punarvasu, Hasta, Mūla, Pūrvabhādra, Aśvinī, Viśākhā and Rohiṇī will prove auspicious.

[This verse gives a general rule to the effect that Mars does good to the world when he transits through or rises in the above asterisms. This must be taken in conjunction with what the author has stated in the previous verse.]

विपुलविमलमूर्तिः किंशुकाशोकवर्णः
स्फुटरुचिरमयूखस्तप्तताम्रप्रभाभः ।
विचरति यदि मार्गं चोत्तरं मेदिनीजः
शुभकृदवनिपानां हार्ददश्च प्रजानाम् ॥१३॥

If Mars being possessed of a large and bright form, red colour resembling the Kiṁśuka and Aśoka flowers, brilliant and charming rays and lustre like that of red-hot molten copper, should move along the Northern Path (or to the north of the star he is in), he would prove beneficial to the kings and bring peace and joy to the subjects.

[Cf. गर्ग—

यास्याादिपितृपर्यन्तं नवर्क्षं मार्गमुत्तरम् ।
भाग्यादिनैर्ऋतान्तं तु मध्यमं मार्गमुच्यते ॥
आषाढाद्याश्विनान्तं तु दक्षिणं समुदाहृतम् ।
सौम्यमार्गस्थितो भौमः प्रजानामुपकारकः ॥
मध्यमे मध्यफलदो याम्ये तु भयदः स्मृतः ॥

In these verses Sage *Garga* speaks of the *Northern*, the *Middle* and the *Southern Path* for Mars. The nine stars beginning from Bharaṇī come under the *Northern Path*, the nine from Pūrvaphalgunī come under the *Middle Path*, and lastly the nine stars from Pūrvāṣāḍha under the *Southern Path*. It is also an astrological principle that a planet situated to the north of an asterism gives good results. The metre is मालिनी.]

———

बुधचारः ॥७॥

Chapter VII—Mercury's Transit

नोत्पातपरित्यक्तः कदाचिदपि चन्द्रजो व्रजत्युदयम् ।
जलदहनपवनभयकृद्धान्यार्घक्षयविवृद्ध्यै ॥१॥

Never does Mercury reappear after his eclipse by the Sun unaccompanied by any unusual (portentous) phenomenon. Generally at such times he creates danger to the people through water, fire or wind, and causes extraordinary fluctuations in the prices of food grains.

[Mercury's movements must be studied by astrologers and economists for predicting market trends in certain periods.

Cf. the समाससंहिता—

उदयं याति शशिसुतो नोत्पातविवर्जितः कदाचिदपि ।
पवनाग्निसलिलभयदो धान्यार्घवृद्धिक्षयकृद्वा ॥

also वृद्धगर्ग—

अवर्षे कुरुते वर्षं वर्षे वर्षं न गच्छति
भये च कुरुते क्षेमं सर्वत्र प्रतिलोमगः ॥

also कश्यप—

नाकस्माद्दर्शनं याति विनोत्पातेन सोमजः ।
भयवातातपहिमैरर्घवृद्धिक्षयादिभिः ॥]

विचरञ्छ्रवणधनिष्ठाप्राजापत्येन्दुवैश्वदेवानि ।
मृद्नन् हिमकरतनयः करोत्यवृष्टिं सरोगभयाम् ॥२॥

When Mercury passes through the stars Śravaṇa, Dhaniṣṭhā, Rohiṇī, Mṛgaśiras and Uttarāṣāḍha and thus cuts them across, he creates drought, diseases and panic.

[Cf. कश्यप—

रोहिणीं वैश्वदेवं च सौम्यवैष्णववासवान् ।
शशिजश्च यदा हन्ति प्रजा रोगैश्च पीडयेत् ॥

Here we have to note the wording 'मृद्नन्' in the text and 'हन्ति' in Kaśyapa's work. This should make us believe that the untoward effects mentioned here would take place only if mercury cuts across the particular asterisms, and not otherwise.]

रौद्रादीनि मघान्तान्युपाश्रिते चन्द्रजे प्रजापीडा ।
शस्त्रनिपातक्षुद्भयरोगानावृष्टिसन्तापैः ॥३॥

When Mercury passes through the five çonstellations beginning with Ārdrā, people will be afflicted as a result of clash of arms, hunger, fright, diseases, drought and sorrow.

[Here the author speaks of the effect of Mercury's movement through some of the stars. But Kaśyapa refers to the cutting of the stars

Cf. कश्यप—

रौद्रादीनि यदा पञ्च नक्षत्राणीन्दुनन्दनः ।
भिनत्ति शस्त्रदुर्भिक्षव्याधिभिः पीड्यते जगत् ॥]

हस्तादीनि चरन् षड्ऋक्षाण्युपपीडयन्गवामशुभः ।
स्नेहरसार्घविवृद्धिं करोति चोर्वी प्रभूतान्नाम् ॥४॥

When Mercury moves through the six stars beginning with Hasta, cutting across them, prices of oils, and juices will shoot up, there will be plenty of food in the country, but the cattle will suffer.

[The word *Sneha* means something that lubricates. So it includes ghee. Rasa means honey, jaggery and such other things.

Cf. कश्यप—

हस्तादीनि चरन् षड्वै नक्षत्राणीन्दुनन्दनः ।
गवामशुभदः प्रोक्तः सुभिक्षक्षेमकारकः ॥

There is a metrical flaw in the first quarter of this verse.]

आर्यम्णं हौतभुजं भद्रपदामुत्तरां यमेशं च ।
चन्द्रस्य सुतो निघ्नन्प्राणभृतां धातुसङ्क्षयकृत् ॥५॥

When Mercury cuts across the stars Uttaraphalgunī, Kṛttikā, Uttarabhādrapada and Bharaṇī, all living beings will be afflicted with diseases arising from the vitiation or diminution of the seven constituent elements of the body viz. muscle, bone, blood, skin, semen, fat and marrow.

[According to Āyurveda the seven elements are : रस, असृक्, मांस, मेदस् अस्थि, मज्जा and शुक्र. According to some there are ten elements including केश, त्वक् and स्नायु.

Cf. कश्यप—

भरणीकृत्तिकार्यम्णमहिर्बुध्नं च चन्द्रजः ।
चरन्धातुविनाशाय प्राणिनां परिकीर्तितः ॥]

आश्विनवारुणमूलान्युपमृद्नन् रेवतीं च चन्द्रसुतः :
पण्यभिषग्नौजीविकसलिलजतुरगोपघातकरः ॥६॥

When Mercury transits afflicting the stars Aśvinī, Śatabhiṣaj, Mūla and Revatī, merchants (merchandise ?), physicians, sailors, substances derived from water, such as pearls, conch shells etc., and horses will come to grief.

[Cf. कश्यप—

रेवतीं वारुणं मूलमश्विनीं चोपमर्दयन् ।
बुधो वणिग्भिषग्वाहाञ्जलोत्थांश्च विनाशयेत् ॥]

पूर्वाहृक्षत्रितयादेकमपीन्दोः सुतोऽभिमृद्नीयात् ।
क्षुच्छस्त्रतस्करामयभयप्रदायी चरञ्जगतः ॥७॥

When Mercury cuts through any one of the three Pūrva stars, (Pūrvaphalgunī, Pūrvāṣāḍha and Pūrvabhādra), people will suffer from hunger, armed conflict, robbers, diseases and panic.

[Cf. the following—

पूर्वात्रये चरन्सौम्यो भेदं कृत्वा यदि व्रजेत् ।
क्षुच्छस्त्रतस्करभयैः करोति प्राणिनां वधम् ॥]

प्राकृतविमिश्रसङ्क्षिप्ततीक्ष्णयोगान्तघोरपापाख्याः ।
सप्त पराशरतन्त्रे नक्षत्रैः कीर्तिता गतयः ॥८॥

Seven courses of Mercury named (i) Prākṛtā, (ii) Vimiśrā, (iii) Saṁkṣiptā, (iv) Tīkṣṇā, (v) Yogāntā, (vi) Ghorā and (vii) Pāpā, have been mentioned in the Tantra (Scientific work) of Sage Parāśara, on the basis of the asterisms.

[The तन्त्र mentioned by our author must be 'पराशरसंहिता'. Some translators have taken the name of the last course to be पापाख्या, while actually it is पापा as shown by वृद्धगर्ग.]

प्राकृतसञ्ज्ञा वायव्ययाम्यपैतामहानि बहुलाश्च ।
मिश्रा गतिः प्रदिष्टा शशिशिवपितृभुजगदेवानि ॥९॥
सङ्क्षिप्तायां पुष्यः पुनर्वसुः फल्गुनीद्वयं चेति ।
तीक्ष्णायां भद्रपदाद्वयं सशाक्राश्वयुक् पौष्णम् ॥१०॥
योगान्तिकेति मूलं द्वे चाषाढे गतिः सुतस्येन्दोः ।
घोरा श्रवणस्त्वाष्ट्रं वसुदैवं वारुणं चैव ॥११॥
पापाख्या सावित्रं मैत्रं शक्राग्निदैवतं चेति ।

The course is known as *Prākṛtā* when Mercury passes through Bharaṇī, Kṛttikā, Rohiṇī or Svātī. It is *Miśrā* when the star is Mṛgaśiras, Ārdrā, Āśleṣā or Maghā. In the course called *Saṁkṣiptā* Mercury transits through Punarvasu, and the two Phalgunīs. The gait is called *Tīkṣṇā* when his transit takes place through the two Bhadrapadās, Jyeṣṭhā, Aśvinī and Revatī. In *Yogāntā* Mercury moves through Mūla, Pūrvāṣāḍha and Uttarāṣāḍha. In *Ghorā* he moves through Śravaṇa, Citrā, Dhaniṣṭhā and Śatabhiṣaj. Lastly in the course known as *Pāpā* Mercury courses through Hasta, Anurādhā and Viśākhā.

उदयप्रवासदिवसैः स एव गतिलक्षणं प्राह ॥१२॥
चत्वारिंशत् त्रिंशद् द्विसमेता विंशतिर्द्विनवकं च ।
नव मासार्द्धं दश चैकसंयुताः प्राकृताद्यानाम् ॥१३॥

The same authority (i.e. sage Parāśara) has given the duration of visibility and combustion of Mercury in the seven courses in terms of days as 40, 30, 22, 18, 9, 15, and 11 days respectively.

[The idea is that if Mercury gets eclipsed or rises in his first course, he will remain invisible or visible for 40 days.

Cf. वृद्धगर्ग—

चत्वारिंशत्प्राकृतायां गतावालक्ष्यते बुधः ।
मासमेकं विमिश्रायां दर्शयित्वास्तमर्हति ॥
अल्पां द्वाविंशतिं सार्द्धं सङ्क्षिप्तामेत्य लक्ष्यते ।
अष्टादशाहं तीक्ष्णायां घोरायां दश पञ्च च ॥
पापायां पादहीनानि तथैकादश तिष्ठति ।
योगान्तिक्यामिन्दुसूनुर्नवाहं लक्ष्यते तथा ॥
चारकालो य एवोक्तः सोमपुत्रस्य भागशः ।
अस्तकालः स एव स्यात्सूर्यमण्डलचारिणः ॥

There is difference of opinion between Parāśara and Vṛddha Garga in that the latter states that in the third (Saṁkṣiptā) course the duration of visibility or otherwise is $22\frac{1}{2}$ days and in the last it is $10\frac{3}{4}$ days. Our author follows Parāśara and says as follows in the समाससंहिता—

प्राकृतविमिश्रसङ्क्षिप्ततीक्ष्णयोगान्तघोरपापाख्याः ।
गतयो लक्षणमासां नोदयदिक्स्थैः स्फुटं भवति ॥
स्पष्टा पराशरमते स्वाती च प्राकृता त्रिभं याम्यात् ।
मिश्रा गतिः शशिशेखरभुजगपितृदेवतासौम्यैः ॥
सङ्क्षिप्ता नाम गतिः पुनर्वसुः फल्गुनीद्वयं पुष्यः ।
तीक्ष्णा भद्रपदाद्यं नक्षत्रचतुष्टयं ज्येष्ठा ॥
मूलत्यृक्षं योगा घोरा श्रवणत्रिभं च सत्वाष्ट्रम् ।
पापाख्या तु विशाखा हस्तो मैत्रं च शशिसूनोः ॥

कश्यप agrees with पराशर and says :

चत्वारिंशत्तथा त्रिंशद्दिनानि द्वौ च विंशतिः ।
अष्टादशार्द्धमासं च दश चैकयुतानि च ॥
नव च प्राकृताद्यासु सोमजस्तूदितस्तथा ।

अस्तं गतः सर्वकालं तिष्ठतीति विनिश्चयः ॥

Next the author gives the effects of these courses.]

प्राकृतगत्यामारोग्यवृष्टिसस्यप्रवृद्धयः क्षेमम् ।

संक्षिप्तमिश्रयोर्मिश्रमेतदन्यासु विपरीतम् ॥१४॥

When Mercury is in his Prākṛtā course, people will enjoy health, happiness, good rains and bumper crops. In the Saṁkṣiptā and Miśrā courses the effects would be of a mixed nature, in the rest they would be quite untoward.

[Cf. गर्ग—

क्षेमारोग्यसुभिक्षेषु लक्षणा प्राकृता गतिः ।

संक्षिप्ता च विमिश्रा च शुभाशुभफलोदये ॥

तीक्ष्णा घोरा च पापा च तथा योगान्तिकापरा ।

एताश्चतस्रः सौम्यस्य दुर्भिक्षाक्षेमलक्षणाः ॥]

ऋज्व्यतिवक्रा वक्रा विकला च मतेन देवलस्यैताः ।

पञ्चचतुर्द्व्येकाहा ऋज्व्यादीनां षडभ्यस्ताः ॥१५॥

According to Devala's view the Ṛjvī or *Direct*, *Ativakrā* or, *Exceedingly Retrograde*, *Vakrā* or *Retrograde* and *Vikalā* or *Deformed* motions of Mercury would come into being when he stays visible for 30 (5×6), 24 (4×6), 12 (2×6) and 6 days (1×6) respectively.

[Sage Devala who himself quotes ancient authorities is quoted here in respect of the four kinds of motions of Mercury. These four names would also apply to the conditions wherein he remains invisible for the different durations. The commentator wants us to understand that the effects of these motions also will last for so many days.]

ऋज्वी हिता प्रजानामतिवक्रार्घं गतिर्विनाशयति ।

शस्त्रभयदा च वक्रा विकला भयरोगसञ्जननी ॥१६॥

Mercury's *Direct* motion is beneficial to people, while his *Exceedingly Retrograde* motion brings about economic ruin of the country through famine. His *Retrograde* motion produces threat of war, while his *Deformed* motion causes panic and diseases.

[Cf. देवल—

दिनानि त्रिंशदुदितस्तिष्ठेद्यदि च सोमजः ।

ऋज्वी गतिः सा विज्ञेया प्रजानां हितकारिणी ॥

चतुर्विंशद्दिनान्येवं यदि तिष्ठेच्च सोमजः ।

अतिवक्रा गतिर्ज्ञेया दुर्भिक्षगतिलक्षणा ॥

अहानि द्वादश यदा बुधस्तिष्ठेत्तथोद्गतः ।

वक्रा गतिः सा विज्ञेया शस्त्रसम्भ्रमकारिणी ॥

षड् दिनानि यदा तिष्ठेदुद्गतः सोमनन्दनः ।
विकला सा गतिर्ज्ञेया भयरोगविवर्द्धिनी ॥
एवमस्तमये सर्वं गतिजं सोमजस्य तु ।
भावाभावाय लोकानां फलं वाच्यं शुभाशुभम् ॥

Next the author gives the effects of Mercury's visibility and disappearance in the different lunar months.]

पौषाषाढश्रावणवैशाखेष्विन्दुजः समाघेषु ।
दृष्टो भयाय जगतः शुभफलकृत्प्रोषितस्तेषु ॥१७॥

If Mercury becomes visible in the lunar months of Pauṣa, Āṣāḍha, Śrāvaṇa, Vaiśākha and Māgha, there will be great danger to the world. But if he remains eclipsed (invisible) during these months, he will prove auspicious.

[According to *Vṛddha Garga* Mercury is seldom visible in the sky in the above-named five months. In the remaining seven months generally he is visible. So the two groups are respectively called *Invisible* and *Visible*. If this rule should be violated, there would be outbreak of cattle disease, drought and famine. For, he says—

वैशाखपौषमाघेषु श्रावणाषाढयोरपि ।
न दृश्यते बुधः प्रायो मासेष्वन्येषु दृश्यते ॥
यदाऽदृश्येषु दृष्टः स्याद् दृश्येषु च न दृश्यते ।
गवां रोगमनावृष्टिं दुर्भिक्षं चापि निर्दिशेत् ॥

See also पराशर—

वैशाखाषाढयोर्माघे पौषश्रावणयोस्तथा ।
बुधो न दृश्यते जातु दृश्येत भयमादिशेत् ॥
पौषे करोति मरकं माघे वातं तथा च सोमसुतः ।
वैशाखे जनमरकमाषाढे श्रावणे च दुर्भिक्षम् ॥

Parāśara gives mortality as the evil effect for the two months Pauṣa and Vaiśākha, storm for Māgha, and famine for Āśāḍha and Śrāvaṇa.]

कार्त्तिकेऽश्वयुजि वा यदि मासे दृश्यते तनुभवः शिशिरांशोः ।
शस्त्रचौरहुतभुग्गदतोयक्षुद्भयानि च तदा विदधाति ॥१८॥

Should Mercury be visible in the lunar months of Kārttika and Āśvina, there would be danger from weapons (or war), robbers, fire, diseases, water and hunger.

[Out of twelve months for seven months Mercury, being visible is disastrous for the world. This may be the reason why Mercury is not considered bad when he is combust, in astrology. The metre is स्वागता.]

रुद्धानि सौम्येऽस्तगते पुराणि यान्युद्गते तान्युपयान्ति मोक्षम् ।
अन्ये तु पश्चादुदिते वदन्ति लाभः पुराणां भवतीति तज्ज्ञाः ॥१६॥

If towns are besieged when Mercury gets eclipsed, they would be freed from the siege when Mercury rises again. According to other scholars besieged cities would be benefited only when Mercury rises in the west.

[Cf. नन्दी—

पश्चार्द्धादुदिते सौम्ये लभते पुररोधकः ।
पुनः प्रागुदिते तस्मिन्पुरमोक्षं विनिर्दिशेत् ॥

According to this authority the besieging army becomes victorious or takes possession of the town when Mercury rises in the west, whereas when he rises again in the east the town would be retaken or freed from the enemy's hold. The metre is इन्द्रवज्रा.]

हेमकान्तिरथवा शुकवर्णः सस्यकेन मणिना सदृशो वा ।
स्निग्धमूर्तिरलघुश्च हिताय व्यत्यये न शुभकृच्छशिपुत्रः ॥ २० ॥

If Mercury appears being possessed of golden hue or of the colour of parrot or is similar in hue to the Sasyaka gem and if his disc is glossy and pretty big, he will prove beneficial to mankind. In the absence of these features he will prove harmful.

[Cf. पराशर—

विमलजलरजतस्फटिकाभः प्रशस्यते ।]

बृहस्पतिचारः ॥८॥

JUPITER'S COURSE

नक्षत्रेण सहोदयमुपगच्छति येन देवपतिमन्त्री ।
तत्सञ्ज्ञं वक्तव्यं वर्षं मासक्रमेणैव ॥१॥

Ascertain the star in which Jupiter reappears after conjunction with the Sun. That year of Jupiter will bear the name of that particular star, and the succeeding years those of the lunar months following it in regular order.

[The jovian year commences with the rising of Jupiter and is called after the asterism in which he reappears. For example, if Jupiter re-emerges after an eclipse in the star kṛttikā, then that year would be called Kārttika. The succeeding years would be Mārgaśīrṣa, Pauṣa etc. Cf. ऋषिपुत्र :—

यत्रोत्तिष्ठति नक्षत्रे सह येन प्रवर्धते ।
संवत्सरः स विज्ञेयस्तन्नक्षत्रविधायकः ॥

also काश्यप :—

संवत्सरे युगे चैव षष्ट्यब्देऽङ्गिरसः सुतः ।
यन्नक्षत्रोदयं कुर्यात्तत्सञ्ज्ञं वत्सरं विदुः ॥
तिष्यादि च युगं प्राहुर्वसिष्ठात्रिपराशराः ।
बृहस्पतेस्तु सौम्यान्ते सदा द्वादशवार्षिकम् ॥
उदेति यस्मिन्मासे तु प्रवासोपगतोऽङ्गिराः ।
तस्मात्संवत्सरो मासो बार्हस्पत्योऽथ गम्यते ॥

also गर्ग :—

प्रवासान्ते सहर्क्षेण तूदितो युगपच्चरेत् ।
तस्मात्कालादृक्षपूर्वो गुरोरब्दः प्रवर्तते ॥
युगानि द्वादशाब्दानि तत्र तानि बृहस्पतेः ।
तत्र सावनसौराभ्यां सावनाब्दो निरुच्यते ॥
एवमाश्वयुजं चैव चैत्रं चैव बृहस्पतिः ।
संवत्सरं नाशयते सप्तत्यब्दशतेऽधिके ॥]

वर्षाणि कार्त्तिकादीन्याग्नेयाद्भद्वयानुयोगीनि ।
क्रमशस्त्रिभं तु पञ्चममुपान्त्यमन्त्यं च यद्वर्षम् ॥ २ ॥

Jupiter's years commence from Kārttika and consist of two asterisms each beginning with Kṛttikā and follow in regular order. However, the 5th, 10th and 11th years comprise each three asterisms.

[Here the word Antya is interpreted as the 12th to the 11th i.e. 10th. If Jupiter rises in kṛttikā or Rohiṇī, his year will be called *Kārttika*; if in Mṛgaśiras or Ārdrā, *Mārgaśirṣa*; if in Punarvasu or Puṣya, *Pauṣa*; if in Āśleṣā or Maghā, *Māgha*; if in Purvaphalgunī, Uttaraphalgunī or Hasta, *Phālguna*; if in Citrā or Svātī, *Caitra*; if in Viśākhā or Anurādhā, *Vaiśākha*; if in Jyeṣṭhā or Mūla, *jyeṣṭha*; if in Pūrvāṣāḍha or Uttarāṣāḍha, *Āṣāḍha*; if in Śravaṇa, Dhaniṣṭhā, or Śatabhiṣaj, *Śrāvaṇa*; if in Pūrvabhādra, Uttarabhādra or Revatī, *Bhādrapada*; and if in Aśvinī or Bharaṇī, *Āśvina*. This shows that only the three months Viz. *Bhādrapada*, *Phālguna* and *Śrāvaṇa*, have three stars each. I cannot understand how the *Āśvina* month which is the 12th in order could have three stars. On the other hand the 10th, viz. *Śrāvaṇa*, has three stars. Our author must have followed some ancient author or he means 10th by the word अन्त्य as given above.

Cf. गर्ग :—

फाल्गुनी चैव हस्तं च चरेद्यदि बृहस्पति : ।
स फाल्गुनोऽब्दः क्रूरः स्याद्धान्यमुच्चाटतां व्रजेत् ॥

श्रावणादीनि च त्रीणि चरेद्यदि बृहस्पतिः ।
श्रावणो नाम सोऽब्दः स्यात्क्षेमसौभिक्षमूर्तिमान् ॥
पूर्वोत्तरे प्रोष्ठपदे चरेद्रेवतिमेव च ।
प्रोष्ठपाद इति ज्ञेयो मध्यमो वत्सरो हि सः ॥

आश्विनं चैव याम्यं च चरेद्यदि बृहस्पतिः ।
संवत्सरः सोऽश्वयुक्स्यात्सर्वभूतहितावहः ॥

नववारा द्विनक्षत्रा गुरोर्द्वादशमासिकाः ।
शेषास्त्रयस्त्रिनक्षत्राः पञ्चमैकादशान्तिमाः ॥

also काश्यप :—

कार्त्तिकादिसमा ज्ञेया द्विनक्षत्रविचारिणा ।
त्रिभं भाद्रपदे ज्ञेयं फाल्गुने श्रावणे तथा ॥]

शकटानलोपजीवकगोपीडा व्याधिशस्त्रकोपश्च ।
वृद्धिस्तु रक्तपीतककुसुमानां कार्त्तिके वर्षे ॥ ३ ॥

In the *Kārttika* year of Jupiter cartmen, persons living by fire, and cattle will suffer. There will also be outbreak of diseases and clash of arms. Red and yellow flowers will grow in abundance.

[Cf. गर्गः—

> कार्त्तिकः प्रचुरातङ्कः क्षुच्छस्त्राग्निभयप्रदः ।
> गोशाकटिकपीडां च करोत्येवमवृष्टिदः ॥]

> **सौम्येऽब्देऽनावृष्टिर्मृगाखुशलभाण्डजैश्च सस्यवधः ।**
> **व्याधिभयं मित्रैरपि भूपानां जायते वैरम् ॥४॥**

In the Mārgaśīrṣa year of Jupiter there will be drought, destruction of crops as a result of pests like wild animals, rats, locusts and birds, outbreak of epidemics and kings' hostilities even with their friends.

[Cf. गर्गः—

> वर्षहन्ता व्याधिकरो मिथो भेदभयावहः ।
> शलभाद्याकुलः सौम्यो दुर्भिक्षभयकारकः ॥]

> **शुभकृज्जगतः पौषो निवृत्तवैराः परस्परं क्षितिपाः ।**
> **द्वित्रिगुणो धान्यार्घः पौष्टिककर्मप्रसिद्धिश्च ॥५॥**

In the Pauṣa year of Jupiter the world will be happy and prosperous, kings will be free from enmity among themselves, the prices of food grains will go up two-fold or three-fold, and preservative work will flourish.

[Bhaṭṭotpala interprets धान्यार्घ etc. as fall in prices of corn. Cf. गर्गः—

> प्रशान्तव्याधिदुर्भिक्षदुर्वर्षाशनितस्करः ।
> सर्वलक्षणसम्पन्नः पौषः संवत्सरोत्तमः ॥]

> **पितृपूजापरिवृद्धिर्माघे हार्दिश्च सर्वभूतानाम् ।**
> **आरोग्यवृष्टिधान्यार्घसम्पदो मित्रलाभश्च ॥६॥**

In the Māgha year of Jupiter people would worship the *manes* (and parents and elders) with greater devotion, and all beings would enjoy happiness and contentment as well as sound health. There would be good rains and good prices for corn ; and people would live with greater amity and cordiality.

[Cf. गर्गः—

> क्षेमारोग्यं सुभिक्षं वर्षणं शिवमेव च ।
> पितृपूजाः प्रवर्तन्ते माघे राज्ञां च सन्धयः ॥

According to this sage the year of Māgha would be notable for treaties among rulers also.]

फाल्गुनवर्षे विन्द्यात्क्वचित्क्वचित्क्षेमवृष्टिसस्यानि ।
दौर्भाग्यं प्रमदानां प्रबलाश्चौरा नृपाश्चोग्राः ॥७॥

In the Phālguna year of Jupiter happiness, rainfall and crops would be sporadic and young women would be afflicted with misfortune. Kings would become cruel and aggressive and robbers would increase enormously.

[Cf. गर्गः—

नारीदौर्भाग्यकृच्चौरः फाल्गुनः सस्यवर्षदः ।
क्वचित्क्षेमं सुभिक्षं च क्वचिदक्षेमकारकः ॥]

चैत्रे मन्दा वृष्टिः प्रियमन्नं क्षेममवनिपा मृदवः ।
वृद्धिश्च कोशधान्यस्य भवति पीडा च रूपवताम् ॥८॥

In the Caitra year of Jupiter rainfall would be scanty, food costly, but people would enjoy happiness and kings would become kind-hearted. Pulses would thrive, but the beautiful would suffer.

[Cf. गर्गः—

मृदुप्रचारा राजानः प्रियमन्नं जनस्य च ।
क्षेमारोग्यं च मृदुता चैत्रवर्षस्तथा मृदुः ॥

The word रूपवतां in the text may mean 'those who live by their physical charm' such as actors and dancing girls.

The beginning of the second half of the verse looks like a Śloka line. The flaw in caesura is quite apparent here.]

वैशाखे धर्मरता विगतभयाः प्रमुदिताः प्रजाः सनृपाः ।
यज्ञक्रियाप्रवृत्तिर्निष्पत्तिः सर्वसस्यानाम् ॥९॥

In the Vaiśākha year of Jupiter both the rulers and the ruled would be devoted to religious practices, happy and free from fear (or troubles). People would be engaged in performing sacrifices and there would be abundant growth of all crops.

[Cf. गर्गः—

ईतयः प्रशमं यान्ति सन्धिं कुर्वन्ति पार्थिवाः ।
वैशाखे तु सस्यजन्या वृष्टयः सम्भवन्ति हि ॥]

ज्येष्ठे जातिकुलधनश्रेणीश्रेष्ठा नृपाः सधर्मज्ञाः ।
पीड्यन्ते धान्यानि च हित्वा कङ्गुं शमीजातिम् ॥१०॥

In the Jyeṣṭha year of Jupiter leaders of classes (castes),

families, wealthy men and trade guilds, kings and those that are well-versed in the laws governing righteous conduct (like judges and wise elders) will be in trouble. All grains except Kaṅgu and those of the Śamī class will suffer.

[सबीजानि is another reading for शमीजातिम्. According to this reading, 'all grains with their seeds' should be affected.
Cf. गर्गः—

वृक्षगुल्मलतासस्यक्षेमवर्षविनाशनः ।
क्रूराज्ञादीप्तिजननो ज्यैष्ठो ज्येष्ठनृपान्तकृत् ॥]

आषाढे जायन्ते सस्यानि क्वचिदवृष्टिरन्यत्र ।
योगक्षेमं मध्यं व्यग्राश्च भवन्ति भूपालाः ॥११॥

In the Āṣāḍha year there will be growth of crops in some places and drought elsewhere. The welfare of the people will be moderate, and kings will become very active and busy.

[योग is the acquisition of things one does not possess, while क्षेम is the protection of what has been acquired.
Cf. गर्गः—

दुर्भिक्षाक्षेमजननश्चाषाढोऽन्योन्यभेदकृत् ।
भूपालयुद्धजननो मध्यमक्षेमकारकः ॥]

श्रावणवर्षे क्षेमं सम्यक् सस्यानि पाकमुपयान्ति ।
क्षुद्रा ये पाखण्डाः पीड्यन्ते ये च तद्भक्ताः ॥१२॥

In the Śrāvaṇa year of Jupiter people will be happy and crops abundant. Heretics and the mea-nminded will be troubled along with their followers.

[Cf. गर्गः—

श्रावणः सस्यसम्पन्नः क्षेमारोग्यकरः शिवः ।
धान्यं समर्घतां याति सम्यग्वर्षति वासवः ॥
क्षुद्रान्पाखण्डिनः सर्वांस्तद्भक्तांश्चोपतापयेत् ॥]

भाद्रपदे वल्लीजं निष्पत्ति याति पूर्वसस्यं च ।
न भवत्यपरं सस्यं क्वचित्सुभिक्षं क्वचिच्च भयम् ॥१३॥

In the Bhādrapada year of Jupiter the produce of creepers like green grams and the first crop of the year will be quite satisfactory. There will be no second crop in the year. Food grains will be in plenty only in some places, and there will be panic or danger in other parts.

[Cf. गर्गः—

प्रौष्ठपात्सस्यजननो नाशयत्यपरं च यत् ।
करोति च क्वचित्क्षेमं क्वचिदक्षेमकारकः ॥]

आश्वयुजेऽब्देऽजस्रं पततिजलं प्रमुदिताः प्रजाः क्षेमम् ।
प्राणचयः प्राणभृतां सर्वेषामन्नबाहुल्यम् ॥१४॥

In the jovian year called Āśvayuja there will be constant rainfall, and the people will enjoy health and happiness. All living beings will grow strong and there will be abundant food for all. [Cf. वृद्धगर्गः—

पर्याप्तसस्यान्नजलक्षेमश्चाश्वयुजः शिवः ।
सम्प्रवृत्तोत्सवः श्रीमान्सर्वकामसुखावहः ॥

Having disposed of the effects of the 12 years of Jupiter, the author now turns to those of jupiter's position, motion, colour etc.]

उदगारोग्यसुभिक्षक्षेमकरो वाक्पतिश्चरन् भानाम् ।
याम्ये तद्विपरीतो मध्येन तु मध्यफलदायी ॥१५॥

Should Jupiter move during his transit to the north of the asterism he is in, he would bestow health, happiness and plenty, while to the south of the star, he would cause contrary results. If he moves in the middle, the effects will be of a mixed nature.

विचरन्भद्वयमिष्टस्तत्सार्द्धं वत्सरेण मध्यफलः ।
सस्यानां विध्वंसी विचरेदधिकं यदि कदाचित् ॥१६॥

If Jupiter moves through two asterisms in the course of a year, he will prove auspicious,; if he covers $2\frac{1}{2}$ stars the effect will be mixed; and if he moves by chance faster and covers more than that, all the crops will be destroyed.

अनलभयमनलवर्णे व्याधिः पीते रणागमः श्यामे ।
हरिते च तस्करेभ्यः पीडा रक्ते तु शस्त्रभयम् ॥१७॥

धूमाभेऽनावृष्टिस्त्रिदशगुरौ नृपवधो दिवा दृष्टे ।
विपुलेऽमले सुतारे रात्रौ दृष्टे प्रजाः स्वस्थाः ॥१८॥

If Jupiter appears with the colour of fire, there will be danger from fire; if with yellow colour, diseases will crop up; if with dark colour, war will break out ; if with green colour, there will be danger from thieves ; if with red colour, danger from weapons; and if with the colour of smoke, the result will be drought. Should Jupiter be sighted during the day, a king will be killed. If Jupiter's orb be large, clear, posited in an auspicious asterism and sighted at night, all the people would be quite happy.

[In the last line नृपाः is another reading for प्रजाः । Many of the colours are said to be bad for Jupiter. In astrology Jupiter's colour is given as golden. So all other colours except golden must be inauspicious for him.

Cf. पराशरः—

कदाचिद्यत्र दृश्येत दिवा देवपुरोहितः ।
राजा वा म्रियते तत्र स देशो वा विनश्यति ॥

In the next verse the *Body of the year* is explained along with its limbs. Effects of planetary conjunction or aspect are also given here.]

रोहिण्योऽनलभं च वत्सरतनुर्नाभिस्त्वषाढाद्वयं
सार्पं हृत्पितृदैवतं च कुसुमं शुद्धैः शुभं तैः फलम् ।
देहे क्रूरनिपीडितेऽग्न्यनिलजं नाभ्यां भयं क्षुत्कृतं
पुष्पे मूलफलक्षयोऽथ हृदये सस्यस्य नाशो ध्रुवम् ॥ १६ ॥

The stars Kṛttikā and Rohiṇī constitute the *Body of the year* (personified); the two Āṣāḍhas are the *navel*; Āśleṣā, the *heart*; and Maghā the *flower*. If these lunar mansions are devoid of malefics, the effect will be beneficial. If the *Body* is afflicted by malefics through conjunction or aspect, there will be danger from fire and wind. If the *navel* is afflicted, there will be threat of famine. If the *flower* is afflicted, destruction of roots and fruits will ensue. Lastly if the *heart* is afflicted, undoubtedly there will be destruction of crops.

[This verse gives clues to find out if the particular year of Jupiter would be well or ill. Just as Time is personified as कालपुरुष, even so here the year is personified as संवत्सरपुरुष. I feel that here the person is to be taken as *female* in view of the *flower*.
Cf. काश्यप :—

कृत्तिका रोहिणी चोभे संवत्सरतनुः स्मृता ।
आषाढाद्वितयं नाभी सार्पं हृत्कुसुमं मघा ॥

क्रूरग्रहहते देहे दुर्भिक्षानलमारुताः ।
क्षुद्भयं तु भवेन्नाभ्यां पुष्पे मूलफलक्षयः ॥
हृदये सस्यहानिः स्यात्सौम्यैः पुष्टिः प्रकीर्तिता ।

The metre is शार्दूलविक्रीडित.

Next he tells us the method of calculating the years of the lustrum or Yuga of five years.]

गतानि वर्षाणि शकेन्द्रकालाद्धतानि रुद्रैर्गुणयेच्चतुर्भिः ।
नवाष्टपञ्चाष्टयुतानि कृत्वा विभाजयेच्छून्यशरागरामैः ॥ २० ॥

लब्धेन युक्तं शकभूपकालं संशोध्य षष्ट्या विषयैर्विभज्य ।
युगानि नारायणपूर्वकाणि लब्धानि शेषाः क्रमशः समाः स्युः । २१ ।

Multiply the number of years that have elapsed since the beginning of the Śālivāhana era by 44. Add 8589 to the product and divide the result by 3750. To the quotient thus obtained add the Śaka years. Divide this by 60 and its remainder by 5. The quotient represents the five-year periods ruled by Viṣṇu and others, and the remainder denotes the number of years that have elapsed in the particular lustrum.

[Let us work out this rule in order to find out the lustrum ruling at present : The current Śaka year (elapsed) 1893 when multiplied by 44 yields 83292. Add 8589 to this product. The result is 91881. By dividing this by 3750 we get a quotient, 24. Add this again to the past Śaka years i.e. 1893. The sum is 1917. By dividing this sum by 60, we get 31 57/60. The remainder 57 gives the past year from Prabhava, which is Āṅgirasa, and the current year Raktākṣa (See also note under verse 22 for the discrepancy). So the current yuga or lustrum is the last one ruled by Bhaga (see verse 23 *infra*). There are 12 yugas or five-year periods whose names are given in verse 23 *infra*. The next verse gives the names of the five years of a yuga. The metre of these and others upto the 37th, except 36, is उपजाति.]

एकैकमब्देषु नवाहतेषु दत्त्वा पृथग्द्वादशकं क्रमेण ।
हृत्वा चतुर्भिर्वसुदेवताद्यान्युडूनि शेषांशकपूर्वमब्दम् ॥२२॥

Place the years of Jupiter obtained according to the previous verse in two places separately. Multiply the first by 9 and divide the other by 12. Add the product of the first and the quotient of the second. Divide the result by 4. The quotient would reveal the particular star counted from Dhaniṣṭha. The remainder would indicate the particular Pāda or quarter of the next star that is occupied by Jupiter.

[To work out the formulae given in verses 20-22 first of all we have to find out the number of jovian years that have elapsed from the beginning of Kali yuga till the beginning of the Śālivāhana era. This is done as follows:—

In a Mahāyuga (i.e. collection of the four yugas) the number of Solar years is $4320000 = 3750 \times 1152$. That of Jupiter for the same period is $4370688 = 3794 \times 1152$. Hence for every 3750 solar years we have 3794 jovial years. Therefore 1 solar year $= \frac{3794}{3750} = 1\frac{44}{3750}$ years of Jupiter. Now we have to find out the number of Jupiter's years past in Kali yuga at the beginning of the Śālivāhana era. For this proceed thus :

The number of solar years past from the beginning of Kali Yuga upto the beginning of the Śaka era is 3179. This should be converted into Jupiter's years: $\frac{3794}{3750} \times 3179$ or $3216\ \frac{1126}{3750}$.

Now it is known that kaliyuga started in the year *Vijaya* (which is the 27th from Prabhava). Therefore, $3216\frac{1126}{3750} + 26$ (26 is the number of years elapsed from Prabhava at the beginning of Kaliyuga) $= 3242\frac{1126}{3750}$. This being divided by 60 gives a remainder $2\frac{1126}{3750}$ which means it is the 3rd year Viz. Śukla, of the cycle of 60 years of Jupiter.

Now coming to the current year of the Śaka era, viz. 1894, the number of jovian years elapsed is $1893 + \frac{44 \times 1893}{3750} + 2\frac{1126}{3750}$ years from the beginning of Prabhava. It is $1893 + 22\frac{792}{3750} + 2\frac{1126}{3750}$ or $1917\frac{1918}{3750}$ which being divided by 60 gives $31\frac{57}{60}$ i.e. 31 cycles of 60 years have passed and in the 32nd cycle 57 years have elapsed. According to this the current cyclic year should be Raktākṣa, the 58th year. However, our Pañcāṅgas, especially the South-Indian ones, name it Virodhikṛt, the 45th year. How did this discrepancy arise? "Originally there was no difference between the Northern and Southern systems of the 60-year jovian cycle. But later on in South India the distinction between the jovian and solar years was ignored and consequently a southern jovian year is the same as a solar year and there is no suppression of a *Saṁvatsara* in a period of 85 or 86 years as is the case with the Northern or true system. It has no connection with the movement of Jupiter, and Pramāthin is regarded as the first year of Kaliyuga as against Vijaya in the Northern system."[1] At present, we are told by the same author on the basis of S.B. Dikshit's findings, the northern year is 12 years in advance of the

(1) Vide "India As Seen In The Bṛhatsaṁhitā"—Ajaya Mitra Shastri, p. 483.

southern one. So by deducting 12 years from 57 got by us, we arrive at 45, which should be taken as the current, and not past *Saṁvatsara* in the southern system. Now divide this 57 by 5 in order to get the yugas and years. We get then 11 yugas and 2 years, which means that it is the *Parivatsara* year in the last yuga known as Bhaga (Sun). The current year would be Idāvatsara ruled by the Moon.

Using the method given in verse 22 for finding the star occupied by Jupiter at the beginning of Śaka year 1893, multiply the result got above viz. 57, by 9 in one place, and divide the same (57) by 12. Add up these results. Then divide the sum by 4. The quotient gives the number of the star occupied by Jupiter, counted from Dhaniṣṭhā. (For, it has been declared that at the commencement of the cyclic year Prabhava Jupiter was in the star Dhaniṣṭhā). Thus 57×9=513, 57÷12=4·75. By adding 513+4·75=517·75. Divide this by 4=517.75÷4=129.4. This means that Jupiter was in the 130th star from Dhaniṣṭhā. So divide 129.4 by 27. The balance is 21 and odd. So Jupiter must have been in the 22nd star from Dhaniṣṭhā i.e. Anurādhā, on 27th March 1971. This is a fact. Cf. also सूर्यसिद्धान्त I. 55 & XIV 17.]

विष्णुः सुरेज्यो बलभिद्धुताशस्त्वष्टोत्तरप्रोष्ठपदाधिपश्च ।
क्रमाद्युगेशाः पितृविश्वसोमशक्रानलाख्याश्विभगाः प्रदिष्टाः ॥२३॥

The lords of the 12 yugas (five-year periods) in the cycle of Jupiter are the following in order: (1) Viṣṇu, (2) Jupiter, (3) Indra, (4) Fire, (5) Tvaṣṭā (one of the Prajāpatis or creators), (6) Ahirbudhnya, (7) the *Manes*, (8) Viśvedevas (the All-Gods), (9) Soma (the Moon), (10) Indrāgnī, (11) the Aśvins, and (12) Bhaga (the Sun).

[Cf. समाससंहिता—

विष्णुगुरुशक्रहुतभुक्त्वष्टाहिर्बुध्न्यपित्र्यविश्वानि ।
सौम्यमथेन्द्राग्न्याख्यं त्वाश्विनमपि भाग्यसंज्ञं च ॥]

संवत्सरोऽग्निः परिवत्सरोऽर्क इदादिकः शीतमयूखमाली ।
प्रजापतिश्चाप्यनुवत्सरः स्यादिद्वत्सरः शैलसुतापतिश्च ॥ २४ ॥

The names of the five years in a lustrum along with their presiding deities are (1) Saṁvatsara with its lord Fire, (2) Parivatsara with the Sun, (3) Idāvatsara with the Moon, (4) Anuvatsara with Prajāpati (creator), and (5) Idvatsara with Rudra.

वृष्टिः समाद्ये प्रमुखे द्वितीये प्रभूततोया कथिता तृतीये ।
पश्चाज्जलं मुञ्चति यच्चतुर्थं स्वल्पोदकं पञ्चममब्दमुक्तम् ॥ २५ ॥

In the first year viz. Saṁvatsara, rainfall will be evenly distributed; in the second year (Parivatsara) the rainfall will be good in the beginning only and not after; in the third year (Idāvatsara) there will be plenty of rain throughout the season; in the fourth year (Anuvatsara) rainfall will be late i.e. at the end of the season; and in the last year (Idvatsara) it will be scanty.

[The four months of Śrāvaṇa, Bhādrapada, Āśvayuja and Kārttika constitute the rainy season. Even distribution of rains means equal distribution in all the four months of the monsoon.]

चत्वारि मुख्यानि युगान्यथैषां विष्ण्वन्द्रजीवानलदैवतानि ।
चत्वारि मध्यानि च मध्यमानि चत्वारि चान्त्यान्यधमानि विन्द्यात् ॥२६॥

Among the 12 yugas the first four viz. Viṣṇu, Jupiter, Indra and Fire, are the foremost and the best ; the four middle ones viz. Tvaṣṭā, Ahirbudhnya, the Manes and Viśvedevas, are moderate, and the last four viz. the Moon Indrāgnī, Aśvins and the Sun, are to be understood as the worst.

[Cf. the समाससंहिता—

चत्वारि युगान्यादौ शुभानि मध्यानि मध्यमफलानि ।
चत्वार्यन्त्यानि न शोभनानि वर्षविशेषोऽत्र ॥]

आद्यं धनिष्ठांशमभिप्रपन्नो माघे यदा यात्युदयं सुरेज्यः ।
षष्ट्यब्दपूर्वः प्रभवः स नाम्ना प्रपद्यते भूतहितस्तदाब्दः ॥२७॥

When Jupiter enters the first quarter of the asterism Dhaniṣṭhā and at the same time rises after getting eclipsed by the Sun, in the month of Māgha, Prabhava, the first year of his cycle of 60 years comes into being and it will be beneficial to all beings.

[The commentator states that the month of Māgha is of the lunar calendar and not of the solar one. For, the lunar Māgha begins when the Sun enters Aquarius and then it is the Solar Phālguna. The condition mentioned in this verse would be satisfied if Jupiter be in 9-23°-21[1] and the Sun in 10-6°-21[1], because Jupiter rises only when there is an interval of 13° between his longitude and the Sun's. In actual experience, however, these three conditions viz. Māgha, Dhaniṣṭhā and Jupiter's rising, may be hard to realise.]

क्वचित्त्ववृष्टिः पवनाग्निकोपः सन्तीतयः श्लेष्मकृताश्च रोगाः ।
संवत्सरेऽस्मिन्प्रभवे प्रवृत्ते न दुःखमाप्नोति जनस्तथापि ॥२८॥

During this year viz. Prabhava, there will be drought, outbreak of fires, storms, the six-fold troubles known as Ītibādhās and phlegmatic ailments in some parts. However, the people in general will not suffer.

तस्माद् द्वितीयो विभवः प्रदिष्टः शुक्लस्तृतीयः परतः प्रमोदः ।
प्रजापतिश्चेति यथोत्तराणि शस्तानि वर्षाणि फलान्यथैषाम् ॥२९॥
निष्पन्नशालीक्षुयवादिसस्यां भयैर्विमुक्तामुपशान्तवैराम् ।
संहृष्टलोकां कलिदोषमुक्तां क्षत्रं तदा शास्ति च भूतधात्रीम् ॥३०॥

Thereafter the second year named *Vibhava* sets in, then Śukla the third year, then Pramoda the fourth year and then Prajāpati the fifth year. These years will yield more and more beneficial effects in their order. In this first yuga of Jupiter the rulers (Kṣatriyas) will govern the country so well that the land would be smiling with abundant paddy, sugarcane, barley and other grains, being rid of all fears, hostilities and the curses of the Kali age, with the subjects quite happy and contented.

आद्योऽङ्गिराः श्रीमुखभावसाह्वौ युवा सुधातेति युगे द्वितीये ।
वर्षाणि पञ्चैव यथाक्रमेण त्रीण्यत्र शस्तानि समे परे द्वे ॥३१॥
त्रिष्वाद्यवर्षेषु निकामवर्षी देवो निरातङ्कभयश्च लोकः ।
अब्दद्वयेऽन्त्येऽपि समा सुवृष्टिः किन्त्वत्र रोगाः समरागमश्च ॥३२॥

In the second yuga of Jupiter the five years are named in order : Aṅgiras, Śrīmukha, Bhāva, Yuvan and Dhātā. Among these the first three will prove auspicious, while the last two will be moderate. In the first three years there will be plenty of rainfall and the people will be free from diseases and fear. In the last two years rains will be moderate, but diseases will crop up and wars will also break out.

शाक्रे युगे पूर्वमथेश्वराख्यं वर्षं द्वितीयं बहुधान्यमाहुः ।
प्रमाथिनं विक्रममप्यथान्यद्वृषं च विन्द्याद्गुरुचारयोगात् ॥३३॥
आद्यं द्वितीयं च शुभे तु वर्षे कृतानुकारं कुरुतः प्रजानाम् ।
पापः प्रमाथी वृषविक्रमौ तु सुभिक्षदौ रोगभयप्रदौ च ॥३४॥

In the third yuga presided over by Indra the years are named in order : *Īśvara*, *Bahudhānya*, *Pramāthin*, *Vikrama* and *Vṛṣa* as a result of Jupiter's transit. The first two years will be very auspicious and will confer on the people the blessings of the Golden Age. The year Pramāthin will be very harmful, while the last two will produce plenty of food but will cause diseases and fear.

श्रेष्ठं चतुर्थस्य युगस्य पूर्वं यच्चित्रभानुं कथयन्ति वर्षम् ।
मध्यं द्वितीयं तु सुभानुसञ्ज्ञं रोगप्रदं मृत्युकरं न तच्च ॥३५॥
तारणं तदनु भूरिवारिदं सस्यवृद्धिमुदितं च पार्थिवम् ।
पञ्चमं व्ययमुशन्ति शोभनं मन्मथप्रबलमुत्सवाकुलम् ॥३६॥

The first year named *Citrabhānu* of the fourth lustrum is considered to be the best, while the second year named *Subhānu* is of moderate effect, as it produces diseases that are not fatal. The third called *Tāraṇa* gives abundant rains, and the fourth named *Pārthiva* makes people happy with abundant crops. The last one called *Vyaya* is said to be auspicious, but it will be marked by the activities of cupid (i.e. there will be many romances) as well as by various festivities.

[The commentator takes the reading नतं च for न तच्च and says that नत is the name of the third year. This is against the traditional list of names. He also omits *Pārthiva*, the fourth year, resorting to the reading मुदितातिपार्थिवम्, which is not very happy. Hence I have rejected it here.

The metre of the last verse is रथोद्धता.]

त्वाष्ट्रे युगे सर्वजिदाद्य उक्तः संवत्सरोऽन्यः खलु सर्वधारी ।
तस्माद्विरोधी विकृतः खरश्च शस्तो द्वितीयोऽत्र भयाय शेषाः । ३७ ।

The first year of the fifth lustrum presided over by Tvaṣṭā is *Sarvajit*. The others are *Sarvadhārin*, *Virodhin*, *Vikṛta* and *khara*. Of these only the second year viz. *Sarvadhārin*, is beneficial, and the rest lead to danger.

नन्दनोऽथ विजयो जयस्तथा मन्मथोऽस्य परतश्च दुर्मुखः ।
कान्तमत्र युग आदितस्त्रयं मन्मथः समफलोऽधमोऽपरः ॥३८॥

In the sixth lustrum presided over by *Ahirbudhnya* the years are named *Nandana*, *Vijaya*, *jaya*, *Manmatha* and *Durmukha*. Of these the first three years are beneficial, while *Manmatha*, the 4th year, is middling, but the last one is utterly baneful.

[The metre is रथोद्धता; so is the next one.]

हेमलम्ब इति सप्तमे युगे स्याद्विलम्बि परतो विकारि च ।
शर्वरीति तदनु प्लवः स्मृतो वत्सरो गुरुवशेन पञ्चमः । ३९ ।
ईतिप्राया प्रचुरपवना वृष्टिरब्दे तु पूर्वे
मन्दं सस्यं न बहुसलिलं वत्सरेऽतो द्वितीये ।
अत्युद्वेगः प्रचुरसलिलः स्यत्तृतीयश्चतुर्थो
दुर्भिक्षाय प्लव इति ततः शोभनो भूरितोयः ॥ ४० ॥

The years composing the 7th yuga of Jupiter presided over by the *Manes* are *Hemalamba*, *Vilambi*, *Vikāri*, *Śarvarī* and Plava. In the first year there will be stormy rains accompanied by the six-fold calamities. In the second year both the rains and crops will be scanty. In the third there will be great havoc caused by floods. In the fourth year there will be famine and in the last year known as Plava there will be good rains and prosperity.

[The metre is मन्दाक्रान्ता.]

वैश्वे युगे शोभकृदित्यथाद्यः संवत्सरोऽतः शुभकृद्द्वितीयः ।
क्रोधी तृतीयः परतः क्रमेण विश्वावसुश्चेति पराभवश्च ॥ ४१ ॥
पूर्वापरौ प्रीतिकरौ प्रजानामेषां तृतीयो बहुदोषदोऽब्दः ।
अन्त्यौ समौ किन्तु पराभवेऽग्निः शस्त्रामयार्तिर्द्विजगोभयं च ॥ ४२ ॥

The years of the 8th lustrum owned by Viśve-devas are *Śobhakṛt* or Śokahṛt, Śubhakṛt, *Krodhin*, *Viśvāvasu* and *Parābhava*. The first two years will be highly beneficial to the people, while the third very troublesome. The last two will be moderate, but the last one, *Parābhava*, will be afflicted with fire, weapons, diseases, sorrow, and danger to Brahmins and cattle.

[For शोभकृत् there is a variant reading viz. शोकहृत्. According to tradition the year Śubhakṛt precedes Śobhakṛt. The metre is उपजाति upto the 45th verse.]

आद्यः प्लवङ्गो नवमे युगेऽब्दः स्यात्कीलकोऽन्यः परतश्च सौम्यः ।
साधारणो रोधकृदित्यथाब्दः शुभप्रदौ कीलकसौम्यसञ्ज्ञौ ॥ ४३ ॥
कष्टः प्लवङ्गो बहुशः प्रजानां साधारणेऽल्पं जलमीतयश्च ।
यः पञ्चमो रोधकृदित्यथाब्दश्चित्रं जलं तत्र च सस्यसम्पत् ॥ ४४ ॥

In the 9th lustrum belonging to the Moon the five years are in order *Plavaṅga*, *Kīlaka*, *Saumya*, *Sādhāraṇa* and *Rodhakṛt*. The two years, *Kīlaka* and *Saumya*, are auspicious and beneficial, while *Plavaṅga* is troublesome to the people in many ways. In the year *Sādhāraṇa* there will be scanty rains and the sixfold troubles will be on the increase. In the fifth year of *Rodhakṛt* rainfall will be sporadic but the crops will flourish.

[The traditional name for *Rodhakṛt* is *Virodhikṛt*.]

इन्द्राग्निदैवं दशमं युगं यत्तत्राद्यवर्षं परिधाविसंज्ञम् ।
प्रमाद्यथानन्दमतः परं यत्स्याद्राक्षसं चानलसञ्ज्ञितं च ॥ ४५ ॥
परिधाविनि मध्यदेशनाशो नृपहानिर्जलमल्पमग्निकोपः ।
अलसस्तु जनः प्रमादिसञ्ज्ञे डमरं रक्तकपुष्पबीजनाशः ॥ ४६ ॥
तत्परः सकललोकनन्दनो राक्षसः क्षयकरोऽनलस्तथा ।
ग्रीष्मधान्यजननोऽत्र राक्षसो वह्निकोपमरकप्रदोऽनलः ॥ ४७ ॥

In the tenth lustrum belonging to Indrāgni the years are named *Paridhāvin*, *Pramādin*, *Ānanda*, *Rākṣasa* and *Anala*. In the year *Paridhāvin* the central country will be destroyed, a king will meet with his end, rain will be scanty and disastrous fires will break out. In *Pramādin* the people will generally be indolent, war will break out and trees which bear red flowers and whose seeds are red will perish. The next year i.e. *Ānanda*, will make every body happy and prosperous. *Rākṣasa* as well as *Anala* is destructive. However, the former will help the growth of summer crops, and the latter will lead to the outbreak of fires and epidemics.

[In the second line Bhaṭṭotpala reads प्रमादिनं विक्रममप्यतोऽन्यत्. In the fifth line also विक्रम: for 'तत्पर:'. As *Vikrama* has already been used for the 4th year of the 3rd lustrum, I think the author could not have used it again. The metre of 46 is औपच्छन्दसिक, and that of 47 रथोद्धता.]

एकादशे पिङ्गलकालयुक्तसिद्धार्थरौद्राः खलु दुर्मतिश्च ।
आद्ये तु वृष्टिर्महती सचौरा श्वासो हनूकम्पयुतश्च कासः ॥ ४८ ॥
यत्कालयुक्तं तदनेकदोषं सिद्धार्थसंज्ञे बहवो गुणाश्च ।
रौद्रोऽतिरौद्रः क्षयकृत्प्रदिष्टो यो दुर्मतिर्मध्यमवृष्टिकृत्सः ॥ ४९ ॥

In the 11th yuga of Jupiter owned by Aśvins the five years are called in order *Piṅgala*, *Kālayukta*, *Siddhārtha*, *Raudra* and *Durmati*. In the first year viz. *Piṅgala*, there will be excessive rains causing havoc to the people, increase of robbers and severe asthmatic complaints that shake the jaws. The second year will be a source of troubles. The third will be highly advantageous and auspicious. The year *Raudra* will be dreadful causing much suffering and destruction. In the year *Durmati* the rainfall will be moderate.

[These verses and the following two are in the उपजाति metre.]

भाग्ये युगे दुन्दुभिसञ्ज्ञमाद्यं सस्यस्य वृद्धिं महतीं करोति ।
उद्गारिसञ्ज्ञं तदनु क्षयाय नरेश्वराणां विषमा च वृष्टिः ॥ ५० ॥
रक्ताक्षमब्दं कथितं तृतीयं यस्मिन्भयं दंष्ट्रिकृतं गदाश्च ।
क्रोधं बहुक्रोधकरं चतुर्थं राष्ट्राणि शून्यीकुरुते विरोधैः ॥ ५१ ॥

In the last lustrum owned by *Bhaga* (Sun) the years are named *Dundubhi, Udgārin* (or Rudhirodgārin), *Raktākṣa*, *Krodha* and (Kṣaya). The first year is helpful to the growth of abundant crops, the second year brings about the ruin of kings and has uneven and irregular rains (or fierce at times). In the third year there will be trouble from tusked animals like boars, and diseases. The fourth year will engender excessive wrath (hatred) and will denude kingdoms through hostilities.

[In the secord line instead of उद्गारि some read भङ्गार. However, the popular name of the year is *Rudhirodgārin*, one which vomits blood.]

क्षयमिति युगस्यान्त्यस्यान्त्यं बहुक्षयकारकं
जनयति भयं तद्विप्राणां कृषीवलवृद्धिदम् ।
उपचयकरं विट्शूद्राणां परस्वहृतां तथा
कथितमखिलं षष्ट्यब्दे यत्तदत्र समासतः ॥५२॥

The last or the fifth year, known as kṣaya, of the last lustrum will create all kinds of loss and destruction, and panic among Brahmins. But the agriculturists will flourish. The Vaiśyas and Śūdras also will prosper; so will robbers and dacoits. Thus have I succinctly described all things pertaining to the cycle of 60 years of Jupiter.

[The author has detached the last year from verse 51 in order to effect a fine finale to the topic of cyclic years. He has compressed in three verses in his समाससंहिता the material he has developed here in 26 verses :

ऐन्द्रे तृतीयमशुभं द्वितीयवर्जानि पञ्चमे तु युगे ।
पित्र्ये युगे तृतीयं चतुर्थमपि पापदं वर्षम् ॥
वैश्वे तृतीयमशुभं शुभदान्युक्तानि चावशेषाणि ।
सौम्ये द्वितीयवर्षं शुभावहं यत्तृतीयं तु ।
प्रथितं शुभमैन्द्राग्नौ तृतीयवर्षं तथाश्विदैवत्ये ।
भाग्ये प्रथमं वर्षं षष्ट्यब्दस्यैष संक्षेपः ॥

The metre is हरिणी.]

अकलुषांशुजटिलः पृथुमूर्तिः कुमुदकुन्दकुसुमस्फटिकाभः ।
ग्रहहतो न यदि सत्पथवर्ती हितकरोऽमरगुरुर्मनुजानाम् ॥ ५३ ॥

Should Jupiter be filled with bright rays all round, be possessed of a large form, white like the lotus, the Kunda jasmine and crystal, be not overpowered by any other planet, and be moving along the right path i.e. to the north of planets and asterisms, he would prove beneficial to the entire mankind.

[Here again the author speaks of Jupiter, the astronomical Jupiter, as having white colour like the lotus, Kunda and crystal.

The metre is an extension of स्वागता with two short syllables instead of a long one in the beginning.]

शुक्रचारः ॥ ६ ॥

Course of Venus

नागगजैरावतवृषभगोजरद्गवमृगाजदहनाख्याः ।
अश्विन्याद्याः कैश्चित्त्रिभाः क्रमाद्वीथयः कथिताः ॥ १ ॥

Nine *avenues* named (1) Nāga (Serpent), (2) *Gaja* (Elephant), (3) *Airāvata* (Indra's elephant), (4) *Vṛṣabha* (Bull), (5) *Go* (cow), (6) *Jaradgava*, (7) *Mṛga* (Deer), (8) *Aja* (Goat), and *Dahana* (Fire) composed of three stars each in regular order beginning with Aśvinī, have been allotted to Venus by some (i.e. Devala and others.)

[According to Devala and Kāśyapa the three stars, Aśvinī, Bharaṇī and Kṛttikā, constitute the Nāgavīthī of Venus. In the same manner other *Avenues* are also formed by other triads of stars in regular order. Our author's own view is given in the 2nd. verse.

Cf. *Devala.*

अश्विन्यादित्रिभाः सर्वा नागाद्या दहनान्तिकाः ।
वीथयो भृगुपुत्रस्य नव प्रोक्ताः पुरातनैः ॥

also *Kāśyapa* :

त्रिष्वश्विन्यादिषु यदा चरति भृगुनन्दनः ।
नागवीयीति सा ज्ञेया प्रथमान्या निबोधत ॥
रोहिण्यादिगजा ज्ञेयाऽदित्याद्यैरावती स्मृता ।
मघाद्या वृषभा ज्ञेया हस्ताद्या गौः प्रकीर्तिता ॥
जारद्गवी विशाखाद्या मूलाद्या मृगवीथिका ।
अजवीथी विष्णुभाद्याऽजाद्या तु दहना स्मृता ॥]

नागा तु पवनयाम्यानलानि पैतामहात् त्रिभास्तिस्रः ।
गोवीथ्यामश्विन्यः पौष्णं द्वे चापि भाद्रपदे ॥२॥

However in my view the *Nāga* avenue of Venus is constituted by the three asterisms Svātī, Bharaṇī and Kṛttikā; and the *Gaja*, *Airāvata* and *Vṛṣabha* by the three succeeding triads of stars, viz. (1) Rohiṇī, Mṛgaśiras, and Ārdrā, (2) Punarvasu, Puṣya and Āśleṣā,

(3) Maghā, Pūrvaphalgunī and Uttaraphalgunī. And the *Govīthī* is composed of the four asterisms Aśvinī, Revatī, Purvabhādra and Uttarabhādra.

जारद्गव्यां श्रवणात्त्रिभं मृगाख्या त्रिभं च मैत्राद्यम् ।
हस्तविशाखात्वाष्ट्राण्यजेत्यषाढाद्वयं दहना ॥ ३ ॥

Similarly the *jaradgava avenue* is composed of three stars Śravaṇa, Dhaniṣṭhā and Śatabhiṣaj; the *Mṛga avenue* of Anurādhā, Jyeṣṭha and Mūla, the *Ajavīthī* of Hasta, Citrā and Viśākhā; and the *Dahana avenue* of the two stars Pūrvāṣāḍha and Uttarāṣāḍha.

[Our author and the ancients are of the same view only in respect of the three Vīthīs, viz. *Gaja*, *Airāvata* and *Vṛṣabha*.]

तिस्रस्तिस्रस्तासां क्रमादुदङ्मध्ययाम्यमार्गस्थाः ।
तासामप्युत्तरमध्यदक्षिणेन स्थितैकैका ॥ ४ ॥

Of these nine *avenues* the first three viz. *Nāga*, *Gaja* and *Airāvata*, are in the *North*; the next three viz. *Vṛṣabha*, *Go* and *jaradgava*, in the *Middle*; and the last three viz. *Mṛga*, *Aja* and *Dahana*, in the *South*. In each triad of *avenues* too the three individual ones are further subdivided into *Northern*, *Middle* and *Southern* respectively.

[In the matter of allotment of stars to the nine *Vīthīs* there are three distinct schools viz. (1) Devala and others, (2) Garga and Varāhamihira, and (3) Parāśara. Between the first school and the second there is complete agreement in respect of only the *Airāvata* and Vṛṣabha *Vīthīs*. There is partial agreement between the two in respect of *Nāga* (only Bharaṇī and Kṛttikā) and of *Mṛga* (only Mūla). Between the Second and third Schools there is full agreement in respect of *Nāga*, *Gaja*, *Go* and *Jaradgava*, and partial agreement in respect of *Airāvata* (with Maghā added) *Vṛṣabha* (with Maghā removed), *Aja* (Viśākhā is the only common feature) and *Dahana* (the two Āṣāḍhas are common) *Mṛga* is completely different in the two Schools. The following chart shows the *Vīthīs* and their constituent asterism according to the three schools. The stars are numbered form Aśvinī.

Serial No.	Names of Vīthīs	I School Devala & others	II School Varāha & Garga	III School Parāśara.
1	Nāga	Stars 1, 2, 3.	Stars 15. 2, 3	Stars. 15, 2, 3
2	Gaja	4, 5, 6,	4, 5, 6	4, 5, 6
3	Airāvata	7, 8, 9	7, 8, 9	7, 8, 9, 10
4	Vṛṣabha	10, 11, 12	10, 11, 12	11, 12
5	Go	13, 14, 15	1, 25, 26, 27	1, 25, 26,27
6	Jaradgava	16, 17, 18	22, 23, 24	22, 23, 24
7	Mṛga	19, 20, 21	17, 18, 19	13, 14,
8	Aja	22, 23, 24	13, 14, 16	16, 17, 18
9	Dahana	25, 26, 27	20, 21	19, 20, 21

Cf. गर्ग :—

कृत्तिका भरणी स्वाती नागवीथी प्रकीर्तिता ।
रोहिण्याद्यास्त्रिभास्तिस्रो गजैरावतवार्षभाः ॥
अहिर्बुध्न्याश्विपौष्णं च गोवीथीति प्रकीर्तिता ।
श्रवणत्रितयं ज्ञेया वीथी जारद्गवीति सा ॥
मैत्रत्रिभा मृगाख्या स्याद्धस्तचित्राविशाखिका ।
अजवीथी तु दहनाषाढायुग्ममिति स्मृता ॥
पूर्वोत्तरा नागवीथी गजवीथी तदुत्तरा ।
ऐरावती ततो याम्या एतास्तूत्तरतः स्मृताः ॥
आर्षभी तु चतुर्थी स्याद्गोवीथी पञ्चमी स्मृता ।
षष्ठी जारद्गवी ज्ञेया तिस्रस्ता मध्यमाश्रिताः ॥

सप्तमी मृगवीथी स्यादजवीथी तथाष्टमी ।
दहना नवमी ज्ञेया दक्षिणं मार्गमाश्रिताः ॥

also समाससंहिता :—

वीथी नागानाम्नी स्वातिर्भरणी च कृत्तिका चैव ।
स्वायम्भुवस्त्रिभाः स्युर्गजवीथ्यैरावती वृषभा ॥
एकपदादिचतुष्कं गोः स्याज्जारद्गवी त्रिभा श्रवणात् ।
मैत्रात्त्रिभं मृगाऽजा हस्तश्चित्रा विशाखा च ॥
द्वे चाषाढे दहना तिस्र उदग्वीथयः क्रमाच्छुभदाः ।
मध्या मध्यास्तिस्रो याम्याः पापा मृगाद्यास्ताः ॥]

वीथीमार्गानपरे कथयन्ति यथास्थितान्भमार्गस्य ।
नक्षत्राणां तारा याम्योत्तरमध्यमास्तद्वत् ॥ ५ ॥

Others (like Sage Kāśyapa) declare these three *Vīthīs* or Avenues for the asterisms as well according as they happen to be to the *North*, in the *Middle* or to the *South* of the ecliptic. Similarly, Venus too is considered to be in the Northern, *Middle* or Southern *Avenue*, if he moves to the north, in the middle or to the south of an asterism, as the case may be.

[This is another definition of the *Vīthīs* for the stars. A planet too may be said to be in a particular *Avenue*, if it occupies the corresponding position relative to the asterism, according to the commentator.

Cf. काश्यप :—

नक्षत्राणां त्रयो मार्गा दक्षिणोत्तरमध्यमाः ।
उदक्स्थास्तारकाः सौम्यो मध्यमो मध्यमाः स्मृतः ॥
दक्षिणा दक्षिणो मार्गो नक्षत्रेषु प्रकीर्तितः ।
नक्षत्रात्सौम्यगः सौम्यमार्गस्थो ग्रह उच्यते ।
दक्षिणे दक्षिणो मार्गो मध्ये मध्य इति स्मृतः ॥]

उत्तरमार्गो याम्यादि निगदितो मध्यमस्तु भाग्याद्यः ।
दक्षिणमार्गोऽषाढादि कैश्चिदेवं कृता मार्गाः ॥ ६ ॥

Yet others (like Sage Garga) have stated that the *Northern Avenue* is constituted by the nine asterisms beginning from Bharaṇī, the *Middle Avenue* by the nine stars beginning from Pūrvaphalgunī, and the *Southern Avenue* by the nine stars beginning from Pūrvāṣāḍhā.

[Cf. *Garga* :—

अश्वयुग्भोगपर्यन्तेऽषाढादौ नवके गणे ।
वर्तमानः सदा क्रूरो दक्षिणे पथि वर्तते ।

शुक्रो निर्ऋतिपर्यन्ते भाग्यादौ नवके गणे ।
वर्तमानश्च मध्यस्थो मध्यमे पथि वर्तते ॥
भरण्यादौ मघान्ते च तृतीये नवके गणे ।
वर्तमानः शुभो ज्ञेय उत्तरे पथि वर्तते ॥]

ज्यौतिषमागमशास्त्रं विप्रतिपत्तौ न योग्यमस्माकम् ।
स्वयमेव विकल्पयितुं किन्तु बहूनां मतं वक्ष्ये ॥७॥

The science of astrology-cum-astronomy has been founded on the intuition of ancient Sages. Hence it is not proper on our part to say which among the divergent views of the Sages are correct and which not. I have, therefore, only quoted here the opinions of many wise men.

[We have seen above a vast number of conflicting opinions regarding the *Vīthīs*. Our author must have felt the necessity to pronounce his judgment on this. But he thought that such a course would not be justified in a field where there is no scientific machinery to prove the correctness or otherwise of a statement. For, all the views quoted above have the scriptural sanctity or authority.]

उत्तरवीथिषु शुक्रः सुभिक्षशिवकृद्गतोऽस्तमुदयं वा ।
मध्यासु मध्यफलदः कष्टफलो दक्षिणस्थासु ॥ ८ ॥

When Venus rises or sets while travelling along the *Northern Avenues*, he will promote prosperity, food crops and all good things; he will produce modrate results while passing through the *Middle Avenues*; and he will bring about disasters while moving in the *Southern* Avenues.

[Cf. **गर्ग** :—

उदयास्तमयं कुर्यान्मार्गमुत्तरमाश्रितः ।
सुभिक्षं च सुवृष्टिं च योगक्षेमं विनिर्दिशेत् ॥
उदयास्तमयं कुर्यान्मध्यमं मार्गमाश्रितः ।
मध्यमं चार्घसस्यं च योगक्षेमं विनिर्दिशेत् ॥
उदयास्तमयं कुर्याद्दक्षिणं मार्गमाश्रितः ।
धान्यस्य सङ्ग्रहं कृत्वा केदारेषु तिलान्वपेत् ॥

According to Parāśara the effects of the movement of Venus through the nine *Avenues* are (1) trouble to those who live by serpents (snake-charmers), (2) suffering of herds of elephants, (3) revolt of the army, (4) affliction of the aged, rich, learned, strong and crops as well as outbreak of phlegmatic troubles, (5) destruction of crops and owners of cattle, (6) trouble to the learned in the Śāstras, (7) diseases among the deer or quadrupeds, crop-diseases and ailments of hermits, (8) fine growth of crops, plentiful rainfall and prosperity to religious students, and (9) destruction of crops, outbreak of fires and diseases caused by the vitiation of bile.]

अत्युत्तमोत्तमोनं सममध्यन्यूनमधमकष्टफलम् ।
कष्टतरं सौम्याद्यासु वीथिषु यथाक्रमं ब्रूयात् ॥ ९ ॥

The transit of Venus through the nine *Avenues* divided into three groups, Northern, Middle and Southern, will produce in order the following results : In the *Nāga Avenue* the results would be exceedingly beneficent, in the *Gaja*, very good, and in the *Airāvata* slight. In the next triad viz. *Vṛṣabha*, *Go* and *Jaradgava* the effects would be in order moderate, middling and slightly harmmful. Lastly in the *Mṛga*, *Aja* and Dahana they would be very bad (or untoward), inauspicious, and exceedingly harmful respectively.

[Next he speaks of six Maṇḍalas or circles of Venus and their effects.]

भरणीपूर्वं मण्डलमृक्षचतुष्कं सुभिक्षकरमाद्यम् ।
वङ्गाङ्गमहिषवाह्लिककलिङ्गदेशेषु भयजननम् ॥ १० ॥
अत्रोदितमारोहेद् ग्रहोऽपरो यदि सितं ततो हन्यात् ।
भद्राश्वशूरसेनकयौधेयककोटिवर्षनृपान् ॥ ११ ॥

The four stars beginning with Bharaṇī, (i.e. Bharaṇī, Kṛttikā, Rohinī and Mṛgaśiras) constitute the first Maṇḍala or circle of Venus. This will produce good effects in the form of plenty of food. However, it will create fear or trouble in the countries of Vaṅga, Aṅga, Mahiṣa, Vāhlika and Kaliṅga. Should another planet pass over Venus after the latter has risen in this circle, it would kill the rulers of the tribes viz. Bhadrāśva, Śūrasena, Yaudheya and Koṭivarṣa.

भचतुष्टयमार्द्राद्यं द्वितीयममिताम्बुसस्यसम्पत्त्यै ।
विप्राणामशुभकरं विशेषतः क्रूरचेष्टानाम् ॥ १२ ॥
अन्येनात्राक्रान्ते म्लेच्छाटविकश्वजीविगोमन्तान् ।
गोनर्दनीचशूद्रान् वैदेहांश्चानयः स्पृशति ॥ १३ ॥

The second *Maṇḍala* consists of the four stars, Ārdrā, Punarvasu, Puṣya and Āśleṣā. It will promote good rains and luxuriant crops. It will, however, be harmful to the Brahmin class, especially to those that are engaged in cruel deeds. Should Venus be attacked or blocked in this *circle* by another planet, Mlecchas, foresters, those that live by dogs (hunters etc.), cattle-owners, the people of Gonarda and Videha, Śūdras and those that are engaged in menial work would be afflicted.

विचरन्मघादिपञ्चकमुदितः सस्यप्रणाशकृच्छुक्रः ।
क्षुत्तस्करभयजननो नीचोन्नतिसङ्करकरश्च ॥ १४ ॥
पित्र्याद्येऽवष्टब्धो हन्त्यन्येनाविकाञ् शबरशूद्रान् ।
पुण्ड्रापरान्त्यशूलिकवनवासिद्रविडसामुद्रान् ॥ १५ ॥

The third *circle* consists of the five asterisms, Maghā, Pūrva and Uttara Phalgunī, Hasta and Citrā. If Venus traverses this *circle* after rising, he will destroy the crops, create the fear of famine (hunger) and thieves, and revolutionize the social order bringing about confusion of the classes. should Venus be attacked by another planet in this circle, he would kill shepherds, Śabaras (a class of hunters), Śūdras, Puṇḍras, people of the western regions, Śūlikas, forest dwellers, Draviḍas and the coastal people.

स्वात्याद्यं भत्रितयं मण्डलमेतच्चतुर्थमभयकरम् ।
ब्रह्मक्षत्रसुभिक्षाभिवृद्धये मित्रभेदाय ॥ १६ ॥
अत्राक्रान्ते मृत्युः किरातभर्तुः पिनष्टि चेक्ष्वाकून् ।
प्रत्यन्तावन्तिपुलिन्दतङ्गणाञ् शूरसेनांश्च ॥ १७ ॥

The three stars, Svāti, Viśākhā and Anurādhā, constitute the fourth *circle*. This produces the sense of security in the minds of people, promotes the interests of Brahmins and Kṣatriyas as well as excellent growth of crops, but causes estrangement among friends. Should Venus be assailed in this circle by another planet, he would kill the chieftain of the Kirātas (hunters), and crush the Ikṣvākus, cave-men, people of Avantī, Pulindas, Taṅgaṇas and Śūrasenas.

ज्येष्ठाद्यं पञ्चर्क्षं क्षुत्तस्कररोगदं प्रबाधयते ।
काश्मीराश्मकमत्स्यान् सचारुदेवीनवन्तींश्च ॥ १८ ॥
अत्रारोहेद् द्रविडाभीराम्बष्ठत्रिगर्तसौराष्ट्रान् ।
नाशयति सिन्धुसौवीरकांश्च काशीश्वरस्य वधः ॥ १९ ॥

The fifth *Maṇḍala* consists of the five stars, Jyeṣṭhā, Mūla, Pūrva and Uttara Āṣāḍha, and Śravaṇa. This will trouble people with hunger, thieves and diseases and afflict the people of Kashmir,

Asmaka, Matsya, Avanti and those living on the banks of the Cārudevī. If Venus is overpowered here by another planet, he will destroy the Draviḍas, Ābhīras, Ambaṣṭhas, Trigartas, Saurāṣṭras, people of Sindhu, Sauvīrakas and the king of Kāśī.

षष्ठं षण्नक्षत्रं शुभमेतन्मण्डलं धनिष्ठाद्यम् ।
भूरिधनगोकुलाकुलमनल्पधान्यं क्वचित्सभयम् ॥ २० ॥
अत्रारोहेच्छूलिकगान्धारावन्तयः प्रपीड्यन्ते ।
वैदेहवधः प्रत्यन्तयवनशकदासपरिवृद्धिः ॥ २१ ॥

The sixth *Maṇḍala* consists of the six stars, Dhaniṣṭhā, Śatabhiśaj, Pūrva and Uttara Bhadrapadā, Revatī, and Aśvinī. It is auspicious and productive of abundant wealth, cattle-wealth and bumper crops, but in some places there will be fear too. If Venus is attacked here by another planet, the Śūlikas and the people of Gāndhāra and Avanti will be tormented; and people of Videha will be killed; but cave-men, Yavanas Śakas and slaves will prosper.

[The *Śūlikas* are assigned to the north-west and south-east divisions (XIV) 23,8). They are also called Cūlikas in the Purāṇas. The Matsya-purāṇa refers to their country as being watered by the river Cakṣu (Oxus). Scholars identify them with the Sogdians living to the north of the Oxus, with the Cālukyas of the Deccan etc. They were also identified with the Śūlikas of Orissa. *Gāndhāra* extended from the Kabul valley to Takṣaśilā and comprised the Rawalpindi and Peshawar districts. The town Puṣkalāvatī is mentioned by our author.

The *Yavanas* were the Greek settlers found in the south-west divison near Nasik.

The *Videha* country comprised the country from Gorakhpur on the Rapti to Darbhanga, with Kosala on the west and Aṅga on the east.

The *Śakas* are mentiond in many inscriptions beginning with that of Rudradāman. They are assigned to the western division. The Agni-purāṇa (LV. 16) assigns them to the south-west of India. They were the descendants of the Scythians who adopted Indian titles such as Kṣatrapa and Mahākṣatrapa.]

अपरस्यां स्वात्याद्यं ज्येष्ठाद्यं चापि मण्डलं शुभदम् ।
पित्र्याद्यं पूर्वस्यां शेषाणि यथोक्तफलदानि ॥ २२ ॥

If Venus rising in the fourth or fifth Maṇḍala happens to be in the western horizon, the results will all be auspicious, and they will be beneficial in the third Maṇḍala, provided he rises in the east. The effects of his transit in other *Maṇḍalas* will be as stated already.

[According to Parāśara the six *Maṇḍalas* are called (1) *Ādya*, (2) *Rohita*, (3) Dāruṇa, (4) Virocana, (5) Urdhvadaṇḍa, and (6) Tīkṣṇa. Unlike Varāhamihira's, Parāśara's third and fourth *Maṇḍalas* contain four stars each. The last two, it is said, contain five stars each. Then, nobody knows what has happened to the star Aśvinī. This sage says that the first four *Maṇḍalas* are said to be *Vāta* (wind) and the last one, Tīkṣṇa, *Vyālamārga* the *Serpent Route*. *Ūrdhvadaṇḍa* minus Śravaṇa is known as *Vaiśvānara* or Fire. So the opinion of Parāśara differs much from Varāhamihira's.

Cf. the समाससंहिता—

भरणीरौद्रमघानिलशक्रधनिष्ठादिसम्प्रवृत्तेषु ।
चारोदयः शुभो मण्डलेषु हित्वैन्द्रचपित्र्याद्ये ।।]

दृष्टोऽनस्तमितेऽर्के भयकृत् क्षुद्रोगकृत्समस्तमहः ।
अर्द्धदिवसे च सेन्दुर्नृपबलपुरभेदकृच्छुक्रः ।। २३ ।।

If Venus becomes visible before the Sun sets, he will create panic; if he is seen throughout the day, famine and diseases will break out; and if seen at midday along with the Moon, there will be discord between the king, his army and the population.

[Cf. पराशर—

ग्रहः सर्वं यदा शुक्रो दृश्यतेऽथ महाग्रहः ।
तदा त्वागन्तुभिर्ग्रामा बाध्यन्ते नगराणि च ।।

The last quarter of the text may also be interpreted as—"The king's army and towns will be vanquished."]

भिन्दन्गतोऽनलर्क्षं कूलातिक्रान्तवारिवाहाभिः ।
अव्यक्ततुङ्गनिम्ना समा सरिद्भिर्भवति धात्री ।। २४ ।।

Should Venus pass cutting the star Kṛttikā, the entire earth will be submerged by rivers carrying waters that overflow the banks and conceal all elevations and depressions on the earth.

प्राजापत्ये शकटे भिन्ने कृत्वेव पातकं वसुधा ।
केशास्थिशकलशबला कापालमिव व्रतं धत्ते ।। २५ ।।

When the wain of Rohiṇī is cut by Venus, the earth would be strewn with the hair and pieces of bones (of the dead), and appear as though she were observing the *Kāpāla* vow to atone for the heinous sin of Brahmin-murder.

[For the vow of Kāpāla see मनुस्मृति XI-72. One who commits the worst crime such as killing a Brāhmaṇa should perform the above vow observing celibacy and penance, covering himself with garlands of skulls, bones, hair etc. for getting rid of the sin. Here the poet speaks metaphorically that the Earth too would look like one observing the vow, since her body would be covered with hundreds of dead bodies, caused by all kinds of visitations of God.

The wain of Rohiṇī is said to be cut by a planet, when it is situated in the 17th. degree of Taurus and has a southern latitude of a little more than two degrees. Cf. ब्रह्मस्फुटसिद्धान्त—

विक्षेपोंऽशद्वितयादधिको वृषभस्य सप्तदशभागे ।
यस्य ग्रहस्य याम्यो भिनत्ति शकटं स रोहिण्याः ॥

also भानुभट्ट—

वृषस्यांशे सप्तदशे विक्षेपो यस्य दक्षिणः ।
अंशद्वयाधिको भिन्द्याद्रोहिण्याः शकटं तु सः ॥]

सौम्यौपगतो रससस्यसंक्षयायोशनाः समुद्दिष्टः ।
आर्द्रागतस्तु कोशलकलिङ्गहा सलिलनिकरकरः ॥२६॥

When Venus comes to *Mṛgaśiras*, he will destroy all juices or tastes and crops; and when he visits *Ārdrā*, he will ruin the Kosala and Kaliṅga countries and produce exceedingly heavy rains.

अश्मकवैदर्भाणां पुनर्वसुस्थे सिते महाननयः ।
पुष्ये पुष्टा वृष्टिर्विद्याधरगणविमर्दश्च ॥२७॥

When Venus is situated in the star *Punarvasu*, the people of Aśmaka and Vidarbha countries will be greatly troubled. When he is in Puṣya, there will be good rains and destruction of the Vidyādharas (the learned ?) in battle.

[Bhaṭṭotpala interprets the word *Vidyādharāṇām*, as *Devayonīnām* meaning demigods. However, since the author is explaining effects of the transit on the denizens of the earth, and not of heaven, that word must stand for some class of human beings of learned men.]

आश्लेषासु भुजङ्गमदारुणपीडावहश्चरन् शुक्रः ।
भिन्दन्मघां महामात्रदोषकृद्भूरिवृष्टिकरः ॥२८॥

When Venus stays in the constellation Āśleṣā, he will cause acute suffering to the people through snakes. But when he pierces the star M*aghā*, he will harm the commanders of elephant-divisions or chief ministers, and ensure copious rains.

[महामात्य is another reading for 'महामात्र'. The piercing or occultation of the junction star of Maghā by a planet is defined by astronomers as follows : "A planet occults the junction star of Maghā (Regulus) when its own rectified latitude, being in the same direction (north), is more than half the latitude, and less than one and a half the latitude of the star." Dr. Kern continues to say : "From this we may deduce that the author of the stanza, (quoted below), whoever he may have been (probably Brahmagupta), had a still more accurate knowledge of the real latitude of Regulus than the Sūrya Siddhānta has, in which the latitude is stated to be 0."

Cf. ब्रह्मस्फुटसिद्धान्त—

छादयति योगतारां मानार्द्धोनाधिकाद्भविक्षेपात् ।
स्फुटविक्षेपो यस्याधिकोनको भवति समदिक्स्थः ॥
विक्षेपेऽन्त्ये सौम्ये तृतीयतारां भिनत्ति पित्र्यस्य ।
इन्दुर्भिनत्ति पुष्यं पौष्णं वारुणमविक्षिप्तः ॥]

भाग्ये शबरपुलिन्दप्रध्वंसकरोऽम्बुनिवहमोक्षाय ।
आर्यम्णे कुरुजाङ्गलपाञ्चालघ्नः सलिलदायी ॥२९॥

Tenanting *Pūrvaphalgunī* Venus destroys Śabaras and Pulindas (two forest tribes), but causes abundant rains. While staying in *Uttaraphalgunī* he gives good rains but ruins the people of Kuru and Pañcāla countries as well as the beings living in the Jāṅgala regions i.e. where there is very little water.

कौरवचित्रकराणां हस्ते पीडा जलस्य च निरोधः ।
कूपकृद्दण्डजपीडा चित्रास्थे शोभना वृष्टिः ॥३०॥

When Venus occupies the star Hasta, the people of the Kuru country as well as artists i.e. painters, will be in trouble, and there will be drought. When he occupies the star Citrā, there will be good rains, but birds and labourers engaged in the sinking of wells will suffer.

स्वातौ प्रभूतवृष्टिर्दूतवणिग्नाविकान्स्पृशत्यनयः ।
ऐन्द्राग्नेऽपि सुवृष्टिर्वणिजां च भयं विजानीयात् ॥३१॥

When Venus passes through Svātī, there will be good rains, but messengers, traders and sailors will be in trouble. In Viśākhā Venus would cause beneficial rainfall as well as threat to merchants.

मैत्रे क्षत्रविरोधो ज्येष्ठायां क्षत्रमुख्यसन्तापः ।
मौलिकभिषजां मूले त्रिष्वपि चैतेष्वनावृष्टिः ॥३२॥

When Venus ts in Anurādhā, there will be hostility among the Kṣatriyas; when he is in Jyeṣṭhā, leaders of Kṣatriyas will be in jeopardy; and when he is in Mūla, druggists (those who deal in medicinal roots) and physicians will be harmed. In addition, there will be drought resulting from his transit through all the three stars (mentioned here).

आप्ये सलिलजपीडा विश्वेशे व्याधयः प्रकुप्यन्ति ।
श्रवणे श्रवणव्याधिः पाखण्डिभयं धनिष्ठासु ॥ ३३ ॥

When Venus passes through the star Pūrvāṣāḍha, aquatic, animals and products will suffer (or people will be troubled by aquatic animals etc.); when he is in Uttarāṣāḍha, diseases will spread; when he is in Śravaṇa, people will suffer from ear-diseases; and when he is in Dhaniṣṭhā, heretics will be in trouble.

शतभिषजि शौण्डिकानामजैकभे द्यूतजीविनां पीडाम् ।
कुरुपाञ्चालानामपि करोति चास्मिन् सितः सलिलम् ॥ ३४ ॥

When Venus is in Śatabhiṣaj, distillers of liquor as well as drunkards will suffer. While passing through Pūrvabhādrapada he afflicts gamblers and the people of Kuru and Pāñcāla countries. However, there will be good rains.

आहिर्बुध्न्ये फलमूलतापकृद्यायिनां च रेवत्याम् ।
अश्विन्यां हयपानां याम्ये तु किरातयवनानाम् ॥ ३५ ॥

While tenanting the star Uttarabhādrapada Venus will destroy roots and fruits; Revatī, travellers and marching troops; Aśvinī, keepers of horses; and Bharaṇī, Kirātas (hunters) and Yavanas.

[See what sage Kāśyapa says on this :

भेदयेत्कृत्तिकां शुक्रो बहुतोयं विमुञ्चति ।
रोहिण्यां मरणं घोरं गृध्राकुलभयाकुलम् ॥
मृगे तु सर्वसस्यानां क्षयं कुर्याद् भृगोः सुतः ।
आर्द्रासु च कलिङ्गानां कोशलानां भयावहः ॥
पुनर्वसौ विदर्भाणां पीडयत्युशनास्तथा ।
पुष्ये पुष्टिं समायान्ति जनाः सस्यानि वृष्टयः ॥
आश्लेषासूशना भेदात्पीडयेद् भुजगैः प्रजाः ।
मघाभेदकरः शुक्रो महामात्रांश्च पीडयेत् ॥

भाग्ये शबरविध्वंसं बहुवृष्टिं प्रमुञ्चति ।
आर्यम्णे तु कुरुक्षेत्रे पाञ्चालांश्चोपतापयेत् ॥
हस्ते चित्रकराणां तु पीडा वृष्टिक्षयो भवेत् ।
सुवृष्टिं कूपकृत्पीडां चित्राभेदं यदा व्रजेत् ॥
स्वातिभेदे सुवृष्टिं च वणिग्नाविकभीतिदः ।
विशाखायां सुवृष्टिं च मैत्रे मित्रं विरुध्यति ॥
ऐन्द्रे पौरविरोधः स्यान्मूले तु भिषजां भयम् ।
आप्ये वैश्वे व्याधिभयं वैष्णवे कर्णवेदना ।
धनिष्ठासु कुकर्मस्थान्वारुणे शौण्डिकक्षयम् ।
प्रोष्ठपादे पूर्वसक्तानहिर्बुध्न्ये फलक्षयः ॥
यायिनां सनृपाणां च पौष्णे ज्ञेयं महद्भयम् ।
अश्विन्यां हयपीडाकृद्भरण्यां कृषिजीविनाम् ॥

According to Parāśara Venus being glossy and full of rays produces rains while tenanting Pūrva and Uttaraphalgunī, Svātī, Viśākhā, the Bhādrapadas, Ārdrā, Bharaṇī and Puṣya. In case he moves to the *north*, in the *middle* or to the *south* of Rohiṇī, Citrā, Viśākhā and Anurādhā, he will cause health and happiness, crops and rainfall to the best advantage, moderate benefit and minimum advantage respectively of the people. If he moves to the north or in the middle of Maghā and Kṛttikā, he will prove beneficial to mankind. Similarly his movement in the middle of the Āṣāḍhas, Punarvasu and Rohiṇī will bring about encirlement of cities by enemies.

In the next verse the author gives the effects of Venus's rising and setting in the different lunar days or Tithis :—]

चतुर्दशीं पञ्चदशीं तथाष्टमीं तामिस्रपक्षस्य तिथिं भृगोः सुतः ।
यदा व्रजेद् दर्शनमस्तमेति वा तदा मही वारिमयीव लक्ष्यते ॥३६॥

When Venus rises or sets on the 8th, 14th or 15th lunar day (new moon) of the dark fortnight, the earth would look as though it were a vast sheet of water i.e. it will be completely submerged in floods.

[Cf. *Kāśyapa*—

कृष्णपक्षे ह्यमावस्याचतुर्दश्यष्टमीषु च ।
उदयं भार्गवः कुर्यात्तदा वृष्टिं प्रमुञ्चति ॥

Sage *Parāśara* gives some more details regarding the months in which he rises or sets thus : If his rising or setting takes place in the month of Kārttika, there will be no rain at all for 90 days. If Venus rises (or sets) during the transit of Jupiter through Kṛttikā, there will be good rain-fall throughout the year. In case the luminaries complete their circuit of the ecliptic (?) at the time of Venus's rising or setting, there will be good rains. Should Venus be tenanting at the time a star or sign that is considered dry or non-rainy, then too there would be rains; and a rain-producing star or sign, surely there would be no rain.

The metre of this verse and others upto the 42nd. is वंशस्थ.]

गुरुर्भृगुश्चापरपूर्वकाष्ठयोः परस्परं सप्तमराशिगौ यदा ।
तदा प्रजा रुग्भयशोकपीडिता न वारि पश्यन्ति पुरन्दरोज्झितम् ॥३७॥

When Jupiter and Venus are situated in the Western and Eastern horizons, being at the same time in opposition (i.e. 180° apart), mankind will be afflicted with diseases, panic and grief and will have no rain at all.

[In the opinion of Bhaṭṭotpala there is no order meant in respect of the quarters occupied by Jupiter and Venus. So either of them can be in the east or west, but it is essential that they should be in the 7th house from each other. He quotes पराशर, ऋषिपुत्र, गर्ग, बृहज्जातक etc. He has come to the conclusion that even the Sages are not unanimous on this subject. Says पराशर—

उदयास्तमयस्थौ तु यदा शुक्रबृहस्पती ।
पूर्वसन्ध्यागतौ स्यातां जनयेतां तदा भयम् ॥

Here this Sage introduces a new rule i.e. both Jupiter and Venus being situated in the eastern horizon.

ऋषिपुत्र speaks differently :

पृष्ठतस्तूशना यत्र पुरस्ताच्च बृहस्पतिः ।
न च कश्चिद्ग्रहो मध्ये बुधो वाप्यथ दृश्यते ॥
एकमार्गसमापन्नौ प्रेक्षमाणौ परस्परम् ।
ते दिशौ पीडिते विन्द्यात् त्रीन्पक्षानभियोजयेत् ॥

Bhaṭṭotpala quotes from the work of Bhadrabāhu, a Jain monk, with the words "तथा च भद्रबाहौ पठ्यते" which indicates a work entitled Bhadrabāhu'. Our commentator must have taken the author's name for that of the work as it often happens in the case of authors of single works e. g. माघ for the शिशुपालवध and भारवि for the किरातार्जुनीय. The following are the verses of the Jain monk :

प्रत्यूषे प्राक्स्थितः शुक्रः पृष्ठतश्च बृहस्पतिः ।
यदाऽन्योन्यं निरीक्षेते तदा चक्रं प्रवर्तते ॥

धर्मार्थकामा लुप्यन्ते प्रस्तावा वार्णसङ्करा: ।
नृपाणां च समुद्योगो यतः शुक्रस्ततो जयः ॥
अवृष्टिश्च भयं रोगो दुर्भिक्षं च तदा भवेत् ।
आढकेन तु धान्यस्य ग्राहकः स्यात्तदा प्रियः ॥
यदा तु पृष्ठतः शुक्रः पुरतश्च बृहस्पतिः ।
यदा वालोकयेतां तौ तावदेव फलं भवेत् ॥

The evil effects of a journey in the direction of Venus are referred to by Kālidāsa in "कामः पुरश्शुक्रमिव प्रयाणे" (कुमार III. 43.)

Cf. also गर्ग—
अन्योन्यमस्तसंस्थौ तु यदि शुक्रबृहस्पती ।
पूर्वसन्ध्यागतौ घोरं जनयेतां महद्भयम् ॥]

यदा स्थिता जीवबुधारसूर्यजाः सितस्य सर्वेऽग्रपथानुवर्त्तिनः ।
नृनागविद्याधरसङ्गरास्तदा भवन्ति वाताश्च समुच्छ्रितान्तकाः ॥३८॥

न मित्रभावे सुहृदो व्यवस्थिताः क्रियासु सम्यग् न रता द्विजातयः ।
न चाल्पमप्यम्बु ददाति वासवो भिनत्ति वज्रेण शिरांसि भूभृताम् ॥३९॥

When Jupiter, Mercury, Mars and Saturn move in advance of Venus, there will be wars among men, serpents and Vidyādharas (a class of demi-gods) and the winds will raze to the ground all things standing erect, such as trees and mountains. Friends too will not remain cordial any longer; Brahmins will not be devoted to their duties; and the God of rain will not give even a drop of water; and he will smash the tops of mountains with his thunderbolt.

[In the following four verses the author discusses separately the effects of the four planets remaining ahead of Venus :]

शनैश्चरे म्लेच्छबिडालकुञ्जराः खरा महिष्योऽसितधान्यशूकराः ।
पुलिन्दशूद्राश्च सदक्षिणापथाः क्षयं व्रजन्त्यक्षिमरुद्गदोद्भवैः ॥ ४० ॥

Should Saturn be the planet in advance of Venus, barbarians, cats, elephants, donkeys, she-buffaloes, boars, black grains, Pulindas; Śūdras and the people of the Southern country would perish through eye-disease and ailments caused by the vitiation of wind.

निहन्ति शुक्रः क्षितिजेऽग्रतः प्रजां हुताशशस्त्रक्षुदवृष्टितस्करैः ।
चराचरं व्यक्तमथोत्तरापथं दिशोऽग्निविद्युद्रजसा च पीडयेत् ॥ ४१ ॥

Should Mars march ahead of Venus, the latter would destroy

human lives by means of fire, weapons (wars), hunger (famine), drought and robbers. He would also destroy completely all movable and immovable objects as well as the Northern-country. He would afflict the quarters with fire, lightning and dust.

बृहस्पतौ हन्ति पुरःस्थिते सितः सितं समस्तं द्विजगोसुरालयान् ।
दिशं च पूर्वां करकासृजोऽम्बुदा गले गदा भूरि भवेच्च शारदम् ॥ ४२ ॥

When Jupiter is ahead of Venus, the latter will destroy all white objects, the abodes of Brahmins, cattle and Gods, as well as the Eastern region. Clouds will pour down plenty of hailstones (instead of rain); and people will be afflicted with throat-diseases, but the autumnal crops will flourish.

[This verse is specially noteworthy for its charming alliteration in both the halves.]

सौम्योऽस्तोदययोः पुरो भृगुसुतस्यावस्थितस्तोयकृ-
द्रोगान् पित्तजकामलांश्च कुरुते पुष्णाति च ग्रैष्मिकान् ।
हन्यात्प्रव्रजिताग्निहोत्रिकभिषग्रङ्गोपजीव्यान् हयान्
वैश्यान्गाः सह वाहनैर्नरपतीन् पीतानि पश्चाद्दिशम् ॥ ४३ ॥

When Mercury, whether setting or rising, is in advance of Venus, the latter will produce copious rains and summer crops. He will also engender diseases caused by the vitiation of bile, and jaundice. In addition, he will destroy recluses, sacrificers, physicians, horses, actors, wrestlers etc., traders, cattle, vehicles, kings, all yellow objects and the western country.

[The metre of this verse is शार्दूलविक्रीडित.]

शिखिभयमनलाभे शस्त्रकोपश्च रक्ते ।
कनकनिकषगौरे व्याधयो दैत्यपूज्ये ।
हरितकपिलरूपे श्वासकासप्रकोपः
पतति न सलिलं खाद् भस्मरूक्षासिताभे ॥४४॥

If Venus appears with the lustre of fire, there will be danger from fire; if he is red in colour, there will be war; if he is golden in hue, diseases will erupt; if he looks green or tawny, people will suffer greatly from asthma and cough; and if he appears grey like ashes, coarse or dark in colour, not a drop of water will fall from the sky.

[The metre is मालिनी.]

दधिकुमुदशशाङ्ककान्तिभृत्स्फुटविकसत्किरणो बृहत्तनुः ।
सुगतिरविकृतो जयान्वितः कृतयुगरूपकरः सिताह्वयः ॥४५॥

Should Venus be possessed of the lustre of curds, Kumuda (a kind of lotus) flower or the Moon, bright and expanding rays, a full and large orb and good motion i.e. not retrograde, and situated to the north of a star or planet, and be free from disturbances like portents, and be victorious in a planetary fight, he would confer the blessings of Kṛta yuga (golden age) on humanity.

[Cf. पराशर—

"हिमकनकरजतशङ्खस्फटिकवैदूर्यमुक्तामधुघृतमण्डकुमुदशशाङ्कच्छविः स्निग्धदीप्तप्रकान्तिप्रकाशः प्रसन्नार्चिरवनिपतिहितकरः प्रशान्तवैरो दुर्भिक्षारोगवृष्टिकरश्च श्यावनीलरूक्षकपिलरक्तध्वस्तदीनाल्पलोष्टसन्निभः शस्त्रवैरव्याधिवर्षान्नक्षयकरः।" In this passage the expression, "प्रशान्त...रश्च" makes little sense. For, if Venus is triumphant in a fight, how could he cause famine, freedom from diseases, and rain ? There might be some mistake in the text.

The metre of the verse is अपरवक्त्र. The following verses are also quoted *possibly* from *Parāśara*:

"कूटाकारनिभः स्निग्धो मार्गस्थो रजतप्रभः।
भार्गवो विस्तृतार्चिश्च प्रजाभावकरः स्मृतः॥"
"प्रावृषि शुक्रः प्राच्यां दिशि स्थितोऽल्पं जलं सृजति नित्यम्।
धान्यं च भूरि कुरुते तृणं च बहु जायते तत्र॥
अपरां निषेव्यमाणः काष्ठां शुक्रो जलं सृजति भूरि।
धान्यं कुरुते चाल्पं तृणं न बहु जायते तत्र॥"

In the first quotation good effects are mentioned, while in the second the presence of Venus in the eastern horizon during the monsoon is said to be not helpful for rainfall but beneficial to crops and grass.]

शनैश्चरचारः ॥ १० ॥

Saturn's Transit

श्रवणानिलहस्तार्द्राभरणीभाग्योपगः सुतोऽर्कस्य ।
प्रचुरसलिलोपगूढां करोति धात्रीं यदि स्निग्धः ॥ १ ॥
अहिवरुणपुरन्दरदैवतेषु सुक्षेमकृन्न चातिजलम् ।
क्षुच्छस्त्रावृष्टिकरो मूले प्रत्येकमपि वक्ष्ये ॥ २ ॥

When Saturn tenants the stars Śravaṇa, Svāti, Hasta, Ārdrā, Bharaṇī and Pūrvaphalgunī, the earth will be flooded with water, provided he is glossy. When he passes through the constellations Āśleṣā, Śatabhiṣaj and Jyeṣṭhā, he will make people happy; but will not cause sufficient rain. Passing through Mūla he brings about hunger or famine, clash of arms and drought. Now I shall give separately the effects of Saturn's passage through the different asterisms.

[Cf. गर्ग—

याम्यवायव्यसावित्ररौद्रश्रवणसंस्थितः ।
भवेत् स्निग्धवपुः सौरो भाग्ये चैवातिवर्षदः ॥
सार्पवारुणमाहेन्द्रनक्षत्रेषु च संस्थितः ।
स्निग्धः सौरः क्षेमकरो नातिवृष्टिं प्रमुञ्चति ॥
क्षुच्छस्त्रावृष्टिदो मूले सूर्यपुत्रः समस्थितः ।]

तुरगतुरगोपचारककविवैद्यामात्यहार्कजोऽश्विगतः ॥
याम्ये नर्तकवादकगेयज्ञक्षुद्रनैकृतिकान् ॥ ३ ॥

When Saturn sojourns in the star Aśvinī, he destroys horses, horsemen, poets, physicians and ministers; and in the star Bharaṇī he harms dancers or actors, musicians or singers, those who play on musical instruments, the wicked and hunters.

बहुलास्थे पीडयन्ते सौरेऽग्न्युपजीविनश्चमूपाश्च ।
रोहिण्यां कोशलमद्रकाशिपाञ्चालशाकटिकाः ॥४॥

When Saturn passes through the star Kṛttikā, those who work on fire i.e. goldsmiths, blacksmiths etc., and army commanders come to grief; and when he passes through Rohiṇī the countries of Kosala, Madra, Kāśī and Pāñcāla as well as cartmen are troubled.

[As I am writing this, Saturn is tenanting Rohiṇī and is retrograde.]

मृगशिरसि वत्सयाजकयजमानार्यजनमध्यदेशाश्च ।
रौद्रस्थे पारतरमठास्तैलिकरजकचौराश्च ॥ ५ ॥

When Saturn sojourns in the star Mṛgaśīrṣa, misfortune befalls the people of the Vatsa country, sacrificers, officiating priests at sacrifices, noble persons and the middle country; and when he tenants the asterism Ārdrā, trouble befalls the people of the Pārata and Ramaṭha countries, oilmongers, washermen and dyers as well as thieves.

[Bhaṭṭotpala reads Pāratara and Maṭha as two countries. It should be Pārata or Pārada and Ramaṭha. One of the synônyms of asafoetida is Rāmaṭha, as it is got from the Ramaṭha country, which according to Kṣīrasvāmin, lies to the north of India. The Paradas are identified with Pardene of Ptolemy in the centre of Gedrosia (Baluchistan).[1] S. Levi's identification of the Ramaṭhas with the country lying between Ghazni and Wakhan seems to be correct.]

आदित्ये पाञ्चनदप्रत्यन्तसुराष्ट्रसिन्धुसौवीराः ।
पुष्ये घाण्टिकघौषिकयवनवणिक्कितवकुसुमानि ॥६॥

When Saturn passes through the star Punarvasu, the people of the Punjab, Saurāṣṭra, Sind and Sauvīra as well as cave-dwellers are harmed; and when he sojourns in the star Puṣya, persons engaged in ringing bells, those who make loud announcements (or those who live in hamlets), Yavanas, Kirātas (traders?), gamblers and flowers are destroyed.

[The commentator construes *Vaṇik* as kirātas. Sometimes Sindhu and Sauvīra are mentioned as one region. It lies between the Jhelum and the Indus. Here Utpala takes them as different names. However, according to Alberuni, Sauvīra stands for Multan and Jahravar. Surāṣṭra corresponds to the Kathiawad peninsula. The word Surat is the corruption af Surāṣṭra. Pratyanta is a bordering country occupied by Mlecchas.]

सार्पे जलरुहसर्पाः पित्र्ये बाह्लीकचीनगान्धाराः ।
शूलिकपारतवैश्याः कोष्ठागाराणि वणिजश्च ॥७॥

When Saturn sojourns in the asterism Āśleṣā, aquatic objects or animals, as well as snakes are destroyed; when he tenants the

1. I.A.I.B. pp. 93-95.

star Maghā, the Bāhlīkas, Cīnas, Gāndhāras, Śūlikas, Pāratas, traders (or Vaiśyas), godowns and Kirātas come to grief.

[Bāhlīka is the modern Bactria or Balkh in the north of Afghanistan. Gāndhāra country extended from the Kabul valley to Takṣaśilā. Śūlikas, otherwise known as Cūlikas, were the people of the north-western part of India. According to the Matsyapurāṇa[1] the country of the Śūlikās is watered by the river Cakṣu (Oxus). Since the author uses both 'Vaiśya' and 'Vaṇijaḥ', they cannot be synonyms. The word 'Vaiśya', therefore, means a tribe of non-Aryan Origin. (See XIV-21 *Infra*). Since the commentator interprets the word 'Vaṇij' as Kirāta a forest tribe—originally the nasal might have been of the dental class. The root 'वन्' means to 'destroy' according to the तत्त्वबोधिनी. Cf also गर्ग—

भुजङ्गकच्छपग्राहनागमत्स्यसरीसृपान् ।
हन्यादर्कसुतस्तिष्ठन्नक्षत्रे सर्पदैवते ॥]

माग्ये रसविक्रयिणः पण्यस्त्रीकन्यकामहाराष्ट्राः ।
आर्यम्णे नृपगुडलवणभिक्षुकाम्बूनि तक्षशिला ॥८॥

If Saturn is situated in the star Pūrvaphalgunī, dealers in juices or articles having the six kinds of tastes, courtesans, virgins and the people of Mahārāṣṭra will suffer; and if he stays in the star Uttaraphalgunī, trouble will befall kings, jaggery, salt, hermits (or mendicants), water and the town of Takṣaśilā.

[The city of Takṣaśilā (Taxila) was an important centre of learning in ancient India. At present the site of the city consists of some villages to the north-west of Rawalpindi.]

हस्ते नापितचाक्रिकचौरभिषक्सूचिका द्विपग्राहाः ।
बन्धक्यः कौसलका मालाकाराश्च पीडयन्ते ॥९॥

When Saturn stays in the star Hasta, barbers, potters, oil-manufacturers etc., thieves, physicians, tailors (needle-workers), elephant-catchers (or elephants and crocodiles), harlots, the people of the Kosala country and garland-makers (florists) come to harm.

चित्रास्थे प्रमदाजनलेखकचित्रज्ञचित्रभाण्डानि ।
स्वातौ मागधचरदूतसूतपोतप्लवनटाद्याः ॥१०॥

When Saturn sojourns in the asterism Citrā, trouble befalls women, writers, painters and painted vessels. When he is in Svāti, rhapsodists (or bards or the people of Magadha), spies, couriers, charioteers or story-tellers, sailors, actors, musicians etc. are affected.

1. I.A.I.B. pp. 100-101.

ऐन्द्राग्नाख्ये त्रैगर्तचीनकौलूतकुङ्कुमं लाक्षा ।
सस्यान्यथ माञ्जिष्ठं कौसुम्भं च क्षयं याति ॥११॥

When Saturn stays in the star Viśākhā, the people of Trigarta (i.e. Jālandhara), Cīna, Kulūta (Kullu in the upper valley of the Beas), saffron, lac, crops, madder and safflower are destroyed.

मैत्रे कुलूततङ्गणखसकाश्मीराः समन्त्रिचक्रचराः ।
उपतापं यान्ति च घाण्टिका विभेदश्च मित्राणाम् ॥१२॥

When Saturn passes through the star Anurādhā, the people of Kulūta, the Taṅgaṇas, the Khasas, the Kashmirians, ministers, those that work with wheels such as potters, oil-makers etc., and those that beat gongs or bell-makers are afflicted; and friends get estranged.

[The Taṅgaṇas were an aboriginal tribe living in the north-eastern region of India.

Bhaṭṭotpala says that the Khasas are mountain-dwellers. Their country lay on the south and west of Kashmir. Re. मित्रभेद see IX 16 *supra*.]

ज्येष्ठासु नृपपुरोहितनृपसत्कृतशूरगणकुलश्रेण्यः ।
मूले तु काशिकोशलपाञ्चालफलौषधीयोधाः ॥१३॥

When Saturn tenants the asterism Jyeṣṭhā, trouble befalls kings, their preceptors, those that receive royal patronage or honour, war veterans (i.e. great heroes), groups or seminaries, elite families and trade guilds; and when he stays in Mūla, the people of Kāśī, Kosala and Pāñcāla, fruits, herbs and warriors come to grief.

[The star Jyeṣṭhā is presided over by Indra, leader of Gods. Hence if this star is tenanted by the malefic planet, Saturn, all those who are at the top are adversely affected. Originally the country of Pañcāla consisted of two parts, the Northern and Southern, with the Ganges as the dividing line and with Ahicchatra and Kāmpilya as their respective capitals.]

आप्येऽङ्गवङ्गकोशलगिरिव्रजा मगधपुण्ड्रमिथिलाश्च ।
उपतापं यान्ति जना वसन्ति ये ताम्रलिप्त्यां च ॥१४॥

When Saturn occupies the star Pūrvāṣāḍha, the people of Aṅga, Vaṅga, Kosala, Girivraja, Magadha, Puṇḍra, the city of Mithilā and the town of Tāmralipti get troubles.

[Girivraja must be the capital of Kekaya. Tāmralipti is the same as Tamluk in the Midnapur district of Bengal.]

विश्वेश्वरेऽर्कपुत्रश्चरन् दशार्णान्निहन्ति यवनांश्च ।
उज्जयिनीं शबरान् पारियात्रिकान् कुन्तिभोजांश्च ॥१५॥

When Saturn moves through the star Uttarāṣāḍha, he destroys the people of the Daśārṇa, the Yavanas, Ujjayinī, the Śabaras, those who live on the Pāriyātra mountain, and the Kuntibhojas.

[Daśārṇa was a famous country in the ancient times. Kātyāyana speaks of that region in his Vārttika "Pravatsara..." Kālidāsa celebrates it in his Meghadūta in "कतिपयदिनस्थायिहंसा दशार्णाः" It lies to the east of Vidiśā on the bank of the river Dhasan. The Kuntibhojas were a people and their country too was called after them. The Pāriyātra mountain forms the western part of the Vindhya range.]

श्रवणे राजाधिकृतान् विप्राग्र्यभिषक्पुरोहितकलिङ्गान् ।
वसुभे मगधेशजयो वृद्धिश्च धनेष्वधिकृतानाम् ॥१६॥

Saturn, tenanting the asterism Śravaṇa, destroys king's officers, eminent Brahmins, physicians, priests and the people of Kaliṅga; and while dwelling in the star Dhaniṣṭhā, he causes the victory of the king of Magadha and the prosperity of treasurers, bankers and the like.

साजे शतभिषजि भिषक्कविशौण्डिकपण्यनीतिवृत्तीनाम् ।
आहिर्बुध्न्ये नद्यो यानकराः स्त्रीहिरण्यं च ॥१७॥

When Saturn occupies the stars Śatabhiṣaj and Pūrvabhadrapadā, physicians, poets, drunkards, traders and politicians are afflicted; and when he stays in Uttarabhadrapadā, rivers, those who dwell on river-banks, carriage-makers, carpenters etc., women and gold are destroyed.

रेवत्यां राजभृताः क्रौञ्चद्वीपाश्रिताः शरत्सस्यम् ।
शबराश्च निपीड्यन्ते यवनाश्च शनैश्चरे चरति ॥१८॥

When Saturn moves in Revatī, king's proteges, inhabitants of the Krauñca Dvīpa, autumnal crops, the Śabaras and Yavanas come to have difficult times.

[The commentator quotes here an extensive prose passage of Parāśara describing the effects of Saturn's stay in the different asterisms. I shall give only the differences, if any, in the approaches of our author and Sage Parāśara. The former starts with Aśvinī, while the sage with Kṛttikā. According to the Sage *Kṛttikā* holding Saturn would afflict among others the Śūrasenas, women and brewers. In *Rohiṇī* he troubles the people of Aṅga and maidens as well. In *Punarvasu* he afflicts widows in addition. In *Puṣya* he troubles those who are in charge of weights and measures, messengers and sea-faring people also. In Maghā he harms in addition oilmen, physicians (Vaidyas instead of Vaiśyas given by Varāhamihira), the Daradas and artisans. In *Uttaraphalgunī* the queen, her children, sesamum, and the people of *Kūrcaghara* and Darśa are also affected. Under Hasta washermen also are mentioned. Under *Viśākhā* yellow flowers as well as war-mongers too are affected. Under *Śravaṇa Agnideśa* also is affected. In *Dhaniṣṭhā* he afflicts lords of wealth, Our author gives only good effects under this star.

In *Śatabhiṣaj* those who live by harlots, robbers and heretics are also afflicted, but not poets and politicians. In *Pūrvaproṣṭhapadā* the people of Draviḍa, Karṇāṭa, Cola, Pāṇḍya and Siṁhala countries as well as the residents of Mahendranagara are afflicted. In *Uttara-bhadrapadā* pulses and those who are in charge of rivers are harmed.

Towards the end of the chapter he changes the metre and the following three verses are in three different metres. In the next verse the author discusses the effects of the mutual positions of Jupiter and Saturn.]

यदा विशाखासु महेन्द्रमन्त्री सुतश्च भानोर्दहनर्क्षयातः ।
तदा प्रजानामनयोऽतिघोरः पुरप्रभेदो गतयोर्भमेकम् ॥१६॥

When Jupiter tenants the star Viśākhā and Saturn Kṛttikā, there will be dreadful unrest and violence among the subjects; and when these two planets occupy one and the same constellation, the capital will be stormed.

[Cf. पराशर—

कृत्तिकासु शनैश्चारी विशाखासु बृहस्पतिः ।
तिष्ठेद्यदा तदा घोरः प्रजानाम्नयो भवेत् ॥
एकं नक्षत्रमासाद्य दृश्यते युगपद्यदि ।
अन्योन्यभेदं जानीयात्तदा पुरनिवासिनाम् ॥

Similarly the conjunction of Saturn and Jupiter (which is called गुरुचण्डालयोग in astrology) in the dual Rāśis is considered harmful. See what देवल says:

मीने धनुषि कन्यायां मिथुने सगुरुः शनिः ।
तिष्ठेद्यदा तदा घोरः प्रजानामनयो भवेत् ॥

The metre of the verse is उपेन्द्रवज्रा.]

अण्डजहा रविजो यदि चित्रः क्षुद्भयकृद्यदि पीतमयूखः ।
शस्त्रभयाय च रक्तसवर्णो भस्मनिभो बहुवैरकरश्च ॥२०॥

If Saturn should appear with many colours, he would destroy birds (or fishes); if he be possessed of yellowish rays, he would cause the threat of famine (or famine and fear); if he be blood-red, there would be war; and if he be ash-coloured (i.e. grey), all the subjects would rise in revolt in a dangerous way.

[Cf. पराशर

नीलपीतः क्षुधे । रक्तभस्मचित्रवर्णः शस्त्रवैरकरोऽण्डजाभिहन्ता । यद्वर्णस्तद्वर्णविनाशी भवति ।

The metre is दोधक.]

वैडूर्यकान्तिविमलः शुभकृत्प्रजानां
बाणातसीकुसुमवर्णनिभश्च शस्तः ।
यं चापि वर्णमुपगच्छति तत्सवर्णान्
सूर्यात्मजः क्षपयतीति मुनिप्रवादः ॥२१॥

Saturn becomes auspicious and beneficial to people, if he is possessed of the bright lustre of Vaidūrya gem (*Lapis lazuli* or beryl); so is he if he resembles in colour either the Bāṇa flower (which is jet black) or the Atasī flower (which is deep blue). Whatever colour—white, red, yellow or black—he attains, he will destroy the corresponding class of people, in the opinion of the Sages such as Garga.

[The colours assigned to the four classes, Brāhmaṇas, Kṣatriyas, Vaiśyas and Sūdras, are respectively white, red, yellow and black. Cf. गर्ग—

भवत्यर्कात्मजे रूक्षे श्यावपीतारुणप्रभे ।
तदात्मकानां भावानां क्षुच्छस्त्राग्निकृतं भयम् ॥

and पराशर—

पाण्डुः स्निग्धोऽमलः श्यामो विस्तृतार्चिः शनैश्चरः ।
मार्गस्थश्च प्रसव्यश्च नक्षत्राद्धित इष्यते ॥

The metre of the verse is वसन्ततिलका.]

केतुचारः ॥११॥

Chapter XI—On Comets

गार्गीयं शिखिचारं पाराशरमसितदेवलकृतं च ।
अन्यांश्च बहून्दृष्ट्वा क्रियतेऽयमनाकुलश्चारः ॥१॥

I am now explaining in a perspicuous manner the movements of comets, after seeing the works of the Sages Garga and Parāśara and of the masters Asita, Devala and a host of others, bearing on this subject.

[Though the achievements of the ancient Sages in respect of astronomical observations may not be quite up-to-date from the point of modern science, yet they must be adjudged as highly satisfactory and analytical, considering the time and facilities under which the ancients had to labour. They must have observed the comets appearing at different times and parts of the sky and their effects, and come to certain conclusions in a scientific manner. We have to admire this scientific attitude of these people. While discussing the phenomena called comets Al-Beruni says that the theories and methods of the Hindus are very lengthy and very subtle. In his opinion these comets do not seem to have much astronomical significance, inasmuch as he treats of this subject as an astrological matter. Chidambara Iyer quotes some scientific opinion in his translation of this work: "What then is a comet according to the latest scientific researches ? The spectroscope has pretty well solved the query. It consists, first, of a more or less solid nucleus of fire, blazing and glowing; second, of vast masses of incandescent gas, constituting the luminous head; third, solid materials, constituting the tail, which are ponderable, which reflect the Sun's light and are carried along by the influence of the nucleus; fourth, an immense prolongation of the tail in the nature of attenuated volumes of gas. The solid materials of a comet, it is believed, consist of stones and sand, particles ground by ceaseless attrition. The proof of this is the concession of most astronomers that meteoric showers are shreds and patches of cometic matter, dropped from the tail, and these meteors are stones. The genesis of comets is found to be in the explosion of planetary bodies, a theory not without good scientific authority.

Arage estimates that there are 17,000,000 of these fiery wanderers within the orbit of Neptune, and Lambert regards 500,000,000 as a moderate estimate for those in the solar system. All the astronomers agree that they are scattered through space as profusely as the fish in the seas. The Orbit of the Earth is overwhelmed in a fine network of cometary orbits, and our globe is like a lost child in a forest full of wild beasts."

"A comet is a cloud of meteors surrounded (at times) by a gaseous envelope moving around the sun," wrote German astronomer Nicholaus Richter in 1868. No longer is that true, says Thomas O'Toole (Sunday St. 24-12-72). Astronomers once thought there were fewer than 500 observable comets in the Solar System. Telescopic observation alone has doubled the number of observable comets, and some scientists now believe there are millions of comets wandering about the Solar System, most of them invisible to man because of their distance from the sun. "Every once in a while one gets perturbed in toward the sun by a stellar or planetary disturbance", explains Maurice Dubin of the U.S. National Aeronautics and Space Administration. "This is the only time we see any of these comets." They are the largest, perhaps most puzzling bodies in the Solar System.

The comet Encke was found surrounded by a cloud of hydrogen gas six million miles across. The comet Bennet had a hydrogen envelope which was 15 times the size of the sun. Comets were long felt to be mixtures of ice and dust.]

दर्शनमस्तमयो वा न गणितविधिनास्य शक्यते ज्ञातुम् ।
दिव्यान्तरिक्षभौमास्त्रिविधाः स्युः केतवो यस्मात् ॥२॥

It is not possible to determine by calculation the rising or setting of the comets, since there are three categories of comets as *Celestial*, *Atmospheric* and *Terrestrial*.

[As the comets are strange phenomena in the nature of portents, they cannot have any fixed timings of rising and setting. For, a portent is a sudden occurrence that augurs well or ill; and if it can be ascertained by mathematical calculations, it ceases to be an augury or portent.

In the next verse the author gives a method for detecting the Ketu.]

अहुताशेऽनलरूपं यस्मिंस्तत्केतुरूपमेवोक्तम् ।
खद्योतपिशाचालयमणिरत्नादीन् परित्यज्य ॥३॥

In places where, despite the absence of fire, there is still the appearance of fire, Ketu's presence is recognized, save for the presence of glow-worms, phosphoric lights on graves, gems, crystals, marble pieces and the like.

[पिशाचालय is construed as यक्षस्थानम् by Utpala.]

ध्वजशस्त्रभवनतरुतुरगकुञ्जराद्येष्वथान्तरिक्षास्ते ।
दिव्या नक्षत्रस्था भौमाः स्युरतोऽन्यथा शिखिनः ॥४॥

The *Atmospheric* Ketus are those that are sighted on flagstaffs, weapons, buildings, trees, horses, elephants and such other quadrupeds. The *Celestial* ones are seen amidst the constellations, and the *Terrestrial* ones are those that do not come under either of the two categories.

शतमेकाधिकमेके सहस्रमपरे वदन्ति केतूनाम् ।
बहुरूपमेकमेव प्राह मुनिर्नारदः केतुम् ॥५॥

Some Sages like Parāśara speak of 101 Ketus, while others such as Garga of 1000 Ketus. However, Sage Nārada declares that there is only one Ketu which appears in many forms and places.

[According to पराशर there are 101 Ketus, of which 16 were born of the breath of Death, 12 of the Sun, 10 of Rudra's wrath at the destruction of Dakṣa's sacrifice, 7 of Pitāmaha (creator), 15 are the sons of Sage Uddālaka, 17 were born of the foreheads of Sages Marīci and Kaśyapa, 5 of Prajāpati's laughter, 3 of fire, 1 of smoke, 14 were born along with the Moon when the ocean was churned for nectar, and lastly one was born of Brahman's anger. See what गर्ग says:

अतीतादयचाराणामशुभानां च दर्शने ।
आगन्तूनां सहस्रं स्याद् ग्रहाणां तन्निबोध मे ॥

Cf. नारद also:

दिव्यान्तरिक्षगो भौम एकः केतुः प्रकीर्तितः ।
शुभाशुभफलं लोके ददात्यस्तमयोदयैः ॥

Next the author gives his own opinion:]

यद्येको यदि बहवः किमनेन फलं तु सर्वथा वाच्यम् ।
उदयास्तमयैः स्थानैः स्पर्शैराधूमनैर्वर्णैः ॥६॥

What difference does it make whether there is a single Ketu or many ? Under any circumstance, its effects ought to be declared through the positions of its appearance and setting, contact with planets or asterisms, smoky mantle and colours.

[Here the author shows himself to be a practical thinker, not a mere theorist. What are required for our practical purpose are the particular part of the sky in which a Ketu appears or disappears and the effects that accrue to the people. Similarly one ought to observe their colours, smoky nature and contact with planets or stars. For, each one of these circumstances is supposed to yield a particular result.]

यावन्त्यहानि दृश्यो मासास्तावन्त एव फलपाकः ।
मासैरब्दांश्च वदेत्प्रथमात्पक्षत्रयात्परतः ॥७॥

The effects of Ketu would be felt for so many months as the number of days during which it remains visible. Similarly its effects would last for so many years as the number of months during which it remains visible. However, the effects in all cases would come to pass only after the first three fortnights of its appearance.

[Bhaṭṭotpala refers to a contrary interpretation of the second half of this verse by some: "अत्र केचिद् व्याख्याविप्रतिपत्ति प्रदर्शयन्ति..." According to this interpretation the meaning would be: "If the Ketu remains visible for not more than three fortnights, the effects would be felt for so many months as the number of days it is visible; and if it is visible beyond three fortnights, the years of its effects would correspond to the number of months it is visible. To prove the incorrectness of this interpretation Utpala quotes the words of both गर्ग and वृद्धगर्ग. The above wrong construction must have been taken by Al-Biruni who too goes wrong, as he says, "If the appearance of a comet lasts longer than 1½ months, subtract from it 45 days. The remainder represents the months of its influence."

Now see what गर्ग says:

यावन्त्यहानि दृश्यस्तावन्मासान् फलं भवेत् ।
मासांस्तु यावद् दृश्येत तावतोऽब्दांश्च वैकृतम् ॥

त्रिपक्षात्परतः कर्म पच्यतेऽस्य शुभाशुभम् ।
सद्यस्कमुदिते केतौ फलं नेहाऽऽदिशेद् बुधः ॥

Cf. also वृद्धगर्ग :

यावतो दिवसांस्तिष्ठेत्तावन्मासान् विनिर्दिशेत् ।
त्रिपक्षात्परतश्चापि कर्म केतोः प्रपच्यते ॥

तस्मात्कालात्परं ब्रूयात्फलमस्य शुभाशुभम् ।
सद्यस्कमुदिते केतौ फलं नेहाऽऽदिशेद् बुधः ॥

See also the author's समाससंहिता—

केचित्केतुसहस्रं शतमेकसमन्वितं वदन्त्येके ।
नारदमत एकोऽयं त्रिस्थानसमुद्भवो विविधरूपः ।
दिव्यग्रहर्क्षजातास्तीव्रफला मन्दफलकरा भौमाः ।
प्राणिध्वजादितुङ्गेषु चान्तरिक्षा न चात्यशुभाः ॥
उदयास्तमयाऽऽधूमनसंयोगाकारमार्गदिग्यातैः ।
फलनिर्देशो दिवसैर्मासा मासैस्तु वर्षाणि ॥

All Ketus are not evil. There are some which augur well for the world.]

ह्रस्वस्तनुः प्रसन्नः स्निग्धस्त्वृजुरचिरसंस्थितः शुक्लः ।
उदितोऽथवाभिवृष्टः सुभिक्षसौख्यावहः केतुः ॥८॥

If a Ketu (comet) be short, slender, clear, glossy, straight, white and visible but for a short while, and if its appearance be immediately followed by a rain, there would be abundance of food crops and happiness.

[There is another reading "उदितो वाप्यभिदृष्टः" which, of course, has not been noticed by the commentator.]

उक्तविपरीतरूपो न शुभकरो धूमकेतुरुत्पन्नः ।
इन्द्रायुधानुकारी विशेषतो द्वित्रिचूलो वा ॥९॥

A comet whose form is contrary to what has been described above, is considered as a Dhūmaketu—a portentous comet—that has risen; and it is disastrous in its effects, all the more so when it resembles the rainbow or is possessed of two or three crests.

[Cf. समाससंहिता—

अचिरस्थितोऽभिवृष्टस्त्वृजुः स्मितः स्निग्धमूर्तिरुदगुदितः ।
ह्रस्वस्तनुः प्रसन्नः केतुर्लोकस्य भावाय ॥
न शुभो विपरीतोऽतो विशेषतः शक्रचापसङ्काशः ।
द्वित्रिचतुश्चूलो वा दक्षिणसंस्थश्च मृत्युकरः ॥

In this abridged work the author introduces a new element viz. rising in the north or south. It may be in the northern or the southern sky, or to the north or south of a planet or asterism.

Next he describes in the following verses upto verse 52 the thousand Ketus with their effects, mentioned by Sage Garga.]

हारमणिहेमरूपाः किरणाख्याः पञ्चविंशतिः सशिखाः ।
प्रागपरदिशोर्दृश्या नृपतिविरोधावहा रविजाः ॥१०॥

There are 25 comets named Kiraṇas, born of the Sun, resembling a pearl-necklace, gems or gold. They are possessed of crests and appear in the east and west. They are disastrous to the rulers of the land.

[Cf. गर्ग—

शुद्धस्फटिकसङ्काशमृणालरजतप्रभाः ।
मुक्ताहारसुवर्णाभाः सशिखाः पञ्चविंशतिः ॥
किरणाख्या रवेः पुत्रा दृश्यन्ते प्राग्दिशि स्थिताः ।
तथा चापरभागस्था नृपतेर्भयदाश्च ते ॥

The commentator adds here a note to the effect that only one of the 25 comets appears at a time, and not all at once. This rule applies to all groups of comets.]

शुकदहनबन्धुजीवकलाक्षाक्षतजोपमा हुताशसुताः ।
आग्नेय्यां दृश्यन्ते तावन्तस्तेऽपि शिखिभयदाः ॥११॥

There are 25 other comets born of the fire and resembling the parrot (blue and yellow), the fire, the Bandhujīva flower (which is deep red), lac and blood in colour. They make their appearance in the South-east and portend fire-disasters.

[These comets are the children of the fire whose direction is the South-east.

Cf. गर्ग—

नानावर्णाग्निसङ्काशा दीप्तिमन्तो विचूलिनः ।
सृजन्त्यग्निमिवाकाशात्सर्वे ज्योतिषनाशनाः ॥
तेऽग्निपुत्रा ग्रहा ज्ञेया लोकेऽग्निभयवेदिनः ।
आग्नेय्यां दिशि दृश्यन्ते पञ्चविंशत्प्रकीर्तिताः ॥]

वक्रशिखा मृत्युसुता रूक्षाः कृष्णाश्च तेऽपि तावन्तः ।
दृश्यन्ते याम्यायां जनमरकावेदिनस्ते च ॥१२॥

There are 25 yet other comets born of Death, possessed of crooked crests, rough and dark in colour. They appear in the south and portend extensive mortality of human beings.

[Cf. गर्ग—

कृष्णा रूक्षा वक्रशिखा दृश्यन्ते याम्यदिक्स्थिताः ।
पञ्चविंशा मृत्युसुताः प्रजाक्षयकराः स्मृताः ॥]

दर्पणवृत्ताकारा विशिखाः किरणान्विता धरातनयाः ।
क्षुद्भयदा द्वाविंशतिरैशान्यामम्बुतैलनिभाः ॥१३॥

There are 22 comets born of the Earth, which are round like mirror, devoid of crest and possessed of rays. They resemble the water or oil, appear in the North-east and portend famine.

[Cf. गर्ग—
समस्तवृत्ता विशिखा रश्मिभिः परिवारिताः ।
अम्बुतैलप्रतीकाशा द्वाविंशद्भूसुताः स्मृताः ॥
ऐशान्यां दिशि दृश्यन्ते दुर्भिक्षभयदास्तु ते ॥]

शशिकिरणरजतहिमकुमुदकुन्दकुसुमोपमाः सुताः शशिनः ।
उत्तरतो दृश्यन्ते त्रयः सुभिक्षावहाः शिखिनः ॥१४॥

There are three Ketus, born of the Moon, which are white like the rays of the Moon, silver, snow, white lotus or the round jasmine and which appear in the North and are conducive to plenty of food crops.

[Cf. गर्ग—
चन्द्ररश्मिसवर्णाभा हिमकुन्देन्दुसप्रभाः ।
त्रयस्ते शशिनः पुत्राः सौम्याशास्थाः शुभावहाः ॥]

ब्रह्मसुत एक एव त्रिशिखो वर्णैस्त्रिभिर्युगान्तकरः ।
अनियतदिक्सम्प्रभवो विज्ञेयो ब्रह्मदण्डाख्यः ॥१५॥

There is a single Ketu known as Brahmadaṇḍa (Rod of Brahman), born of the creator, and possessed of three colours and three crests. There is no fixed direction for its appearance, but it is dreadful in its effect, in that it forebodes destruction of the entire world.

[Cf. गर्ग—
एको ब्रह्मसुतः क्रूरस्त्रिवर्णस्त्रिशिखान्वितः ।
सर्वास्वाशासु दृश्यः स्याद् ब्रह्मदण्डः क्षयावहः ॥]

शतमभिहितमेकसमेतमेतदेकेन विरहितान्यस्मात् ।
कथयिष्ये केतूनां शतानि नव लक्षणैः स्पष्टैः ॥१६॥

I have thus delineated 101 comets. I shall next describe distinctly the remaining 899 comets with all their characteristics.

सौम्यैशान्योरुदयं शुक्रसुता यान्ति चतुरशीत्याख्याः ।
विपुलसिततारकास्ते स्निग्धाश्च भवन्ति तीव्रफलाः ॥१७॥

There are 84 comets called *Caturaśīti* (meaning 84) that are the children of Venus. They are of the form of large and bright stars as well as glossy in appearance. They appear in the North and North-east and produce very dire consequences.

[According to Garga these comets are called *Visarpaka* that rise in the East, for says he—

स्थूलैकतारकाः श्वेताः स्नेहवन्तश्च सप्रभाः ।
अर्चिष्मन्तः प्रसन्नाश्च तीव्रेण वपुषान्विताः ॥
एते विसर्पका नाम शुक्रपुत्राः पुरोदयाः।
अशीतिश्चतुरश्चैव लोकक्षयकराः स्मृताः ॥]

स्निग्धाः प्रभासमेता द्विशिखाः षष्टिः शनैश्चराङ्गरुहाः ।
अतिकष्टफला दृश्याः सर्वत्रैते कनकसंज्ञाः ॥१८॥

Glossy (clear) and lustrous are the 60 comets, having two crests each, that are the children of Saturn. They are called *Kanaka* (golden), appear in all directions and produce disastrous effects.

[Cf. गर्ग—

सुस्निग्धा रश्मिसंयुक्ता द्विशिखाः सप्ततारकाः ।
षष्टिस्ते कनका घोराः शनैश्चरसुता ग्रहाः ॥]

विकचा नाम गुरुसुताः सितैकताराः शिखापरित्यक्ताः ।
षष्टिः पञ्चभिरधिका स्निग्धा याम्याश्रिताः पापाः ॥१९॥

There are 65 comets named *Vikaca*, having a single white star each, bereft of the crest, which are the children of Jupiter. They are glossy, appear in the south and are dreadful in effect.

[Cf. गर्ग—

शुक्लाः स्निग्धाः प्रसन्नाश्च महारूपाः प्रभान्विताः ।
एकतारा वपुष्मन्तो विशिखा रश्मिभिर्वृताः ॥
एते बृहस्पतेः पुत्राः प्रायशो दक्षिणाश्रयाः ।
नामतो विकचा घोराः पञ्चषष्टिर्भयावहाः ।]

नातिव्यक्ताः सूक्ष्मा दीर्घाः शुक्ला यथेष्टदिक्प्रभवाः ।
बुधजास्तस्करसञ्ज्ञाः पापफलास्त्वेकपञ्चाशत् ॥२०॥

Mercury's children named *Taskara* (Thieves), numbering 51 are faint, slender, long and white. They may appear in any direction and are harmful in effect.

[Cf. गर्ग—

अरुन्धतीसमा रूक्षाः केचिदव्यक्ततारकाः ।
सपाण्डुवर्णाः श्वेताभाः सूक्ष्मा रश्मिभिरावृताः ॥
एते बुधात्मजा ज्ञेयास्तस्कराख्या भयावहाः ।
एकाधिकास्ते पञ्चाशदथोत्पथचरा ग्रहाः ॥]

क्षतजानलानुरूपास्त्रिचूलतारा: कुजात्मजा: षष्टि: ।
नाम्ना च कौङ्कुमास्ते सौम्याशासंस्थिता: पापा: ॥२१॥

The sons of Mars are 60 in number and are called *Kauṅkuma*. They resemble blood and fire, are possessed of three crests as well as three stars each, and appear in the north. They are productive of disastrous effects.

[Cf. गर्ग—

त्रिशिखाश्च त्रिताराश्च रक्ता लोहितरश्मय: ।
प्रायशश्चोत्तरामाशां सेवन्ते नित्यमेव ते ॥
लोहिताङ्गात्मजा ज्ञेया ग्रहा: षष्टि: समासत: ।
नामत: कौङ्कुमा ज्ञेया राज्ञां सङ्ग्रामकारका: ॥]

त्रिशत्त्र्यधिका राहोस्ते तामसकीलका इति ख्याता: ।
रविशशिगा दृश्यन्ते तेषां फलमर्कचारोक्तम् ॥२२॥

There are 33 comets well known as *Tāmasakīlakas* (Dark Shafts) that are the children of Rāhu. They are seen on the discs of the Sun and the Moon. Their effects have been already described in the chapter on the 'Sun's Transit'.

[These Dark shafts might be the prototypes of the modern solar flares and sun-spots. The ancients must have observed these appearing on the solar orb.

Cf. गर्ग—

कृष्णाभा: कृष्णपर्यन्ता: सङ्कुला: कृष्णरश्मय: ।
राहुपुत्रास्त्रयस्त्रिंशत्कीलकाश्चातिदारुणा: ॥
रविमण्डलगाश्चैते दृश्यन्ते चन्द्रगास्तथा ॥

Cf. also पराशर—

अपर्वण्येव दृश्यन्ते ह्यङ्गिर:काककीलका: ।
रवेरेवाङ्गिरा मध्ये ह्युभयो: काककीलकौ ॥
अङ्गिरा: सरथो धन्वी दृश्यते पुरुषाकृति: ।
काक: कालाकृतिर्घोरस्त्रिकोणो वापि लक्ष्यते ॥
मण्डलं कीलके मध्ये मण्डलस्यासितो ग्रह: ।
महानृपविरोधाय यस्यर्क्षे तस्य मृत्यवे ॥

According to sage Parāśara these are three comets named *Aṅgiras*, *Kāka* and *Kīlaka*, of which the first appears only on the solar orb, while the other two on both the orbs. The first appears like a human being armed with a bow and seated in a chariot. *Kāka*, which is black (like Yama) and triangular in form, is of dreadful effects. *Kīlaka*, which is black and circular in form, brings about hostilities among mighty kings and death of those whose natal star is occupied by the luminary at the time. See also III, 7-10 *supra*.]

विंशत्याधिकमन्यच्छतमग्नेर्विश्वरूपसंज्ञानाम् ।
तीव्रानलभयदानां ज्वालामालाकुलतनूनाम् ॥२३॥

There is another group of 120 comets known as *Viśvarūpa*, born of Agni (Fire). Their forms are filled with rows of flames. They produce terrible fire-disasters.

[Cf. गर्ग quoted under verse 11 *supra*, and instead of the 4th. line have the following :

विंशं ग्रहशतं घोरं विश्वरूपेति नामतः ॥

From the different numbers of the two sets of comets born of Agni it is clear that they are not identical. The former set has no specific name, while the latter is called Viśvarūpa.]

श्यामारुणा वितारश्चामररूपा विकीर्णदीधितयः ।
अरुणाख्या वायोः सप्तसप्ततिः पापदाः परुषाः ॥२४॥

There are 77 comets, called Aruṇa, born of the Wind, which are dark-red in colour, rough, without any starry form, but looking like the chowries and possessed of scattered rays. They produce disastrous consequences.

[Cf. **गर्ग**—

अतारररूपप्रतिमा धूमरक्तसवर्णिनः ।
वातरूपा इवाभान्ति शुष्कविस्तीर्णरश्मयः ॥
सप्ततिः सप्त चैवान्ये वायुपुत्रान्प्रचक्षते ।
लोकविध्वंसना रूक्षा नामतस्त्वरुणा ग्रहाः ॥]

तारापुञ्जनिकाशा गणका नाम प्रजापतेरष्टौ ।
द्वे च शते चतुरधिके चतुरस्रा ब्रह्मसन्तानाः ॥२५॥

There are 8 comets known as *Gaṇaka*, sons of Prajāpati, that look like a cluster of stars. There are 204 comets named *Caturasra* (Square), born of Brahman. All these produce only untoward results.

[The commentator tells us that wherever no direction of comets is mentioned it should be understood that they may appear in any direction.

Cf. गर्ग—

तारापुञ्जप्रतीकाशास्तारामण्डलसंस्थिता: ।
प्राजापत्या ग्रहास्त्वष्टौ गणका भयवेदिनः ॥
त्र्यस्रा वा चतुरस्रा वा सशिखाः श्वेतरश्मयः ।
द्वे शते चतुरश्चैव ब्रह्मजा भयदाश्च ते ॥]

कङ्का नाम वरुणजा द्वात्रिंशद्वंशगुल्मसंस्थानाः ।
शशिवत्प्रभासमेतास्तीव्रफलाः केतवः प्रोक्ताः ॥२६॥

Kaṅka is the name of the 32 comets born of Varuṇa, having the appearance of a clump of bamboos, and being possessed of moon-like lustre. They produce dire consequences.

[Cf. गर्ग—

वंशगुल्मप्रतीकाशा महान्तः पूर्णरश्मयः ।
काकतुण्डनिभैश्चापि रश्मिभिः केचिदावृताः ॥
मयूखानुत्सृजन्तीव सुस्निग्धाः सौम्यदर्शनाः ।
एते कष्टफलाः प्रोक्ता द्वात्रिंशद्वारुणा ग्रहाः ॥]

षण्णवतिः कालसुताः कबन्धसञ्ज्ञाः कबन्धसंस्थानाः ।
पुण्ड्राभयप्रदाः स्युर्विरूपताराश्च ते शिखिनः ॥२७॥

The sons of Kāla, numbering 96, are called Kabandhas and have the form of a truncated human body. They have no distinct starry bodies and prove beneficial only to the Puṇḍras.

[Cf. गर्ग—

तारापुञ्जविरूपाश्च कबन्धाकृतिसंस्थिताः ।
पीतारुणसवर्णाश्च भस्मकर्पूररश्मयः ॥
कालपुत्राः कबन्धाश्च नवतिः षट् च ते स्मृताः ।
लोके मृत्युकरा घोराः पुण्ड्राणामभयप्रदाः ॥]

शुक्लविपुलैकतारा नव विदिशां केतवः समुत्पन्नाः ।
एवं केतुसहस्रं विशेषमेषामतो वक्ष्ये ॥२८॥

There are 9 comets born of the intermediate quarters, having a single, broad and white star. Thus have I described the 1000 comets. I shall now mention their special characteristics.

[These 9 comets are visible only in the intermediate directions and produce only evil effects.

Cf. गर्ग—

शुक्लैकतारा विपुला विदिक्पुत्रा नव ग्रहाः ।
विदिक्षु संस्थितास्ते च दृश्यन्ते भयदायकाः ॥

In this connection the commentator remarks that only a few of these thousand Ketus become visible to human eyes. Hence the author gives below the peculiarities of these visible ones.]

उदगायतो महान् स्निग्धमूर्तिरपरोदयी वसाकेतुः ।
सद्यः करोति मरकं सुभिक्षमप्युत्तमं कुरुते ॥२९॥

There is a big comet named Vasāketu which has an elongated glossy body stretched towards the north. It rises in the west. Its appearance coincides with dreadful mortality, but it leads to very good growth of food crops in the land.

तल्लक्षणोऽस्थिकेतुः स तु रूक्षः क्षुद्भयावहः प्रोक्तः ।
स्निग्धस्तादृक् प्राच्यां शस्त्राख्यो डमरमरकाय ॥३०॥

There is one named Asthiketu, endowed with all the characteristics of Vasāketu, but is rough and capable of causing famine. There is another Ketu named Śastra, which is similar to the previous one, but glossy and rising in the east. It leads to war and pestilence.

[*Parā ara* gives some more details about these comets : "एते षड्विंशतिरुदयैः फलमावेदयन्ति । तान् नामतो रूपतः फलतः कालतोऽभिधास्यामः । तत्र भार्गवास्त्रय उदयं यान्ति । एकैकशो वसास्थिशस्त्रकेतवः । तत्र वसाकेतुः स्निग्धो महानुदगायतशिखस्त्रिशद्वर्षशतं प्रोष्य सम्प्लवे युगे पश्चिमोदितः सद्यो मरकफलः सौभिक्षकरस्तु । रूक्षोऽस्थिकेतुरसौ भिक्षुकतुल्यप्रवासकालफलः । पूर्वेण स्निग्ध एव न शस्त्रकेतुः । राजविरोधमरकफलः समो रूक्षः" ।]

दृश्योऽमावास्यायां कपालकेतुः सधूम्ररश्मिशिखः ।
प्राङ्नभसोऽर्द्धविचारी क्षुन्मरकावृष्टिरोगकरः ॥३१॥

There is a comet named Kapālaketu, which is visible during the Am ivāsyā—new moon—in the east. Its rays and crest are of smoky colour and it traverses half the heavens. It produces famine, pestilence, drought and diseases.

[Cf. पराशर—

अथादित्यजानां कपालकेतुरुदयतेऽमावास्यायां पूर्वस्यां दिशि सधूम्रार्चिशिखो नभसोऽर्द्धचरो दृश्यते । पञ्चविंशवर्षशतं प्रोष्य त्रींश्च पक्षानमृतजस्य कुमुदकेतोश्चारान्ते स दृष्ट एव दुर्भिक्षानावृष्टिव्याधिभयमरणोपद्रवान् सृजति । जगति यावतो

दिवसान् दृश्यते तावन्मासान् मासैर्वत्सरान्पञ्चप्रस्थं च शारदधान्यार्घं कृत्वा प्रजानामुपयुङ्क्ते ।। From these statements of the Sage we come to know that Vasāketu, Asthiketu and Śastraketu are included among the sons of Śukra (Venus). The first of these makes its appearance once in every 3,000 years. Kapālaketu is one of the children of the Sun. It appears once in every 2500 years.]

प्राग्वैश्वानरमार्गे शूलाग्रः श्यावरूक्षताम्रार्चिः ।
नभसस्त्रिभागगामी रौद्र इति कपालतुल्यफलः ।।३२।।

Raudra is another comet, rising in the east, whose effects are similar to those of Kapālaketu. It traverses in the Ḍahanavīthi (IX-1,3). Its crest is in the form of a trident, and its flame grey, rough and red. It traverses a third of the sky.

[Cf. वृद्धगर्ग—

ज्येष्ठामूलमनुराधा या वीथी सम्प्रकीर्तिता ।
तां च वीथीं समारुह्य केतुश्चेत्क्रीडते भृशम् ।।
दक्षिणाभिनतां कृत्वा शिखां घोरां भयङ्करीम् ।
शूलाग्रसदृशीं तीक्ष्णां श्यावताम्रारुणप्रभाम् ।।
पूर्वेण चोदितश्चैष नक्षत्राण्युपधूमयेत् ।
घोरं प्रजासु सृजति फलं मासे त्रयोदशे ।।
त्रिभागं नभसो मत्वा ततो गच्छत्यदर्शनम् ।
यावतो दिवसांस्तिष्ठेत्तावद्वर्षाणि तद्भयम् ।।
शस्त्राग्निभयरोगैश्च दुर्भिक्षमरणैर्हताः ।
पूर्यमाणाः प्रजाः सर्वा विद्रवन्ति दिशो दश ।।

Cf also पराशर—

अथ दक्षयज्ञरुद्रक्रोधोद्भवः कलिकेतुस्त्रीणि वर्षशतानि नव च मासान् प्रोष्योदयते पूर्वेण वैश्वानरमार्गे ह्यमृतजस्य मणिकेतोश्चारान्ते श्यावरूक्षताम्रारुणां शूलाकारसदृशीं शिखां कृत्वा नभसस्त्रिभागचारी स शस्त्रभयरोगदुर्भिक्षानावृष्टिमरकैर्यावन्मासान् दृश्यते तावद्वर्षाणि त्रिभागशेषां प्रजां कृत्वार्घं च शारदधान्यमाढकमस्तं व्रजति ।।]

अपरस्यां चलकेतुः शिखया याम्याग्रयाङ्गुलोच्छ्रितया ।
गच्छेद्यथा यथोदक् तथा तथा दैर्घ्यमायाति ।।३३।।
सप्तमुनीन्संस्पृश्य ध्रुवमभिजितमेव च प्रतिनिवृत्तः ।
नभसोऽर्द्धमात्रमित्वा याम्येनास्तं समुपयाति ।।३४।।
हन्यात्प्रयागकूलाद्यावदवन्तीं च पुष्करारण्यम ।
उदगपि च देविकामपि भूयिष्ठं मध्यदेशाख्यम् ।।३५।।

अन्यानपि च स देशान् क्वचित्क्वचिद्धन्ति रोगदुर्भिक्षैः ।
दश मासान्फलपाकोऽस्य कैश्चिदष्टादश प्रोक्तः ॥३६॥

There is another Ketu named *Calaketu*, which appears in the western direction, and is possessed of a crest, raised a digit high, with its tip turned towards the south. As it moves towards north its length increases. It touches the Seven Sages i.e. towards the Great Bear, as well the Pole Star and the star Abhijit, and turns back after travelling only half the length of the sky and then sets in the south. When this comet makes its appearance, people in the area lying between the banks of the Prayāga (near Allahabad) and the town of Avantī as well as the forest of Puṣkara will be destroyed. In the northern region too people will come to grief as far as the Devikā river; and those who live in the Madhyadeśa (Middle Country) will be killed in large numbers. In other countries too people will perish here and there as a result of diseases and famine. These effects will be felt for ten months. According to others they will be experienced for 18 months. In all cases the period is to be counted after three fortnights of the appearance of a comet.

[Cf. गर्ग—

क्षुच्छस्त्रमरकव्याधिभयैः सम्पीडयेत् प्रजाः ।
मासान्दश तथाष्टौ च चलकेतुः सुदारुणः ॥

also पराशर—

अथ पैतामहश्चलकेतुः पञ्चदशवर्षशतं प्रोष्योदितः पश्चिमेनाङ्गुलिपर्वमात्रां शिखां दक्षिणाभिगतां कृत्वा जलकेतोश्चारान्ते नभसस्त्रिभागमनुचरन् यथा यथा चोत्तरेण व्रजति तथा तथा शूलाग्राकारां शिखां दर्शयन् ब्रह्मनक्षत्रमुपसृत्य मनाग् ध्रुवं ब्रह्मराशिं सप्तर्षीन् स्पृशन् नभसोऽर्द्धमात्रं दक्षिणमनुक्रम्यास्तं व्रजति । स स्वर्गे दारुणकर्मा । स्वर्गप्राप्तत्वादेव च कृत्स्नमभिहिनस्ति लोकम् । अपि च भूमिं कम्पयित्वा दश मासान्मध्यदेशे भूयिष्ठं जनपदमनवशेषं कुरुते । तेष्वपि क्वचित्क्वचिच्छस्त्रदुर्भिक्षव्याधिमरकभयैः क्लिश्नात्यष्टादश मासानिति ॥]

प्रागर्द्धरात्रदृश्यो याम्याग्रः श्वेतकेतुरन्यश्च ।
क इति युगाकृतिरपरे युगपत्तौ सप्तदिनदृश्यौ ॥३७॥

स्निग्धौ सुभिक्षशिवदावथाधिकं दृश्यते क नामा यः ।
दश वर्षाण्युपतापं जनयति शस्त्रप्रकोपकृतम् ॥३८॥

There is another comet named *Śvetaketu*, whose crest is turned to the south, and which rises in the east at midnight. There is yet another comet named *Ka* in the form of a yoke, which rises in the west. Both these can be seen at the same time for a period of seven days. They are glossy i. e. very bright, and lead to prosperity and happiness, if sighted. Should, however, the comet *Ka* be visible for more than seven days, there would be great disaster caused by wars for ten years.

[Cf. पराशर—

अथौद्दालकः श्वेतकेतुर्दशोत्तरं वर्षशतं प्रोष्य भटकेतोश्चारान्ते पूर्वस्यां दिशि दक्षिणाभिनतशिखोऽर्द्धकाले दृश्यः । तेनैव सह द्वितीयः कः प्रजापतिपुत्रः पश्चिमेन ग्रहकेतोर्यूपसंस्थायी युगपद् दृश्यते । तावुभौ सप्तरात्रदृश्यौ दशवर्षाणि प्रजाः पीडयन्ते (पीडयतः) । कः प्रजापतिपुत्रो यद्यधिकं दृश्यते तदा दारुणतरं प्रजानां शस्त्रकोपं कुर्यात्तथैव स्नेहवर्णयुक्तौ क्षेमारोग्यसुभिक्षदौ भवतः ॥]

श्वेत इति जटाकारो रूक्षः श्यावो वियत्त्रिभागगतः ।
विनिवर्ततेऽपसव्यं त्रिभागशेषाः प्रजाः कुरुते ॥३९॥

The comet called *Śveta* is rough, black and of the form of matted locks. After traversing a third of the sky it turns back in the sinistral way. It destroys two-thirds of the population.

[There should not be any confusion between the two comets, Śvetaketu and Śveta. According to Parāśara the former is the son of Sage Uddālaka and the latter of Sage Kaśyapa.

Cf. पराशर—

अथ काश्यपः श्वेतकेतुः पञ्चदशवर्षशतं प्रोष्यैन्द्रांशः सहजस्य पद्मकेतोश्चारान्ते श्यावरूक्षो नभसस्त्रिभागमाक्रम्यापसव्यं निवृत्योर्ध्वं प्रदक्षिणजटाकारशिखः । स यावन्मासान् दृश्यते तावद्वर्षाणि सुभिक्षमावहति । मध्यदेश आर्यगणानामौदीच्यैश्च भूयिष्ठं बहुशस्त्रिभागशेषां प्रजामवशेषयति ॥]

आरूक्षया तु शिखया दर्शनमायाति कृत्तिकासंस्थः ।
ज्ञेयः स रश्मिकेतुः श्वेतसमानं फलं धत्ते ॥४०॥

There is another comet named *Raśmiketu* which appears near the constellation Kṛttikā with an ash-coloured crest. It produces effects similar to those of the comet Śveta.

[Cf. पराशर—

अथ रश्मिकेतुर्विभावसुजः प्रोष्य वर्षशतमावर्तकेतोश्चारान्ते उदितः कृत्तिकासु धूम्रशिखः श्वेतकेतोः सदृशफलः ॥]

ध्रुवकेतुरनियतगतिप्रमाणवर्णाकृतिर्भवति विष्वक् ।
दिव्यान्तरिक्षभौमो भवत्ययं स्निग्ध इष्टफलः ॥४१॥

सेनाङ्गेषु नृपाणां गृहतरुशैलेषु चापि देशानाम् ।
गृहिणामुपस्करेषु च विनाशिनां दर्शनं याति ॥४२॥

There is another comet known as *Dhruvaketu*, whose movements, dimensions, colour and shape are not regular (i.e. indefinite). It travels in all directions and may be seen in the upper regions of the sky, in the intermediate space or on the earth. It gives good effects, if it is clear and soft. If it be seen on the military equipments of kings, on houses, trees or mountains of countries, and on the house-hold articles such as vessels, ladles and winnowing baskets of house-holders, the concerned persons would meet with their end.

[The second verse should be taken as giving an exception to the rule given in the first viz. स्निग्ध इष्टफलः. Alberuni wrongly translates the word उपस्करेषु.

Cf. पराशर—

अथानियतदिक्कालरूपवर्णप्रमाणसंस्थानो ध्रुवकेतुः पराभवमिष्यतां देशानां राज्ञां जनपदानां च वृक्षपुरपर्वतवेश्मध्वजपताकाशस्त्रवर्मायुधावरणरथनागोष्ट्रपुरुषशयनासनभाण्डेषु वा दृश्यते । स एव च स्निग्धो विमलः प्रदक्षिणशिखो गोगजाजनागवीथीश्चोत्तरेण व्रजन् सुभिक्षं क्षेमारोग्यं चावहति । दशैकविंशतिद्वि (त्रि) षष्टिशतधा वा दर्शनमिच्छन्ति मुनयो ध्रुवकेतोः । तस्य प्रागुदयनिमित्तानि—अवनिचलनम् । अग्नेः प्रभामान्द्यम् । प्रधूपनं दिशाम् । शीतोष्णविपर्ययः । अतिरूक्षवायुसम्भवश्च ॥

कुमुद इति कुमुदकान्तिर्वारुण्यां प्राक्शिखो निशामेकाम् ।
दृष्टः सुभिक्षमतुलं दश किल वर्षाणि स करोति ॥४३॥

The comet named *Kumuda* of white lustre, with its crest turned to the east becomes visible for a single night in the west. It is said that it will produce unique peace and plenty in the countries it is sighted for a period of ten years to come.

[Cf. पराशर—

अथामृतजः कुमुदो मणिः । जलोद्भवः पद्मः । आवर्तः । ऊर्मिः । शङ्खः । हिमः । रक्तः । कुक्षिः । कामः । विसर्पणः । शीतश्चेति । तत्र कुमुदकेतुर्वसाकेतोश्चारसमाप्तौ वारुण्यां दर्शनमुपैति गोक्षीरविमलस्निग्धप्रभां पूर्वेणाभिनतां शिखां कृत्वैकरात्रचरः । स दृष्ट एव सुभिक्षमुत्पादयति । दशवर्षाणि प्रजानामविरोधं च । प्रतीच्यानां च मुखरोगारोचकप्रतिश्यायपाण्डुरोगजननैः प्रजा बाधत इति ॥]

सकृदेकयामदृश्यः सुसूक्ष्मतारोऽपरेण मणिकेतुः ।
ऋज्वी शिखास्य शुक्ला स्तनोद्गता क्षीरधारेव ॥४४॥

उदयन्नेव सुभिक्षं चतुरो मासान् करोत्यसौ सार्द्धान् ।
प्रादुर्भावं प्रायः करोति च क्षुद्रजन्तूनाम् ॥४५॥

The comet named *Maṇiketu* is in the form of a tiny little star, rising in the west and visible only once for a period of only three hours. Its crest is straight and white like a streak of milk ejected from the breast. Even as it appears, it causes abundant food for $4\frac{1}{2}$ months; but it also helps the abnormal appearance of harmful creatures such as reptiles, venomous creatures and the like.

[Cf. पराशर—

मणिकेतुरपि कपालकेतोश्चारावसाने प्रतीच्यामुदयमुपयाति । सूक्ष्मोऽरुन्धतीतारकामात्रः क्षीरप्रसेककान्त्या पूर्वाभिनतया स्निग्धशिखया शर्वर्यमिकयामदृश्यः । स उदयात्प्रभृत्यर्द्धपञ्चमान् मासान् क्षेमसुभिक्षमुत्पादयति । क्षुद्रजन्तूनां प्रादुर्भावं करोत्यतिमात्रकालदृष्टः ॥

According to this Sage the enormous growth of lower creatures i.e. pests, is conditional on the comet appearing for a greater length of time.]

जलकेतुरपि च पश्चात्स्निग्धः शिखयापरेण चोन्नतया ।
नव मासान् स सुभिक्षं करोति शान्तिं च लोकस्य ॥४६॥

There is another comet called *Jalaketu*, which is spotless in form, and is possessed of a crest raised towards the west. It rises also in the west. It causes good crops as well as peace among people for nine months.

[Cf. पराशर—

अथ जलकेतुः पैतामहजस्य चलकेतोर्नवमासावशिष्टे कर्मणि कृतं प्रवर्तयति । पश्चिमेनोदितः स्निग्धः सुजातोऽनुपश्चिमाभिनतशिखः । स च नव मासान् क्षेमसुभिक्षारोग्याणि प्रजाभ्यो धत्ते । अन्यग्रहकृतानां चाशुभानां व्याघातायेति ॥]

भवकेतुरेकरात्रं दृश्यः प्राक् सूक्ष्मतारकः स्निग्धः ।
हरिलाङ्गूलोपमया प्रदक्षिणावर्त्तया शिखया ॥४७॥

यावत एव मुहूर्तान् दर्शनमायाति निर्दिशेन्मासान् ।
तावदतुलं सुभिक्षं रूक्षे प्राणान्तिकान् रोगान् ॥४८॥

Bhavaketu which is a glossy i.e. bright, little star, is visible in the east only for one night. It has a crest resembling the lion's tail and curling to the right. It causes unique abundance of food crops for as many months as the number of Muhūrtas (a muhūrta=48 minutes) it remains visible. Should, however, it be rough, it would cause fatal diseases to mankind.

[Cf. पराशर—

अथ जलकेतोः कर्मसमाप्तावूर्म्यादयः शीतान्ता अष्टौ प्रादुर्भवन्ति । ते त्रयोदशचतुर्दशाष्टादशवर्षान्तरिता दृश्यन्ते । स्निग्धाः सुभिक्षक्षेम्या विपर्यया विपरीताः । क्षुद्रजन्तूनां वधाय । तेषामष्टानां कर्मण्यतीते भवकेतुर्दृश्यते पूर्वेणैकरात्रम् । या कृत्तिकानामग्रतमा तारा तत्प्रमाणया स्निग्धयाऽरूक्षाभया सिंहलाङ्गूलसंस्थानया प्रदक्षिणनताग्रया शिखयोदितः । स यावन्मुहूर्तान्दृश्यते तावन्मासान् भवत्यतीव सुभिक्षाय । रूक्षः प्राणहराणां रोगाणां प्रादुर्भावायेति ॥]

अपरेण पद्मकेतुर्मृणालगौरो भवेन्निशामेकाम् ।
सप्त करोति सुभिक्षं वर्षाण्यतिहर्षयुक्तानि ॥४९॥

Another comet named *Padmaketu* which is as white as the fibre of the lotus stalk, rises in the west and is visible for one night. Its appearance heralds abundance of food as well as happiness for seven years without interruption.

[Cf. पराशर—

अथ पद्मकेतुः श्वेतकेतुफलसमाप्तौ पश्चिमेनाह्लादयन्निव मृणालकुमुदाभया शिखयैकरात्रचरः । सप्त वर्षाण्यभ्युच्छ्रितं हर्षमावहति जगतः ॥]

आवर्त इति निशार्द्धे सव्यशिखोऽरुणनिभोऽपरे स्निग्धः ।
यावत्क्षणान् स दृश्यस्तावन्मासान् सुभिक्षकरः ॥५०॥

The comet named *Āvarta* appearing at midnight in the west is glossy and ruddy in colour and possessed of a crest turned to the right or south. It will bring about peace and plenty for mankind for so many months as the number of Muhūrtas it remains visible.

[Cf. पराशर—

अथावर्तकेतुः श्वेतकेतोः कर्मण्यतीतेऽपरस्यामर्द्धरात्रे शङ्खावदातोऽरुणाभया प्रदक्षिणनताग्रया शिखयोदितः । स यावन्मुहूर्त्तान् दृश्यते तावन्मासान् भवत्यतीव सुभिक्षं नित्ययज्ञोत्सवं जगत् ॥]

पश्चात्सन्ध्याकाले संवर्तो नाम धूम्रताम्रशिखः ।
आक्रम्य वियत्त्र्यंशं शूलाग्रावस्थितो रौद्रः ॥५१॥

यावत एव मुहूर्त्तान् दृश्यो वर्षाणि हन्ति तावन्ति ।
भूपाञ्शस्त्रनिपातैरुदयर्क्षं चापि पीडयति ॥५२॥

The comet named *Saṁvarta* with its crest smoky and coppery in colour, appears in the west at sunset. It occupies a third of the sky and looks as though situated on the points of a trident. It is dreadful in effect, as it afflicts kings with wars and strifes for so many years as the number of Muhūrtas it remains visible, and creates trouble for those persons in whose natal star the comet appears.

[Here the author gives a general principle of mundane astrology but also one of horoscopy. For, a malefic comet, like an eclipse, rising in a person's natal asterism augurs ill for him.

Cf. गर्ग—

येषां नक्षत्रविषये रूक्षः सज्वाललोहितः ।
दृश्यते बहुमूर्तिश्च तेषां विन्द्यान्महाभयम् ॥
अवर्षं शस्त्रकोपं च व्याधिं दुर्भिक्षमेव च ।
कुर्यान्नृपतिपीडाश्च स्वचक्रपरचक्रतः ॥
यत्रोत्तिष्ठति नक्षत्रे प्रवासं यत्र गच्छति ।
धूपयेद्वा स्पृशेद्वापि हन्याद्देशांस्तदाश्रितान् ॥
यस्याभिषेकनक्षत्रं जन्मभं कर्मभं तथा ।
देशर्क्षं पीडयेद्वापि स शान्त्युपरमो भवेत् ॥
स्निग्धः प्रसन्नो विमलः प्रदक्षिणशिखस्तथा ।
दृश्यते येषु देशेषु शिवं तेषु विनिर्दिशेत् ॥
गगनार्द्धचरः सद्यः प्रधानदेशान्विनाशयेदचिरात् ।
निखिलगगनानुचारी त्रैलोक्यविनाशकः केतुः ॥

(The last verse in the Āryā metre does not appear to be Garga's).

Cf. also पराशर—

अथ संवर्तो वर्षसहस्रमष्टोत्तरं प्रोष्य पश्चिमेनास्तं गते सवितरि सन्ध्यायां दृश्यते तन्वीं ताम्ररूक्षां शूलाभां धूम्रं विमुञ्चन्तीं दारुणां शिखां कृत्वा नभसस्त्रिभागमाक्रम्य । स यावन्मुहूर्तान् निशि तिष्ठति तावद्वर्षाणि परस्परं शस्त्रैर्घ्नन्ति पार्थिवाः । यानि नक्षत्राणि धूपयति यत्र चोदेति तानि दारुणतरं पीडयति । तदाश्रितांश्च देशानिति ॥

In the following verses the author states the evil effects of certain asterisms being afflicted by the malignant comets.]

ये शस्तास्तान् हित्वा केतुभिराधूपितेऽथवा स्पृष्टे ।
नक्षत्रे भवति वधो येषां राज्ञां प्रवक्ष्ये तान् ॥५३॥

I shall now explain the fatal consequences of the asterisms of kings being eclipsed by the tails of comets or touched by them, except by the beneficent ones.

[We have seen in the preceding verses that some comets like *kumuda*, *Maṇiketu*, *Jalaketu*, *Bhavaketu*, if glossy, *Padmaketu* and *Āvarta* are auspicious and augur peace and plenty in the land. However, the rest produce different untoward effects. The comets especially the evil ones, are seen emitting smoke from their tails. If a person's natal star is thus tarnished by this smoke, he will have hard times ahead. Similarly kings and countries that are assigned to such asterisms, will have different unpleasant experiences.]

अश्विन्यामश्मकपं भरणीषु किरातपार्थिवं हन्यात् ।
बहुलासु कलिङ्गेशं रोहिण्यां शूरसेनपतिम् ॥५४॥

When the star Aśvinī be affected by a comet by its touch or smoke, it would destroy the king of the Aśmakas; if it be the star Bharaṇī, the king of the *Kirātas* would meet with his end; if it be Kṛttikā, the Kaliṅga ruler would come to grief; and if it be Rohiṇī, the chief of the Śūrasenas would suffer.

[The *Aśmaka* country is differently identified by different scholars. Our author refers to this several times. It lies in the north-western part of India. During Alexander's time the Aśmaka territory "comprised part of Swat and Buner and extended eastwards as far as the Indus and had its capital at the town of Maśakāvatī." The Kirātas were a people in the south-west and north-east divisions of India. They are mentioned in the *Periplus* and by Ptolemy. The Śūrasenas were a people living near Mathurā.]

औशीनरमपि सौम्ये जलजाजीवाधिपं तथार्द्रासु ।
आदित्येऽश्मकनाथान् पुष्ये मगधाधिपं हन्ति ॥५५॥

When the asterism Mṛgaśiras is afflicted by an evil comet (by smoke or touch), the king of the Uśīnaras will fare ill; when the affected star is Ārdrā, the chief of fishermen will suffer; when it is Punarvasu, the rulers of the Aśmaka people will come to grief, and when the asterism thus affected is Puṣya, the king of Magadha will get into trouble.

[The Uśīnaras are supposed to have lived to the north of the Kurus, possibly between the Chenab and the Ravi. Bhaṭṭotpala interprets the word जलजाजीव as ग्रामदेशवासिन: i.e. rural people; but the author means only those who live by catching and selling fish, oysters, shells and the like.]

असिकेशं मौजङ्गे पित्र्येऽङ्गं पाण्ड्यनाथमपि भाग्ये ।
औज्जयिनिकमार्यम्णे सावित्रे दण्डकाधिपतिम् ॥५६॥

If the affected asterism be Āśleṣā, the chief of the Asikas would be destroyed; if it be Maghā, the ruler of Aṅga would meet with his end; if it be Pūrvaphalgunī, the Pāṇḍya king would quit the world; if it be Uttaraphalgunī, the governor of Ujjain would be afflicted; and if it be Hasta, the lord of the Daṇḍaka forest would be destroyed.

[The state of Aṅga is very ancient being mentioned in the *Atharvaveda* (V-22.14), the *Aitareya Brāhmaṇa* (VIII-22). During the time of the Buddha its capital was Campā. This country is mentioned in the Rāmāyaṇa also (I.23). Regarding Asikadeśa many theories are held : Some read Mūṣikanagara in its stead. So some locate it to the west of Kaliṅga. Others take it as Ṛṣika. Even this is not accepted by scholars owing to geographical anomalies.]

चित्रासु कुरुक्षेत्राधिपस्य मरणं समादिशेत्तज्ज्ञः ।
काश्मीरककाम्बोजौ नृपती प्राभञ्जने न स्तः ॥५७॥

If the affected asterism be Citrā, a wise astrologer should predict the death of the ruler of Kurukṣetra; and if it be Svātī, the kings of Kāśmīra and Kāmboja would quit the world.

[Kāmboja is an ancient place mentioned by Yāska (I.2.1.4) and Kālidāsa (Raghu. IV). From the latter's reference it is clear that it is situated near the Himalayas. The areas of Pamir and Badakshan are supposed to represent the ancient Kāmboja country.]

इक्ष्वाकुरलकनाथश्च हन्यते यदि भवेद्विशाखासु ।
मैत्रे पुण्ड्राधिपतिर्ज्येष्ठासु च सार्वभौमवधः ॥५८॥

If the afflicted asterism be Viśākhā, the chiefs of the Ikṣvākus and of the city of Alakā would be killed; if it be Anurādhā, the chief of the Puṇḍras would be exterminated; and if it be Jyeṣṭhā, an emperor would meet with his end.

[The commentator construes the word सार्वभौमवधः as कान्यकुब्जाधिपतेर्मरणम्. Does it mean that Kānyakubja was the capital of an empire during the time of our commentator? Our author refers to Puṇḍra frequently. It corresponds to North Bengal with Puṇḍranagara as its capital.]

मूलेऽन्ध्रमद्रकपती जलदेवे काशिपो मरणमेति ।
यौधेयकार्जुनायनशिबिचैद्यान् वैश्वदेवे च ॥५९॥

If the affected asterism be Mūla, the kings of Āndhra and Madraka (Madra) countries would come to grief; if it be Pūrvāṣāḍhā, the king of Kāśī would die; and if it be Uttarāṣāḍhā, rulers of the Yaudheyas, Arjunāyanas, Śibis and Cedi would be killed.

[*Madra* is the name of a people and their country. This name was famous both in the Brāhmaṇa period and in the period of the Mahābhārata. Mādrī, the younger queen of Pāṇḍu, was the daughter of the king of Madradeśa. It is in the north-west of India. In the Mahābhārata it is spoken of as a part of the Vāhīka country. It covered the territory between the Ravi and the Jhelum. The *Arjunāyanas* are also an ancient people descended from the Pāṇḍava prince Arjuna. Some trace their origin to Kārtavīryārjuna. These are to be assigned to the northern division. This name occurs in the Gaṇa of Pāṇini IV. 2.53. Historians opine that the country of the Arjunāyanas lay within the triangle of Delhi-Jaipur-Agra. The Śibis are also a very ancient people. Some claim their identity with the *Śivas* of the Ṛgveda (VII. 18.7). Our author includes the Śibi country among the Southern states (XIV-12). According to the Jātakas there were two Śibi settlements, one with its capital at Ariṣṭapura and the other at Jetuttara. These differing accounts only prove that the Śibis were constantly changing their settlements. The Cedi is an ancient country, whose king was Śiśupāla of the Mahābhārata fame. The modern Baghelkhand and adjoining regions roughly comprised the ancient Cedi country.]

हन्यात्कैकयनाथं पाञ्चनदं सिंहलाधिपं वाङ्गम् ।
नैमिषनृपं किरातं श्रवणादिषु षट्स्विमान् क्रमशः ॥६०॥

If the afflicted asterisms be Śravaṇa, Dhaniṣṭhā, Śatabhiṣaj, Pūrvabhādrapadā, Uttarabhādrapadā and Revati, rulers of Kekaya, the land of the five rivers, Siṁhala, Bengal, the Naimiṣa forest and Kirātas respectively would be killed.

[The *Kekaya* country lies in the northern division. This name is immortalized in the Rāmāyaṇa because of Daśaratha's third queen. Its capital was Girivraja. The country comprised the districts of Jhelum, Shahpur and Gujarat. The country of the five rivers is the Panjāb in the western division. Siṁhala is the well-known island of Ceylon. The Naimiṣāraṇya occupies a hallowed place in the pages of the Mahābhārata and Purāṇas. It is near the Nimsar Railway Station situated to the north-west of Lucknow on the left bank of the Gumti. The *Kirātas*, according to our author (XIV. 18-30) belong to the south-west and north-east divisions. According to Kālidāsa (Raghu. IV. 76) they lived in the Brahmaputra valley. Their descendants are still found in the Morung, west of Sikkim.]

उल्काभिताडितशिखः शिखी शिवः शिवतरोऽतिवृष्टो यः ।
अशुभः स एव चोलावगाणसितहूणचीनानाम् ॥६१॥

A comet whose crest has been struck by a meteor will prove beneficial. It would be all the more auspicious and beneficent, should its rising be followed immediately by heavy rains. However, it would be unfavourable to the people of Cola, the Afghans, the white Huns and the Chinese.

[Albiruni has misread the word शिवतरो as शिवतरोः meaning Śiva's tree. अतिदृष्ट instead of अतिवृष्ट is the reading adopted by Utpala. He interprets it as 'उदितमात्र एव दृष्टः' seen as soon it has risen. He takes सित-as a distinct people. But our author takes सित-as only an adjective as he says elsewhere (XVI. 37) श्वेतहूण.]

नम्रा यतः शिखिशिखाभिसृता यतो वा
ऋक्षं च यत् स्पृशति तत्कथितांश्च देशान् ।
दिव्यप्रभावनिहतान् स यथा गरुत्मान्
भुङ्क्ते गतो नरपतिः परभोगिभोगान् ॥६२॥

Note the direction in which a comet's crest is bent or curved as well as to which it is projected and the asterism that is touched by it. All the countries situated in those quarters as well as those coming under the particular asterism in question will be overrun by a mighty monarch of matchless valour, and the territories, enjoyed previously by other kings, brought under control, even as Garuḍa (the Vāhana—vehicle of Lord Viṣṇu) kills by his super-human prowess the great (or inimical) serpents, and eats their bodies.

[A beautiful simile involving Śleṣa—pun is employed in this verse couched in the वसन्ततिलका metre. The Countries etc. that are affected are mentioned in Chapters XIV and XV *infra*.

Cf. पराशर—

यस्यां दिशि समुत्तिष्ठेत्तां दिशं नाभियोजयेत् ।
यतः शिखा यतो धूमस्ततो यायान्नराधिपः ॥
प्रतिलोमे यतः केतोर्जयार्थी याति पार्थिवः ।
सामान्यवाहनबलः स नाशमधिगच्छति ॥
दृष्ट्वा षोडश वासरान्न शुभदः कैश्चित्प्रदिष्टः शिखी
सर्वारम्भफलप्रदो हि नियतं चैत्रेऽथवा माधवे ।
ऋक्षं यत्परिभुक्तपीडितहतं यच्चाऽऽशिखाभेदितं
तत्सर्वं परिवर्ज्यं शुद्धमपरं पाणिग्रहे वास्तुषु ॥

The last verse is patently an interpolation by a scholar interested in electional astrology,

Another interpolated passage speaks of 105 Ketus, of which 10 are Varuṇa's children, 24 of the Sun, 18 of Kubera, 9 of Yama, 24 of Fire and 20 of Wind. When a child of Varuṇa rises (and that is in the months of Śrāvaṇa and Bhādrapada i.e. the rainy season), there will be heavy floods and prices will be normal (or may soar high ?). The sons of the Sun rise during the next two months of autumn and dry up all wells, tanks and rivers. Consequently cattle and other animals will perish; there will be drought, famine and panic. In the next two months the children of fire rise and bring about destruction of territories by fire, thefts of valuables, flight of people in panic and outbreak of diseases. The sons of Yama rise in the months of Māgha and Phālguna. Consequently there will be terrible famine and destruction of all grains. Kubera's sons rise in the months of Caitra and Vaiśākha and herald good rains commensurate with the appearance of clouds, performance of sacrifices and such other religious rites everywhere, and happiness, peace and plently in the land. Vāyu's sons rise any time during the two months of Jyeṣṭha and Āṣāḍha. As a result of this banks of clouds will be scattered by strong winds, tops of trees and mansions will be swept off and rulers will be engaged in hostilities.

I have already quoted some scientific opinions about the comets at the beginning of this chapter, Here I am quoting some relevant scientific facts from Thomas Heath's "The Twentieth Century Atlas of Popular Astronomy: Comets consist of a hazy, luminous head, accompanied by a long train of light, known as the tail. The head usually contains a bright star-like point called the nucleus, the most condensed part of the comet's substance. Round this appears the coma, shading out from the nucleus and forming with it the head. The tail, the least substantial part, emanates from the coma and stretches out into space in a direction opposite to that of the sun. Some of the smaller comets show no trace of a tail. As the comets approach nearer the sun the tail makes its appearance. The tail is usually directed away from the sun. According to some astronomers the sun exerts both the force of attraction and repulsion on the comet according to the density of its parts. The main body of the comet is thus kept moving in its orbit about the sun, while the lighter particles are driven away from the sun to form the tail. Professor Bredichin of Moscow Observatory has come to the conclusion that the repulsive force exerted by the sun's electrical condition has resulted in the formation of three distinct types of tails. In the first type the tail is long and pretty straight and is probably formed of hydrogen. In the second type the tails are curved to some extent, and are of moderate length. In the third type the tails are comparatively short and still more curved and brush-like in appearance. These tails are probably composed of particles of iron and other metals. Some of these brighter comets have two or even three tails.

Newton proved that the movements of comets, like those of the planets, are governed by the attraction of the sun, and moved generally in an orbit which was practically a parabola with the sun at the focus. There are several instances of comets breaking up into two or more fragments. Thus we see an intimate connection between comets and meteors. There are eighteen periodic comets whose orbits reach out close to the orbit of Jupiter, two to Saturn, three to Uranus and six to Neptune.... In 1811 there appeared one of the most splendid comets. Its tail stretched over 25° of the sky and measured in absolute length about 100 million miles. The great comet of 1843 was seen in broad daylight in the vicinity of the sun. Its tail measured 150 m. miles in length. ..The star Arcturus (Svātī) was seen shining with unimpaired brilliancy through the densest part of Donati's comet of 1858 (pp. 99-104).

Chart Of Comets I

1	2	3	4	5	6	7
:	Born of	No.	Form and Description	Direction in which they appear	With or without Crest and its description	Effects, good and bad
ıa	The Sun	25	Resemble pearl neck-lace, gems or gold	East or West	With crests	Hostility among kings
utāḥ	Fire	25	Resemble parrots, fire, Bandhujīva flower, lac or blood	South-east	Without crest (according to Garga)	Danger from fire
ısutāḥ	Death	25	Rough and dark	South	With crooked crests	Pestilence
āsutāḥ	Earth	22	Round like mirror and radiant, resembling water or oil	North-east	Without crests	Famine
tāḥ	Moon	3	Resemble moonlight, silver, snow, lotus or jasmine	North	——	Plenty of food
ıadaṇḍa	Brahman	1	With three colours	Any direction	With three crests	destruction of the world

1	2	3	4	5	6	7
ıuraśīti or sarpaka arga)	Venus	84	Glossy and of the form of large white stars	North or north-east.	——	Dreadful effects
ınaka	Saturn	60	Glossy and lustrous	Any direction	With two crests each.	Dire consequences
kaca	Jupiter	65	Glossy, having a single white star	South	Without crests	Untoward effects
ıskara	Mercury	51	Faint, very slender, long and white	Any quarter	——	Do
ıuṁkuma	Mars	60	Resemble blood or fire	North	With three crests	Malefic. Wars (Garga)
masakīlaka	Rāhu	33	Black, resemble crow, truncated body or weapon	Appear on the Sun & Moon at times other than new and full Moon	——	All kinds of bad effects : famine, theft, wars, diseases, king's death, storm etc. (sometimes good on the Moon)
śvarūpa	Fire	120	Surrounded by rows of flames	——	Without crests (Garga)	Fire- disasters

1	2	3	4	5	6	7
ruṇa	Wind	77	Dark-red, without starry form, like chowries, rough and with scattered rays	Any direction	—	Dreadful in effect
aṇaka	Prajāpati	8	Resemble a cluster of stars	—	—	—do—
aturasra	Brahman	204	Triangular or square, with white rays	—	With crest (Garga)	—do—
aṅka	Varuṇa	32	Shine like the Moon and resemble a cluster of bamboos	—	—	—do—
abandha	Kāla (Death)	96	Resemble truncated bodies, but without stars, yellow or red in colour	—	—	Produce mortality but beneficial to the Puṇḍras
idiksutāḥ	Intermediate Quarters	9	With one large, white star	In the intermediate directions	—	Malefic

* *Tāmasakīlakas* —In my opinion these things may stand comparison with the modern sun-spots and solar flares discovered by astronomers with the help of powerful telescopes. Hence it would be useful for us to know what the scientists mean by these phenomena. Thomas Heath describes them as follows: When a telescope of moderate power is used, it will be found that there are dark spots on the surface of irregular form and of different sizes, sometimes arranged in groups, sometimes separated by intervals at different parts of the disc. In the neighbourhood of spots smaller bright patches of light are seen, more luminous than the general surface. These are called faculae or torches

These spots are seen sometimes to split into two or more and sometimes to coalesce to form one. They also move from the eastern edge and disappear on the western edge, crossing the disc in a period of about twelve days Their movements are sometimes in straight paths and at others in curved ones. The solar spots and their influence on our surroundings would grip the imagination of scientists until the mystery is solved.... Alexander Wilson of Glasgow had shown that the spots were cavities in the sun's surface. Even this view has not been accepted.

In 1843 Schwabe of Dessau discovered the number of spots appearing was subject to a periodic fluctuation in a period of more than eleven years. Dr. Rudolph Wolf of Berne proved that the eleven year period corresponds exactly with the period which has been shown to exist in the frequency of magnetic disturbances in the earth's surface. Many other manifestations of the working of nature on the earth and in its atmosphere have practically shown a periodicity similar to that of the sun-spots. *But the attempts to trace a connection between the sun spots and the phenomena of weather, or the price of corn have not been so successful as the probability of such a connection might have led one to expect.*

Chart of Comets II

1	2	3	4
Name	Description, Characteristics etc.	Direction in which it appears	Effects
Vasāketu	Big, glossy, elongated towards the north	West	Fatal diseases, but abundant food
Asthiketu	Do. Rough	West	Famine
Śastraketu	Glossy, big	East	War and pestilence
Kapālaketu	With rays and crest smoky-traversing half the heavens	East on the New Moon day	Famine, pestilence, drought and diseases
Raudraketu	With trident-like crest, and flame rough, grey and red—traverses $\frac{1}{3}$ sky	In the Dahanavīthī in the east	—do—
Calaketu	Its crest, one inch raised, is turned to the south; its length increases as it moves northward, touches the great Bear and Pole star, Abhijit, travels $\frac{1}{2}$ sky and sets in the South.	West	Effects are felt for 10 or 18 months. Destruction of people from Prayāga to Ujjain & Puṣkara, Madhyadeśa, Devikā river in the north etc. famine etc.
Śvetaketu	Its crest is turned to the south. Glossy or otherwise	East at midnight to be seen for 7 days	If glossy-good crops and peace and prosperity
Ka	Has the form of a yoke glossy or otherwise.	West to beseen withthe previousone for 7days	Do. If visible for more than 7 days, war & distress for 10 years
Śveta	Rough, black, resembles matted locks, travels $\frac{1}{3}$ sky, retreats in anti-clockwise manner	—	Destroys $\frac{2}{3}$ population
Raśmiketu	Has ash-coloured crest	Appears near the star Kṛttikā	--do--

1	2	3	4
hruvaketu	Its motion, size, colour & shape are irregular. Sometimes glossy	Travels in three worlds.	Beneficial if glossy. Death of kings if seen on their equipments, of people if seen on their houses, vessels etc.
ımudaketu	White like lotus, with its crest stretched in the east	In the west only for one night.	Excellent-crops for 10 years
aṇiketu	A tiny little star with a straight, white crest	In the west visibleonce for three hours only.	Brings with its rising good-crops for 4½ months, but growth of reptiles etc.
laketu	Glossy with a crest raised towards the west	West	Place and plenty for nine months
ıavaketu	A tiny, glossy star, with a crest turned to the right resembling a lion's tail	In the east for one only night	Abundance of food for so many months as the number of Muhūrtas it is visible. If it is rough, fatal diseases will crop up.
ıdmaketu	As white as the fibre of lotus-stalk	In the west only for one night	Good crops and happiness for 7 years
vartaketu	Glossy or red with crest turned to the south	In the west atmidnight	Abundant focd for as many months as the number of Muhūrtas it remains visible
ṁvarta tu	Of dreadful appearance, resembles a trident, with a crest that is smoky and coppery in colour—occupies a third of the sky	Appears in the west at sunset	Kings are destroyed by wars for as many years as the number of Muhurtas it is visible. It affects persons whose natal star is occupied by it.

अगस्त्यचारः ॥ १२ ॥

Chapter XII—Canopus

मानोर्वर्त्मविघातवृद्धशिखरो विन्ध्याचलः स्तम्भितो
वातापिर्मुनिकुक्षिभित् सुररिपुर्जीर्णश्च येनासुरः ।
पीतश्चाम्बुनिधिस्तपोऽम्बुनिधिना याम्या च दिग्भूषिता
तस्यागस्त्यमुनेः पयोद्युतिकृतश्चारः समासादयम् ॥१॥

The following is a brief description of the course of sage Agastya (Canopus), who is an ocean of penance (*i.e.* spiritual powers), who purifies the waters, by whom was suppressed the Vindhya mountain whose peaks grew so high as to obstruct the Sun's passage, by hom the demon Vātāpi who tore the stomachs of sages was eaten and digested, who drank away the ocean, and who adorns the southern direction.

[This verse is from the समाससंहिता by our author. This is in the शार्दूलविक्रीडित metre.]

समुद्रोऽन्तः शैलैर्मकरनखरोत्खातशिखरैः
कृतस्तोयोच्छित्त्या सपदि सुतरां येन रुचिरः ।
पतन्मुक्तामिश्रैः प्रवरमणिरत्नाम्बुनिवहैः
सुरान् प्रत्यादेष्टुं मितमुकुटरत्नानिव पुरा ॥२॥

That sage suddenly made the ocean appear extremely charming by drying up its waters, in days of yore, through the mountains (such as the Maināka which were exposed) situated in its interior whose peaks were scooped out by the claws of crocodiles (sharks, whales etc.), and which had streams of water and excellent gems and jewels falling down along with pearls, as though to out-shine the Gods that have only a limited number of gems on their crowns.

[According to the Purāṇic story the sage Agastya drank the ocean in a sip in order to expose the demons lying concealed within it. The metre is शिखरिणी.]

येन चाम्बुहरणेऽपि विद्रुमैर्भूधरैः समणिरत्नविद्रुमैः ।
निर्गतैस्तुरगैश्च राजितः सागरोऽधिकतरं विराजितः ॥३॥

Though he (*i.e.* the sage) deprived the ocean of its waters, still he made it more beautiful by means of the (exposed) mountains which were devoid of trees but were bedecked with excellent gems and corals and of the serpents that emerged from them in long rows.

[This verse looks beautiful as a result of the figure of speech called यमक where the word विद्रुमैः as well as राजितः appears twice though in a different sense. The metre of this and the following verse is स्वागता.]

प्रस्फुरत्तिमिजलेभजिह्मगः क्षिप्तरत्ननिकरो महोदधिः ।
आपदां पदगतोऽपि यापितो येन पीतसलिलोऽमरश्रियम् ॥४॥

Though the ocean was reduced by him to a pitiable condition being drained off, yet it was raised to celestial glory, as it exhibited the glittering (or struggling) whales, water-elephants and serpents as well as heaps of gems that were scattered about.

[The commentator interprets the first compound as applying to the world of Gods as well : That world possesses denizens some of whom move about riding whales, some others reside inside water, some ride elephants, some move with retrograde motion and some go about throwing gems.]

प्रचलत्तिमिशुक्तिजशङ्खचितः सलिलेऽपहृतेऽपि पतिः सरिताम् ।
सतरङ्गसितोत्पलहंसभृतः सरसः शरदीव बिभर्त्ति रुचम् ॥५॥

Though the waters were taken away, still it came to possess, as it were, the charm of a lake in autumn with its waves, white lotuses and swans, as a result of its being filled with floundering whales, pearl-oysters and conch-shells.

[रुचिम् is another reading for रुचम्. The word शुक्तिज may also be construed as 'Pearls'. The metre is तोटक.]

तिमिसिताम्बुधरं मणितारकं स्फटिकचन्द्रमनम्बुशरद्द्युति ।
फणिफणोपलरश्मिशिखिग्रहं कुटिलगेशवियच्च चकार यः ॥६॥

The sage transformed the ocean into the sky, as it had white clouds in the form of whales, stars in the form of gems, the Moon in the form of crystal gem, the autumnal splendour in the form of the waterless bed and comets (Ketus) in the form of the rays of the gems on the hoods of the serpents.

[The poet has employed a fine, complete metaphor in addition to alliteration. The metre is द्रुतविलम्बित.]

The poet now proceeds to describe in prose the Vindhya mountain and its treatment at the hands of the sage.

दिनकररथमार्गविच्छित्तयेऽभ्युद्यतं यच्चलच्छृङ्गमुद्भ्रा-
न्तविद्याधरांसावसक्तप्रियाव्यग्रदत्ताङ्कदेहावलम्बा-
म्बरात्युच्छ्रितोद्धूयमानध्वजैः शोभितम्,
करिकटमदमिश्ररक्तावलेहानुवासानुसारिद्विरेफावलीनो-
त्तमाङ्गैः कृतान् बाणपुष्पैरिवोत्तंसकान् धारयद्भिर्मृगेन्द्रैः
सनाथीकृतान्तर्दरीनिर्झरम् ।
गगनतलमिवोल्लिखन्तं प्रवृद्धैर्गजाकृष्टफुल्लद्रुमत्रासवि-
भ्रान्तमत्तद्विरेफावलीहृष्टमन्द्रस्वनैः शैलकूटैस्तरक्षर्क्ष-
शार्दूलशाखामृगाध्यासितैः,
रहसि मदनसक्तया रेवया कान्तयेवोपगूढं सुराध्या-
सितोद्यानमम्भोशनानन्नमूलानिलाहारविप्रान्वितं विन्ध्य-
मस्तम्भयद्यश्च तस्योदयः श्रूयताम् ॥७॥

Listen, ye, now to the rising of that sage (Agastya or Canopus), who stemmed the Vindhya Mountain, which threatened to obstruct the course of the Sun's carriage by raising its peaks; which was beautified with flags hoisted aloft in the form of the clothes hanging and waving from the bodies of the Vidyādhara damsels, who clinging to the shoulders of their confused lovers eagerly seated them on their own laps; which possessed streams inside the caves occupied by lions whose heads were covered with bees following the smell caused by their tasting of the blood mixed with ichor on the heads of the elephants and consequently were wearing ornamental wreaths of Vāṇa flowers, as it were, on their heads; which was scratching, as it were, the firmament with its raised peaks that had the sonorous sound of the humming of the swarms of intoxicated bees that were scattered being shaken by the falling trees in bloom pulled down by elephants and which (peaks) contained hyenas, bears, tigers and monkeys; which is embraced closely by the river Revā (Narmadā) having the Madana trees growing on her banks, as by his beloved engaged in amorous sport; whose gardens are occupied by Gods; and where dwell Brāhmaṇas (sages) who live on water, roots, air and nothing.

[In these descriptions of the Vindhya mountain the poet displays his rare poetic gifts, employing his knowledge of geography and the Purāṇas. He uses with consummate skill the figures of speech, both of sound and sense, such as alliteration, Śleṣa, Upamā, Virodhābhāsa, Utprekṣā etc. and poetic excellences *viz.* sweetness, perspicuity and brilliance. This is a Daṇḍaka with four quarters conforming to the rules of the Surāmadaṇḍaka (See वृत्तरत्नाकर, footnote on page 72).]

उदये च मुनेरगस्त्यनाम्नः कुसमायोगमलप्रदूषितानि ।
हृदयानि सतामिव स्वभावात्पुनरम्बूनि भवन्ति निर्मलानि ।।८।।

At the appearance of sage Agastya (Canopus) the waters that are polluted (in the rainy season) by their contact with mud become clear once again spontaneously, just as the minds (of men) that are corrupted by association with the wicked become pure at the sight of the virtuous.

[Sanskrit poets are fond of comparing the human mind to water. An agitated mind is likewise compared to agitated or turbid water.

Cf. रघुवंश IV. 21.

प्रससादोदयादम्भः कुम्भयोनेर्महौजसः ।
रघोरभिभवाशङ्कि चुक्षुभे द्विषतां मनः ।।

The metre is औपच्छन्दसिक.

Next the poet describes autumn in 4 verses.]

पार्श्वद्वयाधिष्ठितचक्रवाकामापुष्णती सस्वनहंसपङ्क्तिम् ।
ताम्बूलरक्तोत्कषिताग्रदन्ती विभाति योषेव शरत्सहासा ।।९।।

The autumn which nurtures a row of cackling swans flanked on both sides by ruddy geese, shines like a smiling damsel whose front teeth are smeared with the red tinge of betel leaves.

[It is a poetic convention to say that the swans being tortured by rains repair to the Mānasa lake and return to the plains in autumn. Here the comparison is between the autumn wherein the white row of swans flanked by red cakravākas and a beautiful woman whose white laughter is flanked by two sets of reddened teeth. Many poets like Bhāsa and Kālidāsa have described autumn.

सरित्सहासा is another reading which makes the comparison more appropriate. The metre is उपजाति.]

इन्दीवरासन्नसितोत्पलान्विता शरद्भ्रमत्षट्पदपङ्क्तिभूषिता ।
सभ्रूलताक्षेपकटाक्षवीक्षणा विदग्धयोषेव विभाति सस्मरा ।।१०।।

The autumn which possesses white lotuses flanked by blue lilies and which is adorned with rows of hovering bees, looks as charming as a clever woman in love casting side-long glances with dancing brows.

[Instead of शरद्, सरिद् is the reading in some editions. Here the blue lilies are compared to the dark pupils of the eyes, white lotuses to the white eye balls and the moving bees to the moving brows and glances. The metre is a mixture of इन्द्रवंशा. and वंशस्थ.]

इन्दोः पयोदविगमोपहितां विभूतिं
द्रष्टुं तरङ्गवलया कुमुदं निशासु ।
उन्मीलयत्यलिनिलीनदलं सुपक्ष्म
वापी त्रिलोचनमिवासिततारकान्तम् ॥११॥

The pond having the bracelets of waves opens at night the lilies on whose petals rest the bees, as its eyes with dark pupils and beautiful lashes, as though to witness the Moon's splendour caused by the disappearance of the monsoon clouds.

[Here too the poet indulges in a fine imagery *i.e.* poetic fancy coupled with metaphor and pun. There is also the excellence named Samādhi or pathetic fallacy. One could find here also Dhvani or suggestion of a love-lorn woman eagerly looking at her lover's charming face after a long separation.

The metre is वसन्ततिलका.]

नानाविचित्राम्बुजहंसकोककारण्डवापूर्णतडागहस्ता ।
रत्नैः प्रभूतैः कुसुमैः फलैश्च भूर्यच्छतीवार्घमगस्त्यनाम्ने ॥१२॥

The Earth offers worship, as it were, to sage Agastya with abundant gems, flowers and fruits held in the hands *viz.* the pools, filled with various kinds of lotuses, swans, ruddy geese and ducks.

[When a venerable person visits a house, the lady of the house offers him worship. Here Mother Earth worships sage Agastya at his arrival or rising. Here too the poet uses his poetic skill.

The metre is इन्द्रवज्रा.]

सलिलममरपाज्ञयोज्झितं यद्घनपरिवेष्टितमूर्त्तिभिर्भुजङ्गैः ।
फणिजनितविषाग्निसम्प्रदुष्टं भवति शिवं तदगस्त्यदर्शनेन ॥१३॥

The water which is released at the command of the Rain-god Indra by the serpents whose bodies are wrapt up in the clouds, and which is polluted by the fire of poison emitted by them, becomes pure and wholesome at the appearance of sage Agastya.

[The idea of serpents vitiating the waters in the clouds is an ancient Ṛgvedic symbolism, where the cloud or serpent is said to impound the waters or Indra's cattle. Sometimes the same cloud is spoken of as the fortress of the demon Vṛtra.

For a scientific explanation of the Indra-Vṛtra fight see Yāska's Nirukta, II-14.

It is a fact that in the rainy season river waters get muddy and polluted. They become pure only in autumn.

The metre is पुष्पिताग्रा.]

स्मरणादपि पापमपाकुरुते किमुत स्तुतिभिर्वरुणाङ्गरुहः ।
मुनिभिः कथितोऽस्य यथार्घविधिः कथयामि तथव नरेन्द्रहितम् ॥१४॥

Sage Agastya, son of Varuṇa, removes sin through mere remembrance; how much more when he is invoked ! I shall now explain the mode of worshipping him for the benefit of kings as it has been propounded by ancient sages like Garga.

[It is true that Albiruni takes our author to task for mixing science with religion. However, the objection would become untenable if we remembered the cultural background of our author as well as the nature of the work called Saṁhitā, which should rise to the status of an encyclopaedia of knowledge. This verse is notable for its fine metre, which is Toṭaka, and graceful diction.]

संख्याविधानात्प्रतिदेशमस्य विज्ञाय सन्दर्शनमादिशेज्ज्ञः ।
तच्चोज्जयिन्यामगतस्य कन्यां भागैः स्वराख्यैः स्फुटभास्करस्य ॥१५॥

The time of rising of Agastya-Canopus—for each country should be determined by calculation and announced by an astronomer. Now, for Ujjain, it takes place when the Sun's true position is 7° short of Sign Virgo (Kanyā).

[Colebrook comments on this verse and quotes XIV 39, 40 from the Pañcasiddhāntikā :

विषुवच्छायार्धगुणा पञ्चकृतिस्तत्कलास्ततश्चापम् ।
छायात्रिसप्तकयुतं दशभिर्गुणितं विनाड्यस्ताः ॥
ताभिः कर्कटकाद्याद्यल्लग्नं तादृशे सहस्रांशौ ।
याम्याशावनितामुखविशेषतिलको मुनिरगस्त्यः ॥

"Multiply half the length of the equinoctial shadow by 25; take from this product, expressed in minutes, the corresponding arc; add the length of the shadow multiplied by 21; multiply by 10; this gives the number in Vināḍıs. At this number, reckoning from the beginning of Cancer, stands the Sun when Agastya rises in the south, like a mark on the front of a damsel."

Cf. समाससंहिता

सप्तभिरंशैः कन्यामप्राप्ते रोमके तु दिवसकरे ।
दृश्योऽगस्त्योऽवन्त्यां तत्समपूर्वापरेऽप्येवम् ॥

This and the following verses are in इन्द्रवज्रा metre.]

ईषत्प्रभिन्नेऽरुणरश्मिजालैर्नैशेऽन्धकारे दिशि दक्षिणस्याम् ।
सांवत्सरावेदितदिग्विभागे भूपोऽर्घमुर्व्यां प्रयतः प्रयच्छेत् ॥१६॥

कालोद्भवैः सुरभिभिः कुसुमैः फलैश्च
रत्नैश्च सागरभवैः कनकाम्बरैश्च ।
धेन्वा वृषेण परमान्नयुतैश्च भक्ष्यै-
र्दध्यक्षतैः सुरभिधूपविलेपनैश्च ॥१७॥

When the nocturnal darkness is just pierced by the mass of Aruṇa's rays, the king being pure should offer worship to the sage, in the south on the earth with fragrant flowers and fruits of the season, gems got from the sea, gold, garments, milch cows, bulls, Pāyasa (milk porridge). eatables, curd, coloured rice, fragrant incense and ointments, at a place pointed out by the astronomer.

[Here the poet enumerates the articles that are used in the worship of Deities. The metre of the second verse is वसन्ततिलका.]

नरपतिरिममर्घं श्रद्दधानो ददानः
प्रविगतगददोषो निर्जितारातिपक्षः ।
भवति यदि च दद्यात्सप्तवर्षाणि सम्य-
ग्जलनिधिरशनायाः स्वामितां याति भूमेः ॥१८॥

Should a king offer this worship (to the sage) with faith at heart, he would be free from all ailments, and defeat the entire host of his enemies. And if he should offer the worship for a period of seven years continuously according to rules, he would become the unrivalled monarch of the entire earth girded by the ocean.

[The worship of Agastya is prescribed for kings. There are other rituals also like the worship of the Banner of Indra (cf. Chapter XLIII), Nīrājana of horses etc. (chapter XLIV) and Puṣyasnāna (cf. XLVIII). The number 7 plays an important role in Indian religious belief.

The metre is मालिनी. This verse is remarkable for its fine diction and alliteration.]

द्विजो यथालाभमुपाहृतार्घः प्राप्नोति वेदान् प्रमदाश्च पुत्रान् ।
वैश्यश्च गां भूरि धनं च शूद्रो रोगक्षयं धर्मफलं च सर्वे ॥१९॥

A Brāhmaṇa who worships Agastya according to his means would be blessed with a good knowledge of the Vedas, good wives and sons; a Vaiśya would become rich in cattle; and a Śūdra would become very wealthy. All persons in general who offer this worship would be free from diseases and get the merits of virtuous or religious deeds.

[Having mentioned the merits of this worship accruing to kings the author takes up the other three classes in this verse. This reminds us of the फलश्रुति given in the रामायण : "पठन् द्विजो वागृषभत्वमेयात्स्यात्क्षत्रियो भूमिपतित्वमेयात्...।"

The metre is उपजाति.]

> रोगान् करोति परुषः कपिलस्त्ववृष्टि
> धूम्रो गवामशुभकृत्स्फुरणो भयाय ।
> माञ्जिष्ठरागसदृशः क्षुधमाहवांश्च
> कुर्यादणुश्च पुररोधमगस्त्यनामा ॥२०॥

If Agastya is rough, he causes diseases; if russet, drought; if smoky, harm to cattle; if throbbing, fear or danger; if red like madder, famine and wars; and if tiny, siege of the city.

[Finally the author gives the effects of Agastya's appearance, colour etc. The metre is वसन्ततिलका.]

> शातकुम्भसदृशः स्फटिकाभस्तर्पयन्निव महीं किरणाग्रैः ।
> दृश्यते यदि तदा प्रचुरान्ना भूर्भवत्यभयरोगजनाढ्या ॥२१॥

If Canopus shines like gold or crystal and appears to refresh, as it were, the earth with the tips (streams) of his rays, the earth will abound in food, making the people happy and prosperous.

[किरणौघैः is another reading. Utpala interprets the word शातकुम्भ as silver For he says :—

> शातकुम्भशब्दः सुवर्णरजतयोर्द्वयोरपि वाचकः ।

Cf. गर्ग—

> शङ्खकुन्देन्दुगोक्षीरमृणालरजतप्रभः ।
> दृश्यते यद्यगस्त्यः स्यात् सुभिक्षक्षेमकारकः ॥
> वैश्वानरार्चिप्रतिमैर्मांसशोणितकर्दमैः ।
> रणैर्भयैश्च विविधैः किञ्चिच्छेषायते प्रजा ॥]

> उल्कया विनिहतः शिखिना वा क्षुद्भयं मरकमेव विधत्ते ।
> दृश्यते स किल हस्तगतेऽर्के रोहिणीमुपगतेऽस्तमुपैति ॥२२॥

If Agastya be struck by a meteor or comet, there would certainly be danger of famine and pestilence. It is said that Canopus rises when the Sun is stationed in the asterism Hasta and sets when the Sun goes to Rohiṇī.

[This verse the author employs only to give expression to the traditional view with regard to Agastya's rising and setting. This is borne out by the expression. "स किल...". The commentator too expresses the same idea :

"यद्यप्यत्र गणितसाम्यं न भवति तथाप्याचार्येण पूर्वशास्त्रदृष्टत्वात्कथितम् ।" For the author has specifically stated thus in the पञ्चसिद्धान्तिका. (See notes under verse 15 *supra*) पराशर too makes the traditional statement : "हस्तस्थे सवितर्युदेति रोहिणीसंस्थे प्रविशति : He continues thus—अथास्य त्रिविधश्चारोदयकालो दृष्टः—आश्वयुग्बहुलाष्टमीपञ्चदश्योः कार्त्तिकाष्टम्यां वा । तत्राश्वयुग्बहुलोदितः सुवृष्टिक्षेमान्नसम्पत्करः । वर्णैश्चावेदयति । अग्निपरुषरूक्षाभो रोगाय कपिलो वृष्टिनिग्रहाय । धूमाभो गवामभावाय । माञ्जिष्ठः कुङ्कुमच्छविः क्षुच्छस्त्रदः । नीलोऽतिवर्षाय । संवृतः पुररोधाय । स्पन्दनो भयाय ।
अपि च—

हन्यादुल्का यदागस्त्यं केतुर्वाप्युपधूपयेत् ।
दुर्भिक्षं जनमारश्च तदा जगति जायते ॥
सुस्निग्धवर्णः श्वेतश्च शातकुम्भसमप्रभः ।
मुनिः क्षेमसुभिक्षाय प्रजानामभयाय च ॥

The metre is स्वागता.]

सप्तर्षिचारः ॥१३॥

Chapter XIII—*Course of The Seven Sages*

संकावलीव राजति ससितोत्पलमालिनी सहासेव ।
नाथवतीव च दिग्यैः कौबेरी सप्तभिर्मुनिभिः ॥१॥

ध्रुवनायकोपदेशान्नरिनर्तीवोत्तरा भ्रमद्भिश्च ।
यैश्चारमहं तेषां कथयिष्ये वृद्धगर्गमतात् ॥२॥

I shall now expound, according to the view of the Sage Vṛddha (Senior) Garga, the movements of the Seven Seers (the Great Bear), through whom the northern region shines as though bedecked with a pearl necklace, like a maiden with a smiling countenance wearing a garland of white lotuses, by whom she appears to have a lord (or husband), and by whose circular movements the northern quarter seems verily dancing at the instruction of the leader, viz., the Pole-Star.

[The author who is a born poet cannot resist the overtures of his muse and bursts into fine poetry at the sight of the beautiful line of seven stars looking like a pearl necklace which he must have enjoyed on several nights. He employs in this verse simile, metaphor and poetic fancy.

Cf. भट्टब्रह्मगुप्त—

ध्रुवयोर्बद्धं सव्यगममराणां क्षितिजसंस्थमुडुचक्रम ।
अपसव्यगमसुराणां भ्रमति प्रवहानिलक्षिप्तम् ॥]

आसन्मघासु मुनयः शासति पृथ्वीं युधिष्ठिरे नृपतौ ।
षड्द्विकपञ्चद्वियुतः शककालस्तस्य राज्ञश्च ॥३॥

The Seven Sages were stationed in the asterism Maghā when king Yudhiṣṭhira was ruling over the earth. The commencement of the Śaka era took place 2526 years after the period of that monarch.

[There is difference of opinion among scholars with regard to the interpretation of शककालः. According to some it means the beginning of the Vikrama era, and according to others the Śālivāhana era, and some others hold that it refers to the Buddha era. The year of the Mahābhārata War ranges from 950 B.C. to 3201 B.C. in the opinions of different scholars from Pargiter to Mankad. On the basis of the planetary positions mentioned in the Great Epic as as well as the day of Bhīṣma's departure i.e. 8th Tithi ruled by the star Rohiṇī in the bright fortnight of the lunar month Māgha at noon at the commencement of the winter solstice, astronomers have fixed the commencement of the Kaliyuga at 3102 B.C. and the Great War at 3138 B.C. For according to the मत्स्यपुराण Kaliyuga started on the very day that the Lord Kṛṣṇa closed His incarnation. According to the Epic itself Śrīkṛṣṇa's departure took place 36 years after the War. If we deduct the number 2526 from the date of king Yudhiṣṭhira, 3138, we get 612 B.C. as the commencement of the Śakakāla referred to by our author. Thus we come across a great hurdle in accepting the above date, 3138 B.C., assigned to the Great War or Yudhiṣṭhira, the latter having been crowned at the end of the 18-day war. If the Śakakāla of Varāhamihira refers to the Vikrama era, then Yudhiṣṭhira's period would be 2582 B.C.; on the other hand if it be Śālivāhana era, the year would be 2448 B.C. Vide I. A. 1. B. P. 8-11.

Cf. वृद्धगर्ग—

कलिद्वापरसन्धौ तु स्थितास्ते पितृदैवतम् ।
मुनयो धर्मनिरताः प्रजानां पालने रताः ॥]

एकैकस्मिन्नृक्षे शतं शतं ते चरन्ति वर्षाणाम् ।
प्रागुदयतोऽप्यविवराहृजून्नयति तत्र संयुक्ताः ॥४॥

The Sages traverse through each lunar mansion for a period of 100 years. Whichever constellation makes them conspicuous when they rise to the east of it, in that they are said to be situated.

[The second line has a variant reading :

प्रागुत्तरतश्चैते सदोदयन्ते ससाध्वीकाः ।

This is clearer in sense and flawless in construction. This reading might have been suggested by some earlier commentator. This would mean : "These Sages accompanied by the chaste Arundhatī always rise in the north-east." But then the two readings express different ideas viz. the direction of rising and the constellation in which they are posited at the time.

Cf. कश्यप—

शतं शतं तु वर्षाणामेकैकस्मिन् महर्षयः ।
नक्षत्रे निवसन्त्येते ससाध्वीका महातपाः ॥]

पूर्वे भागे भगवान्मरीचिरपरे स्थितो वसिष्ठोऽस्मात् ।
तस्याङ्गिरास्ततोऽत्रिस्तस्यासन्नः पुलस्त्यश्च ॥५॥

पुलहः क्रतुरिति भगवानासन्ना अनुक्रमेण पूर्वाद्यात् ।
तत्र वसिष्ठं मुनिवरमुपाश्रितारुन्धती साध्वी ॥६॥

Among the Sages the revered Marīci is situated in the east; to his west is Vasiṣṭha, to his west is Aṅgiras; to his west is situated Atri; and close to him is Pulastya. Next to him are in order Pulaha and Kratu. Arundhatī, the paragon of virtue, is close to the great Sage Vasiṣṭha among them.

उल्काशनिधूमाद्यैर्हता विवर्णा विरश्मयो ह्रस्वाः ।
हन्युः स्वं स्वं वर्गं विपुलाः स्निग्धाश्च तद्वृद्ध्यै ॥७॥

When these Sages (the Great Bear) are attacked by meteors, thunderbolts, smoke and the like, or when they become pale, devoid of rays or tiny, they will destroy severally their own dependencies (as stated blow), whereas they help the same to prosper, if they appear large and bright.

[Cf. वृद्धगर्ग—

उल्कया केतुना वापि धूमेन रजसापि वा ।
हता विवर्णाः स्वल्पा वा किरणैः परिवर्जिताः ॥
स्वं स्वं वर्गं तदा हन्युर्मुनयः सर्व एव ते ।
विपुलाः स्निग्धवर्णाश्च स्ववर्गपरिपोषकाः ॥

Their Vargas are enumerated in the following 4 verses.]

गन्धर्वदेवदानवमन्त्रौषधिसिद्धयक्षनागानाम् ।
पीडाकरो मरीचिर्ज्ञेयो विद्याधराणां च ॥८॥
शकयवनदरदपारतकाम्बोजांस्तापसान् वनोपेतान् ।
हन्ति वसिष्ठोऽभिहतो विवृद्धिदो रश्मिसम्पन्नः ॥९॥
अङ्गिरसो ज्ञानयुता धीमन्तो ब्राह्मणाश्च निर्दिष्टाः ।
अत्रेः कान्तारभवा जलजान्यम्भोनिधिः सरितः ॥१०॥
रक्षःपिशाचदानवदैत्यभुजङ्गाः स्मृताः पुलस्त्यस्य ।
पुलहस्य तु मूलफलं क्रतोस्तु यज्ञाः सयज्ञभृतः ॥११॥

When Marīci is hurt, he is said to harm the Gandharvas,

Gods, demons, spells, herbs, angels, Yakṣas, Nāgas and Vidyādharas. Vasiṣṭha, when hurt, proves harmful to the Śakas, Yavanas, Daradas, Pāratas, Kāmbojas, hermits and those living in forests; when radiant, he bestows prosperity. Scholars, intelligent men and Brahmins are mentioned as belonging to the domain of Aṅgiras; and foresters, aquatic products, the ocean and rivers are assigned to Atri. Giants, devils, demons, Daityas and serpents are said to belong to Pulastya; roots and fruits to Pulaha; and sacrifices and sacrificers to Kratu.

[In these verses different classes of beings, tribes and articles are mentioned as coming under the influence of the Seven Sages. For a detailed treatment of geographical jurisdiction of the planets, asterisms and quarters the following three chapters may be referred to.

Cf. also वृद्धगर्ग—

देवदानवगन्धर्वा सिद्धपन्नगराक्षसाः ।
नागा विद्याधराः सर्वे मरीचेः परिकीर्तिताः ॥
यवनाः पारताश्चैव काम्बोजा दरदाः शकाः ।
वसिष्ठस्य विनिर्दिष्टास्तापसा वनमाश्रिताः ॥
धीमन्तो ब्राह्मणा ये च ज्ञानविज्ञानपारगाः ।
रूपलावण्यसंयुक्ता मुनेरङ्गिरसः स्मृताः ॥
कान्तारजास्तथाम्भोजा अत्रेर्ये सरिदाश्रिताः ।
पिशाचा दानवा दैत्या भुजङ्गा राक्षसास्तथा ॥
पुलस्त्यस्य विनिर्दिष्टाः पुष्पं मूलं फलं च यत् ।
तत्सर्वं पुलहस्योक्तं यज्ञा यज्ञभृतश्च ये ॥
क्रतोरेव विनिर्दिष्टा वेदज्ञा ब्राह्मणास्तथा ।]

———

कूर्मविभागः ॥१४॥

Chapter XIV—*Division of Globe*

नक्षत्रत्रयवर्गैराग्नेयाद्यैर्व्यवस्थितैर्नवधा ।
भारतवर्षे मध्यप्रागादिविभाजिता देशाः ॥१॥

In Bhāratavarṣa the central region and other countries in regular order beginning with those situated in the east are assigned to the nine triads of stars beginning with Kṛttikā.

[The central region is ruled by the three stars Kṛttikā, Rohiṇı and Mṛgaśiras, the countries to the east by the next triad and so on. By Bhāratavarṣa what is meant is the land lying to the south of Meru. This is the last of the nine Varṣas.

Cf. गर्ग—

कृत्तिकाद्यैस्त्रिनक्षत्रैर्भवर्गैर्नवभिः क्षितिः ।
कल्पिता मध्यदेशादौ प्रागादिक्रमयोगतः ॥
कृत्तिकाद्यस्त्रिनक्षत्रो मध्यदेशे गणो यदा ।
पापैरुपहतो हन्ति मध्यदेशाखिलांस्तदा ॥
रौद्रादिको हन्ति पूर्वां सार्पाद्यः पूर्वदक्षिणाम् ।
आर्यम्णाद्यस्तथा याम्यां स्वात्याद्यो दक्षिणापराम् ॥
ज्येष्ठाद्यः पश्चिमामाशां वैश्वाद्यश्चापरोत्तराम् ।
वारुण्याद्यो हन्ति सौम्यां पौष्णाद्यः शूलिनो दिशम् ॥]

भद्रारिमेदमाण्डव्यसाल्वनीपोज्जिहानसंख्याताः ।
मरुवत्सघोषयामुनसारस्वतमत्स्यमाध्यमिकाः ॥२॥

माथुरकोपज्योतिषधर्मारण्यानि शूरसेनाश्च ।
गौरग्रीवोद्देहिकपाण्डुगुडाश्वत्थपाञ्चालाः ॥३॥

साकेतकङ्ककुरुकालकोटिकुकुराश्च पारियात्रनगः ।
औदुम्बरकापिष्ठलगजाह्वयाश्चेति मध्यमिदम् ॥४॥

To the central region belong the following countries: Bhadra, Arimeda, Māṇḍavya, Sālva, Nıpa, Ujjihāna, Saṁkhyāta, Marwar (desert land), Vatsa, Ghoṣa, those of the Yamunā and Sarasvatī, Matsya, Mādhyamika, Mathurā, Upajyotiṣa, Dharmāraṇya (holy place), Śūrasena, Gauragrīva, Uddehika, Pāṇḍu, Guḍa (or (Pāṇḍu-guḍa?) Aśvattha, Pāñcāla, Sāketa (or Ayodhyā) Kaṅka, Kuru, Kālakoṭi, Kukura, Pāriyātra mountain, Udumbara, Kapiṣṭhala and Hastināpura.

[Alberuni speaks thus of the Kūrma-cakra : "Their astronomers and astrologers divide the directions according to the lunar stations, ...and the figure which represents this division is similar to a tortoise. Therefore it is called *Kūrma-cakra* i.e. the tortoise-circle or the tortoise-shape (I 296-97)." The *Mārkaṇḍeya Purāṇa* (LVIII 80-81) lays down certain propitiatory rituals for the affliction of asterisms and planets ruling a country. This division of India into nine parts is a very ancient device. In the Purāṇas the country is divided into seven regions viz. Madhyadeśa, Udīcya, Prācya, Dakṣiṇāpatha, Aparānta, Vindhyavāsinaḥ and Parvatāśrayiṇah. Rājaśekhara divides Kumāradvīpa in his *Kāvyānuśāsana* into five *deśas*. Both in the *Atharvaveda* (XIX 17.1-9) and the *Aitareya Brāhmaṇa* (VIII 14) this five-fold division is met with.

Many of the places or countries mentioned in these lists cannot be identified with certainty. It is doubtful whether Varāhamihira himself was acquainted with all these. According to Kern Bhadra is a class of *blessed* people. Pāṇḍuguḍa is one word, according to the commentator, but according to Alberuni and Kern it is Pāṇḍu and Guḍa. The *Udumbara* region is included in the Gurdaspur district.

Matsya country is mentioned prominently in the *Mahābhārata*. Virāṭa was its king. The Pāṇḍavas lived in disguise for one year as servants of this king. The *Sālva* country is connected with Matsya. "Sālva comprised the territory extending from Alwar to north Bikaner with Sālvapura, probably modern Alwar, as its principal city."[1] *Ujjihāna* is the same as Uḍḍiyāna, which is corrupted into Urain in Monghyr district, near Kiul, according to N.L. Dey Vogel identifies it with Ujjhana near Bhikdeo in the Kanpur District. According to another opinion it is identical with the Ujhāni town in Badaun district. *Kapiṣṭhala* is said to be identical with the modern Kaithal in the Karnal district. Alberuni calls it Kavital. *Mādhyamikas* are the inhabitants of the country Madhyamikā identified with Nagarī near Chitor in Rajasthan. The Vatsas are an ancient

1. Vide *India As known to Pāṇini*, p. 55.

people whose monarch was Udayana with his capital Kauśāmbī, modern Kosam on the Yamunā. *Uddehika* is identified by Alberuni with a place situated near Bazana, eighty miles from Kanauj. Bazana is said to have been the capital of Gujarat. The *Udumbara* territory is said to have comprised Pathankot, the eastern part of the Kangra Valley and the Hoshiarpur district. *Dharmāraṇya*, according to the Mahābhārata (III. 82.46), is the same as Kaṇvāśrama (Kansawa near Kota). The *Sārasvatas* are the people living on the banks of the Sarasvatī river. At present there is a small stream called Sarsuti, rising in the hills of Sirmur in the Sevaliks and emerging into the plains at Ad-Badri in Ambala.

Our author places Pāñcāla in Madhyadeśa, but originally it lay to the north and west of Delhi from the foot of the Himālayas to the river Chambal. The Gaṅgā divided it into Uttara and Dakṣiṇa Pāñcāla. According to Parāśara the Madhyadeśa includes what is called Āryāvarta. From this we have to deduce that in ancient India the land lying between the two mountains, the Himālayas and the Vindhya, was designated as Madhyadeśa.

In this connection Sage Parāśara gives a graphic description of Jambūdvīpa and its subdivisions as follows :

चत्वारिंशोत्तरं योजनसहस्रं जम्बूद्वीपस्तत्र पूर्वादापश्चिमार्णवमपगाढाः षण्महागिरयः। हिमवान् हेमकूटो निषधो नीलः श्वेतः शृङ्गवांश्च । शतं सहस्राणामितरेषां षष्टिसहस्राणि काञ्चनमयानां गिरीणां चत्वारिंशन्महानद्यश्चत्वार उदधयः। कुनदीनां षष्टिसहस्राणि या महार्णवमनुप्रविशन्ति। एकनवती राज्यानामेकोनशतं कुराज्यानां दश जाङ्गलानि मरवोऽष्टावशीतिः (अष्टाविंशतिः) कच्छास्तावन्त एव द्वीपाः। पञ्च जनपदसहस्राणि। तत्र कृत्तिकादीनि त्रीणि मध्यदेशेऽस्मिन्वर्षे भवन्त्यार्द्रादीनि त्रीणि त्रीण्युक्तवर्जं क्रमात्पूर्वादिष्वष्टासु दिक्षु। दिङ्नक्षत्रेषूपसृष्टेषु दिग्जनपदानामेवोपतापो भवति, विशेषतस्तु शूरसेनमगधकलिङ्गावन्तिसौवीरसैन्धवहाररभूतिमन्दकुणिन्दाधिपतीनाम्। अतः परं दिग्जनपदान् व्याख्यास्यामः।

अथ मध्यदेशे आर्यावर्त इति य आख्यायते तत्र जनपदाः—शूरसेनोद्देहिकपाण्डुगुडाश्वत्थनीपकाञ्चनकौरवौत्तमज्योतिषभद्रारिमेदमाध्यमिकसाल्वसाकेतमत्स्यकपिष्ठलचक्रदौलेपमाण्डव्यपाण्डुनगरगौरग्रीवपारियात्रिककुकुरराज्यौदुम्बरयामुनगजाह्वयोज्जिहानकालकोटिमाथुरोत्तरदक्षिणपाञ्चालकुरुक्षेत्रधर्मारण्यसारस्वताः ॥]

अथ पूर्वस्यामञ्जनवृषभध्वजपद्ममाल्यवद्गिरयः।
व्याघ्रमुखसुह्मकर्वटचान्द्रपुराः शूर्पकर्णाश्च ॥५॥

खसमगधशिबिरगिरिमिथिलसमतटोड्राश्ववदनदन्तुरकाः।
प्राग्ज्योतिषलौहित्यक्षीरोदसमुद्रपुरुषादाः ॥६॥

उदयगिरिभद्रगौडकपौण्ड्रोत्कलकाशिमेकलाम्बष्ठाः ।
एकपदताम्रलिप्तककोसलका वर्धमानाश्च ॥७॥

To the east are situated the seven mountains viz. Añjana, Vṛṣabhadhvaja, Padma, Mālyavān, Śibira, Udayagiri and Mekala, the river Lauhitya, the milky ocean, the Vyāghramukhas (people whose face resembles the tiger's), Suhmas, Karvaṭas, those of Candrapura, Śūrpakarṇas (whose ears resembled winnowing basket), Khasas, Magadha country, Mithilā, Samataṭa, Orissa, the Aśvavadanas (a tribe whose face resembled the horses), the Danturakas (possibly a people with protruding teeth), Prāgjyotiṣa, Cannibals, the Bhadras, Gauḍas, Pauṇḍras, Utkala, Kāśī, the Ambaṣṭhas, the one-footed people, those of Tāmralipti, Kosala and Burdwan.

[The Lauhitya is identified with the Brahmaputra. A tributary of this river is even now called Lohit. *Mālyavān* is identified by Pargiter with the hills near Kupal, Mudgal and Raichur. Our author locates this in the eastern region. The *Udayagiri* may be the mythical Rising Mountain or the one near Bhuvaneshwar in Orissa.

In this section we come across the names of many tribes like the Ambaṣṭhas. According to Manu an Ambaṣṭha is the offspring of a Brāhmaṇa father and a Vaiśya mother. In our text it means a territory peopled by this tribe. They are also mentioned in the south-western division (verse 17 *infra*). Alexander's historians refer to them as living in the northern part of Sind and on the lower Chenab. In the Mahābhārata they are spoken of along with the north-western tribes such as the Śibis and Kṣudrakas. They are also mentioned by Ptolemy as living in the Vindhya region.

Suhma is mentioned both in the Mahābhārata and the Raghuvaṁśa (IV. 35-36). Kālidāsa locates it to the west of Vaṅga. According to Daṇḍin Tāmralipti, modern Tamluk in the Midnapur district, was included in the Suhma country.

The *Khasas* are found both in the eastern and northern divisions. The country of these people was included in the hill-states of Rājapurī and Lohāra They are represented by modern Khakkas in Kashmir.

Magadha originally comprised the districts of Patna and Gaya in Bihar. In the Ṛgveda (III 53.14) its name is Kīkaṭa, but in the Atharvaveda (V. 22.14) it is called Magadha itself.

Samataṭa is associated with Ḍavāka (Nogong district of Assam) and Kāmarūpa (Assam) in Samudragupta's Allahabad Praśasti. In the time of the Khaḍga rulers Karmmānta (modern Kamta near Comilla) was the capital of Samataṭa.

Prāgjyotiṣa is the region around Gauhati. According to the Raghuvaṁśa (IV. 81) it lay on the other bank of the Lauhitya. Hemacandra tells us in his *Abhidhānacintāmaṇi* (IV. 22) that this place is the same as Kāmarūpa.

Pauṇḍra corresponds to North Bengal with its capital at Mahasthan in the Bogra district.

Gauḍaka comprised the present Murshidabad district. Sometimes it means the whole of Bengal. Others hold that Western Bengal came to be called Gauḍa from the city of the same name.

Cf. पराशर—

अथ पूर्वस्यां माल्यवच्छिबिराञ्जनपद्मवृषभध्वजोदयशिखरिदन्तुरकाः काशि-कोशलमिथिलमेकलोत्कलपुण्ड्रकर्वटसमतटोड्रगौडकभद्रद्रविडसुह्मताम्रलिप्तप्राग्ज्योतिष-वर्द्धमानवाजिमुखाम्बष्ठपुरुषादकर्णिकोष्ठाधिश्रोत्रव्याघ्रमुखलौहित्यार्णवक्षीरोदार्णवमी-नाशनकिरातसौवीरमहीधरा विवसनैकपादोदयानुवासिनश्चेति ॥]

आग्नेय्यां दिशि कोसलकलिङ्गवङ्गोपवङ्गजठराङ्गाः ।
शौलिकविदर्भवत्सान्ध्रचेदिकाश्चोर्ध्वकण्ठाश्च ॥८॥

वृषनालिकेरचर्मद्वीपा विन्ध्यान्तवासिनस्त्रिपुरी ।
श्मश्रुधरहेमकुड्यव्यालग्रीवा महाग्रीवाः ॥९॥

किष्किन्धकण्टकस्थलनिषादराष्ट्राणि पुरिकदाशार्णाः ।
सह नग्नपर्णशबरैराश्लेषाद्ये त्रिके देशाः ॥१०॥

In the south-east are situated Kosala, Kaliṅga, Vaṅga, Upavaṅga, Jaṭharāṅga, Śūlikas, Vidarbha, Vatsa, Āndhra, Cedi, the Ūrdhvakaṇṭhas (high-necked ones), the island of Vṛṣa, Nālikeradvīpa (the Cocoa-nut Island), Carmadvīpa, the inhabitants of the Vindhya range, Tripurī, the Śmaśrudharas (the bearded ones), Hemakuḍya, the Vyālagrīvas (the serpent-necked), the Mahāgrīvas (long-necked ones), Kiṣkindha, Kaṇṭakasthala, the territory of the Niṣādas (aborigines), the Purikas, Daśārṇa, the naked Śabaras and Parṇa-śabaras (those wearing leaves). All these places come under the jurisdiction of the triad beginning with Āśleṣa.

[The *Kosala* country has been already assigned to the east. Here it is placed in the south-east as well. This means that its territorial boundaries extended from the east to the south-east considerably. The people of Kosala are called Kosalaka or Kausalaka. For, our author uses both the forms. The eastern Kosala roughly corresponds to the present Oudh. During the period of Śrī Rāma's sons, Kuśa and Lava, Kosala country was divided into two territories viz. Uttara and Dakṣiṇa Kosala with their capitals at Śrāvastī and Kuśasthalī respectively. As the name indicates Kuśa's capital must have been named after him. Our author tells us (in LXXX-6) that the diamonds mined in Kosala have the lustre of the Śirīṣa flower.]

Kaliṅga comprised the districts of Puri and Ganjam. It was this country that Aśoka conquered.

Vaṅga is mentioned by Kālidāsa (Raghu. IV-36) as situated in the delta formed by the Gaṅgā and the Brahmaputra. According to Pargiter it comprised the districts of Murshidabad, Nadia, Jessore, parts of Rajshahi, Pabna and Faridpur.

Upavaṅga has been identified with the central area of the eastern part of the delta of the Gaṅgā. According to Alberuni Jaṭharāṅga consists of two territories viz. Jaṭhara and Aṅga.

The *Śūlikas* are called Cūlikas in the Purāṇas. In the Matsyapurāṇa this country is said to be watered by the Cakṣu (Oxus). A branch of the Śūlikas that migrated to Orissa is to be identified with the Śulkis. P.C. Bagchi connects the Śūlikas with the Cālukyas of the Deccan.

Vidarbha comprised modern Berar and the territory between the rivers Varadā and Waingaṅgā. Ācārya Daṇḍin praises the Vaidarbhī style as containing all the ten literary excellences. In ancient times it was a famous country where lived distinguished scholars and poets. Damayantī, consort of Nala, hailed from this country.

The *Cedi* country roughly corresponds to modern Baghelkhand and adjoining regions.

Tripurī was the capital of the Kalacuris.

Kaṇṭakasthala is identified with the ancient Kaṇṭakaśaila, modern Ghaṇṭaśāla.

The *Niṣādas* are identified by some with the Bhils. The Mahābhārata (III. 130.4) mentions Vinaśana or the place of the disappearance of the Saraswatī as the gate of Niṣādarāṣṭra. It places a Niṣāda settlement between Matsya and the Chambal (II. 31. 4-7).

Purika was situated at the foot of the mountain Ṛkṣavat (Satpura), according to the Harivaṁśa.

Kiṣkindha was the capital of Vālin and later of Sugrīva. It is the hilly region in the vicinity of the Hampi ruins of Vijayanagar in the Bellary district. The Ṛṣyamūka mountain where Sugrīva is said to have taken refuge is visible from the Virūpākṣa temple at Hampi.

Daśārṇa is the region east of Vidiśā watered by the river Daśārṇā, modern Dhasan. Kālidāsa has paid his tribute to this country in his Meghadūta : "कतिपयदिनस्थायिहंसा दशार्णाः ।" The grammarian Kātyāyana has included this word in a Vārttika.

Śabaras are an aboriginal tribe. In the Matsya and Vāyu Purāṇas they are mentioned as inhabitants of Dakṣiṇāpatha. In the south they are found in almost all States, while in the north they are found to the south-west of Gwalior and Narwar and in southern Rajputana. Nagna and Parṇa-śabaras are two subdivisions of these forest tribes. The latter group of Śabaras is still called in South Kanara district by the name *Soppu Koragas*, meaning *leaf-Koravas*.]

अथ दक्षिणेन लङ्काकालाजिनसौरिकीर्णतालिकटाः ।
गिरिनगरमलयदर्दुरमहेन्द्रमालिन्द्यभरुकच्छाः ॥११॥

कङ्कटकङ्कणवनवासिशिबिकफणिकारकोङ्कणाभीराः ।
आकरवेणावर्तकदशपुरगोनर्दकेरलकाः ॥१२॥

कर्णाटमहाटविचित्रकूटनासिक्यकोल्लगिरिचोलाः ।
क्रौञ्चद्वीपजटाधरकावेर्यो रिष्यमूकश्च ॥१३॥

वैदूर्यशङ्खमुक्तात्रिवारिचरधर्मपट्टनद्वीपाः ।
गणराज्यकृष्णवेल्लूरपिशिकशूर्पाद्रिकुसुमनगाः ॥१४॥

तुम्बवनकार्मणेयकयाम्योदधितापसाश्रमा ऋषिकाः ।
काञ्चीमरुचीपट्टनचेर्यार्यकसिंहला ऋषभाः ॥१५॥

बलदेवपट्टनं दण्डकावनतिमिङ्गिलाशना भद्राः ।
कच्छोऽथ कुञ्जरदरी सताम्रपर्णीति विज्ञेयाः ॥१६॥

Now in the south are situated Laṅkā, the Kālājinas, Saurikīrṇas, Tālikaṭas, Girinagara, the mountains Malaya, Dardura,

Mahendra and Mālindya, the Bharukacchas, the Kaṅkaṭas, Kaṅkaṇas, Vanavāsi (modern Banavāsi in North Kanara district), the Śibikas, Phaṇikaras, Koṅkaṇas, Ābhīras, the mine-region, the Veṇā river, the Āvartakas, Daśapura, the Gonardas, Kerala, Karṇāṭaka, the Mahāṭavi (the Great Forest), Citrakūṭa hill, Nasik, Kollagiri (a hill of that name), the Colas, the Krauñca island, the Jaṭādharas (those that have matted locks), the Kāverī river, Ṛṣyamūka mountain, the mines of beryl, conch shells and pearls, Atri's hermitage, the mariners, Dharmapattana (Dharmapuri ?), the islands, Gaṇarājya, Kṛṣṇa, Velluru, the Piśikas, the Śūrpa mountain, mount Kusuma, Tumbavana (a forest), the Kārmaṇeyakas, the Southern Ocean, Tāpasāśrama (a place abounding in hermitages), the Ṛṣikas, Kāñcī, Marucīpaṭṭana, Ceryāryakas (or Ceryas *i.e.* people of Cera or Kerala, kingdom, and the Āryakas), the Siṁhalas, Ṛṣabhas, Baladevapaṭṭana (the modern Valarpatnam in Malabar ?), Daṇḍakā forest, the whale-eaters, the Bhadras, Cutch, elephant caves (where they are caught) and the Tāmraparṇī river.

[We have to find out the reason for the separate mention of *Laṅkā* and *Siṁhala*. Fleet suggests "Laṅkā seems to denote here not the island of Ceylon, but its capital city, because it provides the Hindu prime meridian.]

Kālājina, which is also spelt as Kālāñjana, is identical with Kālañjara, according to Fleet. According to a Purāṇic verse, "सप्तव्याधा दशार्णेषु मृगाः कालाञ्जने गिरौ...," which is recited at Śrāddhas, it is a mountain of some religious importance. We cannot be sure of its location. It may be a mountain in the south abounding in Kṛṣṇamṛgas, a type of spotted dear, whose skins are used for various religious purposes such as the Upanayana.

Saurikīrṇas : Kern splits this word as Sauri and Kīrṇa and identifies the former with the Sorae or Colas of Ptolemy.

Tālikaṭa is identified by Fleet with Talikot in the Bijapur district. A.M. Shastri feels that it would be more appropriate to identify it with Talakāḍu in Mysore, the celebrated capital of the Gaṅgas. In my view Talikot is preferable.

Girinagara is the modern Junagadh, which is immortalized by the Girnar inscription of Rudradaman I.

Bharukaccha is the modern Broach which was Barygaza to the Greeks.

Malaya and *Dardura* are twin mountains in the south. The

former stands for the southern part of the western Ghats from the Nilgiris to Cape Comorin. In the Mahābhārata (Droṇa 23.70-72) it is associated with the Pāṇḍyas. Dardura is identified with the Nilgiris or Palni Hills. Kālidāsa compares these two mountains to the bosoms of Earth

Mahendra "embraces the entire chain of hills extending from Ganjam to Tinnevelly." Kālidāsa associates it with Kalinga (Raghu. VI. 54). In the Rāmāyaṇa Hanūmān is described as flying across the ocean from the summit of this mountain.

Ābhīras are supposed to have entered India from eastern Iran about the second century B.C. They were also considered to be Śūdras. They must have migrated later to the south from the north. In the second and third centuries of the Christian era they were occupying important political positions in Gujarat and Nasik.

Ākara is identified by Kern with modern Khandesh. The word occurs in the inscription of Rudradaman I. Therein it denotes eastern Malwa. The name is still preserved in Agar, 35 miles north east of Ujjain.

Veṇā is the modern Waingaṅgā, a tributary of the Godāvarī.

Daśapura, which is mentioned by Kālidāsa, as well as in the inscription of the *Guild of Silk-weavers*, has been identified with the modern Mandasor.

The *Śibis* are identified by some with the *Śivas* of the Ṛgveda, which is not convincing. There is a Śibijātaka written by Ārya-śūra. These Jātakas know of two Śibi settlements with their capitals at Ariṣṭapura and at Jetuttara, Jattaraur of Alberuni, modern Nagari, 11 miles north of Chitor. Fa-hian locates the scene of the *Sibijātaka* at Shorkot in the Punjab. Thus it cannot be said with certainty who and where exactly these Śibis were in the south. It is possible that some branches of them might have migrated to the south.

Gonarda is said to be the birth place of Patañjali. It is also mentioned in the Mārkaṇḍeya Purāṇa. In the Suttanipāta it has been placed between Ujjayinī and Vidiśā. However, Patañjali was not a south-Indian.

The Ṛṣikas are spoken of along with Vidarbha, Mahiṣaka, Aśmaka and Anūpa, according to the Rāmāyaṇa and the Mahābhārata.

Cf. पराशर—

अथ दक्षिणस्यां विन्ध्यकुसुमापीडदर्दुरमहेन्द्रशूर्पवत्समलयमालिन्द्यावन्तिसाम्बवतिदशपुरैककच्छभरुकच्छर्द्धिवनवासोपगिरिभद्रगिरिनगरदण्डकगणराज्यत्रिराजकर्कोटकञ्चनतिमिङ्गिलाहाररिष्यमूकतापसाश्रमशङ्खमुक्ताप्रवालवैदूर्याकरोद्वक्त्रात्रिवारिचरार्णवचोलककौवेरकावेरिकपाशिकधर्मपट्टनपट्टिकाशक्तृष्णवेल्लूरताम्रपर्णनार्मदगोनर्दचाञ्चीकपट्टनतालिकटसौरिकीर्णसहकारिवेणातटतुम्बवनकालाजिनद्वीपकर्णिकारशिबिकोङ्कणचित्रकूटकर्णाटमहाटविकान्ध्रकोल्लगिरिनासिक्यकार्मणेयकावेर्वारुकवेधिनिकबलदेवपट्टनक्रौञ्चद्वीपसिंहलाः परमतदर्दुरमलयमरीचित्रकूटशिखरालङ्कृतालङ्कारशूर्पपर्वतकुञ्जरदरीसम्भोगवतिनृणां गिरिसाराश्रमाः ॥]

नैऋर्त्यां दिशि देशाः पह्लवकाम्बोजसिन्धुसौवीराः ।
वडवामुखारवाम्बष्ठकपिलनारीमुखानर्ताः ॥१७॥

फेणगिरियवनमार्गरकर्णप्रावेयपारशवशूद्राः ।
बर्बरकिरातखण्डक्रव्यादाभीरचञ्चूकाः ॥१८॥

हेमगिरिसिन्धुकालकरैवतकसुराष्ट्रबादरद्राविडाः ।
स्वात्याद्ये भत्रितये ज्ञेयश्च महार्णवोऽत्रैव ॥१९॥

In the south-west are situated the following countries. Those of the Pahlavas, Kāmbojas, Sindhu-Sauvīras, Vaḍavāmukhas, Aravas, Ambaṣṭhas, Kapilas, Nārīmukhas, Ānartas (Northern Gujarat), the Pheṇagiri, Yavanas, Mārgaras, Karṇaprāveyas, Pāraśavas, Śūdras, Barbaras, Kirātas, Khaṇḍas, Kravyādas (eaters of raw meat), Ābhīras, Cañcūkas, the Hemagiri, the Indus, the Kālakas, the Raivataka mountain, the Surāṣṭras, the Bādaras, the Draviḍas, and the great ocean. These come under the triad of stars headed by Svātī.

[*Pahlavas* are identified with the Parthians, who are known to have occupied parts of north-western India in a few centuries before and after Christ. Rudradāman's inscription mentions a Pahlava named Suviśākha, as the governor of Ānarta and Surāṣṭra.

Kāmboja is mentioned by Kālidāsa (Raghu IV) and in the Mahābhārata (VII 4.5). Hence it is located by scholars to the south of Kashmir; and its western boundaries might have extended to Kafiristan. Yāska refers (I.2.1.4) to the particular usage of the root *Śav* in the sense of 'to go' among the Kāmbojas. It is learned that this peculiarity is still current in the Galcha-speaking areas of Pamir and Badakhshan. It is possible that during the period of Varāhamihira there might have been a settlement of the Kāmbojas in the south-western region of India.

Sindhu-Sauvīra is identified with Sindh-Sagar Doab, the region between the Jhelum and the Indus. In the Junagadh inscription also the two parts appear as one geographical entity. According to the *Kāmasūtra* Sindhudeśa lay to the west of the Indus.

Alberuni states that Sauvīra denotes Multan and Jahravar. In Sanskrit the word *Sauvīra* is used in the sense of 'sour gruel', 'jujube fruit', and 'antimony'. It is also used in combination as in *Sauvīrāñjana*. It is possible that in ancient times great heroes and warriors hailed from this region. Hence the name. *Ānarta* is mentioned in the Girnar inscription. According to the Mahābhārata (II. 14-50) Kuśasthalī or Dvārakā was situated in Ānarta.

Pheṇagiri is placed near the mouth of the Indus by Monier-Williams.

Karṇaprāveya is synonymous with *Karṇa prāvaraṇa* mentioned in the Rāmāyaṇa (IV. 40.26) according to Kern.

Pāraśava is the son of a Brāhmaṇa by a Śūdra woman. Here it is identified with Persia. In chapter LXXXI-2, 5 this country is said to be the producer of excellent pearls.

The *Śūdras* are associated with the Ābhīras and are located in West Rajputana near Vinaśana, according to the Mahābhārata (II. 32.10; IX.37.1). Alexander's historians call them Sodrai who lived between the Indus and the Sutlej above the junction of the five rivers near Mithankot and south of the district of Multan. They had their capital on the Indus.

The *Barbaras* are located in the region about the port of Barbaricum situated on the middle mouth of the indus, according to the Periplus. The *Mārkaṇḍeyapurāṇa* (LVII. 39) places the Barbara country in the Sindhu valley.

The *Cañcūkas* are identified by some with the Chenchus, a hill tribe, living in the Śrīśailam area of Andhra Pradesh.

Hemagiri may be identical with Kanakagiri near Mysore.

Raivataka is a hill opposite Mt. Girnar. Sometimes it is identified with the Girnar mountain itself, which is believed to be birthplace of Neminātha and regarded as one of the five great *Tīrthas* of the Jainas. In the Junagadh inscription of Skandagupta, it is said to be the source of the river Palāśinī.

Surāṣṭra corresponds to the Kathiawad peninsula. Surat is a corruption of this name. The author of the *Periplus* calls it Syrastrene.

Badara is identified by Cunningham with modern Eder. In the time of Yuan Chwang Badarī was a large kingdom bounded by Ajmer and Ranthambhor on the north, by the Loni and the Chambal on the east and west and the Malwa frontier on the south, and extending from the mouth of the river Banas in the Ran of Cutch to the Chambal near Mandasor.

Draviḍa or Dramiḍa is usually regarded as the Sanskritized form of Tamil. Kern feels that Varāhamihira means by this term some Dravidian tribe in the west, perhaps the Brahui in Baluchistan who belong to the Dravidian stock.

Cf. पराशर—

अथ प्रत्यग्दक्षिणस्यां सुराष्ट्रमहाराष्ट्रसिन्धुसौवीरशूद्राभीरद्रविडकनकखण्डसिन्धुकालकफेणगिरिरैवतकनर्तकबाह्लीकयवनपह्लवमार्गरारवरथकाराम्बष्ठकालाजकर्णप्रवरगिरिवासिनोऽतः परं महार्णवोऽर्वकोपजोऽग्निर्वडवामुख इति ॥]

अपरस्यां मणिमान् मेघवान् वनौघः क्षुरार्पणोऽस्तगिरिः ।
अपरान्तकशान्तिकहैहयप्रशस्ताद्रिवोक्काणाः ॥२०॥

पञ्चनदरमठपारततारक्षितिजृङ्गवैश्यकनकशकाः ।
निर्मर्यादा म्लेच्छा ये पश्चिमदिक्स्थितास्ते च ॥२१॥

In the west are the Maṇimat and Meghavat mountains, Vanaugha (Vast Forest), Mount Kṣurārpaṇa, Astagiri, the Aparāntakas, Śāntikas, Haihayas, Mount Praśasta, the Vokkāṇas, the Punjab, Ramaṭhas, Pāratas, Tārakṣiti, the Jṛṅgas, Vaiśyas, Kanakas, Scythians (or Gold-Sythians ?) and all the lawless tribes of barbarians living in the west. All these are ruled by the three stars, Jyeṣṭhā, Mūla and Pūrvāṣāḍha.

[*Aparāntakas* are the people living on the western borders near the Sahya mountain. Kālidāsa mentions (Raghu. IV. 53) the kings of this country.

The *Haihayas* were a branch of the Yādavas. They were divided into five clans, viz., Vītihotra, Bhoja, Avanti, Tuṇḍikera, and Tālajaṅgha. The Kalacuris of Central India were also called Haihayas. The Haihaya country, which was also called Anūpa, comprised the region round Māhiṣmatī.

Vokkāṇa has been identified with Wakhan.

Ramaṭha is the country whence asafoetida was obtained. Hence it was called Rāmaṭha. S. Levi places it between Gazni and Wakhan.

The *Pāratas* are identified with Ptolemy's Pardene in the centre of Geḍrosia (Baluchistan).

Kanaka is identified by Dey with Travancore. Kern takes this word as an epithet of Śaka and translates the compound as Gold-Scythians.

Śakas are located in the south-west of India, in the Agnipurāṇa (LV. 16). Apart from the Scythian rulers of north-western India Śaka Kṣatrapas and Mahākṣatrapas of the lineage of Bhūmaka and Caṣṭana are known to have ruled over western India in the early centuries of the Christian era. In the Allahabad inscription they are said to have paid homage to Samudragupta.

Mlecchas, according to Kern, are foreigners or barbarians. In II. 15 *supra* the Greeks are spoken of as Mlecchas. In Alberuni's time the term was used to denote the Arabs.

Cf. पराशर—

अथ पश्चिमायां दिशि मणिमान् क्षुरार्पणो मेघवान् वनौघः। चक्रवदस्तगिरि-प्रशस्तमण्डिताऱः । पञ्चनदकाशिब्रह्मवसतितारक्षितिपारतशान्तिकशिबिरमठजृङ्गि-वायव्यगुडवासिजहैहयसत्कङ्कताजिकहूणपार्श्ववैतककवोक्काणाः । अन्ये च गिरिवन-वासिनस्त्यक्तधर्मदण्डमर्यादा म्लेच्छजातयः ॥]

दिशि पश्चिमोत्तरस्यां माण्डव्यतुषारतालहलमद्राः ।
अश्मककुलूतहलडाः स्त्रीराज्यनृसिंहवनखस्थाः ॥२२॥

वेणुमती फल्गुलुका गुलुहा मरुकुच्छचर्मरङ्गाख्याः ।
एकविलोचनशूलिकदीर्घग्रीवास्यकेशाश्च ॥२३॥

In the northwest are situated the Māṇḍavyas, Tuṣāras, Tālas, Halas, Madras, Aśmakas, Kulūtas, Halaḍas, the Kingdom of Women, Nṛsiṁha forest, the Khasthas, the river Veṇumatī, Phalgulukas, Guluhas, Marukucchas, Carmaraṅgas, the one-eyed tribe, Śūlikas, the long-necked ones, long-faced ones and long haired ones. These are ruled by the three stars headed by Uttarāṣāḍhā.

(मरुकुच्च is another reading. कोशाश्च is the other reading in some editions.)

Māṇḍavya is identified with the people of Madavika known from an early copper coin. Māṇḍavi of the *Mahāmāyūri* is sometimes identified with Mandawar, 8 miles north of Bijnor, or with Māṇḍavyapura (Mandor near Jodhpur), which might have been their capital.

The *Tuṣāras* are Ptolemy's Tochari who are said to be under the subjugation of the Bactrians and are described as "the most distinguished." According to Stein, the Turkhāra (Tuṣāra) country comprised the upper Oxus Valley including Balkh and Badakhshan. It corresponds to the Tukharistan of the Arab writers.

Halaḍa is translated by Kern as Lahaḍa. He suggests that it may be Lahara, mentioned in the *Rājataraṅgiṇī*. It is a borderland between Kashmir and Dardistan.

Madras are a people living in a part of the Vāhīka country, according to the Mahābhārta (Karṇaparvan Chs. 44 and 45). It covered the extensive territory between the Ravi and the Jhelum. It had two wings, the eastern and the western. Those of the northern division are the Uttara-Madras who lived beyond the Himālayan range.

Aśmaka, according to Bhaṭṭasvāmin, commentator of the Arthaśāstra, is identical with Mahārāṣṭra. T.W. Rhys Davids thinks that the Aśmaka country was originally situated immediately to the north-west of Avanti and that the settlement on the Godāvarī was a later colony. However, Kern suggests that it is more plausible to identify the Aśmaka of our text with the Assakenoi of the Greek writers. In Alexander's time the Aśmaka territory comprised part of Swat and Buner and extended eastwards as far as the Indus and had its capital at the town of Massaga (or Maśakāvatī).

Kulūta is also placed in the north-east. It is the famous Kullu in the upper valley of the Beas. Yuan Chwang calls it Kiu-lu-to. The Kulūtas are mentioned by the author of the Mudrārākṣasa.

Strīrājya, a kingdom of women, was known to Yuan Chwang as an amazonian kingdom in the Himālayan valley of the Sutlej. Dey states that it was 'a country in the Himālaya immediately on the north of Brahmaputra, which has been identified with Garwal and Kumaun ' Atkinson tells us that a woman named Pinchu ruled over the Nu-wang tribe in Eastern Tibet, and the people in each successive reign chose a woman for their sovereign. Vātsyāyana (II. 5.27) mentions a *Strīrājya*, which Yaśodhara places to the west of Vaṅga.

The *Agnipurāṇa* (LV. 17) mentions it as a country in the west of India.

Cf. पराशर—

अथ पश्चिमोत्तरस्यां दिशि गिरिमतिवेणुमतिरलमतिफल्गुलुकमाण्डव्यैकनेत्रमरुकुच्चतुषारतालमल्लहलडहलातर्वदिलीनविलीनदीर्घकेशग्रीवान्याङ्गशरगविषवेषशूलिकगुलुहाः । परमतः स्त्रीराज्यमिति ॥]

उत्तरतः कैलासो हिमवान् वसुमान् गिरिर्धनुष्मांश्च ।
क्रौञ्चो मेरुः कुरवस्तथोत्तराः क्षुद्रमीनाश्च ॥२४॥

कैकयवसातियामुनभोगप्रस्थार्जुनायनाग्नीध्राः ।
आदर्शान्तर्द्वीपित्रिगर्ततुरगाननाः श्वमुखाः ॥२५॥

केशधरचिपिटनासिकदासेरकवाटधानशरधानाः ।
तक्षशिलपुष्कलावतकैलावतकण्ठधानाश्च ॥२६॥

अम्बरमद्रकमालवपौरवकच्छारदण्डपिङ्गलकाः ।
माणहलहूणकोहलशीतकमाण्डव्यभूतपुराः ॥२७॥

गान्धारयशोवतिहेमतालराजन्यखचरगव्याश्च ।
यौधेयदासमेयाः श्यामाकाः क्षेमधूर्ताश्च ॥२८॥

In the north lie the Kailāsa, Himavat, Vasumat, Dhanuṣmat, Krauñca, Meru (all mountains), the Uttara Kuru country, the Kṣudramīnas, Kaikayas, Vasātis, Yāmunas, Bhogaprastha, the Arjunāyanas, Āgnīdhras, Ādarśas, Antardvīpins, Trigarta, the Turagānanas (horse-faced people), the Śvamukhas (dog-faced people), Keśadharas (the hairy ones) Cipiṭanāsikas (flat-nosed tribe) Dāserakas, Vāṭadhānas, Śaradhānas, Taxila, Puṣkalāvata, Kailāvata, Kaṇṭhadhānas, Ambarāvatas, Madrakas, Malwa, Pauravas, Kacchāras, Daṇḍapiṅgalakas, Māṇahalas, Huns, Kohalas, Śītakas, Māṇḍavyas, Bhūtapura, Gāndhāra, Yaśovati (town), Hematālas, Kṣatriyas, Khacaras, Gavyas, the Yaudheyas, Dāsameyas, Śyāmākas and Kṣemadhūrtas. These are ruled by the triad of stars beginning with Śatabhiṣaj.

[The mountain *Krauñca* has been identified with that part of the Kailāsa mountain on which Lake Mānasa is situated.

Meru is identified by some with a part of the Himālayas. According to others it is the highland of Tartary, north of the Himālayas. B.C. Law identifies it with Rudra Himālaya in Garhwal where the Ganges rises, and regards it as identical with the Mount Meros of Arrian. According to another view, Meru denotes the Pamir range in Central Asia.

Uttara-Kuru is the country beyond the Himālayan range, probably in the land of Kashmir (*Pareṇa himavantam*, Ait. Brā. VIII. 14). It is the same as Ottorokorrha of Ptolemy. The land is represented as an earthly paradise.

The *Kekaya* country lay beyond the Beas and had its capital at Girivraja which is identified with Girjaak or Jalalpur on the

Jhelum. Roughly speaking, it comprised the districts of Jhelum, Shahpur and Gujarat.

Vasātis are the Ossadioi of Alexander's historians, settled in the region between the Indus and Jhelum, comprising Rawalpindi. Vasāti is mentioned in the *Mahābhāṣya* (IV. 2.52) and the *Mahāmāyūrī*.

The *Arjunāyanas* are identified by Fleet with the Kalacuris who trace their descent from Kārtavīrya Arjuna. But according to the Kāśikā (II. 4.66) they were discended from the Pāṇḍava hero Arjuna. The find-spots of their coins indicate that their country, known as Arjunāyanaka, lay within the triangle of Delhi-Jaipur-Agra.

Ādarśa is the place where the Sarasvatī disappears. So the word, meaning the country or its people, is derived from *Adarśa*. It was regarded as the western boundary of Āryāvarta. According to another view, it lay not far from the ancient kingdoms of Srughna and Trigarta (Kangra).

Trigarta denotes the country drained by the three rivers, Ravi, Beas and Sutlej. It comprised the whole of the upper Doab between the Ravi and Sutlej. Hemacandra identifies Trigarta with Jālandhara.

Cipiṭanāsikas are those with Mongolian features such as flat nose. The *Periplus* mentions a people called Cirrhadae with flattened nose, who, according to Schoff, were a Bhoṭa tribe, whose descendants, still called Kirāta, live in the Morung, west of Sikkim.

Dāserakas may be an aboriginal tribe. Pāṇini (IV. 1.131) derives the word from Dāsī, a slave woman.

The *Vāṭadhānas* are located, according to the *Mārkaṇḍeya-purāṇa*, between the Bāhlikas and Ābhīras. According to Pargiter, Vāṭadhāna was a country on the eastern side of the Sutlej, southwards from Ferozepur. Dey identifies it with Bhatnair. In the Mahābhārata (II. 32.8) mention is made of a Vāṭadhāna settlement near Madhyamikā, modern Nagari, in Rajputana.

Takṣaśilā comprised the villages of Shahḍheri, Sir-kap, Sirsukh and Kacheha-kot at a short distance to the north-west of Rawalpindi.

Puṣkalāvata has been identified with Charsadda, about 17 miles north-east of Peshawar.

Ambara is explained by Utpala as Ambarāvata.

Mālava Fleet observes, 'Varāhamihira places them too much to the north, as they are undoubtedly the people of Malwa, from whom...the Vikrama era derived its origin.' It is possible that our author refers here to a northern settlement of the Mālavas who lived between the lower Ravi and the Chenab in the 4th century B.C.

The *Pauravas* or Purus lived on the eastern bank of the Jhelum including the Gujarat district. In the 4th century B.C., when Alexander invaded India, Porus, probably the Pūru chief, was ruling over the region between the rivers Jhelum and Chenab. King Duṣyanta is said to be a descendant of Pūru.

Hūṇas are often mentioned by classical writers such as Kālidāsa and Bāṇa. Prabhākaravardhana is styled 'Lion to the Huṇa deer'. Skandagupta had to encounter the Hūṇas. Yuan Chwang says that Bālāditya, son of Tathāgatagupta, imprisoned and later released the Hūṇa chief Mihirakula. Having been expelled from central India, the Hūṇas seem to have confined themselves to Kashmir and Gandhāra.

Gāndhāra extended from the Kabul valley to Takṣaśilā and comprised the Rawalpindi and Peshawar districts. Our author mentions two towns of Gāndhāra viz. Takṣaśilā and Puṣkalāvatī (modern Charsadda), situated to the east and west respectively of the Indus. Gandharvadeśa seems to be the original name of Gandhāra (Rāmāyaṇa VII. 101.11).

The *Rājanyas* must be the same as the Kṣatṛiyas or Xathroi of the Greek writers. The Hoshiarpur region was perhaps their homeland. Later they seem to have migrated to Mathurā. It is reasonable to suppose that each of the four Varṇas had its own original homeland.

Yaudheyas are first mentioned by Pāṇini (V. 3.117). Their coins ranging from the second century B.C. to the fourth century A.D. have been found in Eastern Punjab and in the region between the Sutlej and the Yamunā. They lived on both banks of the Sutlej along the Bhawalpur frontier which is known as Johiyawar, a name reminiscent of the Yaudheyas.

Śyāmakas are identified by Levi with Chō-mi of Sungyun etc. It is also identified by some with Chitral.

Cf. पराशर—

अथोत्तरस्यां हिमवान् क्रौञ्चो मधुमान् कैलासो वसुमानुत्तरोत्तरस्यां मद्रपौरव-यौधेयमालवशूरसेनराजन्यार्जुनायनत्रैगर्तकैकयक्षुद्रमाचेलूकमत्स्यवसातिदर्भफलाफलप्रस्त-

लक्ष्मधूर्त्तशाकलदाशधानहव्यमुरदण्डगव्यशरधानदासेरकवाटधानान्तर्द्वीपिगान्धारवव-न्धिषुवास्तुतक्षशिलालवणवतिपुष्कलावतियशोवतिमणिवतिश्यामाकखचरकोहलकनगर-शरभूतपुरकैरातकादर्शकान्तारदण्डपिङ्गलमाण्डव्ययामुनेयमाणहलहूणहेमतालाश्वमुखा हिमवद्वसुमत्कैलासक्रौञ्चात् परमभिजना इति ।।]

ऐशान्यां मेरुकनष्टराज्यपशुपालकीरकाश्मीराः ।
अभिसारदरदतङ्गणकुलूतसैरिन्ध्रवनराष्ट्राः ।।२९।।

ब्रह्मपुरदार्वडामरवनराज्यकिरातचीनकौणिन्दाः ।
मल्लाः पटोलजटासुरकुनटखसघोषकुचिकाख्याः ।।३०।।

एकचरणानुविद्धाः सुवर्णभूर्वसुधनं दिविष्ठाश्च ।
पौरवचीरनिवासित्रिनेत्रमुञ्जाद्रिगान्धर्वाः ।।३१।।

In the north-east lie Meruka, Naṣṭarājya (lost kingdom), the Paśupālas (protectors of cattle), Kīra, Kashmir, the Abhisāras, Daradas, Taṅgaṇas, Kulūtas, Sairindhras, Vanarāṣṭra (forest empire), Brahmapura, the Dārvas, Dāmaras, Vanarājya (forest kingdom), Kirātas, Cīna, the Kauṇindas, Bhallas, Paṭolas Jaṭāsuras, Kunaṭas, Khasas, Ghoṣas, Kucikas, one-footed men, the Anuviddhas, Suvarṇabhū (gold region), Vasudhana, Diviṣṭhas (situated in heaven), Pauravas, bark-clad people, Trinetras (three-eyed ones), Mount Muñja and the regions of the Gandharvas. These come under the triad of stars beginning with Revatī.

[For **अनुविद्धाः** there is a variant reading as **अनुविश्वाः** and for **वसुधनम्, वसुवनम्.**

The *Kīras* are mentioned in a number of epigraphic records. Their country comprised the territory near Baijnath in the Kangra valley. A Chamba copperplate inscription mentions Kīras between Durgaras (Dongras) and Trigartas.

Abhisāra is identified by Dr. Stein with the tract of the lower region and hills between the Jhelum and Chenab including the state of Rājapura (Rajauri) in Kashmir.

Darada is Dardistan north of Kashmir on the upper Indus. Sir Aurel Stein identifies its capital Daratpurī with modern Gurez. The seats of the Daradas extend from Chitral and Yasin across the Indus region of Gilgit, Chilas and Bunji to the Kishangaṅga valley in the immediate north of Kashmir.

The *Taṅgaṇas* are Ptolemy's Tanganoi whose territory stretched from the Ramgaṅga river to the upper Sarayū. They were one of the aboriginal tribes which the Āryans, while pushing their conquests to the east of the Gaṅgā and Yamunā, drove back into the Himālayas or towards the Vindhyas. The Ṭonk Rajputs of Rohilkhand and the Dangayas are said to be the present representatives of the Taṅgaṇas.

Brahmapura is mentioned in the Agnipurāṇa. Cunningham identifies it with Variat-pattan on the Ramgaṅga river. Yuan Chwang mentions it as a country which lay in the Garhwal and Kumaun region.

Dārva is closely associated with Abhisāra and these together roughly comprised the Punch and Naushera region between the Jhelum and the Chenab.

Dāmaras are identified by Wilson with a fierce intractable tribe inhabiting the mountains to the north of Kashmir.

The *Cīnaraṭṭha* is identified with the Himavantapadesa in the Pali *Sāsanavaṁsa*. B.C. Law places it in the Himālayas beyond Cilāta or Kirāta. Kern translates it into 'the Chinese'.

Paṭola, according to Kern, is Palola, and a corruption of the word *Palvala*. He suggests that by Palola is meant the eastern part of the Tarai near Cooch-Bihar.

Suvarṇabhū is sometimes identified with Ptolemy's Golden Khersonese or the delta of the Irawadi forming the province of Pegu. But it may include also Malaysia and the islands of eastern archipelago.

The subject-matter of this chapter has been summarized by Varāhamihira in his समाससंहिता thus :—

भत्रयमाग्नेयाद्यं मध्यं प्राक्प्रभृति च प्रदक्षिणतः ।
कथयामि प्रविभागं रौद्रात् प्रागादिदेशानाम् ॥
मध्यमुदक्पाञ्चाला वङ्गा यमुनान्तरं कुरुक्षेत्रम् ।
उदगपि च परियात्रात् परमथवाऽयोग्यमत्स्याश्च ॥
सारस्वतयामुनवत्सघोषसंख्याननीपमाण्डव्याः ।
भद्रारिमोदनैमिषसाल्वोपज्योतिषाश्वत्थाः ॥
औदुम्बरोऽथ कुकुरोज्जिहानगजसाह्वकङ्कपाण्डुगुडाः ।
माध्यमिकोद्देहिककालकोटिकापिष्ठलाश्चेति ॥
मध्येऽयं प्रविभागः शेषर्क्षाणां तथादिशेद्देशान् ।
प्रख्यातदेशमध्यानन्यांश्चैवाभिधास्यामि ॥
आर्द्रादिकाशिकोशलमिथिलोत्कलवर्धमानपाण्ड्योड्राः ।
लौहित्यमगधसमतटमेककलाम्बष्ठताम्रलिप्ताख्याः ॥

आश्लेषाद्ये त्रिपुरी निषादराष्ट्राणि चेदिकदशार्णाः ।
शूलिकविन्ध्यान्तःस्था वत्सान्ध्रविदर्भकालिङ्गाः ।
आर्यम्णाद्ये चैदिककोङ्कणवनवासिकोल्लगिरिमलयाः ।
उज्जयिनीभरुकच्छा दिशा च याम्यार्णवो यावत् ।।
स्वात्याद्ये सिन्धुसौवीरकापिलवनितास्यामार्गरानर्ताः ।
बर्बरयवनसुराष्ट्रककाम्बोजद्रविडरैवतकाः ।।
ज्येष्ठादितोऽपरान्तकशकहैहयजृङ्गपाञ्चनदकतकाः ।
निर्मर्यादा म्लेच्छाः शान्तिकवोक्काणवैश्याश्च ।।
विश्वेश्वरादिशूलिकतालतुषारैकनेत्रमाण्डव्याः ।
स्त्रीराज्यचर्मरङ्गाश्मकलडहारुहकफाल्गुलुकाः ।।
शतभिषगाद्ये केकयगान्धारादर्शयामुनाग्नीध्राः ।
दासेयचिपिटनासार्जुनायना दण्डपिङ्गलकाः ।।
पौष्णाद्ये काश्मीरत्रिगर्तदरदाभिसारचीनखसाः ।
तङ्गणकिरातकीरा ब्रह्मपुरजटासुराश्चेति ।।

Cf. also पराशर—

अथ प्रागुत्तरस्यां कौलूतब्रह्मपुरकुणिन्ददिवादिनपारतनष्टराज्यवनराष्ट्रवैम-कैणभल्लसिंहपुरचामरतङ्गणसार्यकपर्वतककाश्मीरदरददर्वाभिमुरजटासुरपटोलसैरिन्ध्र-कुचिन्तनकिरातपशुपालचीनसुवर्णभूमिदेवस्थलदेवोद्यानानि ।।]

वर्गैराग्नेयाद्यैः क्रूरग्रहपीडितैः क्रमेण नृपाः ।
पाञ्चालो मागधिकः कालिङ्गश्च क्षयं यान्ति ।।३२।।
आवन्तोऽथानर्तो मृत्युं चायाति सिन्धुसौवीरः ।
राजा च हारहौरो मद्रेशोऽन्यश्च कौणिन्दः ।।३३।।

When the nine triads of stars beginning with the group of three stars viz. Kṛttikā, Rohiṇi and Mṛgaśiras, are afflicted by malefic planets, the kings of the following nine countries will in their order be destroyed :—Pāñcāla, Magadha, Kaliṅga, Avantī, Ānarta, Sindhu-sauvīra, Hārahaura, Madra and Kuṇinda.

[In these verses our author puts countries under stars different from those mentioned previously in this chapter. For example, he places Avanti in the south, but actually it should belong to the north where Mālwa is situated. Though both Ānarta and Sindhusauvīra belong to the south-west, he puts the latter in the west. King Hārahaura is mentioned here for the first time. The *Hārahaura* country is supposed to be the land lying between the Indus and the Jhelum and the Gandgarh mountain and the salt range.]

———

नक्षत्रव्यूहः ॥१५॥

Chapter XV—*Stellar Rulership*

आग्नेये सितकुसुमाहिताग्निमन्त्रज्ञसूत्रभाष्यज्ञाः ।
आकरिकनापितद्विजघटकारपुरोहिताब्दज्ञाः ॥१॥

The star Kṛttikā presides over the following : White flowers, Brāhmaṇas who maintain and worship the sacred fire daily, knowers of the sacred hymns and sacrificial rules, grammarians, miners, barbers, Brāhmaṇas, potters, priests and astrologers.

[In the preceding chapter the author gives the rulership of the nine triads of stars over the nine regions or quarters and the peoples and countries situated therein. In this chapter he gives various things and types of persons that are ruled by the 27 asterisms severally. Rulership of the four Varṇas or classes is separately given in 28-29 *infra*.]

रोहिण्यां सुव्रतपण्यभूपधनियोगयुक्तशाकटिकाः ।
गोवृषजलचरकर्षकशिलोच्चयैश्वर्यसम्पन्नाः ॥२॥

The following are ruled by Rohiṇī : Observers of vows, merchandises, kings, wealthy persons, Yogins, cartmen, cows, bulls, aquatic animals, husbandmen, mountains and men in authority.

[Bhaṭṭotpala construes the word Paṇya as Paṇyavṛttayaḥ *i.e.* merchants.]

मृगशिरसि सुरभिवस्त्राब्जकुसुमफलरत्नवनचरविहङ्गाः ।
मृगसोमपीथिगान्धर्वकामुका लेखहाराश्च ॥३॥

The following are allotted to the constellation Mṛgaśiras : Fragrant articles, garments, aquatic products, flowers, fruits, gems, foresters (or forest-dwellers), birds, beasts, those who partake of Soma juice (in sacrifices), musicians, lovers and carriers of letters.

रौद्रे वधबन्धानृतपरदारस्तेयशाठ्यभेदरताः ।
तुषधान्यतीक्ष्णमन्त्राभिचारवेतालकर्मज्ञाः ॥४॥

Murderers (or executioners), animal-catchers, liars, adulterers, thieves, rogues, creators of discord, cereals, cruel persons, charmers, sorcerers and those well versed in the art of raising goblins—all these are assigned to star Ārdrā.

आदित्ये सत्यौदार्यशौचकुलरूपधीयशोऽर्थयुताः ।
उत्तमधान्यं वणिजः सेवाभिरताः सशिल्पिजनाः ॥५॥

Under Punarvasu are placed the truthful, generous, pure (clean), high-born, handsome, intelligent, famous, the rich, best varieties of cereals (like the Kalama paddy), merchants, servants and artisans.

[Bhaṭṭotpala construes *Vaṇijaḥ* as *Kirātāḥ* here as well as in V. 40.]

पुष्ये यवगोधूमाः शालीक्षुवनानि मन्त्रिणो भूपाः ।
सलिलोपजीविनः साधवश्च यज्ञेष्टिसक्ताश्च ॥६॥

Under Puṣya come barley, wheat, rice, sugarcane, forests, ministers, kings, fishermen and the like, virtuous men and those that are engaged in big and small sacrifices.

अहिदेवे कृत्रिमकन्दमूलफलकीटपन्नगविषाणि ।
परधनहरणाभिरतास्तुषधान्यं सर्वभिषजश्च ॥७॥

To Āśleṣā are assigned artificial things, bulbs, roots, fruits, insects, reptiles, poison, robbers, cereals and all classes of physicians.

[In Āyurveda many types of Cikitsā-treatment—such as Śalya, Sālākya, Kāyacikitsā etc. are mentioned.]

पित्र्ये धनधान्याढ्याः कोष्ठागाराणि पर्वताश्रयिणः ।
पितृभक्तवणिक्शूराः क्रव्यादाः स्त्रीद्विषो मनुजाः ॥८॥

The following are ruled by Maghā : People rich in gold (money) and corn, granaries, mountaineers, those who are devoted to parents or the *manes*, traders, heroes, carnivorous beings and women-haters.

[The commentator takes the word Koṣṭhāgāra to mean Vipulagrāmāḥ, large villages.]

प्राक्फल्गुनीषु नटयुवतिसुभगगान्धर्वशिल्पपण्यानि ।
कर्पासलवणमाक्षिकतैलानि कुमारकाश्चापि ॥९॥

The following are presided over by *Pūrvaphalguni* : Actors, young women, amiable persons, musicians, artists, commodities, cotton, salt, honey, oil and boys.

आर्यम्णे मार्दवशौचविनयपाखण्डिदानशास्त्ररताः ।
शोभनधान्यमहाधनकर्मानुरताः समनुजेन्द्राः ॥१०॥

Star *Uttaraphalguni* signifies kind-hearted persons, the pure in conduct, modest, heretics, charitable persons and the learned, fine-corn (like the Kalama rice), very rich men, those who are devoted to their duties, and kings.

हस्ते तस्करकुञ्जररथिकमहामात्रशिल्पिपण्यानि ।
तुषधान्यं श्रुतयुक्ता वणिजस्तेजोयुताश्चात्र ॥११॥

Hasta rules thieves, elephants, those who travel in chariots, elephant-drivers, artisans, commodities, cereals, men learned in the Vedas, traders and men of prowess.

त्वाष्ट्रे भूषणमणिरागलेख्यगान्धर्वगन्धयुक्तिज्ञाः ।
गणितपटुतन्तुवायाः शालाक्या राजधान्यानि ॥१२॥

Citrā presides over persons skilled in making ornaments, jewellery (or jewel-examiners), dyeing (or painting), writing, singing and perfumery, as well as mathematicians, weavers, ophthalmic surgeons and king's corn.

स्वातौ खगमृगतुरगा वणिजो धान्यानि वातबहुलानि ।
अस्थिरसौहृदलघुसत्त्वतापसाः पण्यकुशलाश्च ॥१३॥

Under the jurisdiction of Svātī are placed birds, beasts, horses, traders, grains that cause lot of wind (like Bengal gram), unsteady friends, feeble characters, ascetics and connoisseurs of wares.

[Instead of *Paṇya* some texts read *Vanya*. That should be translated as those who are experts in forest-products.]

इन्द्राग्निदैवते रक्तपुष्पफलशाखिनः सतिलमुद्गाः ।
कर्पाससमाषचणकाः पुरन्दरहुताशभक्ताश्च ॥१४॥

Viśākhā rules trees that bear red blossoms and fruits, sesamum, green gram, cotton, black gram, Bengal gram and men devoted to Indra and Agni.

मैत्रे शौर्यसमेता गणनायकसाधुगोष्ठियानरताः ।
ये साधवश्च लोके सर्वं च शरत्समुत्पन्नम् ॥१५॥

Anurādhā rules men of prowess, heads of corporations, friends of the virtuous, lovers of assemblies, tourists (or lovers of carriages), all honest persons in the world and all things that grow in autumn.

पौरन्दरेऽतिशूराः कुलवित्तयशोऽन्विताः परस्वहृतः ।
विजिगीषवो नरेन्द्राः सेनानां चापि नेतारः ॥१६॥

To Jyeṣṭhā belong great battle heroes, those who are noted for pedigree, wealth and fame, thieves, kings who are intent on conquests and commandants.

मूले भेषजभिषजो गणमुख्याः कुसुममूलफलवार्ताः ।
बीजान्यतिधनयुक्ताः फलमूलैर्ये च वर्तन्ते ॥१७॥

Mūla rules medicines, physicians, leaders of groups, those who deal in flowers, roots and fruits, seeds, exceedingly wealthy persons and those who live only on fruits and roots.

आप्ये मृदवो जलमार्गगामिनः सत्यशौचधनयुक्ताः ।
सेतुकरवारिजीवकफलकुसुमान्यम्बुजातानि ॥१८॥

Pūrvāṣāḍha presides over people that are tender-hearted, navigators, fishermen, aquatic animals etc., the truthful, pure and wealthy, constructors of bridges, those who live by water, and aquatic flowers and fruits.

विश्वेश्वरे महामात्रमल्लकरितुरगदेवतासक्ताः ।
स्थावरयोधा भोगान्विताश्च ये तेजसा युक्ताः ॥१९॥

Elephant drivers, wrestlers, elephants, horses, devotees of Gods, immovable things like trees, warriors, persons enjoying pleasures, and men of valour—all these come under Uttarāṣāḍha.

श्रवणे मायापटवो नित्योद्युक्ताश्च कर्मसु समर्थाः ।
उत्साहिनः सधर्मा भागवताः सत्यवचनाश्च ॥२०॥

To Śravaṇa belong jugglers, the ever-active, the efficient, the energetic, the righteous, devotees of Lord Viṣṇu and the truthful.

वसुभे मानोन्मुक्ताः क्लीबाचलसौहृदाः स्त्रियां द्वेष्याः ।
दानाभिरता बहुवित्तसंयुताः शमपराश्च नराः ॥२१॥

Dhaniṣṭhā rules the following : Men without pride, eunuchs, fast friends, men who are hated by women, charitable persons, the very wealthy, and peaceful (or self-controlled) persons.

[Instead of क्लीबाचल there is another reading viz. क्लीबाश्चल. In the latter case the meaning would be just the opposite.]

वरुणेशे पाशिकमत्स्यबन्धजलजानि जलचराजीवाः ।
सौकरिकरजकशौण्डिकशाकुनिकाश्चापि वर्गेऽस्मिन् ॥२२॥

The following come under the star Śatabhiṣaj : Snarers, anglers, aquatic products, and dealers in fish etc., boar-hunters, washermen, distillers and fowlers.

आजे तस्करपशुपालहिंस्रकीनाशनीचशठचेष्टाः।
धर्मव्रतैर्विरहिता नियुद्धकुशलाश्च ये मनुजाः ॥२३॥

Under Pūrvabhādrapada are placed thieves, cowherds, murderous persons, niggards and those engaged in despicable and roguish activities, those who are devoid of virtuous or religious observances and those that are clever in single combat.

आहिर्बुध्न्ये विप्राः क्रतुदानतपोयुता महाविभवाः।
आश्रमिणः पाखण्डा नरेश्वराः सारधान्यं च ॥२४॥

Brāhmaṇas, those that are engaged in sacrifices, charity and penance, very wealthy persons, recluses, heretics, monarchs and valuable corn—all these are ruled by Uttarabhādrapada.

पौष्णे सलिलजफलकुसुमलवणमणिशङ्खमौक्तिकाब्जानि।
सुरभिकुसुमानि गन्धा वणिजो नौकर्णधाराश्च ॥२५॥

Revatī rules aquatic products as well as fruits and flowers, salt, gems, conch shell, pearls, lotuses, perfumes, flowers (or fragrant flowers), traders and sailors (or helmsmen).

अश्विन्यामश्वहराः सेनापतिवैद्यसेवकास्तुरगाः।
तुरगारोहा वणिजो रूपोपेतास्तुरगरक्षाः ॥२६॥

Aśvinī rules horse-dealers, commandants, physicians, attendants, horses, horse-riders, merchants, handsome persons and horse-grooms.

[The commentator interprets *Vaṇijaḥ* as Kirātāḥ, Krayavikrayaniratāḥ.]

याम्येऽसृक्पिशितभुजः क्रूरा वधबन्धताडनासक्ताः।
तुषधान्यं नीचकुलोद्भवा विहीनाश्च सत्त्वेन ॥२७॥

Bharaṇī rules those that feed on blood and flesh, cruel men, those that are engaged in killing, imprisoning and beating others, cereals, low-born persons, and those who are deviod of courage (character or nobility).

[In the following three verses the author alludes to the groups of stars that rule the classes or Varṇas.]

पूर्वात्रयं सानलमग्रजानां राज्ञां तु पुष्येण सहोत्तराणि।
सपौष्णमैत्रं पितृदैवतं च प्रजापतेर्भं च कृषीवलानाम् ॥२८॥
आदित्यहस्ताभिजिदाश्विनानि वणिग्जनानां प्रवदन्ति तानि।
मूलत्रिनेत्रानिलवारुणानि भान्युग्रजातेः प्रभविष्णुतायाः ॥२९॥

सौम्यैन्द्रचित्रावसुदैवतानि सेवाजनस्वाम्यमुपागतानि ।
सार्पं विशाखा श्रवणो भरण्यश्चण्डालजातेरभिनिर्दिशन्ति ॥३०॥

The three Pūrvas viz. Pūrvaphalgunī, Pūrvāṣāḍha and Pūrvabhādrapada, and Kṛttikā rule the Brāhmaṇa class. The three Uttaras *i.e.* Uttaraphalgunī, Uttarāṣāḍha and Uttarabhādrapada, and Puṣya own the Kṣatriya class. Revatī, Anurādhā, Maghā and Rohiṇī rule husbandmen. Vaiśyas are ruled by Punarvasu, Hasta, Abhijit and Aśvinī. Mūla, Ardrā, Svātī and Śatabhiṣaj belong to the powerful class of cruel men. Mṛgaśiras, Jyeṣṭhā, Citrā. and Dhaniṣṭhā own the servant class. Āśleṣā, Viśākhā, Śravaṇa and Bharaṇī rule the outcasts.

[Here the author divides human beings into the wellknown five classes including the outcasts and two more classes viz. husbandmen, and cruel persons. The last category is likely to include all unruly elements in society who may violate all norms of civilized society. Utpala interprets. वणिग्जनानाम् as किरातलोकानाम् in verse 29.

These verses are in उपजाति metre.

In the next two verses definition and effect of *Upahata* are given.]

रविरविसुतभोगमागतं क्षितिसुतभेदनवक्रदूषितम् ।
ग्रहणगतमथोल्कया हतं नियतमुषाकरपीडितं च यत् ॥३१॥

तदुपहतमिति प्रचक्षते प्रकृतिविपर्यययातमेव वा ।
निगदितपरिवर्गदूषणं कथितविपर्ययगं समृद्धये ॥३२॥

A lunar mansion is said to be *Upahata* or *Afflicted* when it is tenanted by the Sun or Saturn, when it is spoilt by Mars either by cutting through or by retrogradation in it, when it gets involved in an eclipse, when it is struck by a meteor, or when it is manifestly crushed by the Moon; or when something unnatural happens to it. When a constellation is thus *afflicted*, all the people and things coming under its jurisdiction will be harmed Otherwise they will prosper.

[In mundane astrology this subject matter will be of great use. As we consider the effects of transits of different planets with reference to an individual's natal Moon, even so transit-effect can be gauged for different groups of persons as well as articles according to the method enunciated in this chapter as elsewhere. Utpala explains the word *Bhedana* as cutting through, or covering.

उषाकरपीडितम् is explained thus : यस्य नक्षत्रस्य चन्द्रमा योगतारका-भेदेन ग्राच्छादनं मध्यगमनं दक्षिणभागगमनं वा करोति तदुषाकरपीडितम् ।

Cf. कश्यप—

शनैश्चरस्य सूर्यस्य सद्दक्षं भोगमागतम् ।
धरित्रीतनयेनापि भिन्नं वक्रप्रदूषितम् ॥
राहुग्रस्तमथोल्काभिर्हतमुत्पातदूषितम् ।
चन्द्रेण पीडितं यच्च प्रकृतेरन्यथास्थितम् ॥
तच्चोपहतकं विन्द्यान्नक्षत्रं हन्ति सर्वदा ।
स्ववर्गमन्यथा नित्यं पुष्णाति निरुपद्रवम् ॥

The metre is वैतालीय. It is a pleasing practice of our author that he changes the metre at the end of chapters as it is the case of the Mahākāvyas.]

———

ग्रहभक्तियोगः ॥१६॥

Chapter XVI—*Planetary Rulership*

प्राङ्नर्मदार्द्धशोणोड्रवङ्गसुह्माः कलिङ्गबाह्लीकाः ।
शकयवनमगधशबरप्राग्ज्योतिषचीनकाम्बोजाः ॥१॥

मेकलकिरातविटका बहिरन्तःशैलजाः पुलिन्दाश्च ।
द्रविडानां प्रागर्द्धं दक्षिणकूलं च यमुनायाः ॥२॥

चम्पोदुम्बरकौशाम्बिचेदिविन्ध्याटवीकलिङ्गाश्च ।
पुण्ड्रा गोलाङ्गूलश्रीपर्वतवर्द्धमानानि ॥३॥

इक्षुमतीत्यथ तस्करपारतकान्तारगोपबीजानाम् ।
तुषधान्यकटुकतरुकनकदहनविषसमरशूराणाम् ॥४॥

भेषजभिषक्चतुष्पदकृषिकरनृपहिंस्रयायिचौराणाम् ।
व्यालारण्ययशोयुततीक्ष्णानां भास्करः स्वामी ॥५॥

The Sun presides over the eastern half of the Narmadā district, the Sone, Orissa, Vaṅga, Suhma, Kaliṅga, Balkh, Śakas (Scythians), Yavanas, Magadha, Śabaras, Prāgjyotiṣa, Cīna, Kamboja, Mekala, Kirātas, Viṭakas, people in and outside mountains, Pulindas, eastern half of the Draviḍa country, the south bank of the Yamunā, Campā, Udumbara, Kauśāmbī town, Cedi, Vindhya forest, Kaliṅga, Puṇḍra, Golāṅgūlas, Śrīparvata, Burdwan, river Ikṣumatī, robbers (or the country of the robbers), Pāratas, wilderness, herdsmen, seeds, cereals, pungent substances, trees, gold, fire, poison (a kind of medicine), heroes, medicines, physicians, quadrupeds, husbandmen, kings, evil-doers, those who march for conquests, thieves, serpents, woods, men of repute and bitter articles or men of cruel disposition.

[The author uses the words तस्कर and चोर here. The commentator says तस्करो देशो जना वा and चोरास्तस्कराः ।]

The *Mekala* mountain is usually identified with the Maikal range in the Gondwana in Madhya Pradesh including the Amara-Kaṇṭaka which is the source of the Narmadā.

The *Viṭakas* are, according to Kern, the same as the Utsava-saṅketas and the Lampākas of the महाभारत.

Campā or Campakāvatī or Campāvatī was an ancient city on the Ganges. It was the capital of the Aṅgas and identified with the modern Bhagalpura.

Śrīparvata is identified with the Nallamalais of the Kurnool district in Andhra Pradesh, extending all along the Krishna in a westerly direction, on the basis of a Nagarjunakonda inscription. It is sometimes identified with the Siriṭana of the Nasik cave inscription of Vāsiṣṭhīputra Puḷumāvi.

Ikṣumatī river is now called Ikhan or Kālindī, a tributary of the Gaṅgā, flowing through Kumaun, Rohilkhand and the district of Farrukhabad. The old town of Saṅkāśya was situated on its bank. It is the same as the Oxymagis of Arrian.

Cf. काश्यप—

प्रागर्द्धं नर्मदायाश्च शोणः शबरमागधाः ।
उड्रा वङ्गा कलिङ्गाश्च बाह्लीका यवनाः शकाः ।
काम्बोजा मेकलाः सुह्माः प्राग्ज्योतिषकिरातकाः ।
चीनाः सर्वे सुशैलेयाः पार्वता बहिरन्तजाः ॥
यमुनाया याम्यकूलं कौशाम्ब्यौदुम्बराणि च ।
विन्ध्याटवी च पुण्ड्राश्च वर्द्धमानाश्च पर्वताः ॥
श्रीपर्वतश्चेदिपुरं गोलाङ्गूलं तथैव च ।
इक्षुमत्याश्रिता ये च जनाः शूरा मदोत्कटाः ॥
कान्तारमथ गोपाश्च कन्दरास्तस्करास्तथा ।
समरे विषमाः शूरास्तरवः कटुका अपि ॥
चतुष्पदा भेषजं च धान्यं वा भिषजस्तथा ।
अरण्यवासिव्यालाश्च कार्षका बालकास्तथा ॥
गौरपत्यं च किञ्जल्कं पुंसज्ञा ये च जन्तवः ।
सर्वेषां भास्करः स्वामी तेजस्तेजस्विनामपि ॥]

गिरिसलिलदुर्गकोसलभरुकच्छसमुद्ररोमकतुषाराः ।
वनवासितङ्गणहलस्त्रीराज्यमहार्णवद्वीपाः ॥६॥

मधुररसकुसुमफलसलिललवणमणिशङ्खमौक्तिकाब्जानाम् ।
शालियवौषधिगोधूमसोमपाक्रन्दविप्राणाम् ॥७॥

सितसुभगतुरगरतिकरयुवतिचमूनाथभोज्यवस्त्राणाम् ।
शृङ्गिनिशाचरकार्षकयज्ञविदां चाधिपश्चन्द्रः ॥८॥

The Moon presides over mountain-fortresses, natural water-barriers, Kosala, Bharukaccha, the ocean, Romans, Tocharians, Vanavāsins (forest-dwellers or people of Banavāsi), Taṅgaṇa, Hala, Strīrājya, the islands of the great ocean, sweet things, flowers, fruits, water, salt, jewels, conch shells, pearls, aquatic products, rice, barley, herbs, wheat, drinkers of Soma juice, Kings called Ākranda (in the cycle of 12 kings they occupy the position next to the Pārṣṇigrāha), Brāhmaṇas, white objects (like silver), beloved persons, horses, lovers, young women, commandants, eatables, clothes, horned animals, demons, agriculturists and persons learned in the sacrificial lore.

[In this section we find some of the characteristics of planets mentioned in Bṛhajjātaka etc. being repeated. See also उत्तरकालामृत[1] V 25-54. It is interesting to note that our author brings the Romans under the tutelage of the Moon, whereas Kāśyapa does not mention them in his list.

Cf. काश्यप—

पर्वता जलदुर्गाश्च कोशलास्तङ्गणा हलाः ।
स्त्रीराज्यं भरुकच्छश्च तुषारा वनवासिनः ॥
मौक्तिकं मणिशङ्खाब्जमौषधं कुसुमं फलम् ।
द्वीपा महार्णवे ये च मधुरा लवणादयः ॥
गोधूमाः शालयः शृङ्गिकार्षकाश्च यवा अपि ।
सोमपा ब्राह्मणा ये च यज्ञज्ञास्तु सुरासवम् ॥
स्त्रीसौभाग्यसमेताश्च लास्यहास्येक्षितानि च ।
निशाचराधिपश्चन्द्रो हृष्टानां च प्रकीर्तितः ॥]

शोणस्य नर्मदाया भीमरथायाश्च पश्चिमार्द्धस्थाः ।
निर्विन्ध्या वेत्रवती सिप्रा गोदावरी वेणा ॥९॥

मन्दाकिनी पयोष्णी महानदी सिन्धुमालतीपाराः ।
उत्तरपाण्ड्यमहेन्द्राद्रिविन्ध्यमलयोपगाश्चोलाः ॥१०॥

द्रविडविदेहान्ध्राश्मकभासापरकौङ्कणाः समन्त्रिषिकाः ।
कुन्तलकेरलदण्डककान्तिपुरम्लेच्छसङ्करिणः ॥११॥

नासिक्यभोगवर्धनविराटविन्ध्याद्रिपार्श्वगा देशाः ।
ये च पिबन्ति सुतोयां तापीं ये चापि गोमतीसलिलम् ॥१२॥

1. See Uttarakālāmṛta ed. V.S. Sastri & revised by M.R. Bhat, pp. 159 to 173.

नागरकृषिकरपारतहुताशनाजीविशस्त्रवार्तानाम् ।
आटविकदुर्गकर्वटवधिकनृशंसावलिप्तानाम् ॥१३॥
नरपतिकुमारकुञ्जरदाम्भिकडिम्भाभिघातपशुपानाम् ।
रक्तफलकुसुमविद्रुमचमूपगुडमद्यतीक्ष्णानाम् ॥१४॥
कोशभवनाग्निहोत्रिकधात्वाकरशाक्यभिक्षुचौराणाम् ।
शठदीर्घवैरबह्वाशिनां च वसुधासुतोऽधिपतिः ॥१५॥

Mars presides over the countries situated in the western half of the Sone, Narmadā and Bhīmarathā, Nirvindhyā, Vetravatī, Siprā, Godāvarī, Venā, Gaṅgā, Payoṣṇī, Mahānadī, Sindhu, Mālatī, Pārā, Uttarapāṇḍya, those who live near mount Mahendra, Vindhya and Malaya, Cola, Draviḍa, Videha, Āndhra, Aśmaka, Bhāsāpara, Koṅkaṇa, Mantriṣika, Kuntala, Kerala, Daṇḍaka, Kāntipura, Mlecchas, half-castes, Nasik, Bhogavardhana, Virāṭa, the countries by the side of the Vindhya mountains, people living on the banks of the Tāpī (Tapti) and the Gomatī (Gumtee), town-dwellers, farmers, Pāratas, persons who live by fire (such as goldsmiths), warriors, foresters, forts, Karvaṭas, slayers, cruel men, arrogant persons, kings, boys, elephants, hypocrites, infanticides, shepherds, red fruits and flowers, corals, army generals, jaggery, liquor, bitter things (like the Neem or merciless persons), treasury, keepers of the sacred fire, mines, Buddhist monks, thieves, rogues vindictive and gluttonous persons.

[Verse 12 is omitted in some editions. The word डिम्भाभिघात is interpreted in another manner by the commentator : अशस्त्रः कलहो डिम्भः, तत्राभिघातः ।

Bhīmarathā is the modern Bhīmā, a tributary of the Kṛṣṇā. It is also called Bhaimarathī.

Mahānadī rises in the Amarakaṇṭaka range, flows through Orissa and falls into the Bay of Bengal.

Nirvindhyā is identified with the Nevuz, a tributary of the Chambal between the Betwa and the Kali-Sindh in Malwa. Kālidāsa refers to it in his Meghadūta (I. 28-9).

Vetravatī is the modern Betwa, a tributary of the Yamunā.

Siprā is a tributary of the Chambal into which it falls a little below Sitamau. The city of Ujjain is situated on its bank.

Śoṇa is the modern Sone which falls into the Gaṅgā near Patna. Megasthenes calls it Erannaboas (Hiraṇyavāha) at whose junction with the Gaṅgā was situated Pāṭaliputa, the celebrated Maurya capital.

Payoṣṇī is identified by Cunningham with the Pahoj, a tributary of the Yamunā between the Sindh and Betwa. According to others it is to be identified with the Paisuni or Paisundi in Bundelkhand.

Pārā or Pāravatī is a tributary of the Chambal rising in Bhopal. The old town of Padmāvatī (modern Pawaya) was situated at the confluence of the Pāravati and Sindhu.

Tāpi, modern Tāptī, rises in the Satpura hills and falls into the Arabian Sea.

There are altogether 16 names of rivers coming under the jurisdiction of Mars.

Cf. काश्यप—

महेन्द्रविन्ध्यमलयाः सिप्रा वेणा महानदी ।
गोदावर्या नर्मदाया भीमायाः पश्चिमा दिशः ॥

चेदिकाः कौङ्कणा दुर्गा द्रविडा वेत्रवन्नदी ।
मन्दाकिनी पयोष्णी च मालती सिन्धुपारकाः ॥

पाण्ड्याश्चोत्तरदेशस्था विदेहान्ध्राश्मकास्तथा ।
भासापराः कुन्तलाश्च केरला दण्डकास्तथा ॥

नागराः पौरवाश्चैव कार्षकाः शस्त्रवृत्तयः ।
हुताशनाजीविनो ये कुञ्जराः पशुपास्तथा ॥

साङ्ग्रामिका नृशंसाश्च सङ्कराश्चोपघातकाः ।
कुमारा भूमिजस्योक्ता दाम्भिकास्तस्करास्तथा ॥]

लोहित्यः सिन्धुनदः सरयूर्गाम्भीरिका रथाख्या च ।
गङ्गाकौशिक्याद्याः सरितो वैदेहकाम्बोजाः ॥१६॥

मथुरायाः पूर्वार्द्धं हिमवद्गोमन्तचित्रकूटस्थाः ।
सौराष्ट्रसेतुजलमार्गपण्यबिलपर्वताश्रयिणः ॥१७॥

उदपानयन्त्रगान्धर्वलेख्यमणिरागगन्धयुक्तिविदः ।
आलेख्यशब्दगणितप्रसाधकायुष्यशिल्पज्ञाः ॥१८॥

चरपुरुषकुहकजीवकशिशुकविशठसूचकाभिचाररताः ।
दूतनपुंसकहास्यज्ञभूततन्त्रेन्द्रजालज्ञाः ॥१९॥

आरक्षकनटनर्तकघृततैलस्नेहबीजतिक्तानि ।
व्रतचारिरसायनकुशलवेसराश्चन्द्रपुत्रस्य ॥२०॥

Mercury presides over the river Lauhitya, Indus, Sarayū, Gambhīrikā, Rathākhyā (i.e. one named Rathā. Is it Bhīmarathā?), Gaṅgā, Kauśikī and other rivers (such as Vipāśā, Sarasvatī and Candrabhāgā), Videha, Kāmboja, the eastern half of Mathurā, the Himalayas, Gomanta hill (or cattle-owners) and Citrakūṭa (the people living in these regions), Saurāṣṭra, bridges, water-routes, merchandise, cave-men, hillmen, reserviors, mechanics, songesters, writers (or copyists), jewel-experts, dyers, perfume-makers, painters, grammarians, mathematicians, decorators, experts in the preparation of elixirs of life, artisans, (such as carpenters, masons, blacksmiths and potters), spics, jugglers, infants, poets, imposters, talebearers, those engaged in black magic, messengers, eunuchs, buffoons, those that are proficient in demonology and magic, policemen, actors, dancers, ghee, oil, oil-seeds, bitter things, observers of vows (like Brahmacārins), chemists (who prepare good tonics) and mules.

[*Kauśikī* river may be the modern Kusi flowing into the Gaṅgā through the district of Purnea in Bihar, or the Kusiara of Sylhet (Bangla Desh) flowing through the area known as Pañcakhaṇḍa.

Gambhīrā, mentioned by Kālidāsa in the Meghadūta (I. 40), is a tributary of the Yamunā above the Chambal flowing east from Gangapur through eastern Rajputana.

Cf. काश्यप—

चित्रकूटगिरी रम्यो हिमवान् कौशिकी तथा ।
मथुरायाश्च पूर्वार्द्धं लोहित्यः सिन्धुरेव च ॥

गाम्भीरिका च सरयू रथाख्या गण्डकी नदी ।
गान्धर्वा लेखहाराश्च तथोदाराश्च कृत्रिमाः ॥

वैदेहाः सर्वजलजाः काम्बोजाश्च सुराष्ट्रिकाः ।
गन्धयुक्तिविदो ये च सौगन्धिरदलेपनाः ॥

सुवर्णरजतं रत्नं मातङ्गतुरगादि यत् ।
पौरा जनपदाः सौम्याः सोमपुत्रवशे स्थिताः ॥]

सिन्धुनदपूर्वभागो मथुरापश्चार्द्धभरतसौवीराः ।
स्त्रुघ्नौदीच्यविपाशासरिच्छतद्रू रमठशाल्वाः ॥२१॥

त्रैगर्तपौरवाम्बष्ठपारता वाटधानयौधेयाः ।
सारस्वतार्जुनायनमत्स्यार्द्धग्रामराष्ट्राणि ॥२२॥

हस्त्यश्वपुरोहितभूपमन्त्रिमाङ्गल्यपौष्टिकासक्ताः ।
कारुण्यसत्यशौचव्रतविद्यादानधर्मयुताः ॥२३॥

पौरमहाधनशब्दार्थवेदविदुषोऽभिचारनीतिज्ञाः ।
मनुजेश्वरोपकरणं छत्रध्वजचामराद्यं च ॥२४॥

शैलेयकमांसीतगरकुष्ठरससैन्धवानि वल्लीजम् ।
मधुररसमधूच्छिष्टानि चोरकश्चेति जीवस्य ॥२५॥

To Jupiter belong the eastern part of the Indus, the western half of Mathurā, the Bharatas, Sauvīras, Srughnas, Northern People, the Vipāśā river, the Śatadru, the Ramaṭhas, Sālva, Trigartas, Pauravas, Ambaṣṭhas, Pāratas, Vāṭadhānas, Yaudheyas, Sārasvatas, Arjunāyanas, half the rural provinces of Matsya, elephants, horses, royal priests, kings, ministers, those who are engaged in auspicious ceremonies and preparation of tonics, those who are compassionate, truthful, pure, pious, learned, charitable and righteous, citizens, rich men, grammarians, philologists, Vedic scholars, sorcerers, politicians, royal equipments (weapons etc.), umbrellas, banners, Chowries etc., benzoin, Jaṭāmāṁsī, Tagara, costus, mercury, rock salt, beans, sweet juices, bees-wax and Coraka perfume.

[*Srughna* is identified with the modern village of Sugh on the old Jumna near Jagadhari.

Vipāśā is Beas. It was also known as Ārjīkīyā in the Ṛgveda (VIII. 3.6).

Cf. काश्यप—

त्रैगर्तसिन्धुसौवीराः शतद्रूमथुरे अपि ।
स्रुघ्नोदीच्यविपाशाश्च पारताम्बष्ठकास्तथा ॥
राजा पुरोहितो मन्त्री माङ्गल्यं पौष्टिकं व्रतम् ।
कारुण्यं कर्म सिद्धानां विद्याशौचतपस्विनाम् ॥
मत्स्याश्च वाटधानाश्च यौधेयाश्चार्जुनायनाः ।
सारस्वताश्च रमठा हस्त्यश्वध्वजचामराः ॥
शब्दार्थविदुषः पौरा नीतिज्ञाः शीलसंयुताः ।
मांसीतगरकुष्ठं च शैलेयं लवणं रसाः ॥
मधुरस्वादवल्लीजं विप्राणां चाधिपो गुरुः ॥

Both Kāśyapa and Vārāhamihira have committed a grammatical error in using the word Viduṣah in the sense of scholars, nominative plural.

The Vārāṇaseya edition reads verse 25 as शैलेयकुष्ठ..." which is short of one Mātrā in the second Pāda.]

तक्षशिलमार्त्तिकावतबहुगिरिगान्धारपुष्कलावतकाः ।
प्रस्थलमालवकैकयदाशार्णोशीनराः शिबयः ॥२६॥

ये च पिबन्ति वितस्तामिरावतीं चन्द्रभागसरितं च ।
रथरजताकरकुञ्जरतुरगमहामात्रधनयुक्ताः ॥२७॥

सुरभिकुसुमानुलेपनमणिवज्रविभूषणाम्बुरुहशय्याः ।
वरतरुणयुवतिकामोपकरणमृष्टान्नमधुरभुजः ॥२८॥

उद्यानसलिलकामुकयशःसुखौदार्यरूपसम्पन्नाः ।
विद्वदमात्यवणिग्जनघटकृच्चित्राण्डजास्त्रिफलाः ॥२९॥

कौशेयपट्टकम्बलपत्रौर्णिकरोध्रपत्रचोचानि ।
जातीफलागुरुवचापिप्पल्यश्चन्दनं च भृगोः ॥३०॥

The following come under the jurisdiction of Venus : Taxila, Mārtikāvata, Bahugiri, Gāndhāra, Puṣkalāvata, Prasthala, Malwa, Kaikaya, Daśārṇa, Uśīnara, Śibi, those who dwell on the banks of the Vitastā, Irāvatī and Candrabhāgā, chariots, silver, mines, elephants, horses, elephant-drivers, wealthy persons, fragrant things, flowers, unguents, gems, diamond, ornaments, lotuses, couches, leading personalities (bride-grooms), young men, young damsels, aphrodisiacs, those who enjoy sumptuous and sweet food, gardens, baths, lovers, those that are endowed with fame, happiness, generosity and charming personality, scholars, ministers, merchants, potters, different varieties of coloured birds (or pictures and birds ?), the three fruits (viz. Cardamom, Clove and Kakkola), fine silk, woollen rugs, bleached silk, Lodhra (whose powder is used as a cosmetic), Patra (the scented skin of a fruit), Coca, nutmeg, Agaru, Vacā, Pippalī and sandalwood.

[*Mārtikāvata* is a country, according to Utpala. This name may have been derived from Mṛttikāvata which may be identical with *Mṛttikāvarapura* mentioned in the Viṣṇupurāṇa (IV. 13.7). The Bhojas appear to have got the name Mātrikāvara as a result of their living in this town. Dey identifies it with the ancient Sālvapura, modern Alwar, or with Merta in Marwar. But in the opinion of Wilson it is more appropriate to identify the place with the country of the Bhojas by the side of the Parṇāśā (Banas) in Malwa.

Vitastā is the Jhelum, one of the five streams of the Punjab.

Irāvatī is the modern Ravi, the Hydraotes of Greek writers.

Candrabhāgā is the modern Chenab, the largest of the five streams of the Punjab.

Cf. काश्यप—

चन्द्रभागां वितस्तां चैरावतीं च पिबन्ति ये ।
पुष्करावतकैकेया गान्धारप्रस्थलास्तथा ॥

दशार्णा मालवास्तक्षशिला मौक्तिकमेव च ।
धनाढ्याः कुञ्जरा अश्वाः प्रस्थल च विलेपनम् ॥

सुरूपसुभगोद्यानकामुकाः कामचारिणः ।
वेसरा मधुरा हृद्या सलिलाशयजीविनः ॥

तरुणा योषितः क्रीडाविदुषो जनगोष्ठिकाः ।
चित्राण्डजाश्च कौशेयं पत्रोर्णं काशिकोशिकाः ॥

पिप्पल्यश्चन्दनं जातीफलमामलकानि च ।
गन्धपत्रस्य लोध्रस्य शुक्रश्चाधिपतिः स्मृतः ॥]

आनर्तार्बुदपुष्करसौराष्ट्राभीरशूद्ररैवतकाः ।
नष्टा यस्मिन् देशे सरस्वती पश्चिमो देशः ॥३१॥
कुरुभूमिजाः प्रभासं विदिशा वेदस्मृती महीतटजाः ।
खलमलिननीचतैलिकविहीनसत्त्वोपहतपुंस्त्वाः ॥३२॥
बान्धनशाकुनिकाशुचिकैवर्त्तविरूपवृद्धसौकरिकाः ॥
गणपूज्यस्खलितव्रतशबरपुलिन्दार्थपरिहीनाः ॥३३॥
कटुतिक्तरसायनविधवयोषितो भुजगतस्करमहिष्यः ।
खरकरभचणकवातलनिष्पावाश्चार्कपुत्रस्य ॥३४॥

Saturn presides over the Ānartas, Arbuda (Mt. Abu.), Puṣkara, Saurāṣṭra, Ābhīras, Śūdras, people living in or near the Raivataka mountain, the country where the river Sarasvatī disappears, the western country, inhabitants of Thaneswar, Prabhāsa, Vidiśā, the river Vedasmṛtī, those that live on the banks of the river Mahī, rogues, the slovenly, unrighteous persons, oilmongers, cowards, eunuchs, gaolers and prisoners, fowlers, impure fellows, fishermen or sailors, deformed persons, aged ones, boar-hunters, leaders of corporations, those that have fallen from their vows, Śabaras, Pulindas, the penurious, pungent and bitter substances, tonics, widows, serpents, thieves, she-buffaloes, donkeys, camels, Bengalgram, pulses that cause flatulence and Niṣpāva pulse.

[*Puṣkara* is mentioned in V. 68 and *Puṣkarāraṇya* in XI. 35. It is identified with Pokhar near Ajmer. It is a famous place of pilgrimage.

Veda-smṛtī is identified with the Besula in Malwa. In the Bhīṣma parvan of the महाभारत it is called वेदस्मृता.

The river *Mahī* rises in the Pāriyātra mountain, has a south-western course upto Banswara wherefrom it turns south and passing through Gujarat drains into the Gulf of Cambay.

Cf. काश्यप—

अर्बुदो रैवतगिरिः सौराष्ट्राभीरकास्तथा ।
सरस्वतीपश्चिमाशा प्रभासं कुरुजाङ्गलम् ॥

आनर्तशूद्रा विदिशा खलतैलिकनीचकाः ।
वेदस्मृती सौकरिकाः मलिनाश्च महीतटम् ॥

दुःशीलशाकुना हीनाः पशुबन्धनकास्तथा ।
पाखण्डिनश्च वैतण्डा निर्ग्रन्था शबराः कृशाः ॥

विरूपाः कटुतिक्तानि रसायनविषादिनः ।
पुलिन्दतस्कराः सर्पा महिषोष्ट्रखराः शुनी ॥

चणका वातला वल्लाः पुंस्त्वसत्त्वविवर्जिताः ।
काकगृध्रशृगालानां वृकाणां च प्रभुः शनिः ॥]

गिरिशिखरकन्दरदरीविनिविष्टा म्लेच्छजातयः शूद्राः ।
गोमायुभक्षशूलिकवोक्काणाश्वमुखविकलाङ्गाः ॥३५॥

कुलपांसनहिंस्रकृतघ्नचौरनिःसत्यशौचदानाश्च ।
खरचरनियुद्धवित्तीव्ररोषगर्त्ताश्रया नीचाः ॥३६॥

उपहतदाम्भिकराक्षसनिद्राबहुलाश्च जन्तवः सर्वे ।
धर्मेण च सन्त्यक्ता माषतिलाश्चार्कशशिशत्रोः ॥३७॥

Rāhu rules over the inhabitants of mountain-peaks, dens and caves, barbarian tribes, Śūdras, jackal-eaters, the Śūlikas, Vokkāṇas, Kinnaras, crippled persons, those who disgrace their lineage, cruel persons, ungrateful men, thieves, untruthful, dirty and miserly persons, donkeys, spies, duelists, wrathful persons, those who live in pits (or children in the womb), evil-doers, reprobates, hypocrites, giants, all sleepy beings, lawless or unrighteous persons, blackgram and sesamum.

[गर्ताश्रयाः is read as गर्भाश्रयाः in some editions. From the reading in the समाससंहिता it is clear that the author's version can be only the latter.

Cf. काश्यप—

बुभुक्षितास्तीक्ष्णरोषा विभिन्नाः कुलपांसनाः ।
नीचा म्लेच्छोत्सादकाश्च गर्तस्थाः पारदारिकाः ॥
सत्यधर्मविहीनाश्च गिरिस्थाः कन्दराश्रिताः ।
प्रतापसत्यहीनाश्च शृगालादा महाशनाः ॥
तिलाश्च बाहुयुद्धज्ञा माषाश्चौराः खराश्चराः ।
यज्ञान् हिंसन्ति ये नित्यं राहुस्तेषामधीश्वरः ॥]

गिरिदुर्गपह्लवश्वेतहूणचोलावगाणमरुचीनाः ।
प्रत्यन्तधनिमहेच्छव्यवसायपराक्रमोपेताः ॥३८॥
परदारविवादरताः पररन्ध्रकुतूहला मदोत्सिक्ताः ।
मूर्खा धार्मिकविजिगीषवश्च केतोः समाख्याताः ॥३९॥

Ketu presides over mountain strongholds, the Pahlavas, White Huns, Colas, Afghans, deserts, Chinese, cavemen (or borderland), the wealthy, highly ambitious persons, energetic men, those endowed with prowess, adulterers, quarrelsome people, those who take pleasuse in others' difficulties, those that are puffed up with pride, fools, unrighteous persons and those that are intent on subjugating others.

[Our author refers to the White Huns in XI-61 also. Since he uses *Śveta* and *Sita*, synonyms of white, it is clear that neither of these words is the name of a country or people.

Cf. काश्यप—

प्राकाराभ्युच्छ्रिताः शृङ्गगिरिस्था विजिगीषवः ।
प्रत्यन्तवासाभिरताः परच्छिद्रविशारदाः ॥
मूर्खा विज्ञानहीनाश्च निर्मर्यादा नरास्तथा ।
परदाररता नीचाः केतोरिति विनिर्दिशेत् ॥

Cf. also the समाससंहिता of our author—

भानोरङ्गकलिङ्गवङ्गयवनाः श्रीपर्वताः पारता
बाह्लीकोत्कटसुह्मशोणमगधाः प्राङ्नर्मदाधीशकाः ।

कौशाम्बी शबरान्ध्रपौण्ड्रयवना याम्याश्रिता मेकला-
श्रीनोदुम्बरवर्धमानविकटाश्चम्पेक्षुमत्याश्रिताः ।।

जलपर्वतदुर्गकोशला वनिताराज्यतुषारतङ्गणाः ।
वनवासहलाः सरस्वती शीतांशोर्भरुकच्छरोमकाः ।।

क्षितिजस्य महानदी पयोष्णी वेणा वेत्रवती च मालती ।
मलयद्रविडाश्मकान्ध्रचोला भीमार्धे त्वपरे च ये स्थिताश्च ।।

पारेविन्ध्यं पश्चिमः शोणभागो गोदावर्याः कूलमद्रिर्महेन्द्रः ।
सिप्रा सिन्धुर्भूमिजस्येति देशा वैदेहाख्याः कोङ्कणाः केरलाश्च ।।

सौम्यस्य सौराष्ट्रिकभोजदेशा गङ्गाश्रिताश्चोत्तरकूलनद्यः ।
विन्ध्यार्द्धमन्त्यं मथुरापुरस्तात्सुवास्तुसिन्ध्वद्रिगुहाश्रिताश्च ।।

जीवस्य सारस्वतमत्स्यशाल्वाः प्राक्सिन्धुभागो मथुरापरार्द्धम् ।
स्त्रुघ्नः शतद्रू रमठा विपाशा त्रैगर्तयौधेयकपारताश्च ।।

देशा भृगोस्तक्षशिला वितस्ता गान्धारकाः कैकयमालवाश्च ।
दाशार्णकौशीनरचन्द्रभागाश्चेद्याह्वसिप्रास्थलकालकाख्याः ।।

सरस्वती यत्र गता प्रणाशं वेदस्मृती मालवकाः सुराष्ट्राः ।
पाश्चात्यदेशा विदिशा मही च सौरेः स्मृताः पुष्करमर्बुदश्च ।।

राहोः कृतघ्नकुलपांसननीचशूद्रा वोक्काणशूलिकनियुद्धविदुग्रकोपाः ।
गोमायुभक्षगिरिदुर्गनिवासिनश्च गर्भस्थहिंसपरदाररताः खलाश्च ।।

शिखिनो वनसंस्थितावगाणा मरुभूपल्लवचोलहूणचीनाः ।
व्यवसायपराक्रमोपपन्नाः परदारानुरता मदोत्कटाश्च ।।]

उदयसमये यः स्निग्धांशुर्महान् प्रकृतिस्थितो
यदि च न हतो निर्घातोल्कारजोग्रहमर्दनैः ।
स्वभवनगतः स्वोच्चप्राप्तः शुभग्रहवीक्षितः
स भवति शिवस्तेषां येषां प्रभुः परिकीर्तितः ।।४०।।

A planet proves favourable to those (persons and objects) whose lord he is declared to be, if, at rising, he be large, of glossy rays, and in his natural state, if no portentous thunder, meteors, dust or planetary conflict afflict him, and if he be posited in his own house, exaltation or be aspected by benefics.

[Bhaṭṭotpala interprets उदय as क्षितिजात्प्रत्युद्गमकाले which means the daily rising as against the re-emergence of a planet after being eclipsed by the Sun. In my view the author's intention is to convey the latter sense.

As the chapter is coming to a close, the metre is changed. It is हरिणी here].

> **अभिहितविपरीतलक्षणे क्षयमुपगच्छति तत्परिग्रहः ।**
> **डमरभयगदातुरा जना नरपतयश्च भवन्ति दुःखिताः ॥४१॥**
>
> **यदि न रिपुकृतं भयं नृपाणां स्वसुतकृतं नियमादमात्यजं वा ।**
> **भवति जनपदस्य चाप्यवृष्ट्या गमनमपूर्वपुराद्रिनिम्नगासु ॥४२॥**

If a planet is possessed of signs contrary to those mentioned above, his dependency (countries, people and things) will suffer; the people and the rulers will be afflicted by battles, panic and diseases. In case the kings have no danger from their enemies, there will certainly be trouble for them from their own sons or ministers. Moreover, in consequence of drought, the people of the country-side will repair to towns, mountains and rivers which they had never visited before.

[The second verse here is construed by Utpala in a different way: स्वसुतकृतमात्मीयपुत्रकृतं वा नियमान्निश्चयादमात्यजं मन्त्रिकृतं वा भयं न भवति ।... एषां मध्यादन्यतमो न भवति तदा जनपदस्य लोकस्यापि यथा तथा भयं भवति...। This line of argument appears to be unwarranted in view of the word नियमात् employed by the author.

Cf. गर्ग—

> स्निग्धरश्मिविशालश्च प्रकृतिस्थश्च यो ग्रहः ।
> ग्रहयुद्धरजोधूमनिर्घातोल्काघनाहतः ॥
> स यदा स्वोच्चराशिस्थो मित्रभे स्वगृहेऽपि वा ।
> स्थितः शुभग्रहैर्दृष्टः स पुष्णाति परिग्रहम् ॥
> स्वमन्यथा हन्ति वर्गं जननाशं करोति च ।
> नृपाणां भयदः प्रोक्तस्त्ववृष्टिभयकारकः ॥

The metres of the verses are वैतालीय and पुष्पिताग्रा respectively].

———

ग्रहयुद्धाध्यायः ॥१७॥

Chapter XVII—Planetary Wars

युद्धं यथा यदा वा भविष्यमादिश्यते त्रिकालज्ञैः ।
तद्विज्ञानं करणे मया कृतं सूर्यसिद्धान्तात् ॥१॥

How and when a planetary war will take place according to the teachings of the sages who know the past, present and future, has been explained by me in the astronomical treatise viz. Pañcasiddhāntikā, on the basis of the Sūryasiddhānta.

[सूर्यसिद्धान्ते is another reading for सूर्यसिद्धान्तात्. Our author frequently alludes to his previous works like the पञ्चसिद्धान्तिका, बृहज्जातक etc.

In the following verse the cause and varieties of planetary warfare are explained.]

वियति चरतां ग्रहाणामुपर्युपर्यात्ममार्गसंस्थानाम् ।
अतिदूराद् दृग्विषये समतामिव सम्प्रयातानाम् ॥२॥

आसन्नक्रमयोगाद्भेदोल्लेखांशुमर्दनासव्यैः ।
युद्धं चतुष्प्रकारं पराशराद्यैर्मुनिभिरुक्तम् ॥३॥

When the planets move in the sky along their orbits lying over one another, they appear to our eyes to move on even surface or plane, as a result of their great distance (from the earth). According to the degree of their seeming approachment, there are four kinds of *war* as stated by Parāśara and other sages, viz. *Bheda* (occultation, cleaving), *Ullekha* (grazing), *Aṁśumardana* (clashing of the rays) and *Apasavya* (passing southward).

[Planetary warfare has been treated of by many ancient sages such as Parāśara, Garga, Kāśyapa and Vajra, according to the commentator. When two planets appear to have a single orb on account of their apparent over-lapping, the fight is called *Bheda*. In this the orb of the lower planet obstructs completely the upper one. When the rims of the two orbs graze each other, it is called *Ullekha*. When the rays of two planets situated closely appear to be clashing with one another, it is *Aṁśumardana*. When a planet covering another moves towards the south, it is *Apasavya* (see notes under XVIII-1 *infra*). Bhaṭṭotpala appears to confuse सव्य and अपसव्य, as he says : "अपसव्यः प्रदक्षिण उच्यते ।" But this is against the statements of the sages. He quotes a verse which distinguishes *Yuddha*, *Samāgama*, *Ullekha* and *Bheda* : "हस्तमात्रं भवेद्युद्धं बाहुमात्रं समागमः । वितस्तिमात्रमल्लेखो भेदश्चैव निरङ्गुलः ॥" ऋषिपुत्र says in this connection :

दक्षिणेनापसव्यं स्यादुत्तरेण प्रदक्षिणम् ।
ग्रहाणां चन्द्रमा ज्ञेयो नक्षत्राणां तथैव च ॥

Vṛddhagarga explains how the planets' mutual अपसव्य and प्रदक्षिण positions are to be determined :

ग्रहाणां विजये भङ्गे नक्षत्राणां च संश्रये ।
कथं प्रदक्षिणं ज्ञेयमपसव्यं तथैव च ॥

नक्षत्राणां ग्रहाणां वा यदा तूत्तरगः शशी ।
तत्प्रदक्षिणमित्याहुर्भवेत् क्षेमसुवृष्टये ॥

नक्षत्राणां ग्रहाणां वा यदा दक्षिणतो व्रजेत् ।
अपसव्यं तदैव स्यादवृष्टिभयलक्षणम् ॥

Bhaṭṭotpala adds here that though the definition of *Apasavya* is the same with respect to all planets, yet in the case of the planetary war named *Apasavya* it is different i.e. it means सव्य. Dr. Kern says : "The *Apasavyam* or *Asavyaṁ yuddham* takes place when the interval is somewhat less than a degree; at a greater interval there is no conflict." Ṛṣiputra and others speak of 15 kinds of war.

Cf. पराशर—

भेदनमारोहणमुल्लेखनं रश्मिसंसर्गश्चेति ग्रहयुद्धं चतुर्विधमाचक्षते कुशलाः । तेषां पूर्वात् पूर्वो गरीयान् ।

Cf. गर्ग—

छादनं रोधनं चैव रश्मिमर्दस्तथैव च ।
अपसव्यं ग्रहाणां च चतुर्धा युद्धमुच्यते ॥

Cf. also काश्यप—

सर्वग्रहेभ्यः शीघ्रेन्दुस्ततस्तस्यैव चात्मजः ।
भार्गवो रविभौमौ च जीवो मन्दः शनैश्चरः ॥

शीघ्रगा मन्दगाश्चैते काले त्वेकर्क्षगामिनः ।
ततो योगो भवेदेषां यतोंऽशत्वैकमाश्रिताः ॥

उपर्युपरिसंस्थास्ते दृश्यन्ते युगपत् स्थिताः ।
भेदोल्लेखांशुमदश्चिापसव्यश्च तथापरः ॥
चतुष्प्रकारः संयोगो युद्धे तु दिविचारिणाम् ॥]

भेदे वृष्टिविनाशो भेदः सुहृदां महाकुलानां च ।
उल्लेखे शस्त्रभयं मन्त्रिविरोधः प्रियान्नत्वम् ॥४॥

अंशुविरोधे युद्धानि भूभृतां शस्त्ररुक्क्षुदवमर्दाः ।
युद्धे चाप्यपसव्ये भवन्ति युद्धानि भूपानाम् ॥५॥

When the *Bheda* (occultation) type of warfare takes place, there will be failure of rains, and discord among friends and big families. At the *Ullekha* (grazing) type of war there will be danger from clash of arms, ministers will be at loggerheads among themselves or with the king, and food will be very dear. When the third type of war (clashing of rays) takes place, there will be wars among kings and general destruction by the sword, diseases and famine. At the last type of conflict *i.e.* Apasavya, kings will be engaged in wars.

[Dr. Kern remarks : "This is not difficult to understand, for the Moon leaving, in her eastward course, a planet or star at her own right (*i.e.* standing north from the planet or star), may be said to make a *Pradakṣiṇa*; standing to the south, *i.e.* leaving a planet or star at her left, she makes an *Apasavya*. Thus Apasavya means, "from the left, at the left", and, in a special application, "at the southside," but from this, it does not necessarily follow that *apasavya* originally was simply the opposite of *savya* "left". Yet it cannot be doubted that they have taken *apasavya* as the reverse of *savya*, or, in other words, that *apa* was understood to mean, not "from the side" but "not"; therefore *asavya* was considered to be simply synonymous with *apasavya*. Moreover, *Savya* has got the meaning of "right", precisely the reverse of its most common acceptation, viz. "left".

"Not to be confounded with this acceptation of *savya* is its use in augury. Applied to augural birds, etc., *savya* is strictly and properly "left", but as birds first appearing from the left of the observer move in the direction of his right, and keep him at their own right *savya*, "left", and *pradakṣiṇa*, 'moving to the right', imply the same, without being the same. Utpala remarks : सर्वं एव शकुनादयो यातुर्वामपार्श्वादग्रत आगत्य दक्षिणपार्श्वेणाक्रामन्ति यत् तत् प्रदक्षिणं सव्यञ्च । एत-

द्विपरीतं दक्षिणपार्श्वाद्वामपार्श्वं गमनं यत्तदपसव्यम् । In astronomical works, *savya* "moving (revolving) toward the right" and *apasavya* "moving toward the left, is common enough; *e.g.* Sūrya Siddhānta XII-55; Siddhānta Śiromaṇi, Golādhyāya 3-51, Āryabhaṭīya IV-16."

While answering an objection to the effect that there can be only three kinds of planetary conflict, the commentator says : The signs of defeat of a planet are (i) being placed to the south of the other planet, (ii) rough appearance, (iii) trembling, (iv) loss of colour or lustre, (v) deformity, (vi) being super-imposed by the other, (viii) tiny form, and (viii) retreating. Those of victory are: (i) to be stationed to the north of the other, (ii) glossiness, (iii) largeness, etc. Though a planet is placed to the south, if it is endowed with the marks of triumph, given above, it should be declared to be victorious. So, whatever effects have been prescribed for a victorious planet stationed to the north, should be said for a victorious planet though placed to the south. This is the purpose of mentioning this variety separately.]

रविराक्रन्दो मध्ये पौरः पूर्वेऽपरे स्थितो यायी ।
पौरा बुधगुरुरविजा नित्यं शीतांशुराक्रन्दः ॥६॥

केतुकुजराहुशुक्रा यायिन एते हता घ्नन्ति ।
आक्रन्दयायिपौराञ्जयिनो जयदाः स्ववर्गस्य ॥७॥

The Sun standing in the meridian is called Ākranda i.e. an ally who comes to the rescue being situated behind the Pārṣṇigrāha, when he is in the east *i.e.* in the forenoon, he is called the *Paura*, a king staying inside the town; and in the west *i.e.* in the afternoon, he is termed the *Yāyin*, one who marches against the enemy. Mercury, Jupiter and Saturn are always *Pauras*, while the Moon is always the *Ākranda*. Ketu, Mars, Rāhu and Venus are *marching* planets. All the planets known as the *Ākranda*, *Yāyin* and *Paura* when hurt, will destroy severally kings coming to the rescue, marching and staying in town. When such planets are victorious, they bestow victory on their own classes of kings.

[In Sanskrit literature 12 kinds of kings are mentioned. Among them the *Vijigiṣu* occupies the hub of the wheel. *Ākranda* is next to the *Pārṣṇigrāha* behind the *Vijigīṣu.* In case *Pārṣṇigrāha* attacks the central king from behind, the *Ākranda* who is behind the former could help the chief king by attacking the attacker *Yāyin* and *Paura* are general terms meaning one who attacks or marches, and one who defends the town respectively. These names do not occur in the list of 12 kings.

The luminaries do not participate in planetary wars. Still they are mentioned here in view of their affliction by meteors etc.]

पौरे पौरेण हते पौराः पौरान् नृपान् विनिघ्नन्ति ।
एवं याय्याक्रन्दा नागरयायिग्रहाश्चैव ।।८।।

When a planet called *Paura* is overpowered by another of the same description, kings defending their towns would kill others in the same situation. The same applies to *Yāyin* and *Ākranda* planets and kings. When there is a conflict between *Paura* and *Yāyin* planets, the victorious will bestow victory on its own class of kings.

[Cf. पराशर—
तेषां तज्जयाद्विजयो वधाद् वधोऽन्योन्यभेदाद् भेदः साम्यात् साम्यम् ।

In the next verse the symptoms of a defeated planet are given.]

दक्षिणदिक्स्थः परुषो वेपथुरप्राप्य सन्निवृत्तोऽणुः ।।
अधिरूढो विकृतो निष्प्रभो विवर्णश्च यः स जितः ।।९।।

A planet is said to be defeated when it is situated to the south of the other, is rough, quivering, retreating without actually coming in contact with the other, small, mounted upon, of unnatural appearance, without brilliance and colourless.

[Here nine marks of defeat are listed, but *Parāśara* has one more, viz. *Abhihata* or struck.

Cf. गर्ग—

अरश्मिर्लोहितः श्यामः परुषः सूक्ष्म एव च ।
अपसव्यगतो यश्च चक्रान्तःपतितस्तथा ।।
च्युतः स्थानाद्धतो यश्च प्रतिस्तब्धस्तथैव च ।
निष्प्रभो विकृतश्चापि जवेनाभिहतश्च यः ।।
अप्राप्य वा निवृत्तो यो वेपनः कृष्ण एव च ।
लक्षणैः सप्तदशभिर्ग्रहं विन्द्यात् पराजितम् ।।

Though the sage speaks of 17 marks, yet we can count only 16. To solve this difficulty we may have to change the reading of जवेन into जवोनोऽभिहतः. Then we get one more mark i.e. one bereft of speed.]

उक्तविपरीतलक्षणसम्पन्नो जयगतो विनिर्देश्यः ।
विपुलः स्निग्धो द्युतिमान् दक्षिणदिक्स्थोऽपि जययुक्तः ॥१०॥

A planet possessed of characteristics contrary to those mentioned above should be considered as victorious i.e. when it is large, glossy and brilliant, even though it may be placed in the south.

[Cf. गर्ग—

द्युतिमान् रश्मिसम्पन्नः प्रसन्नो रजतप्रभः ।
बृहद्रूपधरश्चैव यः समेत्य ग्रहो भवेत् ॥
प्रभावर्णाधिको यश्च ग्रहमावृत्य तिष्ठति ।
तादृशं जयिनं विन्द्याद् ग्रहं ग्रहसमागमे ॥

In this connection Utpala remarks, "एतत् शुक्रस्य प्रायः सम्भवति ।" He quotes in support पुलिशाचार्य—

"सर्वे जयिन उदक्स्था दक्षिणदिक्स्थो जयी शुक्रः ।"

From this we can infer that generally the palm is given to a planet that is situated in the north, but in the case of Venus it is the reverse.]

द्वावपि मयूखयुक्तौ विपुलौ स्निग्धौ समागमे भवतः ।
तत्रान्योन्यं प्रीतिर्विपरीतावात्मपक्षघ्नौ ॥११॥

When both the planets at conjunction are radiant, large and glossy, they being in love with each other conduce to their respective parties (Ākranda etc.) establishing peace and friendship between them; while in the contrary case they destroy the kings over whom they preside.

[Here the word विपरीतौ means—if both of them are devoid of radiance, small, and rough.]

युद्धं समागमो वा यद्यव्यक्तौ स्वलक्षणैर्भवतः ।
भुवि भूभृतामपि तथा फलमव्यक्तं विनिर्देश्यम् ॥१२॥

If, owing to the indistinctness of the indications, it cannot be determined whether a conflict or conjunction is taking place, the effects accruing to the kings on earth too should be declared to be equally uncertain.

[War takes place among the non-luminaries, while *Samāgama* (conjunction) is between the Moon and one of the non-luminaries. At a planetary war sometimes it may not be possible to determine the victor owing to the absence of distinct indications, e.g. when both are radiant, large and glossy. Similarly, at a conjunction it may not be possible to find out if the Moon is either to the north or south of the other planet (non-luminary). If she passes through the other, the effect of *cleaving* should be prescribed and not of conjunction.]

गुरुणा जितेऽवनिसुते बाह्लीका यायिनोऽग्निवार्ताश्च ।
शशिजेन शूरसेनाः कलिङ्गशाल्वाश्च पीड्यन्ते ॥१३॥

सौरेणारे विजिते जयन्ति पौराः प्रजाश्च सीदन्ति ।
कोष्ठागारम्लेच्छक्षत्रियतापश्च शुक्रजिते ॥१४॥

When Mars is defeated by Jupiter, the Bāhlīkas, marching kings and persons living by fire (such as goldsmiths, cooks etc.) will come to grief. When he is vanquished by Mercury, the Śūrasenas, Kaliṅgas and Śālvas will suffer. When he is defeated by Saturn, kings defending a town will become victorious, but the subjects will be harmed. When he is defeated by Venus, granaries, Mlecchas and Kṣatriyas will suffer.

भौमेन हते शशिजे वृक्षसरित्तापसाश्मकनरेन्द्राः ।
उत्तरदिक्स्थाः क्रतुदीक्षिताश्च सन्तापमायान्ति ॥१५॥

गुरुणा जिते बुधे म्लेच्छशूद्रचौरार्थयुक्तपौरजनाः ।
त्रैगर्तपार्वतीयाः पीड्यन्ते कम्पते च मही ॥१६॥

रविजेन बुधे ध्वस्ते नाविकयोधाब्जसधनगर्भिण्यः ।
भृगुणा जितेऽग्निकोपः सस्याम्बुदयायिविध्वंसः ॥१७॥

When Mercury is defeated by Mars, trees, rivers, ascetics, the Aśmakas, kings, people living in the north and sacrificers will come to grief. When he is conquered by Jupiter, the Mlecchas, Śūdras, thieves, wealthy men, citizens (defenders of towns), Traigartas and mountain-dwellers will be affected, and there will be an earthquake. When he is vanquished by Saturn, sailors, warriors, aquatic products, rich persons and pregnant women will suffer. When he is overpowered by Venus, there will be destruction by fire and ruin of corn, clouds and marching monarchs.

जीवे शुक्राभिहते कुलूतगान्धारकैकया मद्राः ।
शाल्वा वत्सा वङ्गा गावः सस्यानि पीड्यन्ते ॥१८॥

भौमेन हते जीवे मध्यो देशो नरेश्वरा गावः ।
सौरेण चार्जुनायनवसातियौधेयशिबिविप्राः ॥१९॥

शशितनयेनापि जिते बृहस्पतौ म्लेच्छसत्यशस्त्रभृतः ।
उपयान्ति मध्यदेशश्च संक्षयं यच्च भक्तिफलम् ॥२०॥

When Jupiter is vanquished by Venus, the Kulūtas, Gāndhāras, Kaikayas, Madras, Śālvas, Vatsas, Vaṅgas, cattle and corn will be affected. When he is overcome by Mars, the middle country, kings and cows will suffer. When he is defeated by Saturn, the Arjunāyanas, Vasātis, Yaudheyas, Śibis and Brāhmaṇas will be harmed. When he is defeated by Mercury, the Mlecchas, truthful men, soldiers and the middle country will be ruined. In addition, those people and things belonging to Jupiter (vide XVI. 21-25 *supra*) will also be destroyed.

[Though the author mentions भक्तिफल- effect of planetary rulership—only with reference to Jupiter and Venus, it is to be understood that the dependencies of all defeated planets will be adversely affected, as a general rule. For, he makes this point clear in the last verse below i.e. 27].

शुक्रे बृहस्पतिजिते यायी श्रेष्ठो विनाशमुपयाति ।
ब्रह्मक्षत्रविरोधः सलिलं च न वासवस्त्यजति ॥२१॥

कोसलकलिङ्गवङ्गा वत्सा मत्स्याश्च मध्यदेशयुताः ।
महतीं व्रजन्ति पीडां नपुंसकाः शूरसेनाश्च ॥२२॥

कुजविजिते भृगुतनये बलमुख्यवधो नरेन्द्रसङ्ग्रामाः ।
सौम्येन पार्वतीयाः क्षीरविनाशोऽल्पवृष्टिश्च ॥२३॥

रविजेन सिते विजिते गणमुख्याः शस्त्रजीविनः क्षत्रम् ।
जलजाश्च निपीड्यन्ते सामान्यं भक्तिफलमन्यत् ॥२४॥

When Venus is defeated by Jupiter, the marching monarch will meet with his end; Brāhmaṇas and Kṣatriyas will be at loggerheads, and there will be no rain; the Kosalas, Kaliṅgas, Vaṅgas, Vatsas, Matsyas, the Middle country, eunuchs and the Śūrasenas will suffer severely. When he is defeated by Mars, commandants of armies will be murdered, and kings will be locked up in wars. When he is overcome by Mercury, mountaineers will be afflicted; and there will be great scarcity of milk and rainfall. When he is vanquished by Saturn, leaders of corporations, military men, Kṣatriyas and aquatic animals (and products) will be harmed. Moreover, the general effects due to planetary rulership (mentioned in XVI. 26-30) will also come to pass.

असिते सितेन निहतेऽर्घवृद्धिरहिविहगमानिनां पीडा ।
क्षितिजेन तङ्गणान्ध्रोड्रकाशिबाह्लीकदेशानाम् ॥२५॥

सौम्येन पराभूते मन्देऽङ्गवणिग्विहङ्गपशुनागाः ।
सन्ताप्यन्ते गुरुणा स्त्रीबहुला महिषकशकाश्च ॥२६॥

When Saturn is overcome by Venus, prices increase, and snakes, birds and proud persons suffer. When he is defeated by Mars, the Taṅgaṇa, Āndhra, Uḍra, Kāśi and Bāhlīka countries will be afflicted. When he is defeated by Mercury, the Aṅgas, merchants, birds, cattle (quadrupeds) and elephants will suffer. And when he is hurt by Jupiter, countries where women are in a majority, the Mahiṣakas and Scythians will be troubled.

अयं विशेषोऽभिहितो हतानां कुजज्ञवागीशसितासितानाम् ।
फलं तु वाच्यं ग्रहभक्तितोऽन्यद्यथा तथा घ्नन्ति हताः स्वभक्तीः ॥२७॥

Thus have been described the special effects of the defeat of Mars, Mercury, Jupiter, Venus and Saturn. The general effects, however, are to be declared as explained in the chapter dealing with planetary rulership. The more a planet is stricken, the more will it harm everything belonging to it.

[What the author means is that the general effects of victory or defeat will accrue to the people, countries and animals as well as things enumerated in the previous chapter. What is given here is only the special character of the effects for each planet.

The metre is उपेन्द्रवज्रा.]

शशिग्रहसमागमाध्यायः ॥१८॥

Chapter XVIII—Conjunction of the Moon with Planets or Stars

भानां यथासम्भवमुत्तरेण यातो ग्रहाणां यदि वा शशाङ्कः ।
प्रदक्षिणं तच्छुभदं नृपाणां याम्येन यातो न शिवः शशाङ्कः ॥१॥

When the Moon moves, wherever possible, to the north of stars or planets i.e. keeps them to her right side, it is called her dextral movement and augurs well for kings (or mankind). If she moves to the south of them, she does not bring happiness to them.

[शुभकृन्नराणां is another reading in the second half of the verse.

"यथासम्भवं" is explained by the commentator thus : It is only in the case of the star or planet that is nearby. This generally happens in the case of those stars whose Vikṣepa is equal to or less than that of the Moon; for example, Kṛttikā, Rohiṇī, Puṣya, Maghā, Citrā, Viśākhā, Anurādhā, Jyeṣṭhā, Śatabhiṣaj and Revatī. In the case of those that are situated far away, e.g. Svāti, Śravaṇa, Dhaniṣṭhā etc., she cannot move to their north. The declination of Svāti is 37° north, while the Moon's 4.5°. Hence she moves always to its south. On the other hand, she moves always to the north of those stars whose southern declination is greater than hers. The same rule holds in the case of Mars and other planets.

Cf. ऋषिपुत्र and वृद्धगर्ग under XVII. 2-3. The metre is उपजाति.]

चन्द्रमा यदि कुजस्य यात्युदक्पार्वतीयबलशालिनां जयः ।
क्षत्रियाः प्रमुदिताः सयायिनो भूरिधान्यमुदिता वसुन्धरा ॥२॥

Should the Moon move to the north of Mars, mountaineers and the mighty would be victorious; Kṣatriyas and marching monarchs would be happy; and the earth would rejoice with abundant corn.

[The metre is रथोद्धता.]

उत्तरतः स्वसुतस्य शशाङ्कः पौरजयाय सुभिक्षकरश्च ।
सस्यचयं कुरुते जनहार्दि कोशचयं च नराधिपतीनाम् ॥३॥

When the Moon traverses to the north of Mercury, she confers victory on the king defending the town, plenty of food, and corn as well as happiness on the people, and enrichment of treasuries of kings.

[The metre is दोधक.]

बृहस्पतेरुत्तरगे शशाङ्के पौरद्विजक्षत्रियपण्डितानाम् ।
धर्मस्य देशस्य च मध्यमस्य वृद्धिः सुभिक्षं मुदिताः प्रजाश्च ॥४॥

When the Moon moves to the north of Jupiter, prosperity will dawn on kings defending their towns, Brāhmaṇas, Kṣatriyas, learned men, righteousness or religion, and the middle country. There will be plenty of food and happiness among the people.

[The metre is उपजाति.]

भार्गवस्य यदि यात्युदक् शशी कोशयुक्तगजवाजिवृद्धिदः ।
यायिनां च विजयो धनुष्मतां सस्यसम्पदपि चोत्तमा तदा ॥५॥

When the Moon is to the north of Venus, those who have hoarded wealth, elephants and horses will flourish, marching chiefs and archers will be victorious and there will be a bumper harvest.

[The metre is रथोद्धता.]

रविजस्य शशी प्रदक्षिणं कुर्याच्चेत्पुरभूभृतां जयः ।
शकबाह्लिकसिन्धुपह्लवा मुद्भाजो यवनैः समन्विताः ॥६॥

Should the Moon traverse to the north of Saturn, kings defending a town would win victory, and the Scythians, Bāhlīkas, people of Sindhu, Pahlavas and Yavanas would be happy.

[The metre is वैतालीय.]

येषामुदग्गच्छति भग्रहाणां प्रालेयरश्मिर्निरुपद्रवश्च ।
तद्द्रव्यपौरेतरभक्तिदेशान् पुष्णाति याम्येन निहन्ति तानि ॥७॥

If the Moon moves to the north of a star or planet, herself remaining free from affliction, she proves beneficent to the substances, kings defending towns or marching chiefs as the case may be, and countries assigned to the particular star or planet. In case she moves to the south of the same, she will destroy all the above-named things belonging to it.

[The metre is इन्द्रवज्रा.]

शशिनि फलमुदक्स्थे यद् ग्रहस्योपदिष्टं
भवति तदपसव्ये सर्वमेव प्रतीपम् ।

इति शशिसमवायाः कीर्तिता भग्रहाणां
न खलु भवति युद्धं साकमिन्दोर्ग्रहर्क्षैः ॥८॥

Thus have been described the effects of the Moon's conjunction with stars and planets to the effect that all the results declared for the Moon's standing to the north of a planet become null and void when she moves to its south. The Moon has no conflict whatsoever with any planet or star.

[The Sun's conjunction with any planet is called the latter's *Eclipse*; the Moon's, *Samāgama*; and that of the non-luminaries among themselves, *Conflict*.

Cf. आचार्य विष्णुचन्द्र—

दिवसकरेणास्तमयः समागमः शीतरश्मिसहितानाम् ।
कुसुतादीनां युद्धं निगद्यतेऽन्योन्ययुक्तानाम् ॥

Here Bhaṭṭotpala ridicules those who have spoken of the Sun's victory and defeat, as being utterly ignorant of astronomy.

The metre is मालिनी.]

ग्रहवर्षफलाध्यायः ॥१९॥

Chapter XIX—Planetary Years and Effects

[Bhaṭṭotpala reminds us that Varāhamihira had promised in the पञ्चसिद्धान्तिका I-22 that he would treat of the effects of years and months in this work :—

वर्षे यद्यस्य फलं मासे च मुनिप्रणीतमालोक्य ।
तत्तद्वृत्तैर्वक्ष्ये होरातन्त्रोत्तरविधाने ॥

In this connection Dr. Kern remarks thus :—

"It is not known which source has been chiefly used by our author in this particular instance; thus much, however, is certain that long before his time Greek horoscopy had been introduced into India."

None can doubt the sincerity and honesty of Varāhamihira inasmuch as he mentions the authorities, both ancient Indian and foreign, for his statements. In the above verse quoted from the *Pañcasiddhāntikā* he expressly states that the वर्षफल and मासफल were expounded by ancient sages (मुनिप्रणीतम्) who must be Garga, Parāśara, Kāśyapa, Devala etc. He also pays tribute to the scholarship of the Yavanas (vide II. 14). From this we are not justified in inferring that everything in astrology and astronomy here was borrowed from the Greeks. It is true that our author adds many Greek terms such as Kriya, Tāvuru and Jutuma to the names prevalent in India.]

सर्वत्र भूर्विरलसस्ययुता वनानि
दैवाद् बिभक्षयिषुदंष्ट्रिसमावृतानि ।
नद्यश्च नैव हि पयः प्रचुरं स्रवन्ति
रुग्भेषजानि न तथातिबलान्वितानि ॥१॥

तीक्ष्णं तपत्यदितिजः शिशिरेऽपि काले
नात्यम्बुदा जलमुचोऽचलसन्निकाशाः ।
नष्टप्रभर्क्षगणशीतकरं नभश्च
सीदन्ति तापसकुलानि सगोकुलानि ॥२॥

हस्त्यश्वपत्तिमदसह्यबलैरुपेता
बाणासनासिमुशलातिशयाश्चरन्ति ।
घ्नन्तो नृपा युधि नृपानुचरांश्च देशान्
संवत्सरे दिनकरस्य दिनेऽथ मासे ॥३॥

The state of things in a year, month or day presided over by the Sun will be as follows : Everywhere the earth will yield very little crop; the forests will be infested with hungry tusked animals as a visitation, there will be very little water flowing in the rivers; medicines will not have their potency. Even in winter the Sun will be extremely warm; clouds, though resembling mountains, will not pour down sufficient rain; the Moon and the clusters of stars in the sky will lose their brilliance; groups of hermits and cattle will languish. Kings accompanied by their followers as well as irresistible forces consisting of the divisions of elephants, horses and foot-soldiers, and armed with mighty bows, swords and staves, will go about destroying the countries in wars.

[Cf. यवनेश्वर—

अब्दाश्रयं लक्षणमीरितं यद् ग्रहस्वभावप्रभवं जनानाम् ।
तदेव तन्मासदिनर्त्तुषूक्तं तदीश्वरस्थानविकल्पितं च ॥

दिवाकराब्दे रणविग्रहोग्रक्षितीश्वरस्तीव्रविषज्वराग्निः ।
अवर्षशुष्कद्रुमशुष्कसस्यप्रचण्डवह्न्युग्रविषाक्षिरोगाः ॥

The reading of the second verse appears to be slightly corrupt. Cf. also समाससंहिता—

तीक्ष्णोऽर्कः स्वल्पसस्यश्च गतमेघोऽतितस्करः ।
बहूरगव्याधिगणो भास्कराब्दो रणाकुलः ॥

Utpala has quoted relevant verses from the पञ्चसिद्धान्तिका I.8-10; 17-19 under II-6 where lords of years, months etc. are mentioned. For a clear method refer to श्रीपतिपद्धति, pp. 40-42 (V.S.S. Edn.).

Unless otherwise stated the metre employed in this chapter is वसन्ततिलका].

व्याप्तं नभः प्रचलिताचलसन्निकाशै-
र्व्यालाञ्जनालिगवलच्छविभिः पयोदैः ।
गां पूरयद्भिरखिलाममलाभिरद्भि-
रुत्कण्ठितेन गुरुणा ध्वनितेन चाशाः ॥४॥

तोयानि पद्मकुमुदोत्पलवन्त्यतीव
फुल्लद्रुमाण्युपवनान्यलिनाविताानि ।
गावः प्रभूतपयसो नयनाभिरामा
रामा रतैरविरतं रमयन्ति रामान् ॥५॥

गोधूमशालियवधान्यवरेक्षुवाटा
भूः पाल्यते नृपतिभिर्नगराकराढ्या ।
चित्यङ्किता क्रतुवरेष्टिविघुष्टनादा
संवत्सरे शिशिरगोरभिसम्प्रवृत्ते ॥६॥

During the year presided over by the Moon, the sky will be covered with clouds which resemble moving mountains, which possess the colour of snakes, collyrium, bees and buffaloes' horn, and which fill the entire earth with pure water and the quarters with their deep thunder that produces pangs of separation in the minds of lovers. The waters (of lakes etc.) will be adorned with lotuses and lilies, trees blossoming and bees humming in the gardens; cows will yield abundant milk; and charming ladies will always be delighting their handsome lovers with amorous sports. Kings will rule over the earth justly and properly and enable the latter to yield a rich harvest of wheat, paddy, barley, Kalama rice and sugar-cane, and be enriched with excellent towns and mines as well as marked with sacrificial altars, and resounding with Vedic chants at big and small sacrifices.

[उत्कण्ठकेन is another reading for उत्कण्ठितेन. These verses are marked by an extra-ordinary felicity of diction and elegant imagery. The author's poetic talents appear to brush aside his scientific restraints and assert themselves giving a literary relief to the reader whose mind must be rigid with scientific ideas. The alliteration in these verses, especially in verse No. 5, is particularly pleasing.

Cf. यवनेश्वर—

सम्पन्नसस्यक्षुपशष्पशालिप्ररूढगुल्मो बहुवर्षधारः ।
रत्नौषधिस्नेहपटुप्रसेकश्चान्द्रो रतिस्त्रीसुखवर्धनोऽब्दः ॥

also समाससंहिता—

बहुवर्षातिसस्यश्च गवां क्षीरप्रदायकः ।
चन्द्राब्दः कामिनामिष्टश्चित्यङ्कितमहीतलः ॥]

वातोद्धतश्चरति वह्निरतिप्रचण्डो
ग्रामान्वनानि नगराणि च सन्दिधक्षुः ।
हाहेति दस्युगणपातहता रटन्ति
निःस्वीकृता विपशवो भुवि मर्त्यसङ्घाः ॥७॥

अभ्युन्नता वियति संहतमूर्तयोऽपि
मुञ्चन्ति न क्वचिदपः प्रचुरं पयोदाः ।
सीम्नि प्रजातमपि शोषमुपैति सस्यं
निष्पन्नमप्यविनयादपरे हरन्ति ॥८॥

भूपा न सम्यगभिपालनसक्तचित्ताः
पित्तोत्थरुक्प्रचुरता भुजगप्रकोपः ।
एवंविधैरुपहता भवति प्रजेयं
संवत्सरेऽवनिसुतस्य विपन्नसस्या ॥९॥

During the year ruled by Mars most violent fires fanned by the wind will spread out threatening to consume villages, forests and towns; crowds of men ruined by the depredations of hordes of robbers and deprived of their properties and cattle, will cry out, "Alas ! Alas !", throughout the land. Though the clouds may appear thick and piled up in the sky, nowhere will they pour down sufficient rain. Even the crops that grow in the low-lying lands will wither away. Even if they should grow, they would be snatched away by robbers. Kings would not be interested in governing their countries properly. Bilious ailments would be on the increase; there will be great trouble from snakes and the people will be afflicted by various calamities such as destruction of food crops.

[कुत्रचिद् is the reading adopted by some in the place of न क्वचिद् and निम्ने instead of सीम्नि.

Cf. यवनेश्वर—

रणप्रचण्डक्षितिपोऽल्पसस्यो विशुष्कवारिद्रुमशष्पशीर्णः ।
अङ्गारकाब्दः प्रचुरोरगाग्निरातङ्कचौर्यक्षुदवृष्टिदुष्टः ॥

and समाससंहिता—

अग्नितस्कररोगाढ्यो नृपविग्रहदायकः ।
गतसस्यो बहुव्यालो भौमाब्दो बालहा भृशम् ॥]

मायेन्द्रजालकुहकाकरनागराणां
गान्धर्वलेख्यगणितास्त्रविदां च वृद्धिः ।

पिप्रीषया नृपतयोऽद्भुतदर्शनानि
दित्सन्ति तुष्टिजननानि परस्परेभ्यः ॥१०॥

वार्त्ता जगत्यवितथाविकला त्रयी च
सम्यक्चरत्यपि मनोरिव दण्डनीतिः ।
अध्यक्षरस्वभिनिविष्टधियोऽपि केचि-
दान्वीक्षिकीषु च परं पदमीहमानाः ॥११॥

हास्यज्ञदूतकविबालनपुंसकानां
युक्तिज्ञसेतुजलपर्वतवासिनां च ।
हार्दि करोति मृगलाञ्छनजः स्वकेऽब्दे
मासेऽथवा प्रचुरता भुवि चौषधीनाम् ॥१२॥

During the year, month or day presided over by Mercury fortune will smile on those who are proficient in the art of jugglery, hypnotism and magic, mines, townsmen, musicians, painters, accountants (or mathematicians) and fighters. Kings will be eager to exchange wonderful gifts creating joy among themselves with the idea of cultivating friendship. Rearing of cattle, agriculture and trade will thrive through sincere efforts. Vedic studies will be in full swing. Justice will be administered scrupulously by kings as by Manu himself. Some will be engaged in spiritual discipline, and others in the science of logic, desiring to attain the supreme state (of Mokṣa or liberation). Jesters, envoys, poets, children, eunuchs, perfumers, and those who live near bridges, water and mountains will be happy. There will be abundant growth of herbs in the land.

[All the persons and things mentioned in this chapter are to be understood to be ruled by the respective planets. For example, Mercury has been described in astrology as an expert in singing, dancing, comics, mathematics etc.

Cf. यवनेश्वर—

सन्धानदानप्रयतक्षितीशः स्वाध्यायतीर्थाध्वरभीर्द्विजोघः ।
निराधिरुङ्मध्यमसस्यवर्षो बौधः सुहृत्स्नेहविवर्धनोऽब्दः ॥

I prefer the reading : अध्वरधीर्द्विजोघः ।

See also समाससंहिता —

ब्रह्मक्षत्रस्य सस्यानां जनानां च कलाविदाम् ।
वृद्धिप्रदोऽब्दो बौधस्तु भूपसाम्यकरः क्षितौ ॥]

ध्वनिरुच्चरितोऽध्वरे द्युगामी विपुलो यज्ञमुषां मनांसि भिन्दन् ।
विचरत्यनिशं द्विजोत्तमानां हृदयानन्दकरोऽध्वरांशभाजाम् ॥१३॥

क्षितिरुत्तमसस्यवत्यनेकद्विपपत्त्यश्वधनोरुगोकुलाढ्या ।
क्षितिपैरभिपालनप्रवृद्धा द्युचरस्पर्द्धिजना तदा विभाति ॥१४॥

विविधैर्वियदुन्नतैः पयोदैर्वृतमुर्वीं पयसाभितर्पयद्भिः ।
सुरराजगुरोः शुभे तु वर्षे बहुसस्या क्षितिरुत्तमर्द्धियुक्ता ॥१५॥

During the auspicious year ruled by Jupiter the deep sounds produced in sacrifices by expert priests chanting Vedic hymns will go up to heaven continually rending the hearts of evil spirits and delighting the hearts of the gods partaking of the offerings. The earth will abound in excellent crops, be rich in elephants, horses, foot-soldiers, wealth and large herds of cattle, and be very prosperous owing to the all-round protection given by her rulers, as if, her people vied with the denizens of heaven. The sky will be covered with numerous towering clouds that regale the earth with their water. The earth will be blessed with plenty of crops and great prosperity.

[The commentator raises a question, अत्र तु किमर्थं शुभग्रहणम्, meaning, why should the author qualify the year as *auspicious* ! The reason is : All the years of the sixty-year cycle are not auspicious, there being some with untoward effects. For, in VIII. 48-52 the effects of the years Piṅgala, Kālayukta, Raudra, Rudhirodgārin, Raktākṣa etc. are said to be very bad, whereas those of Prabhava, Vibhava, Śukla, Pramoda are auspicious. Hence, only those auspicious years of Jupiter will be able to generate good effects, and not the rest.

I feel that the very form and structure of the *Saṁhitā* gives the author ample opportunities to exhibit his poetic talents. For, the ideas given in three verses are effectively condensed by him in an anuṣṭubh śloka in his abridged work given below :

बहुयज्ञोऽतिसस्यश्च गोगजाश्वहितस्तथा ।
पुरन्दरगुरोरब्दो बहुसस्यप्रदः शिवः ॥

Cf. यवनेश्वर—

सुवर्षयज्ञोत्सवसम्प्रदानो नीरुग्व्यथो धर्मपरावनीशः ।
स्फीतान्नपानैर्बहुसस्यकर्मा गुरोः स्वकर्मप्रयतप्रजोऽब्दः ॥

The metre of these verses is औपच्छन्दसिक.]

शालीक्षुमत्यपि धरा धरणीधराभ-
धाराधरोज्झितपयःपरिपूर्णवप्रा ।
श्रीमत्सरोरुहततताम्बुतडागकीर्णा
योषेव भात्यभिनवाभरणोज्ज्वलाङ्गी ॥१६॥

क्षत्रं क्षितौ क्षपितभूरिबलारिपक्ष-
मुद्घुष्टनैकजयशब्दविराविताशम् ।
संहृष्टशिष्टजनदुष्टविनष्टवर्गां
गां पालयन्त्यवनिपा नगराकराढ्याम् ॥१७॥

पेपीयते मधु मधौ सह कामिनीभि-
र्जेगीयते श्रवणहारि सवेणुवीणम् ।
बोभुज्यतेऽतिथिसुहृत्स्वजनैः सहान्न-
मब्दे सितस्य मदनस्य जयावघोषः ॥१८॥

During the year presided over by Venus the earth will be rich in rice and sugarcane, with its surface filled with water poured out by mountain-like clouds, and bedecked with lakes whose waters are filled with charming lotuses, and consequently will shine like a damsel whose limbs are resplendent with lustrous ornaments. Kings will make the quarters resound with the loud cries of victory, having destroyed the mighty hosts of their enemies, and will rule over the earth rich in towns and mines, making the virtuous happy and contented and extirpating all the hordes of wicked persons. Young men will, in the vernal season, drink wine frequently in the company of their sweet-hearts; people will constantly sing melodious songs to the accompaniment of flute and lute; men will enjoy often feasts in the company of their guests, friends and kinsmen; and the cries of victory of the God of Love will be heard everywhere.

[Here too the author shows himself as an erudite scholar and skilled poet, using fine alliterative language and rare grammatical expressions.

Cf. यवनेश्वर —

पर्याप्तसौख्यस्फुटसस्यमेघः प्ररूढवल्लीवरशष्पपुष्पः ।
कामप्रकामक्षितिपो मुदाढ्यः शौक्रोऽङ्गनाहर्षवसुप्रदोऽब्दः ॥

also the समाससंहिता—

सस्याढ्यो धर्मबहुलो गतातङ्को बहूदकः ।
कामिनां कामदः कामं सिताब्दो नृपशर्मदः (शर्मदः सदा) ॥]

उद्वृत्तदस्युगणभूरिरणाकुलानि
राष्ट्राण्यनेकपशुवित्तविनाकृतानि ।
रोरूयमाणहतबन्धुजनैर्जनैश्च
रोगोत्तमाकुलकुलानि बुभुक्षया च ॥१६॥

वातोद्धताम्बुधरवर्जितमन्तरिक्ष-
मारुग्णनैकविटपं च धरातलं द्यौः ।
नष्टार्कचन्द्रकिरणातिरजोऽवनद्धा
तोयाशयाश्च विजलाः सरितोऽपि तन्व्यः ॥२०॥

जातानि कुत्रचिदतोयतया विनाश-
मृच्छन्ति पुष्टिमपराणि जलोक्षितानि ।
सस्यानि मन्दमभिवर्षति वृत्रशत्रु (त्रो-)
र्वर्षे दिवाकरसुतस्य सदा प्रवृत्ते ॥२१॥

When Saturn holds sway over a year, countries will be torn by many battles of unruly bands of robbers, and deprived of their cattle and wealth, with vast multitudes of people crying piteously as a result of the murder of their near and dear ones, and of hunger and fell diseases. The sky will be denuded of clouds driven by the wind, all the trees with their branches broken down will cover the earth; the sky will not be illuminated by the rays of the luminaries, being covered with a dense mass of dust. Tanks and lakes will dry up; and rivers will be very tiny. In some parts, crops will perish for want of water, in others they grow being watered by artificial means; and (or as) the Rain-god will yield but little rain.

[Cf. यवनेश्वर—

तुष्टाल्पवर्षः प्रबलानिलाग्निर्विपन्नसस्यश्चलितक्षितीशः ।
मृत्युक्षुधातङ्कभयोपजुष्टः शनैश्चरोऽब्दः पशुशूद्रगोघ्नः ॥

I feel, it must be सृष्टाल्पवर्षः ।

See also the समाससंहिता—

दुर्भिक्षमरकं रोगान् करोति पवनं तथा ।
शनैश्चरोऽब्दो दोषांश्च विग्रहांश्चैव भूभुजाम् ॥

संवत्सरोक्तं सकलमृतुमासायनेषु च ।
फलं ग्रहस्य वक्तव्यं बलयुक्तस्य नान्यथा ॥]

अणुरपटुमयूखो नीचगोऽन्यैर्जितो वा
न सकलफलदाता पुष्टिदोऽतोऽन्यथा यः ।
यदशुभमशुभेऽब्दे मासजं तस्य वृद्धिः
शुभफलमपि चैवं याप्यमन्योन्यतायाम् ॥२२॥

Should a planet be tiny in appearance, with faint rays, be posited in his depression or be defeated by another, he would not yield any good result (in his year, month or day). If he be otherwise i.e. big, brilliant, posited in his own or any other good house, or victorious in war, he would bring about great progress and prosperity. If both the lords of the year and month be inauspicious or malefic, then their evil effects would be aggravated in the particular month. On the other hand, if both be benefic, the good effects would be heightened. If one of them be good and the other bad, the result would be trifling.

[Cf. देवल—

बली वर्षपतिः पुष्टं फलं यच्छति शोभनम् ।
विबलश्च तथानिष्टं वर्षमासदिनात्मकम् ॥

The metre is मालिनी.]

———

ग्रहशृङ्गाटकाध्यायः ॥२०॥

Chapter XX—*The Planetary Triangle*

यस्यां दिशि दृश्यन्ते विशन्ति ताराग्रहा रवि सर्वे ।
भवति भयं दिशि तस्यामायुधकोपक्षुधातङ्कैः ॥१॥

The direction in which all the non-luminaries become visible after they emerge from combustion, or are eclipsed by the sun will be afflicted with famine, war and diseases.

[In addition to the subject-matter of this verse, the author discusses the effects of some peculiar dispositions of the planets. All these have a bearing on the health and happiness of mankind as well as on their political and social behaviour.

Cf. काश्यप—

भूमिपुत्रादयः सर्वे यस्यामस्तमिते रवौ ।
दृश्यन्तेऽस्तमये वापि यत्र यान्ति रवेस्ततः ॥
दुर्भिक्षं शस्त्रकोपं च जनानां मरकं भवेत् ।
अन्योन्यं भूमिपाः सर्वे विनिघ्नन्ति प्रजास्तथा ॥]

चक्रधनुःशृङ्गाटकदण्डपुरप्रासवज्रसंस्थानाः ।
क्षुदवृष्टिकरा लोके समराय च मानवेन्द्राणाम् ॥२॥

The configurations named *Cakra* (Discus), *Dhanus* (Bow), *Śṛṅgāṭaka* (Triangle), *Daṇḍa* (Staff), *Pura* (Town), *Prāsa* (Dart) and *Vajra* (Thunderbolt), produce famine and drought in the country and promote war among kings.

[Cf. काश्यप—

विहायोक्तं च संस्थानं दृश्यन्ते वै ग्रहा यदा ।
तदा न तत्फलं ब्रूयाल्लोके नाशुभदाश्च ते ॥]

यस्मिन् खांशे दृश्या ग्रहमाला दिनकरे दिनान्तगते ।
तत्रान्यो भवति नृपः परचक्रोपद्रवश्च महान् ॥३॥

Note the particular direction of the sky in which a group of planets is sighted at sunset. There will be another king and great trouble from foreign armies in the country corresponding to that quarter.

[This does not refer to the emergence of planets after eclipse, but their sight in a group at sunset in a particular direction.]

यस्मिन्नृक्षे कुर्युः समागमं तज्जनान् ग्रहा हन्युः ।
अविभेदिनः परस्परममलमयूखाः शिवास्तेषाम् ॥४॥

When planets combine in any asterism, people ruled by that asterism (*vide XIV & XV supra*) will be killed. But when they are radiant and do not occult each other, they will prove beneficent to the same people.

[Cf. the समाससंहिता—

सर्वे यदा दिनकरं विशन्ति कुर्युर्ग्रहास्तदा पीडाम् ।
क्षुच्छस्त्रभयातङ्कैरपरैश्च परस्पराघातैः ॥
प्रत्यर्चिषः प्रसन्नाः सम्भृतकिरणाः प्रदक्षिणावर्ताः ।
सुस्निग्धामलतनवः क्षेमसुभिक्षावहास्ते स्युः ॥]

ग्रहसंवर्तसमागमसम्मोहसमाजसन्निपाताख्याः ।
कोशश्चेत्येतेषामभिधास्ये लक्षणं सफलम् ॥५॥

I shall now describe the characteristics and effects of the six planetary combinations, viz. *Saṁvarta* (concourse), *Samāgama* (Gathering), *Sammoha* (Tarnishing), *Samāja* (Meeting), *Sannipāta* (Encounter) and *Kośa* (Fellowship).

एकर्क्षे चत्वारः सह पौरैर्यायिनोऽथवा पञ्च ।
संवर्तो नाम भवेच्छिखिराहुयुतः स सम्मोहः ॥६॥

पौरः पौरसमेतो यायी सह यायिना समाजाख्यः ।
यमजीवसङ्गमेऽन्यो यद्यागच्छेत्तदा कोशः ॥७॥

उदितः पश्चादेकः प्राक् चान्यो यदि स सन्निपाताख्यः ।
अविकृततनवः स्निग्धा विपुलाश्च समागमे धन्याः ॥८॥

If four or five planets designated as *Pauras* (defenders of town) and *Yāyins* (marching ones) congregate in one and the same constellation, the yoga (combination) is termed *Saṁvarta* or *Concourse*. If in the above combination Rāhu or Ketu should find a place, it would be named *Sammoha* or *Tarnishing*. When a planet called *Paura* is combined with another of the same category, or when one named

Yāyin is joined with another of the same calling, it is termed *Samāja* or *Meeting*. When a third planet joins the combination of Jupiter and Saturn, it is called *Kośa* or *Fellowship*. If two planets, one rising heliacally in the east and the other in the west, join together in the same asterism, it is called *Sannipāta* or *Encounter*. Any conjunction of planets other than the above five is called *Samāgama* or *Gathering*, in which the effect would be always auspicious, if the concerned planets be large, resplendent and natural in appearance.

[Cf. the समाससंहिता—

ग्रहकोशसन्निपातौ संवर्तसमागमौ समाजश्च ।
सम्मोहश्चेति तेषां लक्षणमस्तात्समादेश्यम् ॥

सूर्यजगुरुसंयोगे द्वावप्येकोऽपर: समागच्छेत् ।
स हि भवति कोशसञ्ज्ञो दुर्भिक्षभयावहो लोके ॥

एक उदित: प्रतीच्यामपर: प्राच्यां ग्रहोदितो यदि च ।
अन्योन्यमथोस्राभिर्विलिखेत्स हि सन्निपाताख्य: ॥

सह पौरेण च पौरो यायी सह यायिना ग्रहो यश्च ।
दृश्येत समायुक्त: स समाजाख्य: समुद्दिष्ट: ॥

अथ यायिनागराख्याश्चत्वार: पञ्च वा सह भवेयु: ।
एकर्क्षे संवर्त: शिखिराहुयुत: स सम्मोह: ॥]

समौ तु संवर्तसमागमाख्यौ सम्मोहकोशौ भयदौ प्रजानाम् ।
समाजसंज्ञे सुसमा: प्रदिष्टा वैरप्रकोप: खलु सन्निपाते ॥६॥

The effects of the two Yogas *Saṁvarta* and *Samāgama* are moderate; *Sammoha* and *Kośa* are dangerous to people; in *Samāja* the year will be highly beneficial; and *Sannipāta* there will certainly be great hostilities among men.

[Cf. काश्यप—

संवर्तसङ्गमौ मध्यौ सम्मोहो भयद: स्मृत: ।
कोशश्चानिष्टफलद: समाजाख्य: सुमध्यम: ॥
सन्निपाते महावैरमन्योन्यमुपजायते ॥

In the समाससंहिता our author gives greater details regarding the effects and positions of planets in these Yogas in the several Vīthīs mentioned in IX *supra*:

संवर्तसमागमयोः साम्यं मोहे भयानि कोशे च।
सुसमा समाजसञ्ज्ञे वैराण्यथ सन्निपाताख्ये ॥
दुर्भिक्षरोगतस्करशस्त्रावृष्टिक्षुधं ग्रहाः कुर्युः ।
आनलवीथ्यां ज्ञेया अजवीथ्यां नेत्रपरिहानिः ॥
शस्त्रभयं मृगवीथ्यां जारद्गव्यां क्षुधं च रोगांश्च।
पशुनाशं गोवीथ्यामृषभाख्यायां च नृपपीडा ॥
सुसुभिक्षमिरावत्यां गजवीथ्यां च क्रतूत्सवामोदाः ।
अतिजलमोक्षं कुर्युर्नागाख्यायां च सर्वे तु ॥
ग्रहोदये प्रवासे च सोमसूर्यग्रहे तथा ।
विचार्य वीथीमार्गांश्च लोके ब्रूयाच्छुभाशुभम् ॥]

गर्भलक्षणम् ॥२१॥

Chapter XXI—PREGNANCY OF CLOUDS

अन्नं जगतः प्राणाः प्रावृट्कालस्य चान्नमायत्तम्
यस्मादतः परीक्ष्यः प्रावृट्कालः प्रयत्नेन ॥१॥

As food forms the very life of living beings, and as food is dependent on the monsoon, it should be investigated carefully.

[All our scriptures beginning from the Vedas and Upaniṣads proclaim that food is the Supreme Being for the majority of human beings. Gradually they realize that they are neither the body, nor the vital airs, nor the mind, nor the intellect, nor the bliss, but something beyond all these which, the sages say, is *Anirvacanīya*—inexplicable—and should be realized by oneself for oneself in one's own self. But, as Kālidāsa says "शरीरमाद्यं खलु धर्मसाधनम्", the highest spiritual experience cannot be achieved without a sound body, which, of course, is built up and maintained by proper, Sāttvika, food. This food can be had only if the monsoon is effective. So says the *Bhagavadgītā* (III-14) "अन्नाद्भवन्ति भूतानि पर्जन्यादन्नसम्भवः ।" See also तै. उप. III.-2. This science of meteorology was developed in ancient India by sages like Garga, Parāśara, Kāśyapa, Ṛṣiputra and Siddhasena. This and the following seven chapters deal with topics connected with meteorology—rain and weather.]

तल्लक्षणानि मुनिभिर्यानि निबद्धानि तानि दृष्ट्वेदम् ।
क्रियते गर्गपराशरकाश्यपवज्रादिरचितानि ॥२॥

After going through the characteristics expounded by ancient sages such as Garga, Parāśara, Kāśyapa, Vajra (Bādarāyaṇa, Asita and Devala) in their works, I am now explaining the properties of the rainy season.

दैवविदविहितचित्तो द्युनिशं यो गर्भलक्षणे भवति ।
तस्य मुनेरिव वाणी न भवति मिथ्याम्बुनिर्देशे ॥३॥

The prediction of an astrologer, who observes attentively day and night the symptoms of pregnancy of the clouds, will never be falsified, like that of a sage, when he determines the rainfall.

[अविहितचित्तो is another reading. cf. II. 5.]

किं वातः परमन्यच्छास्त्रं ज्यायोऽस्ति यद्विवित्वैव ।
प्रध्वंसिन्यपि काले त्रिकालदर्शी कलौ भवति ॥४॥

Is there a science superior to this (astrological) science, by knowing which alone one gets the power of visualizing the past, present and the future even in this Kali age which destroys all good things ?

केचिद्वदन्ति कार्त्तिकशुक्लान्तमतीत्य गर्भदिवसाः स्युः ।
न च तन्मतं बहूनां गर्गादीनां मतं वक्ष्ये ॥५॥

Some teachers like Siddhasena declare that the days of pregnancy begin soon after the full-moon of Kārtika month; whereas the opinion of the majority is opposed to this. Hence I shall give the opinion of sage Garga and others (like Vasiṣṭha, Parāśara, Ṛṣiputra and Kaśyapa).

[The commentator spells the word Kaśyapa and not Kāśyapa. It is, therefore, surmised that both these names refer to the same sage.

Cf. सिद्धसेन—

शुक्लपक्षमतिक्रम्य कार्त्तिकस्य विचारयेत् ।
गर्भाणां सम्भवं सम्यक् सस्यसम्पत्तिकारणम् ॥]

मार्गशिरःसितपक्षप्रतिपत्प्रभृति क्षपाकरेऽषाढाम् ।
पूर्वां वा समुपगते गर्भाणां लक्षणं ज्ञेयम् ॥६॥

The symptoms of pregnancy are to be detected when the Moon passes through the asterism Pūrvāṣāḍha beginning from the first day of the bright fortnight of the Mārgaśīrṣa month.

[Cf. गर्ग—

शुक्लादौ मार्गशीर्षस्य पूर्वाषाढाव्यवस्थिते ।
निशाकरे तु गर्भाणां तत्रादौ लक्षणं वदेत् ॥

also कश्यप—

सितादौ मार्गशीर्षस्य प्रतिपद्दिवसे तथा ।
पूर्वाषाढागते चन्द्रे गर्भाणां धारणं भवेत् ॥]

यन्नक्षत्रमुपगते गर्भश्चन्द्रे भवेत्स चन्द्रवशात् ।
पञ्चनवते दिनशते तत्रैव प्रसवमायाति ।।७।।

The foetus formed during the Moon's stay in a particular constellation will be released 195 (solar) days thereafter, when the Moon passes through the same constellation according to the laws of her revolution.

[The commentator discusses whether the days are to be counted according to the civil calendar or the lunar calendar, and comes to the conclusion that it is the former. In support of this he quotes "युगवर्षमासपिण्डं रविमानं साधिमासकं चान्द्रम्···" (पञ्चसिद्धान्तिका I. 16).

Cf. also the समाससंहिता—

पौषासितपक्षाद्यैः श्रावणशुक्लादयो विनिर्द्देश्याः ।
सार्द्धैः षड्भिर्मासैर्गर्भविपाकः स नक्षत्रे ।।]

सितपक्षभवाः कृष्णे शुक्ले कृष्णा द्युसम्भवा रात्रौ ।
नक्तंप्रभवाश्चाहनि सन्ध्याजाताश्च सन्ध्यायाम् ।।८।।

The foetuses formed in the bright fortnight will be released in the dark fortnight and *vice versa*, those formed in the daytime will come out at night and *vice versa*, and those that are formed at dawn in the evening and *vice versa*.

[Cf. गर्ग—

दिवा भवति यो गर्भो रात्रौ स इति पच्यते ।
शुक्लपक्षे समुद्भूतः कृष्णे पक्षे च वर्षति ।।
पौर्णमास्यामथोत्पन्नः सोऽमावास्यां प्रवर्षति ।
अमावास्यां समुद्भूतः पूर्णमास्यां प्रवर्षति ।।
पूर्वसन्ध्यासमुद्भूतः पश्चिमायां प्रवर्षति ।
पश्चिमायां समुद्भूतः पूर्वसन्ध्यां प्रवर्षति ।।
पूर्वाह्णे यः समुद्भूतः पश्चाद्रात्रौ प्रवर्षति ।
निशायां पश्चिमे यश्च स पूर्वाह्णे प्रसूयते ।।
दिनार्द्धे तु समुत्पन्नः स निशार्द्धे प्रसूयते ।।]

मृगशीर्षाद्या गर्भा मन्दफलाः पौषशुक्लजाताश्च ।
पौषस्य कृष्णपक्षेण निर्दिशेच्छ्रावणस्य सितम् ।।९।।

माघसितोत्था गर्भाः श्रावणकृष्णे प्रसूतिमायान्ति ।
माघस्य कृष्णपक्षेण निर्दिशेद्भाद्रपदशुक्लम् ।।१०।।

फाल्गुनशुक्लसमुत्था भाद्रपदस्यासिते विनिर्देश्याः ।
तस्यैव कृष्णपक्षोद्भवास्तु ये तेऽश्वयुक्शुक्ले ॥११॥

चैत्रसितपक्षजाताः कृष्णेऽश्वयुजस्य वारिदा गर्भाः ।
चैत्रासितसम्भूताः कार्तिकशुक्लेऽभिवर्षन्ति ॥१२॥

The foetuses of clouds formed in the bright fortnight of the Mārgaśīrṣa and Pauṣa months are of little consequence. Those formed in the dark half of Pauṣa would be delivered in the bright half of Śrāvaṇa. Similarly, those that are formed in the light half of Māgha would yield rain in the dark half of Śrāvaṇa. For clouds formed in the dark half of Māgha the period of delivery is the light half of Bhādrapada. Likewise, those formed in the light half of Phālguna would have their delivery in the dark half of Bhādrapada. Those formed in the dark half of Phālguna would come out in the bright fortnight of Āsvina. Clouds formed in the light and dark halves of Caitra would be delivered in the dark half of Āśvina and the bright half of Kārtika respectively.

[The commentator observes that as far as this chapter of pregnancy of clouds is concerned the counting of lunar months should start with the light half of Caitra, but the dark half of the same month will be called that of Vaiśākha, as is the practice in northern India.

Cf. गर्ग—

माघेन श्रावणं विन्द्यान्नभस्यं फाल्गुनेन तु ।
चैत्रेणाश्वयुजं प्राहुर्वैशाखेन तु कार्त्तिकम् ॥
शुक्लपक्षेण कृष्णं तु कृष्णपक्षेण चेतरम् ।
रात्र्यह्नोश्च विपर्यासं कार्यं काले विनिश्चयम् ॥
पराशरस्याप्येवं मतम् ॥]

पूर्वोद्भूताः पश्चादपरोत्थाः प्राग्भवन्ति जीमूताः ।
शेषास्वपि दिक्ष्वेवं विपर्ययो भवति वायोश्च ॥१३॥

Clouds formed in the east will pour down rain in the west and *vice versa*. The same rule holds good in the case of the other pairs of quarters. In the same manner, the winds too are reverse at the two periods.

[Clouds formed in the north will pour down in the south and *vice versa*. Treat similarly the pairs of quarters north-east and south-west, north-west and south-east. If the wind blows towards the east at the time of formation of the foetus, then it will blow towards the west at the time of delivery.

Cf. पराशर—

अथ माघेन श्रावणं फाल्गुनेन भाद्रपदं चैत्रेणाश्वयुजं वैशाखेन तु कार्त्तिकं शुक्लेन कृष्णं कृष्णेन शुक्लं दिवसेन रात्रिं रात्र्या दिवसं गर्भाः प्रवर्षन्ति ॥]

ह्लादिमृदूदक्शिवशक्रदिग्भवो मारुतो वियद्विमलम् ।
स्निग्धसितबहुलपरिवेषपरिवृतौ हिममयूखार्कौ ॥१४॥

पृथुबहुलस्निग्धघनं घनसूचीक्षुरकलोहिताभ्रयुतम् ।
काकाण्डमेचकाभं वियद्विशुद्धेन्दुनक्षत्रम् ॥१५॥

सुरचापमन्द्रगर्जितविद्युत्प्रतिसूर्यका शुभा सन्ध्या ।
शशिशिवशक्राशास्थाः शान्तरवाः पक्षिमृगसङ्घाः ॥१६॥

विपुलाः प्रदक्षिणचराः स्निग्धमयूखा ग्रहा निरुपसर्गाः ।
तरवश्च निरुपसृष्टाङ्कुरा नरचतुष्पदा हृष्टाः ॥१७॥

गर्भाणां पुष्टिकराः सर्वेषामेव योऽत्र तु विशेषः ।
स्वर्तुस्वभावजनितो गर्भविवृद्ध्यै तमभिधास्ये ॥१८॥

The following are the good symptoms at the conception of clouds : A delightful and cool breeze from the north, north-east or east; a clear sky; the Sun and the Moon encircled by a glossy, bright and thick halo: the sky covered with large, bulky, smooth, needle-like or razor-like, red clouds or having the colour of the eggs of crows (i.e. bluish) or of the peacock's neck, with the moon and the stars shining brightly; an auspicious twilight—morning or evening—accompanied by rainbow, good rumbling of thunder. lightning and a mock sun; groups of birds and animals crying pleasantly in the north, north-east or east and not facing the Sun; the planets being large, beaming brightly and moving to the north of the asterisms and unhurt; trees with their sprouts unimpaired, and men and quadrupeds happy. These symptoms nourish all the embryos. There are, however, some special characteristics tending to the growth of the foetuses and arising from the peculiar nature of the several seasons which I shall now explain.

[These marks are the general symptoms of a good rainfall. These ought to be observed from the beginning of the bright half of Mārgaśīrṣa to the end of Vaiśākha. In addition to the above there are some special seasonal symptoms which are explained in the following four verses.

Cf, पराशर—

अथ गर्भसंस्थासु माघादिषु चतुर्षु मासेषु या शुचौ धारणा। नभोनभस्यौ प्रावृट् तस्या अनु वर्षा येषु प्रसवन्ति। तत्र चापाभ्रविद्युत्स्तनयित्नुवर्षाणि गर्भास्तांल्लक्षयेत्प्रशस्तानप्रशस्तांश्च। प्रशस्ताभाश्च यस्मिन् काले सूर्येन्दुनक्षत्राश्रयाणां वर्षालिङ्गानां प्रादुर्भावः। पञ्चरूपता गर्भाणां धारणा मासेन शुद्धिः॥]

पौषे समार्गशीर्षे सन्ध्यारागोऽम्बुदाः सपरिवेषाः।
नात्यर्थं मृगशीर्षे शीतं पौषेऽतिहिमपातः॥१९॥

माघे प्रबलो वायुस्तुषारकलुषद्युती रविशशाङ्कौ।
अतिशीतं सघनस्य च भानोरस्तोदयौ धन्यौ॥२०॥

फाल्गुनमासे रूक्षश्चण्डः पवनोऽभ्रसम्प्लवाः स्निग्धाः।
परिवेषाश्चासकलाः कपिलस्ताम्रो रविश्च शुभः॥२१॥

पवनघनवृष्टियुक्ताश्चैत्रे गर्भाः शुभाः सपरिवेषाः।
घनपवनसलिलविद्युत्स्तनितैश्च हिताय वैशाखे॥२२॥

The auspicious symptoms in the months of Mārgasīrṣa and Pauṣa are a red glow of the horizon at dawn and sunset, clouds with halos, not much cold in Mārgaśīrṣa and not too thick frost in Pauṣa; in Māgha, a strong wind, the Sun and the Moon dim by mist, bitter cold, and the Sun rising or setting, accompanied by clouds; in the month of Phālguna, a rough and violent storm, glossy floating banks of clouds, an incomplete halo round the Sun or the Moon, and the Sun russet or red; in the Caitra month the foetuses being formed along with wind, clouds, rain and halos are of good augury; and in Vaiśākha, those that are attended by clouds, wind, rain, lightning and thunder, are beneficial.

[Cf. काश्यप—

शीतमभ्रं तथा वायुश्चन्द्रार्कपरिवेषणम्।
माघे मासि परीक्षेत श्रावणे वृष्टिमादिशेत्॥

फाल्गुने चात्र सङ्घातं वृष्टिस्तनितमेव च।
पुरोवाताश्च ये प्रोक्ता मासि भाद्रपदे शुभम्॥

बहुपुष्पफला वृक्षा वाताः शर्करवर्षिणः।
शीतवर्षं तथाभ्राणि चैत्रेणाश्वयुजं वदेत्॥

वहन्ति मृदवो वाताः पुरः शीघ्र प्रदक्षिणाः।
वैशाखे तानि रूपाणि कार्त्तिके मासि वर्षति॥

Cf. also the समाससंहिता—

शस्तानि मृगान्मासाच्छीतर्हिमवायुमेघकृतानि ।
स्तनिततडिज्जलमारुतघनतापान्यतिशयं तु वैशाखे ।।
कृष्णेन शुक्लपक्षः सितेन कृष्णो निशा दिनोत्थेन ।
रात्र्याह्नः सन्ध्यायां सन्ध्यादिग्व्यत्ययाज्जलदाः ।।]

मुक्तारजतनिकाशास्तमालनीलोत्पलाञ्जनाभासः ।
जलचरसत्त्वाकारा गर्भेषु घनाः प्रभूतजलाः ।।२३।।

तीव्रदिवाकरकिरणाभितापिता मन्दमारुता जलदाः ।
रुषिता इव धाराभिर्विसृजन्त्यम्भः प्रसवकाले ।।२४।।

Clouds that resemble pearls and silver, or Tamāla flower, blue lily and collyrium, in colour, and are shaped like aquatic animals, will possess abundant water in their embryo. Those clouds which are scorched by the fierce rays of the Sun and fanned by a gentle breeze will pour down, at the time of delivery, torrential rains, as if they were angry.

[The words रुषिताः and धाराभिः give rise to what is called शब्दशक्तिमूलध्वनि or suggestion based on the power of word : They suggest enraged warriors cutting the throats of their enemies with their swords.

Cf. the समाससंहिता—

पृथुघनबहुला जलचरसत्त्वान्विताः शुभा गर्भाः ।
स्निग्धसितबहुलपरिवेषपरिवृतौ हिमकरोष्णकरौ ।।
नृखगमृगा मुदिता निरुपहतास्तरवः ।
वियदमलं च यदा भवति तदा सुसमा ।।
स्निग्धतडित्प्रतिसूर्यकमत्स्यशक्रधनुःप्रथमापरमध्ये ।
शान्तरवा मृगपक्षिमनुष्याः शक्रशशीश्वरदिक्पवनश्च ।।]

गर्भोपघातलिङ्गान्युल्काशनिपांसुपातदिग्दाहाः ।
क्षितिकम्पखपुरकीलककेतुग्रहयुद्धनिर्घाताः ।।२५।।

रुधिरादिवृष्टिवैकृतपरिघेन्द्रधनूंषि दर्शनं राहोः ।
इत्युत्पातैरेतैस्त्रिविधैश्चान्यैर्हतो गर्भः ।।२६।।

The following are the symptoms of miscarriage of the foetus: Fall of meteors, thunderbolt (or lightning), dust-storm, false fire in the quarters, earthquake, appearance of city-like formations in the sky, Tāmasakīlakas, Ketu, planetary fight, portentous thunder, unnatural phenomenon in the rain, such as the appearance of blood, a cross-bar of clouds at sunset or sunrise (vide XLVII. 19 *infra*), rainbow and an eclipse (lunar or solar). By these and similar portents of three kinds viz. celestial, atmospheric and terrestrial, a foetus gets destroyed.

[Cf. गर्ग—

अश्मवर्षं तमोवर्षं मांसशोणितवर्षणम् ।
उल्कानिर्घातकम्पश्च वज्रपातस्तथैव च ॥
परिवेषाः परिघयो वासवस्य धनूंषि च ।
अनभ्रस्तनितं वर्षं दिशां दाहस्तथैव च ॥
अनार्तवं पुष्पफलं वारणीयेषु वर्षणम् ।
ग्रहयुद्धेषु घोरेषु हतान् गर्भान् विनिर्दिशेत् ॥

also पराशर—

तेषां ग्रहाणामुदयास्तमयोल्कानिर्घाताशनिपातगन्धर्वनगरदिग्दाहार्करश्मिवर्णविकारभूचलनप्रादुर्भावो वर्षास्ववर्षाय ॥]

स्वर्त्तुस्वभावजनितैः सामान्यैर्यश्च लक्षणैर्वृद्धिः ।
गर्भाणां विपरीतैस्तैरेव विपर्ययो भवति ॥२७॥

Signs, exactly the reverse of those, both general and special for any particular season, by which the growth of a foetus is assured, produce contrary results.

भद्रपदाद्वयविश्वाम्बुदेवपैतामहेष्वथर्क्षेषु ।
सर्वेष्वृतुषु विवृद्धो गर्भो बहुतोयदो भवति ॥२८॥

A foetus that is formed when the Moon is situated in any of the five lunar mansions, viz. Pūrvāṣāḍhā, Uttarāsāḍhā, Pūrvabhadrapadā, Uttarabhadrapadā and Rohiṇī, in any season will yield copious rains.

शतभिषगाश्लेषार्द्रास्वातिमघासंयुतः शुभो गर्भः ।
पुष्णाति बहून् दिवसान् हन्त्युत्पातैर्हतस्त्रिविधैः ॥२९॥

An embryo that is formed when the Moon occupies Śatabhiṣaj, Āśleṣā, Ārdrā, Svāti or Maghā proves beneficial and develops (or rains) for many days, while being stricken with three-fold portents (terrestrial, atmospheric and heavenly), it is destroyed.

[The समाससंहिता explains the three-fold portents thus :

दिव्यं ग्रहक्षजातं भुवि भौमं स्थिरचरोद्भवं यच्च ।
दिग्दाहोल्कामारुतपरिवेषाद्यं वियत्प्रभवम् ॥

Cf. also गर्ग—

प्राजापत्यं मघाश्लेषा रौद्रं चानिलवारुणम् ।
आषाढाद्वितयं चैव तथा भद्रपदाद्वयम् ॥
नक्षत्रदशकं चैतद्यदि स्याद्ग्रहदूषितम् ।
न गर्भाः सम्पदं यान्ति योगक्षेमं न कल्पते ॥
उल्कयाभिहतं वापि केतुना वाप्यधिष्ठितम् ॥
न गर्भाः सम्पदं यान्ति वासवश्च न वर्षति ॥]

मृगमासादिष्वष्टौ षट् षोडश विंशतिश्चतुर्युक्ता ।
विंशतिरथ दिवसत्रयमेकतमर्क्षेण पञ्चभ्यः ॥३०॥

Foetuses that are formed when the Moon is in conjunction with any of the aforesaid asterisms during the months of Mārgaśīrṣa, Pauṣa, Māgha, Phālguna, Caitra and Vaiśākha, will yield rain for 8, 6, 16, 24, 20 and 3 days respectively after 195 days.

[Cf. ऋषिपुत्र—

माघे षोडशसंख्यास्तु षोडशाष्टौ च फाल्गुने ।
विंशतिश्चैत्रमासे तु त्रयश्चेन्द्राग्निदैवते ॥
अष्टौ सौम्येऽथ षट् पौषे संख्यास्तासु च वर्षति ॥]

पञ्चनिमित्तैः शतयोजनं तदर्द्धार्द्धमेकहान्यातः ।
वर्षति पञ्चनिमित्ताद्रूपेणैकेन यो गर्भः ॥३१॥

If an embryo is formed to the accompaniment of the five phenomena or symptoms, viz. wind, water, lightning, thunder and cloud, it will pour rain over an area of 100 Yojanas and for every symptom less, over half the extent of the previous one; but if it is accompanied by only one symptom, the rainfall will be over five Yojanas around.

द्रोणः पञ्चनिमित्ते गर्भे त्रीण्याढकानि पवनेन ।
षड् विद्युता नवाभ्रैः स्तनितेन द्वादश प्रसवे ॥३२॥

If the formation of foetus is accompanied by the five symptoms the quantity of rainfall will at the season amount to a Droṇa; if by wind, three Āḍhakas; if by lightning, six Āḍhakas; if by clouds, nine Āḍhakas; and if by thunder, twelve Āḍhakas.

[A Droṇa=200 Palas. An Āḍhaka=1/4 Droṇa or 11 oz. Avoir. Parāśara says that an Āḍhaka is the capacity of a circular vessel whose diameter is 20 Aṅgulas and depth 8 Aṅgulas.

Cf. पराशर—

आढकांश्चतुरो द्रोणमपां विन्द्यात्प्रमाणतः ।
धनुष्प्रमाणं मेदिन्या विन्द्याद् द्रोणातिवर्षणम् ॥
समे विंशाङ्गुलानाहे द्विचतुष्काङ्गुलोच्छ्रिते ।
भाण्डे वर्षति सम्पूर्णे ज्ञेयमाढकवर्षणम् ॥

See also XXIII-2 *infra*.

Cf. वृद्धगर्ग—

वाते तु आढकं विन्द्यात् स्तनिते द्वादशाढकम् ।
नवाढकं तथाभ्रेषु द्योतितेषु षडाढकम् ॥
निमित्तपञ्चकोपेते द्रोणं वर्षति वासवः ॥]

क्रूरग्रहसंयुक्ते करकाशनिमत्स्यवर्षदा गर्भाः ।
शशिनि रवौ वा शुभसंयुतेक्षिते भूरिवृष्टिकराः ॥३३॥

If the star at which a cloud-foetus is formed be afflicted by malefic planets, there would be a rain of hail stones, thunderbolt and fish, in the season. If, at that time, the Sun or the Moon be posited in this star and be conjoined with or aspected by benefics, there would be copious rain.

गर्भसमयेऽतिवृष्टिर्गर्भाभावाय निर्निमित्तकृता ।
द्रोणाष्टांशेऽभ्यधिके वृष्टे गर्भः स्रुतो भवति ॥३४॥

If there be excessive rain at the time of the formation of foetuses without any apparent cause, there would result destruction of the foetuses. Should the amount of rainfall exceed 1/8 of a Droṇa, there would be miscarriage of the foetus.

[The causes of rain are listed in the following verse occurring in XXVIII. 20 *infra*.

प्रायो ग्रहाणामुदयास्तकाले समागमे मण्डलसङ्क्रमे च ।
पक्षक्षये तीक्ष्णकरायनान्ते वृष्टिर्गतेऽर्के नियमेन चार्द्राम् ॥]

गर्भः पुष्टः प्रसवे ग्रहोपघातादिभिर्यदि न वृष्टः ।
आत्मीयगर्भसमये करकामिश्रं ददात्यम्भः ॥३५॥

If a full-grown embryo does not yield rain at the time of delivery owing to planetary and other evil influences, it will rain mixed with hail-stones at the time of the next formation of pregnancy.

[Our author has explained in VI-10, 11 *supra* how Mars afflicts the clouds and destroys rain. What is the exact meaning of आत्मीयगर्भसमये ? The commentator clarifies it with the words "पुन: पुरस्ताद् द्वितीयगर्भग्रहणकाले ' i.e. when there are symptoms of conception after this affliction. In other words, there will be a rain mixed with hailstones at the next conception. This would mean that there will be both a delivery and a formation of foetus almost at the same time.]

काठिन्यं याति यथा चिरकालधृतं पयः पयस्विन्याः ।
कालातीतं तद्वत्सलिलं काठिन्यमुपयाति ॥३६॥

Just as the milk of a milch cow grows thick and hard if kept too long, even so does the water kept beyond its time.

[*Scientific explanation of rain, hail* etc. :—

Water is evaporated or turned into water vapour and mixed with the atmosphere, at the surface of any sheet of water, and even over the land, where a considerable amount of water is evaporated by day from the surface of vegetation...condensation is the opposite of evaporation. In the atmosphere the condensation of water into drops takes place, not by the molecules of water-vapour collecting together, but by the collection of the molecules of water-vapour on a particle of dust of a particular type. These dust particles are named *nuclei of condensation*, which act as foundations for the water-drops in clouds or rain. Before the water-vapour in the atmosphere can condense on the nuclei, the air must be saturated or nearly saturated.

Cloud floats, while rain falls. Cloud-drops fall too. Rain-drops also vary in size; the drops in light drizzle have a diameter of about eight thousandths of an inch, and fall at a rate of about $2\frac{1}{4}$ feet per second; the drops in heavy rain average about 1/16 inch in diameter and fall about 17 feet in a second.

Rain is formed by the ascent of damp air. Its temperature falls at first at the rate of about $5\frac{1}{2}$°F. for every 1000 feet of ascent. When the amount of water-vapour present is just sufficient to saturate it, condensation takes place in the form of rain or snow.... If a warm current of air clashes against the flank of a cold current, rain associated with the depressions is formed. This depression is to be regarded as a battle-field where warm and cold currents of air clash.

When the condensation of water-vapour from a current of ascending damp air takes place at temperatures above freezing point, the precipitation is in the form of rain.

When water-drops are formed in a rising current of air, and are carried up beyond the level at which they are formed, they do not freeze immediately, but remain at first in the form of liquid water. They probably begin to freeze when their temperature falls below about—10°C, or 14°F. The raindrop then freezes into a soft-core of white ice. Drops of water at a temperature below freezing point freeze on to the falling core. In freezing they trap some air within the ice, so that the coating will be white ice. As a result of its journey the hailstone will have an inner core of soft ice, then a coating of white ice, and outside this a coating of clear ice.... Large hailstones can form only when there are violent ascending currents in the atmosphere. Further, the clouds must extend to a great height at which the temprature is —20°C.

(Cf. "Weather Science for Everybody" by David Brunt, pp 58-67.)

Though modern science is able to explain the formation of clouds, rain, hailstones and to distinguish the types of clouds, it is unable to say for how many days the water-vapour would remain in the atmosphere in the form of cloud before condensing and falling as rain. According to science, which re-echoes Yāska's remark of warfare in respect of radiation and cloud, there are many mysteries in the atmosphere such as the crystal of snow. Like the sages scientists distinguish mainly four types of clouds viz. *Cirrus*, *Stratus*, *Cumulus* and *Nimbus*. The behaviour of the elements is beyond human ken. Nobody can say whether the water-vapour of today will fall down tomorrow as rain. So it is better for scholars to understand and test the principles enunciated by the sages for predicting weather, rain and crops.]

पवनसलिलविद्युद्गर्जिताऽभ्रान्वितो यः
स भवति बहुतोयः पञ्चरूपाभ्युपेतः ।
विसृजति यदि तोयं गर्भकालेऽतिभूरि
प्रसवसमयमित्वा शीकराम्भः करोति ॥३७॥

An embryo which is accompanied by the five concomitant signs, viz. wind, rain, lightning, thunder and clouds, will yield copious rains at the appropriate time. On the other hand, if an embryo pours down excessive rain even at its conception, it will produce only a drizzle at the time of delivery.

[This verse occurring in the समाससंहिता has been incorporated into the text by Bhaṭṭotpala for the reason that Varāhamihira generally closes a chapter with a verse in a longer metre, the metre here being मालिनी].

गर्भधारणाध्यायः ॥२२॥

Chapter XXII—Retention of Embryo

ज्यैष्ठसितेऽष्टम्याद्याश्चत्वारो वायुधारणा दिवसाः ।
मृदुशुभपवनाः शस्ताः स्निग्धघनस्थगितगगनाश्च ॥१॥

The four days commencing from the 8th lunar day of the light half of Jyeṣṭha month are sustained by the winds, and will prove beneficial, if they be attended with soft and auspicious breeze, and if the sky be covered with glossy clouds.

[The idea is that the four days mentioned here are helpful in retaining the embryo by means of the winds. Hence the days are called *Vāyudhāraṇas*. The word शभ is construed by the commentator as 'the wind blowing from the north, north-east and east'.]

तत्रैव स्वात्याद्ये वृष्टे भचतुष्टये क्रमान्मासाः ।
श्रावणपूर्वा ज्ञेयाः परिस्रुता धारणास्ताः स्युः ॥२॥

If in the same month and fortnight there be rain in the four lunar mansions beginning with Svāti, the four months commencing from the Śrāvaṇa would in order be retainers of rain, i.e. there would be no rain in the several months corresponding to the stars in which there is rain.

[If there is rain in the star Svāti, there will be no rain in the month of Śrāvaṇa; if there is rain in the star Viśākhā, no rain in Bhādrapada; if there is rain in Anūrādhā, no rain in Āśvina; and if in Jyeṣṭhā, no rain in Kārtika.

Cf. काश्यप—

ज्येष्ठस्य शुक्लाष्टम्यां तु नक्षत्रे भगदैवते ।
चत्वारो धारणाः प्रोक्ता मृदुवातसमीरिताः ॥
नीलाञ्जननिभैर्मेघैर्विद्युत्स्थगितमारुतैः ।
विस्फुलिङ्गरजोधूम्रैश्छन्नौ शशिदिवाकरौ ॥
एकरूपाः शुभा ज्ञेया अशुभाः सान्तराः स्मृताः ।
अनार्यैस्तस्करैर्घोरैः पीडा चैव सरीसृपैः ॥

ततः स्वात्यादिनक्षत्रैश्चतुर्भिः श्रावणादयः ।
परिपूर्णाः शुभास्ताः स्युः सौम्याः शिवसुभिक्षकाः ॥
स्वातौ तु श्रावणं हन्याद्वृष्टेऽथेन्द्राग्निदैवते ।
भाद्रपदे त्ववृष्टिः स्यान्मैत्रे चाश्वयुजे स्मृता ॥
ऐन्द्रे तु कार्त्तिके त्वेवं वृष्टे वृष्टिं निहन्ति च ।
एतेषु यदि नो वृष्टिस्तदा सौभिक्षलक्षणम् ॥]

यदि ताः स्युरेकरूपाः शुभास्ततः सान्तरास्तु न शिवाय ।
तस्करभयदाश्चोक्ताः श्लोकाश्चाप्यत्र वासिष्ठाः ॥३॥

If those four days of retention be of the same condition, the effect would be happy. If they be dissimilar, they would prove disastrous and cause danger from robbers. The following verses of Sage Vasiṣṭha prove this statement.

सविद्युतः सपृषतः सपांसूत्करमारुताः ।
सार्कचन्द्रपरिच्छन्ना धारणाः शुभधारणाः ॥४॥
यदा तु विद्युतः श्रेष्ठाः शुभाशाः प्रत्युपस्थिताः ।
तदापि सर्वसस्यानां वृद्धिं ब्रूयाद्विचक्षणः ॥५॥
सपांसुवर्षाः सापश्च शुभा बालक्रिया अपि ।
पक्षिणां सुस्वरा वाचः क्रीडा पांसुजलादिषु ॥६॥
रविचन्द्रपरीवेषाः स्निग्धा नात्यन्तदूषिताः ।
वृष्टिस्तदापि विज्ञेया सर्वसस्यार्थसाधिका ॥७॥
मेघाः स्निग्धाः संहताश्च प्रदक्षिणगतिक्रियाः ।
तदा स्यान्महती वृष्टिः सर्वसस्याभिवृद्धये ॥८॥

The days of retention of the embryo will be efficacious, if they are accompanied by lightning, water-drops, dust-storm, and the luminaries hidden by clouds. If there be beautiful flashes of lightning emanating from the auspicious quarters (east, north and north-east), a wise astrologer should predict very good growth of all crops. If there be rain with dust-storm, or if children be engaged in happy sports, the cries of birds be pleasant and their sport be in dust, water and the like, if the luminaries be surrounded by halos that are glossy and not broken, then too there would be good rain helping the growth of all crops. If the clouds be glossy, collected together and moving in a clockwise manner, there would be heavy rains tending to the growth of all crops.

[These five verses are quoted by our author from the work of Sage Vasiṣṭha. Most of the ancient sages wrote in the *Śloka* metre.]

प्रवर्षणाध्यायः ॥२३॥

Chapter XXIII—Rainfall

ज्येष्ठ्यां समतीतायां पूर्वाषाढादिसम्प्रवृष्टेन ।
शुभमशुभं वा वाच्यं परिमाणं चाम्भसस्तज्ज्ञैः ॥१॥

Should there be rain in the lunar mansions beginning with Pūrvāṣāḍhā after the full Moon in the month of Jyeṣṭha, astrologers should judge the quantity of rainfall as well as the good and bad effects thereof.

[The amount of rain observed on these days would enable the rain-forecasters to predict the exact quantity of rainfall for the entire season. शुभ and अशुभ have been interpreted by the commentator as 'good effects for rain' and 'bad effects for absence of rain'.

Cf. गर्ग—

ज्येष्ठे मूलमतिक्रम्य मासि प्रतिपदग्रतः ।
वर्षासु वृष्टिज्ञानार्थं निमित्तान्युपलक्षयेत् ॥]

हस्तविशालं कुण्डकमधिकृत्याम्बुप्रमाणनिर्देशः ।
पञ्चाशत्पलमाढकमनेन मिनुयाज्जलं पतितम् ॥२॥

The quantity of rainfall should be determined with the help of a gauge whose diameter is one cubit. When this vessel contains 50 Palas, it will measure one Āḍhaka.

[According to Parāśara quoted under XXI.32 an Āḍhaka= 17600/7 cubic Aṅgulas. We have already seen that an Āḍhaka is 1/4 Droṇa.

Cf. the समाससंहिता—

ज्येष्ठस्य पौर्णमासीमतीत्य भूमुद्रया यथा वृष्टे।
आप्याद्यैर्जलमानं मागधमानेन हस्तमिते ॥

This statement of our author proves the great advance made by Magadha in trade and culture. Hence the weights and measures used in Magadha must have become famous throughout India.]

येन धरित्री मुद्रा जनिता वा बिन्दवस्तृणाग्रेषु ।
वृष्टेन तेन वाच्यं परिमाणं वारिणः प्रथमम् ॥३॥

The quantity of rainfall should be gauged on the day ruled by any of the rain-producing asterisms (headed by Pūrvāṣāḍhā), when there is rain for the first time, through the amount of rain by which the earth is cleared of dust or drops of water are made to appear on the tips of blades of grass.

[The prospect of rainfall in the season is to be determined through the rain water that falls for the first time in any asterism. In other words, it is the star of the initial rain which is the pivot for the prospect of rainfall throughout the season or in the coming months as explained in chapter XXI.]

केचिद्यथाभिवृष्टं दशयोजनमण्डलं वदन्त्यन्ये ।
गर्गवसिष्ठपराशरमतमेतद् द्वादशान्न परम् ॥४॥

Some sages like Kaśyapa are of opinion that if there be rain in a certain area at the beginning, there will be good rain in the same place throughout the season; while others like Devala maintain that if there be rain over an area of ten Yojanas, there would be good rain during the whole season. But, according to sages Garga, Vasiṣṭha and Parāśara good rain should be predicted only if the rainfall be over an area that is not less than twelve Yojanas.

[Cf. काश्यप—

प्रवर्षणे यथा देशं वर्षणं यदि दृश्यते ।
वर्षाकालं समासाद्य वासवो बहु वर्षति ॥

also देवल—

प्रवर्षणे यदा वृष्टं दशयोजनमण्डलम् ।
वर्षाकालं समासाद्य वासवो बहु वर्षति ॥

and गर्ग—

आषाढादिषु वृष्टेषु योजनद्वादशात्मके ।
प्रवृष्टे शोभनं वर्षं वर्षाकाले विनिर्दिशेत् ॥]

येषु च भेष्वभिवृष्टं भूयस्तेष्वेव वर्षति प्रायः ।
यदि नाप्यादिषु वृष्टं सर्वेषु तदा त्वनावृष्टिः ॥५॥

In whichever stars there is rain at the beginning, there will generally be rain once again under the same stars in the season. If there be no rain at all in any of the asterisms beginning with Pūrvāṣāḍhā at the time of delivery, then there would be no rain in the season.

हस्ताप्यसौम्यचित्रापौष्णधनिष्ठासु षोडश द्रोणाः ।
शतभिषगैन्द्रस्वातिषु चत्वारः कृत्तिकासु दश ॥६॥
श्रवणे मघानुराधाभरणीमूलेषु दश चतुर्युक्ताः ।
फल्गुन्यां पञ्चकृतिः पुनर्वसौ विंशतिर्द्रोणाः ॥७॥
ऐन्द्राग्न्याख्ये वैश्वे च विंशतिः सार्पभे दश त्र्यधिकाः ।
आहिर्बुध्न्यार्यम्णप्राजापत्येषु पञ्चकृतिः ॥८॥
पञ्चदशाजे पुष्ये च कीर्तिता वाजिभे दश द्वौ च ।
रौद्रेऽष्टादश कथिता द्रोणा निरुपद्रवेष्वेते ॥९॥

Should there be rain in any one of the asterisms, viz. Hasta, Pūrvāṣāḍhā, Mṛgaśiras, Citrā, Revatī and Dhaniṣṭhā, the quantity of rainfall in the season would be 16 Droṇas; in Śatabhiṣaj, Jyeṣṭhā and Svāti, it would be 4 Droṇas; in Kṛttikā, 10 Droṇas; in Śravaṇa, Maghā, Anurādhā, Bharaṇī and Mūla, 14 Droṇas; in Pūrvaphalgunī, 25 Droṇas; in Punarvasu, 20 Droṇas; in Viśākhā and Uttarāṣāḍhā, 20 Droṇas; in Āśleṣā, 13 Droṇas; in Uttarābhādrā, Uttaraphalgunī and Rohiṇī, 25 Droṇas; in Pūrvābhādrā and Puṣya, 15 Droṇas; in Aśvinī, 12 Droṇas; and Ārdrā, 18 Droṇas. These quantities should be predicted, provided the concerned lunar mansions are not hurt in any way.

[In this section the author gives the amount of rainfall to be predicted for the season on the basis of rain in the several asterisms at the beginning. It is to be borne in mind that the stars should not be under any affliction.

Cf. the समाससंहिता—

दशयुक्ता द्विकृतखतिथिरसाष्टदिग्विषयरामजलतिथिभिः ।
तिथिरसरसैश्च विरसाः सदशकृताः षड्विहीनाश्च ॥
जलषट्कदशकसहिता जलरसयुक्ताः षड्नाश्च ।
विषयतिथिषट्कसहिताश्चाश्विन्यादिषु जलद्रोणाः ॥]

रविरविसुतकेतुपीडिते भे क्षितितनयत्रिविधाद्भुताहते च ।
भवति च न शिवं न चापि वृष्टिः शुभसहिते निरुपद्रवे शिवं च ॥१०॥

Should a lunar mansion be afflicted by the Sun, Saturn or Ketu, (i.e. by presence in it), or be hurt by Mars (by retrograde motion, cleaving through or by cutting the Yogatārā) or by the three-fold portents, there would be no prosperity to mankind, nor would there be any rain in the season. On the other hand, if the asterism be unhurt and conjoined with benefics, beneficial effects would follow.

[Cf. गर्ग—

सूर्यसौराहते वाच्यं नक्षत्रे भौमघातिते ।
उत्पातैस्त्रिविधैर्वापि राहुणा केतुनापि वा ॥
अवृष्टिमशुभं विन्द्याद्विपरीते शुभं वदेत् ॥

The metre is पुष्पिताग्रा as it is the last verse in the chapter.

Kauṭilya's Arthaśāstra, II-24 (p. 68 Jolly's edition) deals with the amount of rainfall in different countries as well as with the planetary causes therefor :

"षोडशद्रोणं जाङ्गलानां वर्षप्रमाणमध्यर्धमानूपानाम् । देशवापानामर्धत्रयोदशाश्मकानां त्रयोविंशतिरवन्तीनाममितमपरान्तानां हैमन्यानां च कुल्यावापानां च कालतः । तस्योपलब्धिर्बृहस्पतेः स्थानगमनगर्भाधानेभ्यः शुक्रोदयास्तमयचारेभ्यः सूर्यस्य प्रकृतिवैकृताच्च । सूर्याद् बीजसिद्धिः । बृहस्पतेः सस्यानां स्तम्बकरिता । शुक्राद् वृष्टिरिति ।

त्रयः सप्ताहिका मेघा अशीतिः कणशीकराः ।
षष्टिरातपमेघानामेषा वृष्टिः समाहिता ॥
वातमातपयोगं च विभजन्यत्र वर्षति ।
त्रीन् करीषांश्च जनयंस्तत्र सस्यागमो ध्रुवः ॥"

Further on this section treats of seed-treatment as well.]

———

रोहिणीयोगाध्यायः ॥२४॥

Chapter XXIV—The Moon's Conjunction with Rohiṇī

कनकशिलाचयविवरजतरुकुसुमासङ्गिमधुकरानुरुते ।
बहुविहगकलहसुरयुवतिगीतमन्द्रस्वनोपवने ॥१॥
सुरनिलयशिखरिशिखरे बृहस्पतिर्नारदाय यानाह ।
गर्गपराशरकाश्यपमयाश्च यान् शिष्यसङ्घेभ्यः ॥२॥
तानवलोक्य यथावत् प्राजापत्येन्दुसम्प्रयोगार्थान् ।
स्वल्पग्रन्थेनाहं तानेवाभ्युद्यतो वक्तुम् ॥३॥

I shall now explain briefly the good and bad effects of the Moon's conjunction with the star Rohiṇī, having studied them as expounded by Garga, Parāśara, Kāśyapa and Maya to their numerous pupils, and as instructed originally by Bṛhaspati to Sage Nārada in the celestial garden on the summit of the Meru, which resounded with the humming of the bees clinging to the flowers on the trees growing in the caves of the golden rocks that resound with the twitterings of numerous birds as well as the melodious strains of music of heavenly damsels.

[The *Rohiṇī-yoga* should not be mistaken for the Moon's monthly conjunction with the star Rohiṇī. This takes place only once in the year i.e. when she is in contact with this star in the dark fortnight of the lunar month of Āṣāḍha.

Shri Chidambara Iyer remarks in this connection : "These prefatory remarks clearly shew that what follow are important scientific truths in the eyes of Hindu astronomers : that the weather indications of one single day in a year should form the subject of so much calculation with the Hindus in determining the future agricultural prospect of the land, while to the inexperienced eye of a western man of science, the day appears as indifferent or otherwise as any other day of the year argues that modern science is still far behind in her investigations of the laws of nature."]

प्राजेशमाषाढतमिस्रपक्षे क्षपाकरेणोपगतं समीक्ष्य ।
वक्तव्यमिष्टं जगतोऽशुभं वा शास्त्रोपदेशाद् ग्रहचिन्तकेन ॥४॥

योगो यथानागत एव वाच्यः स धिष्ण्ययोगः करणे मयोक्तः ।
चन्द्रप्रमाणद्युतिवर्णमार्गैरुत्पातवातैश्च फलं निगद्यम् ॥५॥

An astronomer should carefully observe the Moon's conjunction with the asterism presided over by the creator (i.e. Rohiṇī) in the dark fortnight of Āṣāḍha and then predict good or bad effects to mankind according to the injunctions of the Śāstras (scientific works). The method of finding out by calculation future conjunction of the Moon with the asterism Rohiṇī has been explained by me in my astronomical treatise *Pañcasiddhāntikā* under the head of "Conjunction with Fixed Stars". The effects, however, should be declared as deduced from the Moon's size, brightness, colour, direction and from portents and winds occurring at the time.

[Cf. the पञ्चसिद्धान्तिका, XIV. 33 :—

बुद्ध्वा शशिविक्षेपं कृत्वा ताराशशाङ्कविवरं च ।
संसाध्य च वक्तव्यः पश्चात्ताराससमायोगः ॥

This is yet another reference to the प. सि. which clearly proves that Varāhamihira had already written that work. However, he refers to the Bṛhat Saṁhitā in the प. सि. XV. 10 in respect of Rāhu.

These verses and many of the succeeding ones are in the इन्द्रवज्रा or उपजाति metre.]

पुराबुदग्यत् पुरतोऽपि वा स्थलं त्र्यहोषितस्तत्र हुताशतत्परः ।
ग्रहान् सनक्षत्रगणान् समालिखेत् सधूपपुष्पैर्बलिभिश्च पूजयेत् ॥६॥

सरत्नतोयौषधिभिश्चतुर्दिशं तरुप्रवालापिहितैः सुपूजितैः ।
अकालमूलैः कलशैरलङ्कृतं कुशास्तृतं स्थण्डिलमावसेद् द्विजः ॥७॥

A Brāhmaṇa should go to a place north or east from the town, stay there for three days fasting and worshipping the Sacred Fire, draw a diagram of the planets and stars, and worship them with oblations coupled with incense and flowers. He should also occupy the bare ground strewn with the sacred grass, adorned at the four corners with waterpots, not blackened at the bottom, containing gems, water and herbs, covered above with the sprouts of trees, and kept clean and smeared with sandal paste.

[Cf. गर्ग—

नगरादुपनिष्क्रम्य दिशं प्रागुत्तरां शुचिः ।
विविक्ते प्रस्थले देशे देवतायतनेऽपि वा ।।
राज्ञा नियुक्तो दैवज्ञः कृतशौचो जितेन्द्रियः ।
निमित्तकुशलो धीरः शुक्लाम्बरसमावृतः ।।
उपवासमथातिष्ठेदष्टमीं संयतव्रतः ।
ततोऽष्टम्याः परे यस्मिन् दिने संयुज्यते शशी ।।
प्राजापत्येन च ततो निमित्तान्युपलक्षयेत् ।।

The metre of these verses is वंशस्थ.]

आलभ्य मन्त्रेण महाव्रतेन बीजानि सर्वाणि निधाय कुम्भे ।
प्लाव्यानि चामीकरदर्भतोयैर्होमो मरुद्वारुणसोममन्त्रैः ।।८।।

He should then sanctify all sorts of seeds with the hymns of Mahāvrata and immerse them in the water containing gold and sacred grass in the pot. Then he should perform a Homa (fire-worship) with the hymns invoking the Maruts, Varuṇa and the Moon.

[The commentator refers to a variant reading to मरुत् as चरुः, which is evidently wrong.]

श्लक्ष्णां पताकामसितां विदध्याद्दण्डप्रमाणां त्रिगुणोच्छ्रितां च ।
आदौ कृते दिग्ग्रहणे नभस्वान् ग्राह्यस्तया योगगते शशाङ्के ।।९।।

He should hoist a flag of very fine yarn and black colour, four cubits in length, on a staff 12 cubits high. After understanding thoroughly the different directions, he should ascertain the direction of the wind through the movement of the streamer, at the Moon's conjunction with Rohiṇī.

[1 Daṇḍa = 1 Dhanus = 4 Cubits.

चतुर्हस्तो धनुःस्मृतः ।
धनुर्दण्डो युगं नाली तुल्यान्येतान्यथाङ्गुलैः ।।

The method of finding out the quarters is explained in the प. सि. IV. 19 :—

शङ्कुचतुर्विस्तारे वृत्ते छायाप्रवेशनिर्गमनात् ।
अपरैन्द्रीदिक्सिद्धिर्यवाच्च याम्योत्तरे साध्ये ।।

The use of a flag for ascertaining the direction of the wind is a matter to be specially taken note of, because even at modern meteorological stations some kind of mechanical vane is employed.

We may also remember what Kālidāsa says about the wind and a fine flag in the Śākuntala :

"चीनांशुकमिव केतोः प्रतिवातं नीयमानस्य ।"

The commentator has explained the प. सि. verse for fixing the directions thus : On a piece of ground which is made level through water-level draw a circle with a string whose length is 24 Aṅgulas. Then the diameter will be 48 Aṅgulas or 4 times the height of the gnomon. Fix the gnomon at the centre of the circle. Make a mark on the part of the circumference where the shadow of the gnomon falls when the Sun is in the eastern horizon. That will give you the western quarter. Similarly make a mark in the afternoon. That will give the eastern point. Now join these two points. Now with the two points on the circumference as the centre with the same radius draw two circles on either side. The two points of intersection represent the north and south. By joining the two points you get the north-south line. This is how दिक् साधन is done. Now with the aid of a flag you can easily find out the direction of wind.

तत्रार्द्धमासाः प्रहरैर्विकल्प्या वर्षानिमित्तं दिवसास्तदंशैः ।
सव्येन गच्छञ्छुभदः सदैव यस्मिन् प्रतिष्ठा बलवान्स वायुः ॥१०॥

For purposes of determining the times of rainfall, each watch of the day (3 hour-period) should be considered as a fortnight, and its subdivisions as days. If the wind blows round from the east to the south and so on i.e. in a clockwise manner, it augurs always prosperity to the world i.e. good rains and bumper crops. When two contrary winds blow, that which is stronger alone should be considered as more powerful, and it is from this wind that prediction should be made.

[In a day and night there are eight watches or Praharas. Generally rains occur in the four months beginning with the lunar month of Śrāvaṇa. Now these four months have eight fortnights. Hence it is possible to equate the eight watches with the eight fortnights. One should observe the behaviour of the wind throughout the day when the Moon is tenanting the star Rohiṇī. Suppose the wind blows sinistrally in the fourth watch of the day i.e. from 3 p.m. to 6 p.m. roughly, the rainfall in the 4th fortnight i.e. the dark half of Bhādrapada, will be unfavourable. To get at the prospects of rain on any particular day, take 1 hour as equivalent of 5 days and a period of 12 minutes as equal to 1 day.

Here the commentator refers to another reading तेनात्र मासा: ्रार्द्धमासा: which would mean that the four watches of the day of the night) alone are to be considered for prognostication. ıis case one watch is equal to one month. It is understandable watching the movement of the flag at night is extremely diffi- Bhaṭṭotpala says that the latter reading is preferable in the of Varāha's assertion that he is following in the footsteps of ;a, Parāśara and others whose opinion agrees with this reading.

Cf. गर्ग—

तदहश्चोदयादूर्ध्वं चतुर्धाहो विभज्य च ।
हिताहितार्थं मासानां चतुर्णामुपलक्षयेत् ॥

same Sage follows this rule of one watch=one month in the :akra :

दिनार्द्धमथवा वायुर्द्वौ मासौ तत्र वर्षति ।
चतुर्भागेन मासं तु शक्रोऽत्यर्थं प्रवर्षति ॥
पूर्वे चैवार्द्धदिवसे पूर्वौ मासौ तु वर्षति ।
अह्नस्तु पश्चिमे भागे पश्चिमौ द्वौ तु वर्षति ॥
अथ पूर्वं व्यतिक्रम्य भागं तत्पश्चिमं ततः ।
मध्याह्ने वाति चेद्वायुर्मध्यौ मासौ तु वर्षति ॥
भाद्रपदोऽश्वयुक् चैव मासावेतौ तु मध्यमौ ।
एतयोरपि निर्देश्या वर्षारात्रस्य सम्पदः ॥

Cf. also ऋषिपुत्र—

दिनार्द्धं वाति चेद्वायुः पूर्वं पश्चिममेव वा ।
मासाद्वयं तदा वर्षो विभागः पूर्वपश्चिमे ॥
समग्रं दिवस वायुर्यदि वाति सुलक्षणः ।
मासास्तु श्रावणाद्या ये तेषां सम्पद्धिर्निर्दिशेत् ॥
वायन्त मारुत चापि यो वायुः प्रतिवायति ।
तत्र यो बलवान् वायुस्तस्यैव फलमादिशेत् ॥

word प्रतिष्ठा in the text is interpreted by some as 'the wind ·ing at sunset', but Utpala rejects this meaning.]

वृत्ते तु योगेऽङ्कुरितानि यानि सन्तीह बीजानि धृतानि कुम्भे ।
येषां तु योंऽशोऽङ्कुरितस्तदंशस्तेषां विवृद्धि समुपैति नान्यः ॥११॥

When the Moon is in conjunction with Rohiṇī, find out which of ;eeds immersed in the water-vessel and what percentage of them, sprouted. Only those grains and none else will flourish during the year, and also to the extent shown by the percentage of sprouting grains.

शान्तपक्षिमृगराविता दिशो निर्मलं वियदनिन्दितोऽनिलः ।
शस्यते शशिनि रोहिणीगते मेघमारुतफलानि वच्म्यतः ॥१२॥

During the Moon's conjunction with Rohiṇī the following auguries are considered beneficial: The quarters resounding with the pleasant cries of birds and beasts, not facing the Sun; the sky being clear and the breeze, not vitiated. I shall now explain the effects of the clouds and the wind.

[Cf. गर्ग—

योगे ह्यनुद्धता वाता ह्लादयन्तः सुखप्रदाः ।
प्रदक्षिणाः श्रेष्ठतमाः पूर्वपूर्वोत्तरा इति ॥

The metre is रथोद्धता.]

क्वचिदसितसितैः सितैः क्वचिच्च क्वचिदसितैर्भुजगैरिवाम्बुवाहैः ।
वलितजठरपृष्ठमात्रदृश्यैः स्फुरिततडिद्रसनैर्वृतं विशालैः ॥१३॥
विकसितकमलोदरावदातैररुणकरद्युतिरञ्जितोपकण्ठैः ।
छुरितमिव वियद्घनैर्विचित्रैर्मधुकरकुङ्कुमकिंशुकावदातैः ॥१४॥

The following are happy auguries relating to the clouds : The sky in some places is to be covered with large banks of black and white clouds, in others with white ones and in some others with dark ones as with huge serpents whose bellies and backs alone are visible in their coils and whose moving tongues are represented by the flashes of lightning (in the clouds). It should look as though the sky were adorned with clouds, some of which are as white as the interior of lotus-blossoms, whose fringes are tinged by the rays of the rising Sun, which may be dark like bees, yellow like saffron, red like the Kiṁśuka flower, and white, and which consequently have a large variety of colours.

[This description of clouds would remind a modern reader of the various types of clouds distinguished by scientists. Here the poet combines both sound and sense effectively with the aid of figures of speech. Here the metre is पुष्पिताग्रा which looks very charming in descriptions of this type.]

असितघननिरुद्धमेव वा चलिततडित्सुरचापचित्रितम् ।
द्विपमहिषकुलाकुलीकृतं वनमिव दावपरीतमम्बरम् ॥१५॥

Or, the sky being studded with dark clouds and beautified with dashing streaks of lightning and the rain-bow, looks verily like a forest on fire, which is teeming with herds of elephants and bisons.

[The metre is अपरवक्त्र.]

अथवाञ्जनशैलशिलानिचयप्रतिरूपधरैः स्थगितं गगनम् ।
हिममौक्तिकशङ्खशशाङ्ककरद्युतिहारिभिरम्बुधरैरथवा ॥१६॥

Or, it (the sky) is blocked by clouds that resemble the mass of boulders of the collyrium mountain, or by those that set at naught the lustre of snow, pearls, conch-shells and the rays of the Moon.

[The metre is तोटक.]

तडिद्धेमकक्ष्यैर्बलाकाग्रदन्तैः स्रवद्वारिदानैश्चलत्प्रान्तहस्तैः ।
विचित्रेन्द्रचापध्वजोच्छ्रायशोभैस्तमालालिनीलैर्वृतं चाब्दनागैः ॥१७॥

Or, it is filled with elephants in the form of clouds, which are as dark as Tamāla and the bees, which have lightning representing the golden trappings, cranes representing the tusks in front, pouring rain standing for ichor, moving fringes for the trunks, and the multi-coloured rainbows for the majestic banners held aloft.

[The description, the alliteration, the metaphor and the dancing metre भुजङ्गप्रयात—all these make up the charm of this verse which is an excellent specimen of our author's literary art. We hear Kālidāsa's echo in these lines.]

सन्ध्यानुरक्ते नभसि स्थितानामिन्दीवरश्यामरुचां घनानाम् ।
वृन्दानि पीताम्बरवेष्टितस्य कान्ति हरेश्चोरयतां यदा वा ॥१८॥

Or, when there are in the sky that is crimson at twilight, clusters of clouds, which, bearing the dark hue of lilies, rob, as it were, Lord Kṛṣṇa, clad in his yellow silken garment, of his beauty.

सशिखिचातकदर्दुरनिःस्वनैर्यदि विमिश्रितमन्द्रपटुस्वनाः ।
खमवतत्य दिगन्तविलम्बिनः सलिलदाः सलिलौघमुचः क्षितौ ॥१९॥

Should the deep and distinct peal of thunder of clouds be followed by the cries of peacocks, Cātaka birds and frogs, and the clouds hang low at the horizon having spread throughout the firmament, there would be a torrential downpour on the earth.

[The metre is द्रुतविलम्बित. The conditions mentioned in this verse are familiar to village elders who prognosticate rain from the atmospheric conditions.]

निगदितरूपैर्जलधरजालैस्त्र्यहमवरुद्धं द्व्यहमथवाहः ।
यदि वियदेवं भवति सुभिक्षं मुदितजना च प्रचुरजला भूः ॥२०॥

Should the sky be covered for three, two or one day at a stretch with banks of clouds of the above description, there would be abundant food, the people would be happy and contented and there would be plenty of water in the land.

[Cf. गर्ग—

दधिरौप्यामलक्रौञ्चताम्राभारुणसन्निभाः ।
शुककौशेयमाञ्जिष्ठास्तपनीयसमप्रभाः ॥
अच्छिन्नमूलाः सुस्निग्धाः पर्वताकारसन्निभाः ।
घना घनाः प्रशस्यन्ते विद्युत्स्तनितसङ्कुलाः ॥

Cf. also पराशर—

रोहिणीयोगे पुनः प्रदक्षिणो मृदुर्मारुतः स्नेहवन्ति चाभ्राणि विद्युच्छक्रचापालङ्कृतानि स्वादुसुरभिविमलशिशिरतावृद्धिश्चाम्भसां वृष्टिक्षेमसुभिक्षाय। यावतो दिवसान् निमित्तप्रादुर्भावानुबन्धस्तावद्वर्षाणि सुभिक्षक्षेमम् । आसप्तरात्राद् बिलवासिनां बिलेभ्यो निष्क्रमणं स्त्रीपुरुषबालानां प्रमोदः पक्षिणां क्षीरपुष्पफलवृक्षसेवनं तरूणामच्छिद्रपत्रता पुरपौरहिताय ॥

Cf. also the समाससंहिता—

आषाढबहुलपक्षे शिशिरकरे रोहिणीसमायुक्ते ।
यदि गगनममलमत्यन्ततीक्ष्णरश्मिः सहस्रांशुः ॥
सलिलगुरुनभ्रजलधरतडिल्लतालोलरञ्जितदिगन्तः ।
अमितमलभेकचातककादम्बविमिश्रमाकाशम् ॥
क्षितितनयरविजरहितः स्फटिकनिभश्चन्द्रमा निरुत्पातः ।
मरुतश्च पूर्वपूर्वोत्तरोत्तराः शान्तमृगविहगाः ॥

The metre is कुसुमविचित्रा.]

Next he speaks of the characteristics of unproductive and harmful clouds.

रूक्षैरल्पैर्मारुताक्षिप्तदेहैरुष्ट्रध्वाङ्क्षप्रेतशाखामृगाभैः ।
अन्येषां वा निन्दितानां स्वरूपैर्मूकैश्चाब्दैर्नो शिवं नापि वृष्टिः ॥२३॥

There would neither be prosperity nor rain in the land, should the clouds be rough and small, tossed about by the wind, have the shapes of camels, crows, dead bodies, monkeys or other inauspicious creatures, and be silent.

[Cf. गर्ग—

छिन्नमूलाश्च वृक्षाश्च शुष्का वाष्पाकुलीकृताः ।
पापसत्त्वानुकाराश्च मेघाः पापफलप्रदाः ॥

The metre is शालिनी.]

विगतघने वा वियति विवस्वानमृदुमयूखः सलिलकृदवम् ।
सर इव फुल्लं निशि कुमुदाढ्यं खमुडुविशुद्धं यदि च सुवृष्ट्यै ॥२२॥

If the Sun should shine with burning rays in a cloudless sky and the sky at night with bright stars look blooming like a lake with lily blossoms, there would be plentiful rain.

[The metre is कुसुमविचित्रा.]

Next he speaks of the effects of the clouds appearing in the different directions.

पूर्वोद्भूतैः सस्यनिष्पत्तिरब्दैराग्नेयाशासम्भवैरग्निकोपः ।
याम्ये सस्यं क्षीयते नैर्ऋतेऽर्द्धं पश्चाज्जातैः शोभना वृष्टिरब्दैः ॥२३॥

वायव्योत्थैर्वातवृष्टिः क्वचिच्च पुष्टा वृष्टिः सौम्यकाष्ठासमुत्थैः ।
श्रेष्ठं सस्यं स्याणुदिक्सम्प्रवृद्धैर्वायुश्चैवं विक्षु धत्ते फलानि ॥२४॥

If the clouds rise in the east, there will be good crops; in the south-east, there will be outbreak of fires; in the south, crops will decay; in the south-west, only partial growth of crops; in the west, good rains; in the north-west, stormy and sporadic rain; in the north, very fine and full rain; and in the north-east, bumper crops. The same effects should be predicted of the wind also arising in the several directions.

[The metre again is शालिनी.]

उल्कानिपातास्तडितोऽशनिश्च दिग्दाहनिर्घातमहीप्रकम्पाः ।
नादा मृगाणां सपतत्रिणां च ग्राह्या यथैवाम्बुधरास्तथैव ॥२५॥

Fall of meteors, flashes of lightning, thunderbolts, false fires in the quarters, portentous rumblings in the sky, earthquakes and the cries of birds and beasts produce the same effects as the clouds do under the above conditions i.e. directions.

नामाङ्कितैस्तैरुदगादिकुम्भैः प्रदक्षिणं श्रावणमासपूर्वैः ।
पूर्णैः स मासः सलिलस्य दाता स्रुतैरवृष्टिः परिकल्पनीया ॥२६॥

The four water-vessels beginning with the one kept at the northern end should be designated as the four months beginning with Śrāvaṇa in the dextral order. If any of the pots be full of water, the particular month signified by that pot will have good rain. On the other hand, if any one be empty, that month would have no rain. The amount of rain will have to be estimated on the basis of the quantity of water left in the pots.

[Cf. गर्ग—

सौम्ये तु श्रावणं विन्द्यात् पूर्वे भाद्रपदं वदेत् ।
दक्षिणेऽश्वयुजो ज्ञेयः पश्चिमे कार्त्तिकं विदुः ॥
सर्वे कुम्भाः सुपूर्णाः स्युरभग्नाः कान्तिसंयुताः ।
चतुरो वार्षिकान् मासान् सर्वान् वर्षति वासवः ॥
सर्वस्रुतैरवृष्टिः स्यादर्द्धैर्मध्यमवर्षणम् ।
द्रवैस्तथाविधा वृष्टिर्वक्तव्या जलमानतः ॥]

अन्यैश्च कुम्भैर्नृपनामचिह्नैर्देशाङ्कितैश्चाप्यपरैस्तथैव ।
भग्नैः स्रुतैर्न्यूनजलैः सुपूर्णैर्भाग्यानि वाच्यानि यथानुरूपम् ॥२७॥

Likewise, through other pots bearing the names of kings, countries and other things (such as the four classes etc.) their fortunes, (good, bad or middling) should be predicted according to the conditions of the pots, when they are quite full, broken, drained off or having a little water.

[Cf. काश्यप—

अन्यदेशाङ्किताः कुम्भा भिद्यन्ते च स्रवन्ति च ।
बन्धहीना वितोयाश्च तेऽभियोज्या नृपेण वै ॥

In this verse the sage prescribes a method to find out which of the kings could be attacked and vanquished.]

Next the author speaks of the effects of the Moon's contact with the constellation Rohiṇī.

दूरगो निकटगोऽथवा शशी दक्षिणे पथि यथातथा स्थितः ।
रोहिणीं यदि युनक्ति सर्वथा कष्टमेव जगतो विनिर्दिशेत् ॥२८॥

Should the Moon situated to the south of the star, whether far or near, conjoin with Rohiṇī, there would result terrible disaster to the world.

[The metre is रथोद्धता.]

स्पृशन्नुदग्याति यदा शशाङ्कस्तदा सुवृष्टिर्बहुलोपसर्गा ।
असंस्पृशन् योगमुदक्समेतः करोति वृष्टिं विपुलां शिवं च ॥२९॥

When the Moon touches Rohiṇī while standing in the south, and then moves to the north, there will be good rains accompanied by many disasters. On the other hand, when she moves to the north without touching the constellation, there will be abundant rains and prosperity to mankind.

रोहिणीशकटमध्यसंस्थिते चन्द्रमस्यशरणीकृता जनाः ।
क्वापि यान्ति शिशुयाचिताशनाः सूर्यतप्तपिठराम्बुपायिनः ॥३०॥

When the Moon is posited in the centre of the wain of Rohiṇī, people will roam about shelterless, their children procuring food for them by begging, and drinking water from sun-scorched vessels (as a result of drought and famine).

[The group of six stars constituting Rohiṇī is called *Śakaṭa* or cart. This subject of cleaving the 'Wain of Rohiṇī' has been dealt with in chapter IX.25 *supra* and in notes thereunder.

प्रजाः is another reading for जनाः in the text.

The metre is again रथोद्धता.]

उदितं यदि शीतदीधितिं प्रथमं पृष्ठत एति रोहिणी ।
शुभमेव तदा स्मरातुराः प्रमदाः कामवशेन संस्थिताः ॥३१॥

Should the Moon rise first and Rohiṇī rising later follow her, there would be all-round happiness and prosperity to mankind, but young damsels, stricken with love, would be under the influence of amorous men.

[The metre of this and the following verse is वियोगिनी.]

अनुगच्छति पृष्ठतः शशी यदि कामी वनितामिव प्रियाम् ।
मकरध्वजबाणखेदिताः प्रमदानां वशगास्तदा नराः ॥३२॥

If the Moon should follow Rohiṇī from behind, as a lover does his beloved, men would be under the control of youthful women, being smitten by the shafts of cupid.

आग्नेय्यां दिशि चन्द्रमा यदि भवेत्तत्रोपसर्गो महान्
नैर्ऋत्यां समुपद्रुतानि निधनं सस्यानि यान्तीतिभिः ।
प्राजेशानिलदिक्स्थिते हिमकरे सस्यस्य मध्यश्चयो
याते स्थाणुदिशं गुणाः सुबहवः सस्यार्घवृष्ट्यादयः ॥३३॥

When the Moon stands to the south-east of Rohiṇī, there will be great calamities in the year; when to the south-west, all the crops will be destroyed being afflicted with all kinds of pests; when to the north-west, crops will flourish only moderately; and when to the north-east, there will be many advantages, bumper crops, higher prices, good and timely rains, health and happiness among the people.

[Cf. the समाससंहिता—

उदगपि च तुहिनकिरणः पूर्वोत्तरतोऽथवा स्थितः प्राच्याम् ।
यदि भवति तदा वसुधा भवति विवृद्धा प्रहृष्टजना ॥
उपसर्गोऽनलदिक्स्थे याम्याशासंस्थिते शकटके च ।
किं कष्टैस्तैरुक्तैः श्रुतमात्रैर्यैः कृशो भवति ॥
क्रिमिशुकशलभादिभयं नैर्ऋत्यां नातिपुष्टिरपरेण ।
वायव्याशासंस्थे मध्यं सस्यं कुमुदनाथे ॥

The metre is शार्दूलविक्रीडित.]

ताडयेद्यदि च योगतारकामावृणोति वपुषा यदापि वा ।
ताडने भयमुशन्ति दारुणं छादने नृपवधोऽङ्गनाकृतः ॥३४॥

Should the Moon cut across the brilliant star of the group of Rohiṇī or cover it with her disc, there would be great danger and the king's murder committed by a woman respectively.

[योगतारा is the most prominent or brightest star of a group. For,

सतारागणमध्ये तु या तारा दीप्तिमत्तरा ।
योगतारेति सा प्रोक्ता नक्षत्राणां पुरातनैः ॥

According to Utpala *cutting* means "शृङ्गैकदेशेन स्पृशति" or touching it with a portion of her horn.

The metre of this and of the following verses is रथोद्धता.]

गोप्रवेशसमयेऽग्रतो वृषो याति कृष्णपशुरेव वा पुरः ।
भूरि वारि शबले तु मध्यमं नो सितेऽम्बुपरिकल्पनापरैः ॥३५॥

If at the time of the arrival of the cattle in the evening, there be a bull or a black animal (such as a goat) in front, there would be copious rains in the year; if it be black and white, rains would be moderate; and if it be white, there would be no rain at all. A proportionate estimate of the quantity of rain is to be made with the animals of other colours.

[It is to be remembered that the prognostication referred to in this verse should be made under the circumstances mentioned in the beginning of this chapter and the previous one too.

Cf. गर्ग—

प्राक्प्रवेशे तु यूथस्य पुरतो वृषभो यदा ।
प्रवेशे कृष्णवर्णो वा पशुर्बहुजलप्रदः ॥

कृष्णा तु गौः सुभिक्षाय क्षेमारोग्याय चोच्यते ।
गौर्यांमथ च नीलायां मघ्याः सस्यस्य सम्पदः ॥
अनावृष्टिकरी श्वेता वाताय कपिला स्मृता ।
पाटला सस्यनाशाय रोगाय करटा स्मृता ॥
एकदेशाय शबला चित्रं चित्रा तु वर्षति ।
पाण्डुरा मध्यमाङ्गी वा ग्रीष्मधान्यविवर्द्धनी ॥
कपिला पश्चिमं वर्षं शोणा त्वग्रे प्रवर्षति ॥

See also what पराशर says :—

अथास्तमयवेलायां पुरद्वारमभिगम्य निमित्तान्युपलक्षयेत् । तत्र गोगजाश्वरथ-प्रथमप्रवेशे पुरविजयो वानरखरोष्ट्रनकुलमार्जारप्रवेशे विद्रवो नेत्राङ्गहीनप्रवेशे त्वशनि-भयमिति ॥]

दृश्यते न यदि रोहिणीयुतश्चन्द्रमा नभसि तोयदावृते ।
रुग्भयं महदुपस्थितं तदा भूश्च भूरिजलसस्यसंयुता ॥३६॥

If the Moon in conjunction with Rohiṇī is not visible as a result of the sky being overcast, great danger from diseases is imminent, but the earth will be blessed with plenty of water and bumper crops.

[Here the author-poet does not alter the metre of the last verse.]

———

स्वातियोगाध्यायः ॥२५॥

Chapter XXV—The Moon's Conjunction with Svāti

यद्रोहिणीयोगफलं तदेव स्वातावषाढासहिते च चन्द्रे ।
आषाढशुक्ले निखिलं विचिन्त्यं योऽस्मिन् विशेषस्तमहं प्रवक्ष्ये ॥१॥

The effects of the Moon's conjunction with Svāti and Āṣāḍha are the same as for her conjunction with Rohiṇī. However, the observations should be made in the bright fortnight of the month of Āṣāḍha. I shall now explain the special features of this latter conjunction.

[Cf. पराशर—

सर्व एते योगा मास्याषाढे भवन्ति । तान् दैवज्ञः प्रयतः शुचिरवधारयेत्, स्वातिसंयुते चन्द्रमसि घनस्निग्धस्तनितविद्युन्मालैरम्भोदैर्नभसोऽवच्छादनं सुभिक्षक्षेमाय तद्वत्सर्ववातप्रादुर्भाव इति । उल्कानिर्घातकम्पोपघातैश्च विपर्ययः ॥

Here the metres employed are इन्द्रवज्रा in the first three verses, आर्या, शार्दूलविक्रीडित and अनुष्टुभ्.]

स्वातौ निशांशे प्रथमेऽभिवृष्टे सस्यानि सर्वाण्युपयान्ति वृद्धिम् ।
भागे द्वितीये तिलमुद्गमाषा ग्रैष्मं तृतीयेऽस्ति न शारदानि ॥२॥

वृष्टेऽह्नि भागे प्रथमे सुवृष्टिस्तद्वद्द्वितीये तु सकीटसर्पा ।
वृष्टिस्तु मध्यापरभागवृष्टे निश्छिद्रवृष्टिर्द्युनिशं प्रवृष्टे ॥३॥

If it rains in the first four-hour period of the night when the Moon is in conjunction with the asterism Svāti, all the crops would thrive; if in the second part, sesamum, green gram and black gram would grow splendidly; if in the third part, summer-crops alone would thrive and not the autumnal ones. If it rains in the first part of the day, there would be excellent rains in the year; if in the second, the effect will be the same, but insects and snakes would increase; and if in the third part, the rain would be moderate. If there be rain throughout the day and night, there would be excellent rain in the year.

[Cf. गर्ग—

स्वातियोगे यदा युक्ते पूर्वरात्रे प्रवर्षति ।
ग्रीष्मशारदसम्पन्नां तां समामभिनिर्दिशेत् ॥
रात्रेर्द्विभागमाश्रित्य स्वातियोगेऽभिवर्षति ।
सम्पदो मुद्गमाषाणां तिलानां चावधारयेत् ॥
त्रिभागशेषे शर्वर्याः स्वातियोगेऽभिवर्षति ।
ग्रैष्मं सम्पद्यते सस्यं शारदं तु विनश्यति ॥
अह्नस्तु प्रथमे भागे वर्षाक्षेमसुवृष्टये ।
द्वितीये शोभना वृष्टिर्बहुसस्यसरीसृपाः ॥
अह्नस्तृतीये भागे तु मध्यमां कुरुते समाम् ।
अहोरात्रं यदा वर्षं स्वातियोगे पुरन्दरः ॥
तदा तु चतुरो मासान् सर्वान्वर्षति वासवः ॥]

सममुत्तरेण तारा चित्रायाः कीर्त्यते ह्यपांवत्सः ।
तस्यासन्ने चन्द्रे स्वातेर्योगः शिवो भवति ॥४॥

There is a star named *Apāṁvatsa, Child of Water,* which is situated due north of *Citrā*. When the Moon joins with *Svāti* while staying in the neighbourhood of Apāṁvatsa, the effect will be splendid and beneficial.

सप्तम्यां स्वातियोगे यदि पतति हिमं माघमासान्धकारे
वायुर्वा चण्डवेगः सजलजलधरो वापि गर्जत्यजस्रम् ।
विद्युन्मालाकुलं वा यदि भवति नभो नष्टचन्द्रार्कतारं
विज्ञेया प्रावृडेषा मुदितजनपदा सर्वसस्यैरुपेता ॥५॥

If there be snowfall on the 7th lunar day of the dark fortnight of the month of Māgha during the Moon's stay with *Svāti*, or if the wind be very strong, or if the dark clouds thunder constantly, or if the sky, where the Sun, the Moon and stars become invisible, is filled with wreaths of lightning, one should understand that the rainy season would be rich in all kinds of crops, gladdening mankind.

[This is a fine example of a good, descriptive poetry. We get here a fine description of the rainy-season, with the sound echoing the sense.]

तथैव फाल्गुने चैत्रे वैशाखस्यासितेऽपि वा ।
स्वातियोगं विजानीयादाषाढे च विशेषतः ॥६॥

In the same manner one should consider the effects of the Moon's conjunction with *Svāti* occurring in the month of *Phālguna* or *Caitra* or in the dark half of *Vaiśākha* and especially in the month of *Āṣāḍha*.

[Bhaṭṭotpala writes here : "अनार्षोऽयं श्लोक:". Does he mean by this that the above statement is not borne out by the statements of ancient sages like Garga, or that this verse is not our author's ? The previous verse in the शार्दूलविक्रीडित metre looks like the last verse of the chapter.]

आषाढीयोगाध्यायः ॥२६॥

Chapter XXVI—The Moon's Conjunction with Āṣāḍha

[Whatever effects have been enumerated for the Moon's conjunction with Rohiṇī, all that will apply to her conjunction with Uttarāṣāḍhā on the full Moon of the month of Āsāḍha.

Cf. पराशर—

अतोऽनन्तरमाषाढासंयुक्ते शशिन्यादानविसर्गान्तभगेषु निमित्तानि प्रावृष्याद्यन्तमध्येषु फलन्ति । तत्र सुरभिरनुकूलः स्पर्शवान् मारुतः पूर्वपूर्वोत्तरोऽतिवर्षसस्यकरो नैर्ऋताग्नेययाम्यवारुणवायव्या मध्यसस्यकराः । विपर्ययो विपरीतेषु । वैदूर्यरजतमधुहेमप्रभा सन्ध्या स्निग्धाभ्रवृक्षप्रादुर्भावश्च प्रावृड्वृद्धये । प्राङ्मध्यपश्चाद्भागेष्वाषाढानां योगः शशिनो वर्षासु तत्कालमेव वर्षाय । वैश्वदेवादुत्तरतः शशी वर्षकरो न दक्षिणतः । निर्घातोल्काशनिभूचलनदण्डान्यावग्रहोपतापे सस्यवधो भवति । भवति चात्र—

सोदकं सातपं साभ्रं सविद्युत् स्तनयित्नुमत् ।
प्रवातं च निवातं च प्रशस्तं तदहः स्मृतम् ॥]

आषाढ्यां समतुलिताधिवासितानामन्येद्युर्यदधिकतामुपैति बीजम् ।
तद्वृद्धिर्भवति न जायते यदूनं मन्त्रोऽस्मिन्भवति तुलाभिमन्त्रणाय ॥१॥

At the time of the full Moon in the month of Āṣāḍha take equal weights of several kinds of seeds and keep them for a night being sanctified with the *Mahāvrata* hymn. Those seeds whose weight increases the next day will flourish during the year, whereas those that go down in weight will not. The hymn for sanctifying the balance used for weighing the seeds is the following :

[Cf. गर्ग—

वायव्यवैश्वदेवाभ्या प्राजापत्यस्य चैव हि ।
एषामप्यधिकं चापि रोहिणी नाम याप्यते ॥

See also the समाससंहिता—

तुलिताधिवासितानामन्येद्युर्यदधिक भवति बीजम् ।
आषाढपौर्णमास्यां तद्वृद्धिस्तत्र मन्त्रोऽयम् ॥

The metre is प्रहर्षिणी.]

स्तोतव्या मन्त्रयोगेन सत्या देवी सरस्वती ।
दर्शयिष्यसि यत्सत्यं सत्ये सत्यव्रता ह्यसि ॥२॥

येन सत्येन चन्द्रार्कौ ग्रहा ज्योतिर्गणास्तथा ।
उत्तिष्ठन्तीह पूर्वेण पश्चादस्तं व्रजन्ति च ॥३॥

यत्सत्यं सर्ववेदेषु यत्सत्यं ब्रह्मवादिषु ।
यत्सत्यं त्रिषु लोकेषु तत्सत्यमिह दृश्यताम् ॥४॥

ब्रह्मणो दुहितासि त्वमादित्येति प्रकीर्तिता ।
काश्यपी गोत्रतश्चैव नामतो विश्रुता तुला ॥५॥

The balance should be invoked with the following hymns : "As the Goddess of Speech is verily Truth, you will, O Truth incarnate, show the real truth, since you are dedicated to Truth. May that Truth appear here, the Truth by which the Sun and the Moon, the planets and the hosts of stars rise in the east and set in the west, the Truth which is revealed in all the Vedas, in the Sages rooted in spirituality and in the three worlds. You are the daughter of Brahman (creator), called by the name Ādityā (daughter of Aditi), and descended from the spiritual preceptor, Sage Kaśyapa. You are popularly known as Balance."

[These verses in praise of the Balance are not by our author. They have been reproduced from the works of ancient sages. Hence the commentator says "अथ तं मन्त्रमार्षमाह". Weights, measures and scales must be exact and the same to everybody in the world. They should be trustworthy. Hence the balance and the like were considered sacred in ancient times. Manu, Kauṭilya and others insist on the correctness and infallibility of weights and measures.]

क्षौमं चतुःसूत्रकसन्निबद्धं षडङ्गुलं शिक्यकवस्त्रमस्याः ।
सूत्रप्रमाणं च दशाङ्गुलानि षडेव कक्ष्योभयशिक्यमध्ये ॥६॥

The scale-pans should be made of silk cloth six digits in length and width, fastened with four strings ten digits long and the cord by which the balance is held between the two scales is six digits in length.

[The commentator interprets the word षडेव...as the dimension of the कक्ष्यासूत्र otherwise known as ग्रहणसूत्र. For the length of the beam refer to verse 9 *infra.*

The metre is उपजाति.]

यास्ये शिक्ये काञ्चनं सन्निवेश्यं शेषद्रव्याण्युत्तरेऽम्बूनि चैव ।
तोयैः कौप्यैः सैन्धवैः सारसैश्च वृष्टिर्हीना मध्यमा चोत्तमा च ॥७॥
दन्तैर्नागा गोहयाद्याश्च लोम्ना हेम्ना भूपाः सिक्थकेन द्विजाद्याः ।
तद्वद्देशा वर्षमासा दिशश्च शेषद्रव्याण्यात्मरूपस्थितानि ॥८॥

Gold should be weighed in the right hand pan, while all other articles as well as water (liquids) in the left hand pan. Weigh severally the waters of wells, rivers and lakes. The rain in the year will be meagre, moderate and copious according as well, river and lake water becomes the heaviest. The value of elephants is determined by the amount of ivory they have; of cows, horses and the like (viz. donkeys, camels, goats and sheep), by their hair; of kings, by the amount of gold in their coffers; of Brāhmaṇas etc., as well as of countries, years, months and quarters, by bees-wax; and of other substances, by their actual weight.

[वृद्धिर्हीना is another reading. The metre is शालिनी.]

हैमी प्रधाना रजतेन मध्या तयोरलाभे खदिरेण कार्या ।
विद्धः पुमान् येन शरेण सा वा तुला प्रमाणेन भवेद्वितस्तिः ॥९॥

A golden balance is the best, one of silver is middling. In the absence of the above two, it should be made of Khadira (Acacia catechu) wood, or it should be made of a shaft by which a person is pierced. The length of the balance should be twelve digits.

[An Aṅgula or digit is the space covered by 8 grains of barley placed side by side, or that of three grains placed lengthwise. It is primarily the breadth of a human finger.

This and the following three verses are in उपजाति metre.]

हीनस्य नाशोऽभ्यधिकस्य वृद्धिस्तुल्येन तुल्यं तुलितं तुलायाम् ।
एतत्तुलाकोशरहस्यमुक्तं प्राजेशयोगेऽपि नरो विदध्यात् ॥१०॥

Such substances as appear to have lost weight on being weighed again, would suffer loss; such as have gained in weight would thrive; and such as continue in the same condition would be indifferent. This is termed the 'secret of weighing treasures'. This applies equally to the Moon's conjunction with Rohiṇī too.

[Cf. गर्ग—

येषां प्रणमते सारं ते भवन्ति च नासमम् ।
येषा तु हीयते सारं तेषां नाशं विनिर्दिशेत् ॥
समानि तु समानि स्युस्तुलया तुलितानि तु ॥

also पराशर—

सारसेऽम्भसि सस्यानां राज्ञां च विजयोऽधिके ।
नादेये मध्यमा सम्पत्कनीयस्यचलोदके ॥
यस्यां दिशि भवेन्माल्यमम्लानं शुचिगन्धिमत् ।
तस्यां दिशि विजानीयाद्राज्ञां शिवमनामयम् ॥]

स्वातावषाढास्वथ रोहिणीषु पापग्रहा योगगता न शस्ताः ।
ग्राह्यं तु योगद्वयमप्युपोष्य यदाधिमासो द्विगुणीकरोति ॥११॥

Evil planets (Mars, Saturn, Rāhu and Ketu) posited in Svāti, Uttarāṣāḍhā or Rohiṇī during the Moon's conjunction with any of these, cause havoc in the country. In the case of an intercalary Āṣāḍha month occurring, one should observe devotional fasting on both the occasions.

[Cf. गर्ग—

योगैः पापैरुपहतैः प्रजानामशुभं वदेत् ।
दुर्भिक्षावृष्टिमरकान् सौम्यैः सौभिक्षमादिशेत् ॥

also पराशर—

शुक्रबुधबृहस्पतिसंयोगे शूकधान्यतिलमुद्गविनाशः । सौरस्य मध्यदेशाभावो भौमस्य शस्त्रकोपः । केतोर्भयदुर्भिक्षप्रादुर्भावावग्रहः । रोहिणीमध्यगमनमिन्दोः सुभिक्षक्षेमवृष्टिकरम् ॥]

त्रयोऽपि योगाः सदृशाः फलेन यदा तदा वाच्यमसंशयेन ।
विपर्यये यस्त्विह रोहिणीजं फलं तदेवाम्यधिकं निगद्यम् ॥१२॥

When the effects of the Moon's conjunctions with Rohiṇī, Svāti and Āsāḍhā are the same, whether good or bad, the prediction is to be made accordingly without hesitation. Should the effects be different, those of Rohiṇī alone would prevail.

निष्पत्तिरग्निकोपो वृष्टिर्मन्दाथ मध्यमा श्रेष्ठा ।
बहुजलपवना पुष्टा शुभा च पूर्वादिभिः पवनैः ॥१३॥

If the wind blows from the eight quarters beginning with the east at the time of the Moon's conjunction with Āsāḍhā, the effects would be in order (i) good harvest, (ii) danger from fire, (iii) sparse rain, (iv) moderate rain, (v) very good rain, (vi) copious rain accompanied by winds, (vii) abundant rain, and (viii) highly beneficial rain.

[The author has already referred to this aspect in Chapter XXIV. 24. Hence this is only by way of clarification for the benefit of students.]

वृत्तायामाषाढ्यां कृष्णचतुर्थ्यामजैकपादर्क्षे ।
यदि वर्षति पर्जन्यः प्रावृट् शस्ता न चेन्न ततः ॥१४॥

If, after the full Moon in the month of Āṣāḍha, there is rain on the 4th lunar day of the dark fortnight in the asterism of Pūrvābhadra, the rainy season will prove beneficial; otherwise not.

[This verse is patently spurious. For, Utpala says that it is Anārṣa. The Benares edition puts this verse at the end of वातचक्र.]

आषाढ्यां पौर्णमास्यां तु यद्यैशानोऽनिलो भवेत् ।
अस्तं गच्छति तीक्ष्णांशो सस्यसम्पत्तिरुत्तमा ॥१५॥

If there be a north-easterly wind on the full-moon day of Āṣāḍha at sunset, there would be excellent growth of crops in the season.

[This verse appears as the first of वातचक्र in the Benares edition where the reading is आषाढपौर्णमास्यां.]

वातचक्रम् ॥२७॥

Chapter XXVII—The Wind Circle

[According to Utpala this chapter is spurious, as it is patently redundant. But, he says, this section is found in many books. So he comments for the benefit of students.]

पूर्वः पूर्वसमुद्रवीचिशिखरप्रस्फालनाघूर्णित-
श्चन्द्रार्कांशुसटाकलापकलितो वायुर्यदाकाशतः ।
नैकान्तस्थितनीलमेघपटला शारद्यसंवर्धिता
वासन्तोत्कटसस्यमण्डिततला सर्वा मही शोभते ॥१॥

If on the day of the full Moon in Āṣāḍha an easterly wind blows from the sky, being tossed by the strokes of the tops of the billows of the eastern ocean and mingled with the mass of the mane-like rays of the luminaries, the whole earth will rejoice being enriched by the splendid vernal and autumnal crops, and being covered overhead with groups of dark clouds everywhere.

[The poet, whoever he might be, has tried to come up to the level of our author in poetic fancy and verbal exuberance.

The metre is शार्दूलविक्रीडित. The grammatical form शारद्य is rather unusual. He could have instead used सच्छारदैर्वर्धिता.]

यदाग्नेयो वायुर्मलयशिखरास्फालनपटुः
प्लवत्यस्मिन्योगे भगवति पतङ्गे प्रवसति ।
तदा नित्योद्दीप्ता ज्वलनशिखरालिङ्गिततला
स्वगात्रोष्मोच्छ्वासैर्वमति वसुधा भस्मनिकरम् ॥२॥

When the wind blows with such force as if to break off the peaks of the Malaya mountain, from the south-eastern part of the sky at sunset on the same full-moon day, the earth, blazing continuously with the flames of fire embracing or spreading on its surface, will emit heaps of ashes along with the hot vapour emanating from its own body.

[The poet continues his description in the same strain. His expression प्लवति instead of प्लवमाने is un-Paninian. Here the word

वमति leads to the poetic excellence named समाधि mentioned by Daṇḍin. The metre is शिखरिणी.

यदा वह्नौ वायुर्वहति गगनेऽखण्डिततनुः is another reading.]

तालीपत्रलतावितानतरुभिः शाखामृगान्नर्तयन्
योगेऽस्मिन् प्लवति ध्वनिः सपरुषो वायुर्यदा दक्षिणः ।
तद्वद्योगसमुत्थितस्तु गजवत्तालाङ्कुशैर्घट्टिताः
कीनाशा इव मन्दवारिकणिका मुञ्चन्ति मेघास्तदा ॥३॥

When at the above-named conjunction a very rough and howling south wind blows, making the monkeys dance through the (shaking) leaves of palm trees, bowers of creepers and trees, the clouds rising like the elephants struck by rod and pricked by goad, shed a few drops of water like miserly persons.

[सर्वोद्योगसमुन्नताश्च is another reading in the third line. This and the following verse are in शार्दूलविक्रीडित metre.]

सूक्ष्मैलालवलीलवङ्गनिचयान् व्याघूर्णयन् सागरे
भानोरस्तमये प्लवत्यविरतो वायुर्यदा नैर्ऋतः ।
क्षुत्तृष्णावृतमानुषास्थिशकलप्रस्तारभारच्छदा
मत्ता प्रेतवधूरिवोग्रचपला भूमिस्तदा लक्ष्यते ॥४॥

If at sunset on the full-moon day of Āṣāḍha a south-west wind blows unceasingly tossing up and down in the sea heaps of small cardamoms, averrhoas and cloves, then the earth shrouded by a heavy load of scattered bone-pieces of men who have perished by hunger and thirst, would appear wild and restless like a young woman who has just lost her husband.

[The style is brilliant and imagery vivid in this verse in which we come across the ghastly effects of famine, drought and mortality stalking the land.]

यदा रेणूत्पातैः प्रविचलसटाटोपचपलः
प्रवातः पश्चाच्चेद्दिनकरकरापातसमये ।
तदा सस्योपेता प्रवरनिकराबद्धसमरा
क्षितिः स्थानस्थानेष्वविरतवसामांसरुधिरा ॥५॥

If at sunset on the same day there is a strong gale from the west, raising dust with its striking wings, the earth will be endowed with rich crops, but will have the leading monarchs engaged in sanguinary battles leading to huge masses of marrow, flesh and blood being thrown everywhere.

[Here alliteration is verv prominent. His descriptions of a duststorm and battles are effective.

The metre is शिखरिणी.]

आषाढीपर्वकाले यदि किरणपतेरस्तकालोपपत्तौ
वायव्यो वृद्धवेगः पवनघनवपुः पन्नगार्द्धानुकारी ।
जानीयाद्वारिधाराप्रमुदितमुदितामुक्तमण्डूककण्ठां
सस्योद्भासैकचिह्नां सुखबहुलतया भाग्यसेनामिवोर्वीम् ॥६॥

At sunset on the same day, if the north-westerly wind be very strong, have a dense appearance and resembles mutilated bodies of serpents (or Garuḍa with his wings out-stretched), then it should be understood that the ear h would possess the plenitude of blessings on account of undiluted happiness, caused by the all-round growth of splendid crops and torrents of rain, wherein the frogs rejoice and croak continuously.

[In the second line पन्नगादानुकारी is another reading; where पन्नगाद means Garuḍa. Here too alliteration is patent. The commentator interprets भाग्यसेनां as भाग्यचमूं—the army of blessings. This description suggests a blessed woman whose forehead bears the auspicious mark of Kuṁkuma—saffron. The metre is स्रग्धरा.]

मेरुग्रस्तमरीचिमण्डलतले ग्रीष्मावसाने रवौ
वात्यामोदिकदम्बगन्धसुरभिर्वायुर्यदा चोत्तरः ।
विद्युद्भ्रान्तिसमस्तकान्तिकलनामत्तास्तदा तोयदा
उन्मत्ता इव नष्टचन्द्रकिरणां गां पूरयन्त्यम्बुभिः ॥७॥

If, at the end of summer i.e. on the full-moon day of Āṣāḍha, where the mass of the sun's rays is screened by Mount Meru, a northerly breeze blows, wafting the fragrance of the sweet-smelling Kadamba flowers, then the clouds will flood the earth with water, as though crying madly, and intoxicated by the sight of the spreading illumination caused by flashes of lightning, and destroying the Moon's rays on the earth.

[The metre is शार्दूलविक्रीडित.]

नष्टचन्द्रार्ककिरणं नष्टतारं न चेन्नभः ।
न तां मन्ये यत्र देवो न वर्षति ॥८॥

If the sky be bereft of the rays of the Sun, the Moon and the stars, and if there be no rain, then, I think, the month cannot be called *Bhādrapada.*

[The verse in the Anustubh metre is Anārṣa or spurious according to the commentator.]

ऐशानो यदि शीतलोऽमरगणैः संसेव्यमानो भवेत्
पुन्नागागरुपारिजातसुरभिर्वायुः प्रचण्डध्वनिः ।
आपूर्णोदकयौवना वसुमती सम्पन्नसस्याकुला
धर्मिष्ठाः प्रणतारयो नृपतयो रक्षन्ति वर्णांस्तदा ॥६॥

If the north-easterly wind be cool, scented by the flowers of Punnāga, Agaru and Pārijāta, be sonorous and be enjoyed by groups of celestials, the earth filled with the youth of water would be rich in food crops, and kings would control their rivals and protect all classes of people with the utmost justice.

[This verse in the शार्दूलविक्रीडित metre is not found in the Benares edition. When the poet has qualified the Earth as उदकयौवना, I do not understand why he has not given the epithet as सम्पन्नसस्यांशुका.]

सद्योवर्षणाध्यायः ॥२८॥

Chapter XXVIII—Signs of Immediate Rain

वर्षाप्रश्ने सलिलनिलयं राशिमाश्रित्य चन्द्रो
लग्नं यातो भवति यदि वा केन्द्रगः शुक्लपक्षे ।
सौम्यैर्दृष्टः प्रचुरमुदकं पापदृष्टोऽल्पमम्भः
प्रावृट्काले सृजति न चिराच्चन्द्रवद्भार्गवोऽपि ॥१॥

If, at a query regarding rain, the Moon be posited in the ascendant which happens to be a watery Sign (Cancer, Capricorn or Pisces), or in the 4th, 7th or 10th house from the Lagna in the bright fortnight, there would be copious rain ere long in the monsoon, provided she is aspected by benefics (Mercury, Jupiter and Venus). If she be aspected by malefics in the above yogas, there would be very little rain. (If she be aspected by both benefics and malefics, there would be ordinary rain). In predicting rain, Venus should be treated just like the Moon under similar circumstances.

[Here the commentator raises an objection to the apparent contradiction in the text : The Moon in the Lagna or a Kendra. Is not the Lagna a Kendra ? The author's idea is that the Moon should be only in the Lagna-Kendra in the dark fortnight, whereas in the bright fortnight she may be even in another Kendra, provided it is a Watery Sign, for making the above prediction.

Though all the editions read वर्षा प्रश्ने I feel it is a misprint for वर्षप्रश्ने. For, the word वर्षाः means 'rainy season' which is not intended here as the author mentions it in the 4th line : प्रावृट्काले.

Cf. the समाससंहिता—

वर्षप्रश्ने प्रावृषि जलराशौ कण्टके शशी बलवान् ।
भृगुजो वा शुभदृष्टो बहुजलकृत् स्वल्पदः पापैः ॥

The metre is मन्दाक्रान्ता in this and the following verse.]

आर्द्रं द्रव्यं स्पृशति यदि वा वारि तत्सञ्ज्ञकं वा
तोयासन्नो भवति यदि वा तोयकार्योन्मुखो वा ।
प्रष्टा वाच्यः सलिलमचिरादस्ति निःसंशयेन
पृच्छाकाले सलिलमिति वा श्रूयते यत्र शब्दः ॥२॥

If the questioner touches any wet object, or water or any object having a name similar to that of water (like milk, pearl etc.), or stands near water or is about to do something connected with water, or if at the time the word 'water' is heard in the place, then he should be told that there would be rain almost immediately without any doubt.

[Cf. the समाससंहिता—

आर्द्रद्रव्यं सलिलं जलसंज्ञश्रवणदर्शनान्यथवा ॥]

उदयशिखरिसंस्थो दुर्निरीक्ष्योऽतिदीप्त्या
द्रुतकनकनिकाशः स्निग्धवैदूर्यकान्तिः ।
तदहनि कुरुतेऽम्भस्तोयकाले विवस्वान्
प्रतपति यदि चोच्चैः खं गतोऽतीव तीक्ष्णम् ॥३॥

If, in the rainy season, the Sun, even while rising, cannot be looked at on account of his dazzling brilliance and appear like molten gold, or possess the pure lustre of beryl, or if he burns with intense heat at the Zenith of the sky, there would be rain on the very same day.

[Cf. Kālidāsa's statement: "दिवस इवाभ्रश्यामस्तपात्यये जीवलोकस्य ।"

The metre is मालिनी.]

विरसमुदकं गोनेत्राभं वियद्विमला दिशो
लवणविकृतिः काकाण्डाभं यदा च भवेन्नभः ।
पवनविगमः पोप्लूयन्ते झषाः स्थलगामिनो
रसनमसकृन्मण्डूकानां जलागमहेतवः ॥४॥

The following are the indications of rain: Tasteless water, the sky with the colour of cow's eyes or crow's eggs (white and blue), the quarters being uncontaminated, salt becoming moist, subdued wind, much tumbling of fishes ashore and the repeated croakings of frogs.

[These symptoms are familiar even to rustics of India. The metre of the verse is हरिणी.]

मार्जारा भृशमवनिं नखैर्लिखन्तो
लोहानां मलनिचयः सविस्रगन्धः ।
रथ्यायां शिशुरचिताश्च सेतुबन्धाः
सम्प्राप्तं जलमचिरान्निवेदयन्ति ॥५॥

Immediate rain is indicated by cats scratching the ground vehemently with their nails, accumulation of rust on iron or bronze vessels with the smell of raw meat or fish, and construction of bridges on the roads by children.

[In the third line शिशुनिचिताश्च is another reading.

The metre is प्रहर्षिणी.]

गिरयोऽञ्जनचूर्णसन्निभा यदि वा बाष्पनिरुद्धकन्दराः ।
कृकवाकुविलोचनोपमाः परिवेषाः शशिनश्च वृष्टिदाः ॥६॥

Mountains looking like heaps of collyrium or their caves wrapt in vapour, and haloes round the Moon with the colour of cock's eyes (deep red), are symptoms of rain.

[The commentator says : कृकवाकोर्जलकुक्कुटस्य यादृग् विलोचनम्...

The metre is वियोगिनी.]

विनोपघातेन पिपीलिकानामण्डोपसङ्क्रान्तिरहिव्यवायः ।
द्रुमावरोहश्च भुजङ्गमानां वृष्टेर्निमित्तानि गवां प्लुतं च ॥७॥

Other indications of rain are the following : Ants shifting their eggs without any trouble, mating of snakes, climbing down the trees by snakes and cows' leaping.

[The metre is उपजाति.]

तरुशिखरोपगताः कृकलासा गगनतलस्थितदृष्टिनिपाताः ।
यदि च गवां रविवीक्षणमूर्ध्वं निपतति वारि तदा न चिरेण ॥८॥

If the chameleons perched on the tops af trees fix their gaze on the firmament, and cows (or bulls) look up towards the Sun, there will be rain ere long.

[It is accepted by scientists that certain animals have uncanny powers of fore-knowledge of coming events. Nowadays the police department employs dogs in tracking criminals.

The metre is तामरस.]

नेच्छन्ति विनिर्गमं गृहाद्धुन्वन्ति श्रवणान् खुरानपि ।
पशवः पशुवच्च कुक्कुरा यद्यम्भः पततीति निर्दिशेत् ॥९॥

If the domestic animals like cows are unwilling to go out of the house and shake their ears and hoofs, or if the dogs behave in the same manner, it should be declared that there will be rain soon.

[The author uses the word श्रवण, which is generally used in the neuter gender, in the masculine.

The metre is वैतालीय.]

यदा स्थिता गृहपटलेषु कुक्कुरा रुदन्ति वा यदि विततं वियन्मुखाः ।
दिवा तडिद्यदि च पिनाकिदिग्भवा तदा क्षमा भवति समैव वारिणा ॥१०॥

When dogs stand on the roofs of houses, or bark continuously looking up towards the sky, or when lightning appears in the north-east at day-time, then the earth will be submerged in water.

[The metre is रुचिरा.]

शुककपोतविलोचनसन्निभो मधुनिभश्च यदा हिमदीधितिः ।
प्रतिशशी च यदा दिवि राजते पतति वारि तदा न चिरेण च ॥११॥

When the Moon appears with the red hue of the eyes of a parrot or pigeon or of honey, and when a second Moon shines in the sky, there will be immediate rain.

[The metre is द्रुतविलम्बित.]

स्तनितं निशि विद्युतो दिवा रुधिरनिभा यदि दण्डवत्स्थिताः ।
पवनः पुरतश्च शीतलो यदि सलिलस्य तदाऽऽगमो भवेत् ॥१२॥

If there be peals of thunder at night and blood-red streaks of lightning standing erect like rods at day-time, and if there be a cool breeze blowing from the east, there would soon be rain.

[The metre is वैतालीय.]

वल्लीनां गगनतलोन्मुखाः प्रवालाः
स्नायन्ते यदि जलपांसुभिर्विहङ्गाः ।
सेवन्ते यदि च सरीसृपास्तृणाग्रा-
ण्यासन्नो भवति तदा जलस्य पातः ॥१३॥

If the sprouts of creepers are turned up towards the sky, birds bathe in water or dust, and reptiles or worms are seated on the tips of grass, there will be an immediate fall of rain.

[For the sake of metre the author uses the root ष्णै in आत्मनेपद instead of परस्मैपद.

The metre is प्रहर्षिणी.]

मयूरशुकचाषचातकसमानवर्णा यदा
जपाकुसुमपङ्कजद्युतिमुषश्च सन्ध्याघनाः ।
जलोर्मिनगनक्रकच्छपवराहमीनोपमाः
प्रभूतपुटसञ्चया न तु चिरेण यच्छन्त्यपः ॥१४॥

If the clouds at dawn or twilight possess the same colour as peacocks, parrots, blue-jays or Cātaka birds, or have the lustre of roses and red lotuses and resemble in shape waves, hills, crocodiles, tortoises, or fishes, and are piled up in many layers, they will pour down rain before long.

[Here the poet uses his descriptive powers very effectively. He employs Homeric similes here.

The metre is पृथ्वी.]

पर्यन्तेषु सुधाशशाङ्कधवला मध्येऽञ्जनालित्विषः
स्निग्धा नैकपुटाः क्षरज्जलकणाः सोपानविच्छेदिनः ।
माहेन्द्रीप्रभवाः प्रयान्त्यपरतः प्राग्वाम्बुपाशोद्भवा
ये ते वारिमुचस्त्यजन्ति न चिरादम्भः प्रभूतं भुवि ॥१५॥

If the clouds are as white as chunam or the Moon at the edges as dark as collyrium, or the bees at the centre, glossy, have many layers, dropping particles of water, and are cut up like the steps of a staircase, and being formed in the east sail westward or *vice versa*, they will drench the earth ere long with plentiful rain.

[We can say that the author is engaged in writing a poem on the clouds in this section.

The metre is शार्दूलविक्रीडित.]

शक्रचापपरिघप्रतिसूर्या रोहितोऽथ तडितः परिवेषः ।
उद्गमास्तसमये यदि भानोरादिशेत्प्रचुरमम्बु तदाशु ॥१६॥

If at the time of sunrise or sunset there be a rainbow, a cross bar of clouds, a mock Sun, a straight fragmentary rainbow, flashes of lightning, and haloes round the Sun and the Moon, it should be predicted that there will be plentiful rain in the near future.

[There are three technical terms used in this verse viz. परिघ, रोहित and परिवेष. These are explained in order in XLVII—19, 20 and XXXIV—1 *infra*.

The metre is स्वागता.]

यदि तित्तिरपत्रनिभं गगनं मुदिताः प्रवदन्ति च पक्षिगणाः ।
उदयास्तमये सवितुर्द्युनिशं विसृजन्ति घना न चिरेण जलम् ॥१७॥

If the sky is variegated like the feathers of the Tittira bird, and groups of birds twitter merrily at sunrise or sunset, then the clouds will pour down rain soon by day and night respectively.

[The commentator says "अनार्षोऽयं श्लोकः" i.e. it is spurious, or one not based on ancient authority.

The metre is तोटक.]

यद्यमोघकिरणाः सहस्रगोरस्तभूधरकरा इवोच्छ्रिताः ।
भूसमं च रसते यदाम्बुदस्तन्महद्भवति वृष्टिलक्षणम् ॥१८॥

If the Sun's rays called *Amogha*—Unerring—are stretched upwards like the outstreched arms of the *Setting Mountain,* and if the clouds thunder close to the earth, they are sure signs of heavy rains.

[For the definition of *Amogha* vide XXX-11 and XLVII-20 *infra.* The expression रसते is un-Pāṇinian.

The metre is रथोद्धता.

Cf. the समाससंहिता—

पृच्छाकाले शान्ता वारुणदिक्स्था विहङ्गा वा ।
दर्पणलोहकलङ्को लवणक्लेदोऽतितीक्ष्णकिरणोऽर्कः ॥
पोप्लूयन्ते मत्स्या दिश्यैशान्यां तडिच्च दिवा ।
उत्कर्णपुच्छवदना गावस्तापोऽम्भसां पवननाशः ॥
अञ्जनपुञ्जश्यामा गिरयो बाष्पावृता यदि वा ।
यदि जलपांसुस्नानं विहगानां मैथुनं द्विजिह्वानाम् ॥
वृक्षारोहणमथवा पिपीलिकाण्डोपसङ्क्रान्तिः ।
कृकवाकुशुककपोतकलविङ्कविलोचनोऽर्केन्द्वोः ॥
स्निग्धः परिवेषो वा वियदमलं बालकनिमित्तम् ।
मधुसदृशः शीतांशुः प्रतिचन्द्रः शीतमारुतः पूर्वः ॥
ऊर्ध्वाङ्कुराश्च वल्ल्यः सद्योवर्षाय कीर्त्यन्ते ।
स्निग्धाः समसितरेखा यथाभ्रवृन्दानि कल्पितान्येव ॥
यच्छन्त्यपो मयूखा यदि चेन्दोर्वा रवेर्दीप्ताः ॥

In verse 7 *supra* the author states "द्रुमावरोहश्च भुजङ्गमानां", but in the समाससंहिता he says 'वृक्षारोहणम्'. Even the commentator interprets the former as वृक्षावरोहणम्. I feel that the reading of the समाससंहिता is the correct one inasmuch as the snakes being unable to bear the heat may climb trees in order to get some relief. It is to be noted that snakes generally do not climb trees, except some varieties.

Cf. also पराशर—

बलवत्सु महद्वर्षमल्पेष्वल्पाम्बुशीकरम् ।
मध्येषु मध्यमं ब्रूयान्निमित्तेषु निमित्तवत् ॥
उल्कानिर्घातभूकम्पपांसुवर्षाणि केतवः ।
अपसव्या ग्रहाश्चैव नित्यं वर्षासु वर्षदाः ॥]

प्रावृषि शीतकरो भृगुपुत्रात्सप्तमराशिगतः शुभदृष्टः ।
सूर्यसुतान्नवपञ्चमगो वा सप्तमगश्च जलाऽऽगमनाय ॥१६॥

If the Moon occupying the 7th house from Venus, or the 5th, 7th or 9th house from Saturn, is aspected by benefics during the rainy season, there will be rain soon.

[This verse must be read along with the first verse of this chapter. This is a popular verse often quoted by astrologers.

The metre is दोधक.]

प्रायो ग्रहाणामुदयास्तकाले समागमे मण्डलसङ्क्रमे च ।
पक्षक्षये तीक्ष्णकरायनान्ते वृष्टिर्गतेऽर्के नियमेन चार्द्राम् ॥२०॥

Generally there will be rain at the heliacal rising and setting of the planets, at the conjunction of the non-luminaries with the Moon, at their entering any of the six Maṇḍalas, at the end of a fortnight and a solstice, and undoubtedly when the Sun passes through the asterism *Ārdrā*,

[For an explanation of the *Maṇḍalas vide* IX. 10 to 20 *supra*.

The metre is उपजाति]

समागमे पतति जलं ज्ञशुक्रयोर्ज्ञजीवयोर्गुरुसितयोश्च सङ्गमे ।
यमारयोः पवनहुताशजं भयं ह्यदृष्टयोरसहितयोश्च सद्ग्रहैः ॥२१॥

There will be rain at the conjuction of Mercury and Venus, of Mercury and Jupiter, and of Jupiter and Venus. At the conjunction, however, of Mars and Saturn there will be great peril arising from wind and fire, provided they are neither conjoined with nor aspected by any of the benefics.

[What would happen if at the conjunction of benefics mentioned here, there be malefic aspect or conjunction? Evidently there cannot be a good rain.

The metre is रुचिरा.]

अग्रतः पृष्ठतो वापि ग्रहाः सूर्यावलम्बिनः ।
यदा तदा प्रकुर्वन्ति महीमेकार्णवामिव ॥२२॥

When the planets are about to be eclipsed by the Sun in front or behind (slower planets in front and faster ones behind) they help in turning the earth into an ocean, as it were.

[Since the author has already mentioned this subject in verse 20 *supra*, the special reference to combustion here suggests that when many planets get eclipsed almost simultaneously there will be a near deluge.

प्रविशति यदि खद्योतो जलदसमीपेषु रजनीषु ।
केदारपूरमधिकं वर्षति देवस्तदा न चिरात् ॥२३॥
वर्षत्यपि रटति यदा गोमायुश्च प्रदोषवेलायाम् ।
सप्ताहं दुर्दिनमपि तदा पयो नात्र सन्देहः ॥२४॥

If there be glowworms at night near the clouds, there would be rain ere long flooding all the fields. In spite of rains if jackals howl in the evening, there will not be a drop of rain, though the sky is overcast for a week at a stretch. This is certain.

[These two verses were evidently added after Bhaṭṭotpala had written his *Vivṛti* on this work. In the last verse to get at the intended meaning we have to take the negative particle 'न' with both the preceding and following words.]

———

कुसुमलताध्यायः ॥२९॥

Chapter XXIX—Prognostics from Flowers and Creepers

Regarding plants and prognostics see the 'Reader's Digest', May 1972, pp. 70-72, "Do Plants Have Feelings" by James Lincoln Collier, who refers to the experiments conducted by Backster and other scientists with the polygraph. These experiments show that even modern science has come to believe that plants have feelings, can read man's thoughts and forecast coming events.

फलकुसुमसम्प्रवृद्धिं वनस्पतीनां विलोक्य विज्ञेयम् ।
सुलभत्वं द्रव्याणां निष्पत्तिश्चापि सस्यानाम् ॥१॥

By observing the abundant growth of flowers and fruits of trees, the availability of all things in large quantities at cheap rates should be ascertained; so is the excellent growth of crops.

[The author means to say that by seeing luxuriant growth of flowers or fruits on a certain kind of trees you can predict bumper crops of a particular cereal or pulse. This fact will be clear from the next verse.]

शालेन कलमशाली रक्ताशोकेन रक्तशालिश्च ।
पाण्डूकः क्षीरिकया नीलाशोकेन सूकरकः ॥२॥

Through the (luxuriant growth of flowers and fruits of the) *Śāla* tree, the prospects of the Kalama rice are to be determined; through the red Aśoka, red rice; through the Kṣīrikā, yellow rice; and through the blue Aśoka, hog's rice.

न्यग्रोधेन तु यवकस्तिन्दुकवृद्ध्या च षष्टिको भवति ।
अश्वत्थेन ज्ञेया निष्पत्तिः सर्वसस्यानाम् ॥३॥

Through the banyan tree, the crop of yavaka should be prognosticated; through the ebony tree, the Ṣaṣṭika rice; and through the sacred tree Aśvattha, the growth of all crops in general.

[Ṣaṣṭika is a kind of paddy that ripens in 60 days. *Yavaka* is a corn different from yava. Vide Pāṇini V. 2-3.]

जम्बूभिस्तिलमाषाः शिरीषवृद्ध्या च कङ्गुनिष्पत्तिः ।
गोधूमाश्च मधूकैर्यववृद्धिः सप्तपर्णेन ॥४॥

Through the Jambū fruits (Rose-apples) the growth of sesamum and black gram is ascertained; through the excellent growth of Śirīṣa the success of Priyaṅgu (panic seed) is assessed; through the Madhūka trees, of wheat, and through the Saptaparṇa, of barley.

[Kṣīrasvāmin explains Madhūka thus : गुडवन्मधुराणि पुष्पाण्यस्य गुडपुष्पः । मधुप्रधानो द्रुमः मधुद्रुमः ।]

अतिमुक्तककुन्दाभ्यां कर्पासं सर्षपान् वदेदसनैः ।
बदरीभिश्च कुलत्थांश्चिरबिल्वेनादिशेन्मुद्गान् ॥५॥

The prospects of cotton crop are to be declared from the *Atimuktaka* tree and the *Kunda* jasmine flowers; those of mustard, from the Asana trees; those of horse-gram, from the jujube fruits; and those of green gram, from the *Cirabilva* (black silk-cotton).

अतसी वेतसपुष्पैः पलाशकुसुमैश्च कोद्रवा ज्ञेयाः ।
तिलकेन शङ्खमौक्तिकरजतान्यथ चेङ्गुदेन शणाः ॥६॥

Atasī (linseed) is to be determined from the flowers of the *Vetasa* tree; *Kodrava* (a kind of grain), from the flowers of the *Palāśa* tree; conch shells, pearls and silver, from the *Tilaka* tree; and hemp, from the *Iṅgudī* tree.

करिणश्च हस्तिकर्णैरादेश्या वाजिनोऽश्वकर्णेन ।
गावश्च पाटलाभिः कदलीभिरजाविकं भवति ॥७॥

The welfare and price of elephants should be read from the *Hastikarṇa* trees; those of horses, from the Aśvakarṇa; those of cows from the Pāṭalā trees (trumpet flower); and those of goats and sheep, from the banana plants.

चम्पककुसुमैः कनकं विद्रुमसम्पच्च बन्धुजीवेन ।
कुरवकवृद्ध्या वज्रं वैदूर्यं नन्दिकावर्तैः ॥८॥

The abundance and cheapness of gold is to be inferred from the *Campaka* flowers; those of corals, from the *Bandhujiva* flowers; those of diamonds from the growth of *Kuravaka* trees (crimson variety of amaranth); and those of *Vaidūrya* (beryl) from the *Nandikāvarta* trees.

विन्द्याच्च सिन्धुवारेण मौक्तिकं कारुकाः कुसुम्भेन ।
रक्तोत्पलेन राजा मन्त्री नीलोत्पलेनोक्तः ॥९॥

The prospects of pearls are to be ascertained from the *Sindhuvāra* tree; those of artisans, from saffron; those of the king, from red lotuses; and those of the minister, from blue lilies.

श्रेष्ठी सुवर्णपुष्पात्पद्मैर्विप्राः पुरोहिताः कुमुदैः ।
सौगन्धिकेन बलपतिरर्केण हिरण्यपरिवृद्धिः ॥१०॥

Traders' luck is judged from *Suvarṇapuṣpa* (golden flower); Brāhmaṇas, from lotuses; royal priests, from lilies; the commander-in-chief of the army, from the *Saugandhika* flower; and the increase of gold, from the Arka plant.

आम्रैः क्षेमं भल्लातकैर्भयं पीलुभिस्तथारोग्यम् ।
खदिरशमीभ्यां दुर्भिक्षमर्जुनैः शोभना वृष्टिः ॥११॥

One should infer the happiness of mankind from mangoes; danger, from Bhallātaka; health, from Pīlu; famine from the growth of *Khadira* and *Śamī* trees; and good rain, from the *Arjuna* trees.

पिचुमन्दनागकुसुमैः सुभिक्षमथ मारुतः कपित्थेन ।
निचुलेनावृष्टिभयं व्याधिभयं भवति कुटजेन ॥१२॥

From the flowers of the Neem tree and *Nāgakesara*, abundance of food grains can be predicted; from the wood-apple, wind; from the *Nicula* tree, danger of drought; and from the *Kuṭaja* tree, threat of diseases.

दूर्वाकुशकुसुमाभ्यामिक्षुर्वह्निश्च कोविदारेण ।
श्यामालताभिवृद्ध्या बन्धक्यो वृद्धिमायान्ति ॥१३॥

The thriving of sugar-cane is presaged by the flowers of *Dūrvā* grass and the sacred grass; outbreak of fires, by the *Kovidāra* tree; and the increase and prosperity of concubines, by the growth of the Śyāmā creeper.

यस्मिन् काले स्निग्धनिश्छिद्रपत्राः सन्दृश्यन्ते वृक्षगुल्मा लताश्च ।
तस्मिन्वृष्टिः शोभना सम्प्रदिष्टा रूक्षैश्छिद्रैरल्पमम्भः प्रदिष्टम् ॥१४॥

When trees, bushes and creepers are seen fully packed with green glossy leaves without any interspace, good rains are to be predicted; whereas if the leaves be rough leaving inter-spaces, very little rain should be declared.

[The commentator was silent upto the previous verse about ancient authorities, and now he quotes पराशर under this Śloka :

अच्छिद्रपत्राः सुस्निग्धाः फलपुष्पसमन्विताः ।
निर्दिशन्ति शुभं वृक्षा विपरीतं विगर्हिताः ॥

It is possible that Bhaṭṭotpala had no access to any ancient texts bearing on this subject except the one verse quoted here.

The metre is शालिनी.].

———

सन्ध्यालक्षणाध्यायः ॥३०॥

Chapter XXX—Indications at Dawn and Twilight

अर्द्धास्तमितानुदितात् सूर्यादिस्पष्टभं नभो यावत् ।
तावत् सन्ध्याकालश्चिह्नै रेतैः फलं चास्मिन् ॥१॥

The interval between the periods when the Sun is half-set and when the stars have not yet become distinct, is called a juncture i.e. the evening *twilight*. Similarly that between the periods when the stars have become dim or indistinct and when the Sun is half-risen is called *dawn*. The effects—good and bad—of the *juncture* are to be judged from the following indications.

[Cf. गर्ग—

अहोरात्रस्य यः सन्धिः सा च सन्ध्या प्रकीर्तिता ।
द्विनाडिका भवेत्साधुर्यावदाज्योतिदर्शनम् ॥

According to याज्ञवल्क्य सन्ध्या lasts for one मुहूर्त only.]

मृगशकुनिपवनपरिवेषपरिधिपरिघाभ्रवृक्षसुरचापैः ।
गन्धर्वनगररविकरदण्डरजःस्नेहवर्णैश्च ॥२॥

The effects of *Sandhyā* i.e. juncture, should be determined through the deer, birds, wind, halo round the Sun and the Moon, mock Sun or Moon, a cross-bar of clouds on the Sun's disc at a *juncture*, tree-shaped clouds and rain-bow as well as through the glossiness of an apparent town in the sky, Sun's rays, a rod-like formation caused by the combination of solar rays, clouds and wind, and dust.

[The commentator takes the word स्नेहवर्णैः —by the oily appearance — as applicable to each member of the compound गन्धर्व··· रजसाम्. I may suggest another interpretation by adding स्नेहवर्णैः to the Dvandva as another member. It should then mean : Through ...dust and the colours of oils.]

भैरवमुच्चैर्विरुवन् मृगोऽसकृद्ग्रामघातमाचष्टे ।
रविदीप्तो दक्षिणतो महास्वनः सैन्यघातकरः ॥३॥

A wild animal (or deer) dreadfully howling aloud repeatedly, indicates the destruction of the village. The same facing the Sun, standing to the south of an army and crying aloud, foretells the annihilation of the army.

अपसव्ये सङ्ग्रामः सव्ये सेनासमागमः शान्ते ।
मृगचक्रे पवने वा सन्ध्यायां मिश्रगे वृष्टिः ॥४॥

If at a juncture (dawn or twilight) a flock of deer (or animals) or the wind be to the left of an army (and be facing the Sun), a war would break out; if it be to the right of the army, cries pleasantly (and is not facing the Sun), the two armies would come together; if it be of mixed characteristics, there would be rain.

[The mixed conditions are (i) The flock being to the left of the army but cries pleasantly and is not facing the Sun, and (ii) it being to the right of the army but facing the Sun.]

दीप्तमृगाण्डजविरुता प्राक् सन्ध्या देशनाशमाख्याति ।
दक्षिणदिक्स्थैर्विरुता ग्रहणाय पुरस्य दीप्तास्यैः ॥५॥

If at dawn there be awkward cries of birds and beasts facing the Sun, it forebodes the destruction of the country. If these with their faces glowing in the sun send forth their cries, standing to the south of a city, the latter will be captured by the enemies.

गृहतरुतोरणमथने सपांसुलोष्टोत्करेऽनिले प्रबले ।
भैरवरावे रूक्षे खगपातिनि चाशुभा सन्ध्या ॥६॥

A dawn or twilight would be of disastrous consequences, if at the time a strong and rough wind be blowing, making a howling noise, crushing houses, trees and arches, raising heaps of dust and clouds of earth, and throwing down birds from the sky.

मन्दपवनावघट्टितचलितपलाशद्रुमा विपवना वा ।
मधुरस्वरशान्तविहङ्गमृगरुता पूजिता सन्ध्या ॥७॥

A dawn or twilight would prove auspicious and beneficial, if the leaves of trees be slightly shaken by the impact of gentle breeze or if there be no stir in the wind at all and if animals and birds, not facing the Sun, send forth their melodious cries.

[*Dīpta* and *Śānta* are technical terms. The former means the direction illumined or heated by the Sun, and the latter, just the opposite. So in the forenoon the west and the creatures standing in that direction become *Dīpta*, while the east and those standing there become *Śānta* in the afternoon. For another definition of *Dīpta* *vide* LXXXVI-12 *infra*.]

सन्ध्याकाले स्निग्धा दण्डतडिन्मत्स्यपरिधिपरिवेषाः ।
सुरपतिचापैरावतरविकिरणाश्चाशु वृष्टिकराः ॥८॥

The following things being glossy at a *juncture*, betoken immediate rain : Daṇḍa (a rod-like formation caused by the combination of sun-beams, clouds and wind), lightning, fish-like formations of clouds, a mock sun, a halo, a rainbow, *Airāvata* (a long fragmentary rainbow) and the sun's rays.

[There are many technical terms in this stanza. For *Daṇḍa vide* verse 16 *infra*; for *Paridhi*, and *Airāvata vide* XLVII 19.20; for *Pariveṣa vide* XXXIV-1.]

विच्छिन्नविषमविध्वस्तविकृतकुटिलापसव्यपरिवृत्ताः ।
तनुह्रस्वविकलकलुषाश्च विग्रहावृष्टिदाः किरणाः ॥९॥

The Sun's rays, which are broken off, unequal, discoloured, unnatural, crooked, turned anti-clockwise, slender, short, impaired and soiled (not bright) cause war and drought.

[In the second line there is a metrical error as ह्र in ह्रस्व is taken as a simple consonant while it is actually a conjunct one. According to Piṅgala it is optionally treated as single consonant.]

उद्द्योतिनः प्रसन्ना ऋजवो दीर्घाः प्रदक्षिणावर्ताः
किरणाः शिवाय जगतो वितमस्के नभसि भानुमतः ॥१०॥

The Sun's rays, which are brilliant, pure, straight, long and turned in a clock-wise direction, and which are seen in a bright sky, presage prosperity to the world.

शुक्लाः करा दिनकृतो दिवाविमध्यान्तगामिनः स्निग्धाः ।
अव्युच्छिन्ना ऋजवो वृष्टिकरास्ते त्वमोघाख्याः ॥११॥

The Sun's rays which are white, glossy, unbroken and straight, and which pervade the entire region of the firmament (from the beginning to the end), are termed *Amogha* '*Unerring*'. Such rays indicate good rain.

कल्माषबभ्रुकपिला विचित्रमाञ्जिष्ठहरितशबलाभाः ।
त्रिदिवानुबन्धिनोऽवृष्टयेऽल्पभयदास्तु सप्ताहात् ॥१२॥

Rays that are greyish, tawny, russet, variegated, madder-hued, green and spotted, and stretch all over the sky (and are turned upwards) are productive of drought and some danger after a week.

[In the first line शबला वा is another reading.]

ताम्रा बलपतिमृत्युं पीतारुणसन्निभाश्च तद्व्यसनम् ।
हरिताः पशुसस्यवधं धूमसवर्णा गवां नाशम् ॥१३॥

माञ्जिष्ठाभाः शस्त्राग्निसम्भ्रमं बभ्रवः पवनवृष्टिम् ।
भस्मसदृशास्त्ववृष्टिं तनुभावं शबलकल्माषाः ॥१४॥

Copper-coloured rays of the Sun bring about a general's death; yellow and rosy ones, his misery (or danger from diseases); green ones, the destruction of cattle and crops; smoky ones, the ruin of cows; madder-coloured rays cause trouble through clash of arms and fires; tawny ones, stormy rain; ash-coloured ones, drought; and spotted and greyish ones, slight rain (or emaciation).

[रुग्व्यसनम् is another reading for तद्व्यसनम्. The commentator interprets तनुभावं as *slightness of rain* by supplying the word वृष्टेः. Had it been the author's intention, he would have plainly used the expression तनुवृष्टिम् without harming the metre. Hence I feel that the expression should mean general debility or emaciation of people. In this section the author shows his familiarity with the use of several colours viz. शुक्ल, कल्माष, बभ्रु, कपिल, विचित्र, माञ्जिष्ठ, हरित, शबल, ताम्र, पीत, अरुण, धूम, the colour of बंधूकपुष्प and अञ्जन. Of these the primary colours are white, red, yellow, black, blue and green.]

बन्धूकपुष्पाञ्जनचूर्णसन्निभं सान्ध्यं रजोऽभ्येति यदा दिवाकरम् ।
लोकस्तदा रोगशतैर्निपीड्यते शुक्लं रजो लोकविवृद्धिशान्तये ॥१५॥

If, at a juncture, dust coloured like the Bandhūka flower (blood red) or like the collyrium powder goes up towards the Sun, mankind will then be afflicted by innumerable diseases, whereas white dust, at the time, betokens prosperity, peace and happiness to mankind.

[Cf. पराशर—

बन्धुजीवनिकाशेन तपनीयनिभेन वा ।
उदये रजसा सूर्यः संवृतः शस्त्रमावहेत् ॥
शङ्खचूर्णनिकाशेन रजसा संवृतो रविः ।
राज्ञो विजयमाख्याति वृद्धिं जनपदस्य च ॥

The metre is इन्द्रवंशा.]

रविकिरणजलदमरुतां सङ्घातो दण्डवत्स्थितो दण्डः ।
स विदिक्स्थितो नृपाणामशुभो दिक्षु द्विजादीनाम् ॥१६॥

The combination of the rays of the Sun, clouds and wind, appearing in the form of a *rod*, is called *Daṇḍa*. When the *Daṇḍa* appears in the intermediate directions, harm would come to the kings, while in the cardinal directions, it forebodes evil to Brāhmaṇas, Kṣatriyas, Vaiśyas and Śūdras respectively.

[The cardinal points are reckoned generally from the north in the scheme of the classes. According to other commentators, the rod appearing in any cardinal direction is inauspicious to all twice-born classes in general.]

शस्त्रभयातङ्ककरो दृष्टः प्राङ्मध्यसन्धिषु दिनस्य ।
शुक्लाद्यो विप्रादीन् यदभिमुखस्तां निहन्ति दिशम् ॥१७॥

The Rod seen at dawn, noon and twilight causes danger from weapons i.e., war, and diseases. The same with white, red, yellow and dark colours destroys the four classes in order. It also destroys the particular direction which it faces.

[The commentator says that that part of the Rod which is close to the Sun is called its bottom and the other end its face.]

दधिसदृशाग्रो नीलो भानुच्छादी खमध्यगोऽभ्रतरुः ।
पीतच्छुरिताश्च घना घनमूला भूरिवृष्टिकराः ॥१८॥

If a blue cloud with its top resembling curds, being situated at the Zenith of the sky, screens the Sun, it takes the name of *Abhrataru—Cloud-Tree*. If the clouds are tinged yellow, having a dense bottom, they would produce copious rains.

[The simile दधिसदृशाग्र is tell-tale and happy. To enjoy this one must have seen thick curds. Here the commentator does not say specifically that अभ्रतरु is the name of a particular formation of clouds, but the author's intention is quite clear. Both the types of clouds mentioned here are good for rain.]

अनुलोमगेऽभ्रवृक्षे शमं गते यायिनो नृपस्य वधः ।
बालतरुप्रतिरूपिणि युवराजामात्ययोर्मृत्युः ॥१९॥

If a Cloud-Tree moving in the same direction behind a marching king, disappears suddenly, the king will be killed; while if the same in the form of a young tree (plant) disappears likewise, the prince (heir-apparent) and minister will die.

कुवलयवैडूर्याम्बुजकिञ्जल्काभा प्रभञ्जनोन्मुक्ता ।
सन्ध्या करोति वृष्टिं रविकिरणोद्भासिता सद्यः ॥२०॥

A twilight which has the lustre of blue lily, beryl or lotus-filaments, which is free from strong winds and which is brightened by the Sun's rays, produces rain the same day.

अशुभाकृतिघनगन्धर्वनगरनीहारधूमपांसुयुता ।
प्रावृषि करोत्यवग्रहमन्यर्त्तौ शस्त्रकोपकरी ॥२१॥

A twilight which possesses clouds of inauspicious forms (like those of an ass, a camel, a headless trunk, a crow, a cat etc.), an aerial city, fog, smoke and dust, produces drought in the rainy season, and clash of arms in other seasons.

शिशिरादिषु वर्णाः शोणपीतसितचित्रपद्मरुधिरनिभाः ।
प्रकृतिभवाः सन्ध्यायां स्वर्त्तौ शस्ता विकृतिरन्या ॥२२॥

In the six seasons beginning with *Śiśira* or winter the natural colours of the sky at twilight are in order red, yellow, white, variegated, lotus-coloured (red and white) and crimson (blood-red). Each colour at twilight is beneficial in its own season, and harmful if it is contrary.

[Cf. गर्ग—

वसन्ते मधुवर्णाभाऽथवा रुधिरसन्निभा ।
ग्रीष्मे श्वेता रजोध्वस्ता पांसुवर्णा च शस्यते ॥
नीललोहितशुक्लाभा सन्ध्या वर्षासु वार्षिका ।
माञ्जिष्ठवर्णा शरदि पीयूषाभा च शस्यते ॥
हेमन्ते बभ्रुवर्णा च पिङ्गला चापि पूजिता ।
शिशिरे शोणवर्णा च सन्ध्या क्षेमसुखप्रदा ॥
स्निग्धा प्रसन्ना विमला सप्रभा नाकुलापि वा ।
सन्ध्या यथर्तुवर्णाभा शान्तद्विजमृगा शुभा ॥]

आयुधभृन्नररूपं छिन्नाभ्रं परभयाय रविगामि ।
सितखपुरेऽर्काक्रान्ते पुरलाभो भेदने नाशः ॥२३॥

If a broken cloud presents the appearance of an armed person and is situated close to the Sun, there will be danger to the king from enemies. If a white aerial city (formed by clouds) is approached by the Sun, the besieged town will be victorious; while if it is cut into two by the Sun, the town will be destroyed.

[Bhaṭṭotpala interprets the second line of the verse differently: अर्काक्रान्ते is rendered by him as the aerial city 'by which the Sun is attacked', but the natural interpretation would be—'which is attacked by the Sun'. For, we know that a city is attacked or besieged by an enemy king. पुरलाभः is also rendered differently by him : येन पुरं नगरमाक्रान्तं तस्य लाभो भवति. This is a far-fetched construction. Here पुरलाभ simply means, the victory of the defenders of the city. In the next sentence he reverts to the natural construction as, "अर्केण यदि मध्यात् खपुरं भिद्यते तदा पुरस्य नाशः ।"]

सितसितान्तघनावरणं रवेर्भवति वृष्टिकरं यदि सव्यतः ।
यदि च वीरणगुल्मनिभैर्घनैर्दिवसभर्तुरदीप्तदिगुद्भवैः ॥२४॥

If the Sun be screened on the right side by clouds that are white or white-fringed, there would be rain. The same result would ensue, if he be screened likewise by clouds which resemble bushes of Andropogon grass, and which arise in an unblasted (not heated by the Sun) quarter.

[The metre is द्रुतविलम्बित in this and the following two verses].

नृपविपत्तिकरः परिघः सितः क्षतजतुल्यवपुर्बलकोपकृत् ।
कनकरूपधरो बलवृद्धिदः सवितुरुद्गमकालसमुत्थितः ॥२५॥

A white cross-bar of clouds appearing at sunrise will be disastrous to the king; a blood-red one will ruin the army through internal dissensions; and one with a golden hue will bestow prosperity and victory on the army.

उभयपार्श्वगतौ परिघौ रवेः प्रचुरतोयकरौ वपुषान्वितौ ।
अथ समस्तककुप्परिचारिणः परिघयोऽस्ति कणोऽपि न वारिणः ॥२६॥

If there be mock suns touching the sun on both sides, there would be abundant rain. Should they surround the Sun on all the four sides, not a drop of rain would fall.

ध्वजातपत्रपर्वतद्विपाश्वरूपधारिणः ।
जयाय सन्ध्ययोर्घना रणाय रक्तसन्निभाः ॥२७॥

पलालधूमसञ्चयस्थितोपमा बलाहकाः ।
बलान्यरूक्षमूर्तयो विवर्धयन्ति भूभृताम् ॥२८॥

विलम्बिनो द्रुमोपमाः खरारुणप्रकाशिनः ।
घनाः शिवाय सन्ध्ययोः पुरोपमाः शुभावहाः ॥२९॥

At the two junctures the clouds that resemble a banner, umbrella, mountain, elephant, and horse conduce to the victory of kings as well as the people; while blood-red ones tend to war. Those that look like the mass of smoke rising from straw-fire and are smooth in appearance, cause the prosperity of the armies of kings. Those clouds which hang low, resemble trees, shine brightly with their deep red colour or look like towns, will bestow prosperity.

[The metre is प्रमाणिका.]

दीप्तविहङ्गशिवामृगघुष्टा दण्डरजःपरिघादियुता च ।
प्रत्यहमर्कविकारयुता वा देशनरेशसुभिक्षवधाय ॥३०॥

At a juncture if birds, jackals and beasts that face the Sun cry out, if there be the *Rod*, dust, cross-bar and the like, or if the Sun appears in an unnatural form everyday, the country, king and the crops would be destroyed.

[Cf. पराशर—

"अथ सन्ध्यासु द्वियोजनान्तरे देशे सद्यः फलमादिशेत् । रश्मिसंयुक्तायां तु सप्तरात्रनिवाते निर्मलस्निग्धायां शान्तमृगद्विजायां प्रसन्नायामनुपहतायां सन्ध्यायां योगक्षेमं विन्द्याद्विपर्ययं विपरीतायाम् । श्वेतायां वसुवृद्धि तस्यामेव परिमण्डलायां रक्तायाम् । हरितायां शस्त्रकोपम् । माञ्जिष्ठायामग्निं पीतायां चतुःपाद्रोगं श्यावायां चौरतो भयम् । नीलपीतायामीतिं गवाम् । हरितालवर्णायां प्रथमामात्यस्य शस्त्रेण वधम् । आम्रकोरकवर्णायां वर्षं नीलरक्तायामवग्रहं च कृष्णायामवर्षम् । श्यावकृष्णगौर्यां पशुघातं विन्द्यात् । वातं कपिलायामस्तमितमात्रे सूर्ये याऽतिमात्रप्रकाशा स्यात् प्रभा सा नाम तस्यां वर्षं विन्द्यात् । प्रत्युषसि तद्रूपायामेव राज्ञः सेनापतेर्वा वधः स्यात् । महावर्षं रूप्यवर्णायां च तस्यामेव ताम्रमध्यायां कृष्णायामनृतौ वर्षमृताववग्रहम् । तथा पीतमाञ्जिष्ठा अग्निजीविनां वधाय । लोहितश्यावा चौरवृद्धये । सर्वा एव च त्रिगात्राः पञ्चरागा वा युद्धाय यच्चालोहितेनैव लिम्पेत्तस्य वधाय । स्निग्धा तु गौरी योगक्षेमाय भवति चात्र ।

प्रतिसूर्यः शक्रधनुर्दण्डकः परिवेषणम् ।
तथैरावतमत्स्याश्च स्निग्धा ये चार्करश्मयः ॥
विद्युतो भूरिकाराश्च वर्णा ये च प्रदक्षिणाः ।
सन्ध्यासु यदि दृश्यन्ते सद्यो वर्षणलक्षणम् ॥

Cf. also काश्यप—

दिनरात्र्यन्तरं सन्ध्या सूर्यस्यार्द्धं प्रदृश्यते ।
यावच्च तावदारभ्य शुभा वाप्यशुभापि वा ॥
नभोऽमलं शुभदिशः पद्मारुणसमप्रभाः ।
मारुतो वाति सुरभिः सुखदो मृदुशीतलः ॥
एषा सन्ध्या शुभा ज्ञेया विपरीताऽशुभा स्मृता ।
रूक्षा च सविकारार्का क्रव्यादखरनादिता ॥
स्निग्धा दण्डपरीवेषा सुरचापविभूषिता ।
क्षिप्रं वर्षप्रदा सन्ध्या जयाऽऽरोग्यविवृद्धिदा ॥

The metre is दोधक.]

प्राची तत्क्षणमेव नक्तमपरा सन्ध्या त्र्यहाद्वा फलं
सप्ताहात्परिवेषरेणुपरिघाः कुर्वन्ति सद्यो न चेत् ।
तद्वत्सूर्यकरेन्द्रकार्मुकतडित्प्रत्यर्कमेघानिला-
स्तस्मिन्नेव दिनेऽष्टमेऽथ विहगाः सप्ताहपाका मृगाः ॥३१॥

Characteristics of a dawn produce their effects—good or bad—at the same moment (i.e., immediately); of the evening, on the same night or in three days; halos, dust and cross-bar of clouds, in a week if not the same day; the Sun-beams (*Amogha* and the like), rainbow, lightning, mock-sun, clouds and wind act in the same manner; birds produce the effects on the 8th day, if not the same day; and beasts, in a week.

[The metre is शार्दूलविक्रीडित.]

एकं दीप्त्या योजनं भाति सन्ध्या विद्युद्भासा षट् प्रकाशीकरोति ।
पञ्चाब्दानां गर्जितं याति शब्दो नास्तीयत्ता केचिदुल्कानिपाते ॥३२॥

A twilight illuminates (and has effect over) a distance of one *yojana* with its gleam; lightning illumines six *yojanas* with its flash; the peal of thunder extends over five *yojanas*; and according to some (i.e., Devala and others), there is no limit for the effect of the fall of meteors.

[Cf. देवल—

सन्ध्या तु योजनं याति विद्युद्भासा षडेव हि ।
मेघशब्दस्तु पञ्चानां योजनानां फलप्रदः ॥
उल्का सर्वत्र फलदा शुभा वाप्यशुभापि वा ॥

The metre is शालिनी.]

प्रत्यर्कसंज्ञः परिधिस्तु तस्य त्रियोजनाभः परिघस्य पञ्च ।
षट्पञ्चदृश्यं परिवेषचक्रं दशामरेशस्य धनुर्विभाति ॥३३॥

The Sun's halo called mock-sun spreads its lustre (as well as influence) over three *yojanas*; a cross-bar of clouds (*Parigha*), over five *yojanas*; a halo, over five or six *yojanas*; and the rainbow shows its effect and lustre for ten *yojanas*.

[The metre is उपजाति.]

दिग्दाहलक्षणाध्यायः ॥३१॥

Chapter XXXI—Glow at the Horizon

दाहो दिशां राजभयाय पीतो देशस्य नाशाय हुताशवर्णः ।
यश्चारुणः स्यादपसव्यवायुः सस्यस्य नाशं स करोति दृष्टः ॥१॥

The fire observed in the quarters, if yellow, forebodes peril to the king; if fiery in colour, the ruin of the country; and if rubicund and accompanied by wind from the left, it will cause destruction of the crops.

[The metre is इन्द्रवज्रा.]

योऽतीव दीप्त्या कुरुते प्रकाशं छायामपि व्यञ्जयतेऽर्कवद्यः ।
राज्ञो महद्वेदयते भयं स शस्त्रप्रकोपं क्षतजानुरूपः ॥२॥

That fake fire which creates illumination and reveals shadow also as the Sun does, owing to its excessive brilliance, portends great calamity to the sovereign. A blood-red one indicates sanguinary wars.

[The fire in the quarters is not a genuine one. It is only an apparent fire.

The metre is इन्द्रवज्रा.]

प्राक् क्षत्रियाणां सनरेश्वराणां प्राग्दक्षिणे शिल्पिकुमारपीडा ।
याम्ये सहोग्रैः पुरुषैस्तु वैश्या दूताः पुनर्भूप्रमदाश्च कोणे ॥३॥

पश्चात्तु शूद्राः कृषिजीविनश्च चौरास्तुरङ्गैः सह वायुदिक्स्थे ।
पीडां व्रजन्त्युत्तरतश्च विप्राः पाखण्डिनो वाणिजकाश्च शार्व्याम् ॥४॥

The fire seen in the east portends evil to Kṣatriyas and to the rulers; in the south-east, to smiths (or artisans) and princes; in the south, to the Vaiśyas and cruel men; in the south-west, to messengers (or ambassadors) and remarried young widows; in the west, to Śūdras and agriculturists; in the north-west, to thieves and horses; in the north, to Brāhmaṇas; and in the north-east, to heretics and merchants.

[पुनर्भू is a virgin widow who is remarried :

"पुनर्भूः सोह्यते भूयो याऽक्षतत्वाद्यथाविधि ॥"

Cf. काश्यप—

प्राच्यां दिशि प्रदीप्तायां श्रेणीनां भयमादिशेत् ।
आग्नेय्यां तु कुमाराणां वैश्यानां दक्षिणे तथा ॥
नैर्ऋत्यां च स्त्रियो हन्ति शूद्रान् पश्चिमतस्तथा ।
वायव्यायां चौरभयं विप्राणामुत्तरे तथा ।
पाखण्डिवणिजां पीडा ह्यैशानी यदि दीप्यते ॥

The metre is the same as before.]

नभः प्रसन्नं विमलानि भानि प्रदक्षिणं वाति सदागतिश्च ।
दिशा च दाहः कनकावदातो हिताय लोकस्य सपार्थिवस्य ॥५॥

A calm sky, glossy and bright stars, breeze blowing in a clock-wise direction, and the blaze in the horizon with the colour of gold, are for the prosperity of mankind and kings.

[This verse, noted for its naturalness and simplicity, proves that the author was an in-born poet worthy of being ranked with Kālidāsa. This reminds us of the latter's verse in the कुमारसम्भव Canto I-23.

The metre is उपेन्द्रवज्रा.]

———

भूकम्पलक्षणाध्यायः ॥३२॥

Chapter XXXII—Signs of Earthquake

क्षितिकम्पमाहुरेके बृहदन्तर्जलनिवासिसत्त्वकृतम् ।
भूभारखिन्नदिग्गजविश्रामसमुद्भवं चान्ये ॥१॥

Some Sages hold that an earthquake is brought about by the huge animals living in the waters of the ocean, while others (like Garga) opine that it is the result of the rest (i e. heaving) that is resorted to by the elephants of the quarters that are tired by the weight of the earth.

[Cf. काश्यप—

वारुणस्योपरि पृथ्वी सशैलवनकानना ।
स्थिता जलजसत्त्वाश्च सक्षोभाश्चालयन्ति ताम् ॥

also गर्ग—

चत्वारः पृथिवीं नागा धारयन्ति चतुर्दिशम् ।
वर्धमानः सुवृद्धश्चातिवृद्धश्च पृथुश्रवाः ॥
वर्धमानो दिशं पूर्वां सुवृद्धो दक्षिणां दिशम् ।
पश्चिमामतिवृद्धस्तु सौम्याशां तु पृथुश्रवाः ॥
नियोगाद् ब्रह्मणो ह्येते धारयन्ति वसुन्धराम् ।
ते श्वसन्ति यदा शान्ताः स वायुः श्वसितो महान् ॥
वेगान्महीं चालयन्ति भावाभावाय देहिनाम् ॥]

अनिलोऽनिलेन निहतः क्षितौ पतन् सस्वनं करोत्यन्ये ।
केचित्त्वदृष्टकारितमिदमन्ये प्राहुराचार्याः ॥२॥

Yet other Sages like Vasiṣṭha declare that it is caused by the atmospheric wind colliding with another and falling to the earth with a booming sound. There are still others like Vṛddhagarga who maintain that it is occasioned by some unseen power (or by the result of the good and bad deeds of human beings). There are some more Sages such as Parāśara who declare as follows :

[The opinions cited in this verse have a semblance of being scientific.

Cf. वसिष्ठ—

यदा तु बलवान्वायुरन्तरिक्षानिलाहतः ।
पतत्याशु स निर्घातो भवेदनिलसम्भवः ॥

तस्य योगान्निपततश्चलत्यन्याहता क्षितिः ।
सोऽभिघातसमुत्थः स्यात्सनिर्घातमहीचलः ॥

The word अदृष्ट in the text also means *fortune*, which is nothing but the resultant of man's *Karma* or action, in previous life.

Vide वृद्धगर्ग—

प्रजा धर्मरता यत्र तत्र कम्पं शुभं वदेत् ।
जनानां श्रेयसे नित्यं विसृजन्ति सुरोत्तमाः ॥

विपरीतस्थिता यत्र जनास्तत्राशुभं तथा ।
विसृजन्ति प्रजानां तु दुःखशोकाभिवृद्धये ॥]

गिरिभिः पुरा सपक्षैर्वसुधा प्रपतद्भिरुत्पतद्भिश्च ।
आकम्पिता पितामहमाहामरसदसि सव्रीडम् ॥३॥

भगवन्नाम ममैतत्त्वया कृतं यदचलेति तन्न तथा ।
क्रियतेऽचलैश्चलद्भिः शक्ताहं नास्य खेदस्य ॥४॥

तस्याः सगद्गदगिरं किञ्चित्स्फुरिताधरं विनतमीषत् ।
साश्रुविलोचनमाननमालोक्य पितामहः प्राह ॥५॥

मन्युं हरेन्द्र धात्र्याः क्षिप कुलिशं शैलपक्षभङ्गाय ।
शक्रः कृतमित्युक्त्वा मा भैरिति वसुमतीमाह ॥६॥

किन्त्वनिलदहनसुरपतिवरुणाः सदसत्फलावबोधार्थम् ।
प्राग् द्वित्रिचतुर्भागेषु दिननिशोः कम्पयिष्यन्ति ॥७॥

In bygone days the Earth, being shaken severely by the winged mountains which flew up and came down heavily, spoke bashfully to the Creator (Brahman) in the assembly of the Gods — "My lord, the name you have given me, namely *Acalā* (Immovable), is falsified by the flying mountains, and I am unable to put up with this suffering." Hearing these words of Mother Earth who was choked with tears and whose lower lip quivered slightly, and observing her down-cast face with tears flowing from her eyes, the Creator spoke thus: "Indra, remove this humiliation of Mother Earth; throw your thunder-bolt and chop off the wings of the mountains." At this, Indra said, 'So be it', and consoled her with the words "Do not fear; but Wind, Fire, myself and Varuṇa will shake you in the four parts of the day and night put together respectively in order to reveal the good and bad effects of actions to the world."

[The story occurring in this section has come down from the Ṛgvedic time to the period of the Kāvyas. In the Indrasūkta (Ṛg. II. 2.2.) Indra is credited to have fixed firmly the earth that was often quaking. Kālidāsa too alludes in his *Kumārasambhava* I-20 to this story. I feel that it is an allegory containing the principles of the early formation of the various celestial bodies including the earth. See also the Rāmāyaṇa V. I. 23-27. सव्रीडा is another reading for सव्रीडम्. Like Kālidāsa our author too uses some obsolete forms, as he employs the expression मा भैः for मा भैषीः.

The commentator refers to another interpretation of the last verse, according to which, both the day and night are divided into four parts each and the four deities mentioned cause earthquake in order in the four parts of the day as well as of the night. This wrong interpretation, says he, is due to the observation made in other Śāstras as follows :—

रात्रौ दिवा च पूर्वाह्णे वायव्यः कम्प उच्यते ।
मध्याह्ने चार्द्धरात्रे च हौताशः कम्प उच्यते ।।
दिवारात्रौ तृतीयेंऽशे माहेन्द्रश्चाभिगीयते ।
चतुर्थे वर्तमानेंऽशे वारुणं निर्दिशेद् बुधः ।।

Against this he quotes पराशर thus :

"तत्र चतुर्षु चतुर्भागेषु दिवानक्तमनिलानलेन्द्रवरुणज कम्पक्रमं विन्द्यात् ।।" also "अद्रिजमतः परं भयमपनयाम्यनिलानलाम्बुपतिमदभिसृष्टाः कम्पाः कदाचिज्जगति हिताहितवेदिनो भविष्यन्तीत्यर्कचन्द्रग्रहणग्रहविकृतचारजांश्च कम्पानाहुः ।।" This shows that earthquakes are caused by eclipses of the luminaries, unnatural phenomena occurring in the planets and special movements of the heavenly bodies.

Cf. also गर्ग—

कृत्वा चतुर्धाहोरात्रं द्विधाहोऽथ द्विधा निशम् ।
देवताश्रययोगाच्च चतुर्धा भगणं तथा ।।
पूर्वे दिनार्द्धे वायव्य आग्नेयोऽर्द्धे तु पश्चिमे ।
ऐन्द्रः पूर्वे च रात्र्यर्द्धे पश्चिमार्द्धे तु वारुणः ।।
चत्वार एवमेते स्युरहोरात्रविकल्पजाः ।।
निमित्तभूता लोकानामुल्कानिर्घातभूचलाः ।]

चत्वार्यर्यम्णाद्यान्यादित्यं मृगशिरोऽश्वयुक् चेति ।
मण्डलमेतद्वायव्यमस्य रूपाणि सप्ताहात् ॥८॥

धूमाकुलीकृताशे नभसि नभस्वान् रजः क्षिपन् भौमम् ।
विरुजन् द्रुमांश्च विचरति रविरपटुकरावभासी च ॥९॥

वायव्ये भूकम्पे सस्याम्बुवनौषधीक्षयोऽभिहितः ।
श्वयथुश्वासोन्मादज्वरकासभवो वणिक्पीडा ॥१०॥

रूपायुधभृद्वैद्याः स्त्रीकविगान्धर्वपण्यशिल्पिजनाः ।
पीड्यन्ते सौराष्ट्रककुरुमगधदशार्णमत्स्याश्च ॥११॥

The stellar circle or group presided over by the Wind-God consists of the seven constellations *viz.*. Uttaraphalgunī, Hasta, Citrā, Svāti, Punarvasu, Mṛgaśīrṣa and Aśvinī, (this means that if there is an earth-quake under any of these seven asterisms, it should be construed as caused by wind). The following symptoms of this circle will appear a week in advance : The quarters will be covered with smoke; a strong wind will blow throwing the dust of the earth breaking down trees; and the Sun will not shine brightly. The effects of an earth-quake of the Wind Circle are the following: Destruction of crops, water, forests and herbs, outbreak of swellings, asthma, lunacy, fever and phlegmatic affections, and trouble to the trading class, courtesans, warriors, physicians, women, poets, musicians, traders, (or commodities). artisans, the Saurāṣṭras, Kurus, Magadha country, Daśārṇa region and the Matsyas.

[Cf. गर्ग—

प्रथमेऽह्नि चतुर्भागे निर्घातोल्कामहीचलाः ।
सौम्यादित्यार्यम्णहस्तचित्रास्वात्यश्विनीषु च ॥
भवन्त्यनिलजाः सर्वे लक्षणान्यवधारय ।
धूमव्याप्ता दिशः सर्वा नभस्वान् प्रक्षिपन् रजः ॥
द्रुमांश्च भञ्जंश्चरति रविस्तपति शीतलः ।
सप्तमेऽहनि कम्पः स्याद्भूमेरनिलसम्भवः ॥

Here the commentator makes a significant observation to the effect that our author has adopted the views of Sage Garga and Ṛṣiputra which differ from those of Vṛddhagarga, Parāśara and Kaśyapa. From this it becomes evident that Garga and Vṛddhagarga are two different persons.

Vide पराशर—

वायव्याभिजिद्वासवाश्वार्यम्णहस्तत्वाष्ट्रेष्वनिलोऽभिकम्पयन् परुषपवननिपातै-

स्तरुकुसुमशष्पसस्यान्युच्छेदयति । उन्मादश्वासश्वयथुविषमज्वरातङ्कक्षुद्विशेषतो भिषग्वणिक्पण्यस्त्रीशिल्पिशूरचित्रकारकविविद्याविवादशीलधूर्तकुरुसारदण्डकवात्समगधसाल्वसौवर्धनपुलिन्दवैदेहसौराष्ट्रनलदकदम्बदशार्णाङ्गवङ्गवर्तिमालवपौरवत्रिगर्तसौवीरयौधेयक्षुद्रकशिविकानभिहन्ति ॥

Chapters XIV & XVI *supra* may be referred to with advantage in this section.]

पुष्याग्नेयविशाखाभरणीपित्र्याजभाग्यसञ्ज्ञानि ।
वर्गो हौतभुजोऽयं करोति रूपाण्यथैतानि ॥१२॥

तारोल्कापातावृतमादीप्तमिवाम्बरं सदिग्दाहम् ।
विचरति मरुत्सहायः सप्तार्चिः सप्तदिवसान्तः ॥१३॥

आग्नेयेऽम्बुदनाशः सलिलाशयसङ्क्षयो नृपतिवैरम् ।
दद्रूविचर्चिकाज्वरविसर्पिकाः पाण्डुरोगश्च ॥१४॥

दीप्तौजसः प्रचण्डाः पीड्यन्ते चाश्मकाङ्गबाह्लीकाः ।
तङ्गणकलिङ्गवङ्गद्रविडाः शबरा अनेकविधाः ॥१५॥

The *Fire Circle* consists of the seven asterisms, Puṣya, Kṛttikā, Viśākhā, Bharaṇī, Maghā, Pūrvabhādrapadā and Pūrvaphalgunī. It reveals its symptoms a week in advance in the following manner: The sky will be filled with falling stars and meteors and will appear aglow as a result of the fire in the horizon; and fire aggravated by the wind will rage over the land. During an earth-quake of the *Fire Circle*, clouds will be destroyed; lakes and tanks will dry up; kings will be at loggerheads with one another; herpes, scab, fever, erysipelas and jaundice will break out; and men of great valour, hot-tempered persons, the Aśmakas, Aṅgas, Bāhlīkas, Taṅgaṇas, Kaliṅgas, Vaṅgas, Draviḍas and hillmen of various tribes will be troubled.

[Cf. गर्ग—

द्वितीयेऽह्नि चतुर्भागे निर्घातोल्कामहीचलाः ।
पित्र्यभाग्याजपुष्याग्निविशाखायमदैवतैः ॥
भवन्त्यनलजास्ते च लक्षणानि निबोध मे ।
तारोल्कापातदिग्दाहैरादीप्तं लक्ष्यते नभः ॥
मरुत्सहायः सप्तार्चिः सप्ताहान्तश्चरत्यपि ।
सप्तमेऽहनि विज्ञेयः कम्पश्चानलसम्भवः ॥

also पराशर—

अग्नीन्द्राग्न्यजयमपितृगुरुभगदैवतेष्वनलोऽभिकम्पयन् वर्षसरित्सरःस्रोतसामपः

क्षपयन् सुखानि रोगारोचकपिटकपाण्डुरुग्ज्वरकिटिभदद्रूदाहकृद्विशेषाद्वातपादकाग्नि-वित्पुलिन्दयवनबाह्लीकवङ्गोष्ट्रासन्त्याश्मकेक्ष्वाकुकुलूततुखारशिबिकत्रिगर्तवैदेहद्रविड-सुराष्ट्रमध्यदेशदशार्णांश्च हिनस्ति ।]

अभिजिच्छ्रवणधनिष्ठाप्राजापत्यैन्द्रवैश्वमैत्राणि ।
सुरपतिमण्डलमेतद्भवन्ति चाप्यस्य रूपाणि ॥१६॥

चलिताचलवर्ष्माणो गम्भीरविराविणस्तडिद्वन्तः ।
गवलालिकुलाहिनिभा विसृजन्ति पयः पयोवाहाः ॥१७॥

ऐन्द्रं स्तुतकुलजातिख्यातावनिपालगणपविध्वंसि ।
अतिसारगलग्रहवदनरोगकृच्छर्दिकोपाय ॥१८॥

काशियुगन्धरपौरवकिरातकीराभिसारहलमद्राः ।
अर्बुदसुराष्ट्रमालवपीडाकरमिष्टवृष्टिकरम् ॥१९॥

The seven asterisms, Abhijit, Śravaṇa, Dhaniṣṭhā, Rohiṇī, Jyeṣṭhā, Uttarāṣāḍhā, and Anurādhā, constitute *Indra's Circle*. Its symptoms are the following : The clouds looking like moving mountains, sending forth loud peals of thunder, containing flashes of lightning and resembling in colour buffaloes' horn, swarms of bees and serpents, will pour down rain. An earthquake occurring in *Indra's Circle* will ruin men of celebrated families and castes, famous persons, kings and heads of corporations. It will also produce dysentery, swelling of the throat, facial diseases and severe vomiting. It will cause trouble to the people of Kāśi, Yugandhara, the Pauravas, Kirātas, Kīras, Abhisāras, Halas, Madras, Arbudas, Surāṣṭra and Mālava countries. It will, however, bring good rains.

[Cf. गर्ग—

निशार्द्धे तु यदा पूर्वे उल्कानिर्घातभूचलाः ।
मैत्रेन्द्रवैश्वश्रवणाभिजिद्रोहिणिवासवैः ॥
स्यादिन्द्रसम्भवः कम्पो लक्षणानि च मे शृणु ।
वर्षन्ति बहवो मेघा वराहमहिषोपमाः ॥
धुन्वन्तो मधुरान् रावान् विद्युद्भासितभूतलाः ।
सप्तमेऽहनि सम्प्राप्ते कम्पः स्यादिन्द्रसम्भवः ॥

also पराशर—

ऐन्द्रवैश्वदेववैष्णवप्राजापत्यसौम्यादित्यमैत्रेषु सुरपतिरवनिमतिचालयन् प्रवृद्धाम्भोदयज्ञधर्मान्नपानोत्सवो जात्यप्रथितकुलाधिपतिसुवास्तुनीचकाश्मीराभिसारप्राच्य-

शककिरातपौरवाच्युतवास्वर्णवमालवपह्लवदण्डककाशिकार्षककैलासमल्ललहवहालानुपतापयति ॥

It is evident that *Parāśara's* circles are constituted differently. For example, his Wind Circle consists of Abhijit and Dhaniṣṭhā, while Garga's Mṛgaśiras and Punarvasu. Similarly there are differences in other Circles also.]

पौष्णाप्यार्द्राश्लेषामूलाहिर्बुध्न्यवरुणदेवानि ।
मण्डलमेतद्वारुणमस्यापि भवन्ति रूपाणि ॥२०॥

नीलोत्पलालिभिन्नाञ्जनत्विषो मधुररावणो बहुलाः ।
तडिदुद्भासितदेहा धाराङ्कुरवर्षिणो जलदाः ॥२१॥

वारुणमर्णवसरिदाश्रितघ्नमतिवृष्टिदं विगतवैरम् ।
गोनर्दचेदिकुकुरान् किरातवैदेहकान् हन्ति ॥२२॥

Varuṇa's Circle is constituted by the seven asterisms, Revatī, Pūrvāṣāḍhā, Ārdrā, Āśleṣā, Mūla, Uttarabhādrapadā and Śatabhiṣaj. Its indications appearing a week before are the following : Huge clouds resembling blue lily, bees and collyrium in colour, rumbling pleasantly, and shining with flashes of lightning, will pour down slender lines of water resembling sharp sprouts. An earthquake of this circle will kill those that are dependent on the seas and rivers; and it will lead to excessive rains. People will also bury the hatchet. It will destroy the Gonardas, Cedis, Kukuras, Kirātas and the people of Videha.

[Cf. गर्ग—

निशायां पश्चिमे भागे निर्घातोल्कामहीचलाः ।
पौष्णाप्यार्द्रोरगा मूलाहिर्बुध्न्यं वरुणं तथा ॥
कम्पो वारुण एभिः स्याच्छृणु तस्यैव लक्षणम् ।
वर्षन्ति जलदास्तत्र नीलाञ्जनचयोपमाः ॥
विद्युद्भासितदेहाश्च मधुरस्वरभूषिताः ।
सप्तमेऽह्नि सम्प्राप्ते कम्पः स्याद्वारुणस्ततः ॥

cf. also पराशर—

"धराभिन्नकेदारपुरनगरप्रबद्धतरुणततजलताक्षुपशष्पसस्यातीसारहिक्काक्षिरोगकृदपि च विशेषतः किरातकाश्मीरापरान्तककौकुरेयशौर्यारकचेदिवत्ससैन्धवोदकयात्रिकोदधिनदनदीसंश्रितांश्च देशानुपहन्ति ॥"

According to this Sage Varuṇa's Circle consists of only six asterisms where Pūrvāṣāḍhā does not find a place.]

षड्भिर्मासैः कम्पो द्वाभ्यां पाकं च याति निर्घातः ।
अन्यानप्युत्पातान् जगुरन्ये मण्डलैरेतैः ॥२३॥

An earthquake bears fruit in six months, and a portentous thunder in two months. Other sages like Garga include other portents also in the above *Circles* for predicting their effects.

[Other portents are—eclipses, fall of meteors and the like. Their effects are to be judged according to the Maṇḍala or *Circle* in which they occur.

Cf. गर्ग—

निर्घातोल्कामहीकम्पाः स्निग्धगम्भीरनिःस्वनाः ।
मेघाः स्तनितशब्दाश्च सूर्येन्दुग्रहणे तथा ॥
परिवेषेन्द्रचापं च गन्धर्वनगरं तथा ।
मण्डलैरेव बोद्धव्याः शुभाशुभफलप्रदाः ॥

Cf. also the समाससंहिता—

आर्यम्णपूर्वं भचतुष्टयं च शशाङ्कमादित्यमथाश्विनी च ।
वायव्यमेतत्पवनोऽत्र चण्डो मासद्वयेनाशुभदः प्रजानाम् ॥
अजैकपादं बहुला भरण्यो भाग्यं विशाखा गुरुभं मघा च ।
क्षुदग्निशस्त्रामयकोपकारि पक्षैस्त्रिभिर्मण्डलमग्निसंज्ञम् ॥
प्राजापत्यं वैष्णवं मैत्रमैन्द्रं विश्वेशं स्याद्वासवं चाभिजिच्च ।
ऐन्द्रं ह्येतन्मण्डलं सप्तरात्रात्कुर्यात्तोयं हृष्टलोकं प्रशान्तम् ॥
आहिर्बुध्न्यं वारुणं मूलमाप्यं पौष्णं सार्पं मन्मथारीश्वरं च ।
सद्यःपाकं वारुणं नाम शस्तं तोयप्रायं हृष्टलोकं प्रशान्तम् ॥

The author states that the time of fruition of an earthquake is six months, but in his abridged Saṁhitā we find him giving two months for the Wind Circle, three fortnights for the Fire Circle, seven days for Indra's Circle and lastly immediate effect for the last one.]

The following three verses also occur in the समाससंहिता, but they are translated because of their importance.

उल्का हरिश्चन्द्रपुरं रजश्च निर्घातभूकम्पककुप्प्रदाहाः ।
वातोऽतिचण्डो ग्रहणं रवीन्द्वोर्नक्षत्रताराग्रणवैकृतानि ॥२४॥
व्यभ्रे वृष्टिर्वैकृतं वातवृष्टिर्धूमोऽनग्निर्विस्फुलिङ्गार्चिषो वा ।
वन्यं सत्त्वं ग्राममध्ये विशेद्वा रात्रावैन्द्रं कार्मुकं दृश्यते वा ॥२५॥
सन्ध्याविकारः परिवेषखण्डा नद्यः प्रतीपा दिवि तूर्यनादः ।
अन्यच्च यत्स्यात्प्रकृतेः प्रतीपं तन्मण्डलैरेव फलं निगाद्यम् ॥२६॥

Other portents are the following : Meteors, aerial city, dust, portentous thunder, earthquake, fires in the quarters, furious winds, eclipses of the luminaries, unnatural phenomena in the case of any star or group of stars, rain without clouds, anything unnatural in the sky, excessive rain (or stormy rain), smoke without fire, flames without sparks, entry of wild animals into a village, sight of a rainbow at night, unnatural phenomena at the junctures, broken halos round the Sun or the Moon, contrary flow of rivers, and sounds of musical instruments in the heavens. The effects of any other phenomenon which is unnatural should be predicted on the basis of the above Maṇḍalas or Circles.

[In the second verse चातिवृष्टि is another reading for वातवृष्टि. The middle one is in शालिनी metre and the rest is इन्द्रवज्रा.

According to *Garga* persons in whose natal asterisms earthquakes and such other portents occur, will have troubles. Hence such persons are advised to perform propitiatory rituals with respect to the Deities in whose Maṇḍalas the portents are observed.]

हन्त्यैन्द्रो वायव्यं वायुश्चाप्यैन्द्रमेवमन्योन्यम् ।
वारुणहौतभुजावपि वेलानक्षत्रजाः कम्पाः ॥२७॥

An earthquake taking place in Indra's Circle counteracts one in Wind's Period and *vice versa*. Similarly one of Varuṇa's Circle will undo the effects of one occurring in the Fire-Period and *vice versa*. Thus the earthquakes of particular *periods* and *circles*, as stated above, cancel each other.

[As we have already seen above i.e., verses 3-7 *supra*, the *periods* are of six-hour duration each, while *circles* are constituted by the asterisms. For example, Indra's *period* is the first half of the night while *Wind Circle* comprises the seven stars Uttaraphalgunī (cf. 8-11 *supra*). If an earthquake occurs in the first half of the night and in Uttaraphalgunī or some other star of its group, it would come under the purview of this verse, and they would cancel each other. If both the Velā and Maṇḍala were to belong to the same authority i.e. Deity, the effect would be doubly strong.

In the opinion of *Garga* if an earthquake were connected with two asterisms belonging to two different Maṇḍalas, the *Velā* or *Period* would take precedence.]

प्रथितनरेश्वरमरणव्यसनान्याग्नेयवायुमण्डलयोः ।
क्षुद्भयमरकावृष्टिभिरुपताप्यन्ते जनाश्चापि ॥२८॥

If there be an earthquake in the Fire Circle and Wind Period or *vice versa* (i.e. Fire Period and Wind Circle), there would be calamities to or death of celebrated monarchs; and people would be tortured by the dread of famine, mortality and drought.

वारुणपौरन्दरयोः सुभिक्षशिववृष्टिहार्दयो लोके ।
गावोऽतिभूरिपयसो निवृत्तवैराश्च भूपालाः ॥ ९ ॥

Should an earthquake occur in the *Varuṇa Circle* and *Indra Period* or *vice versa*, there would be plenty of food crops, prosperity, rain and joy and contentment in the world. Cows would yield milk in abundance and kings sink their differences.

[Cf. काश्यप—

ऐन्द्रश्चानिलजं हन्ति वायव्यश्चापि शक्रजम् ।
आप्यो हौतभुजं हन्ति चाग्निर्वारुणसम्भवम् ॥
वाय्वग्निमिश्रितो यश्च वेलामण्डलसम्भवः ।
दुर्भिक्षव्याधिरोगैस्तु पीड्यन्ते तत्र जन्तवः ।
माहेन्द्रवारुणे यत्र वेलामण्डलसम्भवः ।
सुभिक्षक्षेमधर्माणां तत्र वृष्टिः प्रतिष्ठिता ॥

Cf. also पराशर—

योऽन्यस्मिन्नक्षत्रे भागे चान्यत्र भूचलो भवति ।
स भवेद् व्यामिश्रफलस्तन्मे गदतो निबोध त्वम् ॥
कुरुशाल्वमत्स्यनैषधपुण्ड्रान्ध्रकलिङ्गविन्ध्यपादस्थान् ।
वाय्वाग्नेयः कम्पः सानलजीवान् भजति मैत्र्याम् ॥
प्राच्यशकचीनपह्लवयौधेयकर्पदियक्षवद्गोमान् ।
शरदण्डमगधबन्धकिविनाशनः शक्रवायव्यः ॥
आवन्तिकाः पुलिन्दा विदेहकाश्मीरदरदवासान्ताः ।
बाह्याश्रिताश्च वायव्यवारुणे प्राप्नुयुः पीडाम् ॥
ऐक्ष्वाकवाऽश्मरथ्यान् पटच्चराभीरचीनमरुकुत्सान् ।
ऐन्द्राग्नेयः कम्पो हिनस्ति राज्ञश्च समुदीर्णान् ॥
सरितः सरः समुद्राश्रितांश्च गोनर्दमङ्गनाराज्यम् ।
क्षत्रियगणांश्च हन्यात् कम्पो वरुणाग्निदैवत्यः ॥
काश्याभिसारकाच्युतकच्छद्वीपार्यदेशजाः पुरुषाः ।
गणपूजिताः कुलाग्र्या नृपाश्च वरुणेन्द्रवध्याः स्युः ॥

In the next verse the author speaks of the periods of fruition for other portents :]

पक्षैश्चतुर्भिरनिलस्त्रिभिरग्निर्देवराट् च सप्ताहात् ।
सद्यः फलति च वरुणो येषु न कालोऽद्भुतेषूक्तः ॥३०॥

When the time of fruition of the effects of portents or extraordinary happenings such as throbbing of limbs, and the like has not been specified, they will be felt within two months, provided such happenings take place in the *Wind* Circle; within three fortnights, in the *Fire* Circle; within a week, in *Indra*' Circle; and in the course of the same day, in *Varuṇa*'s Circle.

[Next he speaks of the area or distance over which these circles spread their influence.]

चलयति पवनः शतद्वयं शतमनलो दशयोजनान्वितम् ।
सलिलपतिरशीतिसंयुतं कुलिशधरोऽभ्यधिकं च षष्टितः ॥३१॥

An earthquake occurring in the Maṇḍala of Wind shakes the earth to an extent of 200 Yojanas; one of the *Fire* Circle, 110 Yojanas; one of Varuṇa's, 180 Yojanas; and one of Indra's, 160 Yojanas.

[Cf. काश्यप—

वायव्ये मण्डले नित्यं योजनानां शतद्वयम् ।
दशाधिकमथाग्नेय ऐन्द्रे षष्ठ्याधिकं शतम् ॥
शतं चाशीतिसंयुक्तं वारुणे मण्डले चलेत् ॥

The metre is वैतालीय].

त्रिचतुर्थसप्तमदिने मासे पक्षे तथा त्रिपक्षे च ।
यदि भवति भूमिकम्पः प्रधाननृपनाशनो भवति ॥३२॥

Should there be another earthquake on the 3rd, 4th or the 7th day, or at the end of a month, fortnight or three fortnights, it would cause the destruction of celebrated monarchs.

[Cf. गर्ग—

अर्द्धमासे चतुर्थेऽह्नि तृतीये वाथ सप्तमे ।
कस्मात्पुनर्यदा कम्पो मासे सार्द्धे यदापि वा ॥
उत्पद्यते जने यत्र तत्र विन्द्यान्महद्भयम् ॥

Cf. also पराशर—

स्निग्धस्वनाः प्रदक्षिणानुयायिनोऽम्बुधरा धाराभिषिक्ताः पर्वसु च सर्व एव प्रशस्यन्ते । तीक्ष्णाम्बुवहोऽवनिपतिविग्रहोच्छ्रयाय । त्रिचतुःसप्तरात्रे पक्षमासत्रिपक्षान्तरे प्रततानुकम्पनः प्रवरनरपतिविनाशाय । अपि च शमयन्त्यासप्ताहात् कम्पादिकृतं निमित्तमाश्वेवातिवर्षगोपवासमन्त्रदीक्षाजप्यहवनानि ॥]

———

उल्कालक्षणाध्यायः ॥३३॥

Chapter XXXIII—Signs of Meteors

दिवि भुक्तशुभफलानां पततां रूपाणि यानि तान्युल्काः ।
धिष्ण्योल्काशनिविद्युत्तारा इति पञ्चधा भिन्नाः ॥१॥

The meteors are nothing but the forms of those who fall down after having enjoyed the fruits of their meritorious deeds in Heaven. These meteors are divided into five categories viz. Dhiṣṇya or Ignescent Balls, Meteors, Thunder-bolts, Lightning and Shooting Stars.

[It is a tradition among Indians that those who perform meritorious deeds while living on the earth go to heaven for enjoying their good results. When these are exhausted, the souls come down again to the earth to resume their mundane work. It has also been witnessed that at the departure of great Souls a bright star is seen shooting up towards the heavens.

Vide the Bhagavad Gītā IX-21 "क्षीणे पुण्ये मर्त्यलोकं विशन्ति ।"

Cf. also गर्ग—

स्वास्त्राणि संसृजन्त्येते शुभाशुभनिवेदिनः ।
लोकपाला महात्मानो लोकानां ज्वलितानि तु ॥

and the समाससंहिता—

अस्त्राणि लोकपाला लोकाभावाय सन्त्यजन्त्युल्काः ।
केषाञ्चित्पुण्यकृतां तत्रोल्काविच्युतिः स्वर्गात् ॥

Here Sage Garga's view also is incorporated, while in the text our author mentions the popular view about the meteors.

I feel that the original reading in the first line must have been यानि ता उल्काः according to the rule 'विधेयस्य प्राधान्यम्'].

उल्का पक्षेण फलं तद्वद्धिष्ण्याशनिस्त्रिभिः पक्षैः ।
विद्युदहोभिः षड्भिस्तद्वत्तारा विपाचयति ॥२॥

An Ulkā or meteor and Dhiṣṇyā bear fruit in a fortnight; a thunderbolt, in three fortnights; and lightning as well as Tārā, in six days.

[Cf. the समाससंहिता—

उल्काथ पञ्चरूपा धिष्ण्योल्का विद्युतोऽशनिस्तारा ।
धिष्ण्योल्के पक्षफले तत्त्रिगुणश्चाशनिः षडह्निकेऽन्ये ॥
फलपादकरी तारा धिष्ण्यार्धं पुष्कलं शेषाः ॥]

तारा फलपादकरी फलार्द्धदात्री प्रकीर्तिता धिष्ण्या ।
तिस्रः सम्पूर्णफला विद्युदथोल्काशनिश्चेति ॥३॥

The *Tārā* meteor produces only a quarter of the effects; the Dhiṣṇyā, a half of it; while the remaining three produce their effects in full measure.

अशनिः स्वनेन महता नृगजाश्वमृगाश्मवेश्मतरुपशुषु ।
निपतति विदारयन्ती धरातलं चक्रसंस्थाना ॥४॥

The thunderbolt falls with a deafening sound upon men, elephants, horses, beasts, rocks, houses, trees and domestic animals, revolving like a discus and piercing the surface of the earth.

[Cf. the समाससंहिता—

अशनिः प्राणिषु निपतति दारयति धरातलं बृहच्छब्दा ॥]

विद्युत् सत्त्वत्रासं जनयन्ती तटतटस्वना सहसा ।
कुटिलविशाला निपतति जीवेन्धनराशिषु ज्वलिता ॥५॥

Lightning, which is crooked and extensive, falls suddenly on living beings and heaped up fire-wood, setting them ablaze, causing fright to the animals and producing a rattling sound.

Cf. the समाससंहिता(?)—

विद्युत्तटतटशब्दा ज्वालामालाकुला पतति ॥]

धिष्ण्या कृशाल्पपुच्छा धनूंषि दश दृश्यतेऽन्तराभ्यधिकम् ।
ज्वलिताङ्गारनिकाशा द्वौ हस्तौ सा प्रमाणेन ॥६॥

The *Dhiṣṇyā* is a slender thing with a short tail with a body two cubits long. It resembles burning embers and appears quite distinct over an area of forty cubits.

[Cf. the abridged work :—

धिष्ण्या सिता द्विहस्ता धनूंषि दश याति कृशदेहा ॥]

तारा हस्तं दीर्घा शुक्ला ताम्राब्जतन्तुरूपा वा ।
तिर्यगधश्चोर्ध्वं वा याति वियत्युह्यमानेव ॥७॥

The *Tārā* or shooting star is one cubit long, white, red or slender like the fibre of the lotus-stalk and moves across, up and down the sky, as if being dragged.

[Cf. the abridged work :—

तारा तु हस्तमात्रा यात्यूर्ध्वमधः स्थिता सिता ताम्रा ॥]

उल्का शिरसि विशाला निपतन्ती वर्धते प्रतनुपुच्छा ।
दीर्घा च भवति पुरुषं भेदा बहवो भवन्त्यस्याः ॥८॥

The Ulkā or meteor is broad at the head, having a tiny tail. As it falls down, it grows bigger and bigger. It is $3\frac{1}{2}$ cubits long. There are many varieties of it.

[Cf. the following :

उल्काग्रतो विशाला बहुप्रकारा पुरुषमात्रा ॥]

प्रेतप्रहरणखरकरभनक्रकपिवराहलाङ्गलमृगाभाः ।
गोधाहिधूमरूपाः पापा या चोभयशिरस्का ॥९॥

Those varieties of *Ulkā* that resemble dead bodies, weapons, asses, camels, crocodiles, monkeys, boars, ploughs, wild deer, lizards, snakes and smoke, as well as those that have two heads, are of inauspicious consequences.

ध्वजझषगिरिकरिकमलेन्दुतुरगसन्तप्तरजतहंसाभाः ।
श्रीवृक्षवज्रशङ्खस्वस्तिकरूपाः शिवसुभिक्षाः ॥१०॥

Those that resemble banners, fishes, mountains, elephants, lotuses, the Moon, horses, molten silver, swans, Bilva tree, diamond (or Indra's weapon), conch and the *Svastika* design, lead to prosperity and abundance of food grains.

[Cf. काश्यप—

नरेभतुरगाश्वाश्मवृक्षेषु च पतेत् सदा ।
ज्वलन्ती चक्रवद् दृश्या त्वशनी रावसंयुता ॥
विद्युत्त्रासकरी भीमा शब्दयन्ती तटत्तटा ।
बृहच्छीर्षाऽतिसूक्ष्मा च जीवेषु च पतेत्सदा ॥
धनूंषि दश वा दृश्या सा च धिष्ण्या प्रकीर्तिता ।
ज्वलिताङ्गारसदृशी द्वौ हस्तौ सा प्रमाणतः ॥
पद्मताम्राकृतिश्चैव हस्तमात्रायता गता ।
तिर्यगूर्ध्वमधो याति सोह्यमानेव तारका ॥

उल्का मूर्धनि विस्तीर्णा पतन्ती वर्धते तु सा ।
तनुपुच्छा नृमात्रा तु बहुभेदसमावृता ।।
आयुधप्रेतसदृशी जम्बुकोष्ट्रखराकृतिः ।
धूम्रवर्णा तु पापाख्या विशीर्णा या तु मध्यमा ।।
ध्वजपद्मेभहंसाभा पर्वताश्वसमप्रभा ।
श्रीवृक्षशङ्खसदृशी या चोल्का सा शिवप्रदा ।।]

अम्बरमध्याद् बह्व्यो निपतन्त्यो राजराष्ट्रनाशाय ।
बम्भ्रमती गगनोपरि विभ्रममाख्याति लोकस्य ।।११।।

If they fall in clusters from the middle of the sky, they portend the destruction of the king and the country. If it circles round and round at the zenith of the sky, it indicates unrest and distress among the people.

संस्पृशती चन्द्रार्कौ तद्विसृता वा स भूप्रकम्पा च ।
परचक्रागमनृपभयदुर्भिक्षावृष्टिभयजननी ।।१२।।

If it touches or comes away from the Sun or the Moon and is accompanied by an earthquake, it will lead to an enemy attack, danger to the ruler, famine and trouble from drought.

पौरेतरघ्नमुल्कापसव्यकरणं दिवाकरहिमांश्वोः ।
उल्का शुभदा पुरतो दिवाकरविनिःसृता यातुः ।।१३।।

If an *Ulkā* moves to the left of the Sun and the Moon, it will destroy the defenders of the town and the attacking army respectively; whereas if it issues forth from the Sun and falls in front of a king on the march, it will bestow victory on him.

शुक्ला रक्ता पीता कृष्णा चोल्का द्विजादिवर्णघ्नी ।
क्रमशश्चैतान् हन्युर्मूर्धोरःपार्श्वपुच्छस्थाः ।।१४।।

A meteor being white, red, yellow and black ruins in order the four classes beginning with the Brāhmaṇa. Similarly it harms the four classes in order if it falls with its head, middle part, side and tail foremost.

उत्तरदिगादिपतिता विप्रादीनामनिष्टदा रूक्षा ।
ऋज्वी स्निग्धाखण्डा नीचोपगता च तद्वृद्ध्यै ।।१५।।

A rough meteor that falls in the north, east, south and west bodes evil to the four classes in order beginning with the Brāhmaṇa; while, being straight, glossy, unbroken and falling down from the sky, it tends to the prosperity of the members of the four classes severally.

श्यावारुणनीलासृग्दहनासितभस्मसन्निभा रूक्षा ।
सन्ध्यादिनजा वक्रा दलिता च परागमभयाय ॥१६॥

A meteor that is grey, rosy, blue, crimson, fiery, dark or ashy in colour, rough, visible at a twilight or daytime, crooked and broken, forebodes foreign invasion.

नक्षत्रग्रहघातैस्तद्भक्तीनां क्षयाय निर्दिष्टा ।
उदये घ्नती रवीन्दू पौरेतरमृत्यवेऽस्ते वा ॥१७॥

If a meteor should strike an asterism or a planet, the latter's wards (objects, countries and people) would be ruined. Should it strike the Sun and the Moon at the time of rising or setting, the defenders of the town and the attacking foe respectively would come to grief.

[Cf. काश्यप—

नक्षत्राणि ग्रहाश्चैव यद्युल्काध्वस्तधूमिताः ।
तद्देशनाथनाशाय लोकानां सम्भ्रमाय च ॥

also the समाससंहिता—

उदगादिषु विप्रादीन् सितलोहितकृष्णवर्णाश्च ।
घ्नन्ति ग्रहर्क्षघातैस्तद्भक्तीनां च नाशाय ॥]

भाग्यादित्यधनिष्ठामूलेषूल्काहतेषु युवतीनाम् ।
विप्रक्षत्रियपीडा पुष्यानिलविष्णुदैवेषु ॥१८॥
ध्रुवसौम्येषु नृपाणामुग्रेषु सदारुणेषु चौराणाम् ।
क्षिप्रेषु कलाविदुषां पीडा साधारणे च हते ॥१९॥

If the Yoga-tārā (brightest star) of the asterisms, Pūrvaphalguni, Punarvasu, Dhaniṣṭhā and Mūla be struck by a meteor, young women would be afflicted; if that of Puṣya, Svāti and Śravaṇa be hit, Brāhmaṇas and Kṣatriyas would suffer. When the stars termed *Dhruva—Stable*—and *Saumya—Gentle*—are struck by a meteor, there will be trouble for kings; when those termed *Ugra—Fierce*—and *Dāruṇa—Dreadful*—are struck, thieves will be apprehended and tortured; and when those termed *Kṣipra—Quick*—and *Sādhāraṇa—Moderate* are struck, artists as well as artistes will be in trouble.

[Here we see the asterisms divided into six categories viz. Stable, Gentle, Fierce, Dreadful, Quick and Moderate. The *first* group consists of the three Uttaras and Rohiṇī; the *second,* of Mṛgaśiras, Citrā, Anurādhā and Revatī; the *third,* of three Pūrvas, Bharaṇī and Maghā; the *fourth,* of Ārdra, Āśleṣā, Jyeṣṭhā and Mūla; the *fifth,* of Aśvinī, Puṣya, Hasta and Abhijit; and the *sixth,* of Kṛttikā and Viśākhā. Of course there remain some more asterisms that are not treated of in this context.]

कुर्वन्त्येताः पतिता देवप्रतिमासु राजराष्ट्रभयम् ।
शक्रोपरि नृपतीनां गृहेषु तत्स्वामिनां पीडाम् ॥२०॥
आशाग्रहोपघाते तद्देश्यानां खले कृषिरतानाम् ।
चैत्यतरौ सम्पतिता सत्कृतपीडां करोत्युल्का ॥२१॥
द्वारि पुरस्य पुरक्षयमथेन्द्रकीले जनक्षयोऽभिहितः ।
ब्रह्मायतने विप्रान् विनिहन्याद् गोमिनो गोष्ठे ॥२२॥

Meteors falling on the images of Gods cause disaster to the king and the country; on Indra, to the kings; on houses, to their owners; striking the planets presiding over the several quarters, to the people of the countries situated in those quarters; threshing floor, to agriculturists; a holy (prominent) tree, to respectable people; one falling on the gate of a town will destroy the town itself; on the bolt of a door, the people; on the temple of Brahman, the Brāhmaṇas; and cowpens, their owners.

[For planets ruling the quarters see the बृहज्जातक II-5. We know that countries, peoples etc. are allotted both to the quarters and to the planets in XIV & XVI *supra.* Hence the compound आशाग्रहोपघाते in verse 21 can also be interpreted thus : "When the several quarters as well as the several planets are attacked by meteors, it would spell ruin to the countries, peoples, objects etc. assigned to them severally."]

क्ष्वेडास्फोटितवादितगीतोत्क्रुष्टस्वना भवन्ति यदा ।
उल्कानिपातसमये भयाय राष्ट्रस्य सनपस्य ॥२३॥

If sounds of roaring, clapping hands, instrumental music, songs and loud cries are heard at the time of falling of a meteor, there would be danger to the country and its king.

यस्याश्चिरं तिष्ठति खेऽनुषङ्गो दण्डाकृतिः सा नृपतेर्भयाय ।
या चोह्यते तन्तुधृतेव खस्था या वा महेन्द्रध्वजतुल्यरूपा ॥२४॥

If a meteor having the form of a rod leaves its trail on the sky for a long time, it bodes disaster to the king. So does one that appears to be carried along the sky by a thread, or one that looks like Indra's banner.

[The metre is इन्द्रवज्रा].

श्रेष्ठिनः प्रतीपगा तिर्यगा नृपाङ्गनाम् ।
हन्त्यधोमुखी नृपान् ब्राह्मणानथोर्ध्वगा ॥२५॥
बर्हिपुच्छरूपिणी लोकसङ्क्षयावहा ।
सर्पवत्प्रसर्पती योषितामनिष्टदा ॥२६॥
हन्ति मण्डला पुरं छत्रवत् पुरोहितम् ।
वंशगुल्मवत् स्थिता राष्ट्रदोषकारिणी ॥२७॥
व्यालसूकरोपमा विस्फुलिङ्गमालिनी ।
खण्डशोऽथवा गता सस्वना च पापदा ॥२८॥

A meteor that goes backwards harms traders; crosswise, the queen, with its head downwards, kings; head upwards, Brāhmaṇas; one that resembles the peacock's tail causes the annihilation of the people; one creeping like a snake is ruinous to women; one falling in a circular form destroys the city; in the form of an umbrella, the royal priest; in the form of a bamboo-clump, is harmful to the kingdom; one resembling snakes or hogs or is wreathed in sparks or is broken to pieces and is accompanied by sound, proves destructive.

[Here the author employs a few ungrammatical forms viz. तिर्यगाः, प्रसर्पती, मण्डला.

The metre is समानिका (प्रा. पि. सू. II. 59)].

सुरपतिचापप्रतिमा राज्यं नभसि विलीना जलदान् हन्ति ।
पवनविलोमा कुटिलं याता न भवति शस्ता विनिवृत्ता वा ॥२९॥

A meteor which looks like the rainbow destroys the kingdom; one which disappears in the sky itself ruins the clouds; one moving against the wind in a crooked way or backwards, is harmful.

[The metre comes under त्रिष्टुभ्, but no special name is found. So it is to be called गाथा]

अभिभवति यतः पुरं बलं वा भवति भयं तत एव पार्थिवस्य ।
निपतति च यया दिशा प्रदीप्ता जयति रिपूनचिरात्तया प्रयातः ॥३०॥

A king will have trouble in store from the direction wherefrom a meteor attacks his town or army; but if he marches to that direction in which a meteor falls down ablaze, he will soon vanquish his enemies.

[Cf. काश्यप—

पार्थिवे प्रस्थिते दीप्ता पतत्युल्का महास्वना ।
तां दिशं सिद्ध्यते सिद्धि विजयं लभते चिरात् ॥

अत्र च तात्कालिकलग्नग्रहसंयोगाच्छकुनिरुतश्रवणाच्च फलमूह्यम् ।
Vide the समाससंहिता—

क्रूरग्रहर्क्षलग्नक्षणतिथिकरणप्रभञ्जनैर्दीप्तैः ।
दीप्ताण्डजमृगविरुतैर्निर्घातक्षितिविमर्दैश्च ॥

The metre is पुष्पिताग्रा.]

———

परिवेषलक्षणाध्यायः ॥३४॥

Chapter XXXIV—Characteristics of Halos

संमूर्च्छिता रवीन्द्वोः किरणाः पवनेन मण्डलीभूताः ।
नानावर्णाकृतयस्तन्वभ्रे व्योम्नि परिवेषाः ॥१॥

The rays of the Sun and the Moon turned into a circle by the wind, and reflected in the sky with sparse clouds, become halos possessed of different colours and shapes.

ते रक्तनीलपाण्डुरकापोताभ्राभशबलहरितशुक्लाः ।
इन्द्रयमवरुणनिर्ऋतिश्वसनेशपितामहाग्निकृताः ॥२॥

They attain the following colours—crimson, blue, pale white, dove-coloured, dark, variegated, green and white, when they are caused by Indra, Yama, Varuṇa, Nirṛti, Vāyu, Śiva, Brahman and Agni respectively.

[The Benares edition wrongly takes the reading अम्बुकृताः instead of अग्निकृताः। Bhaṭṭotpala too says: "सोऽपि वरुण कृत एव". In the first line there is also a metrical flaw in the word हरितशुक्लाः. It is possible that the author might have used हरिशुक्लाः or हरितसिताः. The mistake, therefore, must be attributed to the carelessness of the scribe. In the second line too there is an apparent metrical flaw in निर्ऋतिश्वसन, but it is allowed according to prosodical rules. The particular conjunct consonant is called क्रम (Cf. वृत्तरत्नाकर I-10).]

धनदः करोति मेचकमन्योन्यगुणाश्रयेण चाप्यन्ये ।
प्रविलीयते मुहुर्मुहुरल्पफलः सोऽपि वायुकृतः ॥३॥

Kubera produces a halo whose colour is that of the peacock's neck; others produce halos of mixed colours. One that is brought about by Vāyu disappears frequently and produces little effect.

[Cf. काश्यप—

सितपीतेन्द्रनीलाभा रक्तकापोतबभ्रवः ।
शबला बर्हिवर्णाश्च विज्ञेयास्ते शुभप्रदाः ॥
ऐन्द्रयाम्याप्यनैर्ऋत्यवारुणाः सौम्यवह्निजाः ।
हश्याहश्येन भावेन वायव्यः सोऽपि कष्टदः ॥]

चाषशिखिरजततैलक्षीरजलाभः स्वकालसम्भूतः ।
अविकलवृत्तः स्निग्धः परिवेषः शिवसुभिक्षकरः ॥४॥

A halo shining like the blue jay, peacock, silver, oil, milk and water in their order in the six seasons beginning with winter (Śiśira), glossy or clear and in an unbroken circle, conduces to peace and prosperity.

[The natural colours of halos in the six seasons are mentioned here.

Cf. काश्यप—

शिशिरे चाषवर्णश्च वसन्ते शिखिसन्निभः ।
ग्रीष्मे रजतसङ्काशः प्रावृट्तैलसमप्रभः ॥
गोक्षीरसदृशः शस्तः परिवेषः शरत्स्मृतः ।
हेमन्ते जलसङ्काशः स्वकाले शुभदः स्मृतः ॥]

सकलगगनानुचारी नैकाभः क्षतजसन्निभो रूक्षः ।
असकलशकटशरासनशृङ्गाटकवत् स्थितः पापः ॥५॥

One which stays in the sky from morning till evening, shines with many a hue or like blood, and is rough, broken, having the form of a cart, bow or triangle, is of disastrous consequences.

शिखिगलसमेऽतिवर्षं बहुवर्णे नृपवधो भयं धूम्रे ।
हरिचापनिभे युद्धान्यशोककुसुमप्रभे चापि ॥६॥

When the halo resembles the peacock's neck in colour, there will be very heavy rains; when it possesses a number of colours, the king will be killed; when it is of smoke colour, there will be panic; and when it has the colour (the deep red) of the Aśoka flower or of the rainbow, there will be wars.

वर्णेनैकेन यदा बहुलः स्निग्धः क्षुराभ्रकाकीर्णः ।
स्वर्त्तौ सद्यो वर्षं करोति पीतश्च दीप्तार्कः ॥७॥

When a thick and glossy halo possesses the particular single colour assigned for the season and is covered with little razor-like clouds, there will be rain the same day. Similar is a yellow halo accompanied by the fierce Sun.

दीप्तमृगविहङ्गरुतः कलुषः सन्ध्यात्रयोत्थितोऽतिमहान् ।
भयकृत्तडिदुल्काद्यैर्हतो नृपं हन्ति शस्त्रेण ॥८॥

A huge and clumsy halo formed at dawn, noon or sunset accompanied by the cries of wild animals and birds facing the Sun, causes fear; and if it is struck by lightning, meteors and the like (such as portents of terrestrial, mid-regional and celestial kinds), it will cause the king's assassination by weapons.

[Cf. गर्ग—

उदयास्तमयोर्मध्ये सूर्याचन्द्रमसोर्द्वयोः ।
परिवेषः प्रदृश्येत तद्राष्ट्रमवसीदति ॥]

प्रतिदिनमर्कहिमांश्वोरहर्निशं रक्तयोर्नरेन्द्रवधः ।
परिविष्टयोरभीक्ष्णं लग्नास्तमयस्थयोस्तद्वत् ॥६॥

If everyday the Sun and the Moon look blood-red throughout, the king will be slain. The same result will follow, if the luminaries are encircled by halos repeatedly both at rising and setting.

[In the second line there is another reading—लग्नास्तनभःस्थयोः which would mean—when they are rising, in mid-heaven and setting.

Cf. गर्ग—

दिवा सूर्ये परीवेषो रात्रौ चन्द्रे यदा भवेत् ।
एकस्मिश्चेदहोरात्रे तदा नश्यति पार्थिवः ॥
एतेन विधिना नित्यं सप्ताहं परिविष्यते ।
सर्वभूतविनाशः स्यात्तस्मिन्नुत्पातदर्शने ॥

Cf. also the समाससंहिता—

शृङ्गाटकचापविकारसन्निभः परुषमूर्तिरतिबहुलः ।
सकलगगनानुचारी बहुवर्णश्चावलम्बी च ॥
द्वित्रिगुणः खण्डो वा सन्ध्यात्रयमुत्थितो ग्रहच्छादी ।
परिवेषः पापफलो ग्रहरोधी हन्ति तद्भक्तीः ॥
स्निग्धो मधुघृतशिखिचाषपत्रनीलोत्पलाब्जरजतनिभः ।
क्षेमसुभिक्षाय भवेत् परिवेषोऽर्कस्य शशिनो वा ॥]

सेनापतेर्भयकरो द्विमण्डलो नातिशस्त्रकोपकरः ।
त्रिप्रभृति शस्त्रकोपं युवराजभयं नगररोधम् ॥१०॥

A halo consisting of two rings causes danger to the commander of the army, but very meagre clash of arms. One having more than two rings tends to fighting, danger to the prince (yuvarāja) and a siege of the town.

[Cf. गर्ग—

द्विमण्डलपरीवेषः सेनापतिभयङ्करः ।
युद्धे सुदारुणं कुर्याद् दृश्यते मण्डलैस्त्रिभिः ॥]

वृष्टिस्त्र्यहेण मासेन विग्रहो वा ग्रहेन्दुभनिरोधे ।
होराजन्माधिपयोर्जन्मर्क्षे वाऽशुभो राज्ञः ॥११॥

When a planet (Mars, Mercury, Jupiter Venus or Saturn) and a star are encircled by the halo round the Moon, there will be rain within three days, or a war will break out in a month. It would be disastrous to a king, if the lord of his ascendant (at birth) or of his natal sign, or his natal star itself be enclosed within this halo.

[Cf. गर्ग—

त्रीणि यत्रावरुध्येरन्नक्षत्रं चन्द्रमा ग्रहः ।
त्र्यहेण वर्षतीन्द्रश्च मासाद्वा जायते भयम् ॥]

परिवेषमण्डलगतो रवितनयः क्षुद्रधान्यनाशकरः ।
जनयति च वातवृष्टिं स्थावरकृषिकृन्निहन्ता च ॥१२॥
भौमे कुमारबलपतिसैन्यानां विद्रवोऽग्निशस्त्रभयम् ।
जीवे परिवेषगते पुरोहितामात्यनृपपीडा ॥१३॥
मन्त्रिस्थावरलेखकपरिवृद्धिश्चन्द्रजे सुवृष्टिश्च ।
शुक्रे यायिक्षत्रियराज्ञीपीडा प्रियं चान्नम् ॥१४॥
क्षुदनलमृत्युनराधिपशस्त्रेभ्यो जायते भयं केतौ ।
परिविष्टे गर्भभयं राहौ व्याधिर्नृपभयं च ॥१५॥

Saturn being encircled by a halo (round the Moon) destroys base corn such as Priyaṅgu, causes stormy rains, and destroys trees and agriculturists. Mars inside the halo causes sufferings to princes (or boys), commanders of armies, and armies and trouble from fire and weapons. Jupiter in the above situation gives trouble to royal priests, ministers and kings. Mercury inside the halo bestows prosperity on ministers, trees and writers, and produces good rains. Venus in that place causes affliction to marching kings, Kṣatriyas and the queen, and makes food very costly (i.e. causes famine). Ketu in a similar situation would create danger from hunger, fire, mortality, king and weapons. Rāhu brings about trouble to children in the womb, diseases and danger to the king.

[The presence of Rāhu or Ketu inside the *Pariveṣa* cannot be observed, but has to be arrived at by calculation. If there is a halo round the Moon and if the longitudes of Rāhu or Ketu and the Moon are almost the same, we can say that the planet is inside the halo.

Cf. the समाससंहिता—

बलपपुरोहितनरपतिकृषिकृत्पीडा क्रमेण परिविष्टैः ।
कुजगुरुसितार्कपुत्रैः सौम्येन तु मन्त्रिपरिवृद्धिः ॥
केतोः शस्त्रोद्योगो राहोः परिवेषणेन रोगभयम् ।
युद्धक्षुद्भयनृपतेर्नाशं व्याध्यादिभिः क्रमशः ॥]

युद्धानि विजानीयात्परिवेषाभ्यन्तरे द्वयोर्ग्रहयोः ।
दिवसकृतः शशिनो वा क्षुदवृष्टिभयं त्रिषु प्रोक्तम् ॥१६॥
याति चतुर्षु नरेन्द्रः सामात्यपुरोहितो वशं मृत्योः ।
प्रलयमिव विद्धि जगतः पञ्चादिषु मण्डलस्थेषु ॥१७॥

If there be two planets inside the halo around the Sun or the Moon, there would be wars; if there be three planets, famine and drought; if four, the king would die along with his ministers and preceptors; and if five or more, there would be a near-destruction of the universe.

ताराग्रहस्य कुर्यात्पृथगेव समुत्थितो नरेन्द्रवधम् ।
नक्षत्राणामथवा यदि केतोर्नोदयो भवति ॥१८॥

If a non-luminary or an asterism comes to have an independent halo around it, there will be the destruction of the monarch, provided there is no appearance of a Ketu (Comet) at the time.

[Cf. काश्यप—

परिवेषाभ्यन्तरगौ द्वौ ग्रहौ यायिनागरौ ।
युद्धं च भवति क्षिप्रं घोररूपं सुदारुणम् ॥
मण्डलान्तरिताः पञ्च जगतः सङ्क्षयावहाः ।
अथ ताराग्रहस्यैव नक्षत्राणामथापि वा ॥
परिवेषो यदा दृश्यस्तदा नरपतेर्वधः ।
यदि केतूदयो न स्यादन्यथा तद्वदेत्फलम् ॥]

विप्रक्षत्रियविट्शूद्रहा भवेत् प्रतिपदादिषु क्रमशः ।
श्रेणीपुरकोशानां पञ्चम्यादिष्वशुभकारी ॥१९॥

युवराजस्याष्टम्यां परतस्त्रिषु पार्थिवस्य दोषकरः ।
पुररोधो द्वादश्यां सैन्यक्षोभस्त्रयोदश्याम् ॥२०॥
नरपतिपत्नीपीडां परिवेषोऽभ्युत्थितश्चतुर्दश्याम् ।
कुर्यात्तु पञ्चदश्यां पीडां मनुजाधिपस्यैव ॥२१॥

A halo observed on the first four lunar days of a fortnight destroys in order Brāhmaṇas, Kṣatriyas, Vaiśyas and Śūdras; on the 5th, 6th and 7th days, trade guilds, towns and royal treasure respectively; on the 8th lunar day, the yuvarāja; on the 9th, 10th and 11th days, it is harmful to the king; on the 12th, it causes a town to be besieged; on the 13th, mutiny in the army; on the 14th day, danger to the queen; and on the 15th day, to the monarch himself.

नागरकाणामभ्यन्तरस्थिता यायिनां च बाह्यस्था ।
परिवेषमध्यरेखा विज्ञेयाक्रन्दसाराणाम् ॥२२॥
रक्तः श्यामो रूक्षश्च भवति येषां पराजयस्तेषाम् ।
स्निग्धः श्वेतो द्युतिमान् येषां भागो जयस्तेषाम् ।२३॥

The line inside a halo refers to the kings defending a town; one outside it, to the marching kings and the central one, to the two kinds of allies called Ākranda and Āsāra, who come to the rescue of the besieged ones. A line that is blood-red or dark and rough (or impure) denotes defeat to those kings whom it represents, while that which is glossy (clear), white and bright, suggests victory to such kings as are represented by the line.

[The commentator remarks :

"परिवेषे वर्णत्रयेण रेखात्रय दृश्यते प्रायेण । तत्र द्वे रेखे बहिर्वर्तिन्यावतिक्रम्य या स्थिता रेखा साऽभ्यन्तरस्थिता..." *Vide* XVII 6, 7 *infra*.

आक्रन्द is an ally of the marching king and follows his enemy, Pārṣṇigrāha, staying behind the attacker. आसार is explained in the Amaraṭīkā by Kṣīrasvāmin "सैन्यस्य सर्वतो व्याप्तिरासारः, आस्त्रियते येनेत्यासारोऽन्वागच्छद्बलम् ।" (P. 195). Vide the शिशुपालबध II. 64 and *Manu* VII. 207.

इन्द्रायुधलक्षणाध्यायः ॥३५॥

Chapter XXXV—Signs of Rainbows

सूर्यस्य विविधवर्णाः पवनेन विघट्टिताः कराः साभ्रे ।
वियति धनुःसंस्थाना ये दृश्यन्ते तदिन्द्रधनुः ॥१॥

The multi-coloured rays of the Sun, being dispersed by the wind in a cloudy sky, are seen in the form of a bow which is called the Rainbow.

[Here the author shows his knowledge that the Sunlight is composed of 7 colours, which are called 7 horses figuratively. The clouds act as a prism to disperse the sunlight into its component colour.]

केचिदनन्तकुलोरगनिःश्वासोद्भूतमाहुराचार्याः ।
तद्यायिनां नृपाणामभिमुखमजयावहं भवति ॥२॥

Some Sages like Kāśyapa declare that the rainbow is caused by the breath of the descendants of Ananta, the king of serpents. The rainbow appearing in front of marching kings causes their defeat.

[Here the author alludes to the traditional story about the origin of rainbows. Even the sage *Kāśyapa* refers to his predecessors for this belief :

अनन्तकुलजाता ये पन्नगाः कामरूपिणः ।
तेषां निःश्वाससम्भूतमिन्द्रचापं प्रचक्षते ॥]

अच्छिन्नमवनिगाढं द्युतिमत् स्निग्धं घनं विविधवर्णम् ।
द्विरुदितमनुलोमं च प्रशस्तमम्भः प्रयच्छति च ॥३॥

If a rainbow is unbroken, bright, glossy, thick, multi-coloured and touching the earth at both extremities, and if it appears double and behind persons, it is auspicious, and will yield good rains.

[The expression 'द्विरुदितमनुलोमं च' is interpreted otherwise by other commentators : If two rainbows appear in the same direction, not in opposite directions, the result would be beneficial. Our commentator does not approve of this construction.

Cf. ऋषिपुत्र—

द्विरुत्तरमविच्छिन्नं स्निग्धमिन्द्रायुधं महत् ।
पृष्ठतो विजयाय स्याद्विच्छिन्नं परुषं न तु ॥

also नन्दी—

बहुवर्णमविच्छिन्नं द्विरुन्नतं स्निग्धममरपतिचापम् ।
पश्चात् पार्श्वे वापि प्रयाणकाले रिपुवधाय ॥

also बृहस्पति—

नीलताम्रमविच्छिन्नं द्विगुणं सिद्धमायतम् ।
पृष्ठतः पार्श्वयोर्वापि जयायेन्द्रधनुर्भवेत् ॥

also the मयूरचित्रक of गर्ग—

पूर्वस्यां दिशि सङ्ग्रामे भवतीन्द्रधनुर्यदि ।
पश्चिमे च प्रयातानां जयस्तत्र न संशयः ॥
तेषां प्रवृत्ते सङ्ग्रामे पश्चादिन्द्रधनुर्भवेत् ।
पूर्वेण तु प्रयातानां जयस्तत्र न संशयः ॥
येषां प्रवृत्ते सङ्ग्रामे वामपार्श्वे च पृष्ठतः ।
धनुः प्रादुर्भवेदैन्द्रं जयस्तेषां न संशयः ॥
येषां प्रवृत्ते सङ्ग्रामे पुरस्ताद्दक्षिणेन वा ।
धनुः प्रादुर्भवेदैन्द्रं वधं तेषां विनिर्दिशेत् ॥
पश्चिमे तु दिशो भागे भवतीन्द्रधनुर्यदि ।
समेघगगनं स्निग्धं वैदूर्यविमलद्युति ॥
विद्युच्च निर्मला भाति पूर्वे वायुर्यदा भवेत् ।
सप्तरात्रं महावर्षं निर्दिशेद्दैवचिन्तकः ॥]

विदिगुद्भूतं दिक्स्वामिनाशनं व्यभ्रजं मरककारि ।
पाटलपीतकनीलैः शस्त्राग्निक्षुत्कृता दोषाः ॥४॥

A rainbow that is seen in an intermediate quarter, will destroy the lord of that particular region; one seen in a cloudlesss sky will cause pestilence, and one that is pink, yellow and blue will create troubles from war (weapons), fire and famine respectively.

[The lords of quarters mentioned here are not the planets, but are political functionaries viz. king, prince, leader, emissary, merchant, spy, Brāhmaṇa (twice-born) and master of the royal elephants. Vide LXXXVI-34, *infra.*]

जलमध्येऽनावृष्टिर्भुवि सस्यवधस्तरौ स्थिते व्याधिः ।
वल्मीके शस्त्रभयं निशि सचिववधाय धनुरैन्द्रम् ॥५॥

A rainbow seen in the middle of water leads to drought; on

land, to destruction of crops; on a tree, to diseases; on an ant-hill, to danger from weapons (or war); and at night, to the minister's murder.

[Kālidāsa alludes in his मेघदूत to this phenomenon of a rainbow being observed on the tip of an anthill—"वल्मीकाग्रात्प्रभवति धनुः-खण्डमाखण्डलस्य ।"]

वृष्टिं करोत्यवृष्टयां वृष्टिं वृष्टयां निवारयत्यैन्द्रयाम् ।
पश्चात्सदैव वृष्टिं कुलिशभृतश्चापमाचष्टे ॥६॥

A rainbow seen in the east when there is no rain, will produce rain and *vice versa*; one seen in the west always indicates rain.

चापं मघोनः कुरुते निशायामाखण्डलायां दिशि भूपपीडाम् ।
याम्यापरोदक्प्रभवं निहन्यात्सेनापतिं नायकमन्त्रिणौ च ॥७॥

A rainbow seen at night in the east will cause trouble (ill health) to the king; and in the south, west and north, it will destroy in order the commander-in-chief, a great leader and the minister.

[Cf. काश्यप—

अवृष्टौ वर्षणं कुर्यादैन्द्रीं दिशमुपाश्रितम् ।
पश्चिमायां महद्वर्षं करोतीन्द्रधनुः सदा ॥
रात्रौ चेद् दृश्यते पूर्वे भयं नरपतेर्भवेत् ।
याम्यायां बलमुख्यश्च विनाशमभिगच्छति ॥
पश्चिमायां प्रधानस्य सौम्यायां मन्त्रिणो वधः ।
स्निग्धवर्णैर्घनैः शुभ्रैर्वारुण्यां दिशि दृश्यते ॥
बहूदकं सुभिक्षं च शिवं सस्यप्रदं भवेत् ॥

The metre is उपजाति.]

निशि सुरचापं सितवर्णाद्यं जनयति पीडां द्विजपूर्वाणाम् ।
भवति च यस्यां दिशि तद्देश्यं नरपतिमुख्यं न चिराद्धन्यात् ॥८॥

A rainbow seen at night with white, red, yellow and dark hues causes trouble to Brāhmaṇas, Kṣatriyas, Vaiśyas and Śūdras respectively. It will also destroy before long the prominent monarch of that region in the particular direction wherein it is sighted.

[The metre is not named in either Piṅgala's or the Vṛttaratnākara. It comes under त्रिष्टुभ् group. Here I have given a new definition and name : रसकरणैः श्रीर्नयसगगैः स्यात्.]

———

गन्धर्वनगरलक्षणाध्यायः ॥३६॥

Chapter XXXVI—Signs of Aerial City

उदगादिपुरोहितनृपबलपतियुवराजदोषदं खपुरम् ।
सितरक्तपीतकृष्णं विप्रादीनामभावाय ॥१॥

An aerial city appearing in the four quarters beginning with the north is injurious to the royal priests, kings, commanders of armies and Yuvarāja respectively. So is one with white, red, yellow and dark colours to the Brāhmaṇas, Kṣaṭriyas, Vaiśyas and Śūdras respectively.

नागरनृपतिजयावहमुदग्विदिक्स्थं विवर्णनाशाय ।
शान्ताशायां दृष्टं सतोरणं नृपतिजयाय ॥२॥

An aerial city seen in the north confers victory on the kings defending their towns; in the intermediate quarters it will bring about the destruction of persons of mixed castes; and one observed with triumphal arches in a direction not facing the Sun will lead to the victory of kings.

सर्वदिगुत्थं सततोत्थितं च भयदं नरेन्द्रराष्ट्राणाम् ।
चौराटविकान् हन्याद्धूमानलशक्रचापाभम् ॥३॥

One appearing in all directions and at all times indicates danger to kings and countries; and one having the hue or hues of smoke, fire and rainbow will destroy robbers and foresters.

गन्धर्वनगरमुत्थितमापाण्डुरमशनिपातवातकरम् ।
दीप्ते नरेन्द्रमृत्युर्वामे ऽरिभयं जयः सव्ये ॥४॥

An aerial city of pale white colour causes the fall of thunderbolts and storms; if it arises in a blasted quarter, a king will die; if it is to the left (of an army or town), it will cause trouble from enemies; and if to the right, it will confer victory.

[The word दीप्त is a technical term. This is the appellation given to a paarticular quarter among the eight. For details see LXXXVI-12 *infra*.]

अनेकवर्णाकृति खे प्रकाशते पुरं पताकाध्वजतोरणान्वितम् ।
यदा तदा नागमनुष्यवाजिनां पिबत्यसृग्भूरि रणे वसुन्धरा ॥५॥

When an aerial city of various colours and shapes shines in the sky with streamers, banners and gateways, the earth will drink plenty of the blood of elephants, horses and human beings in battle.

[Cf. काश्यप—

बहुवर्णं पताकाढ्यं गन्धर्वनगरं महत् ।
दृष्टं प्रजाक्षयकरं सङ्ग्रामे लोमहर्षणम् ॥

The metre is वंशस्थ.]

प्रतिसूर्यलक्षणाध्यायः ॥३७॥

Chapter XXXVII—Mock Suns

प्रतिसूर्यकः प्रशस्तो दिवसकृदृतुवर्णसप्रभः स्निग्धः ।
वैदूर्यनिभः स्वच्छः शुक्लश्च क्षेमसौभिक्षः ॥१॥

A mock Sun is auspicious, if it is glossy and possessed of the colour appropriate for the Sun in the particular season, if it is similar to beryl in lustre, and is clean and white, it is productive of happiness and plenty.

[Vide III. 23-24. *supra* for the Sun's seasonal colours.]

पीतो व्याधिं जनयत्यशोकरूपश्च शस्त्रकोपाय ।
प्रतिसूर्याणां माला दस्युभयातङ्कनृपहन्त्री ॥२॥

A mock sun that is yellow engenders diseases; one of the colour (red) of the Aśoka flowers leads to clash of arms; and a row of mock suns causes danger from robbers, diseases and murder of kings.

दिवसकृतः प्रतिसूर्यो जलकृदुदग्दक्षिणे स्थितोऽनिलकृत् ।
उभयस्थः सलिलभयं नृपमुपरि निहन्त्यधो जनहा ॥३॥

The mock sun appearing to the north of the Sun causes rain; to the south, a strong wind; on both sides, danger from water (i.e. floods etc.); the same appearing above the Sun destroys the king; and below, the people.

[This verse has already appeared in III as 37 *supra*.

The mock sun is nothing but a reflection of the Sun's disc in the thin clouds near the Sun in the morning hours. This phenomenon may occur in the evening also.

Cf. काश्यप—

यम्ये वातप्रदो ज्ञेय उत्तरे वृद्धिदो रवेः ।
उभयोः पार्श्वयोर्भाति सलिलं भूरि यच्छति ॥

also पराशर—

दीप्ताग्निवर्णः कनकप्रभो वा सन्ध्यासु चेद्भास्करमावृणोति ।
कम्पेत भूः खात्प्रपतेन्महोल्का नृपो विनश्येत्सहितः प्रजाभिः ॥
सन्ध्यासमीपे यदि भास्करस्य दृश्येत माला प्रतिसूर्यकाणाम् ।
सर्पा भवेयुः प्रचुराश्च चौरा रोगाश्च घोरा विविधप्रकाराः ॥
प्रत्यर्कमिन्द्रायुधमत्स्यदण्डाः सविद्युदभ्राशनिवर्षवाताः ।
भवन्त्यभीक्ष्णं दिनरात्रिसन्धौ भयं तदा भूमिपतेर्वधः स्यात् ॥]

———

रजोलक्षणाध्यायः ॥३८॥

Chapter XXXVIII—Indications of Haze

Since Bhaṭṭotpala does not comment upon this chapter, it must have been interpolated after his time.

कथयन्ति पार्थिववधं रजसा घनतिमिरसञ्चयनिभेन ।
अविभाव्यमानगिरिपुरतरवः सर्वा दिशश्छन्नाः ॥१॥

It is said that a king will be killed when all the quarters are covered with dust, resembling the mass of pitch darkness, and making the mountains, cities and trees indistinguishable.

यस्यां दिशि धूमचयः प्राक् प्रभवति नाशमेति वा यस्याम् ।
आगच्छति सप्ताहात् तत्रैव भयं न सन्देहः ॥२॥

There will undoubtedly be danger within a week to that quarter wherein a mass of smoke appears at the first or disappears.

श्वेते रजोघनौघे पीडा स्यान्मन्त्रिजनपदानां च ।
न चिरात्प्रकोपमुपयाति शस्त्रमतिसङ्कुला सिद्धिः ॥३॥

When the mass of cloud-like dust is white, there is trouble in store for ministers and the people alike, and before long there will be a great clash of arms, and normalcy and peace will be restored after a good deal of confusion and suffering.

अर्कोदये विजृम्भति यदि दिनमेकं दिनद्वयं वापि ।
स्थगयन्निव गगनतलं भयमत्युग्रं निवेदयति ॥४॥

Dust appearing prominently, blocking as it were, the entire sky at sunrise for a whole day or two continuously, augurs terrible disaster.

अनवरतसञ्चयवहं रजनीमेकां प्रधाननृपहन्तृ ।
क्षेमाय च शेषाणां विचक्षणानां नरेन्द्राणाम् ॥५॥

Dust appearing in a mass throughout a night tends to the death of a leading king, but confers prosperity on other clever kings.

रजनीद्वयं विसर्पति यस्मिन् राष्ट्रे रजोघनं बहुलम् ।
परचक्रस्यागमनं तस्मिन्नपि सन्निबोद्धव्यम् ।।६।।

When a thick cloud of dust spreads over a kingdom for two nights continuously, it should be understood that the country will be the victim of foreign aggression.

निपतति रजनीत्रितय चतुष्कमप्यन्नरसविनाशाय ।
राज्ञां सैन्यक्षोभो रजसि भवेत् पञ्चरात्रभवे ।।७।।

If dust falls continuously for three or even four nights, food grains and liquids or juicy substances will be destroyed; and if for five nights, there will be mutiny in the armies of kings.

केत्वाद्युदयविमुक्तं यदा रजो भवति तीव्रभयदायि ।
शिशिरादन्यत्रर्त्तौ फलमविकलमाहुराचार्याः ।।८।।

Dust presages extreme danger only when it is not accompanied by the rise of Ketus etc. The sages have declared that the effects would be fully felt only in seasons other than winter.

[Here the interpolator puts the seal of authority by alluding to the opinion of the *ācāryas*.]

———

निर्घातलक्षणाध्यायः ॥३९॥

Chapter XXXIX—Symptoms of Hurricane

पवनः पवनाभिहतो गगनादवनौ यदा समापतति ।
भवति तदा निर्घातः स च पापो दीप्तविहगरुतः ॥१॥

When a gust of wind struck by another dashes against the earth from the sky, a portentous thunder is generated. It is inauspicious when accompanied by the harsh cries of birds facing the Sun.

[Cf. गर्ग—

यदान्तरिक्षे बलवान् मारुतो मारुताहतः ।
पतत्यधः स निर्घातो भवेदनिलसम्भवः ॥]

अर्कोदयेऽधिकरणिकनृपधनियोधाङ्गनावणिग्वेश्याः ।
आप्रहरांशेऽजाविकमुपहन्याच्छूद्रपौरांश्च ॥२॥

आमध्याह्नाद्राजोपसेविनो ब्राह्मणांश्च पीडयति ।
वैश्यजलदांस्तृतीये चौरान्प्रहरे चतुर्थे तु ॥३॥

अस्तं याते नीचान् प्रथमे यामे निहन्ति सस्यानि ।
रात्रौ द्वितीययामे पिशाचसङ्घान् निपीडयति ॥४॥

तुरगकरिणस्तृतीये विनिहन्याद्यायिनश्चतुर्थे च ।
भैरवजर्जरशब्दो याति यतस्तां दिशं हन्ति ॥५॥

At sunrise such a thunder destroys judges, kings, wealthy persons, warriors, women, traders and courtesans; in the first watch of the day, goats, sheep, Śūdras and city-dwellers; in the second, king's servants and Brāhmaṇas; in the third, merchants and clouds; in the fourth, thieves; at sunset, iniquitous persons; in the first watch of the night, crops; in the second, groups of goblins; in the third, horses and elephants; and in the fourth, marching kings. The direction from which issues the dreadful sound like that of a breaking pot, will be destroyed.

[In this section the author gives the effects of the thunder occurring in the different watches of the day and night as well as the direction. What is the sunrise-period ? The commentator answers : "दिनारम्भाद् घटिकाद्वयं यावत् सूर्योदय:"

Cf. the समाससंहिता—

निर्घातोऽह्नोरात्रेण हन्ति नृपपौरभृत्यराष्ट्रजनान् ।
तस्करविप्रांश्चार्कोदयाद्दिशं पतति यस्याम् ॥

also गर्ग—

यदा सूर्योदये प्राप्ते निर्घातः श्रूयते भुवि ।
क्षत्रिया योधमुख्याश्च पीड्यन्तेऽत्र न संशयः ॥
प्रहरांशे तथा वैश्यान् हन्याद् गोजीविनस्तथा ।
परिवृत्ते हरौ वैश्या अपराह्णे तु दस्यवः ॥
नीचचौरांश्च हन्यात् स अस्तमेति दिवाकरे ।
प्रथमे प्रहरे सस्यान्यर्द्धरात्रे तु राक्षसान् ॥
रात्रित्रिभागे वैश्यांश्च प्रत्यूषे चाहितो भवेत् ।
यां दिशं चाभिहन्येत निर्घातो भैरवः स्वनः ॥
तद्देश्यान् हन्ति देशांश्च सर्वदिग्भक्तयस्तथा ॥

सस्यजातकम् ॥४०॥

Chapter XL—Growth of Crops

वृश्चिकवृषप्रवेशे भानोर्ये बादरायणेनोक्ताः ।
ग्रीष्मशरत्सस्यानां सदसद्योगाः कृतास्त इमे ॥१॥

The good and bad yogas, planetary configurations, that have been declared by sage Bādarāyaṇa for the growth of summer and autumnal crops, at the time of the Sun's entry into Scorpio and Taurus respectively, are explained here.

[The prospects of the next summer crops have to be judged from the planetary positions with reference to the ascendant at the time of the Sun's entry into Scorpio. Similarly those of autumnal crops should be gauged at the entry of the Sun into Taurus. In ancient times sage Bādarāyaṇa, who might be identical with or different from the sage *Pārāśarya*, must have been an authority on this subject. Here the commentator remarks that Scorpio or Taurus alone should be taken as the ascendant. This is quite unscientific and unacceptable. For, we could get this ascendant only when the Sun enters the sign, in the morning hours, and not at other times. The correct method would be to calculate the ascendant for the exact time of the Sun's entry into Scorpio or Taurus and then apply Bādarāyaṇa's rules for reading this horoscope. Bhaṭṭotpala's method (based on the ancient rules) be adopted as a rough one.]

भानोरलिप्रवेशे केन्द्रैस्तस्माच्छुभग्रहाक्रान्तैः ।
बलवद्भिः सौम्यैर्वा निरीक्षिते ग्रैष्मिकविवृद्धिः ॥२॥

If at the time of the Sun's entry into Scorpio, the Kendras (angles) from him are occupied by benefics, or if he is aspected (or conjoined with) strong benefics, summer crops will flourish splendidly.

[It is possible that the word 'तस्मात्' in the text means 'from the Sun'. The commentator construes the expression : "सौम्यैर्वा निरीक्षिते" as follows :

Either the angles from the Sun are occupied by benefics, or the Sun is aspected by strong benefics occupying non-Kendra houses. This can happen only in the case of Jupiter and not of Mercury and Venus. Then he adds, "बलवद्भिः सौम्यैर्दृष्टे भानौ युक्ते'. If they are close to the Sun, they would be combust. So he goes on further and says, "यदा सौम्यैर्बलिभिरबलिभिर्वा केन्द्रस्थानानि युक्तानि भवन्ति तदा ग्रैष्मिकसस्यविवृद्धिर्भवति। यदा तु पुनस्त्रिकोणरिपुलाभगाः सौम्या बलिनः पश्यन्ति तदा ग्रैष्मिकस्य विवृद्धिर्भवति।"

Cf. बादरायण—

वृश्चिकसंस्थे सूर्ये सौम्यैर्बलिभिर्निरीक्षिते वृद्धिम्।
तैरेव केन्द्रगैर्वा ग्रीष्मजधान्यस्य निर्दिशेन्महतीम्॥]

अष्टमराशिगतेऽर्के गुरुशशिनोः कुम्भसिंहसंस्थितयोः।
सिंहघटसंस्थयोर्वा निष्पत्तिर्ग्रैष्मसस्यस्य॥३॥

When the Sun tenants Scorpio, and Jupiter and the Moon Aquarius and Leo, or *vice versa*, summer crops will prosper.

अर्कात्सिते द्वितीये बुधेऽथवा युगपदेव वा स्थितयोः।
व्ययगतयोरपि तद्वन्निष्पत्तिरतीव गुरुदृष्ट्या॥४॥

When Venus or Mercury or both are posited in the second or 12th house from the Sun in Scorpio, summer corn will grow well. If, in addition, the Sun be aspected by Jupiter, there would be bumper crops.

[It is clear that there is no place for the ascendant in Bādarāyaṇa's scheme. I have stated above that the method is very rough.

Cf. बादरायण—

सूर्याद् बुधे द्वितीये शुक्रे वा युगपदेव तयोः।
रिप्फगयोरप्येवं निष्पत्तिर्गुरुदृशाऽतीव॥]

शुभमध्येऽलिनि सूर्याद्गुरुशशिनोः सप्तमे परा सम्पत्।
अल्यादिस्थे सवितरि गुरौ द्वितीयेऽर्द्धनिष्पत्तिः॥५॥

When Scorpio is surrounded by benefics i.e. Mercury and Venus, and when the 7th house from the Sun i.e. Taurus, is occupied by Jupiter and the Moon, there will be excellent growth of corn. When the Sun occupies the initial part of Scorpio and Jupiter the second house therefrom, the growth will be only half.

लाभहिबुकार्थयुक्तैः सूर्यादलिगात्सितेन्दुशशिपुत्रैः ।
सस्यस्य परा सम्पत् कर्मणि जीवे गवां चाग्र्या ॥६॥

When Venus, the Moon and Mercury are posited in the 11th, 4th and 2nd houses respectively from the Sun in Scorpio, there will be excellent crop. If in the above planetary configuration Jupiter be in the 10th house i.e. Leo, there would be unique prosperity of cattle.

कुम्भे गुरुर्गवि शशी सूर्योऽलिमुखे कुजार्कजौ मकरे ।
निष्पत्तिरस्ति महती पश्चात्परचक्रभयरोगम् ॥७॥

If at the time of the Sun's entry into Scorpio Jupiter be in Aquarius, the Moon in Taurus, and Mars and Saturn in Capricorn, there would be excellent growth of corn, but later there would be outbreak of diseases and threat of an enemy attack.

मध्ये पापग्रहयोः सूर्यः सस्यं विनाशयत्यलिगः ।
पापः सप्तमराशौ जातं जातं विनाशयति ॥८॥

The Sun occupying Scorpio, being surrounded by malefics on both sides, destroys crops. If there be a malefic in the 7th house, crops would be destroyed even though they may grow well.

[Cf. बादरायण—

क्रूरान्तःस्थः सूर्यो वृश्चिकसंस्थो विनाशयति सस्यम् ।
जातं जातं पापः सप्तमसंस्थो विनाशयति ॥]

अर्थस्थाने क्रूरः सौम्यैरनिरीक्षितः प्रथमजातम् ।
सस्यं निहन्ति पश्चादुप्तं निष्पादयेद्व्यक्तम् ॥९॥

A malefic in the second house from Scorpio, being unaspected by benefics, will destroy the crops sown first; but will enable those sown subsequently to thrive well.

जामित्रकेन्द्रसंस्थौ क्रूरौ सूर्यस्य वृश्चिकस्थस्य ।
सस्यविपत्तिं कुरुतः सौम्यैर्दृष्टौ न सर्वत्र ॥१०॥

Two malefics viz. Mars and Saturn, occupying the 7th and any other angular house from the Sun in Scorpio, will destroy the crops; and if they be aspected by benefics, they would not destroy corn completely or everywhere.

[For benefics to aspect the malefics in Taurus, Mercury and Venus ought to be in Scorpio itself, but Jupiter could be in any one of the following signs, Scorpio, Capricorn and Virgo.

Cf. बादरायण—

सूर्यात्सप्तमसंस्थः पापो यः केन्द्रगश्च हानिकरौ ।
सौम्यग्रहसन्दृष्टौ न तथा सर्वत्र निर्दिष्टौ ॥]

वृश्चिकसंस्थादर्कात् सप्तमषष्ठोपगौ यदा क्रूरौ ।
भवति तदा निष्पत्तिः सस्यानामर्घपरिहानिः ॥११॥

When the two malefics occupy the 6th and 7th houses from the Sun in Scorpio, there will be good growth of crops, but their prices will slump.

[Bhaṭṭotpala misinterprets the expression, अर्घपरिहानिः as बहुमूल्येनाल्पं लभते i.e. things become very costly, whereas it means only fall in prices.]

विधिनानेनैव रविर्वृषप्रवेशे शरत्समुत्थानाम् ।
विज्ञेयः सस्यानां नाशाय शिवाय वा तज्ज्ञैः ॥१२॥

According to this method alone astrologers ought to declare the prosperity or destruction of the autumnal crops, when the Sun enters Taurus.

[Cf. बादरायण—

य एव योगोऽभिहितो वृश्चिकस्थे दिवाकरे ।
वृषेऽपि ते शारदानां चिन्तनीया यथार्थतः ॥]

त्रिषु मेषादिषु सूर्यः सौम्ययुतो वीक्षितोऽपि वा विचरन् ।
ग्रैष्मिकधान्यं कुरुते समर्घमभयोपयोग्यं च ॥१३॥

When the Sun moves through Aries, Taurus or Gemini in conjunction with or being aspected by benefics, summer crops will fetch good price, will be free from pests and be entirely useful.

[उभयोपयोग्यं is another reading which is interpreted by Bhaṭṭotpala as "इहलोके परलोके चोपयुज्यते ।" The word 'समर्घ' is again wrongly construed by him as 'स्वल्पमूल्यम्'.]

कार्मुकमृगघटसंस्थः शारदसस्यस्य तद्वदेव रविः ।
सङ्ग्रहकाले ज्ञेयो विपर्ययः क्रूरदृग्योगात् ॥१४॥

Similarly, the Sun occupying any one of the Signs, Sagittarius, Capricorn and Aquarius in conjunction with or being aspected by benefics, helps autumnal crops to flourish and fetch good price etc. But at the time of harvest, if the Sun be aspected by or conjoined with malefics, contrary effects should be understood for them (i.e. the corn will be very costly, useless and infested with pests).

[Here too the commentator twists the text and construes the expression सङ्ग्रहकाले as विक्रयकाले. But it means only 'the time of harvest.' He adds "विपरीतयोगस्थे सूर्ये विक्रयः कार्यः'. This meaning is not warranted by the text.]

द्रव्यनिश्चयाध्यायः ॥४१॥

Chapter XLI—Classification of Substances

ये येषां द्रव्याणामधिपतयो राशयः समुद्दिष्टाः ।
मुनिभिः शुभाशुभार्थं तानागमतः प्रवक्ष्यामि ॥१॥

I shall now expound, on the authority of the Śāstras, the different Zodiacal Signs that have been declared by ancient Sages (like Kāśyapa) as the rulers of different substances, so that their good and bad effects (on prices etc.) may be understood.

[From the commentary it is clear that Sage Kāśyapa had treated of the subject of commodities and price fluctuations. For this purpose the ancients had allotted different substances to the different Signs of the Zodiac. If the concerned Sign is unafflicted, but well-aspected, the articles will be available in plenty and also fetch good prices.]

वस्त्राविककुतुपानां मसूरगोधूमरालकयवानाम् ।
स्थलसम्भवौषधीनां कनकस्य च कीर्त्तितो मेषः ॥२॥

Sign Aries is considered to rule over cloths, sheep's wool, clothes made of goat's hair, lentils, wheat, resin, barley, herbs growing on land, and gold.

[Cf. काश्यप—

मेषे सुवर्णस्थलजा गोधूमाजाविकास्तथा ।
ग्रहवर्णर्क्षसंयोगे शोभने सफलं भवेत् ॥]

गवि वस्त्रकुसुमगोधूमशालियवमहिषसुरभितनयाः स्युः ।
मिथुनेऽपि धान्यशारदवल्लीशालूककार्पासाः ॥३॥

Sign Taurus controls cloths, flowers, wheat, rice, barley, buffaloes and bullocks. Gemini presides over corn, autumnal creepers like grape vines, lily bulbs and cotton.

[Cf. काश्यप—

वृषे महिषगोवस्त्रशालयः पुष्पसम्भवाः ।
मिथुने धान्यशालूकवल्यः कार्पासशारदम् ॥]

कर्किणि कोद्रवकदलीदूर्वाफलकन्दपत्रचोचानि ।
सिंहे तुषधान्यरसाः सिंहादीनां त्वचः सगुडाः ॥४॥

Sign Cancer rules over paspalum, bananas, Dūrvā grass, fruits, bulbs, fragrant leaves and woody cassia (or cocoanut ?). Sign Leo controls husk-grains, juices, skins of lions etc. and jaggery.

[Cf. काश्यप—

कर्कटे फलदूर्वाश्च कोद्रवः कदली तथा ।
सिंहे धान्यं सर्वरसाः सिंहादीनां त्वचो गुडाः ॥]

षष्ठेऽतसीकलायाः कुलत्थगोधूममुद्गनिष्पावाः ।
सप्तमराशौ माषा यवगोधूमाः ससर्षपाश्चैव ॥५॥

Sign Virgo owns Atasī (common flax), Kalāya corn (peas ?), horse-gram, wheat, green gram and leguminous seeds. Sign Libra rules over black gram, barley, wheat and mustard.

[Cf. काश्यप—

कन्यायां मुद्गनीवारकुलत्थाः सकला यवाः ।
तुले तु यवगोधूममाषाः सिद्धार्थकास्तथा ॥]

अष्टमराशाविक्षुः सैक्यं लोहान्यजाविकं चापि ।
नवमे तु तुरगलवणाम्बरास्त्रतिलधान्यमूलानि ॥६॥

Sign Scorpio owns sugarcane, whatever grows being watered, such as fruits of creepers, iron or bell-metal and goats' and sheep's wool. Sign Sagittarius has horses, salt, weapons, sesamum. corn and roots.

[Cf. काश्यप—

अलिनीक्षुरसं सैक्यमाजं लोहं सकांस्यकम् ।
धान्यं धनुषि वस्त्राणि लवणं तुरगास्तथा ॥]

मकरे तरुगुल्माद्यं सैक्येक्षुसुवर्णकृष्णलोहानि ।
कुम्भे सलिलजफलकुसुमरत्नचित्राणि रूपाणि ॥७॥

Sign Capricorn presides over the shrubs, creepers etc., whatever grows as a result of watering, sugarcane, gold and black metal i.e. iron. Aquarius rules over water-products, fruits, flowers, gems and brilliant things.

[Cf. काश्यप—

मकरे तु सस्यसीसं च सुवर्णगुडधातुजम् ।
कुम्भे कुसुमचित्राणि हंसाश्च जलजास्तथा ॥]

मीने कपालसम्भवरत्नान्यम्बूद्भवानि वज्राणि ।
स्नेहाश्च नैकरूपा व्याख्याता मत्स्यजातं च ॥८॥

Sign Pisces controls such gems as come from testaceous animals, e.g. from the pearl oyster, water-products, diamonds, oils of various kinds, fishes and fish-products.

[Cf. काश्यप—

पद्ममुक्ताफलादीनां द्रव्याणां मीन ईश्वरः ॥]

राशेश्चतुर्दशार्थायसप्तनवपञ्चमस्थितो जीवः ।
द्व्येकादशदशपञ्चाष्टमेषु शशिजश्च वृद्धिकरः ॥९॥
षट्सप्तमगो हानिं वृद्धिं शुक्रः करोति शेषेषु ।
सञ्चयसंस्थाः क्रूराः शुभदाः शेषेषु हानिकराः ॥१०॥

Jupiter occupying the 4th, 10th, 2nd, 11th, 7th, 9th or 5th house from the Sign promotes the interests of those objects that are allotted to that Sign. So does Mercury while occupying the 2nd, 11th, 10th, 5th or 8th house from the concerned Sign. Venus tenanting the 6th and 7th houses from a Sign destroys its objects, while in the rest he promotes their progress. Malefics in the 3rd, 6th, 10th and 11th houses from the concerned Sign prove beneficial while in the rest, harmful.

[Cf.

चतुःसप्तद्विपञ्चस्थो नवदिग्रुद्रगो गुरुः ।
यस्य राशेस्तदुक्तानां द्रव्याणां वृद्धिदः स्मृतः ।
शुक्रः षट्सप्तमस्थो वा हानिकृद्वृद्धिदोऽन्यगः ।
द्व्येकादशदशार्थाष्टसंस्थितः शशिजः शुभः ॥
पापास्तूपचयस्थाश्च वृद्धिं कुर्वन्ति नान्यथा ॥]

राशेर्यस्य क्रूराः पीडास्थानेषु संस्थिता बलिनः ।
तत्प्रोक्तद्रव्याणां महार्घता दुर्लभत्वं च ॥११॥

If strong malefics occupy the Apacaya houses (other than the 3rd, 6th, 10th and 11th) with respect to a particular Sign, the objects assigned to that Sign would become very costly and scarce.

[Cf. काश्यप—

राशेरनिष्टस्थानेषु पापाश्च सबलाः स्थिताः ।
तद्द्रव्याणां नाशकरा दुर्लभास्ते भवन्ति हि ॥]

इष्टस्थाने सौम्या बलिनो येषां भवन्ति राशीनाम् ।
तद्द्रव्याणां वृद्धिः सामर्थ्यं वल्लभत्वं च ॥१२॥

Those articles whose ruling Signs have strong benefics occupy-uspicious Signs therefrom, will thrive well, fetch good prices have great demand.

[For the Iṣṭasthānas for the different benefics *vide* verses 9-10

Cf. काश्यप—

इष्टस्थाने स्थिताः सौम्या बलिनो येषु राशिषु ।
भवन्ति तद्भवानां च द्रव्याणां शुभदाः स्मृताः ॥]

गोचरपीडायामपि राशिर्बलिभिः शुभग्रहैर्दृष्टः ।
पीडां न करोति तथा क्रूरैरेवं विपर्यासः ॥१३॥

Even though a Sign is afflicted by the unfavourable transits from of the benefics, yet no harm would come to the objects rned by it, provided it is aspected by strong benefics. However, esult would be utterly bad if under the unfavourable transits of fics the Sign be aspected by strong malefics.

[The *Gocarapīḍā* or transit-affliction mentioned here refers to enefics occupying houses other than those mentioned in verses d 10. These benefics may aspect the Sign, though they thems may be posited in unfavourable houses. The result of this ct must do some good at least.]

— — —

अर्घकाण्डाध्यायः ॥४२॥

Chapter XLII—Fluctuation of Prices

अतिवृष्ट्युल्कादण्डान् परिवेषग्रहणपरिधिपूर्वांश्च ।
दृष्ट्वाऽमावास्यायामुत्पातान् पौर्णमास्यां च ॥१॥
ब्रूयादर्घविशेषान् प्रतिमासं राशिषु क्रमात्सूर्ये ।
अन्यतिथावुत्पाता ये ते डमरार्त्तये राज्ञाम् ॥२॥

By observing excessive rain, meteor, Rod, halo, eclipse, mock-sun and such other portents on the new-Moon and full-Moon days and also at the Sun's entrance into a new Sign of the Zodiac every month, one should predict fluctuations in the prices of commodities. These portents observed on other days forebode sufferings to kings through wars or bloodshed.

[There are many technical terms in this verse. For Ulkā. Daṇḍa, Pariveṣa and Paridhi see ch. XXXIII-8; XXX-16; XXXIV-1 and XXXVII-1 respectively. From this verse it is clear that the prospects of prices have to be determined through the phenomena occurring on the three critical days viz. new Moon, full Moon and the Sun's entry into a new Sign of the Zodiac. In fact this chapter and the previous two are to be read together for a complete understanding of the prospects for crops and their prices. We find the same sage Kāśyapa being quoted as authority on this subject.

Cf. काश्यप—

उल्कातिवृष्टिर्ग्रहणे सूर्येन्द्वोः परिवेषणम् ।
प्रतिसूर्यादयो येऽन्ये पक्षमासान्तसङ्क्षये ॥
तिथौ निरीक्ष्य चोत्पातान्ब्रूयाल्लोके शुभाशुभम् ।
सुभिक्षदुर्भिक्षकृतान् विशेषोऽत्र विचारतः ॥
प्रतिमासं विधानज्ञो नान्यस्मिन् दिवसे वदेत् ।
अन्यत्र ये भवन्त्येते ते सर्वे नृपदोषदाः ॥]

मेषोपगते सूर्ये ग्रीष्मजधान्यस्य सङ्ग्रहं कृत्वा ।
वनमूलफलस्य वृषे चतुर्थमासे तयोर्लाभः ॥३॥

When the Sun enters Sign Aries one should observe the portents mentioned above, as well as on the Full-Moon and New Moon days, and collect or buy summer corn. He would earn much profit by selling the corn in the fourth month. In the case of forest roots and fruits the observation should be made when the Sun enters Sign Taurus.

मिथुनस्थे सर्वरसान् धान्यानि च सङ्ग्रहं समुपनीय ।
षष्ठे मासे विपुलं विक्रेता प्राप्नुयाल्लाभम् ॥४॥

If one collects all kinds of juice (or juicy things or the six varieties of taste) and corn when the Sun is in Sign Gemini, after observing the portents, and sells them in the sixth month, he will make large profits.

कर्किण्यर्के मधुगन्धतैलघृतफाणितानि विनिधाय ।
द्विगुणा द्वितीयमासे लब्धिर्हीनाधिके छेदः ॥५॥

Similarly one should store up honey, perfumes, oils, ghee and treacle, when the Sun is in Cancer, and sell them in the second month. He will then make cent per cent profit. He will sustain loss if the selling time exceeds or falls short of that period.

सिंहे सुवर्णमणिचर्मवर्मशस्त्राणि मौक्तिकं रजतम् ।
पञ्चममासे लब्धिर्विक्रेतुरतोऽन्यथा छेदः ॥६॥

One should store up gold, gems, skins, armours, weapons, pearls and silver when the Sun is in Leo, and sell them in the 5th month in order to get good profits. Otherwise he will sustain loss.

कन्यागते दिनकरे चामरखरकरभवाजिनां क्रेता ।
षष्ठे मासे द्विगुणं लाभमवाप्नोति विक्रीणन् ॥७॥

If one buys chowries, donkeys, camels and horses when the Sun is in Virgo and sells them in the sixth month, he will get an equal amount as profit.

तौलिनि तान्तवभाण्डं मणिकम्बलकाचपीतकुसुमानि ।
आदद्याद्धान्यानि च वर्षार्द्धाद्द्विगुणिता वृद्धिः ॥८॥

If one should buy cotton cloths, gems, blankets, glass, yellow flowers and corn, when the Sun is in Libra, and sell them in six months, he would make hundred per cent profit.

वृश्चिकसंस्थे सवितरि फलकन्दकमूलविविधरत्नानि ।
वर्षद्वयमुषितानि द्विगुण लाभं प्रयच्छन्ति ॥९॥

One should hoard fruits, bulbs, roots and varieties of gems for two years having secured them during the Sun's transit through Scorpio, and then sell them to get a profit equal to their price.

चापगते गृह्णीयात्कुङ्कुमशङ्खप्रवालकाचानि ।
मुक्ताफलानि च ततो वर्षार्द्धाद् द्विगुणतां यान्ति ॥१०॥

One should buy saffron, conch shell, corals, glass and pearls when the Sun is situated in Sign Sagittarius, and sell them in six months. Then he would get double the amount invested.

मृगघटसंस्थे सवितरि गृह्णीयाल्लोहभाण्डधान्यानि ।
स्थित्वा मासं दद्याल्लाभार्थी द्विगुणमाप्नोति ॥११॥

When the Sun tenants Capricorn or Aquarius one wishing for profit should buy and keep metallic (or iron) vessels and grains and sell them after a month. He would then get double the amount invested.

सवितरि झषमुपयाते मूलफलं कन्दभाण्डरत्नानि ।
संस्थाप्य वत्सरार्द्धं लाभकमिष्टं समाप्नोति ॥१२॥

One should collect roots, fruits, bulbs, vessels and gems when the Sun has entered Sign Pisces, and sell them after six months. He would then get as much profit as he desires.

राशौ राशौ यस्मिन् शिशिरमयूखः सहस्रकिरणो वा ।
युक्तोऽधिमित्रदृष्टस्तत्रायं लाभको दिष्टः ॥१३॥

Profits mentioned above should be declared only when the Sun or the Moon occupying any of the zodiacal Signs is conjoined with or aspected by very friendly planets.

[The commentator is thrown off his guard by the expression, *Adhimitra*, which usually means a planet that is friendly both naturally and temporarily. But in this context it cannot mean any thing other than '*a strong friend*'. For, a temporary friend can neither aspect nor conjoin with a planet, except, of course, Mars aspecting from the 10th and Saturn from the 11th house. In the case of the Sun, Mars can be the friend aspecting him, but he is a malefic. I feel that more than the aspect etc. of friendly planets there should be the aspect etc. of strong benefics.

Cf. काश्यप—

राशौ राशौ स्थितः सूर्यः शशी वा मित्रसंयुतः ।
अधिमित्रेण सन्दृष्टो यथा लाभप्रदः स्मृतः ॥]

सवितृसहितः सम्पूर्णो वा शुभैर्युतवीक्षितः
शिशिरकिरणः सद्योऽर्घस्य प्रवृद्धिकरः स्मृतः ।
अशुभसहितः सन्दृष्टो वा हिनस्त्यथवा रविः
प्रतिगृहगतान् भावान् बुद्ध्वा वदेत्सदसत्फलम् ॥१४॥

The Moon, full or in conjunction with the Sun (on New Moon day) being conjoined with and (or) aspected by benefics, promotes immediately the prices of articles belonging to the particular Sign occupied by her. Similarly, the Sun conjoined with and (or) aspected by malefics, destroys the prices of commodities belonging to that Sign. Thus should one make predictions, good and bad, regarding the price of materials, having duly comprehended the objects belonging to the several Signs of the Zodiac.

[It is understood here that the prices will slump down, if the Moon in either situation is conjoined with or aspected by malefics.

Cf. काश्यप—

अत्रार्कशशिनौ सौम्यैः संयुक्तौ वा निरीक्षितौ ।
शुभग्रहस्थानगतौ सद्योऽर्घस्य विवृद्धिदौ ॥
विपरीतस्थितावेतौ पापयुक्तौ निरीक्षितौ ।
अर्घहानिकरौ प्रोक्तौ मिश्रितौ मध्यमौ स्मृतौ ॥

Here the Sage lays down one more condition for rise in price i.e. the luminary should be in the house of a benefic.

The metre is हरिणी].

इन्द्रध्वजसम्पद् ॥४३॥

Chapter XLIII—Glory of Indra's Banner

In the previous three chapters the author has treated of agricultural and economic matters. Now he takes up for exposition political astrology. What I mean is that the auguries mentioned herein pertain to kings and their kingdoms.

ब्रह्माणमूचुरमरा भगवन् शक्ताः स्म नासुरान् समरे ।
प्रतियोधयितुमतस्त्वां शरण्यशरणं समुपयाताः ॥१॥

Once the celestials submitted to the Creator :—"Oh Lord, we are unable to withstand the demons in battle. Consequently, we have come to you, the protector of the helpless."

देवानुवाच भगवान् क्षीरोदे केशवः स वः केतुम् ।
यं दास्यति तं दृष्ट्वा नाजौ स्थास्यन्ति वो दैत्याः ॥२॥

The Lord replied to the Gods thus :—"Lord Nārāyaṇa reposing on the Milky Ocean will grant you a banner, at sight of which the demons will not be able to face you on the battlefield."

लब्धवराः क्षीरोदं गत्वा ते तुष्टुवुः सुराः सेन्द्राः ।
श्रीवत्साङ्कं कौस्तुभमणिकिरणोद्भासितोरस्कम् ॥३॥

श्रीपतिमचिन्त्यमसमं समं ततः सर्वदेहिनां सूक्ष्मम् ।
परमात्मानमनादिं विष्णुमविज्ञातपर्यन्तम् ॥४॥

तैः संस्तुतः स देवस्तुतोष नारायणो ददौ चैषाम् ।
ध्वजमसुरसुरवधूमुखकमलवनतुषारतीक्ष्णांशुम् ॥५॥

The Gods with Indra as their leader received the Creator's boon and went to the Milky Ocean and eulogized the Lord Nārāyaṇa, consort of Lakṣmī, who had the mark *Śrīvatsa* on His breast, which was brightened by the rays of the Kaustubha gem, who was incomprehensible, peerless, impartial, unknowable to all beings, the Supreme Being, without beginning and end, and all-pervasive. The Lord, being pleased with their invocations, vouchsafed unto them a banner which would prove as the Moon and the Sun respectively to the lotuslike faces of the damsels of the demons and the Gods.

[The Moon is said to be inimical to the lotuses which are delighted at the rising of the Sun. Here the idea is that the banner would enable the celestials to trounce the demons. These verses represent our author's good poetry. Mark the fine alliteration and description in the second line, paradox in the third and *yathāsaṅkhya* in the last line.]

तं विष्णुतेजोभवमष्टचक्रे रथे स्थितं भास्वति रत्नचित्रे ।
देदीप्यमानं शरदीव सूर्यं ध्वजं समासाद्य मुमोद शक्रः ॥६॥

Indra was overjoyed on receiving that banner, which was born of Viṣṇu's effulgence, which shone brilliantly like the blazing Sun in autumn, and which was mounted on a glittering eight-wheeled chariot, bedecked with jewels.

[मुमोद is ungrammatical in form The author might have employed the word तुतोष instead. The commentator too commits a similar mistake by using 'जहर्षे' instead of 'जहर्ष'. The second line that contains a beautiful simile reminds us of Vālmīki's verse, "पोप्लूयमानं शरदीव हंसम्" V. 2-58.

This and the following verse are in उपजाति metre.]

स किङ्किणीजालपरिष्कृतेन स्रक्छत्रघण्टापिटकान्वितेन ।
समुच्छ्रितेनामरराड्ध्वजेन निन्ये विनाशं समरेऽरिसैन्यम् ॥७॥

The Lord of Gods i.e. Indra, put the army of the enemies to death in battle with the help of the banner, which was erected aloft, bedecked with wreaths of little bells, and which bore garlands, umbrellas, bells and ornaments.

[Cf. गर्ग—

असुरास्तं ध्वजं दृष्ट्वा ध्वजतेजःसमाहताः ।
विसंज्ञाः समरे भग्नाः पराभूताः प्रदुद्रुवुः ॥
तान्वज्रेण सहस्राक्षो मासे भाद्रपदेऽसुरान् ।
घातयित्वा सज्येष्ठायामेकरात्रेण वाजिना (हस्तिना) ।
स जित्वा श्रवणे स्वर्गं प्रययौ सद्विजः पथि ॥]

उपरिचरस्यामरपो वसोर्ददौ चेदिपस्य वेणुमयीम् ।
यष्टिं तां स नरेन्द्रो विधिवत् सम्पूजयामास ॥८॥

Thereafter once Indra gave a bamboo flagstaff to the king of

Cedi, named *Uparicaravasu* (who could travel to Heaven from the earth). The king worshipped that according to the sacred laws.

[For the story of Uparicaravasu see the *Mahābhārata* I, 64. V. 16-17.]

प्रीतो महेन मघवा प्राहैवं ये नृपाः करिष्यन्ति ।
वसुवद्वसुमन्तस्ते भुवि सिद्धाज्ञा भविष्यन्ति ॥९॥
मुदिताः प्रजाश्च तेषां भयरोगविवर्जिताः प्रभूतान्नाः ॥
ध्वज एव चाभिधास्यति जगति निमित्तैः फलं सदसत् ॥१०॥

Being pleased with the worship, Indra spoke thus : "Those kings who emulate Vasu will be blessed with wealth and will have their orders obeyed implicitly on earth. Their subjects also will be happy, free from fear and diseases, and have plenty of food. The banner itself will suggest good and bad results in the world through appropriate signs.

[The commentator adds :

"य एवं भगवता दत्तं ध्वजं राजा पूजयिष्यति स एव ध्वजः पूज्यमानो लोके निमित्तैश्चिह्नैः शुभाशुभं दास्यति ।"]

पूजा तस्य नरेन्द्रैर्बलवृद्धिजयार्थिभिर्यथा पूर्वम् ।
शक्राज्ञया प्रयुक्ता तामागमतः प्रवक्ष्यामि ॥११॥

I shall explain on the authority of the Śāstras the method adopted by ancient kings, who aspired for power, prosperity and victory, for worshipping the banner, at the behest of Indra.

तस्य विधानं शुभकरणदिवसनक्षत्रमङ्गलमुहूर्त्तैः ।
प्रास्थानिकैर्वनमियाद् दैवज्ञः सूत्रधारश्च ॥१२॥

The method of preparing Indra's Banner is the following : An astrologer and a carpenter should repair to the forest on an auspicious weekday having a beneficial Karaṇa, asterism and Muhūrta (a period of 48 minutes), when good omens for a journey are observed.

[For an explanation of the Karaṇas see the author's 'Fundamentals of Astrology' p. 185, also C. 1-2 *infra*. The word *Divasa* means both a *Weekday* and a lunar day. Generally Monday, Wednesday, Thursday and Friday are good provided their lords are not weak or afflicted. The lunar days are divided into five groups viz. *Nandā*, *Bhadrā*, *Jayā*, *Riktā* and *Pūrṇā*. An auspicious asterism is one which is other than the *Dāruṇa* (Dreadful) and *Ugra* (Fierce) and one that is *Gentle* and *Common* that is free from malefics. Good omens are curds, coloured rice, flowers etc. In the *Yātrā*, *Karaṇas* other than *Gara*, *Vaṇija* and *Viṣṭi* are recommended. There are 15 *Muhūrtas* in the day and 15 in the night. They are given in the following verse :

शिवभुजगमित्रपितृवसुजलविश्वविरिञ्चिपङ्कजप्रभवाः ।
इन्द्राग्नीन्द्रनिशाचरवरुणार्यमयोनयश्चाह्नि ॥
रुद्राजाहिर्बुध्न्याः पूषादस्रान्तकाग्निधातारः ।
चन्द्रादितिगुरुहरिरवित्वाष्ट्राण्यनिलाख्यका रात्रौ ॥
अह्नः पञ्चदशांशे रात्रेश्चैवं मुहूर्त इति ।
संज्ञा स च विज्ञेयश्छायायन्त्राम्बुभिर्युक्त्या ॥]

उद्यानदेवतालयपितृवनवल्मीकमार्गचितिजाताः ।
कुब्जोर्ध्वशुष्ककण्टकिवल्लीवन्दाकयुक्ताश्च ॥१३॥
बहुविहगालयकोटरपवनानलपीडिताश्च ये तरवः ।
ये च स्युः स्त्रीसञ्ज्ञा न ते शुभाः शक्रकेत्वर्थे ॥१४॥

The following trees are not good for the preparation of Indra's Banner : Those that grow in pleasure gardens, temples, cemeteries, anthills, roads and sacrificial places; those that are very short (i.e. whose growth is stunted), withered at the top, thorny, entwined by creepers and parasitical plants; those that contain nests of numerous birds and hollows, those that have been affected by wind and fire, and those that bear feminine names.

[From the restrictions mentioned we can deduce the ancient's solicitude for fauna and flora. Trees with feminine names are बदरी, etc.

Cf. गर्ग—

प्रोष्ठपादे प्रतिपदि ध्वजार्थं पूर्वतो वनम् ।
गत्वा वृक्षं परीक्षेत वयःसारगुणान्वितम् ॥]

श्रेष्ठोऽर्जुनोऽजकर्णः प्रियकधवोदुम्बराश्च पञ्चते ।
एतेषामेकतमं प्रशस्तमथवापरं वृक्षम् ॥१५॥
गौरासितक्षितिभवं सम्पूज्य यथाविधि द्विजः पूर्वम् ।
विजने समेत्य रात्रौ स्पृष्ट्वा ब्रूयादिमं मन्त्रम् ॥१६॥

The best trees are the following five : Arjuna, Ajakarṇa, Priyaka (Priyaṅgu), Dhava (Lythrum fruticosum) and Udumbara (Glomerous fig-tree). One of these or any other of excellent qualities that has grown on white (or red) or black soil should be selected. A Brāhmaṇa should approach alone in the first part of the night such a tree, worship it according to the rules and recite the following hymn, touching the tree.

यानीह वृक्षे भूतानि तेभ्यः स्वस्ति नमोऽस्तु वः ।
उपहारं गृहीत्वेमं क्रियतां वासपर्ययः ॥१७॥
पार्थिवस्त्वां वरयते स्वस्ति तेऽस्तु नगोत्तम ।
ध्वजार्थं देवराजस्य पूजेयं प्रतिगृह्यताम् ॥१८॥

"Hail to all beings living in this tree ! Salutation to you. May you change your abode after receiving this gift offered by me. O great tree, hail to thee ! The king elects thee for (making) the banner of the Lord of Gods. Kindly accept this worship."

[There is an under-current of deep humanism in this hymn. It has been now established by experiments that trees and creepers respond marvellously to human love. As the horse in the case of a royal horse-sacrifice sacrifices itself for the cause of its king and country, so does the tree for a nobler cause. Hence we cannot but agree with Kālidāsa when he puts in the mouth of the fisherman the following sentiment :

"पशुमारणकर्मदारुणोऽप्यनुकम्पामृदुरेव श्रोत्रियः"]

छिन्द्यात्प्रभातसमये वृक्षमुदक्प्राङ्मुखोऽपि वा भूत्वा ।
परशोर्जर्जरशब्दो नेष्टः स्निग्धो घनश्च हितः ॥१९॥

At dawn, facing the east or north the carpenter should cut the tree. A rough and creaking sound of the axe is not auspicious, but a soft and deep one is beneficial.

नृपजयदमविध्वस्तं पतनमनाकुञ्चितं च पूर्वोदक् ।
अविलग्नं चान्यतरौ विपरीतमतस्त्यजेत् पतितम् ॥२०॥

If the tree falls down unbroken and unbent, and without being entangled in other trees, it will confer victory on the king. So will one that falls with its tip towards the east or north. If it falls down under contrary circumstances, it should be abandoned.

छित्वाग्रे चतुरङ्गुलमष्टौ मूले जले क्षिपेद्यष्टिम् ।
उद्धृत्य पुरद्वारं शकटेन नयेन्मनुष्यैर्वा ॥२१॥

Four digits of the tree at the top and eight digits at the bottom should be cut off, and then the trunk should be put into water. After being taken out it should be carried to the city-gate either through a carriage or by men.

अरभङ्गे बलभेदो नेम्या नाशो बलस्य विज्ञेयः ।
अर्थक्षयोऽक्षभङ्गे तथाणिभङ्गे च वर्द्धकिनः ॥२२॥

If the spokes of the carriage were to be broken when the tree-trunk is put on it or carried by it, the king's army would be shattered (i.e. there would be revolt), if the rim breaks, the army will be destroyed; if the axle, the king's wealth would be lost; and if the axle-pin gives way, the carpenter will come to grief.

भाद्रपदशुक्लपक्षस्याष्टम्यां नागरैर्वृतो राजा ।
दैवज्ञसचिवकञ्चुकिविप्रप्रमुखैः सुवेषधरैः ॥२३॥
अहताम्बरसंवीतां यष्टिं पौरन्दरीं पुरः पौरैः ।
स्रग्गन्धधूपयुक्तां प्रवेशयेच्छङ्खतूर्यरवैः ॥२४॥

On the eighth day of the bright fortnight of the lunar month of Bhādrapada, the king, accompanied by the citizens, royal astrologers, ministers, chamberlains and prominent Brāhmaṇas, all dressed in auspicious garments, should cause *Indra's Standard* covered with a new cloth and beautified with garlands, perfumes and incense, to be brought into the town by the people to the accompaniment of the sounds of conches and musical instruments.

[Cf. गर्ग—

प्रोष्ठपादे सिताष्टम्यां ज्येष्ठायोगे स्वलङ्कृताम् ।
यष्टिं पौरन्दरीं राजा नगरं सम्प्रवेशयेत् ॥

While paraphrasing Garga's ideas our author uses sometimes the very same words as used by the sage. However, here he has omitted one important condition mentioned by the sage viz. the day should synchronize with the asterism Jyeṣṭhā, presided over by Indra. It may be observed that this year, 1972, we get the 8th lunar day with Jyeṣṭhā star after 11.35 A.M. on September 15th.

In the next two verses the author describes the town into which the Standard is carried.]

रुचिरपताकातोरणवनमालालङ्कृतं प्रहृष्टजनम् ।
सम्मार्जितार्चितपथं सुवेषगणिकाजनाकीर्णम् ॥२५॥
अभ्यर्चितापणगृहं प्रभूतपुण्याहवेदनिर्घोषम् ।
नटनर्तकगेयज्ञैराकीर्णचतुष्पथं नगरम् ॥२६॥

The town into which the Banner is brought should be decorated with beautiful flags, triumphal arches and leafy garlands, have happy and gay people, the thoroughfares kept neat and tidy, as well as purified, and filled with gaily dressed courtesans, possess shops that are sanctified, be resounding with the loud chantings of the Puṇyāha and other Vedic hymns, and have the junctions of roads filled with actors, dancers and songsters.

तत्र पताकाः श्वेता भवन्ति विजयाय रोगदाः पीताः ।
जयदाश्च चित्ररूपा रक्ताः शस्त्रप्रकोपाय ॥२७॥

Flags hoisted in the capital, if white, would lead to victory; if yellow, to outbreak of diseases; if variegated, to success; and if red, to clash of arms.

यष्टिं प्रवेशयन्तीं निपातयन्तो भयाय नागाद्याः ।
बालानां तलशब्दे सङ्ग्रामः सत्त्वयुद्धे वा ॥२८॥

If the elephants or other animals carrying the Banner into the town allow it to fall down, there would be danger in store; and if boys clap their hands or if animals fight each other, at that time, there would be fighting.

[The expression प्रवेशयन्तीं is not correct, unless it is taken in the non-causal sense. I suspect that the author might have written प्रवेशयन्तो which must have been mis-spelt by writers. The commentator explains the word नागाद्याः as "आदिग्रहणादश्वमहिषगवादयो गृह्यन्ते ।" I am not sure if buffaloes could be included in this list.]

सन्तक्ष्य पुनस्तक्षा विधिवद्यष्टिं प्ररोपयेद्यन्त्रे ।
जागरमेकादश्यां नरेश्वरः कारयेच्चास्याम् ॥२९॥
सितवस्त्रोष्णीषधरः पुरोहितः शाक्रवैष्णवैर्मन्त्रैः ।
जुहुयादग्निं सांवत्सरो निमित्तानि गृह्णीयात् ॥३०॥

Then the carpenter should plane the trunk (of the tree) and mount it on a platform, so that it is kept horizontally with its tip resting on something. On the 11th lunar day of the same month the king should cause vigil to be observed at night. The royal priest dressed in white clothes and wearing a white turban should offer oblations to the sacred Fire with hymns addressed to Indra and Viṣṇu, while the astrologer should observe the auguries of the sacred fire.

इष्टद्रव्याकारः सुरभिः स्निग्धो घनोऽनलोऽर्चिष्मान् ।
शुभकृदतोऽन्योऽनिष्टो यात्रायां विस्तरोऽभिहितः ॥३१॥

If the sacred fire be fragrant, glossy, thick, full of flames and be possessed of the shape of auspicious objects (such as an umbrella), it would be beneficial. If it be otherwise, the result would be disastrous. This subject (of auguries) has been dealt with by me in detail in the work entitled *Yātrā* (or *Yogayātrā*).

[The reference to the *Yātrā* here shows that our author had already written or planned to write that work. The Bṛhadyātrā or Bṛhadyogayātra was also known as Mahāyātrā and was commented upon by Sūryadeva Somasut. Our author has written an abridged version of this called Svalpayātrā or Ṭikaṇikayātrā. According to Utpala, the *Yogayātrā* is a different work on journeys written by Varāhamihira. Dr. H. Kern had edited its first nine chapters. We are told that the entire work has been published by J.L. Shastri (Vide I.A.I.B. P. 27). Utpala's commentary on this has not yet been published. The *Bṛhadyātrā* also refers to the *Jātaka* as having been already written.

Cf. the योगयात्रा—

कृतेऽपि यत्नेऽपि कृश: कृशानुर्धातव्यकाष्ठाविमुखो नतार्चि: ।
वामे कृतावर्तशिखोऽतिधूमो विच्छिन्नसोत्कम्पविलीनमूर्त्ति: ॥
सिमिसिमायति चास्य हविर्हुतं सुरधनु:सदृश: कपिलोऽथवा ।
रुधिरपीतकबभ्रुहरिच्छवि: परुषमूर्त्तिरनिष्टकरोऽनल: ॥
खरकरभकवानरानुरूपो निगडविभीषणशस्त्ररूपभृद्वा ।
शवरुधिरवसास्थिमज्जगन्धो हुतभुगनिष्टफल: स्फुलिङ्गकृच्च ॥
चर्मविपाटनतुल्यनिनादो जर्जरदर्दुररूक्षरवो वा ।
आकुलयंश्च पुरोहितमर्त्यान् धूमलवैर्न शिवाय हुताश: ॥
हारकुन्दकुमुदेन्दुसन्निभ: सहतोऽङ्गसुखदो महोदय: ।
अङ्कुशातपनिवारणाकृतिहूर्यतेऽल्प उपमानहव्यभुक् ॥
उत्थाय स्वयमुज्ज्वलार्चिरनल: स्वाहावसाने हवि-
र्भुङ्क्ते देहसुखप्रदक्षिणगति: स्निग्धो महान् संहत: ।
निर्धूम: सुरभि: स्फुलिङ्गरहितो घातानुलोमो मृदु-
मुक्तेन्दीवरकाञ्चनद्युतिधरो यातुर्जयं संयति ॥
इष्टद्रव्यघटातपत्रतुरगश्रीवृक्षशैलाकृति-
भेर्यब्दोदधिदुन्दुभीतशकटस्निग्धस्वनै: पूजित: ।
नेष्ट: प्रोक्तविपर्यये हुतवह: स्निग्धो यथाभीष्टद:
सव्येऽङ्गे नृपतेर्दहन्नतिशुभ: शेषं च लोकाद्वदेत् ॥

The author says here, after giving a good deal of details, that whatever has not been included in this description should be understood from the traditions current in society. This science of prognostics of the Sacred Fire is very ancient in that Kālidāsa says in connection

with Raghu's Digvijaya (expedition) :
"प्रदक्षिणार्चिव्यजिन हस्तेनेव जयं ददौ" IV]

स्वाहावसानसमये स्वयमुज्ज्वलार्चिः
स्निग्धः प्रदक्षिणशिखो हुतभुग् नृपस्य ।
गङ्गादिवाकरसुताजलचारुहारां
धात्रीं समुद्ररशनां वशगां करोति ॥३२॥

At the time of the Pūrṇāhuti (final oblation) if the sacred fire blazes forth by itself, is glossy and is full of flames turning to the right, the king will bring under his sway the entire earth with the oceans acting as her girdle and the waters of the Gaṅgā and Yamunā as her beautiful pearl necklaces.

[This verse is a piece of fine poetry with elegant alliteration and brilliant imagery, though the idea contained in it is not new. The metre is वसन्ततिलका.]

चामीकराशोककुरण्टकाब्जवैदूर्यनीलोत्पलसन्निभेऽग्नौ ।
न ध्वान्तमन्तर्भवनेऽवकाशं करोति रत्नांशुहतं नृपस्य ॥३३॥

Darkness will not find any place inside the king's palace, as it will be dispelled by the rays of gems, when the Sacred Fire is of the hue of gold, Aśoka flower, Kuraṇṭa flower, lotus, beryl or blue lily. The idea is that if the Fire shows the above characteristics, the king will soon conquer the entire earth and become very wealthy and happy.

[These verses give an opportunity to the author to show off his poetic powers. The metre is the usual उपजाति. There is also the figure of speech named काव्यलिङ्ग.]

येषां रथौघार्णवमेघदन्तिनां समस्वनोऽग्निर्यदि वापि दुन्दुभेः ।
तेषां मदान्धेभघटावघट्टिता भवन्ति याने तिमिरोपमा दिशः ॥३४॥

Those kings whose sacrificial fire emits sound similar to that of a group of chariots, oceans, clouds, elephants or drums, will in their march darken the quarters, being crowded with hosts of intoxicated elephants.

[In the previous verse the author refers to the auspicious colours of the Fire. Here he refers to its auspicious sounds. The figures are quite patent.

The metre is an उपजाति of the इन्द्रवंशा and वंशस्थ mixed together.]

ध्वजकुम्भहयेभभूभृतामनुरूपे वशमेति भूभृताम् ।
उदयास्तधराधराधरा हिमवद्विन्ध्यपयोधरा धरा ॥३५॥

If the Fire were to look like a banner, pot, horse, elephant or mountain, the concerned kings would bring under their control the whole earth having the rising and setting mountains for her lips and the Himālaya and the Vindhya for her bosoms.

[Here again the shapes presented by the flames are referred to. We see in these verses more of poetry and less of science. The reader will easilv detect in this verse the happy alliterations, puns and metaphors. The word भूभृतां is once repeated; while धरा, four times. The metre is वियोगिनी. It is usual with Sanskrit poets to fancy the Earth as a damsel whose lofty bosoms are the two mountains, the Himālaya and Vindhya. Bhāsa makes these her ear-rings : "हिमवद्विन्ध्यकुण्डलाम् (स्वप्न.)]

द्विरदमदमहीसरोजलाजाघृतमधुना च हुताशने सगन्धे ।
प्रणतनृपशिरोमणिप्रभाभिर्भवति पुरश्छुरितेव भूर्नृपस्य ॥३६॥

If the sacrifice Fire emits the smell of elephant's ichor, mud, lotus, fried grains, ghee or honey, the king will have the earth in front carpeted, as it were, with the rays of the crown-jewels of prostrate potentates.

[Here the reference is to the smell of the sacred fire. The fancy is quite clear here. The metre is पुष्पिताग्रा.]

उक्तं यदुत्तिष्ठति शक्रकेतौ शुभाशुभं सप्तमरीचिरूपैः ।
तज्जन्मयज्ञग्रहशान्तियात्राविवाहकालेष्वपि चिन्तनीयम् ॥३७॥

Whatever good and bad omens, already delineated, are observed from the features of the sacrificial fire on the occasion of the installation of Indra's Banner, should be taken into consideration also at the time of a person's birth, sacrifice, propitiatory ceremonies for the planets, journeys or military expeditions and marriage.

[The idea is that whenever a sacrifice is performed in connection with any ceremony, the omens of the fire would be helpful in predicting the future with reference to that event.

The metre is उपजाति.]

गुडपूपपायसाद्यैर्विप्रानभ्यर्च्य दक्षिणाभिश्च ।
श्रवणेन द्वादश्यामुत्थाप्योऽन्यत्र वा श्रवणात् ॥३८॥

On the 12th lunar day ruling the asterism *Śravaṇa* or any

other asterism, the Banner should be raised and erected, after honouring the Brāhmaṇas with jaggery, sweet-meats, milk porridge and such other dishes as well as with Dakṣiṇās (gifts of money).

[We are told that the Standard of Indra should be brought inside the city on the 8th lunar day and its final erection done on the 12th Tithi. So it is a festival lasting for five days. It would be better if the 5th day had the star Śravaṇa; but the former is more important than the asterism. This reminds us of the rule : मूलेनावाहयेद्देवीं श्रवणेन विसर्जयेत् ।"

Cf. गर्ग—

तत्र श्रवणयोगेन ध्वजोत्थानं प्रशस्यते ।
द्वादश्यां विजये वाश्वमुहूर्त्ते वा दिनेऽथवा ।।]

शक्रकुमार्यः कार्याः प्राह मनुः सप्त पञ्च वा तज्ज्ञैः ।
नन्दोपनन्दसञ्ज्ञे पादोनार्द्धध्वजोच्छ्रायात् ।।३९।।
षोडशभागाभ्यधिके जयविजये द्वे वसुन्धरे चान्ये ।
अधिका शक्रजनित्री मध्येऽष्टांशेन चैतासाम् ।।४०।।

Manu has laid down that seven or at least five minor Standards, called *Indra's Daughters*, should be made by experts. Of these two called *Nandā* and *Upanandā* should measure respectively three-fourths and a half of the height of the main Standard. Four others named *Jayā*, *Vijayā*, and two *Vasundharās* should be taller than the previous one by a sixteenth. In the middle of these, there should be one called *Indra's Mother*, which is taller than the previous one (viz. *Vasundharā*) by an eighth.

[Cf. गर्ग—

दृढकाष्ठकृताः पञ्च सप्त वा लक्षणान्विताः ।
इन्द्रध्वजस्य शोभार्थं कुमारीः कारयेद् द्विजः ।।
अष्टाविंशत्करा यष्टिरष्टहस्ता ततोऽपरा ।
विष्कम्भश्चाङ्गुलैस्तस्याः षड्भिर्द्विगुणितैः स्मृतः ।।
समग्रमनुलोमं वा तक्षं प्राक् शिखयान्वितम् ।
कुर्यादिन्द्रध्वजं शुभ्रं सारदारुमयं शुभम् ।।]

प्रीतैः कृतानि विबुधैर्यानि पुरा भूषणानि सुरकेतोः ।
तानि क्रमेण दद्यात् पिटकानि विचित्ररूपाणि ।।४१।।

The ornaments of various colours and shapes that were put on the celestial Standard by the Gods who were very pleased, in days of yore, should be applied to this Banner also in their order.

[In the following eight verses the author describes the various ornaments (thirteen in number) offered by various Gods headed by Viśvakarmā, in order.]

रक्ताशोकनिकाशं चतुरस्रं विश्वकर्मणा प्रथमम् ॥
रशना स्वयम्भुवा शङ्करेण चानेकवर्णगा दत्ता ॥४२॥
अष्टाश्रि नीलरक्तं तृतीयमिन्द्रेण भूषणं दत्तम् ।
असितं यमश्चतुर्थं मसूरकं कान्तिमदयच्छत् ॥४३॥
मञ्जिष्ठाभं वरुणः षडश्रि तत्पञ्चमं जलोर्मिनिभम् ।
मायूरं केयूरं षष्ठं वायुर्जलदनीलम् ॥४४॥
स्कन्दः स्वं केयूरं सप्तममददाद्ध्वजाय बहुचित्रम् ।
अष्टममनलज्वालासङ्काशं हव्यभुग्वृत्तम् ॥४५॥
वैडूर्यसदृशमिन्द्रो नवमं ग्रैवेयकं ददावन्यत् ।
रथचक्राभं दशमं सूर्यस्त्वष्टा प्रभायुक्तम् ॥४६॥
एकादशमुद्वंशं विश्वेदेवाः सरोजसङ्काशम् ।
द्वादशमपि च निवेशं मुनयो नीलोत्पलाभासम् ॥४७॥
किञ्चिदध ऊर्ध्वनिर्मितमुपरि विशालं त्रयोदशं केतोः ।
शिरसि बृहस्पतिशुक्रौ लाक्षारससन्निभं ददतुः ॥४८॥
यद्यद्येन विभूषणममरेण विनिर्मितं ध्वजस्यार्थे ।
तत्तत्तद्दैवत्यं विज्ञातव्यं विपश्चिद्भिः ॥४९॥

The first ornament made and offered to the Banner by Viśvakarman, the celestial architect, was red like the Aśoka flowers and of quadrangular form; the Creator and Śiva gave severally a girdle of many colours; the third ornament, octangular and bluish-red, was offered by Indra; Yama offered the fourth ornament viz. a dark and lustrous Masūraka (emerald ?); Varuṇa gave the fifth ornament, a hexangular one which was like madder in colour, and resembled the waves of water; Vāyu (the Wind-God) bestowed the sixth gift, viz. an armlet, made of peacock feathers and as dark as the cloud; Lord Skanda gave it his own multi-coloured armlet for the seventh; the Fire-God offered the eighth, a circular ornament as brilliant as the flame of fire; Indra gave another ornament as the ninth, viz. a necklace resembling beryl; one of the Sun-Gods, Tvaṣṭā by name, gave a lustrous ornament looking like the wheel of a chariot, as the tenth; the Viśve-Devas presented the eleventh ornament named *Udvaṁśa*, resembling a lotus; the Sages gave the twelfth ornament called *Niveśa* which shone like the blue lily; and lastly Jupiter and Venus adorned the head of the Banner with the thirteenth ornament with designs at both the ends (or which has a short bottom and tip) and broad at the top and shining like molten red lac. Whatever ornaments were created by the different Gods for the sake of the Banner, are to be taken as being presided over by the respective Deities.

[The presentation of ornaments to the Banner by the Deities is similar to that of ornaments, dress and weapons by different Gods to the Goddess who was specially created to fight the Asura, described in the सप्तशती, otherwise known as the देवीमाहात्म्य.]

ध्वजपरिमाणत्र्यंशः परिधिः प्रथमस्य भवति पिटकस्य ।
परतः प्रथमात् प्रथमादष्टांशाष्टांशहीनानि ॥५०॥

The first ornament has a circumference which is a third of that of the Banner; and each succeeding ornament should be smaller than the preceding one by an eighth.

कुर्यादहनि चतुर्थे पूरणमिन्द्रध्वजस्य शास्त्रज्ञः ।
मनुना चागमगीतान् मन्त्रानेतान् पठेन्नियतः ॥५१॥

One who knows this science of Indra's Banner should fill it with ornaments on the fourth day thereafter i.e. on the 15th lunar day, and chant with devotion the following hymns sung by Manu according to the scriptural tradition.

हरार्कवैवस्वतशक्रसोमैर्धनेशवैश्वानरपाशभृद्भिः ।
महर्षिसङ्घैः सदिगप्सरोभिः शुक्राङ्गिरःस्कन्दमरुद्गणैश्च ॥५२॥
यथा त्वमूर्जस्करणैकरूपैः समर्चितस्त्वाभरणैरुदारैः ।
तथेह तान्याभरणानि योगे शुभानि सम्प्रीतमना गृहाण ॥५३॥
अजोऽव्ययः शाश्वत एकरूपो विष्णुर्वराहः पुरुषः पुराणः ।
त्वमन्तकः सर्वहरः कृशानुः सहस्रशीर्षः शतमन्युरीड्यः ॥५४॥
कविं सप्तजिह्वं त्रातारमिन्द्रमवितारं सुरेशम् ।
ह्वयामि शक्रं वृत्रहणं सुषेणमस्माकं वीरा उत्तरा भवन्तु ॥५५॥

"Accept with a pleased heart these auspicious ornaments on this occasion of the Sacrifice in the same manner as you did, being worshipped with excellent gifts of brilliant forms by Śiva, the Sun, Yama, Indra, the Moon, Kubera, Fire, Varuṇa, groups of great Sages, the Deities presiding over the quarters, nymphs, Venus, Jupiter, Skanda and the multitudes of Gods (or Maruts). Thou art without birth, imperishable, eternal, of immutable form, all-pervading, the Great Boar, the ancient Being, the God of Death, Destroyer of all things, fire, thousand-headed, Indra and the Adorable. I invoke the omniscient, Seven-tongued one (Fire), who is the protector; I invoke the mighty Indra, the ruler of the Gods, the destroyer of Vṛtra, and leader of a mighty army, who protects us carefully. May our heroes (warriors) be crowned with success !"

[This is a beautiful hymn containing the hoary Vedic phrases and ideas. It is quite clear from these and other Vedic hymns that the ancient Sages were in direct communion with the higher cosmic powers which when attuned and channelized helped man to solve his secular and spiritual problems. The last verse is an abridged version of the Ṛk,

"त्रातारमिन्द्रमवितारमिन्द्रं हवे हवे सुहवं शूरमिन्द्रम् ।
हुवे नु शक्रं पुरुहूतमिन्द्रं स्वस्ति नो मघवा धात्विन्द्रः ॥"]

प्रपूरणे चोच्छ्रयणे प्रवेशे स्नाने तथा माल्यविधौ विसर्गे ।
पठेदिमान्नृपतिः सोपवासो मन्त्राञ् शुभान् पुरुहूतस्य केतोः ॥५६॥

The king observing fast should recite the above auspicious hymns in front of the Banner of Indra, when it is decorated, erected, brought into the town, bathed, bedecked with garlands and when it is finally removed.

[The metre is a mixture of इन्द्रवज्रा, उपेन्द्रवज्रा and an unnamed variety of त्रिष्टुभ् which is found in the sacred literature.]

छत्रध्वजादर्शफलार्द्धचन्द्रैर्विचित्रमालाकदलीक्षुदण्डैः ।
सव्यालसिंहैः पिटकैर्गवाक्षैरलङ्कृतं दिक्षु च लोकपालैः ॥५७॥
अच्छिन्नरज्जुं दृढकाष्ठमातृकं सुश्लिष्टयन्त्रार्गलपादतोरणाम् ।
उत्थापयेल्लक्ष्म सहस्रचक्षुषः सारद्रुमाभग्नकुमारिकान्वितम् ॥५८॥

The Standard, bedecked with umbrellas, flags, mirrors, fruits, crescents, multicoloured garlands, banana trunks, sugar-canes, figures of snakes and lion, ornaments, windows and the images of the protectors of the eight quarters in their respective places, should be raised being fastened with strong ropes and hard wooden props on both sides, along with the minor standards called "Indra's Daughters" made of strong and unbroken wood. The arch at the bottom must be fastened with tight nails.

[Utpala translates फल as लाङ्गलम् ploughshare. Under अच्छिन्न-रज्जुम् he remarks :

"इन्द्रध्वजबन्धनार्थमष्टासु दिक्षु अष्टौ रज्जवः कार्याः ।"

and quotes गर्ग—

यथादिशं च रज्ज्वष्टौ मौञ्जीस्रग्दामसंहिताः ।
निग्रहार्थं ध्वजे कार्या निबद्धाश्चेन्द्रमण्डले ।।

मातृका is explained as 'इन्द्रध्वजनिष्पीडनार्थं पार्श्वद्वये मातृकाद्वितयं कार्यम् ।' He explains the word यन्त्रार्गल as : तत्र याः मातृकाः पार्श्वस्थितानि निरन्तराणि काष्ठानि तासां मातृकाणां तिर्यक्कृत्वा यानि काष्ठानि निक्षिप्यन्ते तान्यर्गलाग्रहणेनोच्यन्ते ।

The metres employed are उपजाति and इन्द्रवंशा respectively.]

अविरतजनरावं मङ्गलाशीःप्रणामैः
पटुपटहमृदङ्गैः शङ्खभेर्यादिभिश्च ।
श्रुतिविहतवचोभिः पापठद्भिश्च विप्रै-
रशुभविहतशब्दं सेतुमुत्थापयेच्च ।।५९।।

The king should raise the Standard to the accompaniment of the unceasing shouts of the people drowning the inauspicious sounds through the auspicious benedictions and invocations, the loud sounds of drums, tabors, conchs, kettle-drums etc., and through the repeated loud chantings of Vedic hymns by Brāhmaṇas.

[In the fourth line there is another reading. सुशुभसहितशब्दम्, for अशुभ- which is evidently an emendation by a later scholar.

The metre of this and of the following verse is मालिनी.]

फलदधिघृतलाजाक्षौद्रपुष्पाग्रहस्तैः
प्रणिपतितशिरोभिस्तुष्टवद्भिश्च पौरैः ।
वृतमनिमिषभतुः केतुमीशः प्रजाना-
मरिनगरनताग्रं कारयेद्द्विड्वधाय ।।६०।।

The king should cause the Standard to be erected for the destruction of his enemies, in such a manner that the tip of the Banner points to the city of the enemy, the Banner being surrounded by the citizens who bow their heads in homage and who invoke it with fruits, curds, ghee, fried grains, honey and flowers held in their hands.

[The reading in the second line, तुष्टवद्भिः is adopted by the commentator who construes it as अत्यर्थं स्तुवद्भिः. We are at a loss to find as to how he could get this meaning from the word तुष्टवत्. The correct reading should be सुष्टुवद्भिः. Otherwise we should interpret the word as 'by the happy and content citizens.']

नातिद्रुतं न च विलम्बितमप्रकम्प-
मध्वस्तमाल्यपिटकादिविभूषणं च ।
उत्थानमिष्टमशुभं यदतोऽन्यथा स्या-
त्तच्छान्तिभिर्नरपतेः शमयेत्पुरोधाः ॥६१॥

The raising of the Banner is auspicious if it is neither too slow, nor too fast, not shaky, and if its garlands, decorations and ornaments are not spoiled. If it is otherwise, it forebodes evil, and the royal preceptor should mitigate it through expiatory ceremonies.

[Cf. गर्ग—

अविध्वस्तमनाधूतमद्रुताजिह्ममूर्ध्वगम् ।
इन्द्रध्वजसमुत्थानं क्षेमसौभिक्षकारकम् ॥
निर्घातोल्कामहीकम्पा दीप्ताश्च मृगपक्षिणः ।
उच्छ्रीयमाणे चण्डा वा वायवः स्युर्भयाय ते ॥

The metre is वसन्ततिलका.]

क्रव्यादकौशिककपोतककाककङ्कैः
केतुस्थितैर्महदुशन्ति भयं नृपस्य ।
चाषेण चापि युवराजभयं वदन्ति
श्येनो विलोचनभयं निपतन् करोति ॥६२॥
छत्रभङ्गपतने नृपमृत्युस्तस्करान्मधु करोति निलीनम् ।
हन्ति चाप्यथ पुरोहितमुल्का पार्थिवस्य महिषीमशनिश्च ॥६३॥
राज्ञीविनाशं पतिता पताका करोत्यवृष्टिं पिटकस्य पातः ।
मध्याग्रमूलेषु च केतुभङ्गो निहन्ति मन्त्रिक्षितिपालपौरान् ॥६४॥
धूमावृते शिखिभयं तमसा च मोहो
व्यालैश्च भग्नपतितैर्न भवन्त्यमात्याः ।
ग्लायन्त्युदक्प्रभृति च क्रमशो द्विजाद्यान्
भङ्गे च बन्धकिवधः कथितः कुमार्याः ॥६५॥
रज्जूत्सङ्गच्छेदने बालपीडा राज्ञो मातुः पीडनं मातृकायाः ।
यद्यत्कुर्युश्चारणा बालका वा तत्तत्तादृग्भावि पापं शुभं वा ॥६६॥

The wise opine that there is great danger in store for the king if a carnivorous bird, owl, dove, crow or vulture sits on the Banner. If it be a blue jay, it is dangerous to the Yuvarāja (prince); an eagle sitting on it will prove harmful to the king's eyes. The king will die if the umbrella on the Banner breaks or falls down If honey-bees cling to it, there will be increase of thieves; a meteor falling on it will kill the royal priest; a lightning augurs the queen's death. The fall of a flag on it denotes the queen's exit, while that of an ornament augurs drought. If the Banner should break in the middle, top and bottom, the ministers, king and citizens respectively will meet with their end. When the Banner is covered with smoke, there is danger from fire; when with darkness, mental aberration will be the result. If the figures of snakes fall or break, the minister will come to grief. If portents are sighted in the north and other quarters, Brāhmaṇas and other classes in order will suffer. If any of the minor standards, called 'Indra's Daughters', breaks, courtezans will be killed. Should the ropes snap, there would be trouble to children. If the prop at the bottom breaks, the king's mother will be troubled. Whatever good or bad is done by boys or actors (or wandering ministrels) at the time will have corresponding effects on the people.

[Cf. गर्ग—

प्रहृष्टमनसः सर्वे क्रीडेयुर्मुदिता यदि ।
यदा जलेन गन्धैश्च विन्द्यात् सौभिक्षलक्षणम् ॥
अमेध्यै रक्तकैः केशैर्भस्मना क्रन्दनेन च ।
दुर्भिक्षपीडा विज्ञेया शस्त्रैश्चापि भयं वदेत् ॥

The metres of these five verses are in order वसन्ततिलका, स्वागता, उपजाति, इन्द्रवज्रा and शालिनी].

विनचतुष्टयमुत्थितमर्चितं समभिपूज्य नृपोऽहनि पञ्चमे ।
प्रकृतिभिः सह लक्ष्म विसर्जयेद् बलभिदः स्वबलाभिविवृद्धये ॥६७॥

After worshipping the erected Standard of Indra for four days, the king should discard it on the fifth day (i.e. the first day of the dark fortnight) after due worship in the company of his ministers for the rise of his own power.

[The metre is द्रुतविलम्बित].

उपरिचरवसुप्रवर्तितं नृपतिभिरप्यनुसन्ततं कृतम् ।
विधिमिममनुमन्य पार्थिवो न रिपुकृतं भयमाप्नुयादिति ॥६८॥

Should a king observe this vow (or rule) established by *Uparicaravasu* and followed by other kings without a break, he would not experience any trouble from his enemies.

[The metre is वैतालीय.]

———

नीराजनविधि: ॥४४॥

Chapter XLIV—Lustration Ceremony

[An important item in the worship of Hindu Gods in temples as well as homes is the waving of different kinds of lights before the Deities. This is called आरति in the vernaculars and नीराजन in Sanskrit. Originally it consisted of purificatory rituals. This kind of worship is also offered to kings, warriors, heroes, bridal couple etc. Even royal emblems, horses etc. were recipients of this honour in ancient times. It is done in the month of Kārttika in the autumnal season before kings undertook military expeditions. Actually it is a purificatory ceremony.]

भगवति जलधरपक्ष्मक्षपाकरार्केक्षणे कमलनाभे।
उन्मीलयति तुरङ्गमकरिनरनीराजनं कुर्यात् ॥१॥

When the Lord Nārāyaṇa opens His eyes, *viz.* the Sun and the Moon, with the eye-lashes of the clouds (i.e. when He wakes up from His Yoganidrā or Yogic slumber), the purificatory ceremony, called Nirājana (or Lustration), should be performed for the horses, elephants and warriors.

["Nīrājanā is lustration of arms, a kind of military and religious ceremony performed by kings or generals of armies in the month of Āśvina before they took the field; (it was, so to say, a general purification of the king's Purohita, the ministers, and all the various component parts of the army, together with the arms and implements of war, by means of sacred Mantras)." (Apte Dictionary). This is mentioned by poets like Kālidāsa "वाजिनीराजनाविधौ" (रघु० IV-25) and Śrīharṣa in the Naiṣadha "रराज नीराजनया स राजघ:". Actually the word नीराजनं is derived thus : "नीरेण जलेन अजनं स्पर्शनम्। This is done by house-holders for cows during the Dīpāvalī and for tools etc. during the Dussera. The Lord Viṣṇu is said to go into His yogic slumber on the 11th lunar day of the month of Āṣāḍha and remains in it for four months and wakes up on the *Ekādaśī* of *Kārttika*.]

द्वादश्यामष्टम्यां कार्त्तिकशुक्लस्य पञ्चदश्यां वा ।
आश्वयुजे वा कुर्यान्नीराजनसञ्ज्ञितां शान्तिम् ॥२॥

The purificatory ceremony named lustration should be performed on the 8th, 12th or 15th day of the bright half of the lunar month *Kārttika* or *Āśvina*.

[Bhaṭṭotpala interprets without reason the word पञ्चदश्यां as full Moon or New Moon. Amāvāsyā is not meant here by the author.]

नगरोत्तरपूर्वदिशि प्रशस्तभूमौ प्रशस्तदारुमयम् ।
षोडशहस्तोच्छ्रायं दशविपुलं तोरणं कार्यम् ॥३॥

In the north-east of the town on an auspicious ground a triumphal arch of excellent timber, measuring 16 cubits in height and ten cubits in width, should be erected.

[प्रशस्तदारु is that timber which is used for sacrificial purposes. The jack tree, Devadāru etc. are included in this list.]

सर्जोदुम्बरशाखाककुभमयं शान्तिसद्म कुशबहुलम् ।
वंशविनिर्मितमत्स्यध्वजचक्रालङ्कृतद्वारम् ॥४॥

It is also necessary to have a holy house (meant for propitiatory rites), made of the branches of the Sal tree, Indian fig tree or the Arjuna tree, fully strewn with Kuśa grass and having a door adorned with the figures of fishes, flags and discuses made of bamboo.

प्रतिसरया तुरगाणां भल्लातकशालिकुष्ठसिद्धार्थान् ।
कण्ठेषु निबध्नीयात् पुष्ट्यर्थं शान्तिगृहगाणाम् ॥५॥

With a string dipped in saffron paste, marking nuts, rice, costus and white mustard seeds should be tied to the neck of the horses brought into the holy house for the sake of their prosperity.

[According to the Amarakośa the word प्रतिसर is not used in the feminine, but our author does not regard the rule as sacrosanct.

Cf. काश्यप—

शालिजातकसिद्धार्थान् कुष्ठं भल्लातकं तथा ।
अश्वेषु कण्ठे बध्नीयात्सप्ताहं शान्तिमाचरेत् ॥]

रविवरुणविश्वदेवप्रजेशपुरुहूतवैष्णवैर्मन्त्रैः ।
सप्ताहं शान्तिगृहे कुर्याच्छान्तिं तुरङ्गाणाम् ॥६॥

A propitiatory ceremony should be performed in the *holy house* for the horses for seven days with the Vedic hymns addressed to the

Sun-God, Varuṇa, Viśvedevas, Brahman, Indra and Viṣṇu.

[Cf. काश्यप—

पौष्टिकैर्विविधैर्मन्त्रैः पुरोधा ज्वलनं हुते(वे?)त् ।
हुतान्ते भोजयेद्विप्रान् दक्षिणां विपुलां ददेत् ॥]

अभ्यर्चिता न परुषं वक्तव्या नापि ताडनीयास्ते ।
पुण्याहशङ्खतूर्यध्वनिगीतरवैर्विमुक्तभयाः ॥७॥

The horses that have been worshipped thus ought not to be addressed harshly or beaten. On the other hand, their fears and misgivings ought to be dispelled through the holy sounds of the Puṇyāha hymns, conchs, musical instruments and songs.

प्राप्तेऽष्टमेऽह्नि कुर्यादुदङ्मुखं तोरणस्य दक्षिणतः ।
कुशचीरावृतमाश्रममग्निं पुरतोऽस्य वेद्यां च ॥८॥

When the 8th day dawns, a hermitage covered with the holy grass and tree barks should be constructed to the south of the arch and facing the north. In the front part of this hermitage sacred fire should be installed on a sacrificial altar.

[Cf. काश्यप—

अष्टमेऽह्नि पुरस्कृत्य राजा पौरजनैर्वृतः ।
गच्छेच्छान्तिगृहं हृष्टः शङ्खतूर्यरवैः सह ॥

From the author's description it becomes clear that the *Āśrama* mentioned here is different from the Śāntigṛha, the former being meant for sacrifice, while the latter for the worship of the horses.

Bhaṭṭotpala quotes extensively in this connection from some work dealing with sacrificial altars :

यज्ञे चतुष्षष्टिकरा विवाहे वेदी द्विजानां द्विनरप्रमाणा ।
कार्या ततोऽष्टांशशमक्रमेण राजन्यवैश्यवृषलान्त्यजानाम् ॥

तथा च—

सप्तहस्ता ब्राह्मणानां वेदी यज्ञे प्रकीर्तिता ।
षट्करा क्षत्रियाणां तु वैश्यानां पञ्च कीर्तिता ॥

चतुर्हस्ता तु शूद्राणां विवाहेऽपि विनिश्चिता ।
अलाभे सर्ववर्णानां चतुर्हस्ता प्रकीर्तिता ॥

व्यन्तराणामतो न्यूना निर्दिष्टा मुनिभिः सदा ।
अतो न्यूनाधिका वेदी यजमानस्य मृत्युदा ॥

तथा च—

यज्ञे विवाहे वक्ष्यामि वेदिमानं समासतः ।
त्रिःसप्तहस्तविस्तारा ब्राह्मणानां शुभावहा ॥
क्षत्रियाणां पञ्चदशी वैश्यानां नवसंमिता ।
सप्तहस्ता तु शूद्राणां शिल्पिनां पञ्च कीर्तिता ॥
त्रिहस्ता व्यन्तराणां तु वेदी सर्वत्र कीर्त्तिता ।
भुवोऽपरोधे मर्त्यानां चातुर्वर्ण्यैः प्रकीर्तिता ॥
पञ्चहस्ता कृता वेदी सर्वमाङ्गल्यदायिका ॥

We are told that Varāhamihira himself has given in the following verse the effects of the altars :

वेदी शुभाशुभविधानविधौ प्रदिष्टा
दिक्स्थानमानाभ्यधिका न हीना ।
भ्रष्टा प्रमाणेन करोति भङ्ग
दिग्वक्रसंस्था न च सिद्धिदा स्यात् ॥
प्राग्भागहीना नगरस्य नेष्टा पुरोधसो दक्षिणभागवक्रा ।
नरेन्द्रजायाऽशुभदाऽपरस्यामुदग्बलेशस्य नृपस्य मध्ये ॥]

चन्दनकुष्ठसमङ्गा हरितालमनःशिलाप्रियङ्गुवचाः ।
दन्त्यमृताञ्जनरजनीसुवर्णपुष्प्यग्निमन्थाश्च ॥९॥
श्वेतां सपूर्णकोशां कटम्भराश्रायमाणसहदेवीः ।
नागकुसुमं स्वगुप्तां शतावरीं सोमराजीं च ॥१०॥
कलशेष्वेताः कृत्वा सम्भारानुपहरेद्बलिं सम्यक् ।
भक्ष्यैर्नानाकारैर्मधुपायसयावकप्रचुरैः ॥११॥

Sandalwood, costus, madder, yellow orpiment, red arsenic, Priyaṅgu, Vacā (orris root), Dantī, Guricha, Moruṅga (or antimony ?), turmeric, Suvarṇapuṣpī, Agnimantha (Premua Spinosa), Girikarṇikā (Clitoria), Pūrṇakośā, Kaṭurohiṇī, Trāyamāṇā, Sahadevī, Nāgapuṣpa, Kapikacchu (Cowitch), Śatāvarī and Somarājī—all these sacrificial materials should be put into full pots, and the same collected materials offered properly to the Deities as Bali (food) along with eatables of various kinds, consisting mostly of honey, milk porridge and barley preparations.

[In some editions एताः in the last verse is read as एतान्, thus making it an adjective of सम्भारान्. In the first verse सुवर्णपुष्पाग्नि- is the other reading. A big list of herbs—Oṣadhis—is given here. They are to be put into the Holy Pot which is worshipped. The *Balyupaharaṇa* may also mean the offering of food to the different Deities on the ground, and not necessarily offerings to the fire.]

खदिरपलाशोदुम्बरकाश्मर्यश्वत्थनिर्मिताः समिधः ।
स्रुक्कनकाद्रजताद्वा कर्तव्या भूतिकामेन ॥१२॥

The sacrificial twigs required are of Khadira, Palāśa, Indian fig tree, Kāśmarī and Aśvattha (holy fig tree). One who wishes for prosperity should use the sacrificial ladle made of gold or silver.

पूर्वाभिमुखः श्रीमान्वैयाघ्रे चर्मणि स्थितो राजा ।
तिष्ठेदनलसमीपे तुरगभिषग्दैववित्सहितः ॥१३॥

The king who is possessed of royal power and majesty and is accompanied by a veterinary surgeon and an astrologer, should take his seat on a tiger-skin facing the east in front of the sacred fire.

यात्रायां यदभिहितं ग्रहयज्ञविधौ महेन्द्रकेतौ च ।
वेदीपुरोहितानललक्षणमस्मिंस्तदवधार्यम् ॥१४॥

Whatever symptoms of the altar, priest and fire have been given in my work on *Yātrā* (Journey) in connection with the sacrifices to the planets and Indra's Banner, should be carefully noted and applied to this ceremony as well.

[The commentator quotes profusely from the *Yātrā* in connection with ग्रहयज्ञ thus :

ग्रहयज्ञमतो वक्ष्ये तत्र निमित्तानि लक्षयेद्वेद्याम् ।
भङ्गो मानोनायां दिग्भ्रष्टायामसिद्धिश्च ॥
नगरपुरोहितदेवीसेनापतिपार्थिवक्षयं कुरुते ।
प्राग्दक्षिणापरोत्तरमध्यमभागेषु या विकला ॥

with the पुरोहित thus :—

कम्पोच्छ्वासविजृम्भणप्रचलनस्वेदाश्रुपातक्षुधो-
द्गाराद्यं च पुरोधसः स्मृतिविपच्चानिष्टमन्यच्छुभम् ।
आज्यं केशपिपीलिकामलयुतं सत्त्वावलीढं च य-
त्तन्नेष्टं शुभमन्यथोपकरणं द्रव्याण्यनूनानि च ॥

For the symptoms of the fire see the योगयात्रा quoted under XLIII-31 *supra*.]

लक्षणयुक्तं तुरगं द्विरदवरं चैव दीक्षितं स्नातम् ।
अहतसिताम्बरगन्धस्रग्धूपाभ्यर्चितं कृत्वा ॥१५॥
आश्रमतोरणमूलं समुपनयेत्सान्त्वयञ्छनैर्वाचा ।
वादित्रशङ्खपुण्याहनिःस्वनापूरितदिगन्तम् ॥१६॥

A horse possessing laudable features and an excellent elephant, after being consecrated, bathed and honoured with new white cloths, perfumes, garlands and incense, should be brought slowly with coaxing words under the arch of the hermitage, with the quarters resounding with the noise of musical instruments, conchs and Puṇyāha hymns.

[For the features of horses and elephants see LXVI and LXVII respectively].

यद्यानीतस्तिष्ठेद्दक्षिणचरणं हयः समुत्क्षिप्य ।
स जयति तदा नरेन्द्रः शत्रूनचिराद्विना यत्नात् ॥१७॥
अस्यन्नेष्टो राज्ञः परिशेषं चेष्टितं द्विपहयानाम् ।
यात्रायां व्याख्यातं तदिह विचिन्त्यं यथायुक्ति ॥१८॥

Should the horse or elephant brought into the *Śānti-sadman* (holy house) stand with its right leg uplifted, the king would conquer his enemies ere long without difficulty. Should it stand frightened, it would be harmful to the king. All other activities of elephants and horses indicating good and bad results, which have been dealt with at length in the *Yātrā* should be applied to lustration also according to circumstances.

[For omens through horses and elephants see XCIII. 5.13.14; XCIV. 11, 12 & 13 *infra*.]

पिण्डमभिमन्त्र्य दद्यात्पुरोहितो वाजिने स यदि जिघ्रेत् ।
अश्नीयाद्वा जयकृद्विपरीतोऽतोऽन्यथाभिहितः ॥१९॥

The royal priest should give the horse a rice ball duly sanctified with Vedic hymns. Should the horse smell or eat it, the king would come out victorious; otherwise it would lead to his defeat.

कलशोदकेषु शाखामाप्लाव्यौदुम्बरीं स्पृशेत् तुरगान् ।
शान्तिकपौष्टिकमन्त्रैरेवं सेनां सनृपनागाम् ॥२०॥

The priest should dip a branch of the Indian fig tree in the holy waters of the full pots (already worshipped) and touch the horses with it to the accompaniment of Vedic hymns meant for both expiation and propitiation. The same thing should be repeated for the army, the king and the elephants.

[In mantras and medicines there are two varieties viz. remedial and progressive. Among medicines we have curative ones and those that are tonics meant for improving one's health, one being destructive and the other constructive.]

शान्ति राष्ट्रविवृद्धयं कृत्वा भूयोऽभिचारकर्ममन्त्रैः ।
मृण्मयमरिं विभिन्द्याच्छूलेनोरःस्थले विप्रः ॥२१॥

The expiatory (or remedial) ceremony should be repeated for the prosperity of the kingdom, and then the priest should pierce the heart of the enemy made of clay with a spike, chanting the hymns used in black magic.

खलिनं हयाय दद्यादभिमन्त्र्य पुरोहितस्ततो राजा ।
आरुह्योदक्पूर्वां यायान्नीराजितः सबलः ॥२२॥

Then the priest should give the sanctified bits to the horse. Thereafter the king should mount the horse, receive lustration and proceed towards the north-east along with his army.

[The word उदक्पूर्वां may also be interpreted as 'first to the north'. In this connection we may remember Kālidāsa's statement in the Raghu.

"स गुप्तमूलप्रत्यन्तः शुद्धपार्ष्णिरयान्वितः ।
षड्विधं बलमादाय प्रतस्थे दिग्जिगीषया ॥"

(IV. 26).

and

"स ययौ प्रथमं प्राचीं......"

(IV. 28).]

मृदङ्गशङ्खध्वनिहृष्टकुञ्जरस्रवन्मदामोदसुगन्धिमारुतः ।
शिरोमणिव्रातचलत्प्रभाचयैर्ज्वलन्विवस्वानिव तोयदात्यये ॥२३॥
हंसपङ्क्तिभिरितस्ततोऽद्रिराट् सम्पतद्भिरिव शुक्लचामरैः ।
मृष्टगन्धपवनानुवाहिभिर्धूयमानरुचिरस्रगम्बरः ॥२४॥
नैकवर्णमणिवज्रभूषितैर्भूषितो मुकुटकुण्डलाङ्गदैः ।
भूरिरत्नकिरणानुरञ्जितः शक्रकार्मुकरुचिं समुद्वहन् ॥२५॥
उत्पतद्भिरिव खं तुरङ्गमैर्दारयद्भिरिव दन्तिभिर्धराम् ।
निर्जितारिभिरिवामरैर्नरैः शक्रवत्परिवृतो व्रजेन्नृपः ॥२६॥

The king should proceed under the following happy circumstances : The breeze is scented by the smell of the dripping ichor of elephants that are gladdened by the sounds of tabors and conchs. He shines like the Sun in autumn by the mass of glittering rays of his crest jewels. His beautiful garlands and clothes are shaken by white chowries wafting waves of fine fragrance, just as the Himālaya is surrounded by rows of swans flying hither and thither, carrying with them the fragrant breeze. The king, adorned with his crown, ear-rings and armlets bedecked with gems and diamonds of myriad hues, would resemble Indra's Bow (rainbow) in lustre, being irradiated with the rays of innumerable gems. The king would be accompanied by horses springing up to the sky, as it were, by elephants tearing up, as it were, the earth, and by warriors, who have vanquished their foes, just as Indra is attended upon by the Gods who have defeated their enemies.

[The author cannot resist the temptation of showing off his poetic talents whenever there is an opportunity for it. The similes and fancies he employs here are well known images in Sanskrit literature. Even the diction is appropriate for the theme. मृष्टगन्धपवनानुवाहिभि: reminds us of Kālidāsa's expression, 'ग्राचारपूतं पवनः सिषेवे' (Raghu II-10) and 'यद्वायुरन्विष्टमृगैः किरातैरासेव्यते भिन्नशिखण्डिबर्हः (कुमार. I-15). In the last verse we find traces of Kālidāsa's influence: 'पश्योदग्रप्लुतत्वाद्वियति बहुतरं स्तोकमुर्व्यां प्रयाति' (शाकु. I-7) and 'वप्रक्रीडापरिणतगजप्रेक्षणीयं ददर्श (मेघ० २). शक्रकार्मुकरुचं is another reading.

The first is in वंशस्थ metre and the rest in रथोद्धता.]

सवज्रमुक्ताफलभूषणोऽथवा सितस्रगुष्णीषविलेपनाम्बरः ।
धृतातपत्रो गजपृष्ठमाश्रितो घनोपरीवेन्दुतले भृगोः सुतः ॥२७॥

Or, he should proceed being adorned with diamonds, pearls and ornaments, wearing white garlands, turban, ointment and garments, having the royal umbrella held over his head, and sitting on an elephant, just as planet Venus rides a cloud having the Moon above him.

[Like Kālidāsa in the Raghu (XIII. 76) "तारापतिस्तरलविद्युदिवाभ्रवृन्दम् ।" here our author employs a very charming simile taken from the planetary region.

The metre is वंशस्थ].

सम्प्रहृष्टनरवाजिकुञ्जरं निर्मलप्रहरणांशुभासुरम् ।
निर्विकारमरिपक्षभीषणं यस्य सैन्यमचिरात्स गां जयेत् ॥२८॥

The king whose army consists of soldiers, elephants and horses in a happy mood, is bright with the rays of glittering weapons, is free from unnatural dispositions or evil portents, and is dreadful to the hosts of the enemies, will conquer ere long the whole earth.

[The metre is रथोद्धता].

खञ्जनकलक्षणाध्यायः ॥४५॥

Chapter XLV—The Wagtail

खञ्जनको नामायं यो विहगस्तस्य दर्शने प्रथमे ।
प्रोक्तानि यानि मुनिभिः फलानि तानि प्रवक्ष्यामि ॥१॥

I shall now expound the effects, enunciated by ancient Sages, of the first sighting of the bird called Wagtail in the season.

[The commentator tells us that the Wagtail cannot be seen during the four months beginning with Śrāvaṇa. Many types of this bird are mentioned below.]

स्थूलोऽभ्युन्नतकण्ठः कृष्णगलो भद्रकारको भद्रः ।
आकण्ठमुखात् कृष्णः सम्पूर्णः पूरयत्याशाम् ॥२॥
कृष्णो गलेऽस्य बिन्दुः सितकरटान्तः स रिक्तकृद्रिक्तः ।
पीतो गोपीत इति क्लेशकरः खञ्जनो दृष्टः ॥३॥

A variety of wagtails named *Bhadra*, which has a stout body and a black raised neck, is auspicious. One which is black from the face to the neck is called *Sampūrṇa* (Full) and fulfils one's ambition. The one with dark spots on the neck and white cheeks is named *Rikta* (Empty) and causes disappointment. The one called *Gopīta* which is yellow in colour produces troubles when sighted.

[Cf. काश्यप—

स्थूलोऽभ्युन्नतकण्ठो यो भद्रः कृष्णगलः स्मृतः ।
कृष्णमूर्धा गलान्तं यः स सम्पूर्ण इति स्मृतः ॥
करटान्तौ सितौ यस्य कृष्णो बिन्दुर्गले तथा ॥
स रिक्त इति निर्दिष्टः पीतो गोपीतकः स्मृतः ॥
नामानुरूपेण फलं विहगानां विनिर्दिशेत् ॥]

अथ मधुरसुरभिफलकुसुमतरुषु सलिलाशयेषु पुण्येषु ।
करितुरगभुजगमूर्ध्नि प्रासादोद्यानहर्म्येषु ॥४॥
गोगोष्ठसत्समागमयज्ञोत्सवपार्थिवद्विजसमीपे ।
हस्तितुरङ्गमशालाच्छत्रध्वजचामराद्येषु ॥५॥
हेमसमीपसिताम्बरकमलोत्पलपूजितोपलिप्तेषु ।
दधिपात्रधान्यकूटेषु च श्रियं खञ्जनः कुरुते ॥६॥

A wagtail sighted in the following places tends to prosperity : On trees bearing fragrant flowers and sweet fruits, on holy lakes and rivers, on the heads of elephants, horses and serpents, on temples, gardens and mansions, near cows, cowpens, assemblage of virtuous men, sacrifices, auspicious functions (or festivities , kings and Brāhmaṇas, on elephant-yards, stables, umbrellas, flags, chowries and other royal appendages, near gold, on white cloths, lotuses, blue lilies, worshipped objects, paved and decorated spots, on curd-pots and corn-heaps.

पङ्के स्वाद्वन्नाप्तिर्गोरससम्पच्च गोमयोपगते ।
शाद्वलगे वस्त्राप्तिः शकटस्थे देशविभ्रंशः ॥७॥
गृहपटलेऽर्थभ्रंशो वध्रे वन्धोऽशुचौ भवति रोगः ।
पृष्ठे त्वजाविकानां प्रियसङ्गममावहत्याशु ॥८॥

When the wagtail is seen perched on silt, one will enjoy sweet food; on a heap of cow-dung, excellent milk and milkproducts; on green grass, clothes; on a cart, there will ensue devastation of the country; on the roof of a house, there will be loss of wealth; on a piece of hide, imprisonment; on filth, disease; and on the backs of goats and sheep, immediate union with one's beloved.

महिषोष्ट्रगर्दभास्थिश्मशानगृहकोणशर्कराट्टस्थः ।
प्राकारभस्मकेशेषु चाशुभो मरणरुग्भयदः ॥९॥

If the wagtail is seen sitting on a buffalo, camel, donkey, bones, burial ground, corner of a house, clod of earth, turret, compound wall or a heap of ashes or hair, the result would be disastrous and would cause danger from disease and death.

[अद्रि is another reading for अट्ट.]

पक्षौ धुन्वन्नशुभः शुभः पिबन्वारि निम्नगासंस्थः ।
सूर्योदये प्रशस्तो नेष्टफलः खञ्जनोऽस्तमये ॥१०॥

It is inauspicious, if the wagtail is seen flapping its wings; auspicious, if it is found drinking water from a river; it is beneficial to sight it at sunrise, but in the evening, the result will be harmful.

[वारिवाहस्थः is another reading for निम्नगासंस्थः. The commentator interprets वारिवाह as a channel or tube carrying water. The common meaning, however, is 'cloud'.]

नीराजने निवृत्ते यया दिशा खञ्जनं नृपो यान्तम् ।
पश्येत्तया गतस्य क्षिप्रमरातिर्वशमुपैति ॥११॥

If a king observes at the end of lustration ceremony a wagtail flying in a particular direction and marches against an enemy whose country is situated in that direction, he will surely subjugate that enemy in no time.]

[The wagtail will help a king in throwing his enemy off his guard, because the latter's spies might have brought the news of the intention of the marching king to attack a king living in another direction.

तस्मिन्निधिर्भवति मैथुनमेति यस्मिन्
यस्मिंस्तु छर्दयति तत्र तलेऽस्ति काचम् ।
अङ्गारमप्युपदिशन्ति पुरीषणेऽस्य
तत्कौतुकापनयनाय खनेद् धरित्रीम् ॥१२॥

There will be a treasure underneath the place where the wagtail copulates; mica, where it vomits; and charcoal, where it voids its excrements. To satisfy one's curiosity one may dig the earth in the same place.

[Cf. काश्यप—
मैथुनं कुरुते यत्र तत्र वै निधिमादिशेत् ।
भुक्तं छर्दयते यत्र तत्र काचमधो भवेत् ॥
पुरीषं यत्र कुरुते तत्राङ्गारं विनिर्दिशेत् ॥]

मृतविकलविभिन्नरोगितः स्वतनुसमानफलप्रदः खगः ।
धनकृदभिनिलीयमानको वियति च बन्धुसमागमप्रदः ॥१३॥

The bird being dead, crippled, wounded or diseased produces effects similar to its own condition on the person that sees it. If it comes to roost in one's front, the person will get wealth; if it flies up into the sky, it augurs one's meeting with one's kith and kin.

[The metre is वैतालीय. The expression मृत...रोगित: is grammatically indefensible. It should have been—रोगवान्.]

नृपतिरपि शुभं शुभप्रदेशे खगमवलोक्य महीतले विदध्यात् ।
सुरभिकुसुमधूपयुक्तमर्घं शुभमभिनन्दितमेवमेति वृद्धिम् ॥१४॥

When the king observes an auspicious wagtail in an auspicious place, he should make an offering consisting of fragrant flowers and incense on the ground. By doing so (i.e. by honouring an auspicious omen), he obtains all prosperity and much happiness.

[The metre is पुष्पिताग्रा.]

अशुभमपि विलोक्य खञ्जनं द्विजगुरुसाधुसुरार्चने रतः ।
न नृपतिरशुभं समाप्नुयान्न यदि दिनानि च सप्त मांसभुक् ॥१५॥

Should a king behold an ill-omened wagtail, he would not meet with evil consequences, provided he engages himself in worshipping Brahmins, preceptors, pious men and gods, and also abstains from meat for one full week.

[The metre is वैतालीय.]

आवर्षात्प्रथमे दर्शने फलं प्रतिदिनं तु दिनशेषात् ।
दिक्स्थानमूर्त्तिलग्नर्क्षशान्तदीप्तादिभिश्चोह्यम् ॥१६॥

The effects of the first sight of a wagtail will be felt within a year; and those of the daily sight, before the end of the day itself. The effects must be carefully determined after examining the direction, place, physical features, the Lagna, the asterism, position with respect to the Sun etc.

[Cf. काश्यप—

प्रथमे दर्शने पाकमावर्षात्प्रवदेद् बुधः ।
प्रतिदैवसिके वाच्यं दर्शनेऽस्तमये फलम् ॥

The good quarters are east, north and north-east. The auspicious places are mentioned in verses 4-6 *supra*. The good physical features are found in the *Bhadra* and *Sampūrṇa* types (see verse 2 *supra*). Regarding the ascendant it should be seen whether the sign is owned, occupied and aspected by benefics. Among the asterisms *Dhruva* (Firm) and *Mṛdu* (Tender) are auspicious; *Kṣipra* (Fast), *Cara* (Moving) and *Sādhāraṇa* (Common) are medium, and *Dāruṇa* (Dreadful) and *Ugra* (Fierce) are forbidden or inauspicious. A place is called *Dīpta* or *Śānta* according as it is lighted by the Sun or protected from it. There are other places named *Aṅgāra* (Charcoal) and *Dhūmita* (Smoky) A bird may also be *Dīpta* (Harsh) in its cry. These are explained in detail in LXXXVI etc.]

उत्पाताध्यायः ॥४६॥

Chapter XLVI—Portentous Phenomena

यानत्रेरुत्पातान् गर्गः प्रोवाच तानहं वक्ष्ये ।
तेषां सङ्क्षेपोऽयं प्रकृतेरन्यत्वमुत्पातः ॥१॥

I shall now expound the portents enunciated by Sage Atri and taught by Garga after him. The following is a summary of such portents. Anything that is contrary to nature is called *Utpāta* or Portent.

[Cf. the author's समाससंहिता—

यः प्रकृतिविपर्यासः सर्वः सङ्क्षेपतः स उत्पातः ।
क्षितिगगनदिव्यजातो यथोत्तरं गुरुतरो भवति ॥

There are three kinds of portents viz. terrestrial, atmospheric and heavenly. The science of portents or unnatural occurrences was originally taught by Sage Atri to Sage Garga, who in his turn wrote down details of these in his संहिता.]

अपचारेण नराणामुपसर्गः पापसञ्चयाद्भवति ।
संसूचयन्ति दिव्यान्तरिक्षभौमास्त उत्पाताः ॥२॥

Sins accumulate as a result of bad deeds committed by men. These sins in their turn bring about troubles to them. The three kinds of portents, viz. celestial, atmospheric and terrestrial, foreshadow such troubles.

[Cf. गर्ग—

अतिलोभादसत्याद्वा नास्तिक्याद्वाप्यधर्मतः ।
नरापचारान्नियतमुपसर्गः प्रवर्त्तते ॥]

मनुजानामपचारादपरक्ता देवताः सृजन्त्येतान् ।
तत्प्रतिघाताय नृपः शान्ति राष्ट्रे प्रयुञ्जीत ॥३॥

Displeased with the misdeeds of human beings, the Gods create these portents. The king should cause propitiatory rites to be performed in his kingdom for warding off their evil consequences.

[The effects of both good and bad deeds are indicated by good and bad omens respectively. These Utpātas are the precursors of disasters. Some people argue that remedial ceremonies are quite unnecessary and ineffective in preventing what is destined to happen since the latter is the effect of *Prārabdha* i.e. deeds of previous life that have already begun to yield their effects. If we were to follow this philosophy of fatalism, man would have no impetus to do any work for improving his lot. The *Prārabdha* gives man certain inherent tendencies, no doubt, but he, being a thinking animal, has some amount of freedom to work for his uplift or downfall. Hence the sages of yore found that remedial measure had great significance and could be used for removing hurdles and for constructive purposes.

Cf. गर्ग—

ततोऽपचारान्मर्त्यानामपरज्यन्ति देवताः ।
ते सृजन्त्यद्भुतान् भावान् दिव्यभूम्यन्तरिक्षजान् ॥
त एव सर्वलोकानामुत्पाता देवनिर्मिताः ।
विचरन्ति विनाशाय रूपैः सम्बोधयन्ति च ॥
तान् शास्त्रनिर्गमाद्विप्राः पश्यन्ति ज्ञानचक्षुषा ।
प्रवदन्ति तु मर्त्येषु हितार्थं श्रद्धयान्विताः ॥
ते तु सम्बोधिता विप्रैः शान्तये मङ्गलानि च ।
श्रद्दधानाः प्रकुर्वन्ति न ते यान्ति पराभवम् ॥
ये तु न प्रतिकुर्वन्ति क्रियामश्रद्धयान्विताः ।
नास्तिक्यादथवा कोपाद्विनश्यन्त्यथवाऽचिरात् ॥]

दिव्यं ग्रहर्क्षवैकृतमुल्कानिर्घातपवनपरिवेषाः ।
गन्धर्वपुरपुरन्दरचापादि यदान्तरिक्षं तत् ॥४॥

भौमं चरस्थिरभवं तच्छान्तिभिराहतं शममुपैति ।
नाभसमुपैति मृदुतां शाम्यति नो दिव्यमित्येके ॥५॥

The celestial portents are the unnatural behaviour of planets, and asterism, meteors, thunders, storms and halos; the atmospheric ones are aerial cities, rainbows etc; and the terrestrial ones arise from the moving and stationary objects. The terrestrial portents become ineffective being struck down by remedial measures; the atmospheric ones can be mitigated by expiatory rites, while the celestial ones, according to some, cannot be nullified.

[Cf. गर्ग—

स्वर्भानुकेतुनक्षत्रग्रहताराकंजेन्द्रजम् (जेन्दुजम् ?)।
दिवि चोत्पद्यते यच्च तद्दिव्यमिति कीर्तितम् ॥
वाय्वभ्रसन्ध्यादिग्दाहपरिवेषतमांसि च ।
खपुरं चेन्द्रचापं च तद्विन्द्यादन्तरिक्षजम् ॥
भूमावुत्पद्यते यच्च स्थावरं वाथ जङ्गमम् ।
तदेकदैशिकं भौममुत्पातं परिकीर्तितम् ॥

Cf. also काश्यप—

भौमं शान्तिहतं नाशमुपगच्छति मार्दवम् ।
नाभसं न शम याति दिव्यमुत्पातदर्शनम् ॥

Vide the समाससंहिता—

दिव्यं ग्रहर्क्षजातं भुवि भौमं स्थिरचरोद्भवं यच्च ।
दिग्दाहोल्कापतनं परिवेषाद्यं वियत्प्रभवम् ॥]

दिव्यमपि शममुपैति प्रभूतकनकान्नगोमहीदानैः ।
रुद्रायतने भूमौ गोदोहात् कोटिहोमाच्च ॥६॥

Even the celestial portent might be remedied by enormous gifts of gold, food, cows and lands; by milking cows on the ground in a Śiva temple; and by offering a crore of oblations into the sacred Fire at a sacrifice.

[It is not quite clear what the author means by 'milking on the ground.' It may mean that the milk should not be collected in a vessel, but should be allowed to drench the holy floor of the temple. Or it might mean simply 'in the precincts of a Śiva temple.']

आत्मसुतकोशवाहनपुरदारपुरोहितेषु लोके च ।
पाकमुपयाति दैवं परिकल्पितमष्टधा नृपतेः ॥७॥

The adverse effect of a celestial portent becomes the object of a king's experience in respect of eight individuals or objects, viz. himself, his children, treasury, vehicles (or chariots, horses etc.), his town, his consorts, preceptors and subjects.

[Cf. गर्ग—

पुरे जनपदे कोशे वाहनेऽथ पुरोहिते ।
पुत्रेष्वात्मनि भृत्येषु पश्यते दैवमष्टधा ॥

It may be noted here that Garga puts *servants* in the place of *consorts*. Look also at the sage's passive form of दृश्.]

(1) *Portents through idols of Gods in Temples.*

अनिमित्तभङ्गचलनस्वेदाश्रुनिपातजल्पनाद्यानि ।
लिङ्गार्चायतनानां नाशाय नरेशदेशानाम् ॥८॥

The breaking, moving, sweating, shedding tears, falling, muttering and the like, of Śiva's Emblems, idols of Gods and temples (or holy places), without any cause, forebode the destruction of kings and their countries.

[Cf. गर्ग—

देवतार्चाः प्रनृत्यन्ति वेपन्ते प्रज्वलन्ति वा ।
मुहुर्नृत्यन्ति रोदन्ति प्रस्विद्यन्ति हसन्ति वा ।
उत्तिष्ठन्ति निषीदन्ति प्रधावन्ति पतन्ति वा ।
कूजन्ति विक्षिपन्ते च गात्रप्रहरणध्वजान् ॥
अवाङ्मुखा वा तिष्ठन्ति स्थानात् स्थानं व्रजन्ति वा ।
वमन्त्यग्निं तथा धूमं स्नेहं रक्तं पयो जलम् ॥
प्रसर्पन्ति च जल्पन्ति वा चेष्टन्ते श्वसन्ति वा ।
समन्ताद्यत्र दृश्यन्ते गात्रैर्वापि विचेष्टितैः ॥]

दैवतयात्राशकटाक्षचक्रयुगकेतुभङ्गपतनानि ।
सम्पर्यासनसादनसङ्गश्च न देशनृपशुभदाः ॥९॥

The breaking or falling down of the axle, wheel, yoke, and flag of the car during a temple festival do not augur well for the king and his country. Similarly their being twisted, destroyed and entangled are evil for both.

[सुरयात्रायां is another reading in the place of दैवतयात्रा.]

ऋषिधर्मपितृब्रह्मप्रोद्भूतं वैकृतं द्विजातीनाम् ।
यद्रुद्रलोकपालोद्भवं पशूनामनिष्टं तत् ॥१०॥
गुरुसितशनैश्चरोत्थं पुरोधसां विष्णुजं च लोकानाम् ।
स्कन्दविशाखसमुत्थं माण्डलिकानां नरेन्द्राणाम् ॥११॥
वेदव्यासे मन्त्रिणि विनायके वैकृतं चमूनाथे ।
धातरि सविश्वकर्मणि लोकाभावाय निर्दिष्टम् ॥१२॥
देवकुमारकुमारीवनिताप्रेष्येषु वैकृतं यत्स्यात् ।
तन्नरपतेः कुमारककुमारिकास्त्री परिजनानाम् ॥१३॥
रक्षःपिशाचगुह्यकनागानामेवमेव निर्दिष्टम् ।
मासैश्चाप्यष्टाभिः सर्वेषामेव फलपाकः ॥१४॥

Any unnatural behaviour observed in the images of Sages, Yama (God of Death), the *Manes* and the Creator presages evil to

Brāhmaṇas; one in the idols of Śiva and the protectors of the quarters (eight in number), to the cattle or animals; one in the images of Jupiter, Venus and Saturn, to the priests; one in that of Viṣṇu, to the people at large; one in those of Skanda and Viśākha, to the governors of provinces; one in that of Sage Vyāsa, to the ministers; one in that of Lord Gaṇapati, to the commander of the army; one in those of the Creator and Viśvakarman (celestial architect), foreshadows the destruction of the people. Any uncommon feature seen in the images of sons, daughters, wives, and servants of Gods forebodes disaster to the king's sons, daughters, inmates of the harem and servants respectively. The same result will befall the same kinsmen of the king in order, in case the portent is seen in the idols of the sons, daughters, wives and servants of demons, goblins, Yakṣas and Serpents. All these portents bear fruit in eight months.

[The last verse may also be interpreted as follows : The portents seen in the images of demons, goblins, Yakṣas and Nāgas presage great trouble to the king's sons, daughters, wives and servants respectively.]

बुद्ध्वा देवविकारं शुचिः पुरोधास्त्र्यहोषितः स्नातः ।
स्नानकुसुमानुलेपनवस्त्रैरभ्यर्चयेत्प्रतिमाम् ॥१५॥

मधुपर्केण पुरोधा भक्ष्यैर्बलिभिश्च विधिवदुपतिष्ठेत् ।
स्थालीपाकं जुहुयाद्विधिवन्मन्त्रैश्च तल्लिङ्गैः ॥१६॥

On seeing portents in the idols of Gods, the priest should purify himself both physically and mentally by bath and mental concentration, fast for three days and worship the idols with ablutions, flowers, sandal paste and the like as well as with cloths. He should also propitiate them with the offerings of Madhuparka (a mixture of honey), eatables and other presents, and offer into the Sacred Fire cooked rice, according to the rules, with the Vedic hymns appropriate to the Deities concerned.

[स्थालीपाक is a particular sacrifice performed by house-holders. In that sacrifice the *Caru* or cooked rice, is cooked in an earthen vessel. *Madhuparka* forms part of the reception accorded to distinguished guests, bride-grooms, kings and Gods. It is a sweet drink consisting of five ingredients viz. curd, ghee, water, honey and sugar. The word उपतिष्ठेत् is not grammatically correct.]

इति विबुधविकारे शान्तयः सप्तरात्रं
द्विजविबुधगणार्चा गीतनृत्योत्सवाश्च ।
विधिवदवनिपालैर्यैः प्रयुक्ता न तेषां
भवति दुरितपाको दक्षिणाभिश्च रुद्धः ॥१७॥

Should kings perform properly these expiatory rites for seven days continuously along with the worship of Gods (like Lord Gaṇapati) and groups of learned Brāhmaṇas, who are also honoured with money presents, and also with songs, dance and festivities (as well as vigil at night), whenever they behold any unnatural occurrence in the images of Gods, the evil effects of the portents, being supressed by these rituals etc., would not be experienced by them.

[The author concludes this section after giving the method of atoning for the sins of previous life.

The metre is मालिनी]

(2) *Portents through Fire*

राष्ट्रे यस्यानग्निः प्रदीप्यते दीप्यते च नेन्धनवान् ।
मनुजेश्वरस्य पीडा तस्य च राष्ट्रस्य विज्ञेया ॥१८॥

If there are flames seen without the existence of fire, and if it does not burn brightly even though fed with dry fuel, it forebodes trouble to both the ruler and the ruled (i.e. country).

जलमांसार्द्रज्वलने नृपतिवधः प्रहरणे रणो रौद्रः ।
सैन्यग्रामपुरेषु च नाशो वह्नेर्भयं कुरुते ॥१९॥

If fire is observed on water, flesh or anything wet, it foreshadows the king's death; if on weapons, a sanguinary war; and if the fire goes out in military camps, villages or towns, there will be danger from fire.

[After the invention of matches there is no question of fire going out in modern times. But till about 60 years ago in many Indian homes fire was never allowed to be extinguished. Should a woman find that in her hearth the fire has gone out completely, she would go to the neighbouring house and borrow a few embers.]

प्रासादभवनतोरणकेत्वादिष्वनलेन दग्धेषु ।
तडिता वा षण्मासात् परचक्रस्यागमो नियमात् ॥२०॥

Should temples, houses, triumphal arches, flags and the like be burnt without fire or by lightning, there would undoubtedly be an attack by a foreign army after six months.

[The word आदि in केत्वादि is explained by Utpala as referring to store-room, granary etc.]

धूमोऽनग्निसमुत्थो रजस्तमश्चाह्निजं महाभयदम् ।
व्यभ्रे निश्युडुनाशो दर्शनमपि चाह्नि दोषकरम् ॥२१॥

Should there arise smoke without fire, and dust and darkness spreading in daytime, there would be unprecedented danger. Similarly the disappearance cf stars at night from the cloudless sky as well as the sight of stars in daytime, is very harmful in its effect.

[Cf. गर्ग—

अनिशानि तमांसि स्युर्यदि वा पांसवो रजः ।
धूमश्चानग्निना यत्र तत्र विन्द्यान्महद्भयम् ॥]

नगरचतुष्पादण्डजमनुजानां भयकरं ज्वलनमाहुः ।
धूमाग्निविस्फुलिङ्गैः शय्याम्बरकेशगैर्मृत्युः ॥२२॥

Flames proceeding from towns, animals, birds and human beings are said to be dangerous, according to the wise. Similarly smoke, fire and sparks seen on beds, clothes and hairs will cause the owner's death.

[Cf. गर्ग —

शयनासनयानेषु केशप्रावरणेषु च ।
दृश्यन्ते विस्फुलिङ्गा वा धूमो वा मरणाय तत् ॥]

आयुधज्वलनसर्पणस्वनाः कोशनिर्गमनवेपनानि वा ।
वैकृतानि यदि वायुधेऽपराण्याशु रौद्ररणसङ्कुलं वदेत् ॥२३॥

The blazing, movement, sounding, rushing out of the scabbard, trembling of the sword, or other unnatural phenomena observed in weapons would presage a devastating war leading to utter confusion, in the near future.

[Here the commentator raises an objection : Is not the author, who has already referred to the blazing of Praharaṇa or weapon in verse 19 *supra*, guilty of repetition ? He says that actually there is no repetition. For, according to Nagnajit there are three kinds of Āyudhas or weapons viz. *Praharaṇa*. *Pāṇimukta* (those that are thrown by the hand), and *Yantramukta* (those flung by mechanical device). The first category includes weapons like swords; the second, like discuses; and the third, like stones, arrows, missiles, rods etc. The word *Āyudha* is all-inclusive, wheres *Praharaṇa*, restrictive, meaning only swords, axes etc. Hence there is no fault committed by our respected author. Though there is no difference in the effect, yet the author has mentioned the two words separately in order to suggest the existence of many varieties in weapons.

The metre is रथोद्धता.]

मन्त्रैराग्नेयैः क्षीरवृक्षात्समिद्भिर्होतव्योऽग्निः सर्षपैः सर्पिषा च ।
अग्न्यादीनां वैकृते शान्तिरेवं देयं चास्मिन्काञ्चनं ब्राह्मणेभ्यः ॥२४॥

The expiatory ceremony to be performed for warding off the evil effects of portents of fire etc. consists of a sacrifice to the sacred fire with white mustard seeds, ghee and the twigs got from milky trees, to the accompaniment of hymns addressed to the Fire-God, and of gifts of gold to Brāhmaṇas.

(3) *Portents of Trees*

शाखाभङ्गेऽकस्माद्वृक्षाणां निर्दिशेद्रणोद्योगम् ।
हसने देशभ्रंशं रुदिते च व्याधिबाहुल्यम् ॥२५॥

If the branches of trees break down all on a sudden, it should be predicted that there would be feverish preparations for war; should the trees produce a sound similar to laughing, the country would be ruined; and if they produce a weeping sound, there would be a rich crop of diseases.

राष्ट्रविभेदस्त्वनृतौ बालवधोऽतीव कुसुमिते बाले ।
वृक्षात् क्षीरस्रावे सर्वद्रव्यक्षयो भवति ॥२६॥

If trees put forth flowers and fruits out of season, the country would disintegrate; if very young plants blossom (or bear fruit) luxuriantly, there would be great mortality of children; and if milk flows from trees, all substances will be destroyed.

[Cf. गर्ग—

स्वराष्ट्रभेदं कुरुते फलपुष्पमनार्तवम् ।
बालानां मरण कुर्याद् बालानां फलपुष्पजम् ॥]

मद्ये वाहननाशः सङ्ग्रामः शोणिते मधुनि रोगः ।
स्नेहे दुर्भिक्षभयं महद्भयं निःसृते सलिले ॥२७॥

If wine (or liquor) flows from trees, vehicles (or horses etc.) will be destroyed; if blood, war will follow; if honey, disease will break out; if oil, there will be threat of famine; and if water, there will be great danger.

शुष्कविरोहे वीर्यान्नसङ्क्षयः शोषणे च विरुजानाम् ।
पतितानामुत्थाने स्वयं भयं दैवजनितं च ॥२८॥

If withered trees sprout again, and healthy ones wither away, there will be the destruction of vitality (or powerful persons) and food; and if fallen trees stand erect by themselves, there is the danger of divine visitations.

पूजितवृक्षे ह्यनृतौ कुसुमफलं नृपवधाय निर्दिष्टम् ।
धूमस्तस्मिन् ज्वालाऽथवा भवेन्नृपवधायैव ॥२६॥

The appearance of flowers and fruits on a worshipped tree out of season, or of smoke or flame on it, is considered as a sure sign of the king's destruction.

सर्पत्सु तरुषु जल्पत्सु वापि जनसङ्क्षयो विनिर्दिष्टः ।
वृक्षाणां वैकृत्ये दशभिर्मासैः फलविपाकः ॥३०॥

Walking or talking of trees presages annihilation of the population. The portents of trees bear fruit after ten months.

स्रग्गन्धधूपाम्बरपूजितस्य च्छत्रं विधायोपरि पादपस्य ।
कृत्वा शिवं रुद्रजपोऽत्र कार्यो रुद्रेभ्य इत्यत्र षडेव होमाः ॥३१॥
पायसेन मधुनापि भोजयेद् ब्राह्मणान् घृतयुतेन भूपतिः ।
मेदिनी निगदितात्र दक्षिणा वैकृते तरुकृते हितार्थिभिः ॥३२॥

Putting an umbrella over, the tree should be worshipped with garlands, perfumes, incense and cloths. An imnge of Śiva should be placed under the tree and the hymn called *Rudrādhyāya* chanted repeatedly; and only six oblations made to the Fire with the sacred expression, "Hail to the Rudras". Then the king should feed Brāhmaṇas with milk porridge, honey and clarified butter. In this connection the Dakṣiṇā (votive gift) prescribed by the wise, who are interested in the welfare of the people, to ward off the evil consequences of the portents of trees, is in the form of gifts of land.

[The metres are इन्द्रवज्रा and रथोद्धता.]

(4) *Portents of Crops*

नालेऽब्जयवादीनामेकस्मिन् द्वित्रिसम्भवो मरणम् ।
कथयति तदधिपतीनां यमलं जातं च कुसुमफलम् ॥३३॥

If the stalk of lotus, barley (or wheat, Priyaṅgu etc.), has one or two branches, it forebodes death to its owner. So does a twin flower or fruit.

अतिवृद्धिः सस्यानां नानाफलकुसुमसम्भवो वृक्षे ।
भवति हि यद्येकस्मिन् परचक्रस्यागमो नियमात् ॥३४॥

If the growth of crops is too excessive, and if many varieties of flowers and fruits grow on a single tree, there will undoubtedly be an invasion by a foreign army.

अर्धेन यदा तैलं भवति तिलानामतैलता वा स्यात् ।
अन्नस्य च वैरस्यं तदा तु विन्द्याद् भयं सुमहत् ॥३५॥

When sesamum seeds yield only half the quantity of oil or no oil at all; and when food (and eatables) lose their taste, one should know that there will be great danger ahead.

विकृतकुसुमं फलं वा ग्रामादथवा पुराद्बहिः कार्यम् ।
सौम्योऽत्र चरुः कार्यो निर्वाप्यो वा पशुः शान्त्यै ॥३६॥
सस्ये च दृष्ट्वा विकृतिं प्रदेयं तत्क्षेत्रमेव प्रथमं द्विजेभ्यः ।
तस्यैव मध्ये चरुमत्र भौमं कृत्वा न दोषं समुपैति तज्जम् ॥३७॥

A freakish flower or fruit should be thrown out of the village or town (as part of the expiatory measure). Cooked rice should be offered as oblation to Soma and a goat sacrificed in order to remove the baneful effects of this portent. On detecting any unnatural phenomenon in the crop, the concerned field itself should be gifted away to Brāhmaṇas, first of all, and at the centre of the field, the owner should offer an oblation of cooked rice to the Earth. By so doing he will not experience the evil effects of such portents.

[The metre of the second verse is इन्द्रवज्रा.]

(5) *Portents of Rainfall*

दुर्भिक्षमनावृष्टावतिवृष्टौ क्षुद्भयं परभयं च ।
रोगो ह्यनृतुभवायां नृपतिवधोऽनभ्रजातायाम् ॥३८॥

Drought foreshadows famine; excessive rain, famine and threat of an attack by a foreign foe; untimely rain, disease; and a cloudless rain, the king's death.

शीतोष्णविपर्यासो नो सम्यगृतुषु च सम्प्रवृत्तेषु ।
षण्मासाद्राष्ट्रभयं रोगभयं दैवजनितं च ॥३९॥

Change of weather conditions in the hot and cold seasons, and the improper functioning, of the seasons foreshadow danger to the kingdom, fear of diseases and divine visitations after six months.

[The commentator takes दैवजनितं as an adjective of रोगभय, which would mean—threat of diseases arising from past misdeeds.]

अन्यर्तौ सप्ताहं प्रबन्धवर्षे प्रधाननृपमरणम् ।
रक्ते शस्त्रोद्योगो मांसास्थिवसादिभिर्मरकः ॥४०॥
धान्यहिरण्यत्वक्फलकुसुमाद्यैर्वर्षितैर्भयं विन्द्यात् ।
अङ्गारपांसुवर्षे विनाशमायाति तन्नगरम् ॥४१॥

Continuous rain for seven days in any season other than the monsoon forebodes the death of the chief monarch. Should there be a rain of blood, there would be war; if one of flesh, bones, marrow or the like (i.e. ghee, oil etc.), epidemics; if one of corn, gold, tree-barks, fruits, flowers etc. (i.e. leaves and the like), peril; and if one of burning coal or dust, the particular town would be destroyed.

उपला विना जलधरैर्विकृता वा प्राणिनो यदा वृष्टाः ।
छिद्रं वाप्यतिवृष्टौ सस्यानामीतिसञ्जननम् ॥४२॥

When there is a shower of stones or of freakish animals without clouds, or when there is a spot without any rain whatsoever in spite of excessive rain, the crops would be affected by many pests.

[Vide V 52 and notes thereon *supra.* विकृताः प्राणिनः—ugly creatures—are asses, camels, horses, cats, jackals etc., according to Utpala.]

क्षीरघृतक्षौद्राणां दध्नो रुधिरोष्णवारिणां वर्षे ।
देशविनाशो ज्ञेयोऽसृग्वर्षे चापि नृपयुद्धम् ॥४३॥

If there be a rain of milk, ghee, honey, curds or hot water, the country itself would be devastated; and if there be one of blood, war between kings would ensue.

[This verse is considered by some as an interpolation.]

यद्यमलेऽर्के छाया न दृश्यते दृश्यते प्रतीपा वा ।
देशस्य तदा सुमहद्भयमायातं विनिर्देश्यम् ॥४४॥

If trees etc. do not cast their shadow even when the Sun shines brightly, or if the shadow is in the same direction as the Sun, it should be predicted that great calamity is in store for the country.

व्यभ्रे नभसीन्द्रधनुर्दिवा यदा दृश्यतेऽथवा रात्रौ ।
प्राच्यामपरस्यां वा तदा भवेत् क्षुद्भयं सुमहत् ॥४५॥

If there be rainbow in a cloudless sky by day or night, in the east or west, then there will be great danger from starvation.

सूर्येन्दुपर्जन्यसमीरणानां यागः स्मृतो वृष्टिविकारकाले ।
धान्यान्नगोकाञ्चनदक्षिणाश्च देयास्ततः शान्तिमुपैति पापम् ॥४६॥

When there is a portentous rain, a sacrifice to the Sun, the Moon, Cloud and Wind should be performed, according to ancient authors. If gifts of corn, food, cows and gold are also made to Brāhmaṇas, the sin (that causes these portents) would be obliterated.

(6) *Portents of Water*

अपसर्पणं नदीनां नगरादचिरेण शून्यतां कुरुते ।
शोषश्चाशोष्याणामन्येषां वा ह्रदादीनाम् ॥४७॥

स्नेहासृङ्मांसवहाः सङ्कुलकलुषाः प्रतीपगाश्चापि ।
परचक्रस्यागमनं नद्यः कथयन्ति षण्मासात् ॥४८॥

If rivers recede from a town, or if those that never dry or other places like lakes, dry up, the town would be desolate ere long. If rivers flow carrying oil, blood or flesh, be turbulent or filthy or flow upwards, they presage attack by a foreign enemy after six months.

[ह्रद is a lake which has a perennial spring : "ह्रदो यत्र पातालादुदकमागच्छति स्वयमेव"—remarks the commentator.]

ज्वालाधूमक्वाथारुदितोत्क्रुष्टानि चैव कूपानाम् ।
गीतप्रजल्पितानि च जनमरकायोपदिष्टानि ॥४९॥

The emanation of flames, smoke, foam (boiling), sound of weeping, shouting, singing or talking, from wells is declared as a fore-runner of the mortality of the population.

सलिलोत्पत्तिरखाते गन्धरसविपर्यये च तोयानाम् ।
सलिलाशयविकृतौ वा महद्भयं तत्र शान्तिमिमाम् ॥५०॥

If water springs up from the earth that has not been dug, if water acquires a different smell or taste, and if some unnatural features are seen in tanks etc., there will be great disaster. The following is the expiatory method to be adopted in the above cases.

सलिलविकारे कुर्यात् पूजां वरुणस्य वारुणैर्मन्त्रैः ।
तैरेव च जपहोमं शममेवं पापमुपयाति ॥५१॥

When any unnatural feature is observed with respect to water Varuṇa should be worshipped with Vedic hymns relating to Him and with the same hymns Japa (mental repetition) and Homa (offering of oblations to the sacred fire) should be performed. By doing so, the sin (evil) can be warded off.

(7) *Portents of Births*

प्रसवविकारे स्त्रीणां द्वित्रिचतुष्प्रभृतिसम्प्रसूतौ वा ।
हीनातिरिक्तकाले च देशकुलसङ्क्षयो भवति ॥५२॥

When women give birth to monstrocities, or two, three, four or more children at a time, or when the birth happens to be too premature or over-delayed, ruin will befall the country and the family.

वडवोष्ट्रमहिषगोहस्तिनीषु यमलोद्भवे मरणमेषाम् ।
षण्मासात् सूतिफलं शान्तौ श्लोकौ च गर्गोक्तौ ॥५३॥

Should mares, camels, she-buffaloes, cows and cow-elephants bring forth twins, the former would meet with death. The consequences of such births will come to pass after six months. The following two verses of Sage Garga pertain to its expiation.

[Cf. गर्ग —

अकाले प्रसवे चैव कालातीतेऽथवा पुनः ।
असख्याजनने चैव युग्मस्य प्रसवे तथा ॥

अमानुषाणि काण्डानि सञ्जातव्यञ्जनानि वा ।
अनङ्गा ह्यधिकाङ्गा वा हीनाङ्गाः सम्भवन्ति वा ॥

विमुखाः पक्षिसदृशास्तथार्धपुरुषाश्च वा ।
विनाशं तस्य देशस्य कुलस्य च विनिर्दिशेत् ॥

अप्राप्तवयसे गर्भे द्वौ चतुष्पात् त्रयोऽपि वा ।
अत्युच्चा विनताश्चापि प्रजायन्तेऽन्ययो भवेत् ॥

वडवा हस्तिनी गौर्वा यदि युग्मं प्रसूयते ।
विजन्यं विकृतं वापि षड्भिर्मासैर्नृपक्षयः ॥]

नार्यः परस्य विषये त्यक्तव्यास्ता हितार्थिना ।
तर्पयेच्च द्विजान् कामैः शान्तिं चैवात्र कारयेत् ॥५४॥

चतुष्पदाः स्वयूथेभ्यस्त्यक्तव्याः परभूमिषु ।
नगरं स्वामिनं यूथमन्यथा तु विनाशयेत् ॥५५॥

Such women as give birth to freaks or twins etc. should be removed from the place and left in another country by one who wishes for happiness. He should also please Brāhmaṇas with gifts desired by them, and perform an expiatory ceremony (with the help of priests). As for the quadrupeds, they should be removed from their flock or herd and left in other countries Otherwise they will destroy their own towns, owners and herds.

(8) *Portents of Quadrupeds.*

परयोनावभिगमनं भवति तिरश्चामसाधु धेनूनाम् ।
उक्षाणो वान्योन्यं पिबति श्वा वा सुरभिपुत्रम् ॥५६॥

मासत्रयेण विन्द्यात्तस्मिन्निःसंशयं परागमनम् ।
तत्प्रतिघातायैतौ श्लोकौ गर्गेण निर्दिष्टौ ॥५७॥

Should birds and beasts mate with animals of a different genus, or cows with cows, oxen with oxen, or should a dog suck a calf, the result would be untoward and there would undoubtedly be an invasion by a foreign army in three months. Sage Garga has taught the following two verses for counteracting the evil influences of such portents.

[Bhaṭṭotpala interprets these verses, not on the basis of their wording but on that of Garga's statement given below. Accordingly he says : "Should cows suck each other's udder, or oxen suck each other, or should a dog suck a cow's udder..." How could 'सुरभिपुत्र' mean 'गोस्तन' ?

Cf. गर्ग—

वियोनिषु यदा यान्ति मिश्रीभावः प्रजायते ।
खरोष्ट्रहयमातङ्गा मनुष्या वा न साधु तत् ॥
अकालसक्ता दृश्यन्ते काले च विमदा यदि ।
मातङ्गोष्ट्रहयश्वानः पक्षिणो वा न साधु तत् ॥
धेनुं धेनुः पिबेद्यत्रानडवानं ह्यनडुत्तथा ।
श्वा वा पिबेद्धेनुमथ धेनुः श्वानमथापि वा ॥
प्राप्तेषु त्रिषु मासेषु परचक्रागम वदेत् ॥]

त्यागो विवासनं दानं तत्तस्याशु शुभं भवेत् ।
तर्पयेद् ब्राह्मणांश्चात्र जपहोमांश्च कारयेत् ॥५८॥
स्थालीपाकेन धातारं पशुना च पुरोहितः ।
प्राजापत्येन मन्त्रेण यजेद्बह्वन्नदक्षिणम् ॥५९॥

If such an animal be abandoned or taken to another place, it would remedy the evil effects of the portents and usher in auspicious ones. For this purpose the owner should also worship Brāhmaṇas and cause Japa (silent repetition of Mantras) and Homa (offering of oblation to the Fire) to be performed. The priest should, on this occasion, offer Caru (cooked rice) and a goat (or some other prescribed animal) to the Sacred Fire to propitiate the Creator, to the accompaniment of the chanting of hymns addressed to Prajāpati (Creator), along with large-scale feedings and generous gifts of gold.

(9) *Portents of the Wind.*

यानं वाहवियुक्तं यदि गच्छेन्न व्रजेच्च वाहयुतम् ।
राष्ट्रभयं भवति तदा चक्राणां सादभङ्गे च ॥६०॥

If a carriage moves without a driver (or horses), or does not move even when driven (or dragged) by him (or by them), or if the wheels sink into the earth or break down, there is imminent danger to the kingdom.

[The word यान may also be interpreted as an animal used for riding, such as the horse and elephant. Why are the horses brought under this section dealing with the 'portents of the wind'? According to Vedic literature the horses are presided over by the Wind-God. It is also important to note that the 'speed of Wind' is an exemplar for that of running animals. Likewise, scunds are also carried by the wind.]

गीतरवतूर्यशब्दा नभसि यदा वा चरस्थिरान्यत्वम् ।
मृत्युस्तदा गदा वा विस्वरतूर्ये पराभिभवः ॥६१॥

When sounds of singing and musical instruments are heard in the sky; or when moving objects (like carriages) become stationary, and stationary objects (like trees) move, it augurs death or diseases. When musical instruments produce eerie sounds, there would be defeat at the hands of an enemy.

अनभिहततूर्यनादः शब्दो वा ताडितेषु यदि न स्यात् ।
व्युत्पत्तौ वा तेषां परागमो नृपतिमरणं वा ॥६२॥

If musical instruments produce sounds without being struck, or produce no sounds even when struck, or produce multifarious sounds, there will be an attack by an enemy or the king's death.

गोलाङ्गलयोः सङ्गे दर्वीशूर्पाद्युपस्करविकारे ।
क्रोष्टुकनादे च तथा शस्त्रभयं मुनिवचश्चेदम् ॥६३॥

When the oxen and plough get entangled, when ladles, winnowing baskets etc. (staves, mortars etc.) and cooking utensils exhibit portentous changes, or when these things produce a sound similar to the howling of jackals (or when jackals howl), there will be danger from weapons (i.e. war). The following is the instruction of Sage Garga for remedying the evil effects of this portent.

[The compound दर्वी—can also be interpreted as—"Unnatural changes seen in house-hold appurtenances such as ladles, winnowing baskets etc" Our commentator takes the words separately.]

वायव्येष्वेषु नृपतिर्वायुं सक्तुभिरर्चयेत् ।
आवायोरिति पञ्चर्चो जप्तव्याः प्रयतैर्द्विजैः ॥६४॥

ब्राह्मणान् परमान्नेन दक्षिणाभिश्च तर्पयेत् ।
बह्वन्नदक्षिणा होमाः कर्तव्याश्च प्रयत्नतः ॥६५॥

When these aerial portents are witnessed, the king ought to worship the Wind-God with the flour of barley, and devout and pure Brāhmaṇas should chant repeatedly the five hymns beginning with "*Ā Vāyoḥ*". The king should also please Brāhmaṇas with milk porridge and monetary gifts. Similarly, offerings should be made into the sacred fire with devotion and efforts, along with large-scale feeding of the worthy and generous gifts of gold.

[We are not expected to sit in judgment over the language and expressions of ancient Sages like Garga. A modern editor has pointed out that the word जप्तव्याः is against Pāṇini's rule. For, he must have mistaken the verses for *Varāha's*. Actually these are *Garga's*, whose 'अनड्डुत्' has been ignored by him. Utpala too repeats 'जप्तव्य' in his commentary.]

(10) *Portents of Animals and Birds.*

पुरपक्षिणो वनचरा वन्या वा निर्भया विशन्ति पुरम् ।
नक्तं वा दिवसचराः क्षपाचरा वा चरन्त्यहनि ॥६६॥

सन्ध्याद्वयेऽपि मण्डलमाबध्नन्तो मृगा विहङ्गा वा ।
दीप्तायां दिश्यथवा क्रोशन्तः संहता भयदाः ॥६७॥

If village birds roam in the forest, or jungle birds move about freely in towns or villages or day-birds (like crows) fly at night, or night-birds (like owls) fly at daytime, or if birds or beasts form groups or circles at dawn or dusk, or if they howl in groups facing the Sun, there would be danger ahead.

श्येनाः प्ररुदन्त इव द्वारे क्रोशन्ति जम्बुका दीप्ताः ।
प्रविशेन्नरेन्द्रभवने कपोतकः कौशिको यदि वा ॥६८॥

When eagles appear to be weeping, jackals facing the Sun howl hideously at the city gates, or when a pigeon or owl enters the king's palace, danger is to be apprehended.

[श्वानः is another reading for श्येनाः. It is believed that the howling of a dog resembling moaning presages tragedy in the place.

Cf. गर्ग—

श्येनगृध्रबलाकाश्च वामना मुण्डचारिणः ।
शब्दायन्त इवात्यर्थं प्रदीप्ताः सङ्घशो यदि ॥
रुदन्ति विविधं तदेवाशु विनश्यति ।
यद्यभीक्ष्णं कपोता वा प्रविशन्ति वसन्ति वा ।
राजवेश्मन्युलूका वा तच्छून्यमचिराद्भवेत् ॥]

कुक्कुटरुतं प्रदोषे हेमन्तादौ च कोकिलालापाः ।
प्रतिलोममण्डलचराः श्येनाद्याश्चाम्बरे भयदाः ॥६९॥

गृहचैत्यतोरणेषु द्वारेषु च पक्षिसङ्घसम्पातः ।
मधुवल्मीकाम्भोरुहसमुद्भवश्चापि नाशाय ।।७०।।

Cocks crowing in the evening, cuckoos warbling in the beginning of the dewy season, and vultures and the like (i.e. carnivorous birds) flying in a circle from the right to the left in the sky, forbode danger. Should groups of birds sit on houses, sacred trees, arches and gates, or should honey, anthill or lotus grows in houses etc. (i.e. sacred trees, arches and gates), the place would be devastated.

श्वभिरस्थिशवावयवप्रवेशनं मन्दिरेषु मरकाय ।
पशुशस्त्रव्याहारे नृपमृत्युर्मुनिवचश्चेदम् ।।७१।।

If dogs bring bones or parts of dead bodies into houses, epidemics would break out soon; and if animals and weapons talk like human beings, there would be the king's death. The following remedial measures have been prescribed by the Sage (Garga).

मृगपक्षिविकारेषु कुर्याद्धोमान् सदक्षिणान् ।
देवाः कपोत इति च जप्तव्याः पञ्चभिर्द्विजैः ।।७२।।

सुदेवा इति चैकेन देया गावः सदक्षिणाः ।
जपेच्छाकुनसूक्तं वा मनो वेदशिरांसि च ।।७३।।

For warding off the evil effects of the portents connected with birds and beasts, sacrifices should be performed with liberal gifts of money. Five Brāhmaṇas should also repeat the hymn beginning with the words. "*Devāḥ kapotaḥ*" and the one "*Sudevāḥ...*" (*vide* Vālakhilya 6-4). Or, they may chant repeatedly the Śākuna hymn, the prayer "*Vā Mano...*" or the *Atharvaśiras*. The priests should also be presented with milch cows and liberal gifts of money.

[These two verses must be Garga's, although they are printed as those of Varāhamihira.]

(11) *Portents of Indra's Banner etc.*

शक्रध्वजेन्द्रकीलस्तम्भद्वारप्रपातभङ्गेषु ।
तद्वत्कपाटतोरणकेतूनां नरपतेर्मरणम् ।।७४।।

When Indra's Standard, the cross-bar of a door, pillar, door, door-leaves, arch or flag, falls down or breaks, it foreshadows the king's death.

सन्ध्याद्वयस्य दीप्तिर्धूमोत्पत्तिश्च काननेऽनग्नौ ।
छिद्राभावे भूमेर्दरणं कम्पश्च भयकारी ।।७५।।

Brilliant light at dawn and sunset, smoke rising from the

forest without fire, splitting of the earth without any breach and its tremor are harmful to the people.

पाखण्डानां नास्तिकानां च भक्तः साध्वाचारप्रोज्झितः क्रोधशीलः ।
ईर्ष्युः क्रूरो विग्रहासक्तचेता यस्मिन् राजा तस्य देशस्य नाशः ॥७६॥

The country which is ruled by a king, who is devoted to heretics and atheists, who has forsaken virtuous conduct, is hot-tempered, malicious, cruel and always intent on fighting, will be utterly ruined.

[It is a portent for a country to have a king described in this verse. By inference we can get Varāha's definition of an ideal king.

The metre is शालिनी.]

प्रहर हर छिन्धि भिन्धीत्यायुधकाष्ठाश्मपाणयो बालाः ।
निगदन्तः प्रहरन्ते तत्रापि भयं भवत्याशु ॥७७॥

The place where children strike one another, holding weapons, sticks and stones in their hands and shouting "Strike ! drag ! cut ! break !" will see danger ere long.

[Cf. पराशर—

यदि धनुरसिकाष्ठलोष्टहस्ता पुरशिशवो रणवत्समाचरन्ति ।
प्रहर हर जहीत्युदाहरन्ते भयमचिरात्तुमुलं निवेदयन्ति ।।

According to Pāṇini 'हर छिन्धि' should have been used as 'हरच्छिन्धि'. But then the metre would be spoiled. We can allow such lapses with our author who is a great author, scholar and poet, under the plea, 'निरङ्कुशाः खलु कवयः'.]

अङ्गारगैरिकाद्यैर्विकृतप्रेताभिलेखनं यस्मिन् ।
नायकचित्रितमथवा क्षये क्षयं याति न चिरेण ॥७८॥

A house where figures of monsters or ghosts are drawn with charcoal, red chalk etc., or a picture of the house-owner is drawn with any of the above-named materials, will be destroyed before long.

लूतापटाङ्गशबलं न सन्ध्ययोः पूजितं कलहयुक्तम् ।
नित्योच्छिष्टस्त्रीकं च यद्गृहं तत्क्षयं याति ॥७९॥

A house, which is full of cobwebs, where Gods are not worshipped at dawn and sunset, where there is constant quarrel and where women remain unclean everyday (through their monthly course), will go to rac and ruin.

दृष्टेषु यातुधानेषु निर्दिशेन्मरकमाशु सम्प्राप्तम् ।
प्रतिघातायैतेषां गर्गः शान्ति चकारेमाम् ॥८०॥

If goblins (unearthly beings or evil spirits) are sighted in a place, imminent pestilence should be predicted for it. For averting the evils of these portents Sage Garga has prescribed the following remedial measure.

महाशान्त्योऽथ बलयो भोज्यानि सुमहान्ति च ।
कारयेत महेन्द्रं च माहेन्द्रीं च समर्चयेत् ॥८१॥

The king should perform Great *Śāntis* (expiatory rites), offer food and worship to the Deities and get large quantities of eatables prepared (and distributed among the Brāhmaṇas). He should also worship Mahendra and His consort Indrāṇī.

(12) *Harmless Phenomena*

नरपतिदेशविनाशे केतोरुदयेऽथवा ग्रहेऽर्केन्द्वोः ।
उत्पातानां प्रभवः स्वर्तुभवश्चाप्यदोषाय ॥८२॥

The appearance of portents or unnatural phenomena, at the time of death of a king, devastation of the country by a hostile army, the rising of Ketu (comet) or at a solar or lunar eclipse, and also the sight of those phenomena that are peculiar to the respective seasons, are not harmful.

[It is reported that when great personages cast off their mortal coils, a bright star is seen rising into the heavens. The appearance of a comet itself is a portent, which may be accompanied by other unnatural events. Each season has its own peculiar features which cannot be called portents. Our author quotes profusely Sage Ṛṣiputra on this subject of the peculiar features of the six seasons.]

ये च न दोषाञ्जनयन्त्युत्पातास्तानृतुस्वभावकृतान् ।
ऋषिपुत्रकृतैः श्लोकैर्विद्यादेतैः समासोक्तैः ॥८३॥

Those portents which are generated by the peculiar nature of the seasons and so do not lead to evil consequences, could be understood from the verses of Ṛṣiputra that have been summarized hereunder.

वज्राशनिमहीकम्पसन्ध्यानिर्घातनिःस्वनाः ।
परिवेषरजोधूमरक्तार्कास्तमयोदयाः ॥८४॥
द्रुमेभ्योऽन्नरसस्नेहबहुपुष्पफलोद्गमाः ।
गोपक्षिमदवृद्धिश्च शिवाय मधुमाधवे ॥८५॥

Auspicious are the following portents seen in the spring season constituted by the lunar months of Caitra and Vaiśākha : Thunderbolt, lightning, earth-tremor, bright glare at twilight, sounds of loud thunder, halos, dust, smoke (in forests), the Sun being crimson at the time of rising and setting, the exudation of food, sweet juices, oil and an abundant yield of flowers and fruits on trees and increased sensuality on the part of bulls and birds.

[For details of सन्ध्या *vide* XXX *supra*. The commentator interprets वज्र as lightning, and अशनि as : "अश्मवर्षणम् उल्काभेदो वा ।"]

तारोल्कापातकलुषं कपिलार्केन्दुमण्डलम् ।
अनग्निज्वलनस्फोटधूमरेण्वनिलाहतम् ।।८६।।
रक्तपद्मारुणा सन्ध्या नभः क्षुब्धार्णवोपमम् ।
सरितां चाम्बुसंशोषं दृष्ट्वा ग्रीष्मे शुभं वदेत् ।।८७।।

The following portents seen in summer constituted by Jyeṣṭha and Āṣāḍha, are said to be beneficial : The sky tarnished by shooting stars and falling meteors; the orbs of the luminaries being tawny; blaze and explosion without fire, smoke, dust and a strong wind filling the sky; the twilight red like the red lotus; the sky looking like the ocean with surging waves; and the drying up of the waters of the rivers.

शक्रायुधपरीवेषविद्युच्छुष्कविरोहणम् ।
कम्पोद्वर्तनवैकृत्यं रसनं दरणं क्षितेः ।।८८।।
सरोनद्युदपानानां वृद्ध्यूर्ध्वतरणप्लवाः ।
सरणं चाद्रिगेहानां वर्षासु न भयावहम् ।।८९।।

The following unnatural phenomena are not dangerous in the rainy season : Rainbow, halos, lightning, sprouting of withered trees, tremor, upheaval, unnatural appearances, rumbling and splitting of the earth; rising, flowing upwards and flooding of lakes, rivers and wells respectively; and falling off of mountains and houses.

दिव्यस्त्रीभूतगन्धर्वविमानाद्भुतदर्शनम् ।
ग्रहनक्षत्रताराणां दर्शनं च दिवाम्बरे ।।९०।।
गीतवादित्रनिर्घोषा वनपर्वतसानुषु ।
सस्यवृद्धिरपां हानिरपापाः शरदि स्मृताः ।।९१।।

The following portents in autumn lead to auspicious results : The sight of celestial damsels, spirits, Gandharvas, aerial chariots, marvellous things, and of planets, stars and constellations in the daytime in the sky; sounds of singing and musical instruments in the forests and on mountain plateaus; increase of crops and diminution of water.

शीतानिलतुषारत्वं नर्दनं मृगपक्षिणाम् ।
रक्षोयक्षादिसत्त्वानां दर्शनं वागमानुषी ॥६२॥
दिशो धूमान्धकाराश्च सनभोवनपर्वताः ।
उच्चैः सूर्योदयास्तौ च हेमन्ते शोभनाः स्मृताः ॥६३॥

The following portents in the dewy season are considered beneficial : Cold wind, frost, cries of birds and beasts, sight of demons, Yakṣas and such other invisible beings; aerial voice being heard; the quarters along with the sky, forests and mountains getting darkened with smoke; and the high rising and setting of the Sun.

हिमपातानिलोत्पाता विरूपाद्भुतदर्शनम् ।
कृष्णाञ्जनाभमाकाशं तारोल्कापातपिञ्जरम् ॥६४॥
चित्रगर्भोद्भवाः स्त्रीषु गोऽजाश्वमृगपक्षिषु ।
पत्राङ्कुरलतानां च विकाराः शिशिरे शुभाः ॥६५॥

The following phenomena in winter (Śiśira) are productive of good results : Snowfall, unnatural winds, appearance of deformed and wonderful (superhuman) beings, the sky looking like dark collyrium, and colourful with the fall of stars and meteors; women, cows, goats, horses, beasts and birds giving birth to freakish young ones; and unnatural changes in leaves, sprouts and creepers.

[Bhaṭṭotpala gives an additional meaning to "गोऽजाश्व..." as, "Change in the natural behaviour of cows etc." The unnatural phenomena listed here become natural in the respective seasons as a result of change in the weather conditions.]

ऋतुस्वभावजा ह्येते दृष्टाः स्वर्तौ शुभप्रदाः ।
ऋतोरन्यत्र चोत्पाता दृष्टास्ते चातिदारुणाः ॥६६॥

These portents which are natural to the respective seasons, prove beneficial, if they are seen in their own seasons On the other hand, if they be seen at other times, they would prove dreadful in their effects.

उन्मत्तानां च या गाथाः शिशूनां यच्च भाषितम् ।
स्त्रियो यच्च प्रभाषन्ते तस्य नास्ति व्यतिक्रमः ॥६७॥

The vernacular songs of lunatics, utterances of children and the words of women do not at all go wrong in their effects.

[The words of playing children etc. are of great importance in the sphere of prognostics.]

पूर्वं चरति देवेषु पश्चाच्चरति मानुषान् ।
नाचोदिता वाग्वदति सत्या ह्येषा सरस्वती ॥९८॥

This Supreme Goddess of Speech is always truthful. She does not speak unless she is goaded. For, first She travels among the Gods and then (being goaded by them) goes to the mortals.

[Here we are reminded of the Brāhmaṇa statement, "सत्यसंहिता वै देवाः'. Being wedded to truth the Gods cause portentous words and behaviour to be revealed through all kinds of beings, young and old, human and sub-human. Hence what the author has said in verse 2 of this chapter stands confirmed by this statement. These 15 verses are taken from the work of Ṛṣiputra.]

उत्पातान् गणितविवर्जितोऽपि बुद्ध्वा
विख्यातो भवति नरेन्द्रवल्लभश्च ।
एतत्तन्मुनिवचनं रहस्यमुक्तं
यज्ज्ञात्वा भवति नरस्त्रिकालदर्शी ॥९९॥

Though a person may not be well-versed in astronomic calculations, yet he can become famous and a favourite of monarchs, if he observes (and understands the significance of) the portents carefully. Thus have I explained this secret (of portents) taught by the Sages, by knowing which man can look into the past, present and future.

[In the case of omens etc. intuition plays an important role. In astrology mere knowledge of astronomy and an intellectual grasp of the astrological principles would not be sufficient for predicting correctly one's past, present and future.

The metre is प्रहर्षिणी]

———

मयूरचित्रकम् ॥४७॥

Chapter XLVII—Motley Miscellany

दिव्यान्तरिक्षाश्रयमुक्तमादौ मया फलं शस्तमशोभनं च ।
प्रायेण चारेषु समागमेषु युद्धेषु मार्गादिषु विस्तरेण ॥१॥

भूयो वराहमिहिरस्य न युक्तमेत-
त्कर्तुं समासकृदसाविति तस्य दोषः ।
तज्ज्ञैर्न वाच्यमिदमुक्तफलानुगीति
यद्बर्हिचित्रकमिति प्रथितं वराङ्गम् ॥२॥

स्वरूपमेव तस्य तत्प्रकीर्त्तितानुकीर्त्तनम् ।
ब्रवीम्यहं न चेदिदं तथापि मेऽत्र वाच्यता ॥३॥

In this work I have already dealt with the good and bad effects of the celestial and atmospheric phenomena mostly in connection with the planet's courses, conjunctions, wars, paths etc.. (i.e. Maṇḍalas). Some may find fault with me, saying, "It does not behove Varāhamihira, being noted for brevity, to repeat the same subject." However, scholars of this science ought not to remark that this chapter is a repetition of the effects already expounded, because this chapter, entitled "*Barhicitraka*" or "*Mayūracitraka*" (Peacock's Colours), is a reputed important section of this Saṁhitā (collection). Hence it is the very nature of this section to repeat what has once been explained. And if I exclude this chapter, still they (scholars) would blame me.

[From the nature and contents of this chapter, it looks almost like the concluding section, at sometime, of a part of this work, if not of the entire work.

For the *Divine* and *Atmospheric* see XLVI. 4. For the Mārgas and Maṇḍalas see IX 1-3 and 10-21.

The metres are उपजाति, वसन्ततिलका and प्रमाणिका.]

उत्तरवीथिगता द्युतिमन्तः क्षेमसुभिक्षशिवाय समस्ताः ।
दक्षिणमार्गगता द्युतिहीनाः क्षुद्भयतस्करमृत्युकरास्ते ॥४॥

All the non-luminous planets, being radiant and moving in the northern paths i.e. *Nāga*, *Gaja* and *Airāvata*, confer happiness, peace and plenty; but, being shorn of radiance and moving in the southern avenues viz. *Mṛga*, *Aja* and *Dahana*, they produce threat of famine, theft and mortality.

[Cf. गर्ग—

वर्णवन्तः स्वमार्गस्था नागवीथीविचारिणः ।
यदि ताराग्रहाः सन्ति सर्वलोकहितावहाः ॥
वैश्वानरपथप्राप्ता एकनक्षत्रचारिणः ।
पञ्चताराग्रहाश्चेत्स्युर्विन्द्याल्लोकस्य सङ्क्षयः ॥

The metre is दोधक.]

कोष्ठागारगते भृगुपुत्रे पुष्यस्थे च गिराम्प्रभविष्णौ ।
निर्वैराः क्षितिपाः सुखभाजः संहृष्टाश्च जना गतरोगाः ॥५॥

When Venus occupies the asterism Maghā, and Jupiter Puṣya, kings will be happy and free from mutual hatred, and the people, contented and hale and hearty.

[Cf. गर्ग—

कोष्ठागारगते शुक्रे पुष्यस्थे च बृहस्पतौ ।
विन्द्यात्तदा सुखं लोके शान्तशस्त्रमनामयम् ॥

The metre of this verse has not been named either in Piṅgala's or Kedārabhaṭṭa's work on prosody. However it falls under the category of पङ्क्तिच्छन्दः]

पीडयन्ति यदि कृत्तिकां मघां रोहिणीं श्रवणमैन्द्रमेव वा ।
प्रोज्झ्य सूर्यमपरे ग्रहास्तदा पश्चिमा दिगनयेन पीड्यते ॥६॥

Should the planets barring the Sun hurt (by moving south, covering the chief star of or cutting through) the asterism Kṛttikā, Maghā, Rohiṇī, Śravaṇa or Jyeṣṭha, the countries situated in the west would be torn by troubles.

[Cf. गर्ग—

वैष्णवं पित्र्यमाग्नेयं ज्येष्ठामपि च रोहिणीम् ।
पीडयन्ति यदैतानि राहुषष्ठानुचारिणः ॥
दुर्भिक्षं जायते लोके सस्यमत्र न रोहति ।
शुष्यन्ति सरितः सर्वाः पर्जन्यश्च न वर्षति ॥

The metre is रथोद्धता]

प्राच्यां चेद्ध्वजवदवस्थिता दिनान्ते
प्राच्यानां भवति हि विग्रहो नपाणाम् ।

मध्ये चेद् भवति हि मध्यदेशपीडा
रूक्षैस्तैर्न तु रुचिमन्मयूखवद्भिः ॥७॥

Should the above planets be situated in the form of a banner in the east in the evening, there would be war among the eastern kings; should the formation be in the middle of the sky, there would be misery in the central country, provided the planets are rough and tiny in appearance; and not when they are possessed of bright rays.

[The metre is प्रहर्षिणी.]

दक्षिणां ककुभमाश्रितैस्तु तैर्दक्षिणापथपयोमुचां क्षयः ।
हीनरूक्षतनुभिश्च विग्रहः स्थूलदेहकिरणान्वितैः शुभम् ॥८॥

If they are stationed in the south, the clouds over the Deccan (or the southern country) will be destroyed; and if they come to have small and rough orbs, war will be the result. Good result will follow if they are large and full of bright rays.

[The metre is रथोद्धता]

उत्तरमार्गे स्पष्टमयूखाः शान्तिकरास्ते तन्नृपतीनाम् ।
ह्रस्वशरीरा भस्मसवर्णा दोषकराः स्युर्देशनृपाणाम् ॥९॥

Being endowed with bright rays and stationed in the northern avenues, they bestow peace on the kings of the northern countries. On the other hand, if they are tiny in form and ashy in colour, they cause harm to the rulers of that region.

[Cf. गर्ग—

उत्तरोत्तरमार्गस्था रश्मिमालाधरा ग्रहाः ।
विष्पन्दन्त इवात्यर्थं जयमाहुरुपस्थितम् ॥

The lilting metre is known as रुक्मवती or चम्पकमाला. In the second line the alliteration is happy.]

नक्षत्राणां तारकाः सग्रहाणां धूमज्वालाविस्फुलिङ्गान्विताश्चेत् ।
आलोकं वा निर्निमित्तं न यान्ति याति ध्वंसं सर्वलोकः सभूपः ॥१०॥

Should the stars of the constellations with the planets posited therein be full of smoke, flames and sparks, remain invisible for no reason, the entire population along with their king would be annihilated.

[At the end of the first line आवृताश्चेत् is another reading for अन्विताश्चेत्.

The metre is शालिनी.].

दिवि भाति यदा तुहिनांशुयुगं द्विजवृद्धिरतीव तदाशु शुभा ।
तदनन्तरवर्णरणोऽर्कयुगे जगतः प्रलयस्त्रिचतुष्प्रभृति ॥११॥

When two Moons shine in the sky, Brāhmaṇas will then achieve great prosperity and happiness ere long. Should there be two Suns, Kṣatriyas would engage themselves in warfare; and should there be three or more Suns, there would be dissolution of the world.

[Cf. गर्ग—

द्विचन्द्रं गगनं दृष्ट्वा विन्द्याद्ब्रह्म समुत्थितम् ।
द्वौ वा सूर्यौ यदा स्यातां तदा क्षत्रं विरुध्यति ॥
दृष्ट्वा त्रिचतुरः सूर्याननुदितान् सर्वतो दिशम् ।
शस्त्रेण जनमारेण तद्युगान्तरदर्शनम् ॥

The metre is तोटक.]

मुनीनभिजितं ध्रुवं मघवतश्च भं संस्पृशन्
शिखी घनविनाशकृत् कुशलकर्महा शोकदः ।
भुजङ्गमथ संस्पृशेद् भवति वृष्टिनाशो ध्रुवं
क्षयं व्रजति विद्रुतो जनपदश्च बालाकुलः ॥१२॥

Should a comet touch the Seven Sages (the Great Bear), Abhijit, the Pole Star and Jyeṣṭha, it would destroy the clouds as well as works and people's health, and cause sorrow to them. Should it touch Āśleṣā, there would undoubtedly be drought and consequently the people, troubled by their famished children, would run hither and thither for relief and perish ultimately.

[The metre is पृथ्वी.]

प्राग्द्वारेषु चरन् रविपुत्रो नक्षत्रेषु करोति च वक्रम् ।
दुर्भिक्षं कुरुते महदुग्रं मित्राणां च विरोधमवृष्टिम् ॥१३॥

When Saturn passes through the '*Front Gates*' viz. the seven stars commencing with Kṛttikā, and becomes retrograde, there will be a dreadful and long-drawn famine, drought and hostilities among friends.

[Cf. गर्ग—

विलम्बितगतिः सौरः प्राग्द्वारेषु यदा भवेत् ।
महाभयानि चत्वारि विजानीयात्समन्ततः ॥
अनावृष्टिभयं घोरं दुर्भिक्षं मित्रविग्रहम् ॥

B.G. Tilak has shown in his *Orion* that in the Vedic period and during that of some of the earlier Brāhmaṇas like the शतपथ the

Kṛttikās(Pleiades) never swerved from the east. Hence they were considered the eastern stars.

The metre of this verse is similar to that of verse 5 above, without a name under the पङ्क्ति group.]

रोहिणीशकटमर्कनन्दनो यदि भिनत्ति रुधिरीऽथवा शिखी ।
किं वदामि यदनिष्टसागरे जगदशेषमुपयाति सङ्क्षयम् ॥१४॥

When Saturn, Mars or a comet cuts the wain of Rohiṇī, what shall I say, alas ! For, the whole world will perish, being plunged in the ocean of misery.

[Cf. गर्ग—

रोहिणीशकटं भौमो भिनत्त्यर्कसुतोऽथवा ।
केतुर्वा जगतो ब्रूयात् प्रलयं समुपस्थितम् ॥

This is an अर्धसमवृत्त coined by our author by combining a foot of रथोद्धता with one of प्रियंवदा. Hence it is to be called उपजाति.

See also IX. 25 *supra*.]

उदयति सततं यदा शिखी चरति भचक्रमशेषमेव वा ।
अनुभवति पुराकृतं तदा फलमशुभं सचराचरं जगत् ॥१५॥

When a comet stays visible always or traverses the whole cycle of stars, the whole world with its moving and stationary objects will reap the evil fruit of their past misdeeds (i.e. the whole world will be plunged in the depths of sorrow).

[The metre is वैतालीय.]

धनुःस्थायी रूक्षो रुधिरसदृशः क्षुद्भयकरो
बलोद्योगं चन्द्रः कथयति जयं ज्याऽस्य च यतः ।
गवां शृङ्गो गोघ्नो निधनमपि सस्यस्य कुरुते
ज्वलन् धूमायन्वा नृपतिमरणायैव भवति ॥१६॥

The Moon being rough (unclean ?), blood-red and bow-shaped, presages famine and confrontation of armies, victory going to that side which is situated in the direction of the string of the lunar bow. If the Moon's horns resemble those of cows, cattle and crops will be destroyed; and if she glows or spouts smoke, it is a sure sign of the king's exit from the world.

[The metre is शिखरिणी. I suspect that in the third line the original reading might have been गवांशृङ्गी]

स्निग्धः स्थूलः समशृङ्गो विशालस्तुङ्गश्चोदग्विचरन्नागवीथ्याम् ।
दृष्टः सौम्यैरशुभैर्विप्रयुक्तो लोकानन्दं कुरुतेऽतीव चन्द्रः ॥१७॥

If the Moon be glossy, thick, of even horns, extensive, high in the sky, moving north in the *Nāga* avenue (viz. Bharaṇī, Kṛttikā and Svāti), aspected by benefics, and unaccompanied by malefics, she would confer great joy and happiness on humanity.

[For the *Nāgavīthī* cf. IX. 2 *supra*. Utpala wrongly construes उदक् as उत्तरश्रृङ्गोन्नतः.

The metre is वातोर्मी.]

पित्र्यमैत्रपुरुहूतविशाखात्वाष्ट्रमेत्य च युनक्ति शशाङ्कः ।
दक्षिणेन न शुभः शुभकृत्स्याद्यद्युदक् चरति मध्यगतो वा ॥१८॥

It is inauspicious, if the Moon comes in contact with Maghā, Anurādha, Jyeṣṭhā, Viśākhā and Citrā on the south, while on the north or in the middle, it is auspicious.

[The metre is स्वागता.]

परिघ इति मेघरेखा या तिर्यग्भास्करोदयेऽस्ते वा ।
परिधिस्तु प्रतिसूर्यो दण्डस्त्वृजुरिन्द्रचापनिभः ॥१९॥
उदयेऽस्ते वा भानोर्ये दीर्घा रश्मयस्त्वमोघास्ते ।
सुरचापखण्डमृजु यद्रोहितमैरावतं दीर्घम् ॥२०॥

A line of clouds standing across the Sun at his rising or setting is termed *Bolt*; a second or mock Sun is *Paridhi* or *Halo*; a straight staff (composed of the Sun's rays, clouds and wind) resembling the rainbow is *Rod*; the long rays of the Sun at rising or setting are named *unerring* (*amogha*); a straight and fragmentary rainbow is *Rohita* (Red), and the same, being longer, is termed *Airāvata*.

[*Vide* XXX. 16 and XXXVII. 1-3. The commentator construes ऋजु, which means *straight*, as स्पष्ट, clear.]

अर्धास्तमयात्सन्ध्या व्यक्तीभूता न तारका यावत् ।
तेजः परिहानिमुखाद्भानोरर्धोदयो यावत् ॥२१॥
तस्मिन्सन्ध्याकाले चिह्नैरेतैः शुभाशुभं वाच्यम् ।
सर्वैरेतैः स्निग्धैः सद्यो वर्षं भयं रूक्षैः ॥२२॥

The period after the Sun is half-set and before the stars have appeared is known as *Sandhyā* (evening twilight), and that after the stars have lost their lustre and before the Sun is half-risen is the *morning twilight*. From the above-mentioned symptoms of the two twilights (or junctures) one should predict good or bad effects. If all the features are glossy, there will be rain the same day; if rough, there will be danger.

[*Vide* XXX. 1]

अच्छिन्नः परिघो वियच्च विमलं श्यामा मयूखा रवेः
स्निग्धा दीधितयः सितं सुरधनुर्विद्युच्च पूर्वोत्तरा ।
स्निग्धो मेघतरुर्दिवाकरकरैरालिङ्गितो वा यदा
वृष्टिः स्याद्यदि वार्कमस्तसमये मेघो महाञ्छादयेत् ॥२३॥

If the *Bolt* is unbroken (i.e. full), the sky clear, the Sun's rays (*unerring*) dark and the other rays glossy (clear or bright), the rainbow white, lightning flashing in the north-east, and the tree-shaped cloud glossy or embraced by the Sun's rays all round, there will be rain. The same will happen, if a huge cloud covers the Sun at setting.

[This is a beautiful piece of descriptive poetry. In the third line there is the 'poetic excellence' called *Samādhi*, inasmuch as we get here the idea of a person embracing his friend warmly.

The metre is शार्दूलविक्रीडित.]

खण्डो वक्रः कृष्णो ह्रस्वः काकाद्यैर्वा चिह्नैर्विद्धः ।
यस्मिन्देशे रूक्षश्चार्कस्तत्राभावः प्रायो राज्ञः ॥२४॥

The country where the Sun appears partial, crooked, black, small and rough or marked with the figures of crows and other inauspicious things, will probably lose its monarch.

[Cf. गर्ग—

खण्डो वा कृष्णवर्णो वा ह्रस्वः पिङ्गलकोऽथवा ।
यत्रार्को दृश्यते तत्र राज्ञो मृत्युं विनिर्दिशेत् ॥

The metre is विद्युन्माला.]

वाहिनीं समुपयाति पृष्ठतो मांसभुक् खगगणो युयुत्सतः ।
यस्य तस्य बलविद्रवो महानग्रगैस्तु विजयो विहङ्गमैः ॥२५॥

If groups of carnivorous birds should follow the army of a king wishing to attack his enemy, his army would take to its heels; if the birds fly in front, he would be victorious.

[The metre is रथोद्धता. The desiderative word युयुत्सतः is not quite correct, as the root is आत्मनेपदी. The proper form is युयुत्समानस्य.]

भानोरुदये यदि वास्तमये गन्धर्वपुरप्रतिमा ध्वजिनी ।
बिम्बं निरुणद्धि तदा नृपतेः प्राप्तं समरं सभयं प्रवदेत् ॥२६॥

If at sunrise or sunset an army resembling an aerial city obstructs the Sun's disc, one should predict that the king would be involved in a dangerous war in the near future.

[Cf. गर्ग—

आदित्ये सरथा सेना सन्ध्याकाले यदा भवेत् ।
प्रत्यासन्नं विजानीयाद् भूमिपस्य पराजयम् ॥

It should be remembered that the army mentioned here is not a real one, but an apparent one formed by a peculiar arrangement of the clouds.

The metre is an unnamed variety of त्रिष्टुभ् got by replacing the penultimate long syllable by a short one in the उपस्थिता metre.]

शस्ता शान्तद्विजमृगघुष्टा सन्ध्या स्निग्धा मृदुपवना च ।
पांसुध्वस्ता जनपदनाशं धत्ते रूक्षा रुधिरनिभा च ॥२७॥

A twilight is laudable if it is clear, has gentle breeze blowing and is resounding with the pleasant cries of birds and beasts, not facing the Sun; while one vitiated by dust, rough or red-coloured, will bring about the destruction of the country.

[*Vide* XXX. 3, 5, 7. The metre is मत्ता.]

यद्विस्तरेण कथितं मुनिभिस्तदस्मिन्
सर्वं मया निगदितं पुनरुक्तवर्जम् ।
श्रुत्वापि कोकिलरुतं बलिभुग्विरौति
यत्तत्स्वभावकृतमस्य पिकं न जेतुम् ॥२८॥

Whatever had been expounded in great detail by ancient Sages like Garga has all been explained here by me without committing the fault of repetition. That the crow caws even after hearing the sweet warbling of the cuckoo, is entirely its natural trait and is not done with the idea of defeating the cuckoo.

[This is excellent poetry containing the figure अर्थान्तरन्यास, following in the footsteps of great masters like Kālidāsa. Here the author reveals his humility and eligibility to summarize the ancient teaching in his own humble way. This reminds us of Kālidāsa's statement :

अथवा कृतवाग्द्वारे वंशेऽस्मिन्पूर्वसूरिभिः ।
मणौ वज्रसमुत्कीर्णे सूत्रस्येवास्ति मे गतिः ॥
(रघु. I. 4)

Similarly a later poet, Bhoja, says in his चम्पूरामायण—"किं तर्पणं न विदधाति नरः पितॄणाम् ।"

The metre is वसन्ततिलका.]

Mr. Chidambara Iyer has quoted in his translation of this work some material coming under the purview of Saṁhitā, from some source. I requote the same for the benefit of readers :

There will be famine as long as the course of Jupiter and that of Saturn lie through the end of the signs Meṣa and Vṛścika and through the middle of Vṛṣabha and Siṁha.

During the period when Jupiter and Saturn occupy a single sign of the Zodiac, there would be pestilence, cholera and death among the people.

As long as Jupiter and Venus continue together in a state of disappearance, mankind will suffer from devils, diseases, thieves and enemies.

If the course of Saturn or the retrograde motion of Mars should lie through the signs of Dhanus, Meṣa, Vṛṣabha, Mīna or Siṁha, there would be such deaths among men and animals that only a third of mankind, of elephants, horses, cows and other animals, of birds and of creatures of water would survive.

If the motion of Mars should be an accelerated one, therd would be fear from destructive fires; if he should retrograde and enter another sign, the people would suffer from heat and many families would suffer, and if his course should be through a sign longer than the calculated period, there would be drought in the land and rulers will be at war.

If Jupiter should retrograde or if h's motion should be an accelerated one, and if in this state he should enter another sign, the rivers would not be full; the kings would lose their glory and suffer from diseases.

If Saturn should, after a long direct course, begin to retrograde or have an accelerated motion and in this state enter another sign, there would be diseases, famine and drought in the land and vehicles will suffer destruction.

If, when Jupiter should enter another sign when in his accelerated motion, Saturn should be in his slow motion, Venus should have disappeared, and Mercury should have reappeared, the country would perish.

If Saturn, Mars and Jupiter should be within sight of each other, men with their children would suffer from hunger and from weapons.

If, while the course of the Sun lies through the end of the signs Vṛṣabha, Mithuna, Vṛṣcika and Siṁha, Jupiter and Mars should be in conjunction with it, mankind would suffer from famine, and the deaths would be so many that in the cremation grounds of villages and towns, Piśācas might be seen with hundreds of dead bodies in their mouths.

If two, three or four planets should meet together, people would suffer from death and famine. If five planets should meet, there would also be famine; if six, the chief ruler would run away from his kingdom, and if seven, humanity would come to an end.

If the course of Mars and Saturn through the signs of Karkaṭaka, Siṁha and Mīna should be retrograde or re-retrograde, there would be much suffering on earth. There would also be a scarcity of water and wars in the land; grains would be destroyed and mankind would suffer from robbers.

If Saturn and Rāhu should meet, crops would be injured; commodity would become scarce; husbands and wives would be at strife, there would be drought and famine in the land; cows would suffer death and men would become exceedingly lazy.

If the course of the Sun and the Moon, both of brilliant discs, should lie through the seven asterisms from Kṛttikā, Madhyadeśa would suffer miseries.

If the course of the Sun, the Moon, Mars and Venus should lie through the seven asterisms from Maghā, there would be grief and disease among men and the God of Death would be busy in his wide work of destruction in the southern countries.

If the course of Jupiter, the Moon and Mercury, all of brilliant discs, should lie through the seven asterisms from Anurādhā, the western countries, as far as the sea, as well as the western sea itself with its creatures would suffer miseries.

If the course of the Sun, Venus and Mars should lie through the seven asterisms from Śraviṣṭhā, the northern countries would suffer miseries.

If the benefic planets should appear of the colour of gold, the Brahmins, the Kṣatriyas, the Vaiśyas and the Śūdras would all attend to their respective duties and would become happy.

———

पुष्यस्नानम् ॥४८॥

Chapter XLVIII—Royal Ablution

मूलं मनुजाधिपतिः प्रजातरोस्तदुपघातसंस्कारात् ।
अशुभं शुभं च लोके भवति यतोऽतो नृपतिचिन्ता ॥१॥

The king is the root of the subject tree. Efforts should be made to enhance the king's welfare, since progress and decay of the people are entirely dependent upon the nourishing and injuring respectively of that king-root.

[This is a very significant expression of a patent truth made in a metaphorical language. Here the Subject-tree stands for the entire *state*, called in Sanskrit, Prakṛti. It consists of seven parts viz. the king, ministers, allies, treasury, territory, fortifications and army. By *Prajā*, the author means this *Collective Prakṛti* whose tap root is represented by the king. Varāhamihira's statement is based on the ancient dictum stated by the Great Sage Vyāsa :

"कालो वा कारणं राज्ञो राजा वा कालकारणम् ।
इति ते संशयो मा भूद्राजा कालस्य कारणम् ॥"

and the statement that the king is there for 'प्रजारञ्जन' and 'प्रजारक्षण' and not for 'कामकरण'. Hence the king should conduct himself in the fashion of the tap root, taking sustenance from the earth and distributing it among its different parts.

See also the contrary qualities in XLVI. 76.]

या व्याख्याता शान्तिः स्वयम्भुवा सुरगुरोर्महेन्द्रार्थे ।
तां प्राप्य वृद्धगर्गः प्राह यथा भागुरेः शृणुत ॥२॥

Listen, Ye, to the method of expiation, which had been originally expounded by the Creator to the Preceptor of the Gods for the sake of Indra (the Lord of the Immortals), and which, later, Vṛddhagarga got and imparted to sage Bhāguri.

[We are not in a position to state definitely whether this Bhāguri and the grammarian were one and the same. All rituals are said to have been taught for being performed first for Indra, and then, on that model, for earthly kings. We hear the same thing about King Janamejaya's Coronation and his subsequent Aśvamedha sacrifice as well as world-conquest.

Cf. वृद्धगर्ग –

देवाश्च दितिजैः सार्धं स्पर्धमाना हि मानिनः ।
परस्परं महद्युद्धं चक्रुः सर्वे सुरासुराः ॥
ततो दैत्यगणैः क्रुद्धैर्देवाः सर्वे विनिर्जिताः ।
ततोऽङ्गिराः सुरगुरुर्ध्यानसक्तोऽभवत्पुरा ॥
पुरन्दराभिषेकार्थं बृहस्पतिरकल्पयत् ।
तिष्यमात्मीयनक्षत्रं यस्य देवो बृहस्पतिः ॥
तेन चैवाभिषिक्तश्च देवराजः पुरन्दरः ।
ततो बलसमारूढो नाशयामास दानवान् ॥
देवाश्च हृष्टमनसः पुरीं प्राप्यामरावतीम् ।
पुष्यस्नानं बलतरं तदारभ्य प्रवर्तितम् ॥

I feel बलकरं must have been the original reading.]

पुष्यस्नानं नृपतेः कर्तव्यं दैववित्पुरोधा(धो?)भ्याम् ।
नातः परं पवित्रं सर्वोत्पातान्तकरमस्ति ॥३॥

The royal astrologer and preceptor should give the king a holy bath on a day with which synchronizes the asterism of Puṣya. There is nothing holier than this which puts an end to all the evil effects of portents.

[Hindus believe that on certain holy days like some Full Moons, Saṅkrāntis, eclipses etc. some cosmic forces are released. They are tapped on such occasions for beneficial ends by persons who perform certain rituals on the banks of holy rivers, lakes etc. after bathing therein. Certain holy places stir the imagination of pious people with stored-up impressions of bygone births. Why should, otherwise, people go to the distant Vārāṇasī and bathe in the holy river Gaṅgā that was brought down from Heaven to the earth by King Bhagīratha to purify his ancestors ? I do not think our author could have committed the mistake of using the expression, पुरोधाभ्याम् instead of पुरोधोभ्याम्. The mistake evidently must have been committed by the scribes. The description of the place of the holy bath that follows is splendid, making out the author a great poet.]

श्लेष्मातकाक्षकण्टकिकटुतिक्तविगन्धिपादपविहीने ।
कौशिकगृध्रप्रभृतिभिरनिष्टविहगैः परित्यक्ते ॥४॥
तरुणतरुगुल्मवल्लीलताप्रतानान्विते वनोद्देशे ।
निरुपहतपत्रपल्लवमनोज्ञमधुरद्रुमप्राये ॥५॥

The royal bath should be performed in a forest-region, which is devoid of cordia, beleric myrobalan, thorny, pungent, bitter, and badsmelling trees; which is not frequented by owls, vultures and such other inauspicious birds ; which is full of young trees, shrubs, creepers and bowers, and which consists mostly of beautiful and sweet trees with unspoilt leaves and sprouts.

कृकवाकुजीवजीवकशुकशिखिशतपत्रचाषहारीतैः ।
क्रकरचकोरकपिञ्जलवञ्जुलपारावतश्रीकैः ॥६॥
कुसुमरसपानमत्तद्विरेफपुंस्कोकिलादिभिश्चान्यैः ।
विरुते वनोपकण्ठे क्षेत्रागारे शुचावथवा ॥७॥

Or, it may be done in a pure building in a sacred place in the vicinity of forests that resound with the notes of cocks, jīvas, jīvakas, parrots, peacocks, wood-peckers, blue jays, green pigeons, krakaras, cakoras, Kapiñjalas, Vañjulas, doves, Śrīkaṇṭhas and other birds such as the male cuckoos and bees that are intoxicated by drinking honey.

[The commentator suggests that 'क्षेत्रागारे शुचावथवा' may be taken independently, and not necessarily as an adjunct to 'वनोपकण्ठे'. I think that this interpretation is not quite consistent with what was given in the previous two verses. Having already given 'वनोद्देशे' the author would not repeat the same idea. For, there is no material difference between the two expressions वनोद्देशे and वनोपकण्ठे.]

ह्रदिनीविलासिनीनां जलखगनखविक्षतेषु रम्येषु ।
पुलिनजघनेषु कुर्याद् दृङ्मनसोः प्रीतिजननेषु ॥८॥

Or, it may be performed on the charming laps viz. the sandy banks, that delight the eyes and the heart, that have the marks of nails in the form of aquatic birds, of the courtezans viz. the rivers.

[This is erotic sentiment *par excellence*. It is also a good example of connected रूपक or metaphor. The poet continues the imagery in the following two verses.]

प्रोत्प्लुतहंसच्छत्रे कारण्डवकुररसारसोद्गीते ।
फुल्लेन्दीवरनयने सरसि सहस्राक्षकान्तिधरे ॥९॥

Or it may be done at a lake, which possesses Indra's grandeur on account of its royal umbrella in the form of the flying swans, the loud songs in the form of the cries of ducks, ospreys and cranes, and its numerous eyes in the form of the blue lily blossoms.

[Here the poet employs a full metaphor re-informed by a simile. In all these images we can clearly perceive Kālidāsa's influence. The reader may see the description of the Sarayū (in XIII. Raghu). For हंसच्छन्न we have "“पथा पद्मातपत्रेण भेजे" in the Raghu (IV).]

प्रोत्फुल्लकमलवदनाः कलहंसकलप्रभाषिण्यः ।
प्रोत्तुङ्गकुड्मलकुचा यस्मिन्नलिनीविलासिन्यः ॥१०॥

Or, in a place where there are the sportive damsels viz. lotus-ponds, with their beaming faces of full-blown lotuses, melodious voices of the sweet notes of the royal swans, and hard (or lofty) bosoms of the uplifted buds.

[Here the poet compares the lotus-ponds to charming damsels. The reader may, with advantage, bring to memory Kālidāsa's inimitable verse in the description of Pārvatī :

"आवर्जिता किञ्चिदिव स्तनाभ्यां वासो वसाना तरुणार्क रागम् ।
पर्याप्तपुष्पस्तबकावनम्रा सञ्चारिणी पल्लविनी लतेव ॥"

(V)

In the second line there is another reading : प्रोद्बद्ध, instead of प्रोत्तुङ्ग.]

कुर्याद्गोरोमन्थजफेनलवशकृत्खुरक्षतोपचिते ।
अचिरप्रसूतहुङ्कृतवल्गितवत्सोत्सवे गोष्ठे ॥११॥

Or, it may be done in a cow-pen, which is filled with the drops of foam from the mouths of cows chewing the cud, with cow-dung and with scratches made by their hoofs; and which is pleasing on account of the lowing and frisking of tender calves.

[I am inclined to take the two halves of this verse as independent sentences : In a place which is strewn with the marks of hoofs and drops of foam, or in a cow-pen etc.]

अथवा समुद्रतीरे कुशलागतरत्नपोतसम्बाधे ।
घननिचुललीनजलचरसितखगशबलीकृतोपान्ते ॥१२॥

Or, it may be perfomed on the sea-shore which is teeming with ships that have arrived safely with their cargo of gems and other very valuable things; and whose fringes are variegated with white birds and fishes and the like lurking in the thick bushes of the Nicula trees.

क्षमया क्रोध इव जितः सिंहो मृग्याभिभूयते येषु ।
दत्ताभयखगमृगशावकेषु तेष्वाश्रमेष्वथवा ॥१३॥

Or, it may be done in the hermitages of sages where a lion is subdued by a female deer just as wrath is conquered by forbearance, and where the young ones of birds and the deer roam about freely without any fear.

[The simile in this verse has been suggested by Vālmīki's verse,

"यः समुत्पतितं क्रोधं क्षमयैव निरस्यति ।
यथोरगस्त्वचं जीर्णां स वै पुरुष उच्यते ॥"

(रामा. V. 55-5).]

काञ्चीकलापनूपुरगुरुजघनोद्वहनविघ्नितपदाभिः ।
श्रीमति मृगेक्षणाभिर्गृहेऽन्यभृतवल्गुवचनाभिः ॥१४॥

Or, it may be gone through in a house rendered resplendent by the presence of charming (deer-eyed) women whose gait is impeded by the weight of their heavy hips, girdles and anklets, and whose speech is as pleasing as the warbling of cuckoos.

[This is reminiscent of Kālidāsa's line,

"न दुर्वहश्रोणिपयोधरार्ता भिन्दन्ति मन्दां गतिमश्वमुख्यः ।"

(कुमार. I).]

पुण्येष्वायतनेषु च तीर्थेषूद्यानरम्यदेशेषु ।
पूर्वोदक्प्लवभूमौ प्रदक्षिणाम्भोवहायां च ॥१५॥

It may be done also in holy temples, near holy rivers, in gardens, in attractive regions, in a place where the earth slopes down towards the east or the north, or where the water flows from the left to the right.

[Cf. वृद्धगर्ग—

समुद्रतीरे सोद्याने नदीनां सङ्गमे शुभे ।
महाह्रदेऽथवा तीर्थे देवतायतनेऽथवा ॥
सर्वर्तुकुसुमोपेते वने द्विजवरैर्युते ।
गृहे रम्ये विविक्ते वा पुष्यस्नानं समाचरेत् ॥]

Next the author speaks of the site for this bath.

भस्माङ्गारास्थ्यूषरतुषकेशश्वभ्रकर्कटावासैः ।
श्वाविषमूषकविवरैर्वल्मीकैर्या च सन्त्यक्ता ॥१६॥
धात्री घना सुगन्धा स्निग्धा मधुरा समा च विजयाय ।
सेनावासेऽप्येवं योजयितव्या यथायोगम् ॥१७॥

If the site selected for the holy bath be free from ashes, charcoal, bones, sandy mud, husk, hair, pits, burrows of crabs as well as from burrow-dwelling animals, holes of porcupines and rats and ant-hills, and if it is hard (not hollow), sweet-smelling, glossy (not arid), sweet and even (without ups and downs), it would conduce to victory. The same conditions apply to the case of encampment of armies as well, according to circumstances.

[Here the author and the commentator following him commit two grammatical errors viz. श्वाविध and सुगन्धा. It should have been श्वाविन्मूषक... and सुगन्धि:]

निष्क्रम्य पुरान्नक्तं देवज्ञामात्ययाजकाः प्राच्याम् ।
कौबेर्यां वा कृत्वा बलिं दिशीशाधिपायां वा ॥१८॥
लाजाक्षतदधिकुसुमैः प्रयतः प्रणतः पुरोहितः कुर्यात् ।
आवाहनमथ मन्त्रस्तस्मिन् मुनिभिः समुद्दिष्टः ॥१९॥

The astrologer, minister and the sacrificial priest should set out of the city at night and make food-offerings to the Deities in the east, north or north-east. Then the priest, being pure and prayerful should perform the Āvāhana (invoking the Deity to be present) with fried grains, coloured rice, curds and flowers. The hymn of invocation prescribed by the sages is the following :

[In the first verse the author has not given any finite verb, nor can the singular verb in the second go well with the subject in plural in the first. He could have avoided this error by substituting कुर्युः for कृत्वा.

From the circumstances mentioned here and in subsequent verses we have to conclude that these three persons are to form the advance party to prepare the ground for the holy bath. So the king does not accompany them.]

आगच्छन्तु सुराः सर्वे येऽत्र पूजाभिलाषिणः ।
दिशो नागा द्विजाश्चैव ये चाप्यन्येंऽशभागिनः ॥२०॥
आवाह्यैवं ततः सर्वानिवं ब्रूयात्पुरोहितः ।
श्वः पूजां प्राप्य यास्यन्ति दत्वा शान्ति महीपतेः ॥२१॥

"May all the Gods who wish to be honoured with worship condescend to come here, as well as the quarters, serpents, sages and others that partake of the sacrificial offerings !" Having thus invoked them to be present in the images, the priest should address all of them thus : "Tomorrow you will go back after receiving worship and bestowing peace and prosperity on the king."

आवाहितेषु कृत्वा पूजां तां शर्वरीं वसेयुस्ते ।
सदसत्स्वप्ननिमित्तं यात्रायां स्वप्नविधिरुक्तः ॥२२॥

After offering worship to the Deities that have been invoked to be present, they (the astrologer, minister and priest) should spend the night in the same place in order to find out the good or bad nature of the future revealed by dreams, the rules pertaining to which have been treated of in my work, viz. the *Yatra*.

[Cf. the यात्रा—

दुकूलमुक्तामणिभृन्नरेन्द्रः समन्त्रिदैवज्ञपुरोहितोऽन्तः ।
स्वदेवतागारमनुप्रविश्य निवेशयेत्तत्र दिगीश्वरार्चाम् ॥
अभ्यर्च्य मन्त्रैस्तु पुरोहितस्तामधश्च तस्यां भुवि संस्कृतायाम् ।
दर्भैश्च कृत्वास्तरमक्षतैस्तां लिखेत्समन्तात्सितसर्षपैश्च ॥
ब्राह्मीं सदूर्वामथ नागपुष्पीं कृत्वोपधानं शिरसि क्षितीशः ।
पूजार्घजान् पुष्पफलाभिधानानाशासु दध्याच्चतुरः क्रमेण ॥
यज्जाग्रतो दूरमुदेति दैवमावर्त्य मन्त्रं प्रयतस्त्रिरेतम् ।
लघ्वेकभुग्दक्षिणपार्श्वशायी स्वप्नं परीक्षेत यथोपदेशम् ॥
नमः शम्भो त्रिनेत्राय रुद्राय वरदाय च ।
वामनाय विरूपाय स्वप्नाधिपतये नमः ॥
भगवन् देवदेवेश शूलभृद् वृषवाहन ।
इष्टानिष्टं समाचक्ष्व स्वप्ने स्वप्नस्य शाश्वतम् ।
इष्टमन्त्रांस्ततः स्मृत्वा शिवशक्तिपुरोगमान् ।
अभ्यर्थनां ततस्तस्य कृत्वा सुप्रयतो नृपः ॥
एकवस्त्रे कुशास्तीर्णे सुप्तः प्रयतमानसः ।
निशान्ते पश्यति स्वप्नं शुभं वा यदि वाऽशुभम् ॥]

अपरेऽह्नि प्रभाते सम्भारानुपहरेद्यथोक्तगुणान् ।
गत्वावनिप्रदेशे श्लोकाश्चाप्यत्र मुनिगीताः ॥२३॥

On the morrow, at dawn the required materials possessing the prescribed qualities are to be brought to the same place of worship and offered on the ground; and the following verses bearing on this subject have been imparted by the Sage viz. Vṛddhagarga :

[The idea is that the materials mentioned in the following verses are to be placed in the appropriate compartments of the circular diagram drawn on the ground and then the various Deities worshipped.]

तस्मिन् मण्डलमालिख्य कल्पयेत्तत्र मेदिनीम् ।
नानारत्नाकरवतीं स्थानानि विविधानि च ॥२४॥
पुरोहितो यथास्थानं नागान् यक्षान् सुरान् पितॄन् ।
गन्धर्वाप्सरसश्चैव मुनीन् सिद्धांश्च विन्यसेत् ॥२५॥

ग्रहांश्च सर्वनक्षत्रै रुद्रांश्च सह मातृभिः ।
स्कन्दं विष्णुं विशाखं च लोकपालान् सुरस्त्रियः ॥२६॥
वर्णकैर्विविधैः कृत्वा हृद्यैर्गन्धगुणान्वितैः ।
यथास्वं पूजयेद्विद्वान् गन्धमाल्यानुलेपनैः ॥२७॥
भक्ष्यैरन्नैश्च विविधैः फलमूलामिषैस्तथा ।
पानैश्च विविधैर्हृद्यैः सुराक्षीरासवादिभिः ॥२८॥

On the afore-named ground the learned priest should draw a circle and therein mark the Earth along with the various oceans and the various other regions. He should place serpents, Yakṣas, Gods, the *Manes*, Gandharvas, Nymphs, Sages and Siddhas in their respective compartments. He should also draw in their proper places the planets with all the stars, the Rudras along with the seven Mothers, Skanda, Viṣṇu, Viśākha, the protectors of the quarters and the celestial damsels, with various coloured powders (appropriate to each) that are attractive and sweet-smelling and worship all the deities with perfumes, garlands, scented pastes, eatables and dishes of various kinds as well as with varieties of roots, fruits and meat and attractive drinks such as liquor, milk and wine.

[Bhaṭṭotpala interprets नानारत्नाकरवतीं मेदिनीम् as "बहूनि रत्नानि तत्र स्थापयेदित्यर्थः" i.e. one should place on the ground all kinds of gems. Following him we had translated accordingly in the edition of V.S. Sastri and M.R. Bhat. However, after 25 years I make bold to say that the commentator has not fully comprehended the significance of the occasion. For, the purpose of the *Puṣyasnāna* is to absolve the king of all his sins and enable him to conquer the entire world. For this purpose he should have before him the picture of the whole globe with the oceans and lands as well as the regions inhabited by Nāgas etc. Even the celestial region is depicted in this diagram. Each deity has its appropriate place and colour allotted.]

कथयाम्यतः परमहं पूजामस्मिन्यथाभिलिखितानाम् ।
ग्रहयज्ञे यः प्रोक्तो विधिर्ग्रहाणां स कर्तव्यः ॥२९॥
मांसौदनमद्याद्यैः पिशाचदितितनयदानवाः पूज्याः ।
अभ्यञ्जनाञ्जनतिलैः पितरो मांसौदनैश्चापि ॥३०॥
सामयजुर्भिर्मुनयस्त्वृग्भिर्गन्धैश्च धूपमाल्ययुतैः ।
अश्लेषकवर्णैस्त्रिमधुरेण चाभ्यर्चयेन्नागान् ॥३१॥

धूपाज्याहुतिमाल्यैर्विबुधान् रत्नैः स्तुतिप्रणामैश्च ।
गन्धर्वानप्सरसो गन्धैर्माल्यैश्च सुसुगन्धैः ॥३२॥
शेषांस्तु सार्ववर्णिकबलिभिः पूजां न्यसेच्च सर्वेषाम् ।
प्रतिसरवस्त्रपताकाभूषणयज्ञोपवीतानि ॥३३॥

Now I shall explain the method of worshipping the Deities drawn in their respective places inside the circle or mystic diagram. As for the planets, the same method as expounded in the *Yātrā* in connection with the Planetary Sacrifices should be adhered to. The Dānavas, Daityas and Piśācas are to be worshipped with flesh, rice, liquor etc.; the *Manes* with oil bath, collyrium, sesamum, meat and rice; the sages with the hymns of the Sāma, Yajus and Ṛg Vedas, perfumes, incense and garlands; the Serpents with unmixed colours and the triple sweet—a mixture of honey, ghee and sugar, the Gods with incense, ghee, oblations, garlands, gems, invocations and salutations; the Gandharvas and the nymphs with excellent perfumes and sweet smelling garlands; the remaining Deities (such as Yakṣas) with multi-coloured food-offerings. All the Deities should be worshipped and also strings dipped in saffron-paste, clothes, flags, ornaments and sacred threads placed in their respective compartments.

[Cf. the यात्रा—

यात्रायां ग्रहयज्ञे तत्रार्चा ताम्रमयसवितुः ।
(1) पालाशिकी समिद् वैकङ्कतजाता तथा स्रुक् च ॥
आकृष्णेति च मन्त्रो रक्ता गन्धाः सहागुरुणा ॥
माषातसीतिलाल्वकमुद्गांश्चणकान्विहाय भोज्यविधिः ।
वकुलार्कागस्त्यपलाशशल्यकीकुसुमपूजा च ॥
अष्टशतसस्मितेभ्यो विप्रेभ्यो दक्षिणाऽऽहिताग्निभ्यः ।
देया वृषकनकमही सहस्रकिरणं समुद्दिश्य ॥

(1) It is strange that the editor of the सरस्वतीभवनग्रन्थमाला (९७) claims on page 522, "सर्वेषु पुस्तकेषु 'पालाशिकी स्रुक् च' इति भ्रष्टपाठो वर्तते । अस्माभिर्वैदिकानुसारेण वैकङ्कतजाता तथा' इत्यधिकः पाठो योजितः", since in our 1947 edition, to which the above learned editor refers in his अवतारिका (pp. 18, 19), this addition had already been adopted.]

मण्डलपश्चिमभागे कृत्वाग्निं दक्षिणेऽथवा वेद्याम् ।
आवद्यात्सम्भारान् दर्भान् दीर्घानगर्भांश्च ॥३४॥
लाजाज्याक्षतदधिमधुसिद्धार्थकगन्धसुमनसो धूपः ।
गोरोचनाञ्जनतिलाः स्वर्तुजमधुराणि च फलानि ॥३५॥

सघृतस्य पायसस्य च तत्र शरावाणि तैश्च सम्भारैः ।
पश्चिमवेद्यां पूजां कुर्यात् स्नानस्य सा वेदी ॥३६॥

Fire should be kindled on a sacrificial altar made to the west or to the south of the mystic circle, and all the following necessary sacrificial materials collected on the altar, viz. long (uncut) blades of Darbha grass that do not contain tender sprouts inside, fried grains, ghee, coloured rice, curd, honey, white mustard seeds, perfumes, flowers, incense, Gorocanā (a bright yellow pigment found in the head of a cow), collyrium, sesamum and the sweet fruits of the season, as well as earthen plates filled with ghee and Pāyasa (milk porridge). With these materials got ready worship should be done on the altar to the west of the circle. For, this is the altar recommended for the royal ablution.

[Though the altar for the holy bath may be selected either to the west or south of the mystic diagram, yet the western altar seems to be more powerful for the bath, as the author mentions the पश्चिमवेदी once again at the end. If for some reason the western part is not suitable, then only the southern part should be selected to start with. Vide also verse 75 *infra*.]

तस्याः कोणेषु दृढान् कलशान् सितसूत्रवेष्टितग्रीवान् ।
सक्षीरवृक्षपल्लवफलापिधानान् व्यवस्थाप्य ॥३७॥
पुष्यस्नानविमिश्रेणापूर्णानम्भसा सरत्नांश्च ।
पुष्यस्नानद्रव्याण्यादद्याद्गर्गगीतानि ॥३८॥

In the four corners of the altar should be placed water pots strong and stable with white strings tied round their necks, and sprouts of milky trees and fruits put on their mouths. They should, be filled with water containing the herbs prescribed for this ablution and gems. Then the following materials for the holy bath prescribed by Sage Garga should be brought in.

[Cf. गर्ग—

कलशैर्हेमताम्रैश्च राजतैर्मृन्मयैस्तथा ।
सूत्रसंवेष्टितग्रीवैश्चन्दनागुरुचर्चितैः ॥
प्रशस्तवृक्षपत्रैश्च फलपुष्पसमन्वितैः ।
पुण्यतोयेन सम्पूर्णै रत्नगर्भैर्मनोहरैः ॥]

ज्योतिष्मतीं त्रायमाणामभयामपराजिताम् ।
जीवां विश्वेश्वरीं पाठां समङ्गां विजयां तथा ॥३९॥

सहां च सहदेवीं च पूर्णकोशां शतावरीम् ।
अरिष्टिकां शिवां भद्रां तेषु कुम्भेषु विन्यसेत् ॥४०॥
ब्राह्मीं क्षेमामजां चैव सर्वबीजानि काञ्चनीम् ।
मङ्गल्यानि यथालाभं सर्वौषध्यो रसास्तथा ॥४१॥
रत्नानि सर्वगन्धाश्च बिल्वं च सविकङ्कतम् ।
प्रशस्तनाम्न्यश्चौषध्यो हिरण्यं मङ्गलानि च ॥४२॥

The following herbs and articles should be put into the four holy pots :

The Jyotiṣmatī creeper (a luminous herb), Trāyamāṇā, Abhayā (Harītakī), Aparājitā (Viṣṇukrāntā), Jīvantī, Viśveśvarī, Pāṭhā (Ambaṣṭhā or Vanatiktikā), red madder, Vacā, Sahā (Mudgaparṇī), Sahadevī, Pūrṇakośā, Śatāvarī, Ariṣṭikā, Śivā, Bhadrā, Brāhmī (moonplant), Kṣemā, Ajā, all kinds of seeds, Kāñcanī (turmeric), all auspicious articles (such as curds, coloured rice and flowers) as far as they are available, all herbs, juices of different tastes, gems, all perfumes, Bilva and Vikaṅkata fruits, herbs with auspicious names, gold etc. and auspicious materials.

[In every little object created by God there is some amount of spiritual and physical potency. That is the reason why preparations of herbs called decoctions and other medicines possess both curative and ameliorative powers. In esoteric science too herbs, spells and gems play an important role in this regard. This is due to the fact that objects receive, in addition to having their innate powers, cosmic energy from every other object in the world, especially from the mighty heavenly bodies. If we understand this principle, we can easily appreciate the Moon's appellation, Oṣadhīśa, lord of herbs. The herbs, gems, seeds and minerals used for the Puṣyasnāna along with the powerful Mantras are meant to give a good deal of spiritual strength to the king. Look at the wonderfully significant names of the herbs : Trāyamāṇā meaning protective, Abhayā freedom from fear, Aparājitā never defeated etc.]

आदावनडुहश्चर्म जरया संहृतायुषः ।
प्रशस्तलक्षणभृतः प्राचीनग्रीवमास्तरेत् ॥४३॥
ततो वृषस्य योधस्य चर्म रोहितमक्षतम् ।
सिंहस्याथ तृतीयं स्याद् व्याघ्रस्य च ततः परम् ॥४४॥
चत्वार्येतानि चर्माणि तस्यां वेद्यामुपास्तरेत् ।
शुभे मुहूर्ते सम्प्राप्ते पुष्ययुक्ते निशाकरे ॥४५॥

At first the skin of a bull bearing auspicious marks, which had died of old age, should be spread on the altar with its neck turned to the east. Over this should be spread the red-coloured and unspoilt skin of a fighting bull. Over this a lion's skin and over that a tiger's skin should be put. This should be done in an auspicious Muhūrta when the Moon is in the star Puṣya.

[In Mantraśāstra different skins that are used as seats for meditation etc. are said so give out different types of spiritual vibrations. Lord Śiva is said to have used a tiger-skin seat for His penance : "शार्दूलचर्मव्यवधानवत्याम्."

The excellent features of cows and bulls are given in LXI *infra*.

From verse 44 we understand that in ancient India bull-fighting was one of the popular sports.]

भद्रासनमेकतमेन कारितं कनकरजतताम्राणाम् ।
क्षीरतरुनिर्मितं वा विन्यस्यं चर्मणामुपरि ॥४६॥
त्रिविधस्तस्योच्छ्रायो हस्तः पादाधिकोऽर्धयुक्तश्च ।
माण्डलिकानन्तरजित्समस्तराज्यार्थिनां शुभदः ॥४७॥

A throne made of gold, silver or copper or of any milky tree should be placed on the above-named skins. If the height of the throne is one cubit, one and a quarter, and one and a half cubits, it will prove beneficial to governors of provinces, those who wish to conquer neighbouring kingdoms and those who wish to bring the whole earth under their sway respectively.

अन्तर्धाय हिरण्यं तत्रोपविशेन्नरेश्वरः सुमनाः ।
सचिवाप्तपुरोहितदैवपौरकल्याणनामवृतः ॥४८॥
वन्दिजनपौरविप्रैः प्रघुष्टपुण्याहवेदनिर्घोषैः ।
समृदङ्गशङ्खतूर्यैर्मङ्गलशब्दैर्हतानिष्टः ॥४९॥

After placing some gold inside the throne, the king should sit on it with a jubilant heart, in the company of his ministers, trustworthy friends, preceptors, astrologers, citizens and others having auspicious names; and with bards, citizens and Brāhmaṇas shouting panegyrics and chanting aloud the Punyāha hymn and other Vedic Mantras; and with all evils warded off by the auspicious sounds of tabors, conchs and such other musical instruments.

[The word दैव here stands for दैवज्ञ (astrologer), a part standing for the whole. *Auspicious names* are some of the following : Jayarāja, Siṁharāja etc., which suggest victory and prosperity for the host.]

अहतक्षौमनिवसनं पुरोहितः कम्बलेन सञ्छाद्य ।
कृतबलिपूजं कलशैरभिषिञ्चेत्सर्पिषा पूर्णैः ॥५०॥

Then the priest should cover the king, who is clad in fresh, unwashed silken garments and who has already offered food and worship to the Deities, with a blanket and bathe him with pots filled with ghee.

अष्टावष्टाविंशतिरष्टशतं वापि कलशपरिमाणम् ।
अधिकेऽधिके गुणोत्तरमयं च मन्त्रोऽत्र मुनिगीतः ॥५१॥

The number of pots filled with ghee should be eight, twenty-eight or a hundred and eight. The greater the number of holy pots, the greater will be the efficacy. And the following is the hymn sung by Sage Vṛddha Garga for this occasion.

आज्यं तेजः समुद्दिष्टमाज्यं पापहरं परम् ।
आज्यं सुराणामाहार आज्ये लोकाः प्रतिष्ठिताः ॥५२॥
भौमान्तरिक्षं दिव्यं वा यत्ते कल्मषमागतम् ।
सर्वं तदाज्यसंस्पर्शात् प्रणाशमुपगच्छतु ॥५३॥

Ghee has been declared as power (or vitality); it is the greatest dispeller of sins; it is the food of the celestials; it is ghee on which are established all the worlds. "Whatever sin, terrestrial, atmospheric or celestial, has befallen you, may all that come to an end as a result of this holy ghee coming in contact with your body !"

कम्बलमपनीय ततः पुष्यस्नानाम्बुभिः सफलपुष्पैः ।
अभिषिञ्चेन्मनुजेन्द्रं पुरोहितोऽनेन मन्त्रेण ॥५४॥

Thereafter the preceptor should remove the blanket (from the king's body) and bathe the king with the holy waters meant for the sacred bath, containing fruits and flowers, chanting the following hymns :

सुरास्त्वामभिषिञ्चन्तु ये च सिद्धाः पुरातनाः ।
ब्रह्मा विष्णुश्च रुद्रश्च साध्याश्च समरुद्गणाः ॥५५॥
आदित्या वसवो रुद्रा अश्विनौ च भिषग्वरौ ।
अदितिर्देवमाता च स्वाहा सिद्धिः सरस्वती ॥५६॥
कीर्तिर्लक्ष्मीर्धृतिः श्रीश्च सिनीवाली कुहूस्तथा ।
दनुश्च सुरसा चैव विनता कद्रुरेव च ॥५७॥
देवपत्न्यश्च या नोक्ता देवमातर एव च ।
सर्वास्त्वामभिषिञ्चन्तु दिव्याश्चाप्सरसां गणाः ॥५८॥

नक्षत्राणि मुहूर्त्ताश्च पक्षाहोरात्रसन्धयः ।
संवत्सरा दिनेशाश्च कलाः काष्ठाः क्षणा लवाः ॥५९॥

सर्वे त्वामभिषिञ्चन्तु कालस्यावयवाः शुभाः ।
एते चान्ये च मुनयो वेदव्रतपरायणाः ॥६०॥

सशिष्यास्तेऽभिषिञ्चन्तु सदाराश्च तपोधनाः ।
वैमानिकाः सुरगणा मनवः सागरैः सह ॥६१॥

सरितश्च महाभागा नागाः किम्पुरुषास्तथा ।
वैखानसा महाभागा द्विजा वैहायसाश्च ये ॥६२॥

सप्तर्षयः सदाराश्च ध्रुवस्थानानि यानि च ।
मरीचिरत्रिः पुलहः पुलस्त्यः क्रतुरङ्गिराः ॥६३॥

भृगुः सनत्कुमारश्च सनकोऽथ सनन्दनः ।
सनातनश्च दक्षश्च जैगीषव्यो भगन्दरः ॥६४॥

एकतश्च द्वितश्चैव त्रितो जाबालिकश्यपौ ।
दुर्वासा दुर्विनीतश्च कण्वः कात्यायनस्तथा ॥६५॥

मार्कण्डेयो दीर्घतपाः शुनःशेफो विदूरथः ।
ऊर्वः संवर्त्तकश्चैव च्यवनोऽत्रिः पराशरः ॥६६॥

द्वैपायनो यवक्रीतो देवराजः सहानुजः ।
पर्वतास्तरवो वल्ल्यः पुण्यान्यायतनानि च ॥६७॥

प्रजापतिर्दितिश्चैव गावो विश्वस्य मातरः ।
वाहनानि च दिव्यानि सर्वलोकाश्चराचराः ॥६८॥

अग्नयः पितरस्तारा जीमूताः खं दिशो जलम् ।
एते चान्ये च बहवः पुण्यसङ्कीर्त्तनाः शुभैः ॥६९॥

तोयैस्त्वामभिषिञ्चन्तु सर्वोत्पातनिबर्हणैः ।
यथाभिषिक्तो मघवानेतैर्मुदितमानसैः ॥७०॥

May the Gods bathe thee, and the ancient Siddhas, Brahman, Viṣṇu, Śiva, Sādhyas, groups of Maruts, the Suns (twelve in number), Vasus, Rudras, the great Celestial Physicians, Aditi, the mother of the Gods, Svāhā (wife of Agni), Siddhi, Sarasvatī, Kīrti, Lakṣmī, Dhṛti, Śrī, Sinīvālī (New Moon beginning later in the day), Kuhū (the same beginning right from the dawn), Danu, Surasā, Vinatā, Kadru, consorts of the Gods not mentioned already, and also mothers of the Gods, may all these bathe thee ! May the groups of Divine Nymphs, the stars, Muhūrtas (periods of 48 minutes), Fortnights, Days, Nights, the three junctions, years, the Lords of the Day (the

Sun and other planets), Minutes, Seconds, Moments, Lavas (the sixth part of a twinkling), all these and other auspicious divisions of Time bathe thee! May the Sages wedded to the propagation of the Vedas and engaged in penance, along with their wives and pupils bathe thee! May the celestials who always move about in aerial chariots, groups of Gods, Manus, Oceans, Rivers, the great Serpents, Kimpuruṣas, Vaikhānasas (anchorites), the great Brāhmaṇas (or Sages), Vaihāyasas, the Seven Seers with their wives, the Fixed Places (like Dhruva), Marīci, Atri, Pulaha, Pulastya, Kratu, Aṅgiras, Bhṛgu, Sanatkumāra, Sanaka, Sanandana, Sanātana, Dakṣa, Jaigīṣavya, Bhagandara, Ekata, Dvita, Trika, Jābāli, Kaśyapa, Durvāsas, Durvinīta, Kaṇva, Kātyāyana, Mārkaṇḍeya, Dīrghatapas, Sunaśśepha, Vidūratha, Ūrva (Ūrdhva ?), Saṁvartaka, Cyavana, Atri, Parāśara, Dvaipāyana (i.e. Vyāsa), Yavakrīta, Indra and his younger brother(s), Mountains, Trees, Creepers, Holy Places, Prajāpati, Diti, Cows, the Mothers of the Universe, Divine Vehicles, all the Worlds, the Moving and Stationary Beings, Fires, *Manes*, Asterisms, Clouds, Sky, Quarters, Water—these and many others of auspicious names bathe thee with holy waters capable of destroying all the evil effects of the portents, even as they did Indra, with a happy heart!

इत्येतैश्चान्यैश्चाप्यथर्वकल्पाहितैः सरुद्रगणैः ।
कौष्माण्डमहारौहिणकुबेरहृद्यैः समृद्धया च ॥७१॥

With the above-named hymns and others prescribed in the books on rituals belonging to the Atharva Veda, the eleven Anuvākas (hymns) of the Rudrapāṭha (of the Yajurveda), Kauṣmāṇḍa (six Anuvākas), Mahārauhiṇa, Kubera-hṛdaya and the Samṛddhi Ṛk the above bathing ceremony should be done.

[There is an expiatory sacrifice called *Kūṣmāṇḍa Homa*. The hymns used therein are six in number. *Mahārauhiṇa* is a Mantra. *Kuberahṛdaya* like the *Ādityahṛdaya* is a set of prayers addressed to Kubera.

The कूष्माण्डहोम is performed for atoning for all kinds of heinous sins. There are many methods of performing this ceremony : One method has been taught by Sage Jamadagni and the other by Bodhāyana. The former is simpler without involving पक्वहोम or cooked oblations. The following is the method taught by Jamadagni :—

अथातः सम्प्रवक्ष्यामि कूष्माण्डविधिमुत्तमम् ।
एनसां स्थूलसूक्ष्माणां प्रायश्चित्तं तु वैदिकम् ॥

अकुर्वन् विहितं कर्म निन्दितं च समाचरन् ।
प्रसजंश्चेन्द्रियार्थेषु प्रायश्चित्ती भवेद् द्विजः ॥
केशश्मश्रु वापयित्वा स्नात्वा पुण्यजलाशये ।
प्रतिष्ठाप्य तथैवाग्नि स्वगृह्योक्तविधानतः ।
आज्यभागानन्तरन्तु कूष्माण्डैर्जुहुयाद् द्विजः ।
"यद्देवा"द्यनुवाकैस्तु त्रिभिर्हुत्वाऽऽज्यमन्वहम् ॥
"वैश्वानरा"नुवाकेन तमग्निमुपतिष्ठते ।
"यदित्या"धाय समिधं जयादि प्रतिपद्यते ॥
कर्मादिष्वेव जुहुयात् पूतः स्वर्गं समश्नुते ।
संवत्सरं ब्रह्महा तु मासं वै वीरहा द्विजः ॥
चतुर्विंशतिरात्रीस्तु परिवेत्ता तु दीक्षितः ।
द्वादश त्वग्रदिधिषुः षड्रात्रीः श्यावदन्नपि ॥
तिस्रो रात्रीस्तु कुनखी दीक्षितो भवति द्विजः ।
न मांसमन्नमश्नीयान्नोपेयात्कामिनीमपि ॥
नोपर्यासीत खट्वायां जुगुप्सेतानृताद् द्विजः ।
पयो व्रतं ब्राह्मणस्य यवागूः क्षत्रियस्य च ॥
आमिक्षा चैव वैश्यस्य प्रायश्चित्तार्थमिष्यते ।
सावित्रीञ्च जपेन्नित्यं पवित्राणि च शक्तितः ॥
सर्वेष्वेव व्रतेष्वेवं प्रायश्चित्तार्थमिष्यते ।]

आपोहिष्ठातिसृभिर्हिरण्यवर्णेति चतसृभिर्जप्तम् ।
कार्पासिकवस्त्रयुगं बिभृयात्स्नातो नराधिपतिः ॥७२॥

After undergoing the holy ablution the king should wear a pair of cotton cloths that have been sanctified by the three Mantras of the hymn beginning with '*Āpo hi ṣṭhā*' and by the four beginning with '*Hiraṇyavarṇām*'.

[The Mantra '*Āpo hi ṣṭhā*' is used for purification. This is done daily by every twice-born. 'Hiraṇyavarṇāṁ hariṇīṁ suvarṇarajata-srajām' is the commencement of the Śrīsūkta. The former is meant for purifying the cloths and the latter for conferring prosperity.]

पुण्याहशङ्खशब्दैराचान्तोऽभ्यर्च्य देवगुरुविप्रान् ।
छत्रध्वजायुधानि च ततः स्वपूजां प्रयुञ्जीत ॥७३॥

After sipping water (thrice with Mantras) the king should worship Gods, Preceptors, Brāhmaṇas, his royal umbrella, banner and weapons, when the sounds of conchs and chanting of Puṇyāha hymns flourish; and then he should adore his own guardian Deity (or perform his daily worship).

आयुष्यं वर्चस्यं रायस्पोषाभिरर्ङ्ग्भिरेताभिः ।
परिजप्तं वैजयिकं नवं विदध्यावलङ्कारम् ॥७४॥

Thereupon the king should wear new ornaments conducive to victory, sanctified by the six Mantras beginning with the words 'Āyuṣyam varcasyaṁ rāyaspoṣam...'

गत्वा द्वितीयवेदीं समुपविशेच्चर्मणामुपरि राजा ।
देयानि चैव चर्माण्युपर्युपर्येवमेतानि ॥७५॥
वृषस्य वृषदंशस्य रुरोश्च पृषतस्य च ।
तेषामुपरि सिंहस्य व्याघ्रस्य च ततः परम् ॥७६॥

Going to the second altar, the king should sit on the skins which are to be placed one upon another in the following manner : First the bull's skin is placed, upon this is put that of a cat, upon that, that of an antelope, then that of a spotted deer, upon that the lion's, and lastly the tiger's on the top.

[In verse 34 *supra* the author has told us that an altar should be made either to the west or south. Here he speaks of the other altar. So we have to conclude that if the first altar selected is the western one, then the second would be the southern one, and *vice versa*.]

मुख्यस्थाने जुहुयात् पुरोहितोऽग्निं समित्तिलघृताद्यैः ।
त्रिनयनशक्रबृहस्पतिनारायणनित्यगतिऋग्भिः ॥७७॥

In the chief place i.e. sourhern altar, the priest should make offerings of sacrificial twigs, sesamum, ghee and such other articles (like Śrīphala) into the sacred Fire with hymns addressed to Śiva, Indra, Bṛhaspati, Nārāyaṇa and Vāyu (Wind).

[There is a doubt about the exact meaning of the word, मुख्यस्थान. There are three places mentioned in this scheme viz. the central circle and the western and southern altars. The king sits on the skins spread on the southern altar and the priest performs the Homa in the मुख्यस्थान. I feel that the मुख्यस्थान should be the first altar where the rituals for the पुष्यस्नान were first performed. Of course, the commentator construes the word as 'the southern altar'. Is it not the last and the least important ?]

इन्द्रध्वजनिर्दिष्टान्यग्निनिमित्तानि दैवविद् ब्रूयात् ।
कृत्वाऽशेषसमाप्तिं पुरोहितः प्राञ्जलिर्ब्रूयात् ॥७८॥

The astrologer should explain the auguries of Fire, dealt with in the chapter on 'Indra's Banner' (XLIII. 32 *supra*). After finishing all the rites, the priest should make the following statement with folded hands :

यान्तु देवगणाः सर्वे पूजामादाय पार्थिवात् ।
सिद्धिं दत्वा तु विपुलां पुनरागमनाय च ॥७९॥

"May all the groups of Gods depart from here in order to come again on a subsequent occasion, having now received worship at the hands of the king, and bestowed great success on him."

[This is the usual verse that is recited at the close of worship by the worshipper who rings the bell signifying the end.]

नृपतिरतो दैवज्ञं पुरोहितं चार्चयेद्धनैर्बहुभिः ।
अन्यांश्च दक्षिणीयान् यथोचितं श्रोत्रियप्रभृतीन् ॥८०॥

After this the king should honour the astrologer, priest and others worthy of gifts such as Vedic scholars, with large gifts of money (clothes etc.) according to their merits.

[Cf. गर्ग—(it must be वृद्धगर्ग)

दत्वा वित्तं ब्राह्मणेभ्यो गावो हेमपरिष्कृताः ।
वास्तु युग्यं मही रूप्यं तेभ्यश्च बहुभोजनम् ॥
शङ्खभेरीस्वनैर्दिव्यैर्गीतैश्चैव मनोहरैः ।
सम्प्रविश्य ततो राजा सचिवैः परिवारितः ॥
श्वेतकुञ्जरमारूढः श्वेतमश्वमथापि वा ।
श्वेतचन्दनलिप्ताङ्गः श्वेताम्बरधरः शुभः ॥
पुरस्ताद्विकिरेद्वित्तमाशीर्वादैश्च पूजितः ॥]

दत्वाऽभयं प्रजानामाघातस्थानगान् विसृज्य पशून् ।
बन्धनमोक्षं कुर्यादभ्यन्तरदोषकृद्वर्जम् ॥८१॥

The king should proclaim protection to the subjects, release animals (goats etc.) from the hands of butchers, and order a general amnesty to all prisoners except those who threaten the internal peace of the kingdom.

एतत्प्रयुज्यमानं प्रतिपुष्यं सुखयशोऽर्थवृद्धिकरम् ।
पुष्याद् विनार्धफलदा पौषी शान्तिः परा प्रोक्ता ॥८२॥

If this holy bath be performed every month on the day of the asterism Puṣya, it would bestow happiness, fame, wealth and progress on the king. If it be performed on any other day, it would produce only half the benefits. However, the expiatory ceremony performed on the Full Moon day in the month of Puṣya has been declared to be the foremost in merits.

राष्ट्रोत्पातोपसर्गेषु राहोः केतोश्च दर्शने ।
ग्रहावमर्दने चैव पुष्यस्नानं समाचरेत् ॥८३॥

The royal ablution should be performed whenever a kingdom is afflicted with portents or disasters like epidemics, when there is an eclipse, when a comet is sighted and when there is a planetary war.

नास्ति लोके स उत्पातो यो ह्यनेन न शाम्यति ।
मङ्गलं चापरं नास्ति यदस्मादतिरिच्यते ॥८४॥

There is no portent in the world that is not warded off by this ceremony; and there is no auspicious ritual that surpasses this one.

[Cf. गर्ग—
प्रतिपुष्येण यो राजा स्नायीत विधिपूर्वकम् ।
तस्य राष्ट्रे न सीदन्ति मर्त्या ये जन्तवो भुवि ॥]

अधिराज्यार्थिनो राज्ञः पुत्रजन्म च काङ्क्षतः ।
तत्पूर्वमभिषेके च विधिरेष प्रशस्यते ॥८५॥

This ceremony is highly recommended for the occasion of a king's Coronation, when he aspires for the sovereignty of an empire and when he is anxious for the birth of a son.

महेन्द्रार्थमुवाचेदं बृहत्कीर्तिर्बृहस्पतिः ।
स्नानमायुःप्रजावृद्धिसौभाग्यकरणं परम् ॥८६॥

Bṛhaspati of extra-ordinary fame taught this unique ablution which confers great longevity, prosperity of children and happiness as well as good fortune, for the benefit of Indra.

अनेनैव विधानेन हस्त्यश्वं स्नापयेत्ततः ।
तस्यामयविनिर्मुक्तं परां सिद्धिमवाप्नुयात् ॥८७॥

The king who afterwards bathes his elephants and horses in the same manner, will see them free from all illness and attain great success.

———

पट्टलक्षणम् ॥४६॥

Chapter XLIX—Signs of Crowns

विस्तरशो निर्दिष्टं पट्टानां लक्षणं यदाचार्यैः ।
तत्सङ्क्षेपः क्रियते मयाऽत्र सकलार्थसम्पन्नः ॥१॥

In this chapter I am giving a summary, containing all important subjects, of the characteristics of royal crowns that have been delineated at length by the ancient sages like Kāśyapa.

पट्टः शुभदो राज्ञां मध्येऽष्टावङ्गुलानि विस्तीर्णः ।
सप्त नरेन्द्रमहिष्याः षड् युवराजस्य निर्दिष्टः ॥२॥
चतुरङ्गुलविस्तारः पट्टः सेनापतेर्भवति मध्ये ।
द्वे च प्रसादपट्टः पञ्चैते कीर्तिताः पट्टाः ॥३॥

The crown of a monarch should have an expansion of eight digits in the middle, to confer prosperity on the wearer; that of the chief queen, of seven digits; that of the Yuvarāja (heir-apparent), of six digits; that of the commander of the army, of four digits; and that of the royal protege, of two digits. These are the five types of crowns that have been prescribed.

सर्वे द्विगुणायामा मध्यादर्धेन पार्श्वविस्तीर्णाः ।
सर्वे च शुद्धकाञ्चनविनिर्मिताः श्रेयसो वृद्ध्यै ॥४॥

All the varieties of crowns must have a length double their respective breadth, while their breadth on the sides should be half the central breadth. All of them, made of pure gold, would conduce to increase of prosperity and happiness.

पञ्चशिखो भूमिपतेस्त्रिशिखो युवराजपार्थिवमहिष्योः ।
एकशिखः सैन्यपतेः प्रसादपट्टो विना शिखया ॥५॥

The king's crown has five crests; the Yuvarāja's and the queen's three; the commander's has only one crest, while the protege's crown has no crest at all.

[The crests are knobs on the top of the crown, resembling the *Kalaśas* (small domes) on the top of the temple towers.]

क्रियमाणं यदि पत्रं सुखेन विस्तारमेति पत्रस्य ।
वृद्धिजयौ भूमिपतेस्तथा प्रजानां च सुखसम्पत् ॥६॥

When the gold for the crown is beaten into a sheet if it expands easily, it augurs prosperity and victory to the king, and happiness and wealth to the subjects.

जीवितराज्यविनाशं करोति मध्ये व्रणः समुत्पन्नः ।
मध्ये स्फुटितस्त्याज्यो विघ्नकरः पार्श्वयोः स्फुटितः ॥७॥

A dent or hole in the middle of the crown, when it is under preparation, will bring about loss of life and kingdom. If it breaks in the middle, it should be rejected. One that breaks on the sides will produce hindrances.

[Cf. काश्यप—

क्रियमाणं यदा पत्रं मध्ये स्फुटति भिद्यते ।
तदा नृपभयं प्रोक्तं यस्यार्थे वा प्रकल्पितम् ॥
सुलक्षणं प्रमाणस्थं सुकरं च हितावहम् ।
सुरूपं दर्शनीयं च प्रजानां वृद्धिदं स्मृतम् ॥]

अशुभनिमित्तोत्पत्तौ शास्त्रज्ञः शान्तिमादिशेद्राज्ञः ।
शस्तनिमित्तः पट्टो नृपराष्ट्रविवृद्धये भवति ॥८॥

At the appearance of inauspicious omens, a scholar well-versed in this science should advise proper expiatory rites to the king. A crown, accompanied by laudable symptoms, will lead to the prosperity of both the king and the kingdom.

———

खड्गलक्षणम् ॥५०॥

Chapter L—Signs of Swords

अङ्गुलशतार्धमुत्तम ऊनः स्यात्पञ्चविंशतिः खड्गः ।
अङ्गुलमानाज्ज्ञेयो व्रणोऽशुभो विषमपर्वस्थः ॥१॥

The best sword is one that measures fifty digits, while the smallest one, twenty-five digits. A dent or scratch in an odd digit in the measurement of the sword is to be reckoned as inauspicious.

[If the defect is in an even digit, it would not be inauspicious.]

श्रीवृक्षवर्धमानातपत्रशिवलिङ्गकुण्डलाब्जानाम् ।
सदृशा व्रणाः प्रशस्ता ध्वजायुधस्वस्तिकानां च ॥२॥

Dents or scratches resembling in shape a Bilva tree, Vardhamāna figure, umbrella, Śiva's emblem, ear-ring, lotus, flag, weapon and Svastika mark are all auspicious.

कृकलासकाककङ्कक्रव्यादकबन्धवृश्चिकाकृतयः ।
खड्गे व्रणा न शुभदा वंशानुगताः प्रभूताश्च ॥३॥

The dents resembling a chameleon, crow, heron, carrion-eating bird (like vulture) truncated human body and scorpion, and many dents in the upper part of the blade are ominous.

स्फुटितो ह्रस्वः कुण्ठो वंशच्छिन्नो न दृङ्मनोऽनुगतः ।
अस्वन इति चानिष्टः प्रोक्तविपर्यस्त इष्टफलः ॥४॥

A sword that is broken, too short, blunt, cut at the top, not attractive to the eye and mind, and without resonance, is harmful; whereas one with contrary qualities will yield beneficial results.

क्वणितं मरणायोक्तं पराजयायाप्रवर्तनं कोशात् ।
स्वयमुद्गीर्णे युद्धं ज्वलिते विजयो भवति खड्गे ॥५॥

If the sword sounds by itself, it forebodes the owner's death; if it does not come out even when pulled out, defeat; if it comes out automatically, war; and if it glows, the result would be victory.

नाकारणं विवृणुयान्न विघट्टयेच्च
पश्येन्न तत्र वदनं न वदेच्च मूल्यम् ।
देशं न चास्य कथयेत् प्रतिमानयेन्न
नैव स्पृशेन्नपतिरप्रयतोऽसियष्टिम् ॥६॥

A king ought not to unsheath the sword for no reason, nor brandish it, nor see his own face in it; nor mention its price, nor the place of its origin, nor measure it, nor touch its blade, when he is not pure.

[The rules laid down in this verse are very interesting from the point of esotericism. Some of these rules may with advantage be applied to the gem that is worn for prosperity.

The metre is वसन्ततिलका.]

गोजिह्वासंस्थानो नीलोत्पलवंशपत्रसदृशश्च ।
करवीरपत्रशूलाग्रमण्डलाग्राः प्रशस्ताः स्युः ॥७॥

The following shapes of swords are highly beneficial : One like the cow's tongue, blue lily petal, bamboo leaf, and karavīra leaf. A sword with a pointed or round tip also is auspicious.

निष्पन्नो न च्छेद्यो निकषैः कार्यः प्रमाणयुक्तः सः ।
मूले म्रियते स्वामी जननी तस्याग्रतश्छिन्ने ॥८॥

If a sword happens to be a bit too long, the surplus length should not be cut off, but it should be made to have the required length by rubbing it against a file. If it is cut at the bottom, the owner will die; and if at the tip, his mother.

[Cf. काश्यप—

उत्पन्नो न पुनश्छेद्यो निष्पन्नो यः प्रमाणतः ।
मुष्ट्या भङ्गे म्रियेत्स्वामी तदग्रे तस्य मातरम् ॥
तस्मान्न छेदयेत् खड्गमात्मनोऽशुभदं यतः ।
निघर्षणैः प्रमाणस्थः कार्यो येन शुभो भवेत् ॥]

यस्मिन् त्सरुप्रदेशे व्रणो भवेत्तद्वदेव खड्गस्य ।
वनितानामिव तिलको गुह्ये वाच्यो मुखे दृष्ट्वा ॥९॥

An injury in a particular part of the hilt indicates a similar injury in the corresponding part of the blade of the sword, just as a mole on the face of women suggests the existence of a similar one in their private parts.

अथवा स्पृशति यदङ्गं प्रष्टा निस्त्रिंशभृत्तदवधार्य ।
कोशस्थस्यादेश्यो व्रणोऽस्ति शास्त्रं विदित्वेदम् ॥१०॥

Noting the particular limb touched by the swordsman who questions an astrologer about the existence of injuries in the sword, the latter should declare the injury to exist in the particular part of the sword kept in the sheath, by understanding the following rules thereon.

[The commentator tells us that first of all we have to find out whether there is any injury in the sword, and then in which part. For this the astrologer should find out the ascendant for the time of query. In the chart if there be malefics in angles, he must come to the conclusion that there is injury.]

शिरसि स्पृष्टे प्रथमेऽङ्गुले द्वितीये ललाटसंस्पर्शे ।
भ्रूमध्ये च तृतीये नेत्रे स्पृष्टे चतुर्थे च ॥११॥

नासौष्ठकपोलहनुश्रवणग्रीवांसके च पञ्चाद्याः ।
उरसि द्वादशसंस्थस्त्रयोदशे कक्षयोर्ज्ञेयः ॥१२॥

स्तनहृदयोदरकुक्षीनाभौ तु चतुर्दशादयो ज्ञेयाः ।
नाभीमूले कट्यां गुह्ये चैकोनविंशतितः ॥१३॥

ऊर्वोर्द्वाविंशे स्यादूर्वोर्मध्ये व्रणस्त्रयोविंशे च ।
जानुनि च चतुर्विंशे जङ्घायां पञ्चविंशे च ॥१४॥

जङ्घामध्ये गुल्फे पार्ष्ण्यां पादे तदङ्गुलीष्वपि च ।
षड्विंशतिकाद्यावत्त्रिंशदिति मतेन गर्गस्य ॥१५॥

If the querent touches his head, the dent or injury will be in the first digit of the sword; if the forehead, in the second; if the space between the brows, in the third; if an eye, in the fourth; if the nose, in the fifth; if the lip, in the sixth; if the cheek, in the seventh; if the chin, in the eighth; if the ear, in the ninth; if the neck, in the tenth; if the shoulder, in the eleventh; if the chest, in the twelfth; if the armpits, in the thirteenth; if the breast in the fourteenth; if the heart, stomach, abdomen, and navel, in the fifteenth, sixteenth, seventeenth and eighteenth digits respectively; if the bottom of the navel, hips and the private parts, in the nineteenth, twentieth and twenty-first respectively; if the thighs, in the twenty-second; if between the thighs, in the twenty-third; if the knee, in the twenty-fourth; if the shank, in the twenty-fifth; if between the shanks, ankles, heels, foot and toes, in the twenty-sixth, twenty-seventh, twenty-eighth, twenty-ninth and thirtieth respectively, according to the authority of Sage Garga.

[Cf. गर्ग—

शिरो ललाटं भ्रूमध्यं नेत्रघ्राणकपोलकम् ।
हनुश्रोत्रं तथा ग्रीवा स्कन्धो वक्षश्च कक्षकम् ॥
स्तनौ हृत् क्रोडकुक्षी च नाभिस्तन्मूलमेव च ।
कटिगुह्योरुमध्यं च जानुजङ्घे तयोरधः ॥
गुल्फं पार्ष्णिस्तथा पादमङ्गुलिस्पर्शने ध्रुवम् ।
मूलात् प्रभृति खड्गेऽपि व्रणं त्रिंशाङ्गुलं वदेत् ॥]

पुत्रमरणं धनप्राप्तिर्धनहानिः सम्पदश्च बन्धश्च ।
एकाद्यङ्गुलसंस्थैर्व्रणैः फलं निर्दिशेत्क्रमशः ॥१६॥
सुतलाभः कलहो हस्तिलब्धयः पुत्रमरणधनलाभौ ।
क्रमशो विनाशवनिताप्तिचित्तदुःखानि षट्प्रभृति ॥१७॥
लब्धिर्हानिस्त्रीलब्धयो वधो वृद्धिमरणपरितोषाः ।
ज्ञेयाश्चतुर्दशादिषु धनहानिश्चैकविंशे स्यात् ॥१८॥
वित्ताप्तिरनिर्वाणं धनागमो मृत्युसम्पदोऽस्वत्वम् ।
ऐश्वर्यमृत्युराज्यानि च क्रमात् त्रिंशदिति यावत् ॥१९॥

The results of the injuries in several digits, from the first to the thirtieth, are to be declared in the following order :

(1) Son's death, (2) acquisition of wealth, (3) loss of money, (4) prosperity, (5) imprisonment, (6) birth of a son, (7) quarrel, (8) winning of elephants, (9) death of a son, (10) influx of wealth, (11) death, (12) getting of wife, (13) mental affliction, (14) gain, (15) loss, (16) winning a damsel, (17) murder, (18) progress, (19) death, (20) rejoicing, (21) loss of wealth, (22) acquisition of wealth, (23) lacking happiness, (24) influx of wealth, (25) death, (26) wealth, (27) penury, (28) prosperity or authority, (29) death, and (30) kingship.

[The commentator construes the word, अनिर्वाणं as मृत्युः, but I prefer the meaning 'loss of joy'.]

परतो न विशेषफलं विषमसमस्थास्तु पापशुभफलदाः ।
केचिच्चवफलाः प्रदिष्टास्त्रिंशत्परतोऽप्रमिति यावत् ॥२०॥

Should there be defects beyond the thirtieth digit, the effects thereof would be negligible; but those in the odd and even digits would yield bad and good results respectively. However, according to some Sages (like Parāśara) the injuries beyond the thirtieth digit upto the tip of the sword have no effects whatsoever.

[Cf. गर्ग—

अङ्गुलानि च पञ्चाशत्प्रधानः खड्ग उच्यते ।
तदर्धको निकृष्टः स्यात्तन्मध्ये मध्यमः स्मृतः ॥
विषमाङ्गुलसंस्थो यो व्रणः सोऽनिष्टदः स्मृतः ।
शुभः समाङ्गुलस्थस्तु मध्यगो मध्यमः स्मृतः ॥
त्रिंशद्यावद्विनिर्दिष्टमङ्गुलानां फलं ततः ।
षोडशाङ्गुलगो ज्ञेयो व्रणो मध्यफलप्रदः ॥

also पराशर—

तेषां प्रमाणानि । जघन्यमङ्गुलानि पञ्चविंशतिः । मध्यमं त्रिंशत् । उत्तमं चत्वारिंशत् । अतो हीनमतिरिक्तं वा न धारयेत् । पूर्णात् प्रत्यङ्गुलान्तरितेषु व्रणेष्वनाकृतिषु यावत्त्रिंशदङ्गुलं तावत्क्रमात्फलनियमः । पुत्रनाशोऽर्थागमोऽर्थनाशोऽर्थसञ्चयो गृहदाहो मित्रलाभो व्याधिभयं सुखाप्तिर्ज्ञातिबन्ध आज्ञाप्राधान्यं विपक्षोत्पत्तिर्वाहनलाभः शोकः प्रव्रज्यासुतज्ञातिकुलच्छेदो माहात्म्यबललाभः सन्तापः क्लेशः पुत्रलाभो धनागमः शोकः प्रामाण्यमाधिपत्यमुपभोगो भयं दौर्भाग्यमैश्वर्यं राजपूजेति । परतः सर्वमप्रशस्तं विन्द्यात् ॥]

करवीरोत्पलगजमदघृतकुङ्कुमकुन्दचम्पकसगन्धः ।
शुभदोऽनिष्टो गोमूत्रपङ्कमेदःसदृशगन्धः ॥२१॥
कूर्मवसासृक्क्षारोपमश्च भयदुःखदो भवति गन्धः ।
वैदूर्यकनकविद्युत्प्रभो जयारोग्यवृद्धिकरः ॥२२॥

Auspicious is a sword which smells like the Karavīra flower, blue lily, elephant's ichor, ghee, saffron, round jasmine or Campaka flower, whereas harmful is one that smells like cow's urine, silt or fat. Similarly, one with the smell of tortoise, marrow, blood or salt causes danger and misery; and one with the lustre of beryl, gold and lightning confers victory, health and progress.

इदमौशनसं च शस्त्रपानं रुधिरेण श्रियमिच्छतः प्रदीप्ताम् ।
हविषा गुणवत्सुताभिलिप्सोः सलिलेनाक्षयमिच्छतश्च वित्तम् ॥२३॥
वडवोष्ट्रकरेणुदुग्धपानं यदि पापेन समीहतेऽर्थसिद्धिम् ।
झषपित्तमृगाश्वबस्तदुग्धैः करिहस्तच्छिदये सतालगर्भैः ॥२४॥

The following sword-drinks have been laid down by Śukrācārya (preceptor of the Demons) : One wishing for extra-ordinary opulence should give a drink of blood to the sword; for begetting a virtuous son, a drink of ghee (sacrificial offerings?); for inexhaustible wealth, one of water; for acquiring great wealth by sinful means, one of the milk of mare, camel or elephant; and for cutting the trunks of elephants (in battles), one of fish-bile, and the milk of the deer, horse and goat, mixed with the toddy of palm trees.

[Cf. also पराशर—

अथ पायनानि, क्षीरपायितमरिवधार्थी धारयेत् । तिलतैलारालाभ्यामर्थार्थी । पुत्रार्थी उदकेन । सर्पिषा श्रीकामः । साहसिकः शोणितेन । हस्त्यश्वोष्ट्रक्षीरैः शिलासारच्छेदकामः । अजाक्षीरेण तालवसया मत्स्यवडवाहरिणपित्तेन द्विरदस्कन्धच्छेदकामः । नित्यं चैनं धूपपुष्पगन्धोपहारैरर्चयित्वा शिरस्यपशायिनं कुर्यात् । नावमन्येत न चोच्छिष्टः संस्पृशेत् । नादर्शकी कुर्यात् । नानिमित्तं विवृणुयात् । न क्रीडनायास्य मूलं विवृणुयात् ॥

The metre of the verses is औपच्छन्दसिक.]

आर्कं पयो हुडुविषाणमषीसमेतं
पारावताखुशकृता च युतः प्रलेपः ।
शस्त्रस्य तैलमथितस्य ततोऽस्य पानं
पश्चाच्छितस्य न शिलासु भवेद्विघातः ॥२५॥

A sword rubbed with sesamum oil and then smeared with an unguent prepared with the milky juice of Arka plant mixed with the ashes of sheep's horn, and the excreta of doves and mice, must be given any of the drinks mentioned in the above two verses, and thereafter whetted. Such a sword will not break even against rocks.

[The commentator explains that every weapon should first of all be well massaged with sesamum oil and then the ointment applied to it. Then the weapon should be put in the fire and heated well. After removing the coating, one of the drinks should be given to it.

The metre is वसन्ततिलका.]

क्षारे कदल्या मथितेन युक्ते दिनोषिते पायितमायसं यत् ।
सम्यक् शितं चाश्मनि नैति भङ्गं न चान्यलोहेष्वपि तस्य कौण्ठ्यम् ॥२६॥

An iron weapon treated with a day-old drink made of the burnt powder of bananas (or its ribs) mixed with butter-milk, and then sharpened properly, will not break on stones, nor become blunt on other iron instruments.

[The metre is उपजाति.]

अङ्गविद्या ॥५१॥

Chapter LI—Science of Limbs

[The commentator is of opinion that this chapter may not be by Varāhamihira himself. But he has mentioned this subject as one of the topics that are discussed in the Saṁhitā. Vide II. 18 *supra.* It is quite possible that the original chapter of our author, being lost, might have been rewritten by some scholar before Utpala.]

दैवज्ञेन शुभाशुभं दिगुदितस्थानाहृतानीक्षता
वाच्यं प्रष्टृनिजापराङ्गघटनां चालोक्य कालं धिया ।
सर्वज्ञो हि चराचरात्मकतयाऽसौ सर्वदर्शी विभु-
श्चेष्टाव्याहृतिभिः शुभाशुभफलं सन्दर्शयत्यर्थिनाम् ॥१॥

An astrologer should predict good and bad effects after observing carefully the direction, utterances, place and articles brought at the time, also taking into consideration the movements of the limbs of the questioner with reference to himself or to another person and the particular time of his query. For, Time which is Omniscient, All-powerful, and All-seeing, as It is the Soul (sustainer) of all beings — both movable and stationary — shows good and bad effects through physical movements and utterances of the querents.

[Cf. पराशर—

इह खलु चराचराणां भूतानां कालोऽन्तरात्मा सर्वदा सर्वदर्शी शुभाशुभैर्यः फलसूचकः स विशेषेण प्राणिनां स्वपराङ्गेषु स्पर्शव्याहारेङ्गितचेष्टादिभिर्निमित्तैः फलमभिदर्शयति । तत्प्रयतो दैवज्ञोऽनुग्रहतमतिरवधार्य स्वशास्त्रार्थमनुस्मृत्य यशोधर्मानुग्रहार्थमर्थिनां शुभाशुभानामर्थानां भावाभावमभिनिर्दिशेत् "

तत्र देशे दिशः कालं व्याहारं द्रव्यदर्शनम् ।
अङ्गप्रत्यङ्गसंस्पर्शं समीक्ष्य फलमादिशेत् ॥

The metre in this and the following verse is शार्दूलविक्रीडित.]

स्थानं पुष्पसुहासिभूरिफलभृत्सुस्निग्धकृत्तिच्छदा-
सत्पक्षिच्युतशस्तसंज्ञिततरुच्छायोपगूढं समम् ।
देवर्षिद्विजसाधुसिद्धनिलयं सत्पुष्पसस्योक्षितं
सत्स्वादूदकनिर्मलत्वजनिताह्लादं च सच्छाद्वलम् ॥२॥

An auspicious place for a query is one which is even, covered with the shade of trees that smile with flowers, are laden with fruits, have glossy barks and leaves, are devoid of ill-omened birds and bear auspicious names (e.g. Palāśa, Pippala, banyan etc.); which is the abode of Gods, sages, Brāhmaṇas, virtuous men and Siddhas, which is rich in fragrant flowers and crops, which pleases the heart through the limpidity of its sweet water and which is covered with beautiful green grass.

[Cf. पराशर—

अथ पुष्पितफलितहरितस्निग्धत्वक्पत्रप्रशस्तनामाङ्कितसौम्यद्विजनिषेविततरुच्छायोपगूढे सस्यकुसुमहरितमृदुशाद्वलसक्तमृष्टहृद्यप्रसन्नसलिलावकाशे देवर्षिसिद्धसाधुद्विजावासे प्राङ्मुखोत्तरोत्तरपूर्वाभिमुखो वा यः पृच्छेत्तस्य प्रार्थितार्थोपपत्तिमभिनिर्दिशेत् ॥]

छिन्नभिन्नकृमिखातकण्टकिप्लुष्टरूक्षकुटिलैर्न सत्कुजैः ।
क्रूरपक्षियुतनिन्द्यनामभिः शुष्कशीर्णबहुपर्णचर्मभिः ॥३॥

Inauspicious is a place abounding in trees which are cut, split, worm-eaten, thorny, scorched, coarse, crooked, inhabited by ill-omened birds (e.g. crows, vultures, cranes etc.), bearing despicable names and having many withered leaves and barks that have fallen.

[The metre is रथोद्धता.]

श्मशानशून्यायतनं चतुष्पथं तथाऽमनोज्ञं विषमं सदोषरम् ।
अवस्कराङ्गारकपालभस्मभिश्चितं तुषैः शुष्कतृणैर्न शोभनम् ॥४॥

Equally inauspicious are the following places : Burial ground, a deserted shrine, a place where four roads meet, one that is not pleasing to the heart, rugged, a sandy place, and one that is covered with rubbish, charcoal, potsherds, ashes, husks and dry grass.

[The commentator construes कपालैः as अस्थिशकलैः. The metre is वंशस्थ.]

प्रव्रजितनग्ननापितरिपुबन्धनसौनिकैस्तथा श्वपचैः ।
कितवयतिपीडितैर्युतमायुधमाध्वीकविक्रयैर्न शुभम् ॥५॥

Similarly harmful are the places that are occupied by ascetics, naked persons, barbers, enemies, butchers, dog-eaters (caṇḍālas), gamblers, hermits, sick persons as well as a prison, armoury, apiary or a shop where honey (liquor) is sold.

प्रागुत्तरेशाश्च दिशः प्रशस्ताः प्रष्टुर्न वाय्वम्बुयमाग्निरक्षः ।
पूर्वाह्णकालेऽस्ति शुभ न रात्रौ सन्ध्याद्वये प्रश्नकृतोऽपराह्णे ॥६॥

The best directions for a query are east, north and north-east; north-west, west, south and south-west are unfavourable to the querent. The forenoon is beneficial, while the night, the two twilights and the afternoon are not favourable.

[Cf. पराशर—

छिन्नभिन्नशुष्करूक्षवक्रजन्तुजग्धदग्धकण्टकिक्रव्याद्द्विजनिषेविताप्रशस्तनामाङ्कितपादपच्छाये श्मशानशून्यायतनचत्वरोषररिपुनापितायुधमद्यविक्रयशालासु नैर्ऋताग्नेययाम्यवारुणवायव्याशाभिमुखः प्रचोदयेत्तस्येष्टमर्थमनर्थाय विन्द्यात् ॥

अपि च

वेलाः सर्वाः प्रशस्यन्ते पूर्वाह्णे परिपृच्छताम् ।
सन्ध्ययोरपराह्णे तु क्षपायां तु विगर्हिताः ॥

The metre is इन्द्रवज्रा in this and the following verse.]

यात्राविधाने हि शुभाशुभं यत्प्रोक्तं निमित्त तदिहापि वाच्यम् ।
दृष्ट्वा पुरो वा जनताहृतं वा प्रष्टुः स्थितं पाणितलेऽथ वस्त्रे ॥७॥

The same good and bad results as well as auguries as were mentioned in connection with a king's marching (*vide* XLIII. 12 *supra*) should be taken into consideration here too. The prediction may also be made by observing the articles brought at the time by others, what is in front of the astrologer, or what is in the querent's hand or clothes.

[Cf. पराशर—

यात्राविधाने निर्दिष्टं निमित्त यच्छुभाशुभम् ।
तदेव दृष्ट्वा दैवज्ञो वाञ्छासिद्धि विनिर्दिशेत् ॥]

अथाङ्गान्यूर्वोष्ठस्तनवृषणपादं च दशना
भुजौ हस्तौ गण्डौ कचगलनखाङ्गुष्ठमपि यत् ।
सशङ्खं कक्षांसं श्रवणगुदसन्धोति पुरुषे
स्त्रियां भ्रूनासास्फिग्वलिकटिसुलेखाङ्गुलिचयम् ॥८॥

जिह्वा ग्रीवा पिण्डिके पार्ष्णियुग्मं जङ्घे नाभिः कर्णपाली कृकाटी ।
वक्त्रं पृष्ठं जत्रुजान्वस्थिपार्श्वं हृत्तात्वक्षी मेहनोरस्त्रिकं च ॥९॥

नपुंसकाख्यं च शिरो ललाटमाश्वाद्यसञ्ज्ञैरपरैश्चिरेण ।
सिद्धिर्भवेज्जातु नपुंसकैर्नो रूक्षक्षतैर्भग्नकृशैश्च पूर्वैः ॥१०॥

The following are *masculine* limbs : Thighs, lips, breasts, testicles, feet, teeth, arms, hands, cheeks, hairs, throat, nails, thumbs (or big toes), the frontal bone, armpits, shoulders, ears, anus and joints. The *feminine* ones are the brows, nose, buttocks, folds in the belly, hips, lines on the palm, fingers, tongue, neck, the hind parts of the shanks, heels, shanks, navel, ear-lobes, and the nape of the neck. The *neuter* limbs are the face, back, collar bone, the knees, bones, the sides, heart, palate, eyes, the male genital organ, chest, end of the spine, the head and forehead. Should the querist touch a limb of the first (masculine) group, there would be immediate success in the task undertaken ; should it be one of the second (feminine) group, success could be achieved only after a long time ; while in the last (neuter) group, success would be improbable. Even in the case of the limbs of the first two groups success cannot be predicted in case they (the limbs) are dry, injured, cut or very lean.

[Human limbs are divided here into three groups.

Cf. पराशर—

अङ्गानि मुष्कस्तनपादोरुगुह्यभुजहस्तसमस्तकर्णांसशङ्खदन्तौष्ठाङ्गुष्ठनखगलगण्डकेशसन्धयः पुरुषाख्यानि । भ्रुवौ नासाग्रीवावलयोऽङ्गुलयो लेखा श्रोणिनाभी रसना जङ्घे पिण्डिके पालिस्फिजौ पार्ष्णिः कृकाटिकेति स्त्रीसञ्ज्ञानि ।

शिरो ललाटमुखचिबुकपृष्ठजठरजत्रुजान्वस्थिपार्श्वहृदयकर्णपीठाक्षिमेहनोरस्त्रिकताल्विति नपुंसकाख्यानि ॥

तत्र पुन्नाम स्निग्धमुचितमनुपहतमक्षतमरोगमङ्गं स्पृष्टं दिग्देशकालव्याहारेष्टदर्शनैरुपपन्न प्रष्टुः पृच्छार्थं सकलफलमभिनिवर्तयति । स्त्रीसञ्ज्ञमपि पूर्वोक्तलक्षणयुक्तं यत्नात् कालान्तरेण सफलम् । नपुंसकाख्यमकार्यसिद्धिमनर्थानां वाऽऽगमनं कुर्यात् ॥ अपि च

पुंसञ्ज्ञेष्वाशु सिद्धिः स्यात् स्त्रीसंज्ञेषु चिराद्भवेत् ।
अशुभ त्वेव निर्दिष्टं नपुंसकसनामसु ॥
पुरुषाख्ये नु संस्पृष्टे बाह्ये रूक्षेऽव्रले क्षते ।
नार्थसिद्धिमतो ब्रूयादङ्गविद्याविशारदः ॥

The metres are in order शिखरिणी, शालिनी and उपजाति.]

स्पृष्टे वा चालिते वाऽपि पादाङ्गुष्ठेऽक्षिरुग्भवेत् ।
अङ्गुल्यां दुहितः शोकं शिरोघाते नृपाद्भयम् ॥११॥

If at a query the big toe be touched or shaken, the querist

would suffer from eye-disease. If a finger is touched, his daughter will have grief. If he strikes his head, he will have trouble from the king.

[The author's use of the accusative in 'दुहितुः शोकम्' is hardly defensible, though the commentator supplies the verb 'वदेत्'. For, the author has already used the verb 'भवेत्' with which 'शोकः' would go better.

Cf. पराशर

अथ पृथक् पृथक् फलनिर्देशः। तत्र पादाङ्गुष्ठे प्रचलयन् स्पृष्ट्वा वा पृच्छेत् प्रष्टुश्चक्षुरोगं विनिर्दिशेत्। अङ्गुलिं स्पृष्ट्वा दुहितृशोकं शिरोऽभिहन्यमानं राजतो भयम्॥

The metre is अनुष्टुभ्-श्लोक.]

विप्रयोगमुरसि स्वगात्रतः कर्पटाहृतिरनर्थदा भवेत्।
स्यात् प्रियाप्तिरभिगृह्य कर्पटं पृच्छतश्चरणपादयोजितुः ॥१२॥

If the querist touches his chest, he will have separation from a near and dear one ; if he takes off his cloth from his body, he will undergo some calamity. Should he take a piece of cloth and join his feet together he would attain his cherished object.

[Cf. पराशर—

उरः स्पृष्ट्वा विप्रयोगं स्वगात्राद्वस्त्रमुत्सृजेत्।
तस्यानर्थागमं पादं पादेन संस्पृशेत् पटम्॥
तमभिगृह्य वा पृच्छेद्विन्द्यात् प्रियसमागमम्॥

The metre is रथोद्धता.]

पादाङ्गुष्ठेन विलिखेद् भूमिं क्षेत्रोत्थचिन्तया।
हस्तेन पादौ कण्डूयेत्तस्य दासीमयी च सा ॥१३॥

Should the querist scratch the ground with his big toe, he would be thinking of his fields. If he scratches his feet with the hand, his thought concerns a maid servant.

[Cf. पराशर—

अङ्गुष्ठेन लिखेद् भूमिं क्षेत्रचिन्तां विचिन्तयेत्।
हस्तेन पादौ कण्डूयेत् कुर्याद्दासीकृतां स ताम्॥

The metre is श्लोक.]

तालभूर्जपटदर्शनेंऽशुकं चिन्तयेत् कचतुषास्थिभस्मगम्।
व्याधिराश्रयति रज्जुजालकं वल्कलं च समवेक्ष्य बन्धनम् ॥१४॥

If the querist looks at palm-leaves or birch bark, he must be thinking of fine clothes ; if he stands on hair, husk, bone or ashes, he will be attacked by disease ; and if he stands on, looks at or holds ropes, nets or barks, while asking, he will suffer from imprisonment.

[Cf. पराशर—

तालभूर्जपत्रदर्शने वस्त्रार्थं केशास्थिभस्मान्याक्रम्य व्याधिभयं ब्रूयात् । निगडजालरज्ज्वाश्रित्य वल्कलान्यधिष्ठाय दर्शने वा बन्धनभयम् ॥

The metre is रथोद्धता.]

पिप्पलीमरिचशुण्ठिवारिदैं रोध्रकुष्ठवसनाम्बुजीरकैः ।
गन्धमांसिशतपुष्पया वदेत्पृच्छतस्तगरकेण चिन्तयेत् ॥१५॥
स्त्रीपुरुषदोषपीडितसर्वाध्वसुतार्थधान्यतनयानाम् ।
द्विचतुष्पदक्षितीनां विनाशतः कीर्तितैर्दृष्टैः ॥१६॥

If long pepper, black pepper, dried ginger, cyperus grass, Lodhra, costus, cloth, water, cumin seeds, Gandhamāṁsī, Sonph or Tagara be seen or mentioned at the time, the querist's thoughts would be about a woman's failure, a man's fault, an afflicted person, loss of everything, missing of the passage, loss of children, loss of money, destruction of corn, son's death, loss of bipeds (animals with cloven hoofs), loss of quadrupeds and destruction of landed property respectively.

[Cf. पराशर—

पिप्पलीनां दर्शने प्रदुष्टस्त्रीकृतां चिन्तां मरिचस्य पापपुरुषकृतां शृङ्गवेरस्य मृतचिन्ताम् । अजाज्याः सुतनाशकृतां रोध्रस्यार्थनाशकृतां मुस्तस्य सर्वनाशकृतां कुष्ठस्य सुतनाशकृतां वस्त्रस्यार्थनाशकृतां ह्रीवेरस्य धान्यनाशकृतां तगरस्य भूमिनाशकृतां शतपुष्पया चतुष्पन्नाशाय मांस्या द्विपदनाशकृताम् ॥

In the third line सर्वार्थ is another reading for सर्वाध्व. The metre of the first is रथोद्धता.]

न्यग्रोधमधुकतिन्दुकजम्बूप्लक्षाम्रबदरजातिफलैः ।
धनकनकपुरुषलोहांशुकरूप्योदुम्बराप्तिरपि करगैः ॥१७॥

If the querist holds in his hand the fruits of the banyan tree, Madhuka, Tinduka, Jambū, Plakṣa, mangoes, and jujube, he would gain wealth, gold, servants, iron, silken clothes, silver and copper respectively.

[Cf. पराशर—

अश्वत्थन्यग्रोधफलैर्हस्तस्थैः पृच्छेद्धनागममादिशेत् । मधुकोदुम्बरफलैः काञ्चनागमम् । द्विपदागमं तिन्दुकैः । वस्त्रागमं प्लक्षजैः । रूप्यस्यागममाम्रैः । ताम्रस्यागमं बदरैः । लोहस्यागमं जम्बूकैरिति वा ॥]

धान्यपरिपूर्णपात्रं कुम्भः पूर्णः कुटुम्बवृद्धिकरौ ।
गजगोशुनां पुरीषं धनयुवतिसुहृद्विनाशकरम् ॥१८॥

Should a vessel filled with corn or a pot full of water be seen at the time, the querist's family would prosper. On the other hand, the sight of the dung of elephants, cows and dogs would prove severally destructive to wealth, young women and friends.

[Cf. पराशर—

धान्यपात्रपूर्णोदकुम्भदर्शने कुटुम्बवृद्धिं जानीयात् । हस्तिना द्रव्यागमम् हस्तिशकृतो भ्रंशमैश्वर्यस्य वा । गोमयस्य स्त्रीव्यभिचारम् । शुनः सुहृद्विनाशम् ॥]

पशुहस्तिमहिषपङ्कजरजतव्याघ्रैर्लभेत सन्दृष्टैः ।
अविधनिवसनमलयजकौशेयाभरणसङ्घातम् ॥१६॥

If a cow, elephant, buffalo, lotus, silver and tiger be sighted at the time, the querist would get woollen articles, money, garments, sandal paste, silken clothes and ornaments respectively.

[Cf. पराशर—

महिषस्य क्षौमवस्त्रागमम् । मणिभाण्डस्य गजवाजिनामौर्णिकानाम् । व्याघ्रस्याभरणागमम् । पङ्कजस्य रक्तवस्त्रचन्दनलाभम् । रूप्यस्य कौशेयवस्त्राणाम् ॥]

पृच्छा वृद्धश्रावकसुपरिव्राड्दर्शने नृभिर्विहिता ।
मित्रद्यूतार्थभवा गणिकानृपसूतिकार्थकृता ॥२०॥

If the querist should look at an old Śrāvaka (Kāpālika, a Śaiva monk who wears skulls), his enquiry should be about friends or gambling ; and if at an ascetic of a respectable sect, it would be about a courtesan, king or a woman in confinement.

शाक्योपाध्यायार्हन्निर्ग्रन्थिनिमित्तनिगमकैवर्तैः ।
चौरचमूपतिवणिजां दासीयोधापणस्थवध्यानाम् ॥२१॥

If a Buddhist monk, a teacher, a Jain monk, a naked fakir, a sooth-sayer, a trader of a town, and a fisherman be seen at the time, the querist's thought would be about a thief, commander of army, a merchant, a female servant, a soldier, a shop-keeper and a condemned criminal respectively.

तापसे शौण्डिके दृष्टे प्रोषितं पशुपालनम् ।
हृद्गतं पृच्छकस्य स्यादुञ्छवृत्तौ विपन्नता ॥२२॥

When an ascetic is seen, the querist thinks about a person that has gone abroad ; when a toddy-seller, about tending cattle ; and when a hermit engaged in gleaning corn, about one that has come to grief.

[Cf. पराशर—

निर्ग्रन्थिदर्शने दासीपृच्छा । वृद्धश्रावकदर्शने मिश्रद्यूतकृता वा । शाक्यस्य चौरकृता । परिव्राजकस्य नृपसूतिकागणिकार्था वा । उपाध्यायस्य चमूपतिकृता । नैगमस्य श्रेष्ठिकृता । नैमित्तिकस्य योधार्था । अर्हतो वाणिजिकार्था । उञ्छवृत्तिनो विपन्नार्था । तापसस्य प्रोषितार्था । शौण्डिकस्य पशुपालनार्था । कैवर्तस्य वध्यघातकृता ॥]

इच्छामि प्रष्टुं भण पश्यत्वार्यः समादिशेत्युक्ते ।
संयोगकुटुम्बोत्था लाभैश्वर्योद्भवा चिन्ता ॥२३॥

If a querist uses the expressions, *viz.*, "I should like to ask," "Please tell," "Your honour may see", and "Kindly predict", his thoughts are about some association or meeting, his family, profit and lordship or authority respectively.

निर्दिशेति गदिते जयाध्वजा प्रत्यवेक्ष्य मम चिन्तितं वद ।
आशु सर्वजनमध्यगं त्वया दृश्यतामिति च बन्धुचौरजा ॥२४॥

If he says, "Predict," his thought is about victory or travelling. If he says, "Think out and tell my thoughts", it is about his kinsman ; and if he runs to the astrologer in the midst of a crowd and speaks "Find out quickly", it is about a thief.

[Cf. पराशर—

आदिशार्येत्येवं पृच्छेदैश्वर्यचिन्ताम् । भणेत्युक्ते कुटुम्बकृताम् । इच्छामि प्रष्टुमिति संयोगकृताम् । पश्यत्वार्य इति लाभकृताम् । निर्दिशेत्यध्वकृताम् । जयपृच्छां वा । पृच्छामि तावदाचार्येति वा सम्यक् मां प्रत्यवेक्षस्वेति बन्धुकृताम् । अथ काले निःश्वसनान्तः सहसा बहुजनमध्यगतं दृश्यतामिति पृच्छेदिति चौरचिन्तां जानीयात् ॥

The metre is रथोद्धता.]

अन्तःस्थेऽङ्गे स्वजन उदितो बाह्यजे बाह्य एव
पादाङ्गुष्ठाङ्गुलिकलनया दासदासीजनः स्यात् ।
जङ्घे प्रेष्यो भवति भगिनी नाभितो हृत्स्वभार्या
पाण्यङ्गुष्ठाङ्गुलिचयकृतस्पर्शने पुत्रकन्ये ॥२५॥
मातरं जठरे मूर्ध्नि गुरुं दक्षिणवामकौ ।
बाहू भ्राताऽथ तत्पत्नी स्पृष्ट्वैवं चौरमादिशेत ॥२६॥

If the querist touches an internal limb, the thief must be one belonging to the family ; if an external limb, it is an outsider ; if a big toe, a man-servant ; if a toe, a maid-servant ; if the shanks, a labourer or messenger ; if the navel, his own sister ; if the heart, his own wife ; if a thumb, his son ; if the fingers, his daughter ; if the stomach, his own mother ; if the head, his father or teacher ; and if the right and left arms, his brother and brother's wife respectively. In this manner prediction of theft has to be made from the limb touched by the person.

[Cf. पराशर—

बाह्याङ्गस्पर्शने बाह्यचौरम् । अन्तः स्वकृतम् । तत्र पादाङ्गुष्ठ दासम् । अङ्गुलीषु दासीम् । जङ्घयोः प्रेष्यम् । जठरे मातरम् । हस्ताङ्गुलिषु दुहितरम् । अङ्गुष्ठे सुतम् । नाभ्यां भगिनीम् । गुरु शिरसि । हृदि भार्याम् । दक्षिणबाहौ भ्रातरम् । वामे भ्रातृभार्याम् ॥

The metres are मन्दाक्रान्ता and श्लोक.]

अन्तरङ्गमवमुच्य बाह्यगस्पर्शनं यदि करोति पृच्छकः ।
श्लेष्ममूत्रशकृतस्त्यजत्यथो पातयेत्करतलस्थवस्तु चेत् ॥२७॥
भृशमवनामिताङ्गपरिमोटनतोऽप्यथवा
जनधृतरिक्तभाण्डमवलोक्य च चौरजनम् ।
हृतपतितक्षतास्मृतविनष्टविभग्नगतो-
न्मुषितमृताद्यनिष्टरवतो लभते न हृतम् ॥२८॥

The following are the indications for the non-recovery of the stolen article : The querist touches an external limb after an internal one ; or spits phlegm, passes urine or evacuates the bowels ; or drops something from his hand ; or bends some limb very much and cracks it ; or beholds empty pots carried by people, or thieves ; or hears ominous words such as 'taken away', 'fallen' 'injured', 'forgotten', 'lost', 'broken', 'gone', 'stolen', 'dead' and the like.

[Cf. पराशर—

अभ्यन्तरगं स्पृष्ट्वा बाह्यं स्पृशेन्निर्हरणं वा श्लेष्मपुरीषमूत्रत्यागं कुर्याद्धस्ताद्वा किञ्चित्पातयेत् । गात्राणि वा स्फोटयेत् । क्षतहृतपतितमुषितविस्मृतनष्टकष्टदुष्टानिष्टभग्नगतजीर्णशब्दप्रादुर्भावो वा स्यात् । रिक्तभाण्डतस्कराणां दर्शने न प्रष्टा लाभं विन्द्यात् ॥

The metres are रथोद्धता and कुटक.]

निगदितमिदं यत्तत्सर्वं तुषास्थिविषादिकैः
सह मृतिकरं पीडार्तानां समं रुदितक्षुतैः ।

अवयवमपि स्पृष्ट्वान्तःस्थं दृढं भवदाहरे-
दतिबहु तदा भुक्त्वाऽन्नं संस्थितः सुहितो भवेत् ॥२६॥

All these that have been enumerated already along with husk, bones, poison and the like or with the sound of weeping and sneezing (or injury), forebade death to those that are afflicted by illness. If the querist touches an internal limb and belches aloud, it should be said that he is quite happy after a sumptuous feast.

[In the second line क्षतै: is another reading for क्षुतै:. The metre is हरिणी.

Cf. पराशर—

अथ रोगाभिघातच्छर्दमूत्रपुरीषोत्सर्गे केशास्थिभस्मतुषविषादीनामशुभानां दर्शने तथा छिन्नभिन्नव्यापन्नहतमृतावक्षतजग्धबद्धपाटितरुदितशब्दश्रवणे वा रोगिणां मरणमादिशेत् ॥]

ललाटस्पर्शनाच्छूकदर्शनाच्छालिजौदनम् ।
उरःस्पर्शात् षष्टिकाख्यं ग्रीवास्पर्शे च यावकम् ॥३०॥

If the querist touches his forehead or sees corn with sharp thorns (like paddy), it is to be inferred that he has eaten food consisting of the Ṣaṣtika rice (which ripens in sixty days) ; and if he touches the neck, his food consisted of barley.

The metre is श्लोक.]

कुक्षिकुचजठरजानुस्पर्शे माषाः पयस्तिलयवागवः ।
आस्वादयते चोष्ठौ लिहते मधुरं रसं ज्ञेयम् ॥३१॥

If he touches the abdomen, paps, stomach and knee, he must have eaten black grain (with rice), milk (with rice), sesamum (with rice) and rice gruel respectively ; if he licks his lips, he must have enjoyed sweet dishes.

विसृक्के स्फोटयेज्जिह्वामाम्ले वक्त्रं विकूणयेत् ।
कटुकेऽथ कषायेऽथ हिक्केत् ष्ठीवेच्च सैन्धवे ॥३२॥

If he strikes his tongue against the corner of the mouth, it is to be inferred that the querist had eaten something sour ; if he makes his mouth wry, something pungent ; if he hiccups, something astringent ; and if he spits, something salt.

श्लेष्मत्यागे शुष्कतिक्तं तदल्पं वा क्रव्यादं प्रेक्ष्य वा मांसमिश्रम् ।
भ्रूगण्डौष्ठस्पर्शने शाकुनं तद्भुक्तं तेनेत्युक्तमेतन्निमित्तम् ॥३३॥

If he spits phlegm, it is to be understood that he has eaten a small quantity of something dry and bitter ; if a carnivorous animal is sighted, something mixed with meat; if he touches his brows, temples or lips, food consisting of bird's meat. Thus the signs for predicting the food eaten have been stated.

[The Vārāṇasī edition (1968) reads the second line "श्रुत्वा क्रव्यादं वा प्रेक्ष्य वा मांसमिश्रम् ।" This is evidently not the author's mistake. For, how could he compare only one line of the शालिनी metre, which has only eleven syllables in a quarter, with 13 syllables? The error must have been committed by somebody else. The best reading would be: क्रव्यादं वा प्रेक्ष्य वा मांसमिश्रम्. The meaning of the second वा is 'श्रुत्वा'.

The metre is शालिनी]

मूर्धगलकेशहनुशङ्खकर्णजङ्घं वस्ति च स्पृष्ट्वा ।
गजमहिषमेषशूकरगोशशमृगमहिषमांसयुग्भुक्तम् ॥३४॥

If the querist touches the head, throat, hair, chin, frontal bone, ear, shank and abdomen he must have eaten food mixed with the flesh of elephant, buffalo, sheep, hog, cow, hare, deer and buffalo respectively.

[We can say definitely that this verse is not by Varāhamihira. For, he never violates the metrical rule that in the *Āryā* the 6th Gaṇa must have either a जगण or four short syllables. Hence what I have stated at the beginning of this chapter regarding the authorship of this chapter stands confirmed.]

दृष्टे श्रुतेऽप्यशकुने गोधामत्स्यामिषं वदेद्भुक्तम् ।
गर्भिण्या गर्भस्य च निपतनमेवं प्रकल्पयेत्प्रश्ने ॥३५॥

When an evil omen is seen or heard, the astrologer should state that the querist has eaten the flesh of alligators or fish. In the same manner, the prediction of abortion should be made at a query regarding a pregnant woman, i.e. if there are evil omens at the time of consultation, miscarriage has to be predicted.

[Cf. पराशर—

अथ स्निग्धं दृढमभ्यन्तराङ्ग स्पृष्ट्वोद्गिरन् पृच्छेद् भुक्तमन्नं विन्द्यात् । तत्र ललाटस्पर्शे शूकानां वा शाल्योदनम् । उरसि संस्पृष्टे षष्टिकौदनम् । ग्रीवायां यवान्नम् । जठरे तिलौदनम् । कुक्षौ माषौदनम् । स्तनयोः क्षीरौदनम् । जानुनोर्यावकम् । स्वादयेदोष्ठौ वा परिलिहेत मधुरम् । आविसृक्के जिह्वामपि स्फोटयेदाम्लम् । विकूणयेत् कटुकम् । हिक्केत् कषायम् । निष्ठीवेत्तिक्तम् । शुष्कमल्पं श्लेष्माणमुत्सृजेदतिलवणम् । क्रव्यादानां दर्शने मांसप्रायम् । तत्र भ्रू गण्डजिह्वौष्ठसंस्पर्शने शाकुनम् । हन्वोर्वाराहम् ।

कर्णयोः पार्षदम् । जङ्घयोमर्गिम् । केशानामौरभ्रम् । शङ्खयोर्गव्यम् । वस्तिगलयोर्माहिषम् । मूर्ध्नि कौञ्जरम् । पाटितच्छिन्नभिन्नानां स्पर्शने श्रवणे गोधामत्स्यमांसम् ॥]

पुंस्त्रीनपुंसकाख्ये दृष्टेऽनुमिते पुरःस्थिते स्पृष्टे ।
तज्जन्म भवति पानान्नपुष्पफलदर्शने च शुभम् ॥३६॥

At a query regarding the sex of the child to be born, if a man is seen, inferred, present in front or touched, the birth of a male child should be predicted ; if it is a woman that is seen etc. that of a female child ; and if it is a eunuch or one having a neuter name, a eunuch's birth is to be predicted. The child-birth will be easy and happy, if some drink, food, fruit or flower is seen at the time.

अङ्गुष्ठेन भ्रूवरं वाङ्गुलिं वा स्पृष्ट्वा पृच्छेद्गर्भचिन्ता तदा स्यात् ।
मध्वाज्याद्यैर्हेमरत्नप्रवालैरग्रस्थैर्वा मातृधात्र्यात्मजैश्च ॥३७॥

If a woman touches with her thumb her eye-brow, stomach or finger at a query, she must be thinking of pregnancy. The same prediction should be made when honey, ghee and such other things (i.e good fruits, things having masculine names) or gold, gems and corals (sprouts), or her mother, nurse and child are in front of her.

[Cf. पराशर—

अथ स्त्री भ्रुवौ जठरमङ्गुष्ठेन वाऽङ्गुलिं स्पृष्ट्वा पृच्छेद् गर्भपृच्छां जानीयात् । तथा फलच्छायावृक्षप्रवालाङ्कुरमधुघृतहेमगर्भप्राजापत्ये वा मातृधात्रीपुत्रनिदर्शनशब्दप्रादुर्भावे गर्भपृच्छामेव ॥

The metre is शालिनी.]

गर्भयुता जठरे करगे स्याद्दुष्टनिमित्तवशात्तदुवासः ।
कर्षति तज्जठरं यदि पीठोत्पीडनतः करगे च करेऽपि ॥३८॥

If, at a query about a woman's pregnancy, the querist touches the belly with his or her hand, the woman in question may be pregnant. However, if there should also be bad omens at the time, she may have miscarriage. The same result will have to be predicted, if the querist scratches (or drags) his (or her) stomach owing to the pressure of the seat, or puts one hand on the other.

[The metre is दोधक]

प्राणाया दक्षिणे द्वारे स्पृष्टे मासोत्तरं वदेत् ।
वामेऽब्दौ कर्णं एवं मा द्विचतुर्घ्नः श्रुतिस्तने ॥३९॥

When the querist touches the right nostril, the woman in question may conceive after a month ; when the left nostril or the left ear, after two years ; when the right ear and the breasts, after two months and four months respectively.

[The word घ्राण being neuter in gender, घोणाया would have been proper. The metre is श्लोक.]

वेणीमूले त्रीन् सुतान् कन्यके द्वे कर्णे पुत्रान्पञ्च हस्ते त्रयं च ।
अङ्गुष्ठान्ते पञ्चकं चानुपूर्व्या पादाङ्गुष्ठे पार्ष्णियुग्मेऽपि कन्याम् ॥४०॥

If the querist woman touches the root of her braid, she will give birth to three sons and two daughters ; if the ears, five sons ; if the hands, three sons ; if the little finger, one son ; if the ring finger, two sons ; if the fore-finger, four sons ; if the thumb, five sons. If she touches the big toes or the heels, she will have a single daughter.

[The metre is शालिनी.]

सव्यासव्योरुसंस्पर्शे सूते कन्यासुतद्वयम् ।
स्पृष्टे ललाटमध्यान्ते चतुस्त्रितनया भवेत् ॥४१॥

If she touches her right and left thigh, she will beget two daughters and two sons respectively ; if the middle of the forehead, four sons : and if the end of the forehead, three sons.

[The author always uses सव्य in the sense of 'right' and अपसव्य of 'left'.

Cf. पराशर—

तत्र जठरस्पर्शे गर्भिणीमेवमेव ब्रूयात् । अङ्गुष्ठेन नासास्रोतसि दक्षिणे कुर्याद् मासान्तरेण गर्भग्रहणम् । वामाद् द्विवर्षान्तरेण । कर्णच्छिद्रे मासद्वयेन । वामे वर्षद्वयेन । स्तनयोरङ्गुष्ठेनैव स्पर्शे चतुर्भिर्मासैः । पीठमर्दकं कृत्वा चानन्तरमुदरं कण्डूयेदग्रहस्तं हस्तेनाभिगृह्य वा पृच्छेद् भग्नलोहिकपिठरकुद्दालककुठारस्रुतिचलितपतितभग्नदर्शनशब्दे प्रादुर्भावे वा गर्भपतनं विन्द्यात् । तथान्नपानपुष्पफलपक्षिद्विचतुष्पदानामन्यद्रव्याणां पुंसंज्ञानां दर्शनशब्दप्रादुर्भावे पुञ्जन्म विन्द्यात् । स्त्रीसंज्ञानां स्त्रीजन्म । नपुंसकाख्ये नपुंसकानाम् । पुंसंज्ञमङ्गं संस्पृश्य गर्भिणी पृच्छेत् पुञ्जन्म विन्द्यात् । स्त्रीसंज्ञानां स्त्रीजन्म । नपुंसकाख्येषु नपुंसकानाम् ।

अथ विशेष :—

वेणीमूलमभिगृह्य पृच्छेत्तदा द्वे कन्यके त्रीन्पुत्रान् जनयिष्यसीति ब्रूयात् । ललाटमध्यं स्पृशन्ती चत्वार्यपत्यानि ललाटान्तं त्रीणि । कर्णयोः संस्पर्शे पञ्चापत्यानि । दक्षिणोरुसंस्पर्शे द्वौ पुत्रौ द्वे च कन्यके जनयिष्यसीति । वामस्य तिस्रः कन्या द्वौ पुत्रौ । पादाङ्गुष्ठस्य कन्यकैका । पार्ष्ण्योः कन्यकैकैवेति ॥]

शिरोललाटभ्रूकर्णगण्डं हनुरदा गलम् ।
सव्यापसव्यस्कन्धश्च हस्तौ चिबुकनालकम् ॥४२॥
उरः कुचं दक्षिणमप्यसव्यं हृत्पार्श्वमेवं जठरं कटिश्च ।
स्फिक्पायुसन्ध्यूरुयुगं च जानू जङ्घेऽथ पादाविति कृत्तिकादौ ॥४३॥

If the pregnant woman touches, while enquiring about the possible birth star of her next issue, the head, forehead, brows, ears, cheeks, lower part of chin, teeth, neck, right shoulder, left shoulder, hands, chin, pipe of the neck. chest, right bosom, left bosom, heart, right side, left side, belly, hip, joint of buttocks and anus, right thigh, left thigh, knees, shanks, and feet, she will give birth to a child in any of the asterisms in their order commencing from Kṛttikā.

[Cf. पराशर—

शिरसि संस्पृष्टे कृत्तिकासु जन्म विन्द्यात् । ललाटे रोहिण्याम् । भ्रुवोर्मृग-शिरसि । कर्णयोरार्द्रायाम् । गण्डयोः पुनर्वसौ । हन्वोस्तिष्ये । दन्तयोराश्लेषासु । ग्रीवायां मघासु । दक्षिणांसे प्राक्फल्गुन्याम् । वामांसे उत्तरफल्गुन्याम् । हस्ते हस्तयोः । चिबुके चित्रायाम् । स्वातौ नालके । उरसि विशाखायाम् । दक्षिणस्तनेऽनुराधासु । ज्येष्ठासु वामे । हृदि मूले । दक्षिणपार्श्वे प्रागषाढासु । उत्तराषाढसु परपार्श्वे । जठरे श्रवणे । श्रोण्यां धनिष्ठासु । स्फिग्गुदयोर्वारुणे । दक्षिणोरुणा प्राक्प्रोष्ठपदायाम् । वामेनोत्तरपदायाम् । जानुभ्यां पौष्णे । जङ्घयोरश्विन्याम् । पादयोर्भरण्यामिति ॥

The metres are श्लोक and उपजाति.]

इति निगदितमेतद् गात्रसंस्पर्शलक्ष्म
प्रकटमभिमताप्त्यै वीक्ष्य शास्त्राणि सम्यक् ।
विपुलमतिरुदारो वेत्ति यः सर्वमेत-
न्नरपतिजनताभिः पूज्यतेऽसौ सदैव ॥४४॥

Thus have I explained in clear terms the prognostics of touching the limbs, after carefully examining the treatises on this science, for enabling people to attain their cherished desires. An intelligent and noble astrologer who knows all this, will always be honoured by sovereigns as well as peoples.

[The metre is मालिनी.]

पिटकलक्षणम् ॥५२॥

Chapter LII—Characteristics of Pimples

[This too is supposed to be a spurious chapter. However, Bhaṭṭotpala comments upon it.]

सितरक्तपीतकृष्णा विप्रादीनां क्रमेण पिटका ये ।
ते क्रमशः प्रोक्तफला वर्णानां नाग्रजातानाम् ॥१॥

For the four classes of people beginning with the Brāhmaṇas pimples will be auspicious, if they are in order white, red, yellow and black in colour. These colours are beneficial for the respective classes as well as for those that are below and not for those above them. In other words, a white pimple is good for Brāhmaṇas; white and red for Kṣatriyas; white, red and yellow for Vaiśyas; and white, red, yellow and black for Śūdras.

सुस्निग्धव्यक्तशोभाः शिरसि धनचयं मूर्ध्नि सौभाग्यमारा-
द्दौर्भाग्यं भ्रूयुगोत्थाः प्रियजनघटनामाशु दुःशीलतां च ।
तन्मध्योत्थाश्च शोकं नयनपुटगता नेत्रयोरिष्टदृष्टिं
प्रव्रज्यां शङ्खदेशेऽश्रुजलनिपतनस्थानगा रान्ति चिन्ताम् ॥२॥

Pimples that are glossy and of clear lustre, on the head indicate vast wealth; on the back of the face (i.e. near the hair), good fortune or happiness in the near future; on the two brows, misfortune; in the middle of the brows, meeting with beloved person very soon and bad conduct; on the eye-lids, grief; on the eyes, sight of friends; on the frontal bone, renunciation; and in the area where tears fall down, worries.

[Cf. पराशर—

अथ पिटकाः सितरक्तपीतकृष्णा द्विजादीनां वर्णानां क्रमात् स्थानवर्णविशेषणोत्तरोत्तरफलदा भवन्ति। तत्र मूर्ध्नि सुव्यक्तः सुस्निग्धः सुवर्णोऽभिषेकागमनं कुर्यात्। शिरसि धनागमम्। केशान्ते सौभाग्यम्। ललाटे धनसञ्चयम्। भ्रुवोर्दौर्भाग्यम्। सङ्गमे दौःशील्यमिष्टसङ्गमं च। नेत्रपुटयोः शोकम्। नेत्रयोरिष्टदर्शनम्। शङ्खदेशे प्रव्रज्याम्। चिन्तामश्रुपाते ॥

The metre is स्रग्धरा.]

घ्राणगण्डे वसनसुतदाश्चौष्ठयोरन्नलाभं
कुर्युस्तद्वच्चिबुकतलगा भूरि वित्तं ललाटे ।
हन्वोरेवं गलकृतपदा भूषणान्यन्नपाने
श्रोत्रे तद्भूषणगणमपि ज्ञानमात्मस्वरूपम् ॥३॥

Pimples on the nose and temples bestow clothes and children respectively ; on the lips, good food ; on the lower part of the chin, the same thing i.e. food ; on the forehead, plenty of money ; on the two sides of the jaw-bone, the same result i.e. much wealth ; on the neck, ornaments, good food and drinks ; on the ears, a number of ear-ornaments as well as spiritual knowledge.

[Cf पराशर—

गण्डे सुतलाभम् । नासावंशे वस्त्रलाभम् । चिबुकाधरेष्वोष्ठाधरेष्वन्नम् । अभिहन्वोर्धनागमम् । गले चान्नपानमाभरणं च । शिरःसन्धौ ग्रीवायां चोपघातं शस्त्रेण, कर्णयोस्तद्भूषणमात्मश्रवणं च ॥

The metre is मन्दाक्रान्ता.]

शिरःसन्धिग्रीवाहृदयकुचपार्श्वोरसि गता
अयोघातं घातं सुततनयलाभं शुचमपि ।
प्रियप्राप्तिं स्कन्धेऽप्यटनमथ भिक्षार्थमसकृ-
द्विनाशं कक्षोत्था विदधति धनानां बहुमुखम् ॥४॥

Pimples on the joint of the head cause a hurt from an iron instrument , on the neck, blows ; on the heart and breasts, birth of son ; on the sides, grief ; on the chest, attainment of desired objects; on the shoulders, frequent roamings for begging alms ; and in the armpits, loss of wealth in various ways.

[The metre is शिखरिणी.]

दुःखशत्रुनिचयस्य विनाशं पृष्ठबाहुयुगजा रचयन्ति ।
संयमं च मणिबन्धनजाता भूषणाद्यमुपबाहुयुगोत्थाः ॥५॥

Pimples appearing on the back lead to the destruction of all miseries ; on the arms, to the annihilation of all enemies ; those on the wrists, to restraint or arrest ; and those near the arms, to the acquisition of ornaments and the like.

[विघातं is another reading for विनाशं in the first line. Utpala interprets the last word as "आभरणवस्त्रान्नदानं कुर्वन्ति ।"

Cf. पराशर—

पार्श्वयोः शोकम् । उरसीष्टसङ्गमम् । स्कन्धयोर्भैक्ष्यचर्याम् । कक्षयोरर्थक्षयम् । हृत्स्तनयोः पुत्रलाभम् । पृष्ठे दुःखशमनम् । अरिविनाशं बाह्वोः । प्रबाह्वोराभरणम् । मणिबन्धने नियमनम् ।।

The metre is स्वागता.]

धनाप्ति सौभाग्यं शुचमपि कराङ्गुल्युदरगाः
सुपानान्नं नाभौ तदथ इह चौरैर्धनहृतिम् ।
धनं धान्यं वस्तौ युवतिमथ मेढ्रे सुतनयान्
धनं सौभाग्यं वा गुदवृषणजाता विदधति ।।६।।

Those appearing on the hands, fingers and stomach cause attainment of wealth, good fortune and splendour, and grief respectively ; on the navel, excellent food and drink ; those beneath the navel, loss of wealth by theft ; on the pelvis, wealth and corn ; on the penis, getting a young wife and good sons ; on the anus, wealth ; and on the testicles, fortune and an attractive personality.

[Cf. पराशर—

पाणौ धनागमम् । सौभाग्यमङ्गुलिषु । शोकमुदरे । अन्नपानावाप्ति च नाभौ । चोरैरर्थहरणं तदधरे । धनधान्यावाप्ति वस्तौ । सौभाग्यमर्थलाभं च वृषणयोः । पुत्रजन्म स्त्रीलाभं मेहने । गुदे सौभाग्यम् ।।

The metre is शिखरिणी.]

ऊर्वोर्यानाङ्गनालाभं जान्वोः शत्रुजनात् क्षतिम् ।
शस्त्रेण जङ्घयोर्गुल्फेऽध्वबन्धक्लेशदायिनः ।।७।।

Pimples on the thighs augur the acquisition of vehicles and a wife ; on the knees, loss (or trouble) on account of enemies; on the shanks, hurt from weapons ; and on the ankles, suffering through wandering and imprisonment.

[Cf. पराशर—

यानाङ्गनालाभमूर्वोः । जान्वोरुपरि रिपुघातम् । शस्त्रेण विनाशं जङ्घयोर्गुल्फयोरध्वबन्धपरिक्लेशागमः ।

Both the author of this section and the sage use the word जानु, which is in neuter, in another gender.

The metre is श्लोक.]

स्फिक्पार्ष्णिपादजाता धननाशागम्यगमनमध्वानम् ।
बन्धनमङ्गुलिनिचयेऽङ्गुष्ठे च ज्ञातिलोकतः पूजाम् ।।८।।

Pimples on the buttocks, heels and feet cause loss of wealth, illicit cohabitation (especially with a forbidden person), and long travelling respectively ; on the toes, imprisonment ; and on the big toe, respect of kinsmen.

[The word अङ्गुलिनिचये in the second line has been translated by me as 'on the toes' and *not* as 'on the fingers', because the author has already given the effect of pimples appearing on the fingers in verse 6, as सौभाग्य. Consistently have I translated अङ्गुष्ठ as पादाङ्गुष्ठ i.e., big toe.

Cf. पराशर—

स्फिजोरर्थहरणम् । पार्ष्ण्योरगम्यगमनम् । पादयोरध्वगमनम् । नियमनमङ्गुल्याम् । अङ्गुष्ठेन जातिपूजाम् ॥]

उत्पातगण्डपिटका दक्षिणतो वामतस्त्वभीघाताः ।
धन्या भवन्ति पुंसां तद्विपरीताश्च नारीणाम् ॥९॥

Throbbing, inflammations or boils and pimples appearing on the right side of the body and blows on the left side are auspicious for men, while the same on the opposite side are good for women i.e. throbbing etc., on the left side, and impacts on the right.

इति पिटकविभागः प्रोक्त आमूर्धतोऽयं
व्रणतिलकविभागोऽप्येवमेव प्रकल्प्यः ।
भवति मशकलक्ष्मावर्तजन्मापि तद्व-
न्निगदितफलकारि प्राणिनां देहसंस्थम् ॥१०॥

Thus have I analyzed the effects of pimples on all the parts of the body from head to foot. In the same manner should ulcers and moles be classified. Moles, special marks and hairy circles too appearing on the limbs of human beings produce likewise the results enumerated above.

[Readers can apply the principles enunciated in this chapter to other marks such as moles and hairy circles.

The metre is मालिनी.]

———

वास्तुविद्या ॥५३॥

Chapter LIII—Architecture

Vāstu-śilpa or the science of house-building is very ancient in India. Our author has dealt with this vast science in a single chapter containing 125 verses. The word *Vāstu* means a dwelling. He treats of temple-architecture in LVI and of sculpture in LVIII. It would have been better, had the author put these three chapters in succession.

वास्तुज्ञानमथातः कमलभवान्मुनिपरम्परायातम् ।
क्रियतेऽधुना मयेवं विदग्धसांवत्सरप्रीत्यै ॥१॥

I shall now expound for the delight of learned astrologers the science of house-building which has come down from Brahmā (Creator) through an unbroken succession of sages.

[According to the विश्वकर्मवास्तुशास्त्र the celestial architect got a thorough knowledge of this science from Lord Śambhu. The अपराजितपृच्छा of भुवनदेव (13th century A.D.) speaks of this lore as the gift of the celestial Tree. Another version of the work of Viśva-karman mentions the line of succession of teachers from Lord Śambhu as follows' : Parāśara, Bṛhadratha and Viśvakarman. Dr. Kern remarks in this connection as follows :

"According to Utpala, Garga, etc., more explicit is the statement in a work bearing the title of श्री ब्रह्मोक्तविश्वकर्मप्रकाशिका, where we read,

इति प्रोक्तं वास्तुशास्त्रं पूर्वं गर्गाय धीमते ।
गर्गात्पराशरः प्राप तस्मात्प्राप बृहद्रथः ॥
बृहद्रथाद्विश्वकर्मा प्राप्तवान्वास्तुशास्त्रकम् ।
स विश्वकर्मा जगतो हितायाकथयत्पुनः ॥
वासुदेवादिषु पुनर्भूलोक भक्तितोऽब्रवीत् ।

... ...

अथ स विमलविद्यो विश्वकर्मा महात्मा
सकलगुणवरिष्ठः सर्वशास्त्रार्थवेत्ता ।
सकलसुरगणानां सूत्रधारः कृतात्मा
भवननिवसतां सच्छास्त्रमेतच्चकार ॥

This passage, with many others, shows that Garga, Parāśara, and the like, are more mythological beings, of exactly the same historical value with Brahman, Viśvakarman, Vasudeva. In the opening stanzas of the विश्वक, we find,

यदुक्तं शम्भुना पूर्वं वास्तुशास्त्र पुरातनम् ।।
पराशरः प्राह बृहद्रथाय बृहद्रथः प्राह च विश्वकर्मणे ।
स विश्वकर्मा जगतां हिताय प्रोवाच शास्त्रं बहुभेदयुक्तम् ।।
विश्वकर्मोवाच—
वास्तुशास्त्रं प्रवक्ष्यामि लोकानां हितकाम्यया ।

The Viśvaka seems to be a compilation, for most of the passages quoted by Utpala, either from what he terms किरणाख्यतन्त्र or from Garga, from Bṛhaspati, Viśvakarman himself, Kaśyapa etc., recur in the Viśvaka, a copy of which is in the translator's possession."]

किमपि किल भूतमभवद्रुन्धानं रोदसी शरीरेण ।
तदमरगणेन सहसा विनिगृह्याधोमुखं न्यस्तम् ।।२।।
यत्र च येन गृहीतं विबुधेनाधिष्ठितः स तत्रैव ।
तदमरमयं विधाता वास्तुनरं कल्पयामास ।।३।।

There was, it is said, some Being which obstructed the earth and the sky with its body. The Gods suddenly caught hold of it and laid it upside down. Whichever limbs were held by different Gods had those very Gods as their presiding deities. The Creator ordained that Being to be the House-God of the nature of Gods.

[Cf. बृहस्पति—

पुरा कृतयुगे ह्यासीन्महद्भूतं समुत्थितम् ।
व्याप्यमानं शरीरेण सकलं भुवनं ततः ।।
तद्दृष्ट्वा विस्मयं देवा गताः सेन्द्रा भयावृताः ।
ततस्तैः क्रोधसन्तप्तैर्गृहीत्वा तमथासुरम् ।।
विनिक्षिप्तमधोवक्त्रं स्थितास्तत्रैव ते सुराः ।
तमेव वास्तुपुरुषं ब्रह्मा समभिकल्पये(य)त् ।।]

उत्तममष्टाभ्यधिकं हस्तशतं नृपगृहं पृथुत्वेन ।
अष्टाष्टोनान्येवं पञ्च सपादानि दैर्घ्येण ।।४।।

The king's palace is one of five kinds. The best of them is 108 cubits in width, and the others are 100, 92, 84 and 76 cubits respectively. Their length is greater than the breadth by a quarter (i.e.,135, 125, 115, 105 and 95 cubits).

[Cf. काश्यप—

अष्टोत्तरं हस्तशतं विस्ताराम्नृपमन्दिरम् ।
कार्यं प्रधानमन्यानि तथाष्टाष्टोनितानि तु ॥
विस्तारं पादसंयुक्तं दैर्घ्यं तेषां प्रकल्पयेत् ।
एवं पञ्च नृपः कुर्याद् गृहाणां च पृथक् पृथक् ॥]

षड्भिः षड्भिर्हीना सेनापतिसद्मनां चतुःषष्टिः ।
एवं पञ्चगृहाणि षड्भागसमन्विता दैर्घ्यम् ॥५॥

The five kinds of houses of a commander-in-chief are in order 64, 58, 52, 46 and 40 cubits in width, and their length exceeds the width by a sixth.

The length of the varieties would be in order $74\frac{2}{3}$, $67\frac{2}{3}$, $60\frac{2}{3}$, $53\frac{2}{3}$ and $46\frac{2}{3}$ cubits. The third quarter of the verse, as it is, is faulty being deficient in one Mātrā. It can be rectified by adding तु at the end : एवं पञ्च गृहाणि तु]

षष्टिश्चतुश्चतुर्भिर्हीना वेश्मानि पञ्च सचिवस्य ।
स्वाष्टांशयुतो दैर्घ्यं तदर्धतो राजमहिषीणाम् ॥६॥

The houses of ministers are 60, 56, 52, 48 and 44 cubits in width and their length exceeds their breadth by an eighth. The houses of queens have half the dimensions of the above ones.

[The length of the five kinds would be in order $67\frac{1}{2}$, 63, $58\frac{1}{2}$, 54 and $49\frac{1}{2}$ cubits. The breadth and length of the queens' houses would be : 30 and 33.75 cubits ; 28 and $31\frac{1}{2}$; 26 and $29\frac{1}{4}$; 24 and 27 ; and lastly 22 and 24.75 cubits.]

षड्भिः षड्भिश्चैवं युवराजस्यापवर्जिताऽशीतिः ।
त्र्यंशान्विता च दैर्घ्यं पञ्च तदर्धैस्तवनुजानाम् ॥७॥

The width of the Yuvarāja's houses should be 80, 74, 68, 62 and 56 cubits respectively and their length exceeds the breadth by a third. The dimensions of the houses of the younger princes should be half those of the Yuvarāja's.

[The length of these five varieties would be : $106\frac{2}{3}$, $98\frac{2}{3}$, $90\frac{2}{3}$, $82\frac{2}{3}$ and $74\frac{2}{3}$ cubits in order. The breadth and length of the princes' houses would be 40 and $53\frac{1}{3}$ cubits ; 37 and $49\frac{1}{3}$; 34 and $45\frac{1}{3}$; 31 and $41\frac{1}{3}$; and lastly 28 and $37\frac{1}{3}$ cubits respectively.]

नृपसचिवान्तरतुल्यं सामन्तप्रवरराजपुरुषाणाम् ।
नृपयुवराजविशेषः कञ्चुकिवेश्याकलाज्ञानाम् ॥८॥

The dimensions of the houses of feudatory chiefs, nobles and king's officers would be equal to the difference between the measurements of king's houses and those of the minister's. Similarly the dimensions of the houses of chamberlains, courtesans and artistes would be equal to the difference between the measurements of the houses of the king and the Yuvarāja.

[We have the measurements of the best type of houses for the king as 108 cubits and 135 cubits.

The corresponding figures for the minister's house are 60 and $67\frac{1}{2}$ cubits. So $108-60=48$ cubits ; and $135-67\frac{1}{2}=67\frac{1}{2}$ cubits will be the width and length respectively of the houses for the Sāmantas etc. According to this principle the breadth and length of a chamberlain's house should be 28 and $28\frac{1}{3}$ cubits respectively. This looks rather odd.]

अध्यक्षाधिकृतानां सर्वेषामेव कोशरतितुल्यम् ।
युवराजमन्त्रिविवरं कर्मान्ताध्यक्षदूतानाम् ॥९॥

The houses of all directors and officers (of stables, elephant yards, dairies, royal kitchens etc.) should be of the dimensions of treasure-houses and pleasure-mansions. The difference between the measurements of the houses of Yuvarāja and minister would give those of the houses of heads of industrial workshops and envoys.

[In the second line सामन्त is another reading instead of युवराज which is rejected by Utpala. According to Kullūka (under Manu VII-62) कर्मान्त is इक्षुधान्यादिसङ्ग्रहस्थानम्—a store of grain The measures of treasuries and pleasure-houses are given in verses 14 and 16 *infra.*]

चत्वारिंशद्धीना चतुश्चतुर्भिस्तु पञ्च यावदिति ।
षड्भागयुता दैर्घ्यं दैवज्ञपुरोधसोर्भिषजः ॥१०॥

The five varieties of houses of royal astrologers, preceptors and physicians should measure 40, 36, 32, 28 and 24 cubits in breadth, and their length should exceed the breadth by a sixth.

[Their length would be in order $46\frac{2}{3}$, 42, $37\frac{1}{3}$, $32\frac{2}{3}$ and 28 cubits.]

Next he speaks of the height and number of rooms.

वास्तुनि यो विस्तारः स एव चोच्छ्रायनिश्चयः शुभदः ।
शालैकेषु गृहेष्वपि विस्ताराद्द्विगुणितं दैर्घ्यम् ॥११॥

It is auspicious for houses to have the same height as their breadth. The length of houses with single halls should be double their breadth.

[Cf. काश्यप—

चतुःशालगृहेष्वेवमुच्छ्रायो व्याससम्मितः ।
विस्तारं द्विगुणं दैर्घ्यमेकशालयुतस्य च ॥

Next he speaks of the dimensions of houses for the different classes or Varṇas.]

चातुर्वर्ण्यव्यासो द्वात्रिंशत् सा चतुश्चतुर्हीना ।
आषोडशादिति परं न्यूनतरमतीव हीनानाम् ॥१२॥
सदशांशं विप्राणां क्षत्रस्याष्टांशसंयुतं दैर्घ्यम् ।
षड्भागयुतं वैश्यस्य भवति शूद्रस्य पादयुतम् ॥१३॥

The width of the houses of Brāhmaṇas and other four classes ranges from 32 cubits to 16 cubits, each being reduced by 4 cubits; i.e. Brāhmaṇas have five houses with 32 cubits and below; Kṣatriyas have four with 28 cubits, 24, 20 and 16 cubits for their width; Vaiśyas, three with 24, 20 and 16 cubits; and Śūdras two with 20 and 16 cubits. The lowest class of men (like the Caṇḍālas and Śvapākas) will have houses with much smaller dimensions than these. The length of the houses for the four classes should exceed the breadth by a tenth, eighth, sixth and fourth respectively.

[The length of the five houses for Brāhmaṇas would be in order 35·2, 30·8, 26·4, 22 and 17·6 cubits; for Kṣatriyas, 31·5, 27, 22·5 and 18 cubits; for Vaiśyas, 28, $23\frac{1}{3}$ and $18\frac{2}{3}$ cubits; and for Śūdras, 25 and 20 cubits.

See the किरणाख्यतन्त्र quoted by Utpala :

हस्तद्वात्रिंशता युक्तो विस्तारः स्याद् द्विजालये ।
विस्तारं सदशांशं तु दैर्घ्यं तस्य प्रकल्पयेत् ॥
त्रयाणां क्षत्रियादीनां मानं यत्पूर्वचोदितम् ।
तच्चतुर्भिः करैस्ताक्ष्यं ह्रासयेदनुपूर्वशः ॥
एषामष्टांशषड्भागपाददैर्घ्यं क्रमाद् भवेत् ॥

Next the author mentions the measurements of the treasury and pleasure mansion.]

नृपसेनापतिगृहयोरन्तरमानेन कोशरतिभवने ।
सेनापतिचातुर्वर्ण्यविवरतो राजपुरुषाणाम् ॥१४॥

The dimensions of the treasury and pleasure-mansion would be equal to the difference between those of the royal palace and the commander-in-chief's house. The measure for the houses of king's officers would be equal to the difference between those of the houses of commander-in-chief and one of the four classes. That is, officer belongs to the Brāhmaṇa class, the difference referred to is one between the measure of the commander-in-chief's house and an ordinary Brāhmaṇa's mentioned in the previous two verses; if the officer is a Kṣatriya, we have to subtract the dimensions of a Kṣatriya's house from those of the second house of the Senāpati; if he is a Vaiśya, the subtraction should be done from the measure of the Senāpati's third house; and lastly, if the officer is a Śūdra, the fourth house of the commander-in-chief should be taken.

[The breadth of the treasury and pleasure-house will be 44, 42, 40, 38 and 36 cubits respectively for the five varieties. Now for a Brāhmaṇa officer the measurements are: 32, 30, 28, 26 and 24 cubits; for a Kṣatriya officer, 34, 28, 26 and 24 cubits; for a Vaiśya one, 28, 26 and 24 cubits; and lastly for a Śūdra officer, 26 and 24 cubits.]

Next he gives the measures for the houses of mixed castes :

अथ पारशवादीनां स्वमानसंयोगदलसमं भवनम् ।
हीनाधिकं स्वमानादशुभकरं वास्तु सर्वेषाम् ॥१५॥

The houses of persons of mixed classes such as Pārasavas, sons of Brāhmaṇas by Śūdra women, Bhūrjakaṇṭakas, sons of Brāhmaṇas by Vaiśya women, and Mūrdhāvasiktas, by Kṣatriya women, should have a measure equal to a half of the sum of the measures fixed for the two classes of parents. It is inauspicious for all people to have houses which either exceed or fall short of the fixed measurements.

[The dimensions of a *Pāraśava's* house is equal to $32+20 \div 2=$ 26 cubits; of a Bhūrjakaṇṭaka's $32+24 \div 2=28$ cubits; of a Mūrdhāvasikta's $32+28 \div 2=30$ cubits.

I have taken Utpala's explanation of Bhūrjakaṇṭaka, but according to Manu (X. 21) it is the offspring of a fallen Brāhmaṇa by a woman of the same class,

"व्रात्यात्तु जायते विप्रात्पापात्मा भूर्जकण्टकः ।"]

पश्वाश्रमिणाममितं धान्यायुधवह्निरतिगृहाणां च ।
नेच्छन्ति शास्त्रकारा हस्तशतादुच्छ्रितं परतः ॥१६॥

There is no fixed measurement for the houses of cattle and ascetics as well as for granaries, arsenals, houses of sacred fire and pleasure-houses. However, the authorities on this subject do not approve a height of more than 100 cubits.

[This is an exception to the rule given in verse 11.

Cf. गर्ग—

शतहस्तोच्छ्रितं कार्यं चतुःशालगृहं बुधैः ।
अपि तत्त्वेकशालं तु शुभदं तत्प्रकीर्तितम् ॥]

सेनापतिनृपतीनां सप्ततिसहिते द्विधाकृते व्यासे ।
शाला चतुर्दशहृते पञ्चत्रिंशद्धृतेऽलिन्दः ॥१७॥

Add 70 to the measure for the houses of the king and commander of the army; keep this sum in two places, and divide the one by 14 and the other by 35. The quotients give the measure for the hall and verandah respectively in each case.

[Let us take the best type of king's house whose breadth is 108. Add 70 to this and divide it by 14: $108+70\div14=12\frac{5}{7}$ cubits. This is the measure of the hall. Again divide 108+70 by 35: We get $5\frac{3}{35}$ cubits for the verandah. In the case of the commander's house these are $9\frac{4}{7}$ cubits and $3\frac{29}{35}$ cubits respectively.]

हस्तद्वात्रिंशादिषु चतुश्चतुस्त्रिस्त्रिकत्रिकाः शालाः ।
सप्तदशत्रितयतिथित्रयोदशकृताङ्गुलाभ्यधिकाः ॥१८॥
त्रित्रिद्विद्विद्विसमाः क्षयक्रमादङ्गुलानि चैतेषाम् ।
व्येका विंशतिरष्टौ विंशतिरष्टादश त्रितयम् ॥१९॥

In the houses of Brāhmaṇas and others, measuring from 32 cubits downwards, the halls should have a breadth of 4 cubits 17 digits, 4 cubits 3 digits, 3 cubits 15 digits, 3 cubits 13 digits, and 3 cubits 4 digits respectively. The verandahs of these are in order 3 cubits 19 digits, 3 cubits 8 digits, 2 cubits 20 digits, 2 cubits 18 digits and 2 cubits 3 digits, where the measures gradually decrease.

[In the third line व्यतिक्रमाद् is another reading for क्षयक्रमाद्. The commentator refers to अन्ये, other commentators, who interpret क्षयक्रम as reduction of the digits from the cubits given here. In that case instead of 3c. 19d for the verandah, we would have 2c 5d. This interpretation is rejected on the authority of aged architects.

When the measures of halls and verandahs are given in the case of Brāhmaṇa houses, those for the other classes can be easily got from the second, third and fourth places.]

शालात्रिभागतुल्या कर्तव्या वीथिका बहिर्भवनात् ।
यद्यग्रतो भवति सा सोष्णीषं नाम तद्वास्तु ॥२०॥
सायाश्रयमिति पश्चात् सावष्टम्भं तु पार्श्वसंस्थितया ।
सुस्थितमिति च समन्ताच्छास्त्रज्ञैः पूजिताः सर्वाः ॥२१॥

Outside the house there should be made a foot-path whose breadth must be a third of that of the hall. If the path is in front of the house, the latter is termed "*Soṣṇīṣa*"—one with a turban; if it is behind the house, it is called "*Sāyāśraya*"—Evening Resort; if it is on the two sides, it is designated as "*Sāvaṣṭambha*"—Properly Supported; and if it is laid on all four sides, it is named "*Susthita*"—well-placed. All these types are approved by the authorities on architecture.

[Cf. the किरणाख्यतन्त्र—

य: शालायास्तृतीयांशस्तेन कार्या तु वीथिका ।
यद्यग्रतो भवेद्वीथी सोष्णीषं नाम तद् गृहम् ॥
पश्चात्सायाश्रयं नाम सावष्टम्भं तु पार्श्वयो: ।
समन्ताद्यदि जाता सा तदा सुस्थितमुच्यते ॥]

विस्तारषोडशांश: सचतुर्हस्तो भवेद्गृहोच्छ्राय: ।
द्वादशभागेनोनो भूमौ भूमौ समस्तानाम् ॥२२॥

The height of the first floor (storey) should be a sixteenth of the width increased by four cubits. The height of each of the following upper storeys should be reduced by one-twelfth of the preceding one.

[The height of the first floor of the king's biggest house is $\frac{108}{16}+4=10$ cubits 18 digits. That of the next storey is

$$10-\frac{10c-18d}{12}=9 \text{ cubits } 20\tfrac{1}{2} \text{ digits.}]$$

व्यासात् षोडशभाग: सर्वेषां सद्मनां भवति भित्ति: ।
पक्वेष्टकाकृतानां दारुकृतानां तु न विकल्प: ॥२३॥

The wall of all houses made of burnt bricks should be a sixteenth part of their breadth. There is no restriction regarding the houses made of wood.

[According to this rule, a king's house whose width is 108 cubits, should have walls of 6 cubits 18 digits. In respect of wooden houses there is absolutely no restriction of length, breadth and height.

Cf. गर्ग—

विस्तारषोडशांशेन गृहभित्तिं प्रकल्पयेत् ।
हीनाधिका न कर्तव्या गृहभर्तुर्न शोभना ॥

Also the किरणाख्यतन्त्र—

पक्वेष्टानामयं व्यासो दारुजानां यथेच्छया ।
द्विजाद्येव गृहं कार्यं तत् स्याच्छुभ्रं स्वदिग्गतम् ॥
नवत्रयोदशाद्यैश्च करैर्ज्ञात्वा प्रकल्पयेत् ॥]

एकादशभागयुतः ससप्ततिर्नृपबलेशयोर्व्यासः ।
उच्छ्रायोऽङ्गुलतुल्यो द्वारस्यार्धेन विष्कम्भः ॥२४॥

The breadth of the houses of kings, commanders (and others except the four classes) should be increased by an eleventh part and 70 added to it. This number will give the height of the doors in digits. Their width would be half of their height.

[Applying this rule to the width of the king's house we get $108+\frac{108}{11}+70=187\frac{6}{11}$ digits or 188 digits in round number. This is the height of the door. Half of this i.e. 94 digits, would be its width. Here Utpala commits a small error : Instead of saying : चतुर्णवत्यङ्गुलानि विस्तारः he says नवनवत्यङ्गुलानि...]

विप्रादीनां व्यासात् पञ्चांशोऽष्टादशाङ्गुलसमेतः ।
साष्टांशो विष्कम्भो द्वारस्य त्रिगुण उच्छ्रायः ॥२५॥

In the case of the houses of Brāhmaṇas and other classes the number denoting the breadth in cubits should be divided by 5 and the quotient taken as so many digits. This should be increased by 18. To this should be added an eighth part of itself. That will give the width of the door; and thrice that number will be its height in digits.

[Taking 32 cubits, the width of a Brāhmaṇa's house, we divide it by 5 and get 6 as the quotient. This number is to be taken as 6 digits. Now add 18 to it. We get 24. By increasing this by its own eighth part we get $24+3=27$ digits Tnis is the width of the door. Thrice this will be its height i.e. $27\times3=81$ digits.]

उच्छ्रायहस्तसंख्यापरिमाणान्यङ्गुलानि बाहुल्यम् ।
शाखाद्वयेऽपि कार्यं सार्धं तत् स्यादुदुम्बरयोः ॥२६॥

उच्छ्रायात्सप्तगुणादशीतिभागः पृथुत्वमेतेषाम् ।
नवगुणितेऽशीत्यंशः स्तम्भस्य दशांशहीनोऽग्रे ॥२७॥

The thickness of the two side-frames of the door is as many digits as the number of cubits in its height. One and a half times this gives the thickness of the threshold and the upperblock. The breadth of all the four pieces is an eightieth part of seven times the door-height. An eightieth part of nine times the height (of) gives the width of a pillar at the bottom, and the same reduced by a tenth is its width at the top.

[Here we find two technical terms, शाखा and उदुम्बर. The former is the side-frame and the latter consists of देहली and निटाल, the lower and upper blocks respectively.

We have seen that the height of the door in the king's house is 188 digits, which comes to 8 cubits approximately. So the thickness of the frame would be 8 digits, and that of the threshold and the upper-block, 12 digits. Now $\frac{188 \times 7}{80} = 16\frac{9}{20}$ digits. Hence 16·5 digits would be the breadth of all the four pieces. A pillar on the ground floor of the above house will have a width at the bottom $= \frac{10c.18d. \times 9}{80} = 29$ digits; and its width at the top $= 29 - \frac{29}{10} =$ 26·1 or 26 digits. Its circumference is thrice its width (24 digits make one cubit).]

समचतुरस्रो रुचको वज्रोऽष्टाश्रिर्द्विवज्रको द्विगुणः ।
द्वात्रिंशता तु मध्ये प्रलीनको वृत्त इति वृत्तः ॥२८॥

A pillar that is perfectly square in the middle (barring the two ends) is termed *Rucaka*; one that is octagonal, a *Vajra* or Diamond; one with sixteen sides, a double diamond; one with 32 sides, *Pralīnaka*; and a round is named *Vṛtta* or cylindrical.

[Thus five types of pillars are mentioned here : *Rucaka*, *Vajra*, *Dvivajra*, *Pralīnaka* and *Vṛtta*. All these are said to be auspicious. These names are based on the shape of the middle portion. For, the lower and upper parts will have different *motifs*.

Cf. किरणाख्यतन्त्र—

वेदास्रो रुचकः स्तम्भो वज्राष्टास्रियुतो मतः ।
द्विवज्रः षोडशास्रिः स्याद् द्विगुणास्रिः प्रलीनकः ॥
समन्तवृत्तो वृत्ताख्यः स्तम्भः प्रोक्तो द्विजोत्तमैः ॥]

स्तम्भं विभज्य नवधा वहनं भागो घटोऽस्य भागोऽन्यः ।
पद्मं तथोत्तरोष्ठं कुर्याद् भागेन भागेन ॥२९॥

When the whole pillar is divided into nine equal parts, the first two will belong to the bottom and the last two to the top. They are called *Vahana* or *Support*, *Ghaṭa* or *Pot*, *Padma* or *Lotus*, and *Uttaroṣṭha* or *Upper lip*. Designs and artistic *motifs* can be carved in these parts.

[Utpala says : "उत्तरोष्ठो यत्र शोभार्थं रूपकविशेषाः क्रियन्ते ।" The names *Ghaṭa* and *Padma* are used here because they are actually shaped like them. The commentator refers to some other opinion which makes *Uttaroṣṭha*, the eighth part and *Padma*, the ninth.

Cf. the किरणाख्यतन्त्र—

विभज्य नवधा स्तम्भं कुर्यादुद्वहनं घटम् ।
कमलं चोत्तरोष्ठं तु भागे भागे प्रकल्पयेत् ॥]

स्तम्भसमं बाहुल्यं भारतुलानामुपर्युपर्यासाम् ।
भवति तुलोपतुलानामूनं पादेन पादेन ॥३०॥

The thickness of the main architrave is equal to that of the pillar; above this there are beams and minor beams, whose thickness is three-fourths of that of its immediately preceding one.

[We have seen that a pillar on the ground floor of a king's house has a width of 29 digits at the bottom. This will be the thickness of the main architrave. The thickness of the beam and minor beam would be $29 \times \frac{3}{4}$ digits and $29 \times \frac{3}{4} \times \frac{3}{4}$ digits respectively. The commentator says first :

"भारतुलाया उपरि यदन्यत् काष्ठं दीयते तत्तुलोपतुलासंज्ञम् ।"

Then he adds

"वीप्साकरणात् केचिच्चतस्र इति वर्धयन्ति । भारतुला उपतुला तुलोपतुला चेति ॥"

I feel, however, that they must be तुला and उपतुला.]

अप्रतिषिद्धालिन्दं समन्ततो वास्तु सर्वतोभद्रम् ।
नृपविबुधसमूहानां कार्यं द्वारैश्चतुर्भिरपि ॥३१॥

A house with an unbroken (unrestricted ?) verandah all round is called *Sarvatobhadra* (All-auspicious). This type of house with four doors is beneficial for kings and Gods.

[The four doors are to be in the four directions. What is the special significance of 'अप्रतिषिद्धं?' Does it mean that there is no restriction about its measurements ?

Cf. गर्ग—

अलिन्दानां व्यवच्छेदो नास्ति यत्र समन्ततः ।
तद्वास्तु सर्वतोभद्रं चतुर्द्वारसमायुतम् ॥]

नन्द्यावर्तमलिन्दैः शालाकुड्यात् प्रदक्षिणान्तगतैः ।
द्वारं पश्चिममस्मिन् विहाय शेषाणि कार्याणि ॥३२॥

A house which has verandahs starting from the walls of the halls and going to their respective extremities from left to right is termed *Nandyāvarta*, which should have only three doors leaving off the western one.

[Cf. गर्ग—

प्रदक्षिणां गतैः सर्वैः शालाभित्तेरलिन्दकैः ।
विनापरेण द्वारेण नन्द्यावर्तमिति स्मृतम् ॥]

द्वारालिन्दोऽन्तगतः प्रदक्षिणोऽन्यः शुभस्ततश्चान्यः ।
तस्मिंश्च वर्धमाने द्वारं तु न दक्षिणं कार्यम् ॥३३॥

The front verandah of the main building should extend from the left hall to the right hall. Another verandah is made from there from left to right, and still another beautiful one from there in the same manner. A building with such verandahs is known as *Vardhamāna*, which should not have an entrance in the south.

[Cf. गर्ग—

द्वारालिन्दोऽन्तगस्तेषां ये त्रयो दक्षिणां गताः ।
विहाय दक्षिणं द्वारं वर्धमानमिति स्मृतम् ॥]

अपरोऽन्तगतोऽलिन्दः प्रागन्तगतौ तदुत्थितौ चान्यौ ।
तदवधिविधृतश्चान्यः प्राग्द्वारं स्वस्तिके शुभदम् ॥३४॥

In the *Svastika* type of mansion the western verandah should extend from the left hall to the right one; the other two verandahs (southern and northern) originating from the western verandah should touch the ends in the east, and the fourth one (i.e. eastern one) is held between their bounds. Such a mansion with only an eastern entrance is beneficial.

[Cf. गर्ग—

पश्चिमोऽन्तगतोऽलिन्दः प्रागन्तौ द्वौ तदुत्थितौ ।
अन्यस्तन्मध्यविधृतः प्राग्द्वारं स्वस्तिकं शुभम् ॥]

प्राक्पश्चिमावलिन्दावन्तगतौ तदवधिस्थितौ शेषौ ।
रुचके द्वारं न शुभदमुत्तरतोऽन्यानि शस्तानि ॥३५॥

In the building known as *Rucaka* the eastern and western verandahs touch the ends in the south and north; and touching these two internally there are two more. In this building an entrance in the north is not auspicious, while in the other quarters they are good.

[Cf. गर्ग—

प्राक्पश्चिमावलिन्दौ यावन्तगौ तद्भवौ परौ ।
सौम्यं द्वारं विना यत्स्याद् रुचकाख्यं तु तत्स्मृतम् ॥]

श्रेष्ठं नन्द्यावर्तं सर्वेषां वर्धमानसं च ।
स्वस्तिकरुचके मध्ये शेषं शुभदं नृपादीनाम् ॥३६॥

The *Nandyāvarta* and *Vardhamāna* types of houses are the best for the people of all classes (i.e. Brāhmaṇas etc.); *Svastika* and *Rucaka* are moderate, and the last one viz. *Sarvatobhadra*, is beneficial for kings, ministers etc.

[Utpala gives the plans of these five types of houses which are shown below :

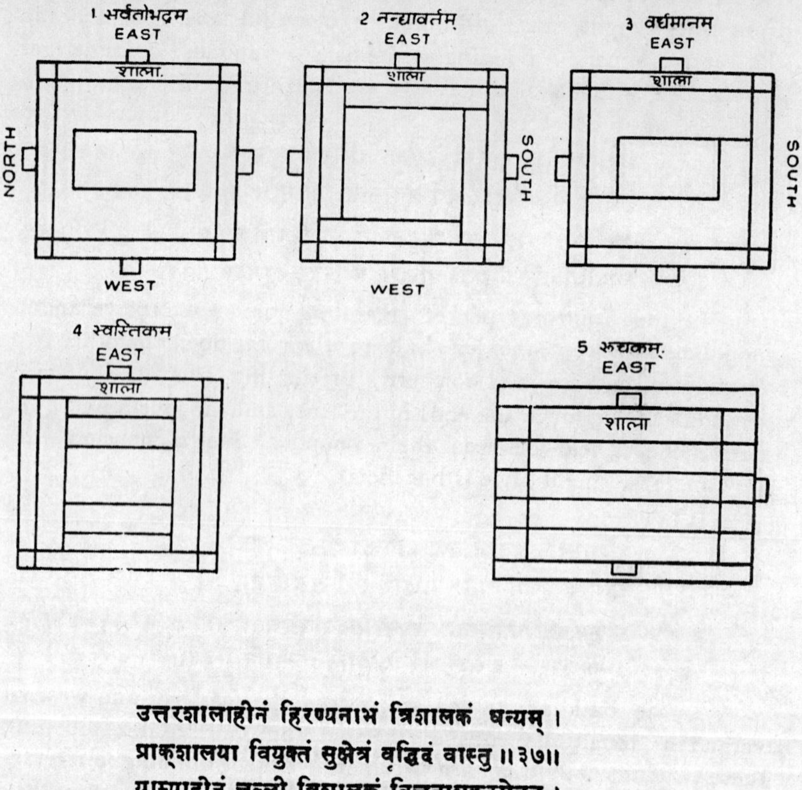

उत्तरशालाहीनं हिरण्यनाभं त्रिशालकं धन्यम् ।
प्राक्शालया वियुक्तं सुक्षेत्रं वृद्धिदं वास्तु ॥३७॥
याम्याहीनं चुल्ली त्रिशालकं वित्तनाशकरमेतत् ।
पक्षघ्नमपरया वर्जितं सुतध्वंसवैरकरम् ॥३८॥

A three-halled house, where the northern hall is absent, is named *Hiraṇyanābha* and fortunate. Similarly, *Sukṣetra* is one where the eastern hall is absent and leads to prosperity. One without the southern hall is designated as *Cullī*, which leads to loss of wealth. Lastly a house devoid of the western hall is named *Pakṣaghna* and is destructive to children, and the cause of hatred.

[Cf. the किरणाख्यतन्त्र—

शस्तं हिरण्यनाभाख्यं हीनं चोत्तरशालया ।
सुक्षेत्र पूर्वतो हीनं शालया वृद्धिदं मतम् ॥
चुल्ली दक्षिणया हीनं धनार्थप्राणनाशनम् ।
यत् स्यादपरया हीनं पक्षघ्नं तत् सुतान्तकृत् ॥

By suitable adjustment of the lines in the first four types of houses we can get these three-halled houses.]

In the following verses the author describes six types of two-halled houses.

सिद्धार्थमपरयाम्ये यमसूर्यं पश्चिमोत्तरे शाले ।
दण्डाख्यमुदक्पूर्वे वाताख्यं प्राग्युता याम्या ॥३९॥
पूर्वापरे तु शाले गृहचुल्ली दक्षिणोत्तरे काचम् ।
सिद्धार्थेऽर्थावाप्तिर्यमसूर्ये गृहपतेर्मृत्युः ॥४०॥
दण्डवधो दण्डाख्ये कलहोद्वेगः सदैव वाताख्ये ।
वित्तविनाशश्चुल्ल्यां ज्ञातिविरोधः स्मृतः काचे ॥४२॥

A two-halled house with only the western and southern halls is known as *Siddhārtha*; one with the western and northern halls *Yamasūrya*; one with the northern and eastern halls, *Daṇḍa*; one with the eastern and southern halls, *Vāta*; one with the eastern and western ones, *Gṛha-cullī* (or Cullī); and one with the southern and northern ones, *Kāca*. The first type of house leads to acquisition of wealth; the second, to the owner's death; the third, to death by being beaten with clubs (or, to punishment and death); the fourth, to constant grief from strife; the fifth, to loss of money; and the sixth, to enmity with kinsmen.

[Instead of दण्डवधो in 41 दण्डवधौ is another reading.

Cf. the किरणाख्यतन्त्र—

सिद्धार्थं तु भवेच्छुभ्रं याम्यापरयुतं यदि ।
पश्चिमोत्तरसंयुक्तं यमसूर्यं तु मृत्युदम् ॥
उदक्पूर्वयुतं यत् स्याद् दण्डाख्यं दण्डकारकम् ।
पूर्वयाम्ययुतं ज्ञेयं वाताख्यं कलहप्रियम् ॥
पूर्वापरयुतं गेहं चुल्लीनामार्थनाशकृत् ।
दक्षिणोत्तरशालाढ्यं काचसंज्ञं विरोधकृत् ॥]

Here the commentator commends the author's exceptional success in summarizing briefly the views of ancient authors like Viśvakarman, Maya and Kāma, who have explained the construction of each type of house in very great detail. For, look at the statement of *Hiraṇyagarbha* about the existence of 64 types or 120 varieties of the houses :

गृहाणां क्रमयोगेन चतुःषष्टिः समासतः ।
अनेकयोगभेदाच्च शतं विंशोत्तरं स्मृतम् ॥

But विश्वकर्मा speaks of 256 varieties of buildings.

एवं शतद्वयं पिण्डं षट्पञ्चाशच्च वेश्मनाम् ।
यथावत् कृत्यजः कृत्स्न उक्तशास्त्रेऽपि यत्नतः ॥

Here Utpala refers to some scholars, who have not rightly understood the meaning of this science of architecture, and thereby cast aspersions on the author's contradictory statements in verses 11 and 16 about the breadth and height of houses, viz. "It is auspicious to have the height of a building equal to its breadth," and "The authorities do not approve of the height to be more than 100 cubits." [The contradiction here is that the king's first house has a width of 108 cubits. If its height were to be 108 cubits, it would be violating the rule of maximum height.] These half-baked scholars, he continues, explain away this difficulty by referring to one as the general rule and to the other as the exception. In fact there is neither in this case. For, in verse 22 our author has given the height of the first floor as 10 cubits 18 digits and of the next floor (storey) as the above reduced by a twelfth.

Viśvakarman has laid down that mighty emperors could have a mansion of 7½ storeys; Brāhmaṇas, 6½; Kṣatriyas 5½; Vaiśyas 4½; and Śūdras 3½ storeys :

यजन्ते राजसूयाद्यैः क्रतुभिर्येऽवनीश्वराः ।
तलैरर्धाष्टमैस्तेषां कारयेद् भवनोत्तमम् ॥
तथार्धसप्तमैरेव विप्राणां कारयेद् गृहम् ।
अर्धषष्ठैः क्षत्रियाणां वैश्यानामर्धपञ्चमैः ॥
त्रिभिः सार्धैश्च शूद्राणां भवनं शुभदं स्मृतम् ॥

The same authority speaks of three kinds of cubits viz., ज्येष्ठ or प्राशय major, मध्यम or साधारण medium, and कनिष्ठ or शम minor :

यवा मध्यान्विता अष्टावङ्गुलं ज्येष्ठमुच्यते ।
सप्त मध्यमसंख्यानामङ्गुलं षट् कनीयसाम् ॥

According to Utpala the minor cubit is adopted by Varāhamihira. Viśvakarman wants the *medium* cubit to be employed in the matter of height of buildings :

साधारणेन हस्तेन परं शूद्रस्य विंशतिः ।
चत्वारिंशच्च वैश्यस्य षष्टिः स्यात् क्षत्रियस्य तु ॥

ब्राह्मणस्य तथाशीतिः शतं च नृपतेः स्मृतम् ।
नातः परतरं नृणामूर्ध्वमानं विधीयते ॥
गन्धर्वसिद्धयक्षाणां धर्मतः समुदाहृतम् ॥

The three kinds of cubits mentioned above represent in order the length of 192, 168 and 144 full-grown barley grains. So 100 *medium* cubits would be equal to 87½ *major* cubits. The total height of the 7½ storeys of a king's house would be 61c. 21d. Here Utpala commits a mistake, because he says the total height is 62·5 cubits.

Viśvakarman lays down that the height of the foundations of best houses should be 2½ cubits. There is restriction regarding the height of the storeys of buildings only with two, three and four halls. In a house of a single hall, the height is equal to its breadth. For, says *Śakra* :—

एकशालं यथाकामं विस्तारं कारयेद् गृहम् ।
गृहमायामहीनं तत्त्वेकशालं प्रचक्षते ॥
गृहविस्तारमाधिक्यं प्राहोत्सर्गस्तु गौतमः ।

According to this the breadth should not exceed the length in a single-halled house. However, should it exceed the length, such houses would be called *Utsargas*, according to *Gautama*. Single-halled houses are not constructed for Brāhmaṇas etc. Such houses are not conducive to longevity, but, if made of straw, they are good.

See what गर्ग says :

अनाजीवकरं सर्वमेकशालमुदाहृतम् ।
अपि शाला तृणमयी कार्या तस्य शुभप्रदा ॥

Viśvakarman (in the वास्तुविश्वकर्मप्रकाश) employs the three kinds of cubits for different constructions :

ग्रामखेटपुरादीनां विभागायामविस्तरान् ।
परिखाद्वाररथ्याश्च स्तम्भान् प्रासादवेश्मनाम् ॥
तेषां निर्गममार्गं च सीमाक्षेत्रान्तराणि च ।
देशान्तरविभागांश्च वासोपवनयोस्तथा ॥
अध्वनः परिमाणं च क्रोशगव्यूतियोजनैः ।
खातक्रकचराशींश्च प्रशयेन प्रमापयेत् ॥
शयनाशनयानानि कर्मदण्डायुधं तथा ।
वापीकूपप्रमाणानि तथा नृगजवाजिनाम् ॥
इक्षुयन्त्रारघट्टांश्च हलयूपयुगध्वजान् ।
आतोया (द्या ?) नि च नावश्च शिल्पिनां चाप्युपस्करान् ॥

पादुके च वृषीं छत्रं चर्मोपकरणानि च ।
मात्रा शमेन हस्तेन नल्वदण्डांश्च मापयेत् ॥

In support of the statement that Varāhamihira uses only the शम or *minor* cubit, the commentator refers to the reading शम or शय in verse 19—'त्रित्रिद्विद्विशमाः'.

In verse 23 the author says that the thickness of the wall should be equal to a sixteenth part of the width of the house, provided it is made of burnt bricks. The mixing together of raw and burnt bricks as well as of new and old ones in the construction of houses is forbidden as shown below :

न नवं पुराणयुक्तं न पक्वमामेन चैव संयोज्यम् ।
अन्यत्र स्खलितशिलाविशीर्णमच्छिन्नसंस्कारात् ॥
(तन्त्रान्तरे)

Hiranyagarbha, however, permits the mixing as follows :—

आमेष्टकास्त्वधश्चेयाः पक्वाश्च चिनुयात्ततः ।
पक्वाश्रिता ह्यधश्चेया यथेष्टमुपरीष्टकाः ॥

The same authority speaks of eight kinds of buildings according to the material used in their construction :

गृहं तु विविधं प्रोक्तं शरीरैस्तु पृथग्विधैः ।
पाषाणैर्निचितं यच्च तद्गृहं मन्दिरं स्मृतम् ॥
पक्वेष्टकं वास्तुनाम भवनं हितमुत्तमम् ।
आमेष्टकं सुमन्तं तु सुधारं कर्दमेन तु ॥
मानस्यं वर्धितं काष्ठैर्वेणुभिर्नन्दनं स्मृतम् ।
वस्त्रैश्च विजयं प्रोक्तं राज्ञां शिल्पिविकल्पितम् ॥
कालिमेति च विज्ञेयमष्टमं तृणजातिभिः ।
उत्तमानि तु चत्वारि गृहाणि गृहमेधिनाम् ॥
सौवर्णं राजतं ताम्रमायसं च प्रकीर्तितम् ।
सौवर्णं पुष्करं नाम राजतं श्रीभवं तथा ॥
ताम्रेण सूर्यमन्तं तु चण्डनाम तथाऽयसम् ॥
देवदानवगन्धर्वयक्षराक्षसकिन्नरैः ।
द्वादशैते प्रकारास्तु गृहाणां नियताः स्मृताः ॥
जातुषं त्वानिलं नाम त्रापुषं वारिबन्धकम् ।
एवञ्जातिषु सर्वासु गृहाणि तु चतुर्दश ॥

But *Maya* rejects these categories and accepts only five :

कटिमं ग्रन्थिमं चैव दायिमं रिपिमं तथा ।
खातिमं च पुरं ख्यातं क्रियाः पञ्चविधा गृहे ॥

The commentator adds :

"सर्व एव विकल्पाः पक्वेष्टकाकृतानां क्रियन्ते, नान्येषाम्। दारुकृतादीनां तु पुनर्देवतानिवेशभोजनदेवागारमहानसादिनिवेशमात्रमेव क्रियते, नान्यदिति। तथा च तन्त्रान्तरे पठ्यते—

तत्र च विसस्यभूमेः परीक्षणं देवतानिवेशश्च ।
तलकोच्छ्रायः कार्यो विधानतो वास्तुपुरुषस्य ॥
शेषाणामपि च तथैव सन्निविष्टक्रिया समुद्दिष्टा ।
भोजनशालासंस्थानलक्षणं चैषु सामान्यम् ॥
नैषां नियमस्तलकोच्छ्रयेषु नायामविस्तरार्थेषु ।
न द्वारेषु न दारुषु न पालिनाडीविभागेषु ॥]

एकाशीतिविभागे दश दश पूर्वोत्तरायता रेखाः ।
अन्तस्त्रयोदश सुरा द्वात्रिंशद्बाह्यकोष्ठस्थाः ॥४२॥

In order to divide the ground-plan of a house into 81 squares draw ten lines from east to west and ten others from north to south. Inside the diagram, thirteen deities are situated, and thirty-two in the outer compartments. Thus, there are 45 deities in this figure. (See diagram 1 under 48 *infra*).

शिखिपर्जन्यजयन्तेन्द्रसूर्यसत्या भृशोऽन्तरिक्षश्च ।
ऐशान्यादिक्रमशो दक्षिणपूर्वेऽनिलः कोणे ॥४३॥
पूषा वितथबृहत्क्षतयमगन्धर्वाख्यभृङ्गराजमृगाः ।
पितृदौवारिकसुग्रीवकुसुमदन्ताम्बुपत्यसुराः ॥४४॥
शेषोऽथ पापयक्ष्मा रोगः कोणे ततोऽहिमुख्यौ च ।
भल्लाटसोमभुजगास्ततोऽदितिर्दितिरिति क्रमशः ॥४५॥

The nine deities situated in the outer compartments beginning with the one at the north-eastern corner and ending with the south-eastern are : Śikhin, Parjanya, Jayanta, Indra, Sūrya, Satya, Bhṛśa, Antarikṣa and Anila (or Anala). Then follow in order Pūṣan, Vitatha, Bṛhatkṣata, Yama, Gandharva, Bhṛṅgarāja, Mṛga and Pitṛ on the south to the south-western corner. Then come regularly in the west Dauvārika, Sugrīva, Kusumadanta, Varuṇa, Asura, Śoṣa, Pāpayakṣman and Roga ending in the north-western corner. Thereafter there are Ahi, Mukhya, Bhallāṭa, Soma, Bhujaga, Aditi and Diti in the north in regular order, the total number being 32.

[Instead of शिखि, अनिल and बृहत्क्षत, शिख, अनल and बृहत्क्षति are the respective variant readings.]

मध्ये ब्रह्मा नवकोष्ठकाधिपोऽस्यार्यमा स्थितः प्राच्याम् ।
एकान्तरात् प्रदक्षिणमस्मात्सविता विवस्वांश्च ॥४६॥
विबुधाधिपतिस्तस्मान्मित्रोऽन्यो राजयक्ष्मनामा च ।
पृथिवीधरापवत्सावित्येते ब्रह्मणः परिधौ ॥४७॥
आपो नामैशाने कोणे हौताशने च सावित्रः ।
जय इति च नैर्ऋते रुद्र आनिलेऽस्यन्तरपदेषु ॥४८॥

Diagram 1 (with 81 squares)

N.E. EAST S.E.

NORTH (left) — SOUTH (right)

शिखी	पर्जन्यः	जयन्तः	इन्द्रः	सूर्यः	सत्यः	भृशः	अन्त-रिक्षः	अनिलः
दितिः	आपः	जयन्तः	इन्द्रः	सूर्यः	सत्यः	भृशः	सावित्रः	पूषा
अदितिः	अदितिः	आप-वत्सः	अर्यमा	अर्यमा	अर्यमा	सविता	वितथः	वितथः
भुजगः	भुजगः	पृथिवी-धरः	ब्रह्मा	ब्रह्मा	ब्रह्मा	विव-स्वान्	बृह-त्क्षतः	बृह-त्क्षतः
सोमः	सोमः	पृथिवी-धरः	ब्रह्मा	ब्रह्मा	ब्रह्मा	विव-स्वान्	यमः	यमः
भल्लाटः	भल्लाटः	पृथिवी-धरः	ब्रह्मा	ब्रह्मा	ब्रह्मा	विव-स्वान्	गन्धर्वः	गन्धर्वः
मुख्यः	मुख्यः	राज-यक्ष्मा	मित्रः	मित्रः	मित्रः	इन्द्रः	भृङ्ग-राज	भृङ्ग-राजः
अहिः	रुद्रः	शोषः	असुरः	वरुणः	कुसुम-दन्तः	सुग्रीवः	जयः	मृगः
रोगः	पाप-यक्ष्मा	शोषः	असुरः	वरुणः	कुसुम-दन्तः	सुग्रीवः	दौवा-रिकः	पिता

N.W. WEST S.W.

In the centre of the diagram Brahman occupies nine compartments; to his east there is Aryaman (in three squares); next to the right of Aryaman there is Savitṛ in a single square at an interval of one division; next to him to the right is Vivasvat; next to him is Indra; then going up to the west of Brahman there are Mitra (in 3 divisions) and Rājayakṣman; then turning to the east, there are Pṛthvīdhara (in 3) and Āpavatsa. In this manner these eight deities are situated on the circumference around Brahman. In the internal north-eastern corner (behind Parjanya), there is Āpaḥ; in the south-eastern corner (between Savitṛ and Anila), Sāvītra; in the south-western corner, Jaya; and in the north-western corner, Rudra.

आपस्तथापवत्सः पर्जन्योऽग्निर्दितिश्च वर्गोऽयम् ।
एवं कोणे कोणे पदिकाः स्युः पञ्च पञ्च सुराः ॥४६॥
बाह्या द्विपदाः शेषास्ते विबुधा विंशतिः समाख्याताः ।
शेषाश्चत्वारोऽन्ये त्रिपदा दिक्ष्वर्यमाद्यास्ताः ॥५०॥

One group consisting of five deities that own one division each viz. Āpaḥ, Āpavatsa, Parjanya, Agni (Śikhin) and Diti, is situated in the north-eastern corner. In the same manner there are five deities in each of the remaining three corners viz., south-east, south-west and north-west. The remaining deities in the outer compartments, 20 in number, own two squares each. The remaining 4 deities headed by Aryaman preside over three squares each (beginning with the east of Brahman).

[In diagram 1 there are altogether 81 squares or compartments owned by 45 deities : In the four outer corners there are $5 \times 4 = 20$ deities having 20 squares i.e. one square each. Then there are 20 deities (5×4) in the four outer quarters, each owning two compartments, which comes to 40 compartments. Then there are four deities in the four inner quarters having three divisions each i.e. 12 divisions. Lastly, *Brahman* who is in the centre of the site, owns or occupies 9 squares.

(i) *Deities ruling over single compartments* :

Śikhin, Parjanya, Diti, Āpaḥ and Āpavatsa; Antarikṣa, Anila Pūṣan, Sāvitra; and Savitā, Mṛga, Pitṛ, Dauvārika, Jaya and Indra; and Pāpayakṣman, Roga, Ahi (serpent), Rudra and Rājayakṣman.

(ii) *Those ruling over two squares* :

Jayanta, Indra, Sūrya, Satya and Bhṛśa; Vitatha, Bṛhatkṣata, Yama, Gandharva and Bhṛṅgarāja; Sugrīva, Kusumadanta, Varuṇa,

Asura and Śoṣa; and Mukhya, Bhallāṭa, Soma, Bhujaga and Aditi.

(iii) *Those ruling over three squares each* :

Aryaman, Vivasvat, Mitra and Pṛthivīdhara.

(iv) Only *one* viz., Brahman holds sway over 9 squares.

Cf. पराशर—

तत्र बहिर्देवताः प्राक्पर्जन्यकरग्रहमहेन्द्ररविसत्यभृशान्तरिक्षपवनाः । दक्षिणतः पूषावितथबृहत्क्षतयमभृङ्गगन्धर्वमृगपितरश्चेति । पश्चिमतो दौवारिकसुग्रीवपुष्पदन्तासुरवारुणयक्षरोगशोषाश्चेति । उदङ्नागराजमुख्यभल्लाटसोमादितिकुबेरनागहुतवहाः । तन्मध्ये ब्रह्मा तत्पुरतोऽर्यमा दक्षिणतो विवस्वान् मित्रः प्रत्युदक् पृथ्वीधर इति । ब्राह्मपदानुषङ्गिणोऽष्टावन्ये । आपापवत्सावैशान्यां सावित्रसवितारावेवाग्नेय्यां जयेन्द्रौ नैर्ऋत्यां रुद्रवायू वायव्यामिति सर्वदेवताः पञ्चचत्वारिंशदिति । तथान्यैः सहैतेषां पदानामसादृश्यम् ॥

Then the commentator quotes the following from some unknown text :

रुद्रा हुताशनश्चैव पिता चानल एव च ।
एते कोणगता देवा एकाशीतिपदे स्थिताः ॥
चतुःषष्टिपदेऽप्येवं पापयक्ष्मात्र न स्थितः ।
एभ्योऽन्ये सदृशा ज्ञेयाः सुराः सर्वपदाश्रिताः ॥]

In the next four verses the author mentions the assignment of these deities to the different limbs of Vāstu-puruṣa (House-God) :

पूर्वोत्तरदिङ्मूर्धा पुरुषोऽयमवाङ्मुखोऽस्य शिरसि शिखी ।
आपो मुखे स्तनेऽस्यार्यमा ह्युरस्यापवत्सश्च ॥५१॥

पर्जन्याद्या बाह्या दृक्श्रवणोरःस्थलांसगा देवाः ।
सत्याद्याः पञ्च भुजे हस्ते सविता च सावित्रः ॥५२॥

वितथो बृहत्क्षतयुतः पार्श्वे जठरे स्थितो विवस्वांश्च ।
ऊरु जानु च जङ्घे स्फिगिति यमाद्यैः परिगृहीताः ॥५३॥

एते दक्षिणपार्श्वे स्थानेष्वेवं च वामपार्श्वस्थाः ।
मेढ्रे शक्रजयन्तौ हृदये ब्रह्मा पिताऽङ्घ्रिगतः ॥५४॥

This Vāstu-puruṣa (House-God) who lies prone on the site, has his head turned towards the north-east. Fire (Agni) is situated on his head; Water (Āpaḥ), on the face; Aryaman, on the breast; Āpavatsa, on the chest; Parjanya, on the eye; Jayanta, on the ear; Indra, on the chest (neck ?); and the Sun, on the shoulder (all these four belong to the outer divisions); the five headed by Satya (i.e.

Satya, Bhṛśa, Antarikṣa, Anila and Pūṣan), on the arm; Savitṛ and Sāvitra, on the hand; Vitatha and Bṛhatkṣata, on the side; Vivasvat, on the stomach; Yama, Gandharva, Bhṛṅgarāja and Mṛga, on the thigh, knee, shank and buttock respectively. The above deities are situated on the limbs of the right side of the Vāstu-puruṣa. Similarly, there are deities on the left side i.e. Pṛthivīdhara, on the left breast; Diti, on the left eye; Aditi, on the left ear; Bhujaga, on the left side of the chest (neck ?); Soma, on the left shoulder; Bhallāṭa, Mukhya, Ahi, Roga and Pāpayakṣman, on the left arm; Rudra and Rājayakṣman, on the left hand; Śoṣa and Asura, on the left side; Mitra, on the left side of the stomach; Varuṇa, on the left thigh; Kusumadanta, on the left knee; Sugrīva, on the left shank; Dauvārika (Door-keeper), on the left buttock; Śakra (Indra) and Jaya, on the genital organ; Brahman, on the heart; and Pitṛ, on the feet.

[In verse 53 ऊरुजानु and जङ्घा would have been better readings instead of ऊरु and जङ्घे. In this figure of the House-God there are nineteen limbs from head to foot, of which *chest* appears in three lists viz. Āpavatsa as mere chest, and then Indra as the right side of it, and Bhujaga as the left side of the chest. Only one deity viz. Pitṛ, is assigned to the feet. The commentator too has erred while allotting deities to the various limbs on the left side : The author has assigned *Vivasvat* to the right side of the stomach, but Utpala has forgotten to assign any deity to its left side. Actually Mitra should be assigned to the left side of stomach. I feel that the original reading in the last line must have been, मेढ्रे शक्रजयौ तौ instead of... जयन्तौ. Another doubt arises in mind as I count the limbs taken by the author i.e. he has not assigned any deity to the neck. So I make bold to suggest that the reading should be, दृक्श्रवणगलस्थलांसगा देवाः in verse 52, as उरःस्थल has been already dealt with. This kind of division of the ground into 81 squares should be resorted to while planning the construction of cities, villages and houses.]

अष्टाष्टकपदमथवा कृत्वा रेखाश्च कोणगास्तिर्यक् ।
ब्रह्मा चतुष्पदोऽस्मिन्नर्धपदा ब्रह्मकोणस्थाः ॥५५॥
अष्टौ च बहिष्कोणेष्वर्धपदास्तदुभयस्थिताः सार्धाः ।
उक्तेभ्यो ये शेषास्ते द्विपदा विंशतिस्ते हि ॥५६॥

Or, by drawing nine lines across and nine vertically we can get 64 squares. Here diagonals should be drawn from corner to corner. In this diagram, Brahman rules over four squares at the centre; and the eight deities situated along the diagonals in the corners near him rule over half a square i.e. Āpaḥ, Āpavatsa, Savitṛ, Sāvitra, Indra, Jaya, Rājayakṣman and Rudra; in the outer corners, Śikhin, Antarikṣa, Anila, Mṛga, Pitṛ, Pāpayakṣman, Roga and Diti, over half a square each; those that are on both sides of these, over one square and a half i.e. Parjanya, Bhṛśa, Pūṣan, Bhṛṅgarāja, Dauvārika, Śoṣa, Nāga (or Ahi), and Aditi; and the remaining twenty, over two squares each.

[Here too Utpala's commentary is sometimes confusing as he omits some names such as *Mṛga* from the second group, and *Pūṣan* and *Aditi* from the last group. Instead of Jaya he states Jayanta in a corner. While enumerating the 20 deities he omits *Sugrīva*. According to this scheme the House-God has 64 parts.

Utpala refers here to some scholars who hold this 64 square scheme to be the biggest one. In this it is probable that the doors are in the corners. Though the author mentions here only quadrangular sites, he speaks of circular, hexagonal, octagonal houses as well as those with ten and sixteen sides or angles, elsewhere (*vide LVI.* 20, 23, 28 *infra*). Sage *Bharata* too speaks of circular and triangular buildings. Then Utpala quotes the following from some other Śāstra :

एकाशीतिपदे क्षेत्रे कर्तव्यं वृत्तपञ्चकम् ।
बाह्ये वृत्तद्वयं यत्तत्पदद्वात्रिंशता युतम् ।।
तृतीयं द्वादशपदं चतुर्थं तु चतुष्पदम् ।
केवलं पञ्चमं कार्यं ब्रह्मा पञ्चस्ववस्थितः ।।
शिख्यादयस्तु द्विपदा बहिर्विष्कम्भसंस्थिताः ।
अर्यमाद्याः सुराः सर्वे पदिकाः परिकीर्तिताः ।।

For an explanation of this see diagram 3.

वृत्तानि चत्वारि समानि कृत्वा वास्तोश्चतुःषष्टिपदस्य सम्यक् ।
अधस्तदर्धेन च सूर्यवेदैर्विभज्यते वृत्तचतुष्टयं च ।।
शिख्यादयश्चैकपदे निविष्टाः पदद्वये चार्यमकादयश्च ।
आपादयश्च त्रिपदाः प्रतिष्ठाश्चतुष्पदश्चात्र पितामहः स्यात् ।।

See diagram 4. Regarding the triangular plan the following quotation gives the details :

त्र्यस्राणि पञ्च क्षेत्राणि त्रिकोणे परिकल्पयेत् ।
प्राची दिगष्टधा कार्या कोणवर्ज्या ततः परे ।।
रविभागविभक्ते ते वास्तुद्वाराणि तानि तु ।
दितिं वायुं जलपतिं कोणेषु त्रिषु विन्यसेत् ।।

ततः शिख्यादिकान्सर्वान् शेषेषु विनिवेशयेत् ।
द्वितीये पूर्ववद् भागाः षोडशद्विगुणास्ततः ॥
तत्रापि कोणत्रितय पूर्वोक्तान् विबुधान् न्यसेत् ।
शेषेषु वास्तुकोष्ठस्थान्सुरांश्च विनिवेशयेत् ॥
क्षेत्रे तृतीये चत्वारि सर्वशाखासु कारयेत् ।
प्राग्गतिर्यमसावित्री सविता च ततः परम् ॥
विवस्वानिन्द्रमित्रौ च जयश्चैव हरस्तथा ।
राजयक्ष्मा भूमिधर आपो वत्सयुतः स च ॥
चतुर्थे पञ्चभिर्भागैः कृत्वा तन्मध्यगस्तथा ।
पितामहो विनिर्दिष्टस्त्र्यस्रक्षेत्रेऽप्ययं विधिः ॥

See diagram 5 for explanation.]

सम्पाता वंशानां मध्यानि समानि यानि च पदानाम् ।
मर्माणि तानि विन्द्यान्न तानि परिपीडयेत्प्राज्ञः ॥५७॥

The meeting points of the longer diagonals and the exact middle points of the squares should be considered as *Vulnerable Points*, which a wise astrologer ought not to hurt.

[Actually the word *Vaṁśa* means 'diagonal', but the author uses the word here in a wider sense i.e. they stand even for the minor lines connecting a few pairs of squares as explained in verse 63 *infra.* In addition to the two main diagonals there are four minor ones. These six bring about nine points of intersection. These minor diagonals are called *Rajjus.* Bhaṭṭotpala seems to have written a work on architecture entitled वास्तुविद्या, wherefrom he quotes here two verses :

रोगाद्वायुं नयेत्सूत्रं पितृतोऽथ हुताशनम् ।
एतत्सूत्रद्वयं प्रोक्तं मुनिभिर्वंशसंज्ञितम् ॥
वितथाच्छोषकं चान्यद् भृशं मुख्यात्तथा नयेत् ।
जयन्ताद् भृङ्गराजाख्यं सुग्रीवमदितेस्तथा ॥
एतच्चतुष्टयं प्रोक्तं रज्जुसंज्ञं मनीषिभिः ॥]

तान्यशुचिभाण्डकीलस्तम्भाद्यैः पीडितानि शल्यैश्च ।
गृहभर्तुस्तत्तुल्ये पीडामङ्गे प्रयच्छन्ति ॥५८॥

Should the *vulnerable points* be hurt by dirty materials, nails, pillars, pegs etc. (with heavy things like stones), they would cause trouble to the owner of the building in the corresponding limbs of his body.

[The limbs of a man correspond to those of the House-God enumerated in verses 51-54.]

कण्डूयते यदङ्गं गृहभर्तुर्यत्र वाऽमराहुत्याम् ।
अशुभं भवेन्निमित्तं विकृतेर्वाग्नेः सशल्यं तत् ॥५६॥

If, at the time of query, the owner of the house scratches a limb, it should be understood that the corresponding part of the house (in contact with the limbs of the Vāstu-puruṣa) has some affliction or hurt. Or, if at the time of offering oblations to the Deities at the sacrifice (connected with the construction of the house) there is some evil omen (such as sneezing, spitting, weeping, howling, or uttering inauspicious words etc.) or unnatural behaviour of the fire (such as sparks, crackling sound, bad odour and the like), those particular limbs of the House-God occupied by the Deities (to whom oblations are offered) should be afflicted with a nail or peg.

धनहानिर्दारुमये पशुपीडा रुग्भयानि चास्थिकृते ।
[लोहमये शस्त्रभयं कपालकेशेषु मृत्युः स्यात् ॥६०॥
अङ्गारे स्तेनभयं भस्मनि च विनिर्दिशेत्सदाग्निभयम् ।
शल्यं हि मर्मसंस्थं सुवर्णरजतादृतेऽप्यशुभम् ॥६१॥
मर्मण्यमर्मगो वा निरुणद्धयर्थागमं तुषसमूहः ।]
अपि नागदन्तको मर्मसंस्थितो दोषकृद्भवति ॥६२॥

If the thorn (or affliction) is wooden, the owner will sustain loss of money; if it is caused by bone. he will have the risk of disease and his cattle will be afflicted; [if it is made of iron, he will have trouble from weapons; and it is skulls or hair, there will be death; if it is charcoal, there is fear of thieves; and if it is ashes, there will be constant danger from fire. The dart, unless it is of the nature of gold or silver, will prove highly dangerous, if it is situated in a vulnerable point. A heap of husk or chaff, whether found in a vulnerable spot or elsewhere, will obstruct the influx of wealth.] Even an ivory peg entrenched in a vulnerable part will cause misery.

[The portion inside the square brackets is not found in some editions.

All kinds of Śalya or thorn except silver and gold are harmful. Ivory, no doubt, is an auspicious thing. Still it is considered here as ruinous. Gold, silver, gems etc., are considered as promoters of the strength and auspiciousness of the foundation.]

रोगाद्वायुं पितृतो हुताशनं शोषसूत्रमपि वितथात् ।
मुख्याद् भृशं जयन्ताच्च भृङ्गमदितेश्च सुग्रीवम् ॥६३॥

तत्सम्पाता नव ये तान्यतिमर्माणि सम्प्रदिष्टानि ।
यश्च पदस्याष्टांशस्तत् प्रोक्तं मर्मपरिमाणम् ॥६४॥

The nine points of intersection of the lines connecting Roga and Anila, Pitṛ and Śikhin, Śoṣa and Vitatha, Mukhya and Bhṛśa, Jayanta and Bhṛṅgarāja, and Aditi and Sugrīva are considered to be the most *Vulnerable Parts*. The measure of the vulnerable part is an eighth part of a square.

पदहस्तसंख्यया सम्मितानि वंशोऽङ्गुलानि विस्तीर्णः ।
वंशव्यासोऽध्यर्धः शिराप्रमाणं विनिर्दिष्टम् ॥६५॥

The breadth of a diagonal is as many digits as the number of cubits each square measures. The breadth of a line (running east-west and north-south of the ten lines in each direction) is one and a half times that of the diagonals.

[शिरा or Vein is the line that runs from east to west or north to south. There are altogether 20 such lines in Diagram 1. Utpala quotes the following verses from another Śāstra or text which happens to be none other than the वास्तुविश्वकर्मप्रकाश—

शान्ता यशोवती कान्ता विशाला प्राणवाहिनी ।
सती च सुमना नन्दा सुभद्रा सुरथा तथा ॥
पूर्वापरा गता ह्येता उदग्याम्याश्रिताः शृणु ।
हिरण्या सुव्रता लक्ष्मीर्विभूतिर्विमला प्रिया ।
जया काला विशोका च तथेन्द्रा दशमी स्मृता ।
धन्या धरा विशाला च स्थिरा रूपा गदा निशा ॥
विभवा प्रभवा चान्याः सौम्ययाम्याश्रिताः शिराः ॥]

सुखमिच्छन् ब्रह्माणं यत्नाद्रक्षेद्गृही गृहान्तःस्थम् ।
उच्छिष्टाद्युपघाताद् गृहपतिरुपतप्यते तस्मिन् ॥६६॥

A house-owner wishing for happiness should guard very carefully Brahman (i.e. the nine squares occupied by Him) situated at the centre of the house. For, His affliction by dirty things like remnants of food, would harm the owner in it.

दक्षिणभुजेन हीने वास्तुनरेऽर्थक्षयोऽङ्गनादोषाः ।
वामेऽर्थधान्यहानिः शिरसि गुणैर्हीयते सर्वैः ॥६७॥

स्त्रीदोषाः सुतमरणं प्रेष्यत्वं चापि चरणवैकल्ये ।
अविकलपुरुषे वसतां मानार्थयुतानि सौख्यानि ॥६८॥

If the House-God is bereft of the right arm, the owner will sustain loss of wealth and misery through women (or disgrace of women); if He is without the left arm, loss of money and corn; if His head is absent, he will fall from all virtues. If His feet are missing, faults of women (or troubles from women), death of sons, and servitude will be the result. On the other hand, if the God is endowed with all the limbs in fine shape, the occupants of the house will be blessed with honour, wealth and happiness.

[After treating of afflictions to the Deity, the author explains the harmful effects of the absence of His limbs. We have seen the different limbs of the Deity in verses 51-54 *supra.*]

गृहनगरग्रामेषु च सर्वत्रैवं प्रतिष्ठिता देवाः ।
तेषु च यथानुरूपं वर्णा विप्रादयो वास्याः ॥६९॥

In the same manner are Deities (Śikhin etc.) situated in the different parts of towns and villages, as in the case of houses. In these places also suitable parts should be allotted to Brāhmaṇas and other classes.

[When villages or towns are planned the same sketch of the Vāstu-puruṣa should be prepared and His limbs marked. The vulnerable parts ought to be guarded there too. People belonging to the four classes should be given house-sites in the appropriate directions in those places]

वासगृहाणि च विन्द्याद्विप्रादीनामुदग्दिगाद्यानि ।
विशतां च यथा भवनं भवन्ति तान्येव दक्षिणतः ॥७०॥

The houses of Brāhmaṇas and other classes should be located in the northern, eastern, southern and western parts respectively of villages and towns. The houses are to be constructed in such a manner that for the people who enter the courtyard the houses lie to their right.

[The four classes are given the four quarters beginning with the north in regular order. The courtyard should be so constructed that when you enter it the house lies to your right : If the house faces the east, the gate leading to the court should be in the north; if it faces the south, the gate should be in the east; if the west, in the south; and if the north, in the west.]

नवगुणसूत्रविभक्तान्यष्टगुणेनाथवा चतुःषष्टेः ।
द्वाराणि यानि तेषामनलादीनां फलोपनयः ॥७१॥

The following are the effects of the doors put up at the 32 outer squares beginning with Śikhin (see diagram No. 1), whether in the plan of 81 compartments or of 64 (diagram No. 2).

अनिलभयं स्त्रीजननं प्रभूतधनता नरेन्द्रवाल्लभ्यम् ।
क्रोधपरतानृतत्वं क्रौर्यं चौर्यं च पूर्वेण ॥७२॥

If the door is put up at Śikhin, Parjanya etc., to Antarikṣa on the east, the respective effects are (1) danger from wind, (2) birth of daughters, (3) immense wealth, (4) royal favour, (5) extreme wrath, (6) falsehood, (7) cruelty and (8) theft.

अल्पसुतत्वं प्रैष्यं नीचत्वं भक्ष्यपानसुतवृद्धिः ।
रौद्रं कृतघ्नमधनं सुतवीर्यघ्नं च याम्येन ॥७३॥

The effects of the door being in the eight places on the south beginning with Anila and ending with Mṛga are in order (1) few children, (2) slavery, (3) mean life, (4) increase of food, drink and children, (5) fierceness, (6) ingratitude, (7) penury and (8) destruction of children and power.

सुतपीडा रिपुवृद्धिर्न सुतधनाप्तिः सुतार्थफलसम्पत् ।
धनसम्पन्नृपतिभयं धनक्षयो रोग इत्यपरे ॥७४॥

The effects of the door being in the 8 places on the west beginning with Pitṛ and ending with Pāpayakṣman are (1) trouble to sons, (2) increase of enemies, (3) no acquisition of wealth or children, (4) prosperity of sons, wealth and fruits, (5) increase of wealth, (6) danger from the king, (7) loss of wealth, and (8) ill health.

वधबन्धो रिपुवृद्धिः सुतधनलाभः समस्तगुणसम्पत् ।
पुत्रधनाप्तिर्वैरं सुतेन दोषाः स्त्रिया नैःस्वम् ॥७५॥

The effects of the door being in the 8 places beginning with Roga and ending with Diti on the north are (1) death or imprisonment, (2) increase of enemies, (3) influx of wealth and birth of sons, (4) possession of all virtues, (5) getting children and wealth, (6) enmity with one's own son, (7) faults of wife, and (8) poverty.

[नैःस्व्यम् would have been a better expression.

On the eastern side the auspicious squares for the doors are Parjanya, Jayanta and Indra; on the southern side, Bṛhatkṣata only;

on the western side, Kusumadanta and Varuṇa; and on the northern side, Mukhya, Bhallāṭa and Soma.

The commentator states here that in spite of the option given by the author in respect of the two plans (of 81 and 64 squares), it is essential to prepare the ground into 81 squares for the construction of houses for kings etc., as well as for the four classes. For, *Viśvakarman* also lays down the same rule in the following words :

राजवेश्मनि वेशश्च गृहादीनि च वर्णिनाम् ।
एकाशीतिपदेनैव शक्रस्थानं च मापयेत् ॥
प्रासादान् विविधान् छन्दांस्तथाऽऽद्यांश्चाष्टमण्डपान् ।
एकाशीतिपदेनैव सर्वनितान् प्रमापयेत् ॥
नगरग्रामखेटादीन् शिबिराणि च भूभृताम् ।
स्थपतिस्तान् शतपदप्रविभागेण मापयेत् ॥

The parts of the plan where doors are to be fixed should be separated in the beginning itself. Only after this the wall should be constructed.

For says *Nandin* :

"भित्तिश्चिन्त्या द्वारे सत्याचार्या व्यवस्यन्ति ।"
आचार्येण समाससंहितानिबन्धने स्पष्टतरं निबद्धम्—
पूर्वाण्यैशान्यां यान्याग्नेय्यां दक्षिणानि जानीयात् ।
द्वाराणि नैर्ऋतात्पश्चिमान्युदक्स्थानि वायव्याम् ॥
आग्नेयमग्निभयदं पार्जन्यं स्त्रीप्रसूतिदं द्वारम् ।
प्रचुरधनदं जयन्तं नृपवल्लभकारि माहेन्द्रम् ॥
सौर्ये क्रोधः प्रचुरः सत्येऽनृतवादितं भृशे क्रौर्यम् ।
चौर्यं तथान्तरिक्षे प्राग्द्वाराणि प्रदिष्टानि ॥
वायव्येऽल्पसुतत्वं प्रैष्यं पौष्णेऽथ नीचता वितथे ।
बह्वन्नपानपुत्रं बृहत्क्षते याम्य अपि रौद्रम् ॥
गान्धर्वे गन्धत्वं नृपचौरभयाय भृङ्गराजाख्यम् ।
मृगमपि सुतवीर्यघ्नं दक्षिणतो द्वारनिर्देशः ॥
पित्र्ये शरीरपीडा दौवारिकसंज्ञिते च रिपुवृद्धिः ।
सुग्रीवे धनहानिः पुत्रधनाढ्यं कुसुमदन्तम् ॥
वारुणमर्थनिचयदं नृपभयदं चासुरं विनिर्दिष्टम् ।
शोषं धनहानिकरं बहुरोगं पापयक्ष्माख्यम् ॥
रोगमुखं वधबन्धदमात्मजवैराभिवृद्धिदं नागम् ।
मुख्यं धनसुतवृद्धिदमनेककल्याणदं च भल्लाटम् ॥

सौम्यं धनपुत्रकरं भौजङ्गे पुत्रवैररिपुवृद्धिः ।
अदितौ स्त्रीदोषाः स्युर्दितौ धनं संक्षयं याति ॥

The above quotation proves conclusively that the north-eastern corner should be reckoned as belonging to the east, the south-eastern to the south, the south-western to the west, and the north-western to the north. It is for this reason that the commentator ridicules the doubting Thomases who express the doubt, "What is the fate of the ninth square in the east ?" Then he quotes with approval the opinion of भगवान् गर्ग—

पूर्वादिक्रमयोगेन हौताशेऽग्निभयं वदेत् ।
पार्जन्ये प्रचुरा नार्यो जायन्ते बहुवित्तता ॥
माहेन्द्रे नृपवाल्लभ्यं सौर्येऽतिक्रोधिता भवेत् ।
सत्येऽनृतत्वं विज्ञेयं क्रूरत्वं तु भृशे भवेत् ॥
अन्तरिक्षे तु विज्ञेयो नित्यं चौर्यसमागमः ।
स्यात् पुत्रकामो वायव्ये पौष्णे प्रेष्यत्वमेव च ॥
नीचत्वं वितथे ज्ञेयं स्याद् बृहाक्षे तु सन्ततिः ।
क्षुद्रकर्मा भवेद्यामे गान्धर्वे कृतनाशनम् ॥
पित्र्ये स्वल्पायुरधनं व्ययं दौवारिके महत् ।
सुग्रीवे धननाशः स्यात्पुष्पदन्ते तु वर्धनम् ॥
वरुणे मुख्यभोगित्वं नृपभङ्गस्तथासुरे ।
नित्यातिरोगता शोषे पापाख्ये पापसञ्चयः ॥
रोगे बन्धवधो नित्यं नागे रिपुभयं महत् ।
मुख्ये धनसुतोत्पत्तिर्भल्लाटे विपुलाः श्रियः ॥
सौम्ये तु धर्मशीलत्वं भौजङ्गे बहुवैरता ।
अदितौ वनितादोषा दितौ तु धनसंक्षयः ॥
पदे पदे कृतं श्रेष्ठं द्वारं सफलदायिकम् ।
पदक्षये कृतं यच्च तद्व्यामिश्रफलप्रदम् ॥

The commentator adds that what Varāhamihira has given here is a general definition and description of houses and doors, but other writers on this subject have mentioned eight House-Gods and their asterisms as well as those of the 32 doors. According to them houses and doors should be constructed on the basis of the strength of the Moon and the asterism (of the deities and doors) known as चन्द्रबल and ताराबल. They speak of eight deities of houses thus :

रिक्तो ध्वजश्च ध्वांक्षश्च सिंहः श्वा वृषभस्तथा ।
वानरो भद्र इत्यष्टौ ज्ञेया वास्तुनरा बुधैः ॥

These deities are found out by calculation thus :

गृहान्तरदिशां मानं सङ्गुण्य च परस्परम् ।
वसुभिर्भागमाहृत्य शिष्टं वास्तुनरं वदेत् ।।

अथवा—

बाह्वोः प्रबाह्वोः संयोगदलमन्योन्यताडितम् ।
वसुभक्तं ततः शेषं सेव्यं वास्तुनरं वदेत् ।।
एतच्चतुरस्रक्षेत्रे ।

अथ वर्तुले—

व्यासं त्रिगुणितं कृत्वा विष्कम्भं तत् समादिशेत् ।
व्यासार्द्धवर्गस्त्रिगुणः फलं स्यात्परिवर्तुले ।।

Here विष्कम्भ means circumference and the value of π is 3.

अथ षडश्रिप्रभृतिषु—

द्विर्न्यस्य परिधेर्वर्गमेकस्मादश्रिजार्धितात् ।
लब्धं संशोध्य परतो भक्त्वा द्वादशभिः फलम् ।।

अथ त्रिकोणे—

बाहुप्रबाहुसंयोगदलघातं त्रिकोणके ।

The idea is that the house-deity is represented by the remainder got, when the area of the site is divided by 8. If the remainder is zero, it is called *Rikta* or Empty; if I *Dhvaja* or Banner and so on :

समशून्यगतो रिक्तो ध्वजश्चैकावशेषके ।
द्वाभ्यां ध्वांक्षस्त्रिभिः सिंहश्चतुर्भिः श्वा प्रकीर्तितः ।।
पञ्चभिर्वृष इत्याहुः षड्भिर्वानर उच्यते।
सप्तभिर्भद्र इत्येतदष्टानां लक्षणं स्मृतम् ।।
रिक्ते सूर्यस्तथाश्लेषा ध्वजे सोमश्च कृत्तिका ।
ध्वाङ्क्षे राहुश्च भरणी सिंहे भौमस्तथा मघाः ।।
बुधः शुनि धनिष्ठा च वृषे जीवश्च रोहिणी ।
भद्रे तु श्रवणः सौरः कपौ शुक्रश्च फाल्गुनी ।।
चन्द्रतारानुकूल्येन कारयेत विचक्षणः ।
विभुर्नश्यति रिक्तेन ध्वजेन विपुलाः श्रियः ।।
ध्वांक्षेण नित्यमुद्वेगः सिंहेन जितशत्रुता ।
अस्थैर्यं सारमेये स्याद्वृषे परितपो ध्रुवः ।।
कपिना चापलं स्त्रीणां नित्यं भद्रेण निर्वृतिः ।।

अथ द्वारनक्षत्राणि—

कृत्तिका भगमैन्द्रं च विशाखा च पुनर्वसुः ।
तिष्यो हस्तस्तथाऽऽर्द्रा च क्रमात् पूर्वेषु निर्दिशेत् ।।

चित्रा विशाखा पौष्णं च नैर्ऋतं यमदैवतम् ।
वैश्वदेवाश्विनं मैत्रं क्रमाद् दक्षिणसंश्रितम् ॥
पित्र्यं प्रोष्ठपदार्यम्णमाषाढं च द्विदैवतम् ।
वारुणाश्विनसावित्रं क्रमात् पश्चिमसंश्रितम् ॥
स्वात्याश्लेषाभिजित्सौम्यं वैष्णवं वासवं तथा ।
याम्यं ब्राह्मं क्रमात्सौम्यद्वारेषु च विनिर्दिशेत् ॥]
मार्गतरुकोणकूपस्तम्भभ्रमविद्धमशुभदं द्वारम् ।
उच्छ्रायाद् द्विगुणमितां त्यक्त्वा भूमिं न दोषाय ॥७६॥

A door being pierced by a road, tree, corner, well, pillar or water-sluice, is inauspicious, but if it is removed to a distance equal to twice its height, there will be no harm done to anybody.

[Cf. भगवान् गर्ग—

द्वारोच्छ्रायद्विगुणितां त्यक्त्वा भूमिं बहिःस्थितः ।
न दोषाय भवेद्वेधो गृहस्य गृहिणोऽथवा ॥

also the समाससंहिता—

स्तम्भतरुभ्रमकोणविद्धं वेधश्च न शुभकरद्वारम् ।
वेधोच्छ्रायाद् द्विगुणां भूमिं त्यक्त्वा न दोषाय ॥

Here the commentator raises a doubt whether the expression *height* refers to the door or the object that pierces or wounds. Here it is Garga's statement, more than that of the समाससंहिता, that dispels the doubt.]

रथ्याविद्धं द्वारं नाशाय कुमारदोषदं तरुणा ।
पङ्कद्वारे शोको व्ययोऽम्बुनिःस्राविणि प्रोक्तः ॥७७॥
कूपेनापस्मारो भवति विनाशश्च देवताविद्धे ।
स्तम्भेन स्त्रीदोषाः कुलनाशो ब्रह्मणोऽभिमुखे ॥७८॥

A door wounded by a road presages the owner's death; by a tree, harm to children; by mire, grief; by a runnel, excessive expenditure of money; by a well, epilepsy; by an idol of God, the owner's destruction; by a pillar, frailty of women; and one facing Brahman, extinction of the family.

[Cf. विश्वकर्मा—

गृहमध्ये कृतं द्वारं द्रव्यधान्यविनाशनम् ।
आवहेत् कलहं शोकं नारीर्वा सम्प्रदूषयेत् ॥

also भारद्वाज—

शिरा मर्माणि वंशाश्च नालमध्यं च सर्वशः ।
विहाय वास्तुमध्यं च द्वाराणि विनिवेशयेत् ॥

Cf. यम—

ब्रह्मस्थाने न विध्येत नागदन्तस्थलानि च ।
मृद्दारुभिर्गवाक्षैश्च मानपानैस्तथैव च ॥
द्वारैश्च भित्तिभिश्चैव शय्याभागैः कथञ्चन ।
स्वामिनो मरणं तत्र महादुःखेन पार्थिव ॥

The commentator raises another doubt here i.e. he has stated in verse 75 that the doors on Bhallāṭa and Soma in the north are highly auspicious, but they face Brahman in the centre, which is forbidden according to this verse. The explanation is that what is given in verse 75 is an exception to the rule given in 78.]

उन्मादः स्वयमुद्घाटितेऽथ पिहिते स्वयं कुलविनाशः ।
मानाधिके नृपभयं दस्युभयं व्यसनमेव नीचे च ॥७६॥

द्वारं द्वारस्योपरि यत्तन्न शिवाय सङ्कटं यच्च ।
आध्यात्तं क्षुद्भयदं कुब्जं कुलनाशनं भवति ॥८०॥

पीडाकरमतिपीडितमन्तर्विनतं भवेदभावाय ।
बाह्यविनते प्रवासो दिग्भ्रान्ते दस्युभिः पीडा ॥८१॥

A door which opens automatically causes lunacy; one that closes likewise, destruction of the family; one that is too big leads to trouble from the king; one that is too low, fear of robbers and misery; one above another as well as one that is too narrow is not conducive to happiness; one that is too broad brings about famine; a crooked door, extinction of the family; one that is pressed very much by the upper block, affliction to the owner; one that is bent inwardly, the owner's death; one bent outwardly, absence from home; and one that is not properly situated in its usual direction, trouble from robbers.

मूलद्वारं नान्यैर्द्वारैरभिसन्दधीत रूपर्द्ध्या ।
घटफलपत्रप्रमथादिभिश्च तन्मङ्गलैश्चिनुयात् ॥८२॥

The principal door ought not to be surpassed by other doors through superior structure and decorative motifs. That door should be embellished profusely with the designs of auspicious objects such as water-pots, fruits, foliage as well as images of Śiva's attendants (and lions, serpents, swans, etc.).

ऐशान्यादिषु कोणेषु संस्थिता बाह्यतो गृहस्यैताः ।
चरकी विदारिनामाऽथ पूतना राक्षसी चेति ॥८३॥

पुरभवनग्रामाणां ये कोणास्तेषु निवसतां दोषाः ।
श्वपचादयोऽन्त्यजात्यास्तेष्वेव विवृद्धिमायान्ति ॥८४॥

In the outer corners beginning with the north-east of a house there dwell evil spirits viz. *Caraki, Vidāri*, Pūtanā and Rākṣasī respectively. Hence those who dwell in these corners of cities, houses and villages come to grief, whereas the outcastes such as Caṇḍālas (who eat dog's meat) alone flourish there.

[Cf. what other works say :

स्कन्दोऽर्यमा जम्बुकाख्यः पिलिपिञ्चस्तथापरः ।
प्राच्यादिदिक्चतुष्के तु निवसन्ति महाग्रहाः ॥

कोणेष्वाचार्योक्ता एव ।

ऐशान्यां चरकी प्रोक्ता स्कन्दः प्राग्भागसंस्थितः ।
हौताशन्यां विदारी च याम्यां चैवार्यमा स्थितः ॥
पूतना नैर्ऋते ज्ञेया जम्बुकः पश्चिमे स्थितः ।
राक्षसी चानिले कोणे पिलिपिञ्चस्तथोत्तरे ॥

Among the outcastes are included cobblers, Pukkasas etc. Pukkasa is the offspring of a Niṣāda by a Śūdra woman. (Manu X. 18).]

याम्यादिष्वशुभफला जातास्तरवः प्रदक्षिणेनैते ।
उदगादिषु प्रशस्ताः प्लक्षवटोदुम्बराश्वत्थाः ॥८५॥

The trees Peepal, banyan, the Indian fig and the holy Aśvattha growing in the south, west, north and east respectively are of untoward effects; while in the north, east, south and west respectively they are beneficial.

[Cf. गर्ग—

वर्जयेत् पूर्वतोऽश्वत्थं प्लक्षं दक्षिणतस्तथा ।
न्यग्रोधं पश्चिमे भागे उत्तरे चाप्युदुम्बरम् ॥
अश्वत्थे तु भयं ब्रूयात् प्लक्षे ब्रूयात्पराभवम् ।
न्यग्रोधे राजतः पीडा नेत्रामयमुदुम्बरे ।
वटः पुरस्ताद् धन्यः स्याद् दक्षिणे चाप्युदुम्बरः ।
अश्वत्थः पश्चिमे भागे प्लक्षस्तूत्तरतो भवेत् ॥]

आसन्नाः कण्टकिनो रिपुभयदाः क्षीरिणोऽर्थनाशाय ।
फलिनः प्रजाक्षयकरा दारूण्यपि वर्जयेदेषाम् ॥८६॥
छिन्द्याद्यदि न तरूंस्तान् तदन्तरे पूजितान्वपेदन्यान् ।
पुन्नागाशोकारिष्टबकुलपनसान् शमीशालौ ॥८७॥

Thorny trees (like the Khadira) in the vicinity of houses cause danger from enemies; milky ones (like the Arka) lead to destruction of wealth; and fruit-bearing ones (like the mango), to loss of children. Even their timber should be avoided in the construction of houses. If these trees (thorny etc.) cannot be cut down, auspicious trees such as Punnāga, Aśoka, Ariṣṭa (Nimba), Bakula (or Kesara), the jack tree, Śamī and Sal should be planted amidst them.

[If there should be any forbidden tree in the vicinity of a house which cannot be removed for some reason or other, an auspicious tree could be planted between the house and the forbidden tree so that the latter becomes farther off. If this is done the untoward effect prescribed for the bad tree could be warded off.]

In the next verse the author discusses the best ground for constructing a house on.

शस्तौषधिद्रुमलता मधुरा सुगन्धा
स्निग्धा समा न सुषिरा च मही नराणाम् ।
अप्यध्वनि श्रमविनोदमुपागतानां
धत्ते श्रियं किमुत शाश्वतमन्दिरेषु ॥८८॥

A ground which is soft, even, of sweet smell and taste, and abounding in excellent herbs, trees and creepers, and not hollow underneath, confers all-round prosperity even on those persons who may take rest on it in order to relieve themselves of the fatigue of their journey, how much more then on those who construct a permanent home on it and live in it ?

[Under commendable herbs are mentioned Jāyā, Jayantī, Jīvantī, Jīvaputrā, etc. The trees should be fit for sacrificial purposes, such as Palāśa, Pippala, etc. The creepers are Śyāmalatā etc. The commentator mentions चूतततयश्च among creepers.

The metre is वसन्ततिलका and the figure of speech अर्थापत्ति.]

In the next two verses the discusses the effects of the neighbouring buildings on a house.

सचिवालयेऽर्थनाशो धूर्त्तगृहे सुतवधः समीपस्थे ।
उद्वेगो देवकुले चतुष्पथे भवति चाकीर्त्तिः ॥८९॥
चैत्ये भयं ग्रहकृतं वल्मीकश्वभ्रसङ्कुले विपदः ।
गर्त्तायां तु पिपासा कूर्माकारे धनविनाशः ॥९०॥

If a minister's house be in the neighbourhood of the house in question, the owner of the latter would sustain loss of wealth; if a rogue's (or gambler's) residence, death of a son; if a temple, mental afflictions; if a crossing of roads, infamy; if a holy tree, danger caused by evil spirits; if a place filled with ant-hills or pot-holes, calamities; if a cave, thirst; and if a piece of ground shaped like a tortoise, loss of money.

[The commentator says that चैत्यवृक्ष, is कल्पवृक्ष. For says the *Purāṇa*—

मन्दरस्य गिरेः शृङ्गे महावृक्षः स केतुराट् ।
आलम्बशाखाशिखरः कदम्बश्चैत्यपादपः ॥

Cf. बृहस्पति—

चैत्यवृक्षेषु भूतेभ्यः कृच्छावासः पुरा ह्ययम् ।
अरतिस्त्वभिवर्धेत निविष्टैः कण्टकिद्रुमैः ॥

Utpala says about गर्ता, "गर्ता प्रसिद्धा चिता..."]

उदगादिप्लवमिष्टं विप्रादीनां प्रदक्षिणेनैव ।
विप्रः सर्वत्र वसेदनुवर्णमथेष्टमन्येषाम् ॥६१॥

If the ground slopes down towards the north, it is beneficial for Brāhmaṇas; towards the east, for Kṣatriyas; towards the south, for Vaiśyas; and towards the west, for Śūdras. However, a Brāhmaṇa may have his dwelling on any of these grounds, but the rest only according to their rank i.e. a Kṣatriya on a ground sloping down towards the east, south or west; a Vaiśya, towards the south or west; and a Śūdra, towards the west only.

In the following four verses the author describes the same methods for testing the suitability of the grounds for the different classes.

गृहमध्ये हस्तमितं खात्वा परिपूरितं पुनः श्वभ्रम् ।
यद्यूनमनिष्टं तत् समे समं धन्यमधिकं यत् ॥६२॥

A pit measuring one cubit in diameter and depth should be dug in the centre of the house-site. If, on filling it with the same earth, the pit is insufficiently filled, it is harmful; if just filled, moderate; and if the earth is more than sufficient, it is blessed.

श्वभ्रमथवाऽम्बुपूर्णं पदशतमित्वाऽऽगतस्य यदि नोनम् ।
तद्धन्यं यच्च भवेत् पलान्यपामाढकं चतुः षष्टिः ॥६३॥

Or, fill the same pit with water and then walking a hundred steps, come back. If the water in the pit has not diminished, the ground is blest. Similarly, it is very favourable, if an Āḍhaka of the earth dug out weighs 64 palas.

[Cf. पराशर—

निमेषशतमतीत्याखातश्वभ्रगतजलगतां चारिणीं समुद्धृतामापूर्यमाणामति-
रक्तां मृदं चतुःषष्टिपलाढकां तुल्यां च ।।]

आमे वा मृत्पात्रे श्वभ्रस्थे दीपवर्तिरभ्यधिकम् ।
ज्वलति दिशि यस्य शस्ता सा भूमिस्तस्य वर्णस्य ।।६४।।

Or, place a lamp inside an unbaked earthen pot in the same pit with four wicks facing the four directions. The site is most beneficial for that class of people which is represented by the direction of the wick.

[The reader is aware of the rule regarding the classes and directions. The north is the direction of Brāhmaṇas. This verse may also be interpreted as follows : Place four lamps in pits in the four directions and observe which lamp burns longest. The तन्त्रसमुच्चय of Kerala mentions this wick-experiment with four lamps in the four driections for testing the site. (See the author's paper entitled "On Architecture in Ancient India" read in the 'Symposium on History of Sciences of India', New Delhi, October 17-20, 1968.)

श्वभ्रोषितं न कुसुमं यस्य प्रम्लायतेऽनुवर्णसमम् ।
तत्तस्य भवति शुभदं यस्य च यस्मिन् मनो रमते ।।६५।।

Place flowers of the four colours, white, red, yellow and dark, assigned to the four classes in the pit at night and observe them on the morrow. That class whose flower has not faded in the pit will flourish on that site. Similarly, any site would be auspicious for a person, provided his heart feels very happy there.

[The last statement is based on a psychological principle. The condition of the mind presages future events and their success or failure. See also LXXV-3 *infra* for a similar idea.

See also **गर्ग**—

या यस्य राशिता भूमेर्भवेत्तु गृहकर्मणि ।
तस्यां श्वभ्रं खनेर्मध्ये हस्तमात्रं समन्ततः ।।
तच्छ्वभ्रं पूरयेत्तेन पांसुना सुविचक्षणः ।
वर्धमाने च वृद्धिः स्याद्धीयमाने विगर्हिता ।।
साम्ये साम्यं विनिर्दिष्टमथवान्यद्विचारणम् ।
पूरयित्वाऽथवा श्वभ्रं मृद्भिः क्रमशतं व्रजेत् ।।

पूर्णं स्यादागमं यावत् सा भूमिस्तु प्रशस्यते ।
तस्मिन् वा धारयेच्छ्वभ्रे चित्रं माल्यमनुक्रमात् ॥
यच्चिरान्म्लायते माल्यं तद्वर्णं तत्र चावसेत् ।
आमे वा मृण्मये पात्रे दीपवर्त्तिचतुष्टयम् ।
यस्यां दिशि प्रज्वलति चिरं तस्यैव सा शुभा ॥]

सितरक्तपीतकृष्णा विप्रादीनां प्रशस्यते भूमिः ।
गन्धश्च भवति यस्यां घृतरुधिरान्नाद्यमद्यसमः ॥९६॥

कुशयुक्ता शरबहुला दूर्वाकाशावृता क्रमेण मही ।
ह्यनुवर्णं वृद्धिकरी मधुरकषायाम्लकटुका च ॥९७॥

A soil that is white, red, yellow and black is beneficial to the Brāhmaṇas, Kṣatriyas, Vaiśyas and Śūdras respectively. Similarly if it smells like ghee, blood, food and liquor, it is good for the four classes in order. It is also favourable for these classes in their order, if it is covered with the four kinds of grass viz. the holy Darbha, Śara, Dūrvā and Kāśa. Likewise, a sweet, astringent, sour and pungent soil bestows prosperity on these classes in order.

[Cf. गर्ग—

मधुरा दर्भसंयुक्ता घृतगन्धा च या मही ।
उत्तरप्रवणा चेति ब्राह्मणानां तु सा शुभा ॥
रक्तगन्धा कषाया च शरवीरेण संयुता ।
रक्ता प्राक्प्रवणा ज्ञेया क्षत्रियाणां तु सा मही ॥
दक्षिणप्रवणा भूमिर्याम्ला दूर्वाभिरन्विता ।
अन्नगन्धा च वैश्यानां पीतवर्णा प्रशस्यते ॥
पश्चिमप्रवणा कृष्णा विकुण्ठा काशसंवृता ।
मद्यगन्धा मही धन्या शूद्राणां कटुका तथा ॥]

What should one do before constructing a house ?

कृष्टां प्ररूढबीजां गोऽध्युषितां ब्राह्मणैः प्रशस्तां च ।
गत्वा महीं गृहपतिः काले सांवत्सरोद्दिष्टे ॥९८॥

भक्ष्यैर्नानाकारैर्दध्यक्षतसुरभिकुसुमधूपैश्च ।
दैवतपूजां कृत्वा स्थपतीनभ्यर्च्य विप्रांश्च ॥९९॥

विप्रः स्पृष्ट्वा शीर्षं वक्षश्च क्षत्रियो विशश्चोरू ।
शूद्रः पादौ स्पृष्ट्वा कुर्याद्रेखां गृहारम्भे ॥१००॥

The owner of land who wishes to construct a house should go at a time prescribed by the astrologer to the worthy site which has been ploughed, where sown seeds have sprouted, and where Brāhmaṇas and cows have stayed for a night, worship the deities with varieties of eatables, curds, coloured rice, fragrant flowers and incense, and honour Brāhmaṇas and architects. Then touching his head, breast, thighs or feet, according as he is a Brāhmaṇa, Kṣatriya, Vaiśya or Śūdra, he (owner) should draw a line (with any object held in the hand) on the ground, at the commencement of the construction of a house.

[The first line gives a few conditions such as ploughed to show that the land is not barren, on the other hand, fertile as well as blessed by cows and Brāhmaṇas. For, the Lord is said to be 'गोब्राह्मणहिताय च'. See the following verse quoted by Utpala on purification of land :

सम्मार्जनेनाञ्जनेन सेकेनोल्लेखनेन वा ।
गवां च सन्निवासेन भूमिः शुध्यति पञ्चभिः ॥]

The following verses give the effects of the line being drawn with various objects.

अङ्गुष्ठकेन कुर्यान्मध्याङ्गुल्याऽथवा प्रदेशिन्या ।
कनकमणिरजतमुक्तादधिफलकुसुमाक्षतैश्च शुभम् ॥१०१॥
शस्त्रेण शस्त्रमृत्युर्बन्धो लोहेन भस्मनाग्निभयम् ।
तस्करभयं तृणेन च काष्ठोल्लिखिता च राजभयम् ॥१०२॥
वक्रा पादालिखिता शत्रुभयक्लेशदा विरूपा च ।
चर्माङ्गारास्थिकृता दन्तेन च कर्तुरशिवाय ॥१०३॥
वैरमपसव्यलिखिता प्रदक्षिणं सम्पदो विनिर्देश्याः ।
वाचः परुषा निष्ठीवितं क्षुतं चाशुभं कथितम् ॥१०४॥

Should the owner draw the line with his thumb, fore-finger, middle finger, or with gold, silver, gem, pearl, curds, fruit, flower or coloured rice (barley), the result would be quite good. On the other hand, should he draw the line with a weapon, he would be killed by a weapon; with a metallic (or iron) piece, he would suffer imprisonment; with ashes, there would be danger from fire; with straw, fear of theft; and with a wooden piece, trouble from the king. A line that is crooked, and drawn with the foot leads to trouble from enemies and misery; so is one that is ugly or not clear; one drawn with a piece of hide, charcoal, bone or tooth would cause disaster to the owner; one drawn in an anti-clock wise direction, hatred; and in a clock-wise direction, prosperity. Harsh words, spitting and sneezing at the commencement are said to be inauspicious.

अर्द्धनिचितं कृतं वा प्रविशन् स्थपतिर्गृहे निमित्तानि ।
अवलोकयेद् गृहपतिः क्व संस्थितः स्पृशति किं चाङ्गम् ॥१०५॥

रविदीप्तो यदि शकुनिस्तस्मिन् काले विरौति परुषरवम् ।
संस्पृष्टाङ्गसमानं तस्मिन् देशेऽस्थि निर्देश्यम् ॥१०६॥

After entering a finished or half-finished house, the architect should carefully look for the auguries and also observe where (i.e. in which limb of the House-God) the house-owner is standing and which part of his body is touching. If at that time a bird, heated by the Sun, cries harshly, it must be predicted that there is a bone of that limb corresponding to the one touched, on the spot.

[The commentator gives here a detailed exposition of the word 'Ravi-dīpta'—'heated by the Sun' : One meaning of Dīptā is that direction opposite to the Sun. Among the eight quarters one becomes *Aṅgāriṇi* or having charcoal, the next *Diptā* or heated, the next to that *Dhūmitā* or smoky, and the remaining five Śāntā or tranquil in each watch of the day or night. For example, from Sunrise till the end of the first watch (i.e, till 9 A M., taking the sunrise to be at 6 A.M.) the *North-East* is termed (1) *Aṅgāriṇi*, the East (2) Dīptā, *South-East* (3) *Dhūmitā* and the remaing five i.e. (4) South, South-West, West, North-West and North, Śāntā. In the next watch i.e. from 9 A.M. to 12 A.M. these designations go to East, S.E., South and S.W., West, N.W., North and N.E. in order. In the same manner the process has to be repeated in the last watches of the day and in the four watches of the night as well.

See the quotation from some other Āgama :

पृच्छाकाले गृहस्वामी यदङ्गं स्पृशति स्वकम् ।
भुवो हस्तप्रमाणेन शल्यं ब्रूयात्तदङ्गजम् ॥]

शकुनसमयेऽथवाऽन्ये हस्त्यश्वश्वादयोऽनुवाशन्ते ।
तत्प्रभवमस्थि तस्मिंस्तदङ्गसम्भूतमेवेति ॥१०७॥

Or, at the time of observing the auguries, if other animals like the elephant, horse and dog, scorched by the Sun, cry, it should be predicted that the particular spot occupied by the owner contains a bone of such an animal, belonging to the limb corresponding to the one touched by him.

सूत्रे प्रसार्यमाणे गर्दभरावोऽस्थिशल्यमाचष्टे ।
श्वशृगाललङ्घिते वा सूत्रे शल्यं विनिर्देश्यम् ॥१०८॥

If at the time of stretching the measuring string or tape there be the braying of a donkey, it indicates the presence of a bone underneath. The same fault or *thorn* should be declared in case the string is crossed by a dog or jackal.

[The Śalya or hurt must be a piece of bone of that class of animals to which the one crossing the line belongs. The bone, of course, would belong to that limb of the animal which corresponds to the one touched by the owner.]

दिशि शान्तायां शकुनिर्मधुरविरावी यदा तदा वाच्यः ।
अर्थस्तस्मिन् स्थाने गृहेश्वराधिष्ठितेऽङ्गे वा ॥१०९॥

If at that time a bird sitting in a *tranquil* quarter, warbles sweetly, it should be understood that there is a hidden treasure on the spot or in the limb of the House-God occupied by the owner.

[The meaning of 'तस्मिन् स्थाने' is—in the place occupied by the bird. The depth will be so many cubits as correspond to the height of the limb touched : "When the ground is dug for laying the foundation the owner should stand up with arms uplifted in the pit. Find out the height of that limb from the bottom of the pit. The depth of the *Śalya* or fault (bone etc.) would be equal to this measure."

Cf. गर्ग—

प्रश्नकाले गृहपतिः कस्मिन्नङ्गे समास्थितः ।
किमङ्गं संस्पृशेद्वापि व्याहरेद्वा शुभाशुभम् ॥
विलोक्य स्थपतिः पूर्वं पश्चाच्छल्यं विचारयेत् ।
शङ्खभेरीमृदङ्गानां पटहानां च निःस्वनाः ॥
दध्यक्षतानां पुष्पाणां फलानां दर्शनानि च ।
प्रष्टुश्च प्रवदेच्छल्यं वास्तुज्ञानविशारदः ॥
दीपदिक्संस्थितः पक्षी विरौति परुषं रवम् ।
स्पृष्टाङ्गसदृशं शल्यं तस्य स्थाने विनिर्दिशेत् ॥
निखनेदवनिं तत्र तदङ्गं ब्रुडते यथा ।
गृहनाथस्य तत्राधः शल्यं निःसंशयं वदेत् ॥
प्रश्नकाले गजो गौर्वा तुरगो गर्दभोऽपि वा ।
उष्ट्रो वा सारमेयो वा मार्जारश्छागरोऽपि वा ॥

यः प्राणी व्याहरेत् तत्र तद्भवं शल्यमादिशेत् ।
प्रमाणं तस्य वक्तव्यं पूर्वोक्तविधिना ततः ॥]

Next he gives some more evil omens and their consequences:

सूत्रच्छेदे मृत्युः कीले चावाङ्मुखे महान् रोगः ।
गृहनाथस्थपतीनां स्मृतिलोपे मृत्युरादेश्यः ॥११०॥

स्कन्धाच्च्युते शिरोरुक् कुलोपसर्गोऽपवर्जिते कुम्भे ।
भग्नेऽपि च कर्मिवधश्च्युते कराद् गृहपतेर्मृत्युः ॥१११॥

If the string snaps, while being stretched, the owner will die; if a peg is driven upside down, a fell disease will afflict him; if the owner or carpenter (architect) forgets anything, he will meet with his end. Should the pot of water, while being brought, fall from the shoulder, the owner would have some cerebral disease; should it be drained away, there would be misery to his family; should it be broken, the labourers would be killed; and should it fall down from the hand, the owner would die.

उत्तरपूर्वे कोणे कृत्वा पूजां शिलां न्यसेत्प्रथमम् ।
शेषाः प्रदक्षिणेन स्तम्भाश्चैवं समुत्थाप्याः ॥११२॥

छत्रस्रगम्बरयुतः कृतधूपविलेपनः समुत्थाप्यः ।
स्तम्भस्तथैव कार्यो द्वारोच्छ्रायः प्रयत्नेन ॥११३॥

In the north-eastern corner of the site a worship should be offered with the necessary materials (such as garlands, scents, incense, cloths, food, gold, liquor, meat etc.) and then, first of all, a stone laid there, and other stones in the remaining (seven ?) quarters in a clock-wise manner. In the same manner should pillars and doors be raised carefully, being decorated with umbrellas, garlands, cloths, incense and ointments.

[Utpala takes the reading दक्षिणपूर्वे first and then refers to the other reading उत्तरपूर्वे. He should have known that nobody would advise a worship to be performed in the South-eastern corner at first.

Cf. गर्ग—

शिलाविन्यासकाले तु सम्भारांश्चोपकल्पयेत् ।
समुद्रजानि रत्नानि सुवर्णं रजतं तथा ।
सर्वबीजानि गन्धांश्च शरान्दर्भांस्तथैव च ।
शुक्लान्सुमनसः सर्पिः केतकीं मधुरोचनाम् ॥

आमिषं च तथा मद्यं फलानि विविधानि च ।
क्षीरोदनं पूर्णकुम्भान् कोणे कोणे प्रदापयेत् ॥
नानाविधानि भक्ष्याणि पानानि विविधानि च ।
हुत्वाग्निं विधिवत्काले मुहूर्ते चोपपादिते ॥
गृहकोणेषु सर्वेषु पूजां कृत्वा विधानतः ।
ततः पुण्याहघोषेण शिलान्यासं प्रकल्पयेत् ॥
ऐशानमादितः कृत्वा प्राग्दाक्षिण्येन विन्यसेत् ।
अनेनैव विधानेन स्तम्भद्वारावरोहणम् ॥
वास्तुविद्याविधानज्ञः कारयेत्सुसमाहितः ।
शिलाविन्यासमन्त्रोऽयं निर्दिष्टो मुनिभिः पुरा ॥
नन्दे नन्दाय वासिष्ठे वसुभिश्च हितप्रजे ।
सुचिरे नन्ददे नन्दे वासिष्ठे रम्यतां गृहे ॥
भद्रे काश्यपदायादे पूजनं भद्रमावह ।
सुभगे सुव्रते देवि गृहे काश्यपि रम्यताम् ॥
जये भार्गवदायादे प्रजानां भद्रमावह ।
भव भूतिकरी देवि गृहे भार्गवि रम्यताम् ॥
सर्वबीजसमायुक्ते सर्वगन्धौषधैर्वृते ।
प्रजापतिसुते देवि सुखदाऽस्तु महीसुते ॥
पूर्णेऽङ्गिरसदायादे पूर्णकामाः प्रजाः कुरु ।
पूजिते परमाचार्ये गन्धमाल्यैरलङ्कृते ॥
अव्यङ्गे चाक्षते पूर्णे मुनेरङ्गिरसः सुते ।
इष्टके त्वं प्रयच्छेष्टं प्रतिष्ठां गृहिणः कुरु ॥
ग्रामस्वामिपुरस्वामिगृहस्वामिपरिग्रहे ।
मनुष्यपशुहस्त्यश्वधनवृद्धिकरी भव ॥

Next the commentator quotes the rules for installing the Śaṅku-peg, from another book on the subject :

स्निग्धादिभूभागसमुत्थितानां न्यग्रोधबिल्वद्रुमखादिराणाम् ।
शमीवटोदुम्बरदेवदारुक्षीरिस्वदेशोत्थफलद्रुमाणाम् ॥
उपोषितः शिल्पिजनस्त्वथैषां मध्यात्तु तीक्ष्णेन कुठारकेण ।
भित्त्वा ततो दिक्पतिनोत्तरस्यां शुभे च लग्ने परिगृह्य शङ्कुम् ॥
करप्रमाणं परतश्चतस्रस्तदर्धमानेन ततोऽनुगृह्य ।
नीत्वा न्यसेत् तांश्च गृहे तु तावद्यावत्प्रतिष्ठासमयोऽस्य शङ्कोः ॥

नन्देति सूक्तिः कथितैशकोणे हुताशनाख्ये सुभगेति चान्या ।
सुमङ्गली नैर्ऋतभागसंस्था भद्रङ्करी मारुतकोणयाता ॥
वृषाश्वपुन्नागपदाङ्कितानां नन्दादिकानां क्रमशः शिलानाम् ।
अखण्डितानां सुदृढीकृतानां सुलक्षणानां ग्रहणं निरुक्तम् ॥
कूर्मोऽथ शेषो हि जनार्दनः श्रीर्ध्रुवश्च मध्ये भवनस्य संस्था ।
द्वाराधिपा दिक्पतयो गजाश्च सम्पूजनीया बलिभिः सुमन्त्रैः ॥
स्नानार्घ्यमाल्याम्बरधूपलेपैर्बल्योपहारैः प्रतिपूज्य शङ्कुम् ।
ध्रुवे शिलायाश्च ततः खनित्वा शङ्कुं प्रतिष्ठाप्य तथा च कुम्भम् ॥
लाजाक्षतव्रीहिसपञ्चगव्यमध्वाज्ययातं परिपूर्य सम्यक् ।
ऋग्भिस्तथैशं विधिवत्प्रकुर्याद्धोमो ध्रुवादुत्तरस्तु कार्यः ॥

अथ लग्नशुद्धिः—

धनुर्वणिग्गोयुगनारिकुम्भे वास्तुप्रतिष्ठाकरणं प्रधानम् ।
एतच्चतुर्थं गृहसंज्ञमृक्षं जलोद्भवं तच्छुभमुद्दिशन्ति ॥
असम्भवे शुक्रशशाङ्कयोगाज्जलाश्रयं प्राहुरतीन्द्रियज्ञाः ।
एषां नवांशेऽन्यगृहे शुभर्क्षे कर्तुर्व्ययाष्टत्रिककोणवर्जे ॥
केन्द्रत्रिकोणज्वलनाख्यलाभार्थावस्थितेष्वीज्यसितेन्दुजेषु ।
गृहं समृद्धं सुदृढं जनाढ्यं व्यये तृतीये ज्ञगुरू समृद्धौ ॥
वाच्यं तथा सूर्यकुजार्कजेषु तृतीयषष्ठायगतेषु नित्यम् ।
शेषेष्वतोऽन्येषु विशेषतस्तु चौराग्निदाहक्षतरोगजाड्यम् ॥
लग्नात्तृतीयाम्बुषडायगेन्दौ कार्यं गृहं स्त्रीधनधान्यदासैः ।
अभीष्टमन्येषु गतोन्यथातो धिष्ण्यं गृहं चात्र गुणातिरिक्तम् ॥
प्रवेश एवं भवनस्य कार्यो विप्रादिकानां यदुदीरितं प्राक् ।
किन्त्वत्र गोजाविकवाहनानां विना स्थिरैः स्वाष्टसमैः प्रवेशः ॥

अथ वैदिकमन्त्राः—

ध्रुवे वास्तुनरे चैव द्वाराणां ग्रन्थिषु स्मृतान् ।
वैदिकांश्चैव मन्त्रांश्च प्रवक्ष्याम्यनुपूर्वशः ॥
कूर्मे मन्त्रमयो यज्ञो वर्धतां बलिकर्मणि ।
शेषे नमोऽस्तु सर्पेभ्य इदं विष्णुर्जनार्दने ॥
तव श्रियः श्रिये यान्तु ध्रुवाद्यास्तु ध्रुवे स्मृतम् ।
सविता श्रियः प्रसविता शङ्कोराहुर्मनीषिणः ॥

अथ शङ्कुदेवताः—

ब्रह्मणे ब्रह्मजज्ञानमर्यम्णे यान्तु अर्यमम् ।
सविता श्रियः प्रसविता तथैवेति विवस्वतः ॥

इन्द्रस्येन्द्रो मयं वाच्यं मित्रे मित्राञ्जनं स्मृतम् ।
तथा मृडानो रुद्रोऽथ रुद्रस्य परिकीर्त्तितम् ॥
भूधराय इहैवैधि रम्भराय हयं महत् ।
प्रोक्ता वास्तुनरस्यैवं देवताश्च त्रयोदश ॥
ये देवा हि चतुर्दिक्षु द्वाराणां मन्त्रसङ्ग्रहे ।
नक्षत्राणां पुरा प्रोक्तं सूक्तीनामधुना शृणु ॥
यो रुद्रोऽग्नौ तु नन्दिन्यामाहुत्यं शुभगाय च ।
सुमङ्गली: सुमङ्गल्या भद्रं कर्णीति भद्रिका ॥
एतेषां बलयो वक्ष्ये हविषं पायसं दधि ।
मोदकाज्यपयोव्रीहिलाजाऽक्षतफलानि च ॥
ध्रुवादुत्तरतो होममनादेश्यं तु कारयेत् ।
तव श्रियादिमन्त्रैस्तु हुवेदाज्यं समाहितः ॥
एवं प्रवेशकाले तु स्थालीपाकसमो हि सः ।
मन्त्रैर्होमस्तु सूक्तीनां पञ्चरङ्ग प्रवाहणः ॥
ये देवादिकरण्डाश्च काण्डात्काण्डात्प्ररोहणम् ।
पाद्यमर्घ्यादिकं यत्तु शान्तिकल्पेन दर्शितम् ।
तदिहापि ग्रहीतव्यं सर्वमेतच्छ्रुतार्थकम् ॥
एवं देवालये शान्तौ दीक्षायज्ञादिसर्वतः ।
स्वतन्त्रोक्तेन वक्तव्यं निर्माणस्य प्रवेशनम् ॥]

विहगादिभिरवलीनैराकम्पितपतितदु:स्थितैश्च तथा ।
शक्रध्वजसदृशफलं तदेव तस्मिन्विनिर्दिष्टम् ॥११४॥

When the pillars and doors are mounted by birds and the like (i.e. reptiles, bees etc.), when they shake, fall or are placed wrongly, the effects will be the same as those prescribed for Indra's Banner.

[Many bad effects have been enumerated in XLIII 62-66 *supra* for Indra's Flag being occupied by vultures, owls etc.]

प्रागुत्तरोन्नते धनसुतक्षयः सुतवधश्च दुर्गन्धे ।
वक्रे बन्धुविनाशो न सन्ति गर्भाश्व दिङ्मूढे ॥११५॥

इच्छेद्यदि गृहवृद्धिं ततः समन्ताद्विवर्धयेत्तुल्यम् ।
एकोद्देशे दोषः प्रागथवाऽप्युत्तरे कुर्यात् ॥११६॥

If the house is raised in the east or north, there will be loss of wealth and children; if it gives out a bad smell, a son will be killed; if it is not straight, death of kinsmen; and if it does not face any particular direction, no children will be born. If one wishes for the prosperity of one's house-hold, one ought to raise the level of the floor uniformly on all sides. If at all there could be any fault anywhere, it should be either in the east or in the north.

[This rule is very important in that it lays down that you cannot have different parts, of one and the same house at different levels. If at all raising the level becomes unavoidable, then it should be done either in the east or north. For, in these two directions the fault seems to be not a serious one.]

प्राग्भवति मित्रवैरं मृत्युभयं दक्षिणेन यदि वृद्धिः ।
अर्थविनाशः पश्चादुदग्विवृद्धिर्मनस्तापः ॥११७॥

If the floor of a house be raised in the east, the owner would be at loggerheads with his friends; if in the south, fear of death; if in the west, loss of wealth; and in the north, mental affliction.

[From this we can realize that the faults accruing from the elevation of the floor in the east and north are not very serious.]

In the next verse he prescribes directions for kitchen etc. in the house:

ऐशान्यां देवगृहं महानसं चापि कार्यमाग्नेय्याम् ।
नैर्ऋत्यां भाण्डोपस्करोऽर्थधान्यानि मारुत्याम् ॥११८॥

In a four-halled house (*Catuśśāla*) the worship-room should be situated in the north-east; kitchen in the south-east; the store-room in the south-west; and the treasure-room and granary in the north-west.

[Cf. the किरणाख्य तन्त्र—

पूर्वस्यां श्रीगृहं प्रोक्तमाग्नेय्यां स्यान्महानसम् ।
शयनं दक्षिणायां च नैर्ऋत्यामायुधाश्रयम् ॥
भोजनं पश्चिमायां च वायव्यां धनसञ्चयम् ।
उत्तरे द्रव्यसंस्थानमैशान्यां देवतागृहम् ॥

According to some schools different types of Vāstu-Puruṣa are to be adopted even for the construction of kitchen, worship-room etc. (See notes under 75 *supra*) :

श्रीगृहेऽत्र ध्वजः कार्यो धूपश्चैव महानसे ।
सिंहो निद्रागृहे कार्यः श्वा कुर्यादायुधाश्रये ॥
वृषो भोजनशालायां कपिर्धान्यगृहे सदा ।
द्रव्यस्थाने सदा भद्रो रिक्तो देवगृहे तथा ॥

Is it possible that धूप stands for ध्वाङ्क्ष ?]

In the next verse he deals with the effects of the existence of water i.e. its source like tank, well, etc., in the different directions.

प्राच्यादिस्थे सलिले सुतहानिः शिखिभयं रिपुभयं च ।
स्त्रीकलहः स्त्रीदौष्ट्यं नैस्व्यं वित्तात्मजविवृद्धिः ॥११९॥

If there is water to the east, south-east, south, south-west, west, north-west, north and north-east of a house, the effects would be (1) loss of children, (2) danger from fire, (3) fear of enemies, (4) quarrel among (or with) women, (5) frailty of women, (6) poverty, (7) increase of wealth, and (8) prosperity of children in order.

[Under verse 75 *supra* I had referred to the ungrammatical expression, नै:स्वम्, which was not made by the author but by the scribe, as the correct word is used in this verse.]

In the next verse he discusses the types of trees that could be used for the construction of houses.

खगनिलयभग्नसंशुष्कदग्धदेवालयश्मशानस्थान् ।
क्षीरतरुधवविभीतकनिम्बारणिवर्जितान् छिन्द्यात् ॥१२०॥

For constructing a house one ought to select for timber, trees other than that are inhabited by birds, that are broken, withered, burnt, that are in temples and burial grounds, milky trees, Dhava (*Lythrum fruticosum*), Vibhītaka (*Beleric myrobalan*), Nimba (Neem) and Araṇi (the tree whose twigs are used for churning out fire for sacrifice).

रात्रौ कृतबलिपूजं प्रदक्षिणं छेदयेद्दिवा वृक्षम् ।
धन्यमुदक्प्राक्पतनं न ग्राह्योऽतोऽन्यथा पतितः ॥१२१॥

A tree that had been worshipped with food, etc. the previous night, should be cut at day-time beginning with the north-eastern part in a clockwise direction. If it falls towards the north or east, it will be blest and beneficial; and one falling elsewhere should be rejected.

[See XLIII 13-20 *supra* in connection with Indra's Banner.

छेदो यद्यविकारी ततः शुभं दारु दगृहौपयिकम् ।
पीते तु मण्डले निर्दिशेत्त ोर्मध्यगां गोधाम् ॥१२२॥
मञ्जिष्ठाभे भेको नीले सर्पस्तथाऽरुणे स टः ।
मुद्गाभेऽश्मा कपिले तु मू कोऽम्भश्च खड्गाभे ॥१२३॥

If the cutting appears natural, the timber is good for being used for a house. If there is a yellowish circle (not natural) in the centre of the cross section of the tree, it should be predicted that there is an alligator inside the tree; if a madder-coloured circle, a frog; if a bluish one, a reptile; if a red one, a chameleon; if it is one with the colour of green gram, a stone; if a tawny one, a rat; and if it is one resembling a sword, water.

[The commentator says that the word खड्गाभे means 'circle as black as the blade of a sword.']

धान्यगोगुरुहुताशसुराणां न स्वपेदुपरि नाप्यनुवंशम् ।
नोत्तरापरशिरा न च नग्नो नैव चार्द्रचरणः श्रियमिच्छन् ॥१२४॥

A person wishing for prosperity ought not to sleep above grains, cows, elders or teachers, fire and deities, nor along the diagonals, nor with the head turned towards the north or west, nor naked, nor with wet feet.

[The Varhśas are nine in number, explained in 63-64 *supra*. This verse looks more like an excerpt from the Dharmaśāstra. A house-holder should not sleep with *Nāga-dantas* (ivory pieces) towards his feet. For says विश्वकर्मा—

शय्यानुवंशविन्यस्ता तुला हन्यात्कुटुम्बिनः ।
कर्तुः शय्या स्वतानस्था नागदन्ताः क्षयावहाः ॥

The metre is स्वागता. The word स्वपेत् is grammatically untenable.]

भूरिपुष्पविकरं सतोरणं तोयपूर्णकलशोपशोभितम् ।
धूपगन्धबलिपूजितामरं ब्राह्मणध्वनियुतं विशेद् गृहम् ॥१२५॥

The owner should enter the house which is strewn with heaps of flowers, decorated with arches, embellished with auspicious pots filled with water, where the Deities of the site have been worshipped with incense, perfumes and offerings of food, and which is resounding with the sound of Brāhmaṇas chanting the Vedas.

[The commentator draws our attention to the fact that the Deities worshipped on this occasion are only those that are in the centre of the diagram 1, and not those in the outer squares, such as Śikhin, Parjanya etc. as well as Aryaman etc. Vide, तन्त्रान्तर (which only means 'some other work') :

ज्येष्ठस्य कर्मसिद्ध्यर्थं नव पञ्चगुणाः सुराः ।
यतस्तत्र वसन्त्येते मूर्धाद्यङ्गेषु कृत्स्नशः ॥

Some more deities external to the 45 mentioned already have been spoken of by *Hiraṇyagarbha* :

देवताः सम्प्रवक्ष्यामि वास्तूनामनुपूर्वशः ।
द्वारे प्रजापतिं विन्द्याद् द्वारदेशे ह्युमापतिम् ॥
बलदेवो यमश्चैव दक्षिणस्यां च संस्थितौ ।
स्कन्दः शेषोऽथ वरुणः पश्चिमायां दिशि स्थितः ॥
आदित्या वसवो रुद्रा उत्तरां दिशमाश्रिताः ।
ब्रह्मा चैव महेन्द्रश्च दिशमैन्द्रीं समाश्रितौ ॥
कीर्तिधृ तिश्च लक्ष्मीश्च वास्तुमध्ये प्रतिष्ठिताः ।
हुत्वाग्निं गृहमध्ये तु दैवतान्यर्चयेद् बुधः ॥
दिगन्तरेषु सर्वेषु दिक्षु चैव यथाक्रमम् ।
कुलदैवतपूजां च कृत्वा च कुलमेधिनाम् ॥
दिक्षु दैवीषु सर्वासु विदिक्षु च यथाक्रमम् ॥

See also तन्त्रान्तर—

बाह्याभ्यन्तरदेवांस्तु वास्तुमध्ये यथास्थितान् ।
तथा च सर्वान् सम्पूज्य विधिनैव पुरोहितः ॥

The metre is रथोद्धता. The commentator says in a verse that he has constructed a boat in the form of his scholiam to enable students to cross the ocean of this science taught by Varāhamihira that they may get the wealth.]

दकार्गलम् ॥५४॥

Chapter LIV—Exploration of Water Springs

[Like the previous chapter, *Water-Divination* is an important and independent science practised in ancient India. Water is available from two sources, viz. the sky and the subterranian region. Our author states that the teachers of the science of the former kind of water i.e. atmospheric, are Baladeva, Garga, Kaśyapa and Devala, while those of the latter i.e. subterranian one, Sārasvata and Manu, whose authority is quoted by Utpala. As far as our present knowledge goes, no work of Sage Manu bearing on *Dakārgala* has been discovered. For this reason Bhaṭṭotpala's commentary assumes special importance. Now what is the exact meaning of this word, *Dakārgala* ? *Daka* is the shorter form of *Udaka* meaning water; and *Argala* stands for bar or bolt. In other words the expression means a branch of science dealing with water locked up or imprisoned in the bowels of the earth. Hence we can take it to represent the *modus operandi* for tapping the underground water resources.]

धर्म्यं यशस्यं च वदाम्यतोऽहं दकार्गलं येन जलोपलब्धिः ।
पुंसां यथाङ्गेषु शिरास्तथैव क्षितावपि प्रोन्नतनिम्नसंस्थाः ॥१॥

एकेन वर्णेन रसेन चाम्भश्च्युतं नभस्तो वसुधाविशेषात् ।
नानारसत्वं बहुवर्णतां च गतं परीक्ष्यं क्षितितुल्यमेव ॥२॥

I shall now expound the science of 'Water-Divination' which leads to religious merit and fame, as it helps men to ascertain the source of water. Just as there are veins in the human body, even so do they exist, some higher up, others lower down, in the earth. Though the water falling from the sky (as rain) possesses the same colour and taste, yet it assumes various colours and tastes owing to the difference in the nature of the soil (where it falls). Hence it should be examined in relation to its environments.

[Cf. verse 104 *infra* for the different tastes of water, and verses 23-26 etc. for Śirās or veins. The metre is उपजाति.]

In the next three verses the author tells us the names and effects of the various veins.

पुरुहूतानलयमनिर्ऋतिवरुणपवनेन्द्रशङ्करा देवाः ।
विज्ञातव्याः क्रमशः प्राच्याद्यानां दिशां पतयः ॥३॥

दिक्पतिसञ्ज्ञा च शिरा नवमी मध्ये महाशिरानाम्नी ।
एताभ्योऽन्याः शतशः विनिःसृता नामभिः प्रथिताः ॥४॥

पातालादूर्ध्वशिराः शुभा चतुर्दिक्षु संस्थिता याश्च ।
कोणदिग्गुत्था न शुभाः शिरानिमित्तान्यतो वक्ष्ये ॥५॥

The Gods who preside over the eight quarters beginning with the east are in order Indra, Fire, Yama (God of death), Nirṛti (demon), Varuṇa (Lord of water), Wind, the Moon and Śiva. The water-veins in the different directions are named after their presiding deities. There is the ninth known as the *Great Vein* in the centre of these. There are hundreds of veins branching off from these and bearing distinct appellations. A vein that comes up from the nether-world is auspicious; so are those that are situated in the four cardinal points, while those in the intermediate quarters are inauspicious. Hereafter I shall explain the characteristics of these veins.

यदि वेतसोऽम्बुरहिते देशे हस्तैस्त्रिभिस्ततः पश्चात् ।
सार्धे पुरुषे तोयं वहति शिरा पश्चिमा तत्र ॥६॥

चिह्नमपि चार्धपुरुषे मण्डूकः पाण्डुरोऽथ मृत्पीता ।
पुटभेदकश्च तस्मिन्पाषाणो भवति तोयमधः ॥७॥

If a rotang tree is seen flourishing in a waterless tract, there will be water at a depth of 7½ cubits at a distance of 3 cubits to the west of the tree. There will be found a westerly vein flowing underneath. At a depth of 2½ cubits the symptoms would be a pale white frog; thereafter, yellow clay and further, a hard stone (which will break only by the application of much heat) and underneath that there will be water.

[*Puruṣa* is the height of a man with his arms raised, which is 120 digits or 5 cubits. Cf. Sage सारस्वत—

निर्जले वेतसं दृष्ट्वा तस्माद् वृक्षादपि त्रयम् ।
पश्चिमायां दिशि ज्ञेयमधः सार्धेन वै जलम् ॥
नरोऽत्र षष्ट्रिद्विगुणा चाङ्गुलानां प्रकीर्तितः।
तत्र खात्वाऽर्धपुरुषं भेकः पाण्डुरवर्णकः ॥
मृत्पीता पुटभेदश्च पाषाणोऽधस्ततो जलम् ।
शिरा पश्चिमदिक्स्थात्र वहतीति विनिर्दिशेत् ॥]

जम्ब्वाश्चोदग्घस्तैस्त्रिभिः शिराधो नरद्वये पूर्वा ।
मृल्लोहगन्धिका पाण्डुरा च पुरुषेऽत्र मण्डूकः ॥८॥

In a waterless place if a Jambū tree is found, an easterly vein can be detected at a depth of ten cubits at a distance of three cubits to the north of the tree. Its signs are : the earth smelling like iron at a depth of five cubits, then pale-white clay, and further a frog.

जम्बूवृक्षस्य प्राग्वल्मीको यदि भवेत् समीपस्थः ।
तस्माद्दक्षिणपार्श्वे सलिलं पुरुषद्वये स्वादु ॥९॥
अर्धपुरुषे च मत्स्यः पारावतसन्निभश्च पाषाणः ।
मृद्भवति चात्र नीला दीर्घं कालं बहु तोयम् ॥१०॥

If there be an ant-hill nearby to the east of a Jambū tree, there would be sweet water at a depth of ten cubits at a distance of three cubits to the south of the tree. When the earth is dug $2\frac{1}{2}$ cubits deep, there will be found fish; next a stone with the colour of a dove; and next blue clay. Underneath this there will be inexhaustible water for a long time.

[Cf. सारस्वत—

जम्बूवृक्षात्पूर्वभागे वल्मीको यदि दृश्यते ।
तरोर्दक्षिणतो हस्तांस्त्रींस्त्यक्त्वाऽधो जलं वदेत् ॥
नरद्वयेऽर्धपुरुषे मत्स्योऽश्मा पक्षिसन्निभः ।
ततोऽपि मृत्तिका नीला ततो मृष्टं जलं वदेत् ॥]

पश्चादुदुम्बरस्य त्रिभिरेव करैर्नरद्वये सार्धे ।
पुरुषे सितोऽहिरश्माञ्जनोपमोऽधः शिरा सुजला ॥११॥

If there be an Indian fig tree in a waterless place (with or without an ant-hill), there would be a vein of good water at a depth of $12\frac{1}{2}$ cubits at a distance of three cubits to the west of the tree. Here the indications are that at depth of five cubits there would be a white snake, then a stone as black as collyrium, and then the vein of water.

उदगर्जुनस्य दृश्यो वल्मीको यदि ततोऽर्जुनाद्धस्तैः ।
त्रिभिरम्बु भवति पुरुषैस्त्रिभिरर्धसमन्वितैः पश्चात् ॥१२॥

श्वेता गोधार्धनरे पुरुषे मृद्धूसरा ततः कृष्णा ।
पीता सिता ससिकता ततो जलं निर्दिशेदमितम् ॥१३॥

If there be an ant-hill to the north of an Arjuna tree, there would be water at a depth of 17½ cubits at a distance of three cubits to the west of the tree. Here the signs are that at a depth of 2½ cubits there will be a white alligator; then at a depth of five cubits, grey clay; then dark, then yellow, then white. and then sandy earth; and beneath that abundant water will be found.

वल्मीकोपचितायां निर्गुण्ड्यां दक्षिणेन कथितकरैः ।
पुरुषद्वये सपादे स्वादुजलं भवति चाशोष्यम् ॥१४॥

रोहितमत्स्योऽर्धनरे मृत् कपिला पाण्डुरा ततः परतः ।
सिकता सशर्कराऽथ क्रमेण परतो भवत्यम्भः ॥१५॥

If there is a Nirguṇḍī tree overgrown with an ant-hill (or with an ant-hill closeby), there will be sweet and never-failing water at a depth of 11¼ cubits at a distance of three cubits to the south of the tree. There will be red fish at a depth of 2½ cubits; then, red-brown clay; next, pale-white clay; then, sand mixed with gravel and beneath that there will be water.

पूर्वेण यदि वदर्या वल्मीको दृश्यते जलं पश्चात् ।
पुरुषैस्त्रिभिरादेश्यं श्वेता गृहगोधिकार्द्धनरे ॥१६॥

If an ant-hill be seen to the east of a jujube tree, water should be declared to exist at a distance of three cubits to the west of the tree at a depth of 15 cubits. When the earth is dug 2½ cubits, a white lizard will be found.

[Cf. सारस्वत—

पूर्वभागं वदर्याश्चेद्वल्मीको दृश्यते जलम् ।
पश्चाद्धस्तत्रये वाच्यं खाते तु पुरुषत्रये ॥
अधःखातेऽर्धपुरुषे दृश्यते गृहगोधिका ।
श्वेतवर्णा ततोऽधःस्थं जलं भवति निर्मलम् ॥]

सपलाशा बदरी चेद् दिश्यपरस्यां ततो जलं भवति ।
पुरुषत्रये सपादे पुरुषोऽत्र च दुण्डुभश्चिह्नम् ॥१७॥

If in a waterless place there be a jujube tree along with a Pālāśa tree, there would be water at a depth of 16¼ cubits at a distance of three cubits to its west. Here the symptom will be a non-poisonous snake at a depth of five cubits.

[Cf. सारस्वत—

पलाशयुक्ता बदरी यत्र दृश्या ततोऽपरे ।
हस्तत्रयादधस्तोयं सपादे पुरुषत्रये ।।
नरे तु दुण्डुभः सर्पो निर्विषश्चिह्नमेव च ।
अधस्तोयं च सुस्वादु दीर्घकालं प्रवाहितम् ।।]

बिल्वोदुम्बरयोगे विहाय हस्तत्रयं तु याम्येन ।
पुरुषैस्त्रिभिरम्बु भवेत्कृष्णो ऽर्द्धनरे च मण्डूकः ।।१८।।

There will be water at a depth of 15 cubits at a distance of three cubits to the south of the place where a Bilva and an Indian fig tree are joined together. The indication in this case is a black frog at a depth of 2½ cubits.

काकोदुम्बरिकायां वल्मीको दृश्यते शिरा तस्मिन् ।
पुरुषत्रये सपादे पश्चिमदिक्स्था वहति सा च ।।१९।।

आपाण्डुपीतिका मृद्गौरसवर्णश्च भवति पाषाणः ।
पुरुषार्धे कुमुदनिभो दृष्टिपथं मूषको याति ।।२०।।

If an ant-hill is seen near (or along with) an opposite-leaved fig tree (Phalgu), there will be a westerly water vein flowing underneath it at a depth of 16¼ cubits. The symptoms are pale yellow clay and white stone; and at a depth of 2½ cubits a white rat will be found.

[The commentator takes तस्मिन् to mean under the very same ant-hill, but elsewhere through out he takes the vein to be at a distance of 3 cubits in a certain direction. I feel that that rule need not be given up in this instance and the meaning would be: 'There will be a vein of water flowing in a westerly direction at a distance of 3 cubits to the west of the ant-hill.]

जलपरिहीने देशे वृक्षः कम्पिल्लको यदा दृश्यः ।
प्राच्यां हस्तत्रितये वहति शिरा दक्षिणा प्रथमम् ।।२१।।

मृन्नीलोत्पलवर्णा कापोता दृश्यते ततस्तस्मिन् ।
हस्तेऽजगन्धको मत्स्यकः पयोऽल्पं च सक्षारम् ।।२२।।

When a Kampillaka tree is seen in a waterless place, there will be a water-vein flowing in a southerly direction at a distance of three cubits to the east of the tree at a depth of 16¾ cubits. The symptoms are blue-clay at first, then dove-colour-clay, and further at a depth of one cubit, there will be a fish smelling like goat, and beneath that a little brackish water.

[Cf. **सारस्वत**—

निर्जले यत्र कम्पिल्लो दृश्यस्तस्मात् करत्रये ।
प्राच्यां त्रिभिर्नरैर्वारि सा भवेद् दक्षिणा शिरा ॥
अधो नीलोत्पलाभासा मृत् कापोतप्रभा क्रमात् ।
हस्तेऽजगन्धको मत्स्यो जलमल्पमशोभनम् ॥]

शोणाकतरोरपरोत्तरे शिरा द्वौ करावतिक्रम्य ।
कुमुदा नाम शिरा सा पुरुषत्रयवाहिनी भवति ॥२३॥

There is a water-vein named Kumudā, which flows at a depth of 15 cubits and at a distance of two cubits to the north-west of a Śoṇāka tree in a waterless tract.

[In the अमरकोश स्योनाक and शोणाक are given as synonyms.]

आसन्नो वल्मीको दक्षिणपार्श्वे विभीतकस्य यदि ।
अध्यर्धे भवति शिरा पुरुषे ज्ञेया दिशि प्राच्याम् ॥२४॥

Should there be an ant-hill closeby to the south of a Beleric Myrobalan tree, there would be a water-vein at a distance of 2 cubits to its east and at a depth of 7½ cubits.

[विभीतकस्य याम्यायां वल्मीको यदि दृश्यते ।
करद्वयान्तरे पूर्वे सार्धे च पुरुषे जलम् ॥]

तस्यैव पश्चिमायां दिशि वल्मीको यदा भवेद्धस्ते ।
तत्रोदग् भवति शिरा चतुर्भिरर्धाधिकैः पुरुषैः ॥२५॥

श्वेतो विश्वम्भरकः प्रथमे पुरुषे तु कुङ्कुमाभोऽश्मा ।
अपरस्यां दिशि च शिरा नश्यति वर्षत्रये ऽतीते ॥२६॥

If the ant-hill be to the west of the same tree, there would be a vein to the north of the tree at a distance of one cubit and at a depth of 22½ cubits. The signs here would be a white reptile (or a scorpion?) at a depth of five-cubits, then a crimson stone, and then there would be a vein of water flowing westward. However, this vein will disappear after three years.

[The commentary does not help us in identifying the विश्वम्भरक which is a creature.]

सकुशासित ऐशान्यां वल्मीको यत्र कोविदारस्य ।
मध्ये तयोर्नरैरर्धपञ्चमैस्तोयमक्षोभ्यम् ॥२७॥

प्रथमे पुरुषे भुजगः कमलोदरसन्निभो मही रक्ता ।
कुरुविन्दः पाषाणश्चिह्नान्येतानि वाच्यानि ॥२८॥

If there is an ant-hill darkened by the holy grass to the north-east of a mountain ebony tree, there will be inexhaustible water at a depth of 22½ cubits between the tree and the ant-hill. The indications mentioned are a snake of the colour of the lotus-calix at a depth of 5 cubits; below that red earth; and lower still a coryndon stone (ruby).

[In the first line सकुशःसित is another reading. But in our previous edition we had adopted the reading given here. This is more sensible than the one where सित appears instead of असित].

यदि भवति सप्तपर्णो वल्मीकवृतस्तदुत्तरे तोयम् ।
वाच्यं पुरुषैः पञ्चभिरत्रापि भवन्ति चिह्नानि ॥२९॥

पुरुषार्धे मण्डूको हरितो हरितालसन्निभो भूश्च ।
पाषाणोऽभ्रनिकाशः सौम्या च शिरा शुभाम्बुवहा ॥३०॥

Should an Echites tree be covered by ant-hills, it should be predicted that there is water at a depth of 25 cubits at a distance of one cubit to its north. The signs are that at a depth of 2½-cubits there would be a green frog, then the earth resembling yellow orpiment, then a stone dark like the cloud, and beneath that a northerly vein carrying good water.

[Cf. सारस्वत—

भुजङ्गगृहसंयुक्तो यत्र स्यात् सप्तपर्णकः ।
ततः सौम्ये हस्तमात्रात् पञ्चभिः पुरुषैरधः ॥
वाच्यं जलं नरार्धे तु मण्डूको हरितो भवेत् ।
हरितालनिभा भूश्च मेघाभोऽश्मा ततः शिरा ॥
उत्तरा सुजला ज्ञेया दीर्घा मृष्टाम्बुवाहिनी ॥]

सर्वेषां वृक्षाणामधः स्थितो दर्दुरो यदा दृश्यः ।
तस्माद्धस्ते तोयं चतुर्भिरर्धाधिकैः पुरुषैः ॥३१॥

पुरुषे तु भवति नकुलो नीला मृत्पीतिका ततः श्वेता ।
दर्दुरसमानरूपः पाषाणो दृश्यते चात्र ॥३२॥

If a frog is seen at the foot of any tree, there will be water at a depth of 22½ cubits at a distance of one cubit to its north. The signs are : a mongoose at a depth of 5 cubits, then blue-clay, yellow, then white clay and next a stone of the form of a frog. (Water will be got underneath that.)

[Cf. सारस्वत—

तरूणां यत्र सर्वेषामधःस्थो दर्दुरो भवेत् ।
वृक्षादुदग्दिशि जलं हस्तात् सार्धैर्नरैरधः ॥
चतुर्भिः पुरुषे खाते नकुलो नीलमृत्तिका ।
पीतश्वेता ततो भेकसदृशोऽश्मा प्रदृश्यते ॥]

यद्यहिनिलयो दृश्यो दक्षिणतः संस्थितः करञ्जस्य ।
हस्तद्वये तु याम्ये पुरुषत्रितये शिरा सार्धे ॥३३॥

कच्छपकः पुरुषार्धे प्रथमं चोद्भिद्यते शिरा पूर्वा ।
उदगन्या स्वादुजला हरितोऽश्माधस्ततस्तोयम् ॥३४॥

Should an ant-hill be found to the south of a Gray Bonduc tree, there would be a water-vein at a depth of 17½-cubits at a distance of 2 cubits to its south. The signs would be : a small tortoise at a depth of 2½-cubits; there would emerge first of all an easterly vein, then another northerly vein of sweet water; then a green stone below; beneath that there would be water.

[It is strange that Utpala construes the word हरितः as शुक्रवर्णः.]

उत्तरतश्च मधूकादहिनिलयः पश्चिमे तरोस्तोयम् ।
परिहृत्य पञ्च हस्तानर्धाष्टमपौरुषान् प्रथमम् ॥३५॥

अहिराजः पुरुषेऽस्मिन् धूम्रा धात्री कुलुत्थवर्णोऽश्मा ।
माहेन्द्री भवति शिरा वहति सफेनं सदा तोयम् ॥३६॥

If there be an ant-hill to the north of a Bassia tree, there would be water at a depth of 37½ cubits at a distance of five cubits to the west of the tree. Here the indications are : first a big snake at a depth of 5 cubits, then tawny clay, next a stone of the colour of horse gram; next there would be an easterly vein carrying always foamy water.

[I feel that कुलुत्थ might be a mistake for कुलत्थ.]

वल्मीकः स्निग्धो दक्षिणेन तिलकस्य सकुशदूर्वश्चेत् ।
पुरुषैः पञ्चभिरम्भो दिशि वारुण्यां शिरा पूर्वा ॥३७॥

If there be a glossy ant-hill covered with holy grass and dūrvā grass to the south of a Tilaka tree, there would be water at a depth of 25 cubits at a distance of 5 cubits to the west of the tree. The water-vein there would be an easterly one.

[Cf. **सारस्वत**—

तिलकाद् दक्षिणे स्निग्धः कुशदूर्वासमायुतः ।
वल्मीकाच्चोत्तरे पञ्च हस्तान् सन्त्यज्य पश्चिमे ॥
नरैः पञ्चभिरम्भोऽधः शिरा पूर्वात्र विद्यते ॥]

सर्पावासः पश्चाद्यदा कदम्बस्य दक्षिणेन जलम् ।
परतो हस्तत्रितयात् षड्भिः पुरुषैस्तुरीयोनैः ॥३८॥

कौबेरी चात्र शिरा वहति जलं लोहगन्धि चाक्षोभ्यम् ।
कनकनिभो मण्डूको नरमात्रे मृत्तिका पीता ॥३९॥

If there be an ant-hill to the west of a Kadamba tree (*Nauclea orientalis*), there would be a northerly vein carrying inexhaustible water with the smell of iron at a depth of $28\frac{3}{4}$ cubits at a distance of 3 cubits to the south of the tree. The signs are : a golden frog at a depth of 5 cubits; and then, yellow clay.

वल्मीकसंवृतो यदि तालो वा भवति नालिकेरो वा ।
पश्चात् षड्भिर्हस्तैर्नरैश्चतुर्भिः शिरा याम्या ॥४०॥

If a palm tree or cocoanut tree be found covered with ant-hills, there would be a southerly water-vein at a depth of 20 cubits at a distance of 6 cubits to the west of the tree.

याम्येन कपित्थस्याहिसंश्रयश्चेदुदग्जलं वाच्यम् ।
सप्त परित्यज्य करान् खात्वा पुरुषाञ्जलं पञ्च ॥४१॥

कर्बुरकोऽहिः पुरुषे कृष्णा मृत् पुटभिदपि च पाषाणः ।
श्वेता मृत् पश्चिमतः शिरा ततश्चोत्तरा भवति ॥४२॥

If there be an ant-hill to the south of a wood-apple tree, there would be water at a depth of 25 cubits at a distance of 7 cubits to the north of the tree. Here the symptoms would be : a variegated snake at a depth of 5 cubits ; then, black clay; then a hard stone;

next white clay; and then there would be a westerly vein and next, a northerly one.

अश्मन्तकस्य वामे बदरी वा दृश्यतेऽहिनिलयो वा ।
षड्भिरुदक् तस्य करैः सार्धे पुरुषत्रये तोयम् ॥४३॥

कर्मः प्रथमे पुरुषे पाषाणो धूसरः ससिकता मृत् ।
आदौ च शिरा याम्या पूर्वोत्तरतो द्वितीया च ॥४४॥

Should there be a jujube tree or an ant-hill to the north of an Aśmantaka tree, there would be water at a depth of $17\frac{1}{2}$ cubits and at a distance of 6 cubits to the north of the Aśmantaka. The signs thereof are: in the first layer of 5 cubits a tortoise, then purple stone, next, clay mixed with sand, then at first a southerly vein and next, a north-easterly one.

वामेन हरिद्रतरोर्वल्मीकश्चेज्जलं भवति पूर्वे ।
हस्तत्रितये सत्र्यंशैः पुम्भिः पञ्चभिर्भवति ॥४५॥

नीलो भुजगः पुरुषे मृत्पीता मरकतोपमश्चाश्मा ।
कृष्णा भूः प्रथमं वारुणी शिरा दक्षिणेनान्या ॥४६॥

If there is an ant-hill to the north of a Dāru Haldi tree, there will be water $28\frac{3}{4}$ cubits down and 3 cubits to the east of the tree. The signs for this are : a blue snake upto a depth of 5 cubits, next yellow clay, then an emerald-like stone, next black earth, then at first a westerly vein and then a southerly one.

[The Haridrādruma is called *Maradarasina* in Kannaḍa. The ordinary *arasina* is turmeric.]

जलपरिहीने देशे दृश्यन्तेऽनूप जानिचिह्नानि ।
वीरणदूर्वा मृदवश्च यत्र तस्मिन् जलं पुरुषे ॥४७॥

भार्ङ्गी त्रिवृता दन्ती सूकरपादी च लक्ष्मणा चैव ।
नवमालिका च हस्तद्वयेऽम्बु याम्ये त्रिभिः पुरुषैः ॥४८॥

If in a waterless place are seen the characteristics of a watery region or soft Vīraṇa grass or Dūrvā, water will be found there at 5 cubits below the earth. Or if a kind of brinjal (?) Trivṛtā (white variety of Teori), Dantī, Sūkarapādī, Lakṣmaṇā and Navamālikā (Double Jasmine) creeper be found to be growing in a place, water will be got at a depth of 15 cubits and two-cubits to the south of these herbs.

[The Benares edition gives the wrong reading 'चेन्निमित्तानि' which spoils the metre. The commentator remarks that भार्ङ्गी and others are 'स्वनामभिः सुप्रसिद्धाः'. It is not clear what भार्ङ्गी means. Is it भार्गी (Bamanaiṭhī) mentioned in the Amarakośa?]

स्निग्धाः प्रलम्बशाखा वामनविकटद्रुमाः समीपजलाः ।
सुषिरा जर्जरपत्रा रूक्षाश्च जलेन सन्त्यक्ताः ॥४६॥

Those trees which are glossy, have long overhanging branches, are very short and very extensive, have water nearby (i.e. there must be water under ground in such places); whereas those that ar hollow, have pale leaves, and are dry, do not indicate water in the neighbourhood.

तिलकाम्रातकवरुणकभल्लातकबिल्वतिन्दुकाङ्कोलाः ।
पिण्डारशिरीषाञ्जनपरूषका वञ्जुलोऽतिबला ॥ ५० ॥

एते यदि सुस्निग्धा वल्मीकैः परिवृतास्ततस्तोयम् ।
हस्तैस्त्रिभिरुत्तरतश्चतुर्भिरर्धेन च नरेण ॥५१॥

If Tilaka (Tilā), Āmrātaka (Spondias), Varuṇa (Tapia), Bhallātaka (Marking Nut tree), Bilva, Tinduka (a sort of ebony) Aṅkola (walnut), Piṇḍāra, Śirīṣa (Siris), Añjana, Parūṣaka, Vañjula (Bayas) and Atibalā are very glossy and covered with ant-hills, there will be water at a depth of 22½ cubits and at a distance of 3 cubits to the north of them.

अतृणे सतृणा यस्मिन् सतृणे तृणवर्जिता मही यत्र ।
तस्मिन् शिरा प्रदिष्टा वक्तव्यं वा धनं चास्मिन् ॥५२॥

If in a grassless place a patch of ground is seen covered with grass, or in a grassy plot, one is seen devoid of it, a vein of water or treasure is to be declared to exist there.

[The commentator refers here to some opinion according to which the depth of the vein also should be considered as in the previous śloka i.e. 4½ Puruṣas.]

कण्टक्यकण्टकानां व्यत्यासेऽम्भस्त्रिभिः करैः पश्चात् ।
खात्वा पुरुषत्रितयं त्रिभागयुक्तं धनं वा स्यात् ॥५३॥

When a thorny tree flourishes in the midst of non-thorny trees and *vice versa*, there will be a treasure or water at a depth of $18\frac{3}{4}$ cubits at a distance of 3 cubits to the west of the tree.

नदति मही गम्भीरं यस्मिंश्चरणाहता जलं तस्मिन् ।
सार्धैस्त्रिभिर्मनुष्यैः कौबेरी तत्र च शिरा स्यात् ॥५४॥

Where the earth being srtuck by feet emits a loud and pleasant sound, a northerly water-vein will be found at the same place at a depth of $17\frac{1}{2}$ cubits.

वृक्षस्यैका शाखा यदि विनता भवति पाण्डुरा वा स्यात् ।
विज्ञातव्यं शाखातले जलं त्रिपुरुषं खात्वा ॥५५॥

Should a single branch of a tree hang low or be colourless, it should be understood that water exists at a depth of 15 cubits under the branch.

फलकुसुमविकारो यस्य तस्य पूर्वे शिरा त्रिभिर्हस्तैः ।
भवति पुरुषैश्चतुर्भिः पाषाणोऽधः क्षितिः पीता ॥५६॥

Where the fruits and flowers of a tree look unnatural (i.e. resemble others), there will be a water-vein flowing 20 cubits below at a distance of 3 cubits to its east. Here the symptoms are: Stone below and yellow clay.

यदि कण्टकारिका कण्टकैर्विना दृश्यते सितैः कुसुमैः ।
तस्यास्तलेऽम्बु वाच्यं त्रिभिर्नरैरर्धपुरुषे च ॥५७॥

If a Kaṇṭakāri (Bṛhatī or Prickly Nightshade) plant is seen devoid of thorns, but with white flowers, there will be water underneath it at a depth of $17\frac{1}{2}$-cubits.

खर्जूरी द्विशिरस्का यत्र भवेज्जलविवर्जिते देशे ।
तस्याः पश्चिमभागे निर्देश्यं त्रिपुरुषैर्वारि ॥५८॥

Should there be a date tree with two tops in a waterless area, water should be declared to exist 15 cubits below at a distance of two cubits to the west of it.

[Cf. सारस्वत—

खर्जूरी द्विशिरस्का स्यान्निर्जले चेत् करद्वये ।
निर्देश्यं पश्चिमे वारि खात्वाऽधः पुरुषत्रयम् ॥]

यदि भवति कर्णिकारः सितकुसुमः स्यात्पलाशवृक्षो वा ।
सव्येन तत्र हस्तद्वयेऽम्बु पुरुषद्वये भवति ॥५९॥

If a Karṇikāra (Barahal) or Palāśa (*Butea Frondosa*) tree bears white flowers (instead of red ones), there will be water two cubits to its south at a depth of 10 cubits.

यस्यामूष्मा धात्र्यां धूमो वा तत्र वारि नरयुगले ।
निर्देष्टव्या च शिरा महता तोयप्रवाहेण ॥६०॥

If steam or smoke arises from the earth, there will be water underneath at 10 cubits; and it should be stated that the vein will yield an abundant supply of water.

यस्मिन् क्षेत्रोद्देशे जातं सस्यं विनाशमुपयाति ।
स्निग्धमतिपाण्डुरं वा महाशिरा नरयुगे तत्र ॥६१॥

If in the region of a field the crops that have grown perish or if the vegetation there is very glossy and exceedingly white, there will be a vein of abundant water on the spot at a depth of 10 cubits.

[The above exposition relates to the availability of water in jungle and watery regions. Hereafter the author treats of water-divination in desert areas.]

मरुदेशे भवति शिरा यथा तथातः परं प्रवक्ष्यामि ।
ग्रीवा करभाणामिव भूतलसंस्थाः शिरा यान्ति ॥६२॥

I shall now expound the possibilities of veins in desert regions. The water-veins run below the earth's surface in the form of camel's neck i.e. syphons).

[The camel's neck is crooked, long and thin. The veins of water in deserts would be very deep and slender.]

पूर्वोत्तरेण पीलोर्यदि वल्मीको जलं भवति पश्चात् ।
उत्तरगमना च शिरा विज्ञेया पञ्चभिः पुरुषैः॥६३॥

विह्नं दर्दुर आदौ मृत्कपिला तत्परं भवेद्धरिता ।
भवति च पुरुषेऽधोऽश्मा तस्य तलेऽम्भो विनिर्देश्यम् ॥६४॥

If there be an ant-hill to north-east of a Pīlu tree, there would be water at a distance of 4½ cubits to the west of the tree and at a depth of 25 cubits. The vein of water would be running in a northerly direction. The signs would be: in the first Puruṣa (5 cubits) a frog, then brown clay, thereafter green clay, then below, a stone and beneath that water (in plenty).

[I do not understand why Utpala says हरिता means शुक्ला. The author does not give in the text the distance of the vein from the tree but Sage Sārasvata, who is quoted by the commentator, gives it as "सरलैश्चतुर्भिर्हस्तैः" which Utpala takes to mean 4½ cubits. If that be correct, the reading ought to be सदलैः instead of सरलैः which must be a printer's devil. Hence I take the liberty of correcting the reading in the following quotation from सारस्वत—

ऐशान्यां पीलुवृक्षस्य वल्मीकश्चेज्जलं वदेत् ।
चतुर्भिः सदलैर्हस्तैः पश्चिमे नरपञ्चमे ॥
प्रथमे पुरुषे भेकः कपिला हरिता च मृत् ।
पाषाणस्य तले सौम्यां शिरां बहुजलां वदेत् ॥]

पीलोरेव प्राच्यां वल्मीकोऽतोऽर्धपञ्चमैर्हस्तैः ।
दिशि याम्यायां तोयं वक्तव्यं सप्तभिः पुरुषैः ॥६५॥
प्रथमे पुरुषे भुजगः सितासितो हस्तमात्रमूर्त्तिश्च ।
दक्षिणतो वहति शिरा सक्षारं भूरि पानीयम् ॥६६॥

If the ant-hill be to the east of the Pīlu tree, there would be water 4½ cubits to the south at a depth of 35 cubits. The signs would be: in the first Puruṣa (5 cubits) a white and black snake of one cubit length; to its south flows a vein with plenty of brackish water.

उत्तरतश्च करीरस्याहिगृहं दक्षिणे जलं स्वादु ।
दशभिः पुरुषैर्ज्ञेयं पुरुषे पीतोऽत्र मण्डूकः ॥६७॥

Should there be an ant-hill to the north of a Karīra (Caril) tree, there would be sweet water 50 cubits below at a distance of 4½ cubits to the south of the tree. The sign at a depth of 5 cubits is a yellow frog.

[The word *Karīra* should not be taken here to mean 'the tender bamboo shoot.' For, it is a desert tree, Maru vṛkṣaḥ, says Kṣīrasvāmin (Amara II-77). He says (in III-174) it is वंशविशेष or a variety of bamboo.

Cf. सारस्वत—

उदक्करीराद्वल्मीको दृश्यते चेज्जलं वदेत् ।
चतुर्भिर्दक्षिणे हस्तैः सार्धैर्दशनरादतः ॥
नरे भेकः पीतवर्णो दृश्यते चिह्नमत्र हि ॥]

रोहीतकस्य पश्चादहिवासश्चेत्त्रिभिः करैर्याम्ये ।
द्वादश पुरुषान् खात्वा सक्षारा पश्चिमेन शिरा ॥६८॥

If there be an ant-hill to the west of a Rohītaka tree, there would be a westerly vein of brackish water 60-cubits underneath at a distance of 3 cubits to the south of the tree.

[According to the *Amarakośa* the tree is Rohitaka. It is otherwise known as प्लीहशत्रु—enemy of spleen]

इन्द्रतरोर्वल्मीकः प्राग्दृश्यः पश्चिमे शिरा हस्ते ।
खात्वा चतुर्दश नरान् कपिला गोधा नरे प्रथमे ॥६९॥

Should there be an ant-hill to the east of an *Indra* tree (Kahuā), there would be a vein of water one cubit to its west at a depth of 70 cubits. The indication is that at a depth of 5 cubits there would be a brown alligator.

[According to the *Amara* (II-46) इन्द्रद्रु is the same as नदीसर्ज and Arjuna. Kṣīrasvāmin states that *Indradru* has three meanings : Kuṭaja Arjuna and Devadāru. It is possible that in the present context it stands for Devadāru which grows on the hills.]

यदि वा सुवर्णनाम्नस्तरोर्भवेद्वामतो भुजङ्गगृहम् ।
हस्तद्वये तु याम्ये पञ्चदशनरावसानेऽम्बु ॥७०॥

क्षारं पयोऽत्र नकुलोऽर्धमानवे ताम्रसन्निभश्चाश्मा ।
रक्ता च भवति वसुधा वहति शिरा दक्षिणा तत्र ॥७१॥

If there is an ant-hill to the north of a Suvarṇaka tree (*Cassia fistula*), there will be brackish water 75 cubits below at a distance of two cubits to the south of the tree. When the earth is dug $2\frac{1}{2}$-cubits, there will be found a mongoose; next copper-coloured stone; then, red earth; then there flows a southerly vein.

बदरीरोहितवृक्षौ सम्पृक्तौ चेद्विनापि वल्मीकम् ।
हस्तत्रयेऽम्बु पश्चात् षोडशभिर्मानवैर्भवति ॥७२॥

सुरसं जलमादौ दक्षिणा शिरा वहति चोत्तरेणान्या ।
पिष्टनिभः पाषाणो मृत् श्वेता वृश्चिको ऽर्धनरे ॥७३॥

If a jujube tree and a Rohita tree are joined together with or without an ant-hill nearby, there will be sweet water 80 cubits below at a distance of 3 cubits to their west. First a southerly vein will come to light and then a northerly one. The signs here are : the stone will be paste-like, next white clay, and at $2\frac{1}{2}$ cubits down a scorpion will be seen.

सकरीरा चेद् बदरी त्रिभिः करैः पश्चिमेन तत्राम्भः ।
अष्टादशभिः पुरुषैरैशानी बहुजला च शिरा ॥७४॥

If a jujube tree be joined with a Karīra tree, there would be a north-easterly vein of copious water at a depth of 90 cubits and at a distance of three cubits to the west of the tree.

पीलुसमेता बदरी हस्तत्रयसम्मिते दिशि प्राच्याम् ।
विंशत्या पुरुषाणामशोष्यमम्भोऽत्र सक्षारम् ॥७५॥

If the jujube tree is combined with a Pīlu tree, there will be an inexhaustible supply of brackish water 100 cubits below to the east of the tree at a distance of three cubits.

ककुभकरीरावेकत्र संयुतौ यत्र ककुभबिल्वौ वा ।
हस्तद्वयेऽम्बु पश्चान्नरैर्भवेत् पञ्चविंशत्या ॥७६॥

If a Kakubha (Indradru?) and a Karīra tree or Kakubha and Bilva (Marmelos) trees are joined together, there will be water 125 cubits below at a distance of two cubits to the west of the trees.

वल्मीकमूर्धनि यदा दूर्वा च कुशाश्च पाण्डुराः सन्ति ।
कूपो मध्ये देयो जलमत्र नरैकविंशत्या ॥७७॥

When the Dūrvā grass (Bent grass) or the holy grass growing on the top of an ant-hill appear pale-white, a well should be sunk in its middle. There will be water in this place at a depth of 105 cubits.

भूमिः कदम्बकयुता वल्मीके यत्र दृश्यते दूर्वा ।
हस्तद्वयेन याम्ये नरैर्जलं पञ्चविंशत्या ॥७८॥

If Dūrvā (Bent grass) is seen on an anthill in a place full of Kadamba trees (Nauclea orientalis), there will be water at a depth of 125 cubits and at a distance of two cubits to the south of the anthill.

[The Kadamba tree is supposed to be dear to Balarāma, because it has the smell of wine We do not know if people were extracting liquor from it. The धन्वन्तरि निघण्टु (V-105) says

"परः कदम्बः प्रावृषेण्यः कादम्बर्यो हलिप्रियः ।
नीपो धूलिकदम्बोऽन्यः सुवासो वृत्तपुष्पकः ॥

This tree has two other names. धाराकदम्ब and राजकदम्ब.]

वल्मीकत्रयमध्ये रोहीतकपादपो यदा भवति ।
नानावृक्षैः सहितस्त्रिभिर्जलं तत्र वक्तव्यम् ॥७९॥
हस्तचतुष्के मध्यात् षोडशभिश्चाङ्गुलैरुदग्वारि ।
चत्वारिंशत्पुरुषान् खात्वाऽश्माऽधः शिरा भवति ॥८०॥

If there is a Rohitaka tree along with three other trees of different types in the centre of three ant-hills forming the apexes of a triangle, there will be water 200 cubits below at a distance of 4 cubits and 16 digits to the north of the centre. When the bottom is reached, there will be stone and beneath that water-vein.

ग्रन्थिप्रचुरा यस्मिन् शमी भवेदुत्तरेण वल्मीकः ।
पश्चात्पञ्चकरान्ते शतार्धसंख्यैर्नरैः सलिलम् ॥८१॥

If there be an ant-hill to the north of a knotty Śamī tree (Saen) there will be water at a depth of 250 cubits at a distance of 5 cubits to its west.

एकस्थाः पञ्च यदा वल्मीका मध्यमो भवेच्छ्वेतः ।
तस्मिन् शिरा प्रदिष्टा नरषष्ट्या पञ्चवर्जितया ॥८२॥

When there are five ant-hills in one and the same place and the central one white, there is said to be a water-vein below the central one at a depth of 275 cubits.

सपलाशा यत्र शमी पश्चिमभागेऽम्बु मानवैः षष्ट्या ।
अर्धनरेऽहिः प्रथमं सवालुका पीतमृत्परतः ॥८३॥

Where there is a Śamī tree joined with a Palāśa (Buteo frondosa) tree, there will be water 300 cubits below at a distance of 5 cubits to its west. Where the earth is dug 2½ cubits, there will be a snake at first, and then yellow clay mixed with gravel.

[Cf सारस्वत—

शमी पलाशसंयुक्ता यत्र स्यात् तत्र पश्चिमे ।
पञ्चहस्ताज्जलं वाच्यं षष्ट्याऽत्र पुरुषैरधः ॥
अत्रार्धपुरुषे सर्पः पीता मृत् स्यात्सवालुका ।
तदधोऽम्भो विनिर्देश्यं दीर्घकालं प्रवाहितम् ॥]

वल्मीकेन परिवृतः श्वेतो रोहीतको भवेद्यस्मिन् ।
पूर्वेण हस्तमात्रे सप्तत्या मानवैरस्तु ॥८४॥

Where there is a white Rohitaka tree surrounded by an ant-hill, there will be water at a depth of 350 cubits and one cubit to the east.

श्वेता कण्टकबहुला यत्र शमी दक्षिणेन तत्र पयः ।
नरपञ्चकसंयुतया सप्तत्याहिर्नरार्धे च ॥८५॥

If there is a white Śamī tree full of thorns, there will be water at depth of 375 cubits and one cubit to the south of the tree. At a depth of 2½ cubits there will be a snake.

[Thus the author refers to a number of desert trees with or without ant-hills in their vicinity as the guiding factors locating water. In modern times tube wells are sunk to get water from very great depths. Here the maximum depth in desert areas is 375 cubits and the minimum is 25 cubits, while elsewhere they are 37½ cubits and 7½ cubits respectively.]

Cf. सारस्वत—

श्वेतातिकण्टका यत्र शमी स्यात् तत्र दक्षिणे ।
हस्तेन पञ्चसप्तत्या नराणां निर्दिशेज्जलम् ॥
खातेऽर्धपुरुषे सर्पो दृश्यतेऽञ्जनसप्रभः ।
सुरसं च जलं ज्ञेयं चिरचारप्रवाहितम् ॥]

मरुदेशे यच्चिह्नं न जाङ्गले तैर्जलं विनिर्देश्यम् ।
जम्बूवेतसपूर्वं ये पुरुषास्ते मरौ द्विगुणाः ॥८६॥

The existence of water in a semi-desert area (where there is little water) should not be predicted on such symptoms as are found in a desert. If the characteristics mentioned viz. Jambū, Vetasa etc., in connection with waterless tracts, are seen in deserts, water should be declared to exist there at twice the depth mentioned.

[The symptoms of Jāṅgala or semi-desert tracts, are mentioned in Verses 6 and 8 *supra*. Sometimes the characteristics of Jāṅgala and Anūpa tracts may be found in desert areas, and *vice versa*, but prediction of water will have to be made on the basis of the type of land. In the former case the measure of the depth should be doubled and in the latter halved.

जम्बूस्त्रिवृता मौर्वी शिशुमारी सारिवा शिवा श्यामा ।
वीरुधयो वाराही ज्योतिष्मती गरुडवेगा च ॥८७॥
सूकरिकमाषपर्णीव्याघ्रपदाश्चेति यद्यहेर्निलये ।
वल्मीकादुत्तरतस्त्रिभिः करैस्त्रिपुरुषे तोयम् ॥८८॥

If a Jambū tree, Trivṛt, Maurvī, Śiśumārī, Sārivā, Śivā, Śyāmā, Vārāhī, Jyotiṣmatī, Garuḍavegā, Sūkarikā, Māṣaparṇī or Vyāghrapadā creeper grows on an ant-hill, there should be water 15 cubits below at a distance of 3 cubits to the north of the ant-hill

[There is a big list of botanical names given here. Except Jambū all are herbs.

In the second line of the first verse there is a metrical flaw, in that the fourth quarter is short of one Mātrā or syllabic instant; and there is a जगण in the 5th Gaṇa. In this verse Varāhamihira uses a new word viz. वीरुधय: which is the plural of वीरुधि, which is not in common usage.]

एतदनूपे वाच्यं जाङ्गलभूमौ तु पञ्चभिः पुरुषैः ।
एतैरेव निमित्तैर्मरुदेशे सप्तभिः कथयेत् ॥८६॥

The above measures apply only to those areas which abound in water; but in a semi-desert region the depth should be 25 cubits. If these indications are found in a desert water should be declared to exist at a depth of 35 cubits.

[This and the previous two verses are meant for illustrating the principle enunciated in verse 86.]

एकनिभा यत्र मही तृणतरुवल्मीकगुल्मपरिहीना ।
तस्यां यत्र विकारो भवति धरित्र्यां जलं तत्र ॥९०॥

Where a patch of ground, otherwise uniform and devoid of grass, trees, ant-hills and bushes, contains some unusual characteristics, there will be water 25 cubits below.

[Cf. सारस्वत—

एकवर्णा मही यत्र वृक्षगुल्मतृणादिभिः ।
वल्मीकैश्चापि रहिता तस्यां तत्र विपर्ययः ॥
पञ्चभिः पुरुषैस्तत्र जलं भूमावधः स्थितम् ॥]

यत्र स्निग्धा निम्ना सवालुका सानुनादिनी वा स्यात् ।
तत्रार्धपञ्चकैर्वारि मानवैः पञ्चभिर्यदि वा ॥९१॥

If the earth is soft (not dry), low, sandy or emitting sound, there will be water in that place at a depth of 22½ or 25 cubits.

स्निग्धतरूणां याम्ये नरैश्चतुर्भिर्जलं प्रभूतं च ।
तरुगहनेऽपि हि विकृतो यस्तस्मात् तद्वदेव वदेत् ॥९२॥

There will be abundant water at a depth of 20 cubits to the south of trees that are very glossy. The same result should be declared if a tree in the midst of a thicket shows uncommon features [water will be found at a depth of 20 cubits to the south of that tree.]

नमते यत्र धरित्री सार्धे पुरुषेऽम्बु जाङ्गलानूपे ।
कीटा वा यत्र विनालयेन बहवोऽम्बु तत्रापि ॥६३॥

Where in a semi-desert or a place full of water the earth goes down being trodden upon, or where numerous insects are seen without their abode, there, will be water at a depth of 7½ cubits.

उष्णा शीता च मही शीतोष्णाम्भस्त्रिभिर्नरैः सार्धैः ।
इन्द्रधनुर्मत्स्यो वा वल्मीको वा चतुर्हस्तात् ॥६४॥

An isolated cold spot in a warm ground or *vice versa* will have water at a depth of 17½ cubits. Where in a semi-desert or watery region a rain-bow, anti-hill or fish is seen, water will be found at the same depth at a distance of four cubits therefrom.

वल्मीकानां पङ्क्त्यां यद्येकोऽभ्युच्छ्रितः शिरा तदधः ।
शुष्यति न रोहते वा सस्यं यस्यां च तत्राम्भः ॥६५॥

If in arow of ant-hills, one is taller than the rest, there is a vein of water four cubits underneath that. Similarly there should be water at the same depth in a spot where vegetation that has grown withers away or does not sprout at all. This rule is applicable to semidesert and watery tracts only. (Another meaning is : at a depth of 17½ cubits at a distance of 4 cubits from that.)

[Cf. सारस्वत—

वल्मीकपङ्क्त्यां यद्योकोऽभ्युच्छ्रितस्तदधो जलम् ।
न रोहते शुष्यते वा यत्र सस्यं चतुष्करात् ॥
जलं तत्रैव निर्देश्यं भूमौ निःसंशयं तदा ॥

Here there is a ticklish problem : In almost all the cases the depth of water is given in Puruṣas and the distance in cubits. However, Bhaṭṭotpala interprets in this verse :

"तदा तदधस्तथोच्छ्रितस्य वल्मीकस्याधस्तले चतुर्भिर्हस्तैः शिरा जलं भवति ।"

When water is said to be just underneath a thing, there is no necessity for mentioning any distance from it. However, the statement of Sage Sārasvata, चतुर्हस्तात्, which is in the Ablative case gives room for doubt whether the reference is to horizontal length or not. In our previous edition (page 477) we have taken it to mean the horizontal distance of 4 cubits. If this be the correct interpretation, we might take the depth from the previous verse, viz. सार्धैस्त्रिभिर्नरैः i.e 17½ cubits.]

न्यग्रोधपलाशोदुम्बरैः समेतैस्त्रिभिर्जलं तदधः ।
वटपिप्पलसमवाये तद्वद्वाच्यं शिरा चोदक् ॥६६॥

If a banyan, Butea Frondosa and Glomerous fig tree, or a banyan and a holy fig tree are found together, there will be water underneath them at a depth of three-cubits; and the vein will be flowing towards the north. [Another meaning :—there will be water underneath at a distance of 3 cubits from them and at a depth of 15 cubits (17½ ?)]

[In the interpretation of this verse too the same doubt persists: The word त्रिभिः may also mean at a depth of 15 cubits. Even Sage *Sārasvata's* words do not help resolve the doubt, for he says :

पलाशोदुम्बरौ यत्र स्यातां न्यग्रोधसंयुतौ ।
वटपिप्पलकौ वाथ समेतौ तदधो जलम् ॥
करैस्त्रिभिरुदक् चाम्भः शिरां बहुजलां वदेत् ॥

The last line may also be construed as : There will be water underneath them at a distance of 3 cubits to the north of the trees : and the vein will be a source of abundant water.]

In the next two verses the author gives effects of sinking wells in the different quarters of a village or town.

आग्नेये यदि कोणे ग्रामस्य पुरस्य वा भवेत्कूपः ।
नित्यं स करोति भयं दाहं च समानुषं प्रायः ॥६७॥
नैर्ऋतकोणे बालक्षयं च वनिताभयं च वायव्ये ।
दिक्त्रयमेतत्त्यक्त्वा शेषासु शुभावहाः कूपाः ॥६८॥

Should there be a well to the south-east of a village or town, it would mostly cause constant fear and danger to men from fire. Should it be situated in the south-west, it would cause infant mortality; and in the north-west, danger to women. Wells sunk in quarters other than these three would lead to auspicious results.

[This may be applied to wells in houses as well. The phrase, समानुषं दाहम्, is interpreted by our commentator as : मनुष्यादि दहति अग्निभयं करोतीत्यर्थः, which is rather far-fetched.]

सारस्वतेन मुनिना दकार्गलं यत्कृतं तदवलोक्य ।
आर्याभिः कृतमेतद्वृत्तैरपि मानवं वक्ष्ये ॥९९॥

Thus have I expounded the subject of water-divination in verses composed in the Āryā metre, having studied the work on the subject written by Sage Sārasvata. Now I shall treat of the same subject in verses composed in the Vṛtta type of metres as taught by Sage Manu.

[As I have mentioned in the beginning of this chapter Manu and Sārasvata had both written on *Dakārgala. Varāhamihira* has summarized the former's in *Vṛtta* and the latter in Āryā. In Sanskrit prosody *Vṛtta* and *Jāti* are the two categories of metres. In the former the Gaṇas viz. म, य, र, स, त, ज, भ, and न are based on certain groups of three syllables, short and long, whereas the latter on Mātrās or syllabic instants. Āryā being Jāti, is based on Mātrāgaṇa.]

स्निग्धा यतः पादपगुल्मवल्ल्यो निश्छिद्रपत्राश्च ततः शिरास्ति ।
पद्मक्षुरोशीरकुलाः सगुण्ड्राः काशाः कुशा वा नलिका नलो वा ॥१००॥

खर्जूरजम्ब्वर्जुनवेतसाः स्युः क्षीरान्विता वा द्रुमगुल्मवल्ल्यः ।
छत्रेभनागाः शतपत्रनीपाः स्युर्नक्तमालाश्च ससिन्दुवाराः ॥१०१॥

विभीतको वा मदयन्तिका वा यत्रास्ति तस्मिन्पुरुषत्रयेऽम्भः ।
स्यात्पर्वतस्योपरि पर्वतोऽन्यस्तत्रापि मूले पुरुषत्रयेऽम्भः ॥१०२॥

There will be a water-vein at a depth of 15 cubits in a place where the trees, bushes and creepers are glossy and densely covered with leaves, (or have leaves without holes) or where land-lotus, Gokṣura or Ṣaḍaṅga, Uśīra, Kula, Guṇḍra, Kāśa, Nalikā or Nala (a kind of grass) grow. Water will be available at the same depth, if the following trees are found : Date trees, Jambū, Arjuna and Vetasa or milky trees, shrubs and creepers, or mushrooms, Hastikarṇa, Nāgakesara, Śatapatra, Kadamba, Karoja and Sinduvāra or Vibhītaka or Madayantikā. Similarly there is water at the same depth at the foot of mountain, if that be surmounted by another mountain.

[According to the commentator the water will be found at the foot of the upper mountain and not of the lower one. Manu's words too do not clarify the point.

Cf. मनु—

गुल्मपादपवल्ल्यः स्युः पत्रैश्चाखण्डितैर्युताः ।
तदधो विद्यते वारि खाते तु पुरुषत्रये ॥
पद्मक्षुरोशीरकुला गुण्ड्रा काशः कुशोऽथवा ।
नलिकानलखर्जूरजम्बूवेतसकार्जुनाः ॥
यत्र स्युर्द्रुमवल्ल्यश्च क्षीरयुक्ताः फलान्विताः ।
छत्रेभनागनीपाश्च शतपत्रविभीतकाः ॥
सिन्दुवारा नक्तमालाः सुगन्धा मदयन्तिकाः ।
यत्रैते स्युस्तत्र जलं खातेऽम्भः पुरुषत्रये ॥
गिरेरुपरि यत्रान्यः पर्वतः स्यात्ततो जलम् ।
तस्यैव मूले पुरुषैस्त्रिभिर्वाऽधो विनिर्दिशेत् ॥

The metre of these verses up to 109 is उपजाति.]

**या मौञ्जिकैः काशकुशैश्च युक्ता नीला च मृद्यत्र सशर्करा च ।
तस्यां प्रभूतं सुरसं च तोयं कृष्णाथवा यत्र च रक्तमृद्वा ॥१०३॥**

There is plenty of sweet water in a place which has Muñja grass, reeds and sacrificial grass, where the earth is blue and mixed with pebbles, and where the earth is black or red.

**सशर्करा ताम्रमही कषायं क्षारं धरित्री कपिला करोति ।
आपाण्डुरायां लवणं प्रदिष्टं मृष्टं पयो नीलवसुन्धरायाम् ॥१०४॥**

A copper-coloured earth mixed with gravel will yield water of astringent taste; red-brown earth makes the water brackish; a pale white earth produces salt-water; and blue earth, sweet water.

**शाकाश्वकर्णार्जुनबिल्वसर्जाः श्रीपर्ण्यरिष्टाधवशिंशपाश्च ।
छिद्रैश्च पत्रैर्द्रुमगुल्मवल्ल्यो रूक्षाश्च दूरेऽम्बु निवेदयन्ति ॥१०५॥**

Śāka, Aśvakarṇa, Arjuna, Bilva, Sarja, Śrīparṇī, Ariṣṭā, (soap-berry tree ?), Dhava (Lythrum fruticosum) and Śiṁśapā trees, other trees, shrubs and creepers being coarse and having leaves full of holes, indicate the existence of water far away.

[This idea has already been referred to in verse 49 *supra.*]

**सूर्याग्निभस्मोष्ट्रखरानुवर्णा या निर्जला सा वसुधा प्रदिष्टा ।
रक्ताङ्कुराः क्षीरयुताः करीरा रक्ता धरा चेज्जलमश्मनोऽधः ॥१०६॥**

The land which has the colour of the Sun, fire, ashes, camel or donkey, is said to be waterless. If the Karīra exudes milk and has red sprouts, and the earth red, there will be water underneath stones.

वैदूर्यमुद्गाम्बुदमेचकाभा पाकोन्मुखोदुम्बरसन्निभा वा ।
भृङ्गाञ्जनाभा कपिलाभवा या ज्ञेया शिला भूरिसमीपतोया ॥१०७॥

A rock that resembles beryl, green gram, cloud, dark gem, ripe fig, bee or collyrium, or is brown, should be understood as having abundant water nearby.

[भङ्गाञ्जनाभा is another reading. The meaning then would be : which looks, when cut, like collyrium.]

पारावतक्षौद्रघृतोपमा या क्षौमस्य वस्त्रस्य च तुल्यवर्णा ।
या सोमवल्ल्याश्च समानरूपा साप्याशु तोयं कुरुतेऽक्षयं च ॥१०८॥

A rock or stone which resembles in colour a pigeon, honey ghee, silken cloth or the *Soma* creeper, yields soon inexhaustible water.

ताम्रैः समेता पृषतैर्विचित्रैरापाण्डुभस्मोष्ट्रखरानुरूपा ।
भृङ्गोपमाङ्गुष्ठिकपुष्पिका वा सूर्याग्निवर्णा च शिला वितोया ॥१०९॥

A rock that is full of red or variegated spots that is pale white or has the colour of ashes, camels, donkeys, the Sun, fire, bee or the flower of the Aṅguṣṭhikā creeper (bluish red), is incapable of giving any water nearby.

चन्द्रातपस्फटिकमौक्तिकहेमरूपा
याश्चेन्द्रनीलमणिहिङ्गुलुकाञ्जनाभाः ।
सूर्योदयांशुहरितालनिभाश्च याः स्यु-
स्ताः शोभना मुनिवचोऽत्र च वृत्तमेतत् ॥११०॥

Stones that possess the colour of or lustre of moonlight, crystal gem, pearl, gold, sapphire, vermilion, collyrium, rays of the rising Sun or yellow orpiment, are auspicious. The following is the authority of Sage Manu on the point, couched in the Vṛtta (Indravajrā) metre.

[The metre is वसन्ततिलका.]

एता ह्यभेद्याश्च शिलाः शिवाश्च यक्षैश्च नागैश्च सदाभिजुष्टाः ।
येषां च राष्ट्रेषु भवन्ति राज्ञां तेषामवृष्टिर्न भवेत् कदाचित् ॥१११॥

These stones, enumerated above, are auspicious and hence ought not to be broken, since they are always tenanted by Yakṣas and Nāgas. Those kings, in whose kingdoms such stones or rocks are found, will never experience drought.

[The metre of this and the following two verses is इन्द्रवज्रा or उपजाति.]

Next the author mentions some methods of breaking stones.

भेवं यदा नैति शिला तदानीं पलाशकाष्ठैः सह तिन्दुकानाम् ।
प्रज्वालयित्वानलमग्निवर्णा सुधाम्बुसिक्ता प्रविदारमेति ॥११२॥

When a stone does not break ever when it is hammered, a fire should be burnt on it with the logs of Palāśa (Butea frondosa) and Tinduka (a sort of ebony) trees until the stone assumes the colour of the fire i.e. red, and then it should be sprinkled with lime water. Then it will break easily.

[According to Utpala सुधा means क्षीर or milk, which is patently wrong. Varāhamihira commits a grammatical error here by using क्त्वा suffix in प्रज्वालयित्वा instead of प्रज्वाल्य.]

तोयं शृतं मोक्षकभस्मना वा यत्सप्तकृत्वः परिषेचनं तत् ।
कार्यं शरक्षारयुतं शिलायाः प्रस्फोटनं वह्निवितापितायाः ॥११३॥

The ashes of the Mokṣaka tree should be boiled in water and mixed with the ashes of reeds. The rock, being heated (as explained in the previous verse), should be sprinkled seven times successively with the decoction. Then it will break.

[The reading we have is श्रितं which is wrong. It should be शृतम्. Hence I have taken the liberty of correcting it. The mistake must have been committed by the scribe, the tree मोक्षक is otherwise known as मणीवक according to Utpala, but the धन्वन्तरिनिघण्टु says :

मुष्कको मोक्षको घण्टामूषको रञ्जकस्तथा ।
क्षारश्रेष्ठो गोलिहश्च द्विविधः श्वेतकृष्णकः ॥ (V. 132).]

तक्रकाञ्जिकसुराः सकुलत्था योजितानि बदराणि च तस्मिन् ।
सप्तरात्रमुषितान्यभितप्तां दारयन्ति हि शिलां परिषेकैः ॥११४॥

Butter-milk, sour gruel and liquor with horse gram and jujube fruits, mixed together, must be kept for seven nights and then poured on the hard rock that has been heated as before. Then it will break.

[I feel that it is not enough if the mixture mentioned here is poured only once. It should be poured seven times, each time after the stone is heated. For, the author uses the plural in परिषेकैः and the word सप्तकृत्वः appears in the previous verse. Utpala, however, does not clarify the point.

The metre is स्वागता.]

नैम्बं पत्रं त्वक् च नालं तिलानां सापामार्गं तिन्दुकं स्याद् गुडूची ।
गोमूत्रेण स्रावितः क्षार एषां षट्कृत्वोऽतस्तापितो भिद्यतेऽश्मा ॥११५॥

The leaves and bark of the Neem tree, sesamum stalks, Apāmārga (a medicinal creeper), Tinduka and Amṛtā creeper should be burnt to ashes. These ashes should be dissolved in cow's urine and poured six times on the stone heated successively. Then it will break.

[Utpala interprets तिलानां नालम् as 'यस्मिन्नभ्यन्तरे कोशाकारे तिला भवन्ति' which would mean the pods of sesamum, but the word नाल means only the *stalk*.

अपामार्ग is called *uttarane* in Kannaḍa. cf. धन्वन्तरि. अपामार्गस्तु शिखरी प्रत्यक्पुष्पी मयूरकः । अधःशय्याथ किणिही दुर्ग्रहः खरमञ्जरी ॥ स एवोक्तः शैखरिको मर्कटी दुरभिग्रहः । पत्रपुष्पी च शिखरः कूटो मर्कटपिप्पली ॥ (I 260-261).

The metre is शालिनी.]

V. 116 Same as L 25.

V. 117 Same as L, 26.

[I do not understand the relevance of these two verses to the subject of breaking a stone. Even the commentator does not explain why the matter pertaining to the sword should be introduced here.

Possibly the author means by repeating these verses to suggest that the unguent and the ashes mentioned there are to be applied to the heated stone for breaking it, or that the sword or hammer may be made more effective in breaking the stone by the application of these unguents etc.]

Next the author treats of the construction of ponds, wells, etc. and their effects.

पाली प्रागपरायताम्बु सुचिरं धत्ते न याम्योत्तरा
कल्लोलैरवदारमेति मरुता सा प्रायशः प्रेरितैः ।
तां चेदिच्छति सारदारुभिरपां सम्पातमावारयेत्
पाषाणादिभिरेव वा प्रतिचयं क्षुण्णं द्विपाश्वादिभिः ॥११८॥

A rectangular tank with its longer banks on the eastern and western sides retains water for a long time, while the one with those sides in the south and north does not, because it is eroded invariably by the strong waves raised by the wind. Should one wish for such a pond (with the long sides on the southern and northen sides owing to exigencies of the land), he would do well to guard its walls against the impact of the water with strong timber or with stones and the like (i.e. with burnt bricks). The bed of the pond or tank should also be made hard by being trampled by elephants, horses, etc.

[The author uses two rare words here, viz. पाली and चय. The former is explained by Utpala as वापी, but actually it means a line i.e. embankment; the latter is not. In the *Amara*, however, we get चय as a synonym of वप्र which is generally used in the sense of an *embankment*, e.g. वप्रक्रीडा. Kṣīrasvāmin, however, says चीयते चयः प्राकाराधारः, which would mean the 'base of the wall'. In the present context it may also be taken to mean 'the joints', which must be made proof against water. In villages the instruments that are used for making the earth hard are heavy wooden pieces with a flat face resembling the elephant's foot.

The metre is शार्दूलविक्रीडित.]

ककुभवटाम्रप्लक्षकदम्बैः सनिचुलजम्बूवेतसनीपैः ।
कुरबकतालाशोकमधूकैर्बकुलविमिश्रैश्चावृततीरम् ॥११६॥

The banks of the tank should be shaded with Arjuna, banyan, mango, pīpal, *nauclia orientalis*, *Hijjal*, *Eugenia*, *Bayas*, or *Bent*, Nīpa (Dhūlikadamba ?) globe amaranth (the crimson variety), Tāla, Aśoka, *Bassia* and Bakula trees.

[Though *Kadamba* and Nīpa are considered as synonyms, here we have to take Nīpa as another variety of *Kadamba*.

The metre is अनवसिता.]

द्वारं च नैर्वाहिक.ेकदेशे कार्यं शिलासञ्चितवारिमार्गम् ।
कोशस्थितं निर्विवरं कपाटं कृत्वा ततः पांसुभिरावपेत्तम् ॥१२०॥

An outlet for the water should be made on one side with the sluice being built of stones; and a panel without apertures, fixed in a frame and fastened to the earth with mud.

[The metre is इन्द्रवज्रा.]

In the next two verses he gives a prescription for purifying water.

अञ्जनमुस्तोशीरैः सराजकोशातकामलकचूर्णैः ।
कतकफलसमायुक्तैर्योगः कूपे प्रदातव्यः ॥१२१॥

A mixture of antimony, and the powder of Bhadramustā (a kind of grass) bulbs, andropogon, Rājakośātaka and myrobalan combined with Kataka nuts should be dropped into a well (for purifying the water).

[About अञ्जन the commentator says : प्रसिद्धो वृक्षविशेषः । सौवीरक इति केचित् । Even the latter word has three meanings: antimony, sour gruel and jujube. The mixture comprises six ingredients.]

कलुषं कटुकं लवणं विरसं सलिलं यदि वाऽशुभगन्धि भवेत् ।
तदनेन भवत्यमलं सुरसं सुसुगन्धि गुणैरपरैश्च युतम् ॥१२२॥

Even the water that is muddy, bitter, saltish, bereft of good taste, and of bad odour, will become clear (pure), of good taste and good smell and endowed with other good qualities]

[The other qualities are said to be freedom from bitter taste and saltishness.

The metre is तोटक.]

Next he speaks of the good asterisms for sinking wells.

हस्तो मघानुराधापुष्यधनिष्ठोत्तराणि रोहिण्यः ।
शतभिषगित्यारम्भे कूपानां शस्यते भगणः ॥१२३॥

The following asterisms are beneficial for sinking wells : Rohiṇī, Puṣya, Maghā, the three Uttaras (Uttaraphalgunī, Uttarāṣādhā and Uttarabhādrapadā), Hasta, Anurādhā, Dhaniṣṭhā and Śatabhiṣaj.

कृत्वा वरुणस्य बलिं वटवेतसकीलकं शिरास्थाने ।
कुसुमैर्गन्धैर्धूपैः सम्पूज्य निधापयेत्प्रथमम् ॥१२४॥

One should, first of all, offer worship with oblations to Varuṇa and erect a peg of banyan or Vetasa tree at the place of the vein, having worshipped it with flowers, perfumes and incense.

मेघोद्भवं प्रथममेव मया प्रदिष्टं
ज्येष्ठामतीत्य बलदेवमतादि दृष्ट्वा ।
भौमं दकार्गलमिदं कथितं द्वितीयं
सम्यग्वराहमिहिरेण मुनिप्रसादात् ॥१२५॥

I have already explained the subject of water born of the clouds (i.e. celestial or atmospheric water) which is judged after the full Moon in the month of Jyeṣṭha (as stated in XXIII *supra*), on the authorty of Baladeva and others. This second method of exploring the subterranian water has now been clearly treated by me, Varāhamihira, by the grace of the Sages (i.e. Sārasvata and Manu).

[This verse is not found in the Benares edition. The metre is वसन्ततिलका.]

[NOTE : *See Chart of Water-Veins and Indicators.*]

वृक्षायुर्वेदाध्यायः ॥५५॥

Chapter LV—Treatment of Trees

This too is an important scientific topic that was cultivated in ancient India. Gardening is closely connected with town-planning, house-building and construction of tanks. Ancient Sages like Kāśyapa and Parāśara have laid down rules about the trees to be planted in gardens, grafting and transplantation of trees as well as diseases of trees and their treatments. Sixteen varieties of Anūpaja (born in watery tracts) trees are mentioned in connection with transplantation and grafting. They have also taught the diagnosis of diseases of trees and their treatment. There are many works of later origin such as the Kṛṣiparāśara, *Abhilaṣitārthacintāmaṇi*, Viśvavallabha of Cakrapāṇimiśra, Vṛkṣāyurveda of Surapāla and the *Upavanavinoda* which deal with many topics such as fertilizers for curing diseases of trees and to produce better yields as well as some wonderful effects. These have been detailed in my Paper, "Fertilizers in Ancient India" read in the International Sanskrit Conference, New Delhi, on 27-3-1972.

प्रान्तच्छायाविनिर्मुक्ता न मनोज्ञा जलाशयाः ।
यस्मादतो जलप्रान्तेष्वारामान् विनिवेशयेत् ॥१॥

Since tanks and the like do not look charming without shade on their sides, one ought to have gardens laid out on the banks of water.

[Vide LIV. 119 where the author has spoken of the necessity for shading the banks of tanks. Both the tanks and gardens are mutually beneficial. That is why charming gardens like the Brindavan Gardens in Mysore have been created near dams and reservoirs in modern India.

The metre upto 18th verse is अनुष्टुभ् or śloka.]

Next he speaks of the *Sesamum-treatment* for the soil.

मृद्वी भूः सर्ववृक्षाणां हिता तस्यां तिलान् वपेत् ।
पुष्पितांस्तांश्च मृद्नीयात्कर्मैतत्प्रथमं भुवः ॥२॥

A soft soil is helpful for all varieties of trees. First of all one ought to sow there sesamum, which must be crushed when in bloom (to mix with the soil). This is the first treatment to be done for the soil.

[The sesamum plants in bloom, when cut into pieces and allowed to mingle with the soil, would become an excellent green manure for preparing the soil for further cultivation. It is also held that if these sesamum crop does not flourish in a field, nothing could be grown there with advantage.

Cf. काश्यप—

दूर्वावीरणसंयुक्ताः सानूपा मृदुमृत्तिकाः ।
तत्र वाप्यः शुभा वृक्षाः सुगन्धिफलशखिनः ॥]

अरिष्टाशोकपुन्नागशिरीषाः सप्रियङ्गवः ।
मङ्गल्याः पूर्वमारामे रोपणीया गृहेषु वा ॥३॥

Ariṣṭa (Neem or soap berry tree), Aśoka, Punnāga and Śirīṣa trees and Priyaṅgu creeper, which are auspicious, should first be planted in gardens as well as near houses.

[Cf. काश्यप—

अशोकचम्पकारिष्टपुन्नागाश्च प्रियङ्गवः ।
शिरीषोदुम्बराः श्रेष्ठाः पारिजातकमेव च ॥
एते वृक्षाः शुभा ज्ञेयाः प्रथमं तांश्च रोपयेत् ।
देवालये तथोद्याने गृहेषूपवनेषु च ॥]

Next he treats of grafting.

पनसाशोककदलीजम्बूलकुचदाडिमाः ।
द्राक्षापालीवताश्चैव बीजपूरातिमुक्तकाः ॥४॥
एते द्रुमाः काण्डरोप्या गोमयेन प्रलेपिताः ।
मूलोच्छेदेऽथवा स्कन्धे रोपणीयाः परं ततः ॥५॥

Grafting may be done in respect of the jack tree, Aśoka, plantain, Eugenia, lemon, pomegranate, grape vine, Pālīvata, Mātuluṅga (citron) and jasmine creeper by smearing a branch with cowdung and transplanting it on the branch of another; or it may be done by cutting off the trunk of a tree and by transplanting it like a wedge on the trunk of another tree. (Here the part when the junction is effected must be covered with a coating of mud).

[Our commentator remarks : अन्यवृक्षस्य मूलोच्छेदं कृत्वा तस्य छिन्नमूलस्योपरि विजातीयो वृक्षो रोपणीयः, which would mean : 'Uproot a tree and transplant a tree of a different type upon it.' This is not the meaning intended by the author, as far as I can judge. The author must have meant that *in case a good tree has been uprooted*, its trunk or branch can be transplanted on the branch of another tree of the same group. If we could have transplantation in respect of two trees of different groups, then we should be able to get jack fruits from one branch and mangoes from another. Even this wonder may be feasible in modern times. The *Abhilaṣitārthacintāmaṇi* refers to many recipes for turning sour or bitter fruits into sweet ones, a tree into a creeper, etc.

Cf. काश्यप—

द्राक्षातिमुक्तको जम्बूबीजपूरकदाडिमाः ।
कदलीबहुलाशोकाः काण्डरोप्याश्च वापयेत् ॥
अन्येऽपि शाखिनो ये च पुष्पिताः फलितास्तथा ।
गोमयेन प्रलिप्ताश्च रोपणीया विवृद्धये ॥]

अजातशाखाञ् शिशिरे जातशाखान् हिमागमे ।
वर्षागमे च सुस्कन्धान् यथादिक्स्थान्प्ररोपयेत् ॥६॥

The grafting should be done in the *Śiśira* season (February-March) for those plants which have not yet got branches; in the *Hemanta* season (December-January) for those that have grown branches; and in the rainy season (August-September) for those that have large branches. The particular direction of the tree that is cut off should be kept up in grafting also.

[The commentator refers to some scholars who prefer the reading : 'जातशाखान् घनागमे । वर्षागर्भे च,' which would mean, the beginning and middle of the monsoon. These readings are to be rejected on the authority of Sage काश्यप, who says :

अजातशाखा ये वृक्षाः शिशिरे तांश्च रोपयेत् ।
जातशाखाश्च हेमन्ते रोपणीया विधानतः ॥
सुस्कन्धाः शाखिनो ये तान् प्रावृट्काले तु रोपयेत् ॥]

घृतोशीरतिलक्षौद्रविडङ्गक्षीरगोमयैः ।
आमूलस्कन्धलिप्तानां सङ्क्रामणविरोपणम् ॥७॥

Trees can be taken to other countries and there grafted on others, if they are smeared from root to the stem with ghee, *andropogon*, sesamum, honey, Viḍaṅga, milk and cow-dung.

[The word सङ्क्रामणविरोपणम् may also be construed thus : Trees thus treated can be safely taken to another place and planted there. Here Utpala quotes a verse without naming, possibly from Sage Kāśyapa :

घृतं क्षीरं तथा क्षौद्रमुशीरतिलगोमयैः ।
विडङ्गलेपनं मूलात् सङ्क्रामणविरोपणम् ॥]

शुचिर्भूत्वा तरोः पूजां कृत्वा स्नानानुलेपनैः ।
रोपयेद्रोपितश्चैव पत्रैस्तैरेव जायते ॥८॥

One should be clean and pure and worship a tree with ablutions and sandal paste etc. and then graft it. Then it will thrive even with the leaves with which its has been grafted.

सायं प्रातश्च घर्मर्त्तौ शीतकाले दिनान्तरे ।
वर्षासु च भुवः शोषे सेक्तव्या रोपिता द्रुमाः ॥९॥

The transplanted (grafted) trees should be watered both in the morning and evening everyday in summer; on alternate days in the cold season; and whenever the soil becomes dry in the rainy season.

जम्बूवेतसवानीरकदम्बोदुम्बरार्जुनाः ।
बीजपूरकमृद्वीका लकुचाश्च सदाडिमाः ॥१०॥
वञ्जुलो नक्तमालश्च तिलकः पनसस्तथा ।
तिमिरोऽम्रातकश्चेति षोडशानूपजाः स्मृताः ॥११॥

Eugenia, Bayas (or Bent), Vānīra, *Nauclea orientalis*, Glomerous fig tree; Arjuna, Bījapūra (citron), grape vine; lemon, pomegranate, Vañjula (spondias), Naktamāla (Gray bonduc), Tilaka, jack, Timira and Āmrātaka are the sixteen trees that grow in a moist soil.

[The distinction between अनूपज, जाङ्गल and मरूद्भव is not absolute, as the author himself has stated that the trees which are generally found in moist soil may at times be found growing in other regions as well.]

Next the author discusses the subject of distance between one tree and another in a garden.

उत्तमं विंशतिर्हस्ता मध्यमं षोडशान्तरम् ।
स्थानात् स्थानान्तरं कार्यं वृक्षाणां द्वादशावरम् ॥१२॥

It is very good, if trees are planted 20 cubits apart; moderate, if 16 cubits apart; and inferior, if 12 cubits apart.

[Cf. काश्यप—

अन्तरं विंशतिर्हस्ता वृक्षाणामुत्तमं स्मृतम् ।
मध्यमं षोडश ज्ञेयमधमं द्वादश स्मृतम् ॥]

अभ्याशजातास्तरवः संस्पृशन्तः परस्परम् ।
मिश्रैर्मूलैश्च न फलं सम्यग्यच्छन्ति पीडिताः ॥१३॥

Trees that have grown quite close to one another and are touching one another with their roots interlocked are tortured, and so do not yield fruits in full measure.

शीतवातातपै रोगो जायते पाण्डुपत्रता ।
अवृद्धिश्च प्रवालानां शाखाशोषो रसस्रुतिः ॥१४॥

Trees get disease from cold weather, strong winds and hot sun. Consequently their leaves become pale-white, sprouts scanty and sickly, branches dry, and their milk oozes out.

[The विश्ववल्लभ of Cakrapāṇimiśra states in VIII that trees get diseases by the vitiation of the three humours, वात, पित्त and कफ (Wind, Bile and Phlegm) (vide, my Paper on 'Fertilizers in Ancient India)]

चिकित्सितमथैतेषां शस्त्रेणादौ विशोधनम् ।
विडङ्गघृतपङ्काक्तान् सेचयेत् क्षीरवारिणा ॥१५॥

Thereafter (i.e. after the trees show symptoms of disease), the trees should be treated. At the outset, the trees should be cleared of ulcers and the like (i.e. whatever is colourless and wet) with a knife. Then a paste made of Viḍaṅga, ghee and silt must be applied to those parts and they should be sprinkled with water and milk. (If this is done, they will be free from disease).

[Cf. काश्यप—

शाखाविटपपत्रैश्च च्छायया वि(र?)हिताश्च ये ।
येऽपि पर्णफलैर्हीना रूक्षाः पत्रैश्च पाण्डुरैः ॥
शीतोष्णवर्षवाताद्यैर्मूलैर्व्यामिश्रितैरपि ।
शाखिनां तु भवेद्रोगो द्विपानां लेखनेन च ॥
चिकित्सितेषु कर्तव्या ये च भूयः पुनर्नवाः ।
शोधयेत्प्रथमं शस्त्रैः प्रलेपं दापयेत्ततः ॥
कर्दमेन विडङ्गैश्च घृतमिश्रैश्च लेपयेत् ।
क्षीरतोयेन सेकः स्याद् रोहणं सर्वशाखिनाम् ॥]

फलनाशे कुलत्थैश्च माषैर्मुद्गैस्तिलैर्यवैः ।
शृतशीतपयःसेकः फलपुष्पसमृद्धये ॥१६॥

When the fruits of a tree are destroyed (prematurely), it should be watered with milk that has been cooled after being boiled, with horse-gram, black gram, green gram, sesamum and barley. Being treated thus, it will have abundant flowers and fruits.

अविकाजशकृच्चूर्णस्याढके द्वे तिलाढकम् ।
सक्तुप्रस्थो जलद्रोणो गोमांसतुलया सह ॥१७॥

सप्तरात्रोषितैरेतैः सेकः कार्यो वनस्पतेः ।
वल्लीगुल्मलतानां च फलपुष्पाय सर्वदा ॥१८॥

For increasing the yield of flowers and fruits of trees, creepers and shrubs, they should be sprinkled constantly with a mixture of an *āḍhaka* (54 Palas) of the powder of the dung of goats as well as of sheep, one *āḍhaka* of sesamum powder, a *prastha* (16 Palas) of wheat particles, a *Tulā* (100 Palas) of beef and a *Droṇa* (256 Palas) of water kept for seven nights. (This is the measure for one tree).

[The commentator quotes the following verses from some text explaining the different weights and measures :

त्रियवं कृष्णलं विद्यान्माषलः पञ्चकृष्णलः ।
ते स्युर्द्वादश लक्षाख्यं सुवर्णमथ षोडश ॥
पञ्चलक्षैश्चतुर्भिस्तु सुवर्णैर्निष्क उच्यते ।
चतुष्पलोऽथ कुडवः प्रस्थः स्यात्तच्चतुष्टयम् ॥
आढकस्तु चतुष्प्रस्थो द्रोणस्तु चतुराढकः ।
मानिका तु चतुर्द्रोणा खारी स्यात्तच्चतुष्टयम् ॥
तुला पलशतं ज्ञेयं भारः स्याद्विंशतिस्तुलाः ।
शुष्कद्रव्येषु संख्येयं चार्द्रेषु द्विगुणा भवेत् ॥

Cf. काश्यप—

अजाविकानां द्वौ प्रस्थौ शकृच्चूर्णं च कारयेत् ।
तिलानामाढकं दद्यात् सक्तूनां प्रस्थमेव च ॥
गोमांसशतमेकं स्याद् द्वे सार्धे सलिलस्य च ।
सप्ताहमुषितैरेतैः सेकं दद्याद् वनस्पतेः ॥
स भवेत्फलपुष्पैश्च पत्रैश्चाङ्कुरितैर्वृतः ॥]

Next the author discusses the topic of treatment of seeds :

वासराणि दश दुग्धभावितं बीजमाज्ययुतहस्तयोजितम् ।
गोमयेन बहुशो विरूक्षितं क्रौडमार्गपिशितैश्च धूपितम् ॥१९॥

मांससूकरवसासमन्वितं रोपितं च परिकर्मितावनौ ।
क्षीरसंयुतजलावसेचितं जायते कुसुमयुक्तमेव तत् ॥२०॥

All seeds should be soaked in milk for ten days, taking them out daily with the hand smeared with ghee. Then they must be rolled many times in cow-dung, fumigated with the flesh of deer and hog; thereafter with flesh and hog's marrow, they should be planted in a soil that has been already prepared (with the sesamum treatment). Being sprinkled with milk and water, they will grow and bloom.

[It is not clear if the author wants us to believe that if the process mentioned in these verses is gone through, the seeds would be accompanied by blossoms even as they sprout. Note the expression used : 'कुसुमयुक्तमेव जायते ।'

The metre here and in the following verse is रथोद्धता.]

तिन्तिडीत्यपि करोति वल्लरीं व्रीहिमाषतिलचूर्णसक्तुभिः ।
पूतिमांससहितैश्च सेचिता धूपिता च सततं हरिद्रया ॥२१॥

Even a tamarind seed will produce a sprout when sprinkled with a compound of the flour of rice, black gram and sesamum and wheat particles along with stale meat, and repeatedly fumigated with turmeric powder.

कपित्थवल्लीकरणाय मूलान्यास्फोतधात्रीधववासिकानाम् ।
पलाशिनी वेतससूर्यवल्ली श्यामातिमुक्तैः सहिताष्टमूली ॥२२॥
क्षीरे शृते चाप्यनया सुशीते तालाशतं स्थाप्य कपित्थबीजम् ।
दिने दिने शोषितमर्कपादैर्मासं विधिस्त्वेष ततोऽधिरोप्यम् ॥२३॥
हस्तायतं तद्द्विगुणं गभीरं खात्वावटं प्रोक्तजलावपूर्णम् ।
शुष्कं प्रदग्धं मधुसर्पिषा तत् प्रलेपयेद्भस्मसमन्वितेन ॥२४॥
चूर्णीकृतैर्माषतिलैर्यवैश्च प्रपूरयेन्मृत्तिकयान्तरस्थैः ।
मत्स्यामिषाम्भस्सहितं च हन्याद्यावद् घनत्वं समुपागतं तत् ॥२५॥
उप्तं च बीजं चतुरङ्गुलाधो मत्स्याम्भसा मांसजलैश्च सिक्तम् ।
वल्ली भवत्याशु शुभप्रवाला विस्मापनी मण्डपमावृणोति ॥२६॥

For making the wood-apple seeds sprout, take the roots of Sārivā, myrobolan, Dhava, Vāśikā (*Justicia*), the branches with leaves also of Vetasa and Sūryavallī, Śyāmā-creeper, and Atimuktaka (eight roots in all), boil them in milk and cool it, and then soak the seeds in this liquid for a period of time equal to that of 100 beats (of the hand). Take them out and after drying them in the sun daily for 30 days, sow them according to the following method :

Dig a pit one cubit in diameter and twice as deep, fill it with milk and water; and burn the pit when it becomes dry. Then smear it (pit) with a mixture of honey, ghee and ashes. Then, first fill it with mud to a height of four digits, then fill it with the flour of black gram, sesamum and barley; again put mud over this to the same height (4 digits). Again fill it with the flour of black gram etc. Pour on it an infusion of fish and water and then pound all this until it becomes a thick mass. Sow the seed at a depth of four digits and sprinkle it with fish-water and flesh-water. Soon will a tendril with excellent sprouts cover the bower in a marvellous manner.

[Utpala says that Śyāmā, according to some, means *Trivṛt.* The author commits two grammatical errors in 23 : For तालशतं he says तालाशतं and स्थाप्य without a preposition is wrong. Here ताल means a *beat* in keeping time in music. The metre is उपजाति except in the last where it is इन्द्रवज्रा.]

शतशोऽङ्कोलसम्भूतफलकल्केन भावितम् ।
एतत्तैलेन वा बीजं श्लेष्मातकफलेन वा ॥२७॥

वापितं करकोन्मिश्रमृदि तत्क्षणजन्मकम् ।
फलभारान्विता शाखा भवतीति किमद्भुतम् ॥२८॥

Any seed being soaked a hunderd times in a paste of Aṅkola fruit or in its oil, or in a paste or oil of Śleṣmātaka (*Sebesten*) fruit, will, when sown in a soil mixed with hail, sprout instantaneously, and what wonder would it be, if its branches were laden with fruits !

[Utpala says that करका is अशनिपात, which, according to the accepted meaning of the term, is wrong. For, says *Amara* :—'वर्षोपलस्तु करका'. I.2.12 The metre is *Śloka.*]

श्लेष्मातकस्य बीजानि निष्कुलीकृत्य भावयेत् प्राज्ञः ।
अङ्कोलविज्जलाद्भिश्छायायां सप्तकृत्वैवम् ॥२९॥

माहिषगोमयघृष्टान्यस्य करीषे च तानि निक्षिप्य ।
करकाजलमृद्योगे न्युप्तान्यह्ना फलकराणि ॥३०॥

A wise man should remove the shell of the Śleśmātaka (Sebesten) seeds, soak them in water mixed with the slimy paste of Aṅkola (*Alangium*) fruits and dry them in shade seven times. Then rub them with buffalo's dung, and lay them in their dry dung.

Being sown thereafter in a soil soaked with hail-water, they will bear fruit in a day.

[Bhaṭṭotpala says that the seeds smeared with buffalo-dung should be kept inside a heap of dry buffalo-dung in a pot until the contents are drenched by hail-water. He construes करकाजल as अशनिपातजल here too. The author enumerates the asterisms suitable for planting trees.

ध्रुवमृदुमूलविशाखा गुरुभं श्रवणस्तथाश्विनी हस्तः ।
उक्तानि दिव्यदृग्भिः पादपसंरोपणे भानि ॥३१॥

The asterisms prescribed by the Seers of transcendental wisdom (such as Garga) for the planting of trees are the three Uttaras, Rohiṇī, Anurādhā, Citrā, Mṛgaśirṣa, Revatī, Mūla, Viśākhā, Puṣya, Śravaṇa, Aśvinī and Hasta.

[Instead of उक्तानि some people have the reading शस्तानि, says Utpala.]

———

प्रासादलक्षणाध्यायः ॥५६॥

Chapter LVI.—Description of Temples.

कृत्वा प्रभूतं सलिलमारामान् विनिवेश्य च ।
देवतायतनं कुर्याद्यशोधर्माभिवृद्धये ॥१॥

One should build a temple in order to enhance one's fame and religious merit, after securing an abundant supply of water through tanks and lakes, laying out fine gardens.

[Generally big tanks are constructed near places of worship for the use of pilgrims and of the temple itself. Gardens are also laid out near temples for shade and for producing a pleasant atmosphere around them as well as for the supply of fragrant flowers for the worship. This verse appears to have been introduced to silence critics who might call in question the author's wisdom in separating this chapter from the one on 'House-Building'.

The first 19 verses are in Śloka metre.]

इष्टापूर्त्तेन लभ्यन्ते ये लोकास्तान् बुभूषता ।
देवानामालयः कार्यो द्वयमप्यत्र दृश्यते ॥२॥

One who wishes to attain to the worlds secured by performing sacrifices and sinking wells and the like, should build a temple, whereby one could attain the fruits of both.

[The commentator quotes the following verses from some work to explain the word इष्टापूर्त्त:

इष्टं यज्ञेषु यद्दानं ततोऽन्यत्पूर्त्तमिष्यते ।
इष्टाभिः पशुबन्धैश्च चातुर्मास्यैर्यजेद् द्विजः ॥
अग्निष्टोमादिभिर्यज्ञैर्यो यजेत स इष्टवान् ।
वापीकूपतडागादिदेवतायतनानि च ॥
अन्नप्रदानमाचार्यैः पूर्त्त इत्यभिधीयते ॥

Cf. also काश्यप—

इष्टापूर्त्तादिभिर्यज्ञैर्यावत्कुर्वन्ति मानवाः ।
अग्निष्टोमादिपशुभिरिष्टं यज्ञं प्रकीर्त्तितम् ॥
वापीकूपतडागादिदेवतायतनानि च ।
स्वर्गस्थितिं सदा कुर्यात् तद्दानं पूर्त्तसंज्ञितम् ॥
देवानामालयः कार्यो द्वयमप्यत्र लभ्यते ॥]

सलिलोद्यानयुक्तेषु कृतेष्वकृतकेषु च ।
स्थानेष्वेतेषु सान्निध्यमुपगच्छन्ति देवताः ॥३॥

Deities reside with pleasure in places which abound in water and gardens, whether natural or otherwise.

[Ancient Sages had their Āśramas or hermitages as well as Gurukulas amidst sylvan grandeur on the banks of big rivers. For, in such surroundings there is a spiritual atmosphere, where the turbulent mind and senses can be subdued without much difficulty. After all, God dwells in His glory where the mind finds tranquillity and contentment.]

सरःसु नलिनीछत्रनिरस्ततरविरश्मिषु ।
हंसांसाक्षिप्तकह्लारवीथीविमलवारिषु ॥४॥
हंसकारण्डवक्रौञ्चचक्रवाकविराविषु ।
पर्यन्तनिचुलच्छायाविश्रान्तजलचारिषु ॥५॥

Gods dwell with pleasure also in (or near) lakes, where the rays of the sun are warded off by the parasol of lotus, whose clear waters contain avenues of white lotuses tossed by the shoulders of swans, which resound with cries of swans, flamingoes, curlews and ruddy geese and which have the aquatic animals resting in the shade of Nicula (*Hijjal*) trees on their banks.

[These lines are reminiscent of the poetry of great masters like Kālidāsa and Vālmīki. Vide सु० कां० XIV. 24-26. The following verses of the महाभारत which explain the places where the Goddess of wealth and beauty dwells are interesting :

सत्यासु नित्यप्रियदर्शनासु सौभाग्ययुक्तासु गुणान्वितासु ।
वसामि नारीषु पतिव्रतासु कल्याणशीलासु विभूषितासु ॥
वसामि फुल्लासु च पद्मिनीषु नक्षत्रवीथीषु च शारदीषु ।
नदीषु हंसस्वननादितासु तपस्विसिद्धद्विजसेवितासु ॥

(Condensed edn. page 451)]

क्रौञ्चकाञ्चीकलापाश्च कलहंसकलस्वराः ।
नद्यस्तोयांशुका यत्र शफरीकृतमेखलाः ॥६॥
फुल्लतीरद्रुमोत्तंसाः सङ्गमश्रोणिमण्डलाः ।
पुलिनाभ्युन्नतोरस्या हंसहासाश्च निम्नगाः ॥७॥

Likewise do they dwell in places where the rivers have large girdles of curlews, sweet voice in the form of the melodious notes of the royal swans; silken *sarees* of the waters, knots of the cloth made of tiny fishes, floral ear-ornaments in the form of trees in bloom on their banks, round buttocks of confluences; lofty bosoms of sand-dunes, and merry laughter in the form of the white swans.

[Here the imagery is excellent as the rivers are spoken as charming damsels. The metaphor employed here is worthy of great poets like Vālmīki and Kālidāsa.

Bhaṭṭotpala reads हंसवासाः instead of हंसहासाः : In my view his reading is not good as it is a repetition. There is an apparent repetition in the text, viz. काञ्ची and मेखला. Actually the latter has to be taken, as suggested by the commentator, in the sense of नीवि or knot of the lady's cloth.]

वनोपान्तनदीशैलनिर्झरोपान्तभूमिषु ।
रमन्ते देवता नित्यं पुरेषूद्यानवत्सु च ॥८॥

They rejoice always in the vicinity of forests, rivers, mountains and waterfalls, as well as in towns abounding in pleasure-gardens.

[Cf. काश्यप—

हरितोज्ज्वलतोयाढ्या वाप्यः पक्षिभिरावृताः ।
वनोपवनमालिन्यो नित्यमुत्फुल्लितद्रुमाः ॥
हंसकारण्डवाकीर्णाः कोकिलालापनादिताः ।
षट्पदागीतमधुरा नृत्यद्भिः शिखिभिर्युताः ॥
तत्र देवा रतिं यान्ति सान्निध्यान्नित्यसंस्थिताः ॥]

भूमयो ब्राह्मणादीनां याः प्रोक्ता वास्तुकर्मणि ।
ता एव तेषां शस्यन्ते देवतायतनेष्वपि ॥९॥

The different kinds of earth recommended for the construction of houses for the different classes of the society are likewise recommended to persons of various classes for constructing temples.

[Vide LIII. 96-97 *supra* for the varieties of soil recommended. This shows that each community or class had its own temple.]

चतुःषष्टिपदं कार्यं देवतायतनं सदा ।
द्वारं च मध्यमं तस्मिन् समदिक्स्थं प्रशस्यते ॥१०॥

The temple site should always be divided into 64 squares. Its central or main gate would be auspicious if situated in one of the four cardinal directions.

[Vide LIII. 55 *supra* and diagram 2 for the subdivision of the site.]

The author next gives the dimensions of temples.

यो विस्तारो भवेद्यस्य द्विगुणा तत्समुन्नतिः ।
उच्छ्रायाद्यस्तृतीयांशस्तेन तुल्या कटिः स्मृता ॥११॥

विस्तारार्धं भवेद् गर्भो भित्तयोऽन्याः समन्ततः ।
गर्भपादेन विस्तीर्णं द्वारं द्विगुणमुच्छ्रितम् ॥१२॥

उच्छ्रायात्पादविस्तीर्णा शाखा तद्वदुदुम्बरः ।
विस्तारपादप्रतिमं बाहुल्यं शाखयोः स्मृतम् ॥१३॥

त्रिपञ्चसप्तनवभिः शाखाभिस्तत्प्रशस्यते ।
अधः शाखाचतुर्भागे प्रतीहारौ निवेशयेत् ॥१४॥

शेषं मङ्गल्यविहगैः श्रीवृक्षैः स्वस्तिकैर्घटैः ।
मिथुनैः पत्रवल्लीभिः प्रमथैश्चोपशोभयेत् ॥१५॥

द्वारमानाष्टभागोना प्रतिमा स्यात् सपिण्डिका ।
द्वौ भागौ प्रतिमा तत्र तृतीयांशश्च पिण्डिका ॥१६॥

The height of a temple should be double its width, and the height of the foundation above the ground consisting of steps (over which the edifice is built) equal to a third of this height. The *Sanctum Sanctorum* should be half the width of the temple. All round it there should be walls. Its door should be one fourth of the *Sanctum Sanctorum* in width and twice as high. The side-frame of the door should have a breadth of a quarter of its height. Similar should be the threshold and the upper block. The thickness of the frames is to be equal to a fourth of their breadth. A door consisting of three, five, seven or nine frames is highly commended. In the lower part, upto a height of a fourth of the doorpost, two images of door-keepers (like Nandin and Daṇḍa) are to be installed, the remaining space being ornamented with the carvings of auspicious birds (like swans and ruddy geese). Bilva trees, Svastika figures, pitchers, couples, foliage, creepers and Śiva's Hosts. The idol with its pedestal ought to be as high as the door diminished by an eighth, of these, the idol being of two parts and the pedestal of one.

[Many technical terms occur here : कटि meaning hip or the flight of steps in the foundation, गर्भ the central shrine, शाखा the side frame, उदुम्बर the threshold and upper block, and पिण्डिका the pedestal. There are twenty types of temples with different dimensions. The *Meru* type has the following dimensions : Breadth=32 cubits, height=64 cubits, height of Kaṭi=$\frac{64}{3}$ cubits; the *sanctum san torum*= 16 cubits; all round there are walls of three cubits thickness, leaving a distance of 1 cubit all around for people to move about. The door is 4 cubits in breadth; its height is 8 cubits; the width of the frame and threshold=2 cubits, its thickness=12 digits; height of the idol =4 cubits and 16 digits; the height of the pedestal=12 cubits and 8 digits.

In verse 13 there is another reading उदुम्बरौ instead of उदुम्बरः. Utpala explains the statement that the door should consist of three, five, seven or nine Śākhās or frames, by pointing out that the total width of the frame should be made up of the width of as many frames as necessary : "शाखाविस्तारस्तिसृभिर्यदि न पूर्यते, तदा पञ्चभिः पूरणीयः,

Cf. काश्यप—

पुरानुसारप्रासादाः कर्तव्याः शुभलक्षणाः ।
नात्युच्चा नातिनीचाश्च समदिक्सूत्रसूत्रिताः ।।
चतुःषष्टि कोष्ठकानां मध्ये च तत्र विन्यसेत् ।
द्वारं च मध्यमं श्रेष्ठं समदिक्स्थं प्रशस्यते ।।
विस्तारद्विगुणोत्सेधः कटिरंशे तृतीयके ।
विस्तारार्धेन तद्गर्भो भित्तयोऽन्यास्तथान्तरे ।।
गर्भाच्चतुर्थभागे च द्वारं तद्द्विगुणोच्छ्रितम् ।
द्वारोच्छ्रायचतुर्भागो विस्तारः शाखयोः स्मृतः ।।
उदुम्बरस्तथैवोक्तः शाखामानेन नित्यशः ।
घनत्वं पादमानेन शाखयोश्च प्रकीर्तितम् ।।
एकशाखास्त्रिशाखा वा पञ्च सप्त नवापि वा ।
द्वारिकास्तत्र शस्यन्ते द्वारिभिर्या त्रकुण्ठिकाः ।।
शाखाचतुर्थभागेऽत्र प्रतीहारौ तु कारयेत् ।
प्रमथैर्विहगैश्चैव जीवजीवजलोद्भवैः ।।
श्रीवृक्षस्वस्तिकैः पद्मैर्हंसैश्चैव मनोरमैः ।
पत्रान्तरे लताशुभैर्ग्रहैर्वैनायकादिभिः ।।
देवं सपिण्डिकं स्थाप्यं द्वाराष्टं शोभितं शुभम् ।
द्वौ भागौ प्रतिमा कार्या तृतीयश्चैव पिण्डिका ।।
स्रवणद्रोणिकाभागो वामे पार्श्वे विधीयते ।
निर्माल्यञ्च निवेद्यं च बलिपूजापमार्जनम् ।।]

मेरुमन्दरकैलासविमानच्छन्दनन्दनाः ।
समुद्गपद्मगरुडनन्दिवर्धनकुञ्जराः ।।१७।।

गुहराजो वृषो हंसः सर्वतोभद्रको घटः ।
सिंहो वृत्तश्चतुष्कोणः षोडशाष्टाश्रयस्तथा ॥१८॥
इत्येते विंशतिः प्रोक्ताः प्रासादाः संज्ञया मया ।
यथोक्तानुक्रमेणैव लक्षणानि वदाम्यतः ॥१९॥

There are twenty types of temples enumerated here by me as follows : (1) Meru, (2) Mandara, (3) Kailāsa, (4) Vimānacchanda, (5) Nandana, (6) Samudga, (7) Padma, (8) Garuḍa, (9) Nandivardhana, (10) Kuñjara (11) Guharāja, (12) Vṛṣa, (13) Haṁsa, (14) Sarvatobhadraka, (15) Ghaṭa, (16) Siṁha, (17) Vṛtta, (18) Catuṣkoṇa, (19) Ṣoḍaśāśri, and (20) Aṣṭāśri. I shall now explain their characteristics in regular order.

तत्र षडश्रिर्मेरुर्द्वादशभौमो विचित्रकुहरश्च ।
द्वारैर्युक्तश्चतुर्भिर्द्वात्रिंशद्धस्तविस्तीर्णः ॥२०॥

Among them, the type of temple known as *Meru* is hexangular, has twelve storeys and internal windows of various kinds. It has four doors or gates in the four directions and is 32 cubits in width. (Its height is 64 cubits).

[Cf. काश्यप—

द्वात्रिंशद्धस्तविस्तीर्णं चतुर्द्वारं षडश्रिकम् ।
भूमिकास्तत्र कर्तव्या विचित्रकुहरान्विताः ॥
द्वादशोपर्युपरिगा वर्तुलाण्डैः समायुताः ।
प्रासादो मेरुसंज्ञः स्याद् निर्दिष्टो विश्वकर्मणा ॥]

त्रिंशद्धस्तायामो दशभौमो मन्दरः शिखरयुक्तः ।
कैलासोऽपि शिखरवानष्टाविंशोऽष्ट भौमश्च ॥२१॥

The *Mandara* too is hexangular, 30 cubits in width, and has ten storeys and domes. *Kailāsa* is similar to this, but has eight floors and is 28 cubits in width.

[The height of *Mandara* would be 60 cubits and of *Kailāsa* 56 cubits.

Cf. काश्यप—

त्रिंशद्धस्तास्तु विस्तीर्णः प्रासादोऽयं द्वितीयकः ।
अष्टभौमश्च कैलासो हस्ताष्टाविंशतिः स्मृतः ।
षडश्रिः शिखरोपेतः प्रासादस्तु तृतीयकः ॥]

जालगवाक्षकयुक्तो विमानसञ्ज्ञस्त्रिसप्तकायामः ।
नन्दन इति षड्भौमो द्वात्रिंशः षोडशाण्डयुतः ॥२२॥

The temple of the *Vimānacchanda* type is hexagonal 21 cubits breadth, and has latticed windows and eight floors. The *Nandana* is similar, but has six storeys and 16 cupolas and is 32 cubits in width.

[Cf. काश्यप—

गवाक्षजालसंयुक्तो विमानश्चैकविंशतिः ।
षडश्रिरष्टभौमश्च प्रासादः स्याच्चतुर्थकः ॥
नन्दनस्तु षडश्रिः स्याद् द्वात्रिंशद्धस्तविस्तृतः ।
षड्भौमः षोडशाण्डस्तु प्रासादः पञ्चमो मतः ॥]

वृत्तः समुद्गनामा पद्माकृतिः शया अष्टौ ।
शृङ्गेणैकेन भवेदेकैव च भूमिका तस्य ॥२३॥

The temple known as *Samudga* is circular in shape, and the *Padma* is shaped like a lotus (with eight petals). Both these measure 8 cubits in width, and have only one storey and one dome.

[The commentator says that the *Samudga* is shaped like a green gram and *Padma* has eight petals.

Cf. काश्यप—

वर्तुलस्तु समुद्गः स्यात्पद्मः पद्माकृतिस्तथा ।
हस्ताष्टकं तु विस्तीर्णौ भूमिका शृङ्गभूषिता ॥]

गरुडाकृतिश्च गरुडो नन्दीति च षट्चतुष्कविस्तीर्णः ।
कार्यस्तु सप्तभौमो विभूषितोऽण्डैस्तु विंशत्या ॥२४॥

The *Garuḍa* is shaped like an eagle with wings and tail. The *Nandin* (i.e. *Nandivardhana*) is like the previous one but without the wings and tail. Both these are 24 cubits broad. They have seven storeys and are adorned with 20 cupolas.

[Cf. काश्यप—

गरुडो गरुडाकारः पक्षपुच्छविभूषितः ।
नन्दी तथाकृतिर्ज्ञेयः पक्षादिरहितः पुनः ॥
कराणां षट्चतुष्कास्तु विस्तीर्णौ सप्तभूमिकौ ।
दशभिर्द्विगुणैरण्डैर्भूषितौ कारयेत्तु तौ ॥]

कुञ्जर इति गजपृष्ठः षोडशहस्तः समन्ततो मूलात् ।
गुहराजः षोडशकस्त्रिचन्द्रशाला भवेद्वलभी ॥२५॥

The *Kuñjara* has the form of the back of a standing elephant, and measures 16 cubits all round from the bottom. It has only one storey. The *Guharāja* type (shaped like a cave) is 16 cubits wide and single-storeyed. Both have their sloping roof with three upper rooms.

[Utpala refers to another reading viz. सुविस्तरो मूलात् in the place of समन्ततो मूलात् ।

Cf. काश्यप—

कुञ्जरो गजपृष्ठाभो हस्ताः षोडश विस्तृतः ।
गुहराजो गुहाकारो विष्कम्भात् षोडश स्मृतः ॥
त्रिचन्द्रशाला वलभी तयोः कार्या सुलक्षणा ।
दशमैकादशावेतो प्रासादौ द्वौ प्रकीर्तितौ ॥]

वृष एक भूमिभृङ्गो द्वादशहस्तः समन्ततो वृत्तः
हंसो हंसाकारो घटोऽष्टहस्तः कलशरूपः ॥२६॥

The temple known as *Vṛṣa* has only one storey and dome, measures 12 cubits in width, and is circular all round. The *Haṁsa* is shaped like a swan with beak, wings and tail, and is 12 cubits broad. It has only one storey. The Ghaṭa is shaped like a pot, 8 cubits broad and single-storeyed and single-domed.

[Cf. काश्यप—

वृषो द्वादशहस्तस्तु समवृत्तैकभूमिकः ।
शृङ्गेणैकेन संयुक्तः प्रासादः परिकीर्तितः ॥
हंसो हंसाकृतिर्ज्ञेयो हस्ता द्वादशविस्तृतः ।
एकभूमिकया युक्तः पक्षपुच्छाद्यलङ्कृतः ॥
घटः कलशरूपस्तु विस्तीर्णोऽष्टकरः स्मृतः ॥]

द्वारैर्युतश्चतुर्भिर्बहुशिखरो भवति सर्वतोभद्रः ।
बहुरुचिरचन्द्रशालः षड्विंशः पञ्चभौमश्च ॥२७॥

The *Sarvatobhadra* has four doors in four directions, many beautiful dormer windows (i.e. upper rooms) and five storeys, its breadth being 26 cubits. (It is square in shape).

[Cf. काश्यप—

शिखरैर्बहुभिर्युक्तश्चतुर्द्वारविभूषितः ।
रुचिरैश्चन्द्रशालैश्च बहुभिः परिवारितः ॥
चतुरस्रः पञ्चभौमः षड्विंशद्धस्तविस्तृतः ।
सर्वतोभद्र इत्युक्तः प्रासादो दशपञ्चमः ॥]

सिंहः सिंहाक्रान्तो द्वादशकोणोऽष्टहस्तविस्तीर्णः ।
चत्वारोऽञ्जनरूपाः पञ्चाण्डयुतस्तु चतुरस्रः ॥२८॥

The *Siṁha*, which is adorned with images of lions, has 12 angles and is 8 cubits broad. The last four viz. *Vṛtta* i.e. circular, *Catuṣkoṇa* i.e. Quadrangular, *Ṣoḍaśāśri* i.e. one with 16 angles, and

Aṣṭāśri i.e. Octagonal, have significant names and are dark inside. All these are single-storeyed except the *Caturasra* (Catuṣkona) which has five domes.

[Bhaṭṭotpala explains the construction of the last four as follows : These dark temples do not have external light entering the interior. Close to the temple walls should be constructed all round and the entrance should be on the western side. The walls should be so constructed with openings in the upper parts that they appear to be rising from the temple structure itself and not away from its. People should enter by the outer gate in the west, go towards the north and coming to the eastern part of the temple, enter it by the door in the east. The idea is that the temple will have only one door in the east, but the outer gate will be in the west. The idol inside the *sanctum sanctorum*, being made of gems, would illumine the interior by means of its effulgence.

Cf. काश्यप—

सिंहः सिंहसमाक्रान्तः कोणैर्द्वादशभिर्युतः ।
विष्कम्भादष्टहस्तः स्यादेका तस्य च भूमिका ॥
वृत्तो वृत्ताकृतिः कार्या संज्ञातुल्यास्तथापरे ।
सान्धकारास्तु सर्वे ते भूमिकैकाः समावृताः ॥
एकाण्डरूपिताः सर्वे पञ्चभिश्चतुरस्रकः ॥]

भूमिकाङ्गुलमानेन मयस्याष्टोत्तरं शतम् ।
सार्द्धं हस्तत्रयं चैव कथितं विश्वकर्मणा ॥२९॥

According to *Maya*, the height of a storey is 108 digits, while according to *Viśvakarman* it is $3\frac{1}{2}$ cubits or 84 digits.

[Cf. मय—

प्रासादभूमिकामानं शतमष्टोत्तरं स्मृतम् ॥

and विश्वकर्मा—

चतुर्भिरधिकाशीतिरङ्गुलानां तु भूमिका ॥]

प्राहुः स्थपतयश्चात्र मतमेकं विपश्चितः ।
कपोतपालिसंयुक्ता न्यूना गच्छन्ति तुल्यताम् ॥३०॥

Learned architects reconcile the above two opinions on the subject : If the height of the crown-work (dove-cot or cornice) be added, the smaller number will be equal to the greater one.

[Utpala says :—कपोतपालिग्रहणेन बहिर्निर्गतानि सिंहमुखानि काष्ठान्युच्यन्ते । तथा चोक्तम्—"कपोतपालिं ब्रुवते विटङ्कं च बहुश्रुताः" तथा च तन्त्रान्तरे पठ्यते —

कपोतपालिरहितं मानं चतुरशीतिकम् ।
भूमिकानां सह तया शतमष्टोत्तरं स्मृतम् ॥
अङ्गुलानामतः साम्यं भूमिकासु प्रकीर्तितम् ॥

This and the previous verse are in *Śloka* metre.]

प्रासादलक्षणमिदं कथितं समासाद्
गर्गेण यद्विरचितं तदिहास्ति सर्वम् ।
मन्वादिभिर्विरचितानि पृथूनि यानि
तत्संस्पृशन् प्रति मयात्र कृतोऽधिकारः ॥३१॥

Thus have I briefly explained the characteristics of temples. All that had been expounded by sage Garga has been incorporated in this chapter. I have derived authority for my statements by following closely the voluminous texts composed by sages Manu and others (like Vasiṣṭha, Maya and Nagnajit).

[The author's statement shows clearly that he has practically summarized what sage Garga had written. He has also seen the large works of Manu and others on this subject. However, our commentator, surprisingly does not quote even a single verse of Garga or Manu. We have to conclude from this that at the time of Utpala their works must have passed into oblivion. Hence he quotes largely from one *Kāśyapa*.

The metre is वसन्ततिलका ।]

वज्रलेपलक्षणाध्यायः ॥ ५७ ॥

Chapter LVII—Preparation of Adamantine Glue.

[The subject of preparation of adamantine glue is closely connected with that of construction of temples, mansions etc., because that was very essential for fixing idols, in constructing walls and the like when cement and other modern materials were unknown. Even now these glues known as *Aṣṭabandha* are prepared in temple premises for fixing or refixing images of Gods. Only one authority viz. Maya, is mentioned by our author.]

आमं तिन्दुकमामं कपित्थकं पुष्पमपि च शाल्मल्याः ।
बीजानि शल्लकीनां धन्वनवल्को वचा चेति ॥ १ ॥

एतैः सलिलद्रोणः क्वाथयितव्योऽष्टभागशेषश्च ।
अवतार्योऽस्य च कल्को द्रव्यैरेतैः समनुयोज्यः ॥ २ ॥

श्रीवासकरसगुग्गुलुभल्लातककुन्दुरुकसर्जरसैः ।
अतसीबिल्वैश्च युतः कल्कोऽयं वज्रलेपाख्यः ॥ ३ ॥

Take the unripe fruits of *Tinduka* (*Diospyros paniculata*) and *Kapittha* (*Feronia elephantum*), flowers of silk cotton (*Morus acedosa*), seeds of *Śallaki* (*Boswellia serrata*), bark of *Dhanvana*, and Vacā (Orris root); boil all of them in a *Droṇa* (256 Palas) and reduce the decoction to an eighth of its original volume (i.e. 32 Palas). Mix the sediments with the following substances, *viz. Śrivāsaka* (a secretion of a tree used as incense, Turpentine?), *Raktabola* (myrrh), Guggulu (*Commiphora roxburghii*), *Bhallātaka* (*Semecarpus anacardium*), *Kundurūka* (*cunduru*, exudation of Deodar?), resin, *Atasi* (*Linum usikatissimum*) and Bilva fruit (*Aegle marmelos*). The resulting paste is termed *Adamantine Glue*.

[Next he mentions the uses of this *Glue*.]

प्रासादहर्म्यवलभीलिङ्गप्रतिमासु कुड्यकूपेषु ।
सन्तप्तो दातव्यो वर्षसहस्रायुतस्थायी ॥ ४ ॥

When this glue, being heated, is used in the construction of temples, mansions, windows, walls and wells as well as in fixing Śiva's Emblems and idols of Gods, it will last for a crore of years.

[Next he gives another composition of this glue.]

लाक्षाकुन्दुरुगुग्गुलुगृहधूमकपित्थबिल्वमध्यानि ।
नागफलनिम्बतिन्दुकमदनफलमधूकमञ्जिष्ठाः ॥ ५ ॥

सर्जरसरसामलकानि चेति कल्कः कृतो द्वितीयोऽयम् ।
वज्राख्यः प्रथमगुणैरयमपि तेष्वेव कार्येषु ॥ ६ ॥

There is another adamantine glue of excellent qualities already mentioned which is also used for the same purpose. It is composed of lac, Kunduru, Guggulu (*Commiphora roxburghii*), soot (collected in the house), wood-apple (*Feronia elephantum*), Bilva (Aegle marmelos) Kernel, fruits of Nāga (*Canthium parviflorum*), Neem (*Azadirachta indica*) Tinduka (*Diospyros paniculata*) and Madana (*Randia dumetorum*). Madhūka (*Cynometra ramiflora*), Mañjiṣṭhā (*Rubia cordifolia*), resin, myrrh and Āmalaka (*Emblica officinalis*).

[There is another reading नागबलाफलतिन्दुक in the place of नागफलनिम्ब. The method of preparation is the same as before. In the next verse he mentions a third variety of glue.]

गोमहिषाजविषाणैः खररोम्णा महिषचर्मगव्यैश्च ।
निम्बकपित्थरसैः सह वज्रतलो नाम कल्कोऽन्यः ॥ ७ ॥

There is a third variety of glue known as *Vajratala* (*Adamantine Surface*) which is constituted by the horns of cows, buffaloes and goats, hair of donkeys, buffalo-hide, cow-hide, Neem fruits, wood apples and myrrh.

[This mixture too should be boiled and reduced as before. In this glue some organic substances are also included.]

Next he mentions a fourth variety of glue taught by *Maya*.

अष्टौ सीसक भागाः कांसस्य द्वौ तु रीतिकाभागः ।
मयकथितो योगोऽयं विज्ञेयो वज्रसङ्घातः ॥ ८ ॥

A compound of eight parts of lead, two of bell-metal, and one of iron rust, has been mentioned by Maya and is to be known as *Vajra-saṅghāta* (Adamantine compound).

[According to Utpala this compound includes other materials as well, but they are to be used in equal quantities. Possibly he means to say that the materials mentioned in the previous verses may also be added to this mixture in equal quantities.

[Cf. मय—

सङ्गृह्याष्टौ सीसभागान् कांसस्य द्वौ तथांशकम् ।
रीतिकायास्तु सन्तप्तो वज्राख्यः परिकीर्तितः ॥]

CHART OF UNDERGROUND WATER SPRINGS

Direction of water veins	*Depth at which water is found*	*Indicators*	*Distance & Directions from Indicators*	*Symptoms underneath*
Westerly vein	7½ cubits	*Vetasa* tree in a waterless tract	3 cubits to the west of the tree	At 2½ cubits depth pale white frog, below that yellow clay & below hard stone, next water
Easterly vein	10 cubits	*Jambū* tree in a waterless place	3c. to the north of the tree	At 5c. below mud smelling like iron, then pale white clay and further down a frog
Sweet water	10 c.	Anthill to the east of a *Jambū* tree	3c. to the south of the tree	At 2½c. depth fish, next dove-coloured stone, next blue clay
Vein of good water	12½ c.	*Udumbara* tree in a waterless tract with or without ant-hill	3c. to the west of the tree	At 5c. depth a white snake and then black stone

Abundant water	$17\frac{1}{2}$ c.	Anthill to the north of *Arjuna* tree	3c. to the west of the tree	At $2\frac{1}{2}$c. below a white alligator, then 5c. below grey clay, then dark, then yellow, then white and then sandy earth
Plenty of sweet water	$11\frac{1}{4}$ c.	Anthill on or nearby a *Nirguṇḍī* tree	3c. to the south of the tree	At $2\frac{1}{2}$c. below red fish, then red-brown clay, neat pale white clay, then sand mixed with gravel
Pure water	15 c.	Anthill to the east of a *Badarī* tree	3c. to the west of the tree	At $2\frac{1}{2}$ c. depth a white lizard
Sweet water	$16\frac{1}{4}$ c.	A *Badarī* tree along with a *Palāśa* tree in a waterless tract	3c. to the west of the tree	At 5c. below a non-poisonous (water) snake
Do.	15c.	A *Bilva* tree and an Indian fig tree be joined together	3c. to the south of the trees	At a depth of $2\frac{1}{2}$ c. a black frog
Westerly vein	$16\frac{1}{4}$ c.	Anthill on a *Phalgu* tree	3c. to the west of the anthill	Pale yellow clay and white stone and at $2\frac{1}{4}$ c. depth a white rat

Vein flowing in a southerly direction	16¼ c.	A *Kampillaka* tree in a waterless place	3c. to the east of the tree	Blue clay, then dove-coloured clay, then 1c. below fish smelling like goat and beneath that a little brackish water
Vein called *Kumudā*	15c.	A *Śoṇāka* tree in a waterless place	2c. to the north of the tree	
	7½c.	Anthill to the south of a *Vibhītaka* tree	2c. to the east of that tree	
A westerly vein which will disappear after 3 yrs.	22½c.	Anthill to the west of a *Vibhītaka* tree	1c. to the north of the tree	A white reptile (scorpion) at 5c. below, next a crimson stone, beneath that water
Abundant water	22½c.	Anthill fully covered with *Darbha* grass to the north-east of a *Kovidāra* tree	Between the tree and ant-hill	A snake with the colour of lotus calis at a depth of 5c., below that red earth and still below a ruby
Northerly vein of good water	25c.	A *Saptaparṇa* tree covered with anthills	1c. to the north of the tree	A green frog at 2½c. depth, next earth like orpiment, then a stone dark like cloud, then water-vein

Water	22½c.	Frog at the foot of any tree	1c. to the north of the tree	A mongoose at 5c. depth, then bluish clay, yellow, then white clay, next a frog like a stone
First an easterly vein, then another northerly one of sweet water	17½c.	Anthill to the south of a *Karañja* tree	2c. to the south of the tree	A small tortoise at 2½c. depth, first an easterly vein, then northerly vein, beneath that a green stone and below that water
Easterly vein	37½c.	Anthill to the north of a *Madhūka* tree	5c. to the west of the tree	At 5c. depth a big snake, then tawny clay, next a stone of the colour of horse-gram, next foamy water
Easterly vein	25c.	Glossy anthill covered with holy grass and *Dūrvā* to the South of a *Tilaka* tree	5c. to the west of the tree	
Northerly vein of plentiful water smelling like iron	28¾c.	Anthill to the west a *Kadamba* tree	3c. to the south of the tree	A golden frog at 5c. depth and then yellow clay

Southerly vein	20c.	A Palm tree or Cocoa-nut tree covered with anthills	6c. to the west of the tree	
First a westerly vein and then northerly one	25c.	Anthill to the south of a *Kapittha* tree	7c. to the north of the tree	A variegated snake at 5c. depth, then black clay, then hard stone, next white clay
First southerly vein and then north-easterly one	$17\frac{1}{2}$c.	A *Badarī* tree or ant-hill to the north of an *Aśmantaka* tree.	6c. to the north of the *Aśmantaka* tree	At 5c. depth a tortoise, then purple stone, next clay mixed with sand, then a southerly vein and below that a North-Easterly one
First a westerly vein and below a south-erly one	$28\frac{3}{4}$c.	Anthill to the North of a *Dāru Haldi* tree	3c. to the east of the tree	A blue snake upto a depth of 5c., next yellow clay, then emerald-like stone, next black earth, then west-erly vein and then a south-erly one
Water	5c.	Characteristics of watery region in a waterless place, or presence of soft *Vīraṇa* grass or *Dūrvā* grass		

Do.	15c.	*Trivṛtā*, *Dantī*, *Sūkara-pādī*, *Lakṣmaṇā* and *Navamālikā* creeper growing in a place	2c. to the south of those herbs	
Do.	Nearby	Glossy trees with long overhanging branches be short and extensive		Contrary indications are: dry and hollow trees with pale leaves
Do.	22$\frac{1}{2}$ c.	If *Tilaka*, *Āmrātaka*, *Varuṇa*, *Bhallataka*, *Bilva*, *Tinduka*, *Aṅkola* etc. are very glossy and covered with anthills	3c. to the north of the trees	
A vein of water or treasure	22$\frac{1}{2}$c.	A grassy patch of ground in a grassless place or *vice versa*.		
Do. Do.	18$\frac{3}{4}$ c.	A thorny tree amidst non-thorny trees or *vice versa*	3c. to the west of the tree	
A northerly vein	17$\frac{1}{2}$c.	Where the earth being stamped by foot emits a loud and pleasant sound	At the same place	

Water	15c.	A single branch of a tree hangs very low or be colourless	Under that branch	
Do.	20c.	Flowers and fruits of a tree look unnatural	3c. to its east	Stone bellow and yelow clay
Do.	17½c.	*Bṛhatī* plant be devoid of thorns, and with white flower		
Do.	15c.	A date tree with two tops in a waterless place	2c. to its west	
Abundant water	10c.	Steam or smoke arising from the earth	Underneath the same place	
Do.	10c.	If in a field the crops perish or if the vegetation is very glossy or white		
Northerly vein with abundant water	25c.	Anthill to the north-east of a *Pilu* tree in a desert place	4½c. to the west of the tree	At 5c. depth a frog, next brown clay, next green clay, then a stone and below that plenty of water

Southerly vein with plenty of brackish water.	35c.	Anthill to the east of a *Pīlu* tree	4½c. to the south	A white & black snake one cubit long upto a depth of 5 cubits
Sweet Water	50c.	Anthill to the north of a *Karīra* tree	4½c. to the south of the tree	A yellow frog upto a depth of 5c.
Westerly vein of brackish water	60c.	Anthill to the west of a *Rohitaka* tree	3c. to the south of the tree	
Water	70c.	Anthill to the east of *Indra* tree	1c. to the west of the tree	At a depth of 5c. a brown alligator
Southerly vein of brackish water	75c.	Anthill to the north of a *Suvarṇaka* tree	2c. to the south of the tree	At a depth of 2½c. a mongoose, next copper-coloured stone, then red earth, then water
Southerly vein first and then a northerly one of sweet water	80c.	*Badarī* and *Rohita* trees joined together with or without anthill nearby	3c. to the west of the trees	Paste-like stone, next white clay and at 2½c. depth a scorpion
North-easterly vein of copious water	90c.	*Badarī* joined with a *Karīra* tree	3c. to the west of the tree	
Plenty of brakish water	100c.	*Badarī* joined with a *Pīlu* tree	3c. to the east of the tree	

Water	125c.	A *Kakubha* tree and a *Karīra* or *Bilva* tree joined together	2c. to the east of the tree	
Do.	105c.	*Dūrvā* or sacred grass growing on anthill appear pale white	A well sunk in its place	
Do.	125c.	*Dūrvā* on anthill in a place full of *Kadamba* trees	2c. to the south of the anthill	
Do.	200c.	A *Rohitaka* tree along with three other trees surrounded by 3 ant-hills	4c. 16 digits to the north of the centre of anthills	First a stone and beneath that a water-vein
Do.	250c.	An anthill to the nor-th of a knotty *Śamī* tree	5c. to the west of the tree	
Do.	275c	If the central one of a group of 5 anthills be white	Below the central anthill	
Do..	300c.	*Śamī* tree joined with a *Palāśa* tree	5c. to its west	At 2½ c. depth a snake, then yellowish clay mixed with gravel

Do.	350c.	A white *Rohītaka* tree surrounded by anthills	1c. to the east	
Do.	375c.	A thorny white *Śamī* tree in a place	1c. to the south of the tree	At 2½c. depth there will be a snake
Do.	15c.	A *Jambū* tree...or *Vyāghrapadā* creeper growing on an anthill	3c. to the north of anthill	
Do.	25c.	If in a uniform ground without grass, anthills etc. there are some unnatural characteristics		
Do.	22½ or 25c.	The ground soft, low, sandy or emitting sound when struck		
Abundant water	20c.	Glossy trees	To the south of the trees	
Do.	Do.	A tree in the midst of a thicket showing uncommon features	Do.	

Do.	7½c.	In a semi-desert or one full of water, the earth sinks being trodden or where numerous inseets are seen without their abode	
Do.	17½c.	An itolated cold spot in a warm ground or *vise versa*	
Do.	Do.	In a semi-desert or watery region a rainbow, anthill or fish be seen	4c. therefrom
Water vein	4 cubits under the tall anthill	In a row of anthills one is taller than the rest	
Do.	17½c.	Where vegetation withers away or does not sprout at all, in a semi-desert or watery tract	4c. therefrom

A northerly vein	3c. (15c. ?)	A banyan tree, *Palāśa* and *Udumbara* be joined together or banyan and holy fig tree together	(3c. from them)
Water	15c.	Where trees, bushes & creepers an glossy with dense leaves—or land lotas, *Uśīra* etc. grow	
Do.	15c.	Date trees, *Jambū*, *Arjuna*, *Vetasa* or milky trees, mushrooms, or *Kadayantikā* grows	
Do.	Do.	A mountain sarmounted by another	At the foot of the mountain
Plenty of Sweet water	?	Where there is *Muñja* grass, reeds, and *Darbha* grass, where the earth is bluish and mixed with pebbles, or where the earth is black or red	

Water that is astringent in taste			Copper-coloured earth mined with gravel	
Brackish water			Red brown earth	
Salt water			Pale white earth	
Sweet water			Bluish earth	
Water underneath stones			Where *Karīra* exudes milk and has red sprouts and the earth is red	
Abundant water		Nearby	A rock resembling beryl, green gram, cloud, dark gem, ripe fig, bee or collyrium, or is brown	
Inexhaustible water			Rock or stone coloured like a pigeon, honey, ghee, silken cloth, or *Soma* creeper	